ALL ABOUT SPACE

VOL. 2 HOUSE 1 CATALOGUE

PARK BOOKS

EDITED BY:
DIETER DIETZ,
MATTHIAS MICHEL
& DANIEL ZAMARBIDE

PHOTOGRAPHY:
DYLAN PERRENOUD

DESIGN:
JONAS VOEGELI

COORDINATING EDITOR:
AGATHE MIGNON

I couldn't tell whether it was the last thing I had heard before the system shutdown had been completed and I had blacked out, or the first thing that came to my mind when I regained consciousness. The sentence just kept echoing in my head:
"Welcome to the real world!" –

The real world looked like a shithole and smelled even worse. I was sitting on a ragged chintz armchair, legs and arms stretched out. I felt a bit dizzy, but apart from that I was pretty much alive and kicking. On the opposite side of a cracked knee-high glass table there was a shabby brown leather couch that somehow looked familiar. So did the naked bulb that dangled from the grey concrete ceiling and lit the room in a somewhat indifferent way. And so did the cheap office desk buried under used dishes and jumbled notepads, the filthy open kitchenette, the crammed wooden racks and bookshelves, the old CP5 stage piano and the battered guitar cases, the overflowing ashtrays, the empty beer and bourbon bottles on the dusty parquet floor. Black velvet curtains were drawn before the windows so that I couldn't see whether it was bright or dark outside.

As soon as I had awakened enough to face it, I had to admit to myself that this couldn't be any other place than my office. My office, my study, my library, my conference room, my living room, my dining room, my bedroom, my storeroom, my recording studio and my video lab all in one. It was part of a two-room social housing flat on the fifth floor of a brand-new municipal apartment building, almost but not quite in downtown Zurich. I had moved in there about four weeks ago. Since it was a two-room flat, there had to be another room, but at that moment I couldn't recall what it looked like or what I was using it for. I couldn't even remember whether it was on the other side of the kitchenette or next to the bathroom.

However, there was one thing that didn't look familiar at all. Through the service hatch of the kitchenette I could see the upper half of a lady's office suit, silvery grey cotton with black borders, very elegant and very clean compared to the rest of the scenery, but definitely out of fashion since ... say ... the late 1940s. The woman who wore it was tall and of rather curvaceous shape, and, judging from the noise, she was making coffee with my Bialetti pot. Her straight and shiny pitch-black hair fell softly over her shoulders as if she had just walked out of a shampoo commercial.

"Excellent performance," she said without looking back at me. "Your results are very encouraging. You can take off the headset now. Try to relax."

Her dark alto voice, purring like a Rolls running at idle in the courtyard of a Beverly Hills mansion, finally called to my mind what this scene was all about. It was all about the so-called *HOUSE 1 Project* which was, for the most part, still a mystery to me on that 15th of December 2015. Her name was Adrienne Fromsett. At least that was the name she had used when she had introduced herself to me some time ago. It was a false name, of course, but that didn't bother me much because in the business I was in a lot of people changed their names more often than their underwear. I would probably had introduced myself under a false name too if she had not already knew my real one. Apart from that, Adrienne Fromsett was quite conspicuously different from my everyday clientele in every conceivable respect.

What actually did bother me was the thing that lay on the cracked glass table. It looked like what you might envision as a tablet computer from the 2030s and provided remote control over the thing that had got entangled in my hair: a set with two earphones and three headbands of some shiny noble metal. I couldn't tell whether it had been minutes or hours ago when that thing had sent me on the strangest trip of my life: a trip into what might be called "my individual world interior". I had been to the "Desolate Lowlands" and the "place where space inventors go", I had been let in on the disclosure and the dissolution, the curse and the morals of space. I had been told about the "Dreamcatcher Hotel Society" and the "Greatest Day For Freedom". I had seen the deep black silent void and the dead space of nothingness, I had been down the rabbit hole, chased by a squadron of black army helicopters, and hiding out in a short story. I had witnessed a theatre performance of Plato's *Republic* and a very sinister speech a certain Mr Shinya Takabayashi gave at a secret meeting on the occasion of the World Economic Forum back in 1987. And I had met the mysterious Spacemaker him- or herself at a Greyhound bus stop in the Mojave Desert. Although I probably could not recollect half of what I had been through, there were quite enough souvenir pictures in my head to fill a novel of 200 pages or more.[1]

The thing that looked like an iPad from a distant future was, according to Miss Fromsett, equipped with some neuro-active virtual reality application by the name of "SPACEMAKER1" based on an incredibly advanced interactive media technology called "MultiCom Sensorama Data Transfer" (MSDT). Allegedly, the technology was designed to induce, retrieve, and reproduce certain states of consciousness by registering, resonating, and amplifying the respective cerebral impulses. Thus, it could be used to trigger or intensify particular neuro-functional processes but not to actually control them. "What you experience during a SPACEMAKER session is principally a product of your own thoughts, memories, fantasies, and emotions," as Miss Fromsett had put it. "The application cannot impose anything specific on your mind, at least not until you have become a reasonably trained space inventor. All it

1 See Dieter Dietz / Matthias Michel / Daniel Zamarbide; *All About Space, Volume 1: The Invention of Space*. Park Books, Zurich, 2016.

does is to stimulate and temporarily prioritise certain combinations of brain activities."

After she had served two cups of black coffee on saucers (heaven knows where she had found those!) and placed them on the glass table, she sat down on the brown leather couch, settled back and crossed her legs, which was quite a daring posture for a woman with the legs of a pole-vaulter wearing a half-length cotton skirt. We just stared at each other for a few minutes, occasionally taking a sip, as if we had been posing for a painter.

To be honest, I liked to stare at her. She was as far from a front-cover beauty as she could possibly be, but she sure was an adventurous sight to see. She probably was in her late thirties, and she was six and a half feet tall at least. Her thin face was covered with scars of all sorts and sizes. It seemed as if they had been intentionally arranged around the wry hooked nose and the big dark savage eyes to fit into some obscene sculptural work of art. The office suit she wore had to be custom-tailored because it was simply unthinkable that anything off the rack could have fitted her peculiar body proportions: slender shoulders contrasted with heavily muscled upper arms, hips like a double garage merged into a wasp waist that was barely visible beneath the pair of monstrous floppy boobs that couldn't possibly be forced into shape by any imaginable type of corsage. However, in spite of all these physical disproportions, she did not appear clumsy at all. Each and every move she made was admirably precise, elegant, and, in a mysterious way, intelligent. She was so obviously and so bizarrely one of a kind, I couldn't help being fascinated. I couldn't help feeling attracted to her.

After a while I broke the silence with a question that seemed to be as good as any to start this conversation.

"How long have I been ... gone?"

"More than twenty minutes," she replied promptly. "As I said: It was an excellent performance."

"It sure felt like days. What exactly do you mean by 'an excellent performance'?"

"On average, a very first SPACEMAKER session is interrupted after three minutes and six seconds, either because the test person falls asleep or cannot stay focused any longer. You lasted twenty minutes on a constantly high concentration level, and you were able to close the session by deliberately initiating a system shutdown. That's an impressive but not exactly unexpected result. My client wouldn't have chosen you if your qualifications for this job were anywhere near the average."

"And what qualifications would that be?"

"Apart from your neurophysiological health condition and your professional experience as a cryptographer, there were two layers of evaluation criteria", she commented in a polished British English with a slight French accent and the distanced politeness of a press conference moderator. "The first layer involved intellectual abilities like cognitive intelligence, levels of education, general knowledge, imagination and memory capacities, urge for comprehension and understanding, social awareness, or independence of ideological influences, whereas the second layer was focused on certain combinations of more psychological characteristics like empathy, emotional stability, situational cleverness, spirit of adventure, inquisitiveness, sexual orientation, humour, resistance to materialistic needs, inclination to desperation and cynicism et cetera."

"Sounds like a profile of the perfect 21st century outcast to me. May I ask whether my 'inclination to desperation and cynicism' has been considered as a favourable characteristic?"

"In combination with some of your other qualifications, I would say yes, it most certainly is a favourable characteristic with regard to what my client expects you to accomplish. Does that answer your question?"

"Maybe. But it certainly does not explain why anyone would make such huge efforts to find a guy for a simple observation job and pay him 250 grand for doing it. But you wouldn't tell me what I really want to know anyway, now would you?"

She slapped on what was meant to be a winsome smile, but given the disfiguration of her face it looked more like a sardonic grin. "We have been through this before, Mr Teller. I'm neither supposed to tell you who my client is at this time nor to undeceive you about the means and resources at his or her disposal." This "his or her" resounded emphatically in my head. The wording had haunted me throughout the excursion into my "individual world interior" due to the inconclusive sex of the ubiquitous Spacemaker figure. "But you should know by now," Miss Fromsett continued, "that these resources are unrestricted enough to execute such an evaluation without even approaching the target persons."

"And unrestricted enough to confront them with a technology that appears to be mere science fiction to a common man like me, I might add."

"Exactly," she said, and the smile vanished from her face. "Besides, it is the common man's practice to overestimate technologies until he gets used to them, but in most cases purportedly 'new' technologies are nothing more than innovative applications or reconfigurations of those that have existed before. What, on the other hand, the common man persistently underestimates is knowledge. All truly new things are based on knowledge, not on technology. Don't you agree?"

She seemed to always have a clever reply to everything. This conversation quite obviously resembled the ones I had had with the black hooded figure during the SPACEMAKER session. Although I was already beginning to put up with it, I still tried to sound as scornful as possible when I asked her: "Do you really want to make me believe that all the weird things I've seen in those twenty minutes were made up by my own mind ... or had already been in there all along? – Do you want to make me believe that there were some prefigured concepts of the aesthetics, the politics, the morals, or the phenomenology of space before I put that headset on? –You can't be serious!"

"Nobody comes even close to understand what the human mind is capable of, at least not to date. So yes, I seriously want you to believe it because it's the truth."

She bended forward to put her cup down on the table, keeping her dark eyes glued to mine. As she sat back again, she suggested jovially: "Why don't you tell me about the weird things you have seen in those twenty minutes?" –

Well, I told her. And although I confined myself to a brief outline, it took me quite a while. She didn't ask questions, she didn't comment on anything, she didn't interrupt me a single time, as if there had been nothing about my account that could have possibly surprised or impressed her in any way. And when I was finished, the only thing she said was: "So you have actually met the Spacemaker in person. That's more than we would ever have expected."

She left no doubt that she was only talking to herself.

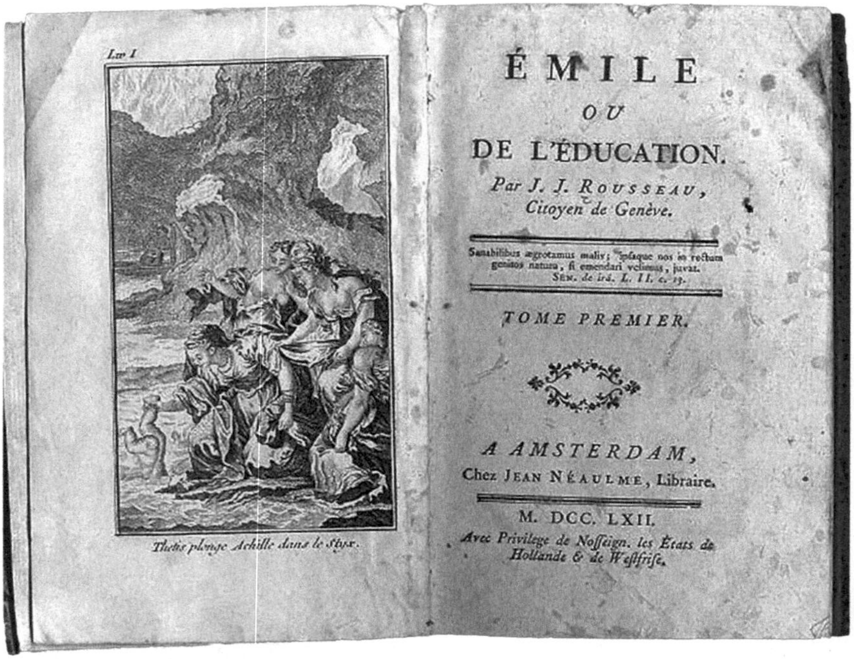

frontispiece to ÉMILE ou DE L'ÉDUCATION, Jean- Jacques Rousseau, 1762

The present book, the HOUSE 1 Catalogue, is the continuation of a journey that took a significant turn in the fundus of the Vidy Theater in Lausanne, in Summer 2015. Sitting with the ALICE team between wigs, costumes, scraps of paper, posters from now and then, and many unidentifiable objects a daring idea came up: why not go beyond simulation in models and drawings, beyond this test-ground so important to the processes of imagining other worlds. The idea was straightforward: to build a house with our first year class of over 200 students.

It was decided and it was set as an experiment. To our knowledge no such large group was ever involved in a design and build process on one singular project in a first year architectural design studio. Can so many individuals collaborate in design and construction to finally erect one house? One house that will house ideas, programs, space for interaction? And truly design it together, based on dialogue, and not on standard competition procedures?

The first volume of the All About Space series of books proposes full immersion in the format of a novel. It is also novel in its scope as an educational device. It is set to reformat – for at least the time spent in reading – a series of givens that we attribute to our existence. In particular to how we think we are in space. The book sets the 'what if' as a strong protagonist in an array of questions with not many causal answers. Questions bound with tremendous energy by many – people. A book that is asking for immersion – for a letting go and readiness for being captured by a narrative that blends me as a reader into another void, bodiless, yet shining through gaps in a screen.

Volume 2, the 'HOUSE 1 Catalogue', is a consequence of that adventure. Consisting of three distinctive parts, all in form of catalogues, this structure is superimposed by a continuing narrative that progresses towards a constellation – provided by HOUSE 1 – where the individual is beginning to face society. The narrative creates a series of links that provide continuity between Volume 1, the Catalogue parts of Volume 2, and the forthcoming volume 3. This frame story aims at explaining and resolving the strange mixture of facts concerning the built house and the fiction of its inhabitation. The first of the three catalogues, the Theory Catalogue, contains a collection of texts written by guests to our studio, reference texts, and student quotes. It resumes the intellectual background of the HOUSE 1 project as a whole. The Construction Catalogue was originally inspired by the 'Sets' structure of the legendary Whole Earth Catalogue but eventually developed in a more focused and documentary direction. It presents abundant and heterogenic material relevant to the conception, the design, and the construction of HOUSE 1. The concluding Inhabitation Catalogue sets up a fictional community of twelve 'archetypical' inhabitants introduced as the 'raw material' of a social community or civilized (that is: 'housed') culture. The characters and events of the twelve short stories are derived from the architecture of HOUSE 1 itself: from its structure, its room constellations, and its all-over appeal. On the other hand, they allegorically combine myths, tales, theories, and historical developments of some of the most influential cultures and civilizations with regard to how they tell the tale of individuals assuming to form a society. Thus, they reveal the congruency of different concepts of social coexistence in different cultural contexts, a congruency that is essentially based on astonishingly common comprehensions of the correlation between mankind and the natural world.

This leads to yet another subtext in this present book. Having read Richard Sennett's book TOGETHER recently was inspiringly revealing to me. Sennett's views on cooperation, dialogical discourse, and the necessity for a negotiation of space of cultural diversity, reflect what we feel are fundamental skills we need to build with young people – not only in architecture. While building up the program for our first year students with our team at ALICE we were not consciously drawing on those thoughts and writings. Then, readingTOGETHER, I felt as if I would be confronted with a theory of what we are trying to do. In our program, negotiation of space, here in a literal sense, was always a key factor in our curriculum. We never gave our students a bare piece of ground or a tabula rasa to play on. We always engaged a framework where parcels would be superimposed, and the notion of owning ground, even for didactic or pedagogical purposes, was excluded. Therefore students were always forced to negotiate between themselves. Building a project at a specific spot in a vertically superimposed matrix condition automatically implies to impact on your neighbors realm. In this sense our own action in appropriating space automatically impacts onto others, onto our surroundings – and reveals both potential and threat. This idea we exercised over a few years in architectural scale models. Now, this year we dared for the first time to test this approach in full scale. The result is HOUSE 1, built on EPFL campus and residing there for 3 months. It traveled thereafter to Versailles to the Versailles School of Architecture and was reassembled in different form in a new collaboration

Alice chooses to follow the white rabbit into its hole and is falling softly. Immersion is fundamental for education. We set curiosity before affirmation, the question before the answer, and listening at equal place to speaking.

Dieter Dietz.

THEORY CATALOGUE

A

When Miss Adrienne Fromsett had approached me for the first time two months earlier in Paris, she had introduced herself as the legal representative of a client who wanted to remain anonymous for the time being. I had been staying in a cheap hotel near the *Abbesses* Métro station for one night, and she just knocked on my door at about two in the morning, dressed up in fishnet stockings and synthetic black leather like a mature mid-range hooker, which certainly was, if meant to be sort of a disguise, quite appropriate with regard to that particular hotel in that particular neighbourhood. She must have known in advance that my French was lousy because she talked to me in English right away. After she had surprised me with her frighteningly accurate comprehension of my course of life in general and my semi-legal activities in particular and after having fairly convinced me that this was not meant to be the end of my career as an undercover data trader but rather the end of my temporary financial problems, she had told me about the "HOUSE 1 Project" and the task her client had chosen me to fulfil. She had outlined it as "part of a scientific research program" that was supposed to be kept confidential as long as there were no valid results to publish.

It had seemed like nothing out of the ordinary at first sight, and having checked into the available information about the implied project on the official website of the *École polytechnique fédérale de Lausanne* (EPFL), Switzerland, I had finally agreed to accept the terms. Those terms were, apart from "a more than reasonable payment": utmost secrecy, an exclusive priority commitment in writing for eight consecutive months commencing the 15th of December 2015, my relocation to a new address in Zurich which would be entrusted to me by Miss Fromsett's client, and my willingness to enhance my cerebral capacities by means of an electronic training program. Miss Fromsett had left my hotel room shortly after four o'clock, six hours later I had passed eight gigabytes of stolen private banking data on two CDs to a middleman who worked for the French tax investigation authorities, and at eleven past twelve I had caught a TGV train to Geneva at the *Gare de Lyon*.

I had met Miss Fromsett a second time in a coffee bar at the Zurich airport a few days before I moved to my new accommodation. She had been dressed, quite appropriately for the occasion, in a simple trouser suit this time. The cause of the meeting was to sign a rental contract for the apartment and a cooperation agreement paper on which the name of her client was hidden beneath a black sticker. We had fixed our next meeting, which was supposed to grant me sort of a "proper project introduction" and to take place at my new residence, on the 15th of December. And here we were, sitting opposite one another, chitchatting and drinking coffee in the early evening of that very same 15th of December, and the so-called *HOUSE 1 Project* seemed to be an even bigger mystery to me than ever before.

"You have second thoughts about this," she said, breaking yet another pondering silence, and looked at me in a strangely compassionate way. "Who would blame you for that?"

Yes, of course, I had second thoughts about it now that I had got acquainted with the so-called "training program" I had committed myself to use regularly in the forthcoming months. And what still made me feel uncomfortable was the amount of money Miss Fromsett's "client" was ready to pay for my services; even more so because the observation job I was supposed to get done was, on the face of it, neither unusual nor especially difficult. Compared to most of the things I had done for a living in recent years, gathering information about some educational project in the department of architecture of a technical university was not even particularly illegal, even if it involved a bit of hacking into protected data servers and communication devices.

"Yes, I do have second thoughts," I voiced my feelings. "There are too many obscurities involved. I still don't have the slightest idea what this 'HOUSE 1' business is all about. During the past weeks I have informed myself about the project at the EPFL, and I can see that building a real house within the framework of an educational project for first semester students in architecture is an extraordinary thing to do. But, to be honest, I would feel much better if I had any idea why your client is so interested in this project and how his extravagant expenses in this allegedly 'scientific' matter can possibly be justified. I'm just trying to calculate my personal risks, you know. And besides, I really don't like the idea of taking trips with this funky high-tech plaything of yours on a regular basis. In short: The more I think about it, the less I want this job."

"I understand, Mr Teller." Once again, her tone of voice had become unmistakably formal. "But as you know, at this time our agreement is not negotiable anymore."

Indeed, legally speaking it wasn't. On the other hand, I reassuringly thought to myself, I definitely was in need of a nest egg. And I had most certainly taken much bigger risks than this many times before. I had acquired and smuggled, encrypted and decrypted all kinds of highly sensitive data for all kinds of legal, illegal, also outright criminal customers and organisations. I had worked for mobsters, jealous wives, political activists, intelligence agencies, and so-called terrorists.

But then again, although I had developed my own advanced encryption techniques, although I had set up a sophisticated system of scrambling programs and fake identities on redirected remote servers, I had unavoidably left my traces all over the Internet, which sure was reason enough to be very careful about the assignments I accepted and the selection of my employers and contacts. After all, this carefulness was not only the reason why I never made a lot of money by my sort of trade but also the reason why I was still in it. In fact, I had always seen to it that I made just as much profit it takes to get by. I seemingly led the life of a typical but not exactly hopeless welfare case, though I had never applied for any social security benefits. It was just a camouflage that provided me with a certain anonymity as well as with a few convenient liberties as long as I was able to maintain the appearance of a 46-year-old unemployable loner with a few corresponding mental issues and a bit of an alcohol problem. And as long as my tax declarations did not raise any suspicion either, of course.

To put it in a nutshell, my situation was not exactly free from worry at the time. Actually, it was pretty dicey and highly contingent to say the least.

Miss Fromsett interrupted my stray thoughts, apparently reading my mind like an open book. "May I suggest that you look at it from a different perspective for once," she said. "Has it ever occurred to you that my client and I may not know exactly what we are looking for and that the risks *we* take by getting *you* involved in this may be just as high as yours? – In other words: Has it ever occurred to you that we might just be in need of *your help*?"

"What are you trying to tell me?"

"I'm trying to say that we have reason to believe that there's more to this remarkable educational project than meets the eye. We have approached you because we think that your *specific qualifications* might be helpful to find out what it is. And because we are quite aware that the 'obscurities' related to this assignment may seem to be all too many from your personal point of view, my client is ready to invest more in your cooperation than you would expect under the given circumstances. Can you follow me so far?"

"So you want me to find some kind of code or encrypted information in the project data?"

"Well, maybe," she replied evasively. "As I said, we do not really know what we are looking for yet."

"Then why don't you give me a hint of what you *think* you're looking for at least?"

"For now, your job is to get a comprehensive idea of the HOUSE 1 project and its progress. We want you to understand it as thoroughly as possible. And we want weekly reports on what you find and what you think about what you have found. We want printouts of these reports sent to a post office box address. A 'simple observation job', as you have liked expressing yourself earlier. And we take it from there."

There was absolutely nothing worth examining about her fingernails, they were neither painted nor manicured, but she examined them anyway. She acted her part pretty well, and there definitely was some power of persuasion in her pointed calmness.

"By the way, Mr Teller," she continued, "I am commissioned to let you know that a quarter of your pay has already been transferred to an offshore account. You have signed a contract with my client. You have accepted the terms, including this new residence of yours. You have absolutely no way of getting out of this before the job is done. Remember, we know everything … well, *almost* everything about you. More than enough to make your life a living hell whenever we think it's appropriate to do so."

"Are you threatening me?"

"Yes, sort of. But you might prefer to take it as a reminder that your options to do a number on us are considerably limited."

"Thank you, Miss Fromsett, that was plain enough," I said debonairly, trying not to sound more impressed than necessary. "I can't deny that I'm already beginning to become fond of your canny answers. How about if we proceed to discuss how and to what end you want me to make use of your fancy 'training program'?" –

She told me that the long-term objective of my training sessions was to learn to make use of the MultiCom Sensorama technology without losing my perception of the outside reality. She told me that it would presumably take me months to develop that capability, but she refused to tell me why I was supposed to acquire it because that information possibly could have "prejudiced the objectiveness of my analysis". She told me that, in the beginning, my exercises should be limited to a one-hour-session per week in order to avoid lasting side effects like insomnia, short-term memory loss, or paranoid hallucinations. Furthermore, she told me that I was to practice exclusively in the second room of my new apartment, which was, for that very purpose, to be kept completely empty, unfurnished, and unused for any other activities until further notice. She showed me a secret compartment hidden beneath the parquet floor of that second room that had been specially designed for safekeeping the futuristic tablet computer and the headset. And, naturally, all my tasks and actions on behalf of her client were to be kept strictly confidential. To be honest, I had expected worse.

When she had finished her instructions she suddenly seemed to be in a hurry to leave. She gave me a business card with a French mobile number embossed on it and said in a tone of voice as if she had been trying to sell a week's holiday in Waikiki: "You can reach me on that number, but don't you dare to try without a good reason. I'll get back to you in time."

She didn't say in time for what, of course. I showed her to the door, and as she turned around to say goodbye something crossed my mind that I had to get off my chest: "Are there others? – I mean, are there any other people who do not know exactly what they're looking for but look for it all the same?"

She smiled vaguely. "To be honest, I would have been very disappointed if you had let me walk out of here without asking that question. Unfortunately, I have no answer to it. We have done everything in our power to keep this mission a secret, but it cannot be ruled out that someone else is pursuing the same lead, of course. In fact, it would be naive not to be alert to the possibility."

"I will do my best to take account of that, Miss Fromsett," I replied and almost cricked my neck when I looked up to smirk at her face. "Oh, and by the way, why did you choose that name?"

"Always trust your intuition, Mr Teller. According to the evaluation report, it is to be considered as one of your most winning traits."

"My intuition tells me that the evaluation report contained a list of my preferred reading. And since Raymond Chandler ranked high on it, you thought that I would particularly like that name, though, for your part, you would not class 'The Lady in the Lake' among his very best work. Anyway, I think the name becomes you."

"Thank you," she said. Her smile changed from vague to almost friendly. And, as if it had actually been a spontaneous idea, she added: "If it's all right with you, call me Adrienne."

She stepped out into the hallway and closed the door behind herself.

And what did I do? – Most probably I went straight back to the living room and poured me a decent drink.

ALICE Y1
AN APPROACH TO TEACHING ARCHITECTURE IN A FIRST YEAR DESIGN STUDIO

The design studio or atelier is one of the central pillars of studies in architecture. Why is this so?

In addition to analytical, empirical, and knowledge-based foundation design also comprises elements of speculation and innovation projecting into the future. This nature of being based in history or the known, while at the same time proposing something yet to be built up and experienced, makes design a discipline asking for logical, analytical capacities and those of invention and innovation alike. In our view, the processes behind the iterations between the known world and the projected possible realities proposed by a new project are at core of the capacities to be established in architectural education. These processes take place in the atelier.

The ALICE y1 first year atelier centers on two axes: on the Conception of space and on the Construction of space. They are taught in alternating blocks of 4 to 7 weeks. The alternating blocks enhance the concept of a parallel approach to the conception and the construction of space: Through immediate exposure of students to creative processes and their tools on the one side; and on the other through intense immersion into making by constructing elements and space at full scale. The Conception of space and the Construction of space thus become complimentary fields of investigation – explored in alternating phases between working in model and drawing scale as well as in full scale.

These parallel moments of exposure are enhanced by a further dimension: Architecture's nature as a social catalyst. Students are exposed to the public and to the city from the very first day of their studies. Here they experience that an architect does not operate alone – nor from above: She or he operates from within. Hence collaboration and discourse are put forward as skills that are fundamental to the profession.

To insure intensity and diversity between the distinct phases, which focus on conception and on construction, the first year curriculum offers a series of lectures and interventions by several lecturers and foresees complimentary exercises, which transfer experience and learning outcomes from former phases into the next. Scale transfer from body to crafted artifact, and from artifact to space thus becomes an iterative process where the students learn to confront imagined, conceived reality with one they physically build themselves. The final project of the first year curriculum will test the student's ability to synthesize acquired knowledge, skills and ideas. Each person will design a room: an Inside. And build it in a group, to construct HOUSE 1.

Built first as PROTOSTRUCTURE – a balloon-frame timber construct holding the genetic code for the future projects – HOUSE 1 is an experimental format for collaborative design and construction. As a physical manifestation of a conceptual framework the PROTOSTRUCTURE federates principles of organizing space and its construction.

HOUSE 1 is also a house. It is the result of a collaboration of 250 first year students and architects. It facilitates spatial appropriation – as a cooperative act by a large group engaged in a continuous process of negotiation, debate and construction. In reference to Richard Sennett's recent book 'Together', strong emphasis is given to the notions of collaboration, dialogical discourse and the negotiation of a space of social difference. The project works as a hypothesis as it materializes these notions in the process of its construction and in its physical spatial parameters.

HOUSE 1 is built on the principles of the idea of protostructure. The PROTOSTRUCTURE, here in the form of an interpreted balloon-frame, translates the notion that constructible ground is always a common – constructible ground is constructed itself. It derives its value from collective acts. This value belongs to the community and shall be shared. Its potentials derive from context, accessibility, infrastructure. The PROTOSTRUCTURE accentuates the fragility of common values and reveals the necessity for discourse, debate, disagreement and agreement. Hence the responsibility to negotiate space is key. Accordingly we do not give our students a bare piece of ground or a tabula rasa to play on. Rather we engage a framework where parcels are replaced by superimposed space, and the notion of owning ground, even for didactic or pedagogical purposes, is excluded. Therefore all actors are bound to negotiate between themselves. Building a project at a specific spot in a vertically superimposed matrix automatically implies to impact on your neighbors spaces. In this sense your own action in appropriating space obviously impacts onto the others, onto your surroundings, and reveals both potential and threat.

HOUSE 1 is programmed as a series of rooms with diverse programmes: 'parvis', 'entrée', stairwell, library, theater, garden, terrace, alcove, lookout etc. – all these programmes are in mutual exchange and in programmatic synergy. Boundaries between projects are zones of negotiation. Accordingly each project is strongly contextualized by the others and will enter into multilayered dialogical discourse with its surroundings. The spatial experience of HOUSE 1 is therefore not that of a homogenous architecture but rather that of an unfolding evolution of a space in question, often still hovering in potentialities, and open for interpretation.

Accademic and Professional Context

With our teaching formats we aim to respond to the challenges of shifts in the profile of the profession of the architect that have emerged in the past three decades. Modes of working that have changed in evolution from earlier models due to globalization and information technologies ask for new and adequate environments for design processes in profession and education. With our interconnected and multifaceted learning environment as well as with our modes of operation from individual to group we prepare young architects for future challenges in profession and academia. While keeping the fundamentals that are essential to the profession of the architect as central in the learning outcomes, the operational and communicational skills that we require will help future professionals and researchers to act in diverse environments and constellations inside and outside of our own discipline. The profile that we aim for contains elements of orthogonality: a fostering of deep and fundamental knowledge in the discipline, with aptness to communicate and operate horizontally at the interstices between professions and fields. With this we aim to foster the most fundamental skill to be acquired for an architect: the capacity to synthesize given problems into novel and innovative design.

The integration of full-scale crafting and real world problems at every stage of the studies in both masters and bachelor is a key feature of our diverse teaching formats. Hence our students are automatically exposed to processes that will not only require their skills as designers who federate the production of space from an elevated perspective that grants a seemingly comprehensive view of the stakes at hand. She or he will also operate from an entirely immersed position – the designer becomes a craftsman, be it in social, political, economical or constructive terms. In such a process-structure the designer or architect will operate from inside, from within.

(HOUSE 1 – the collective artifact forming the kinetic pivot of this book – was built in Spring/Summer 2016 as part of the curriculum of the first year architectural design studio at EPFL. ALICE, the *Atelier de la Conception de l'Espace,* is responsible for the first year design course at the EPFL School of Architecture in Lausanne since 2010.)

DIETER DIETZ
Architect, researcher, and educator based in Zurich and Lausanne. He holds a chair for architectural design at the School of Architecture at EPFL in Lausanne and is principle of dieterdietz.org. Until 2012 he was founding partner of UNDEND architecture Zurich. With the ALICE-laboratory and his office he practices trans-disciplinary design and research crossing the fields of architecture, engineering, the arts, design and spatial culture. He has been educated at ETH in Zurich and at Cooper Union in New York. His current work investigates the nature of architectural space and of insideness as a primary condition where the lives of humans take place. Projects on human habitat, public space and the interior of the city serve as a point of departure for research relating landscape, urban environment and architecture to our embodied existence in space. The projects conducted at ALICE lab and with his practice have been awarded and exhibited internationally. Throughout his work in practice, research and teaching Dieter is convinced that architecture is a social activity that we have to engage in together.

GREAT APES NEVER BUILT HOUSES

Prologue

The following text is a first draft of a longer one that I intend to work on during the coming months of 2017. Although originally it started as a commission that was to appear in a catalogue of an Art Center (Fri-Art, in Fribourg, Switzerland) doing a research on Anti-Art and other Anti's in a diversity of creative domains, it took another turn The text has never been published, simply because not finished. Hopefully it will be, but I must admit that it is taking me to strange and fundamental readings on the most basic (yet so incredibly complex) topic of being in the world as a species.

Why is the following text included in the HOUSE 1 catalogue? Does it have anything to do with the pedagogical exercise that is the subject of this book? Yes, I think so. Its pertinence comes from the questioning of what architecture is, where its limits and limitations are, if it has any as a discipline, and how it should be taught and learnt. HOUSE 1, as you will see in some 470 pages of this book, is about origins. It sits, I believe, at the origins of shelter making. This focus on origins is transmitted most profoundly in the inhabitation catalogue – the last part of this book, where creatures of more complexity than apes and proto-humans literally invade the spaces of HOUSE 1. It is thus not a coincidence that the first year student's exercise is seen by some of us somehow as an initiation rite; a primitive, original endeavour that has the immense power to question what we do as architects. How do we work collectively? For what purpose and with what tools? What do we make, other than drawings and budgets? How do we occupy the land? These are the fundamental questions that we tend to put aside as we lose ourselves in object-making, or in the everyday logistical struggles of running an architectural office.

HOUSE 1 is a house that travels through the imaginary history of our housing origins. This is probably because HOUSE 1 has been thought of and built in the manner of the paintings in the Lascaux caves: With a ambition to fulfil the physical and non-physical world, collectively, and directly on site. Perhaps HOUSE 1 can be compared to those paintings in another way; both offer ways to observe and understand what an existing environment is, and above all, how we relate to it.

Great Apes Never Built Houses

History, whatever discipline it deals with, has its share of black holes: zones of the unknown, where pieces of the whole seem to be missing. There is often a general consensus on untold and unwritten events, spaces or inventions that have contributed extensively to the making of a discipline's official historical storytelling. You have to be a very initiated scholar to dig into the discipline's theoretical digressions to be able to find out whether or not the 'official story' represents just one of many possible stories.

This is no exception in the history of architecture, where the institutional milestones of modernism have remained untouched in writings throughout the twentieth century; From Pevsner's Pioneers of the Modern Movement of 1939 to Jean-Louis Cohen's The Future of Architecture Since 1889 – A Worldwide History (2012). With the exception of more holistic approaches from Leonardo Benevolo's and Michel Ragon, and a very few others, the history of modern architecture remains a history of heroes and their seminal buildings. The famous 1931 image of a group of New York Architects dressed as high-rise buildings for the Beaux-Arts Ball, an image that has been popularised in the architectural milieu by Rem Koolhaas' publication Delirious New York, synthesises remarkably this established trend: A handful of male architects and their singular edifices constitute the main bulk of modern architectural history.

But architecture and its theories go much farther back in time than the construction of modernism. The profoundly anthropocentric topics of the Renaissance treatises are probably 'season two' of the History of Architecture series. This is not necessarily the right place to delve into the incommensurable volumes of writings, hypotheses and theories of such Renaissance scholars as Leon Battista Alberti, Philibert de Lorme, Filarete or Marc-Antoine Laugier in the 18th century, but it is noteworthy to observe that they all refer to the same antique Roman source text, whether it is to agree or disagree with it: Vitruvius' Ten Books on Architecture, the 'season one' of Western architectural theory. In this treatise, Vitruvius explains thoroughly how the 'first man' distinguishes himself from animals by developing his intelligence through empathy, and the crafting of tools. Empathy makes him want to gather with others, and to fabricate the spaces to make this assembly possible. The tools he develops allow him, through construction, to adapt himself more and more efficiently to different climate conditions, conquering nature in the process and opening up opportunities for a new nomadic life. Contrary to the more idyllic views of Ovid, 'Nature' is seen by Vitruvius as a hostile environment, in which man must build in order to protect himself.

Much later, in 1753, the Abbey Marc-Antoine Laugier made a breakthrough in this line of thinking, by getting rid of the classical heritage and referring more directly to models of 'Mother Nature'. Yet the frontispiece of his main work, An Essay on Architecture, depicts what remains a canonical archetype of architecture: the primitive hut. This architectural figure has passed through the ages intact, dominating even today over many other alternative views on the origins of architecture. The primitive hut, in Laugier's terms, represents the original construction that gave birth to architecture: Columns, skin (facade), and above all, roof, constitute the very first attempt of man to construct a shelter.

When I was approached to write this text, the open brief I was given – to write about 'anti-architecture' – really appealed me, in that it sounded extremely odd to my ears. The sound of it, anti-architecture, seemed particularly unfamiliar as a term. Some modest research seams to confirm that there is indeed no established term 'anti-architecture' I found one publication as far as my research has revealed that has used the term: The collection of essays titled Anti-Architecture and Deconstruction (2004), which critiques the late twentieth century deconstructivist movement in architecture. Edited by Nikos A. Salingaros, the book features contributions by cult figures outside mainstream architecture circles, such as the Viennese-born architect and design theorist Christopher Alexander.

However, in considering the vast repository of critical writing on and about architecture, as well as the work of numerous creative practices that have stepped away from traditional building, it seems that no scholar or professional has yet addressed the concept of an anti-architecture in depth. During my quest, the thought became apparent to me that as soon as we start considering the idea of man sheltering himself, there cannot be an 'anti-architecture'. Anti-architecture, when followed through to its logical conclusion, would mean humankind naked, exposed and unprotected in a wild and hostile natural world. In the very moment that when we put a barrier, or shelter, over our heads; we are already inside the idea of architecture.

In my sleepless nights, while turning over this very tricky subject in my mind, I went back to my readings on "great apes": Specifically, Franz deWaal's essays and book "Our Inner Ape" on empathy, and his anti-Darwinistic approach to the question of evolution. I returned to the primitive hut of architectural history, by which architecture could only be seen through an extremely anthropocentric and a posteriori view of the world (particularly at a time, 2 million years ago, where the pithecanthropus erectus shared the word with many other species, without governing over them).

Despite continuous scientific discoveries that clearly blur the limits of our knowledge on prehistoric human evolution, a few facts seem to be quite confirmed by now. 'Human' is the name given to the family of a few species, Homo Sapiens being the one that has prevailed or survived over all of the others. But new species of Human could yet appear, particularly with the intense research being carried out at the moment (the last discovery of a new member of the homo family, Homo Naledi, was made in September 2015 in South Africa). Another certainty is that Homo Sapiens migrated en masse from Africa to the rest of the world (including Australia by sea, in what is currently considered to be the first ever human ocean crossing, and the Americas) between 60 000 and 35 000 years ago. The agricultural revolution happened 15 to 10 000 years ago, beginning humans' sedentary journey: an adventure that brought about the need for permanent houses, and consequently, architecture as defined by the main thinkers and treatises of the discipline.

If the cave paintings of Lascaux can be dated to 17 000 BCE, at approximately the time when sedentary agriculture was beginning, where are the human shelters of a comparative complexity to the art presented on the cave walls? Logically, shouldn't a species that has spent so many thousands, or even millions, of years developing complex cultures have also engineered shelters to protect themselves and each other? Was permanent building not in humankind's agenda?

I hurried to Lascaux during the Christmas of 2016, anxious to see the very new replica of the paintings, recently opened inside a new formalist building made by Norwegian architecture firm Snøhetta, which stands in the fog of the Perigord region in France. The replica is astonishing in its precision: 16 points per millimetre have been accurately reproduced in a brand new artificial cave, a few hundred meters from the original. It is a multifaceted fabrication that mixes very contemporary techniques of 3D moulding, material research (the moulds and surfaces are a multi-layered compound of resin and mineral, the visible mineral layer being a protected patent developed for the Lascaux project) and traditional painting. During a visit, anyone with a basic knowledge of art and techniques can grasp the complexity of these paintings. The first thing that strikes the visitor is the precision of the gestures. There is no improvisation in those stones. It is not the work of a child mind trying to reproduce imaginary animals. The authors of these paintings and engravings were skilled artists. The layers of complexity in those oeuvres is so great that to describe them all in this short essay would be impossible: they contain symbolism that reveals a complex understanding of nature and time, hieroglyphic symbols that describe a proto-written language, the intricate use of existing stone wall geometries to support the story-telling of the painting frescoes; a rich natural pigmentation (that has lived 17 000 years), and scaffolding devices to reach the higher ceilings of the cave. These are just some of the many captivating features of these cave paintings.

A mind like mine, with the tendency to search for architectural parallels, cannot avoid pondering just what kind of architecture could have been achieved by channelling the same complexity of technique and creativity shown in these paintings? And there is further question: why isn't there any trace here of the will to build? Lascaux is of course one case among many, and after all, quite recent in the history of humanity, but it does nonetheless prove that these people had already acquired the capacity to think, project and make great pieces of art collectively. Indeed, it is assumed that some 30 000 years prior to the Lascaux paintings, homo sapiens set foot in Australia (the oldest prehistoric site in Australia, the Malakunanja II rock, is dated to 55 000 BCE). Using floating devices, these people made the first open ocean crossings, yet another indication of sapiens' ability to overcome difficulty with creativity, know-how and collective action.

One might then speculate that for the early sapiens, and other Homos erectus (Heidelbergensis, Fiorensis, Neanderthalis, etc), housing was simply not an issue. The idea of a supporting shelter, built with the purpose of gathering the community under a single roof, did not seem to be a concern of the early humans. Or rather, they found shelter already in what Nature had to offer. Why spend time on house-making when nature already provided the necessary sheltering devices? Man found everything there, and if not, he travelled to obtain it.

If we consider the evolution of humans, from the first Australopithecus 4 million years ago to today, the historical development of architecture as we know it – and as considered by the 20th century scholars – is the equivalent of a single pebble in the Joshua Tree National Park. Not only that, but the subject of architecture as enduring building seems to be completely absent in the investigation of human evolution.

Had the Agricultural revolution not occurred, might there have been the possibility of a global population, naked, and potentially sheltered by a single 'superskin' that would stretch across the world, protecting us from nature and climate? Could this have been the outcome of a world without architecture? No Primitive hut, no Vitruvius, no Alberti. Evidently, this is a thought that our minds might find difficult to swallow; yet there is something quite interesting in approaching the idea of Architecture not as "engineered building", nor as the structure and fabrication of a shelter – concepts that the Renaissance solidly engraved into western architectural thinking. It is still provocative to assert that what is called 'decoration' by many architects and treated as a pejorative term may actually be an architectural gesture, made through the acquisition of precise skills and sensitivities, that appeared long before branch structures and roof-making were claimed to be the origins of architecture.

Architecture could thus be considered as a broader endeavour; one that does not necessarily mean the destruction and replacement of nature, but rather one that might limit itself, as a practice, to the fine observation and modification of existing conditions in its search for a shelter to house populations. It could become a closer friend to Art: that fundamental discipline that has spent so much time, as in Lascaux, simply understanding our environment and deciphering it. Architecture would then become more about maintenance: the conservation of what's around us. We would mount and dismount our camps wherever we go, leaving little trace, erasing our architecture from our passage in a pre.-sedentary model.

If we managed, over millions of years, to do without Architecture, could we not use technology to rethink our relation to the earth? Such a speculative model makes it possible to review our original roots in relation to the contemporary state of being in our limited world. And to review, as well, the all-too-important status that architecture has acquired in our society. Perhaps there is an interesting hypothesis to consider here, as we understand that the two things that made evolution possible were tools (to deal with Nature) and art (to observe and understand Nature), and that only our capacity to use tools and art collectively made homo sapiens different to other humans, allowing us to acquire new skills that other humans did not: those of invention (the production of fictions) and collaboration (the creation of communities).

Anti-architecture cannot possibly exist, since as soon as it begins to appear, it turns itself back into architecture again, like an unsinkable boat turned upside down, bobbing on the water. So: do we either continue floating in the architectural world that we know, or do we sink the whole boat and start again: with no mediating force of architecture at all, but only with our environment, and with the inscribing of our bodies within it?

DANIEL ZAMARBIDE
Architect (FAS – IAUG – SIA | BUREAU A) by education, practicing and questioning continuously the borders of the field. He has developed through the years a particular interest in the protean aspects of Architecture and nourishes his work and research through other domains like philosophy, applied and visual arts as well as cinema. The aim of these explorations is always a way to explore and question Architecture, its potential and large operational possibilities in given situations and for specific people. Engagement is a key preoccupation in his practice, social and political, Architecture being best defined within the realm of public space, which is the best definition of the space where his practice operates. He lives and works between Lisbon and Geneva, where his practice BUREAU A is based, and Lausanne where he teaches at the ALICE Lab at the EPFL.

THE INVENTION OF TOGETHERNESS OR THE APPROPRIATION OF SPACE OR HOW I WOULD LEARN TO STOP WORRYING AND COMPREHEND THE HOUSE

Object

I know exactly what a house is. I know what a house is when I see one, and I know what I'm talking about when I talk about one. That's certainly good enough to handle the everyday demands that are put on my notion of a house as long as I can avoid situations that require a comprehensive understanding. Thus, I have no reason to worry about the fact that a "house" is one of those things of which I know exactly what they are until the very moment I am required to explain them.

However, supposed I actually was requested to explain what a "house" is in a catchy definition, my first attempt would most probably be a technical one, irrespective of my profession or educational background. Like at least nine out of ten adults, I would try to refer to any kind of building that is equipped with certain technical features serving certain purposes, which means that I would intuitively and more or less explicitly base my definition on the fact that a house is *built* or *constructed* according to specific intentions. In other words, I would spontaneously follow the common categorical logic of defining an artefact by first choosing a type of artificial or technical objects ("building") and then attribute a principal purpose or function to it ("providing shelter from adverse environmental influences").

To ascertain the adequacy of the definition (or to enhance its vividness in a dialogical situation) I would probably digress into an enumeration of the most diverse examples I can think of, seeking to illustrate the broadness of possible purposes and appearances of houses, starting out from those that are built for people to live and work in, proceeding to storehouses and representational houses, from doll's houses to cinemas and space stations, from jailhouses to greenhouses to henhouses, and, in case no one would raise any objection, from rabbit holes to bird's nests to beehives and anthills, and so forth. I might end up mentioning a few of the various figurative, metaphoric, and systemic uses of the word in political or educational contexts, in ancestry or astrology etc.

Although I would find this kind of technicity-based strategy of defining a house in almost every available dictionary, although I know that the point of a definition is not to explain things thoroughly but rather to *imply* a reasonable scope of explanations, and although

I would certainly not want to live up to the standards of Aristotle or Wittgenstein, I would not quite be satisfied with it, especially in view of that quasi endless list of very different and differentiable housing purposes and functions which makes me aware of the fact that there are houses I would not exactly or necessarily refer to as "buildings" and vice versa. *This* differentiation is based on criteria that seem to be, if not subjective, at least not perfectly objectifiable. If I replace the term "building" by "construction", the definition may work a little better in this respect (thinking of tents, for example, or cardboard boxes, or cars and – why not? – submarines that definitely comply with basic housing standards), but still, completely apart from this, the figurative uses of the word hint at a notion that significantly goes beyond the mere object.

Admittedly, you always find that "something beyond the mere object" if you're quirky enough to bother and search for it. Mostly (and most trivially), it emerges in the course of unforeseeable and hardly objectifiable *experiences* that set in as soon as the object (e.g. a construction providing shelter) is recognised or basically understood as such; experiences that substantially and continuously extend the object's initial meaning and comprehension. In the case of an artefact, this experiential process leads the way to continuous modification, to possible improvement and refinement of the object itself as well as the notion of it, and with regard to the "house" we even tend to assume that this extension must be (or must have been) significant and eventually complex enough to co-initiate and co-conduct the process of cultural history in general and of civilisation in particular. If that assumption is correct, the notion of a house may well reach not only beyond the object but also beyond any comprehensive technical definition.

The main difference between comprehending something as an object and comprehending it as an experience is that the perspective on an object is basically an "outside" perspective whereas the experiential view allows various "inside" and sometimes "subjective" perspectives whenever that seems appropriate or necessary, albeit by compromising the definitional "objectivity", of course. However, if anything is worth being considered from an inside perspective, it is a house, isn't it? –That may be the reason why many of the definitions in dictionaries skip the all too obvious sheltering function of a house and start out from "a building to live in" or "a building for people to live in". But however essential the inside may be when it comes to understand what a house is, let's not put up with it too easily.

Against the backdrop of all this, a second attempt of defining what a house is would switch from the perspective on a technical or artificial object to a more phenomenological perspective, trying to focus on what the common experience of a house is about. This second attempt is not contrary but rather complementary to the first one insofar that it examines the aspects that have left me a bit unsatisfied with the technicity-based definition. The latter may imply a lot of essential explanations like the way of construction, the shapes, sizes, proportions, the equipment and materialities of houses. It also implies that a house necessarily establishes spatial inside-outside situations, of course, but the comprehension of the interior spaces remains comparatively vague and unspecific, which probably is the main reason why the objective definition calls for an enumeration of examples for different functions and purposes.

Experience

From the "experiential" point of view, a house is most evidently a matter of spatial conception. Hence, if I allow myself to envision the very first men or hominids that ever did (or tried to) build huts or hideouts that fit in the anthropocentric notion of a house, I must take it for granted that they already had developed a considerable comprehension of space before they even thought of it, which is not as trivial as it may seem.[1] Maybe they transferred their experiential concept of trees or caves into a primitive spatial construction, maybe they imitated the housing strategies of animals, maybe they accidentally came across a useful constellation of natural objects providing shelter from the rain, the storm, the cold, or the predators, and subsequently tried to reproduce it using the tools and materials available to them. However, they must have started out from some kind of idea, model, or prefiguration, and that idea must have been

1 See Dieter Dietz / Matthias Michel / Daniel Zamarbide (ed.); *All About Space, Volume 1: The Invention of Space*, chapters I.4. *The Desolate Lowlands* and I.5. *Moonwatcher*. Park Books, Zurich 2016.

based upon or derived from a very simple spatial experience rather than from a subtle technical consideration: the experience that spatial environments can be *purposively* separated into spatial insides and spatial outsides and that, depending on their physical qualities, the former provide shelter from certain adversities of the latter. Needless to say that this experience involves a very essential and radical first step to what might be called a progressive "*appropriation* of space".

Initially, there seems to be little to invoke in favour of this hypothetical very first notion except for its philosophical plausibility. But when I project it onto cultural history in general and the history of architecture in particular, it turns out to capture the house as the aforementioned cultural determinant quite accurately. Not because it is remarkably precise or specific in a definitional sense (quite obviously it is not) but because it embraces the principle features of a house (like walls, roofs, floors, doors, windows etc.) in their specific comprehensive context, both with regard to their relational purposes *and* their practical technical development from the most primitive hut to the state-of-the-art all-inclusive hotel complex with its most sophisticated high-tech equipment. In other words: If I accept the experiential notion of a house as "a construction establishing accessible (and possibly multiple) spatial insides in relation to the respective (and also possibly multiple) spatial outsides" – or, if you prefer: "a construction that allows residing in an *interior* that is intentionally segregated from a relative *exterior*" –, it comes with a few noteworthy additional implications that the technicity-based definition of the mere object initially evades:

— The essentially spatial inside-outside perspective encompasses the notion of a "room" because the notion of a "room" is, if reduced to the max, *nothing but* a spatial inside. Evidently, the list of possible purposes, functions, and features of a room (or a systemic combination of rooms) is virtually endless. In fact it is not only as endless as the list of possible purposes of a house, it is *exactly the same* list that has triggered the dissatisfaction with the definition of the object in the first place. In other words: There is no definitive way to tell whether the room or the house is prior to the other in cognitive or phenomenological terms. They refer to the very same notion.

— Accordingly, the inside-outside perspective explains the subjective differentiation between "houses" and "buildings" in everyday language quite descriptively: We tend to speak of a building (instead of a house) when the context of its interior and its exterior is less obvious, less familiar, less comprehensible, less assessable, less structured, less accessible or simply of less personal interest. In addition, this context brings the multiple transitions and connections between interiors and exteriors into focus: the interfaces, the convergences, the (both technical and aesthetical) conditionings of spatial insides and outsides, all the more because a house normally provides multiple inside-outside situations.

— In like manner, the experiential perspective does not only include the aforementioned tents, cardboard boxes, cars, submarines and the like, it also includes – given that "constructions" can be both of a physical and a cognitive nature – the various ideational, figurative, and systemic applications of the term "house" in an intelligible way: they are generally meant to mark out a certain range or group or configuration of things as an *inclusive* entity (and, implicitly, all "other" things of the same or a comparable kind as excluded).

— Moreover, this point of view most certainly helps to understand the characteristics by which different houses appeal to us differently. What we like or dislike about a house, how we "feel" about it, even how we spontaneously assess its outer appearance is rarely due to an immediate judgement on its objective technicity or its technical features but more often a matter of how these features direct or modulate the experience of relations between interior and exterior spaces. These aspects are (or should be) not only crucial criteria of architectural assessments, but also determine most of the stagings and mise-en-scènes of all kinds of houses in the arts, most obviously (but not only) in visual arts like painting, photography, and film.

Many more of these implications might be added here, but for now, I would like to bring this excursion to a close by referring to an illustrative childhood memory. At an age when understanding things was much more based on experience than on any kind of objectivity, every constellation of natural or artificial objects perceived as an inside-outside situation could serve as a house of considerable complexity whenever a "house" was required for the game I wanted to play. The point is that I did not need to invest much imaginative power in fancying technical or objective details of a house as long as there was a way to get "in there" and as long as the "inside" provided a sufficient feeling of cosiness, safety, or seclusion from the "outside". A table I could crawl under or a configuration of bushes I could hide behind was good enough if nothing better was at hand. And if observations like this do not even come close to the cogency of representative surveys of psychogenetic concept formation, they still seem to tell a lot about the notion of a house in terms of common sense.

Remarkably enough, the two approaches to the idea of a house do not seem to necessarily imply one another, although they are complementary in a rather self-evident way. According to whether you intuitively or deliberately start out from the objective or the explicitly space-related definition, you most probably will stick to the respective point of view without getting aware that something's missing, which becomes quite obvious with regard to the various tales of the history of civilisation that usually introduce the notion of the "house", along with only very few others like "tool" or "language", as an initial determinant of our very idea of culture. As is well known and not really surprising, the story of the house as an object and artefact is unequally more frequent and common than its counterpart, which is almost exclusively and speculatively hinted at by a handful of philosophers, phenomenologists, psychologists, and existentialists. To what extent this is due to the usual focus on technicality and factuality of historiography in general and the cultural concept of progressive mastery of an objectified nature in particular (as against the natural contingency of humanity, the development of ideas and phenomenological comprehensions) would have to be subject of another detailed examination, but it seems not completely inappropriate to say that since the beginning of the Early Modern Age our notion of a "house" has been significantly confined to the Eurocentric aspects of technicity and auctorial artificiality.

However, from the technicity-based perspective, the story of the house as a determinant of cultural history is a simple story of a continuous and seemingly inevitable progress with interruptions due to unfortunate historical incidences. The same goes for the history of architecture, which is quite commonly resumed as a history of basically technical achievements implying cultural consequences, and these increasingly complex(ed) achievements are usually attributed to a genealogy of almost literally monolithic masterminds. On the other hand, if considered from an experiential and explicitly space-related perspective, the same story turns into an erratic and non-linear history of cultural, social, and political processes during which the conceptions of houses are contingent on the history of ideas rather than on the history of technical progress. Both stories are considerably incomplete and deceptive, but complementing each other they certainly come a little closer to a comprehensive and acceptable truth.

Togetherness

Since neither of the two perspectives contradicts the common assumption that the initial purpose of a house is to provide shelter (and since this assumption, although necessarily unprovable, is so perfectly plausible that it would be hard to make a serious stand against it), a brief and pointed outline of a non-historical but consecutive story of the notion of the house, conceptualised in seven stages that integrate both perspectives equally, would most certainly start out from that particular function. It's a story everybody knows, but it is usually told in parts and hardly ever in its entirety.

Shelter

As a construction providing shelter from adverse outer or environmental influences, the house obviously fits into the concept of artefacts and technical means that extend the puny and comparatively miserable bodily outfit of human beings in the sense of prostheses without which these beings would not have the slightest chance of survival. On the other hand, the biological weakness of the human kind advances the development of cognitive capabilities and the urge for abundance and luxuriation alike wherefore the progressing housing strategies certainly serve as a perfect example. Although the first huts and hideouts are constructed in a way that only complies with the most primitive housing requirements, it is quite probable that their sheltering function is gradually and rather rapidly extended: from one-room-interiors to partitions, from outside fireplaces to stoves, from the naked soil to bed installations etc. These first pieces of technical equipment are subject to immediate physical necessities that do not substantially exceed the satisfaction of the basic need for shelter. However, in the *spatial* context of a "house", these necessities inevitably evoke first notions of "privacy" along with respective concepts of "possession".

Home

As soon as a certain amount of effort has been invested to make the house not only a place of shelter but also a "private" (and essentially interior) space of comfort and intimacy, it immediately prompts appropriative attitudes and behaviours. This appropriation is commonly associated with defensive measures and aggression against "outsiders" and "intruders", but it is also the origin of more subtle feelings that relate to the house as a "home". The experience or sentiment of "being at home" is closely linked to highly emotional conceptions of families, tribes, ancestries, shared identities and destinies that are transferred to the house both as a real and a notional object. Under certain conditions, these conceptions are directly and quite naturally extended to its territorial surroundings, eventually to clusters of houses and "villages", finally to countries and so-called "nations": the cognitions of the interior are expanded (or rather: projected) to the exterior of the house, and at this very moment at the latest, the notion of the house irrevocably transcends the bounds of the "mere object".[2]

2 The etymology of the term "house" itself supports this broader scope of the notion in almost all European languages up to the Early Modern Age. As far as the history of the Old Germanic and Old Nordic words "hus" and "hud" ("hut") in particular can be traced back, they denote not only the building but rather the inclusive idea of a building, the territory on which it is built, and its inhabitation in the sense of a "homestead". An original relationship with the ancient Greek word "κευτηοσ", meaning "cave", "gorge", "stable", "lodging", and "place to live", cannot be proven but is considerably probable.

Conceived of as a home, a house is meant to be an inhabited and belonging place, and if it is abandoned, it turns into an "empty space" of the strangest and sometimes rather creepy kind. Phenomenologically speaking, this experience is one of the original common experiences of a species that has given up a nomadic in favour of a sedentary life.

Spirituality

Sooner or later, the abovementioned extension of the experience of a secluded "home", along with the notions of "one's own" and the "strange", must be integrated into the respective spiritual, mythological, and religious comprehensions of the world as a whole, even more so when the contingencies of a hunter-gatherer way of life pass into those of early agricultural communities. Accordingly, the notion of the house is augmented by speculations about the existence and coherence of natural and supernatural phenomena and turns into sort of a cosmological model or principle: a quite descriptive paradigm of the spatial order of things.

Reciprocally, religious, mythological, and cosmological models are integrated into the concept of the house. Houses become "haunted" and "inhabited" by demons and spirits and gods, they are equipped with respective features and insignia, and some of them are specifically designed as "holy" interiors serving the purpose of ritual and meditative communication with superior or supreme forces. In the course of these developments, many metaphysical meanings are attributed to the notion of the house.

Communication

The technical refinement and progressive sophistication of the house – its spatial and functional differentiation and multiplication – provides the human intellect with multiple resonating spaces, so to speak. The differentiated interiors turn into sheltered and protected breeding spaces for differentiated deliberations, opinion formations, and convictions that can be discussed, verified, negotiated, and eventually developed further. The house becomes a greenhouse of all sorts of communication and communicative abilities, which most certainly has a considerable impact on the behaviour of its inhabitants: It does not only advance cognitive capabilities and the accumulation of knowledge, it also leads the way to systematically organised and self-organised cooperation and collaboration. In turn, the strategies of the differentiation of labour produce more common wealth and release the necessary resources for the further acceleration of cultural, technical, and intellectual developments. If the notion of the house has not already become a notion of social and political dimensions before, it certainly does under the influence and pressure of increasing communicative means and activities that advance the conception of specific interiors and exteriors serving the specific purpose of public communication, negotiation, and trading. The respective reorganisations of political powers and hierarchies are reflected in further systemic extensions of the notion of the house.

Creativity

At this point, the different development stages of the notion cannot be subjected to a reasonable consecutive order anymore. Along with the increase and differentiation of communicative activities, the variety of different functions and technical enhancements of different types of private and public and representational houses get more numerous and complex, all the more because they have to meet all the requirements of growing communities. And the more differentiated and complex they get, the more the inhabitants are relieved from activities concerning the primary necessities of life. For the most part, the excess capacities are used for luxurious and creative activities, which leads to even more specifically equipped rooms and houses for handcrafts and artworks, for all sorts of pleasures and entertainments, and for the first tentative steps of specified scientific research.

This explosion of creative potential definitely unleashes human beings as the luxuriating and abundance-driven beings they will be for evermore. They "grow" in almost any conceivable respect, including reproduction, consumption, and claims of space, which is rather conspicuous with regard to the ways they conceive and build their houses.

Common sense

Civilisation is on its way. Economies emerge and go through crises and through flourishing phases. Most of the urges and activities that once were tied to the sheer fight for survival have been "cultivated" or turned into activities of pleasure and luxury. Mortality rates decrease. The claims of additional spaces and resources (including the respective distribution battles) are on the rise, and so are the complexities and complications of continuously growing communities. Wars are conducted to settle these claims, and when the wars are over, contracts and agreements are negotiated and broken again. All these processes are of common interest and impact and therefore based upon common understandings of coexistence and collaboration. And since these understandings originate in the collective experience of included and excluded, shared and divided, complexed and multiplexed spaces, the notion of the house is both explicitly and implicitly applied to most strategies that are mapped out to meet the multiple challenges. The origin of these strategies survives in the many systemic and political notions and terminologies that refer to the house as an eidetic principle of social affairs.

In other words: The "common sense" upon which advanced civilisations are based is essentially grounded in the primeval experience that spatial environments can be purposively separated into respective spatial insides and outsides: in the cognitive appropriation of space that initiates both the process of the *human conditioning of space* and the ideational realisation of the *spatial condition of human beings*.[3] Evidently, they converge on the notion of houses and housings.

3 The so far ultimate inquiry into the spatial conditions of human beings and their conditioning of space is, beyond doubt, Peter Sloterdijk's trilogy *Spheres*: *Bubbles* (1998), *Globes* (1999), and *Foam* (2004), originally edited in German as *Sphären I–III*, Frankfurt a. M. 1998–2004. As the clever aestheticising of the titles suggests, Sloterdijk adopts a phenomenological approach, rooted in Heidegger's thinking and spanning existential, cosmological, and social aspects of the topic on over 2000 pages. His "story" covers all the notional, cognitive, and metaphorical aspects of the cultural and philosophical history of spatial experience, presenting an enormous number of examples, illustrations, interpretations, and applications of human housing strategies, both from a technical and an experiential point of view. However, although he ends up delivering a reasonably critical derivation, description, and analysis of the spatial conditions of contemporary "globalised" societies, he hardly draws any political conclusions. The text itself does not clearly indicate whether this is due to the humbleness of the philosopher, the discursive eclecticism of the postmodernist, or the personal political attitude of the writer. But it most certainly supports the conclusion that we are in urgent need of political (and politically applicable) comprehensions of these spatial conditions.

Society
This common sense is the foundation on which the henceforth "civilised" human beings organise to assume the form of a "society". And, as is obvious as can be, the loss of that foundation will inevitably lead to a society's collapse. The many examples in the history of civilisation could not show more clearly that such collapses are usually preceded by a *notional* regression of the above-mentioned stages. However, *in reality* the complex and fragile structures of organised societies often collapse accidentally and all of a sudden like a house of cards.

Conclusion

Quite obviously, this story, in spite or precisely because of its briefness, is meant to introduce the house as sort of a notional or cognitive vehicle advancing progressive theories and practices of spatial and eventually political *togetherness*. It is based upon the collective experiences of being inside and outside of secluded and permeable spaces, sharing interiors and exteriors, acting and interacting upon them to turn these experiences into useful and productive artefacts. Like most stories of that kind, it is highly idealistic and highly realistic at the same time. It is realistic because it relates to everyday experiences and does not contradict the historically verified processes that we can agree on even in these times of postmodern eclecticisms and opinion-driven whateverisms. On the other hand, it is idealistic because it is mainly focused on the ideas that constitute the accumulated meanings of the term as well as the notion of what a house can possibly be under given conditions. And, of course, the story conveys suggestions and implications about how and to what extent the generic notion of the house applies to present social realities.

In general terms, it implies that the ways of building and using houses indicate or even figure a respective stage of social development. This might seem trivial at first sight but it is not, especially not in the light of comprehending the house as a determinant of cultural history: The story also implies that the stage of social development is not (at least not necessarily) represented in the technical level of development or sophistication (or vice versa). It is rather represented in the level of comprehension and application of (interior and exterior) conditioning of spaces according to social structures and environmental circumstances. To allege an all too suggestive example, the justification of colonialist policies like exploitation, cultural vandalism, and genocide has – not only but substantially – been based on the ignorance with respect to this particular point. And in a broader historical view, it is an inconvenient but rather conspicuous truth that the most technically advanced houses are not necessarily inhabited by the most notionally advanced societies.

In political terms, the story suggests that we have every reason to be careful about the use and abuse of the many implications that come along with the notion of the house. The principal ideas of liberalism and socialism (which go thousands of years farther back than their modern labellings) have always been complementarily and alternately implemented in the development of that notion, at least up to the beginning of the 20th century when both socio-political principles rapidly degenerated into withdrawn contradictory ideologies beyond any reasonable foundation in social realities or on solid philosophical grounds.[4] Liberalism has downgraded its ambitions from the liberty of societies to the freedom and self-righteousness of individuals (which is an un- or even antipolitical attitude by definition), while socialism has elevated its objectives from social development on the basis of common sense to abstract and systemic ideals of mass salvation. Most obviously, neither of the principles has ever been developed far enough to meet the political – never mind the economic – challenges of the globalised world they have envisioned and implemented so effectively. That is why they have remained, against all common sense, so prone to the most dangerous and destructive plague in modern societies. Ironically enough, nationalism, a very natural but necessarily erratic concept at primitive stages of social development, invokes the very same paradigmatic notion as the liberalist and the socialist idea of a society, but as against the latter two, nationalism has always been incompatible by definition with any "global" perspective whatsoever. With regard to the irrevocably "globalised" world that we inhabit since the 18th century, it appears

4 See also *All About Space, Volume 1: The Invention of Space*, chapter IV. *The Politics of Space*. Zurich 2016.

to be reasonable to consider all these seemingly incompatible ideas in the light of their common ground: a political notion of the house that has long ago acquired global implications.

In economical terms, the story involves the fundamental correlation of economy (and economics) with the development of houses and housings; a correlation that goes far beyond the explicit etymological connection. Against this background as well as against the background of the economic principles of markets, it may be deemed maliciously cynical that in most developed countries housing has been systematically subject to economic oppression by institutional means (including, of course, all kinds of financial and real estate speculation). But, completely apart from that, the story of the notion of the house implies a specifically economic idea that could be outlined as the *ecology of appropriated spaces*, which might be worth being developed further.

Last but not least, by implying that the conception and building of houses is not only a matter of technical (and possibly aesthetical) progress but also and even primarily a matter of progressive conditionings of space in general and of living spaces in particular, the story addresses the theories and practices of architecture, which, in its modernistic and highly professionalised manifestations, is quite obviously not interested in both aspects alike. Understandably, architects cherish their artefacts as technical objects, and, of course, they love to talk and think about spaces and spatial qualities. But, as a general rule that becomes rather conspicuous in view of the imageries by which architects usually have their objects represented (in architectural photography, for example), they don't like to grapple with them as *used* and *inhabited* objects and spaces. In this regard and generally speaking on behalf of those who cannot afford to substantially influence the design and equipment of the spaces and buildings they live in, the architectural constructions and conditionings of "spatial insides in relation to their respective spatial outsides" might have quite some room for improvement these days.

In view of this last point, I get back to my initial attempts at defining a house. Did I make any progress in comprehending what a house is by now? –Theoretically, yes. But in these chatty times that allow us to impose any load of theoretical bullshit on a discourse by no other means than educated babble, I sure would appreciate it if I could transfer these theoretical basics into practical application. However, since I am neither an architect nor an estate investor, neither a politician nor an economist or a businessman, my means and resources are considerably limited in this respect. But if they were not, I might think of conceiving and building a house that fulfils all the theoretical criteria except for a particular or definite purpose. I might think of inviting as many people with as many different professional and unprofessional opinions as possible to cooperate on the project. After finishing the construction, I might leave the house to as many inhabitants of as many different interests, provenances, and social backgrounds as possible. I might even think of dismantling and rebuilding it in many different places. And I would just wait and see what happens ... –

Most probably, I would think of calling the house "HOUSE 0".

MATTHIAS MICHEL
Author, communication designer, and lecturer in design, concept development, and political economics. He studied Philosophy, Film, and History of the Arts, taking his degree with a treatise on the "Outlines of a Philosophy of Failure" at the University of Zurich. During the 1990s his work as a writer and researcher shifted from media culture and theory to theory of science and existential philosophy. In 1998 he launched a second career as a media and communication designer, winning several international awards in cooperation with Richard Feurer and Jonas Voegeli, while continuing with his scientific work at the ETH in Zurich. In 2003 he started teaching graphic, editorial, and corporate design at the University of the Arts in Zurich. As an editor and author he is particularly interested in the narrative convergence of these different fields, trying to integrate and synthesise science and fiction, design and literature, philosophy and popular culture towards a coherent history of ideas.

A HOUSE OUT OF NOISE

The beautiful noiseuse is not a picture, is not a representation, is not a work, it is the fount, the well, the black box, that includes, implies, surrounds, that is to say buries, all profiles, all appearances, all representations, the work itself.
Michel Serres, Noise.

In *Noise,* Michel Serres accompanies the writer Balzac through "The Unknown Masterwork", a story found in his work "The Human Comedy." In this story, Poussin, Pourbus, and Frendhofer, three contemporary painters (part-real, part-fictitious), aim at finding the ultimate beauty, the unknown masterwork: *La belle noiseuse.* Through these three characters, Serres unfolds multiple "ways of seeing," exploring what it means to articulate a masterpiece out of noise. I will permit myself to borrow Serres' story in order to unfold an investigation in space that questions precisely what Serres so skillfully addresses: How to articulate yet still preserve the potency of indetermination?

How to talk, then, about space: not as something that "is", but rather in terms of its ability to "potentially be"? Is space a 'thing,' or everything that it is *not* (an orchestration of indexes around a centered void)? Shall we then talk about "everything but space"? With some luck I stumbled upon an adventure, a perfect "object trouvé", or, the first in a series of experiments in space: HOUSE 1. Yet, by applying an archeological stance towards things one finds, the seemingly "already there" can be excavated. This is how the story of this house, which is not just one, but any of them, has been articulated.

Before HOUSE 1 there was something rather than nothing. Not the void, not the absolute blank, but noise, a marine sound of turbulence. A protostructure, like Proteus, god of the sea, "a god of the first water," says Serres, "a god whose name stands at the beginning." Both Proteus and protostructure undertake metamorphoses. According to Serres, "[Proteus] is animal, he can be element, water, or fire. He's inert, he's alive. He's under the beam of the beacon, he's under the veil. He knows. He's a prophet, he possesses the gift of prophecy, but refuses to answer questions. He contains all information, admits no information. He's the possible, he's chaos, he's cloud, he's background noise." Protostructure is unlike infrastructure, as it locally accommodates; yet protostructure is like infrastructure, in that it globally integrates. Protostructure forms a matrix in a placeless space: a matrice, uterus, womb, a pregnant field of the possible, a container of information, of potential form(ation)s, of forms of order.

We depart hence with software: we build with ideas and concepts, for we build only as we inhabit, and we inhabit and build in order to create place, in order to create space. A place is a singular point in the midst of noise, not isolated but "inflated", as Leibniz would have it, inflated and charged by the totality of the world that it expresses. Through these actions, places or units of existence slowly populate the protostructure. I will dare then to say that HOUSE 1 is a house made of houses, each one enclosing universes that talk to each other, and by doing so, recognising the existence of otherness. These houses trace lines and connections, laws of hostility and hospitality between one and the other; and between the individual and the collective.

HOUSE 1 has neither program nor purpose. There is no origin we can claim for it, but rather continuous acts of foundation, contracted only ephemerally and only collectively. Once cities were founded on *civitas*, or contracts establishing the collective will of a community to coexist in the same location. Then, transcending any specific community, there was the *urbs*: a generic condition founded ex-nihilo and reproduced ad infinitum, for its aim was to provide conditions for territorial expansion. HOUSE 1, like the first cities, is contractual: a politicisation of the infrastructural, a customisation of the protostructure through localised acts of acupuncture. Protostructure in Versailles, protostructure in Lausanne, the same (?) but different, they define a world in their own terms both immanently and contractually. Through contracts, we found and we find; we articulate programs as spaces of existence, we politicise what "dwells in the middle", in the interstice, the interior, the *inter-esse*.

HOUSE 1 is monomaterial yet composite. It is an attempt to transform matter into a scope of manners. Its material is not frozen, but a latent cloud of indexes in the world of wood and wooden things. Material becomes experience, only meaningful in relation to its manipulation, to a technical gesture. Your touch would be enough to guide you through its variations, hybridisations, encounters and interruptions. Solid as protostructure, fragile and bouncing on an almost 4.33 silence gap, pixelated in a (cosmic) negative sphere, ephemeral where windows are doors and doors are characters, a textured and striated tendon, white and meandering like a rabbit to be followed. And Alice does so, in a *parcours* from otherness to otherness, timeless and ageless, heterotopic. She looks from within onto a reflecting pond, an existentialist; and from without, onto a floating belvedere, small *Rückenfigur* over the landscape, a romantic. She is now utopian, and greets the sun from a panoptic garden. SImulating the world, she learns from in its phototropic movements with a machine of her own, that of mimicry. Yet, in learning, she creates as much as she destroys. She goes into the dark, sometimes a maze, sometimes a forest; the space outside the grid, outside the law, and from which, uniquely and necessarily, a new law emerges: that of reversal.

HOUSE 1 is tinkered with shamelessly, and is signed by an unspecified author. It has neither object nor subject. It is not about a house, but about the invention of a making. In *De Architecture*, Vitruvius anticipated a three-dimensional system of conception consisting of orthographia (elevation), ichnographia (plan) and scenographia (perspective). "Ichnography." says Serres, "is what is possible or knowable or producible, it is the fount of phenomena. It is the complete chain of the metamorphoses of the marine god Proteus" (or the protostructure and its field of possibilities). In order to access it we recur to the subject, its position, its point of view, its limitations: we create scenographies. "Poussin, Porbus run toward the canvas," tells Serres, "move away, bend over, right and left, up and down, they look for the habitual story line, the usual scenography."

There is a dialog that is shifting and moving, and every time it moves it creates something new. Serres writes: "[Poussin and Porbus] stand so as to see an oblique profile. As if by chance, they shall have a spot where a straight form will appear. Scenography, orthography." Scenographies overlap and a profile emerges like a quasi-object, like a 'quasi-us'. It is the orthography between all and one. The whole thing turns political; orthography establishes the rules for writing well, *civitas* those for living well together. However, the house does not attempt to clarify the voice with which its contracts are evocated. Instead, it draws attention to their evocation, motivated by a principle of unsettled identity. At the very heart of the house, a theatre retells the story over and over, as if part of a Quantum plot. Spectators are being watched, while actors observe the spectators' play. "The thing one gradually comes to find out is that one has no identity that is when one is in the act of doing anything," says Gertrude Stein. "[Masterpieces] are knowing that there is no identity and producing while identity is not. That is what a masterpiece is".

At the end of Serres' story, none of the three players saw the Ichnography only Balzac himself: "And they look, as is their wont, for a space where there is a phenomenon, a space and an incarnation, a cell and knowledge. A representation. And thus, they do not see the ichnography." Balzac secretly signed this masterpiece in a corner of the canvas, namelessly, with a footprint: the Greek *ichnos*, a trace arising from the chaos of tones and colors. The architect is no genius, but a master, re-encountering, attempting, reusing, misinterpreting. The architect speaks architecture as language, and architectonics as the re-articulation of units out of noise, without taking any given vocabulary or measure for granted.

DIANA ALVAREZ-MARIN
Architect, researcher and teaching assistant at the Chair of CAAD of the ETHZ. She is co-author of the book "A Quantum City, Mastering the generic" and is currently involved in the "Quantum City" project, around which she is developing her PhD thesis. Her research work addresses the idea of the indexical city under the light of the abundance of information and computer literacy. Diana graduated with honours from the École Nationale Supérieure d'Architecture et de Paysage de Lille, France in 2007. Her diploma work focused on the shift towards "Metapolisation", in opposition to the widely established idea of "Metropolisation" in the urban discourse. After her diploma, she collaborated with international practices such as Rem Koolhaas' O.M.A. in Rotterdam and group8 in Geneva. She completed the Master of Advanced Studies program in Computer Aided Architectural Design at ETH Zürich (2011–2012) and was a visiting researcher at the Future Cities Laboratory of the Singapore ETH Centre (2013–2016). She loves writing and thinking in both natural and programming languages.

TOGETHER

"Living with people who differ racially, ethnically, religiously or economically – is one of the most urgent challenges facing civil society today. Together argues that cooperation needs more than good will: it is a craft that requires skill, In modern society traditional bonds are waning, and we must develop new forms of secular, civic ritual that make us more skilful in living with others. From medieval guilds to today's social networks, Richard Sennett's visionary book explores the nature of cooperation, why it has become weak and how in can be strengthened."[1]

It is my great pleasure to include three excerpts from this book that is so dear to me. Sennett's account of things, times, places, and the people who made them are so fascinating and dense that each chapter, each page, and every word opens worlds and possible paths into a diversified reading of culture and in what matters for us as we negotiate the process of living together. Sennett's description of Hans Holbein's painting *The Ambassadors*, for example, is for me as exciting as diving into time – where each painted object traces lines toward a multiplicity of potential situations: lines that we ourselves have already become a part of.

Dieter Dietz.

1 Together, The Rituals, Pleasures and Politics of Cooperation, Richard Sennett, London: Penguin Books, 2013, back cover text.

Dialectic and dialogic conversations[2]

There is an analogy between the musical rehearsal and the verbal conversation, but it conceals a puzzle. Much of the actual communication between musicians consists of raised eyebrows, grunts, momentary glances and other non-verbal gestures. Again, when musicians want to explain something, they more frequently show than tell, that is, they play a particular passage to others, leaving the others to interpret what they are doing. I'd be hard pressed to explicate in words exactly what I mean when I say 'perhaps more espressivo'. Whereas, in a conversation, we need to find the words.

Still, the musical rehearsal resembles those discussions, in which the skills of listening to others become as important as making clear statements. The philosopher Bernard Williams writes scathingly about the 'fetish of assertion', that impulse to ram home your case as though its content is all that counts, Listening skills don't figure much in this kind of verbal joust; the interlocutor is meant to admire and so to agree, or to counter with equal assertiveness – the familiar dialogue of the deaf in most political debate.

And, though a speaker may express him-or herself awkwardly, the good listener cannot dwell on the sheer fact of that insufficiency. The good listener has to respond to intent, to suggestion, for the conversation to keep moving forward.

Listening carefully produces conversations of two sorts, the dialectic and the dialogic. In dialectic, as we learned in school, the verbal play of opposites should gradually build up to a synthesis; dialectic starts in Aristotle's observation in the Politics that 'though we may use the same words, we cannot say we are speaking of the same things'; the aim is to come eventually to a common understanding. Skill in practising dialectic lies in detecting what might establish that common ground.

About this skill, Theodore Zeldin writes, in a small, wise book on conversation, that the good listener detects common ground more in what another person assumes than says. The listener elaborates that assumption by putting it into words. You pick up on the

2 Together, The Rituals, Pleasures and Politics of Cooperation, Richard Sennett, London: Penguin Books, 2013, pages 18 to 20.

intention, the context, make it explicit, and talk about it. Another kind of skill appears in the Platonic dialogues, where Socrates proves a very good listener by re-stating 'in other words' what his discussants declare, but the re-statement is not exactly what they have actually said, or indeed intended. The echo is actually a displacement. This is why dialectic in Plato's dialogues does not resemble an argument, a verbal duel. The antithesis of a thesis is not 'you dumb bastard, you are wrong!' Rather, misunderstandings and cross purposes come into play, doubt is put on the table; people then have to listen harder to one another.

Something akin occurs in a musical rehearsal when a player observes, 'don't get what you are doing, does it go like this?' The re-statement makes you think again about the sound, and you may adjust as a result, but not copy what you heard. In everyday conversation, this is the sense of the common phrase 'bouncing ideas off other people'; where these verbal balls land may surprise everyone.

'Dialogic' is a word coined by the Russian literary critic Mikhail Bakhtin to name a discussion which does not resolve itself by finding common ground. Though no shared agreements may be reached, through the process of exchange people may become more aware of their own views and expand their understanding of one another. 'Professor, your top note sounds harsh' inaugurated a dialogic exchange in rehearsing the Schubert Octet. Bakhtin applied the concept of knitted-together but divergent exchange to writers like Rabelais and Cervantes, whose dialogues are just the opposite of the converging agreement in dialectic. Rabelais's characters shoot off in seemingly irrelevant directions which other characters pick up on; the discussion then thickens, the characters spurred on by one another. Sometimes great performances of chamber music convey something akin. The players do not sound entirely on the same page, the performance has more texture, more complexity, but still the players are sparking off one another – as true in classic chamber music as in jazz.

Of course, the difference between dialectic and dialogic conversation is not a matter of either/or. As in Zeldin's version of a dialectical conversation, the forward movement in dialogic conversation comes from paying attention to what another person implies but does not say; as in Socrates' cunning 'in other words', in a dialogic conversation misunderstandings can eventually clarify mutual understanding. The heart of all listening skills, though, lies in picking up on concrete details, on specifics, to drive a conversation forward. Bad listeners bounce back in generalities when they respond; they're not attending to those small phrases, facial gestures or silences which open up a discussion. In verbal conversation, as in musical rehearsal, exchanging is built from the ground up.

Inexperienced anthropologists and sociologists can suffer a peculiar challenge in conducting discussions. They are sometimes too eager to respond, going wherever their subjects lead; they do not argue, they want to show that they are responsive, that they care. A big issue lurks here. A dialogic conversation can be ruined by too much identification with the other person.

The 'Great Unsettling'
How the Reformation Transformed Cooperation[3]

In 1533, Hans Holbein the Younger finished The Ambassadors, which now hangs in London's National Gallery. The painting shows two young men who face forward; between them is a two-tiered table stuffed with things, scientific instruments on the top shelf, a lute, a case of flutes, a hymnal, a mathematics book and a hand-held globe on the bottom. The two young men are arrayed in rich robes, especially the man on the left, his body outlined in white fur edging his robe; an intricate green cloth hangs behind them; an oriental carpet is draped behind the table. Amid this sensuous profusion a disturbing object lies in the foreground: a giant disk floating at an angle, with something obscure on its surface if the painting is looked at straight on; once the viewer moves to the side, this obscure image becomes clarified as a death's head: a skull.

Holbein painted The Ambassadors just as the secular consequences of the Reformation were coming to a head in Britain. Henry VIII, in spearheading this change, was driven less by religious conviction than sexual desire; he wanted a divorce from Catherine of Aragon in order to marry Anne Boleyn, and the Church then as now, forbade divorce. Henry was willing to overthrow the old faith, and embrace new Protestant doctrine, at least nominally, to get his way. The 'ambassadors' in the painting are two young men, Jean de Dinteville and Georges de Selve, envoys sent to England by Catholic France to deal with the havoc caused by Henry VIII's marital troubles, a complex mission since Anne Boleyn had links to the French court. Holbein's painting though, represents much larger changes in early modern society's understanding of cooperation.

The open hymnal on the lower shelf marks one social consequence of the religious schism: the effort in Protestantism to reform religious ritual, so that it is more cooperative. The hymnal is open to two songs written by Martin Luther (on the left 'Come sacred spirit', on the right 'Man, if thou would live a good life and remain with God'). Both hymns celebrate renunciation of the flesh; Henry VIII would

3 Together, The Rituals, Pleasures and Politics of Cooperation, Richard Sennett, London: Penguin Books, 2013, pages 96 to 99.

have been unlikely to sing them fervently. Luther meant these hymns also to serve new church rituals that would bind congregants together more strongly than the old. He used simple words written in the native language congregants spoke, rather than in refined Latin, the language of the clergy; the bibles he used were printed, making them widely accessible. In these ways, Luther sought to strengthen religious community, a community in which all could directly and equally share their faith.

The tools which appear on the top shelf of the table in Holbein's painting signal a change in the organization of workshops. These are the precision tools pilots used to convert information about the heavens into precise mathematical calculations. There is a compound solar viewer used to calculate sunlight and solar time; a sextant used to locate the sun's position in the sky; a nine-sided object resembling a spinning toy, each face etched with circles measuring angles in different ways, used to reckon space in different configurations. All are tools used by navigator-explorers to chart unknown regions of the world, tools with political value, since they would assist Europe's project of conquering new territories, but which the first explorers did not understand very well how to use. These instruments on Holbein's table are products of a new kind of workshop, the technical laboratory, a workshop which would alter how artisans practised cooperation.

Then there are the two young men themselves. They were not in fact professional diplomats, which is odd, since diplomacy was in the process of becoming an organized profession. The profession took form around resident ambassadors, served by a newly articulated bureaucracy of consuls, secretaries and double agents. These young men were envoys called in as auxiliaries during a crisis. Though specialized, the diplomatic profession had a wider resonance in European Culture because of the ways diplomats conducted conversations. Up to about 1500, Latin was the language of European diplomacy as of the clergy; now French began to be spoken as well, a French which combined vernacular, everyday forms of expression with diplomacy's formal codes of address. In the same way that theatrical speech served as a model for discussion in eighteenth-century coffee houses, so in the sixteenth century diplomatic French spread like an ink-blot into ordinary social conversation. Speech which combined the formal and the colloquial migrated from embassies to aristocratic salons; in time, the language of salons migrated further into sitting rooms of bourgeois life.

The spread of diplomatic speech into everyday life may seem a small footnote in the history of European civilization. But it was in fact one sign of a sea-change in sociable behaviour: the shift from chivalry to civility. Chivalric values were woven tight into the fabric of aristocratic life; civilized codes were rooted in professional conduct, a profession requiring skill, a skill that non-professionals could learn and practise. Civility, moreover, generated new ethics of sociability, of how people ought to behave; these ethical standards applied particularly to the practice of cooperation.

Historians are rightly suspicious of strict periods like Medieval, Renaissance and Reformation; these are arbitrary divisions of time. And yet history is not a continuous flow; as in natural time, human history has punctuating moments. Apart from its beauty, The Ambassadors is an iconic painting in that it marks three great changes in European society in the sixteenth century. These were the transformation of rituals in religion; changing practices of material production; and the appearance of a new ethics for sociability. Holbein's painting signals turning points in all three ways people cooperated at the dawn of the modern era.

The artist was not simply a recorder. At the bottom of the canvas, the death's head makes one comment. This skull can be seen only by stepping sideways, a painterly technique called anamorphosis. When looked at from the side all the other objects and the people in the painting become flat and distorted. Death's heads were a traditional symbol of the vanity of human wishes. The lute makes another comment on the times; it has a broken string, another traditional symbol of discord. More novel was the mathematics book, written by Peter Apian in 1527, On Mercantile Calculations, open to a page on 'division'. The effect of all three is unsettling, but Holbein was a painter, not a preacher. Looked at straight on, the people and the objects on the table are arresting and beautiful in themselves; in the same spirit, let's look directly at each element in this great icon.

The Workshop[4]

The navigation equipment on Holbein's table represented a great change in productive life. This was the expansion of workshops organized as guilds to include workshops more like laboratories. This change gathered force during the three generations before Luther nailed his 95 Theses to a church door in 1517, and has endured ever since. Cooperation in the making of new sorts of technologies and things was also an unsettling transition to modernity; it posed the question of how people should cooperate in discovery and experiment – Google Wave's question.

The workshop, as noted in Chapter I, is one of the oldest institutions of human society. One reason it is so old has to do with where artisanal labour gets done. The traces of workshops from six thousand years ago in Mesopotamia show that shared labour had become rooted to one place. Like farming, the artisanal workshop terminated the wandering way of life; while nomadic tribes scavenged, workshops produced their own sustenance. Chinese written records from the second millennium BC predicted that such settled labour would become ever more skilful than the work of nomads, the urban potter a better craftsman than his wandering counterpart. Part of the reason for this belief lay in the artisan's tools, which became ever bigger, heavier and more complicated, and so more difficult to transport. An example is the city potter's wheel, which replaced the itinerant potter's upturned gourd.

If we make a big jump in time up to the medieval period, the articulated skills of the urban craftsman had found a bureaucratic base in guilds. As cities renewed in Europe from the eleventh century on, they transformed the monastic workshop. The economic life of the city depended on producing more than the producers themselves needed. Each city sold the surplus on to people in other cities, inter-city trade becoming ever more important than intra-city commerce. Individual workshops produced the surplus; guilds orchestrated how these goods were fed into the system of trade.

4 Together, The Rituals, Pleasures and Politics of Cooperation, Richard Sennett, London: Penguin Books, 2013, pages 109 to 111.

The workshops had to practise efficient internal coordination if they were to provide for more than local needs. That was in large part a matter of organizing men's time. The monastery day had mixed labour, whether in the garden or in sheltered workshops, with long periods of shared prayer and solitary contemplation, but producing a surplus of things for the trading economy required more sheer hours at the bench. Moreover, innovation of a sort was required in the work itself. The urban workshop developed greater skill in the practice of old crafts. Goldsmithing in the twelfth century and glass-making in the fourteenth evolved new skills, thanks to the appearance of complicated tools. Pottery-making, the most ancient of all crafts, required the same sorts of implements in 1300 as the great potters of antiquity had wielded, but potters now experimented with different sorts of clay. Urban workshops emphasized efficiency, necessary to produce surplus, a subject for which the Old Testament provided no guidance. Still, the spiritual equation did not disappear in the medieval market economy. Labour remained God-sanctioned in principle, the Church remained an authority presiding over economic power. But the monastic refuge ceased to provide an adequate everyday model for social relations in the urban workshop.

Guilds managed conflict between competing workshops, and issued guarantees that goods were genuinely what the makers claimed them to be. Most important, they enforced labour rights protecting workers, especially young workers, from some of the physical abuse and exploitation which occurred in slave or serf communities. Each workshop contained three levels of worker, who all lived on the premises: apprentices whose contracts ran usually for seven years, journeymen whose contracts ran for three, and masters who permanently owned the operation.

These dry elements of structure came to life through the rituals which guilds evolved. In the city's parades and feasts, apprentices carried the guild's flags; all guild members were entitled to wear distinctive, often elaborate clothes. Within each workshop, ritual paid a special kind of tribute to skill. The apprentice presented at the end of his training a piece of work called the chef d'œuvre which showed to the workshop what he could achieve so far. The chef d'œuvre was sometimes then exhibited in the guild hall, to be commented upon by anyone in the city; up the workshop ladder, the journeyman presented a more advanced chef d'œuvre to a community composed only of masters.

The young apprentice or journeyman was not allowed to speak or explain; the maker's personality didn't enter the picture; the rituals aimed at judgement of a man-made object on its own merits, and the object had to speak for itself. Our medieval forebears went about establishing the objective fact of quality through discussions aiming at consensus, though in a peculiar form of speech-act. The standard form of address used for objects was 'you' rather than 'it'. Medieval craft-speech took this verbal locution one step further; the objects were treated as if alive, as though they had been magically transformed into beings with whom one discussed and disputed.

The ritual of the chef d'œuvre may thus seem a kind of spectacle akin to theatrical spectacles in the religious sphere. But there was a big difference. At parades or inside churches, congregants fell silent in the presence of the religious performers; here, the audience spoke up; they were judges rather than spectators. Religion imbued every aspect of medieval life, so that there was no deep schism between how people prayed and how they worked; the workshop emphasized shared critical thinking in these rituals judging the worth of things, however, while religious spectacle did not.

We might imagine, that rituals would prove socially divisive because the judges could decide the work wasn't good enough. But in fact these were win-win exchanges. Most objects made by apprentices and journeymen usually passed the test – in the metal-working trades c. AD 1200 nearly 90 per cent did, in Italian leather trades at the same time about 80 per cent did (these can be only very rough numbers). The makers of things judged not sufficiently 'lively' had a second, and more rarely a third, chance to try again the year following, The pass rate may seem to render test-day a fraud. Not at all. The event exemplifies the classic rite-of-passage ritual: a young person is taken outside himself, exposed to danger, then reconfirmed as a valued member of the community. In medieval craftsmanship, the maker's things took this journey for him.

RICHARD SENNETT
Richard Sennett has explored how individuals and groups make social and cultural sense of material facts – about the cities in which they live and about the labour they do. He focuses on how people can become competent interpreters of their own experience, despite the obstacles society may put in their way. His research entails ethnography, history, and social theory. As a social analyst, Mr. Sennett continues the pragmatist tradition begun by William James and John Dewey.
His first book, The Uses of Disorder [1970] looked at how personal identity takes form in the modern city. He then studied how working-class identities are shaped in modern society, in The Hidden Injuries of Class, written with Jonathan Cobb. [1972] A study of the public realm of cities, The Fall of Public Man, appeared in 1977; at the end of this decade of writing, Mr. Sennett sought to account the philosophic implications of this work in Authority [1980].

At this point he took a break from sociology, composing three novels: The Frog who Dared to Croak [1982], An Evening of Brahms [1984] and Palais Royal [1987]. He then returned to urban studies with two books, The Conscience of the Eye, [1990], a work focusing on urban design, and Flesh and Stone [1992], a general historical study of how bodily experience has been shaped by the evolution of cities.

In the mid 1990s, as the work-world of modern capitalism began to alter quickly and radically, Mr. Sennett began a project charting its personal consequences for workers, a project which has carried him up to the present day. The first of these studies, The Corrosion of Character, [1998] is an ethnographic account of how middle-level employees make sense of the "new economy." The second in the series, Respect in a World of Inequality, [2002] charts the effects of new ways of working on the welfare state; a third, The Culture of the New Capitalism, [2006] provides an overview of change. Most recently, Mr. Sennett has explored more positive aspects of labor in The Craftsman [2008], and in Together: The Rituals, Pleasures and Politics of Cooperation [2012]. The third volume in this trilogy, The Open City, will appear in 2016.

Among other awards, Richard Sennett has received the Hegel and Spinoza Prizes and an honorary degree from the University of Cambridge.
(Source: https://www.richardsennett.com)

0 0 : 0 0

Dieter Dietz (DD)

Bienvenue à cette seconde partie du symposium sur le thème de la pédagogie[1]. Pourquoi avons-nous monté ce programme? Pourquoi le fait de construire un projet avec deux cents personnes propose l'hypothèse principale que nous faisons pour l'enseignement de cette première année?

On discutera quelques questions qui me semblent très importantes: Comment comprendre l'architecture non comme quelque chose qui s'enseigne de manière unilatérale mais justement qui se partage?

Cette discussion, à laquelle ne participeront pas seulement nos experts invités – Diana Alvarez-Marin (DAM), Jeanne Wéry (JW) et Cédric Libert (CL) – mais également toute l'équipe du laboratoire ALICE et bien sûr vous-mêmes [students], sera modérée par Daniel Zamarbide (DZ), à qui je passe la parole.

0 5 : 1 7

DZ

L'idée d'aujourd'hui est que l'on réfléchisse un peu à ce que l'on a fait ensemble. Ensemble, c'est un bien grand mot bien sûr puisque moi-même je n'ai pas construit quoi que ce soit [laughs], mais ensemble quand même puisque nous représentons le lien avec l'institution. On a beaucoup parlé de ce qu'il s'est passé sur le chantier, mais on a aussi constaté une transformation marquante des studios de projet en atelier de production, presque corporative, au sens entrepreneurial du terme. J'aimerais de plus proposer quelques réflexions non pas sur la manière dont on peut, nous, vous "éduquer" mais plutôt comment vous voulez vous éduquer vous-mêmes et quel parcours vous avez envie de faire pour apprendre l'architecture. Suggestion: (...) J'aimerais de plus proposer quelques réflexions – non pas sur notre manière d'enseigner – mais plutôt sur la manière dont vous souhaitez être éduqués et quel parcours vous avez envie de suivre pour apprendre l'architecture. Une bonne partie des personnes présentes ici sortent d'autres écoles où elles ont appris l'architecture de manière très différente, mais nous sommes finalement tous architectes et faisons à peu de choses près la même chose. On enseigne traditionnellement l'architecture de manière très différente, mais alors quels sont les outils? Devons-nous savoir construire, dessiner, réfléchir? Quels sont les acquis que l'on doit posséder à la fin de notre parcours? Quel type d'architecte voulez-vous être? Quel est le métier que vous voulez fabriquer? Ce sont des questions que vous devez vous poser, car il n'y a pas un seul métier d'architecte et l'architecture est une discipline toujours en mutation. Voilà les deux pistes de réflexions que je peux lancer, mais je passe la parole à nos invités.

0 8 : 5 8

CL

Personnellement ce que je trouve saisissant quand je vois un projet comme HOUSE 1, construit par deux cents personnes, c'est la disparition de la notion d'auteur, ou la mort de l'egotrip [sic] de l'architecte. Je pense que c'est un sujet très actuel qu'il est tout à fait valable d'évoquer et que je trouve tout à fait intéressant de projeter comme modèle d'enseignement ou même comme processus. C'est l'idée du faire, la chose s'est fabriquée en se faisant et par l'action de ceux qui l'ont construite. Ce que je trouve intéressant, c'est que c'est justement la fin du modèle comme finalité, la fin des dogmatismes, des mandarinismes aussi parfois, que pose la démarche d'un enseignement expérimental comme celui-là. A l'inverse d'une pédagogie dogmatique, où la finalité est identifiée rapidement et où tout le processus consiste à s'en rapprocher, il n'y a ici qu'un chemin très ouvert qui permet selon moi d'engager un rapport beaucoup plus frontal avec des notions de complexité. Cette

1 The first part took place on June 1st 2016, during the first day of the HOUSE 1 project final critics.

complexité c'est l'état insaisissable du monde qui nous entoure; la modernité attendait de la saisir, la postmodernité a tenté de la saisir et aujourd'hui, au fond, elle est en train de nous échapper de plus en plus. Sur ce constat, il me semble nécessaire de repenser nos démarches d'apprentissage du monde, et l'idée d'un système très ouvert, basé sur une non-finalité, me paraît être opportun. Je conclurai avec ces phrases de John Cage dans lesquelles il associe la démarche expérimentale à un processus dont on ignore fondamentalement la finalité, ce qu'il a toujours appliqué dans sa vie et dans son travail: "I'm trying to be unfamiliar with what I'm doing"; "the highest purpose in life is to have no purpose at all"[2].

11:39

DAM

Il dit aussi: "Nothing is a mistake. There's no win and no fail, there's only make", phrase qui fait partie des dix règles pour étudiants et professeurs[3].

11:49

CL

Oui c'est la troisième que je cherchais. Voilà, je retrouve un peu cet héritage, celui du John Cage performeur, certes musicien, mais aussi professeur, l'homme du Black Mountain College, dans ce que vous faites.

12:05

DZ

Du coup, je vais me permettre d'enchaîner sur le Black Moutain College qui fait, selon moi, partie de ces institutions importantes qui pourraient incarner le contre-exemple de l'EPFL. Je voudrais l'introduire par un artiste particulier, Kenneth Snelson. Vous n'en avez sans doute jamais entendu parler, comme la plupart des gens, puisqu'il s'est fait voler son brevet par un autre personnage que vous connaissez peut-être, qui est Richard Buckminster Fuller. Mais Kenneth Snelson est l'artiste qui a découvert et développé le principe structurel de Tensegrity au Black Mountain College. J'aime l'idée qu'au sein d'une école qui prône une pédagogie purement expérimentale, en manipulant la structure sans but on aboutit à une méthode scientifique de calcul. Tensegrity est un système de tubes métalliques rigides et de câbles qui fonctionne tout autant en tension qu'en compression, et dont Kenneth Snelson faisait des sculptures. Ce système sera repris par Cedric Price et bien sûr par Buckminster Fuller, mais je trouve vraiment intéressant qu'il trouve son origine dans un processus de recherche expérimental et artistique. Le Black Mountain College, pour faire court, est une école qui a vécu assez peu de temps, entre 1933 – ce qui correspond avec la fin du Bauhaus – et 1957. Fondée par Joseph Albers, c'est une école dont la vocation était d'enseigner les arts, l'architecture et la musique, en se basant sur un système de workshop, sans cursus ou formation définie. On y a vu John Cage, Merce Cunningham et Buckminster Fuller pour les plus connus, mais aussi Willen de Kooning ou Robert Motherwell. De brefs passages mais intensément productifs, et comme une utopie, je trouve très intéressant ce lieu d'enseignement qui, comme le Bauhaus avant lui, ne vit que sur une courte période mais laisse des traces fondamentales pour la pédagogie.

15:04

DAM

Moi j'aimerais revenir sur ce que tu as dit en discutant de trois points, trois concepts dans la conception architecturale. Tout d'abord la rencontre. Donc par rapport à ce que tu disais, Picasso disait: "Je ne cherche pas, je trouve"[4]. C'est-à-dire que tu chemines le long d'un processus dont tu ne connais pas l'issue mais tu continues et tu fais avec ce que tu trouves en route, en concevant la vulnéra-

2 John Cage, On Robert Rauschenberg, Artist, and his Work', in Metro, Milan, 1961; John Cage, Silence: Lectures and Writings, Middletown: Wesleyan University Press, 1961.

3 Some Rules for students and Teachers, attributed to John Cage, in Learning by Heart: Teachings to Free the Creative Spirit, Corita Kent and Jan Steward, New-York: Allworth Press, 2008.

4 Attributed to Pablo Picasso, in Les quatre fondamentaux de la psychanalyse, Jacques Lacan, Paris: Editions du Seuil, 1973.

bilité de l'inconnu comme une force. L'apprentissage "en faisant" amène alors à une disposition féconde de l'esprit. D'autre part, la tentative, ou bien le sens du possible, voir toute création comme l'invention d'un "faire", c'est-à-dire sans arriver avec une méthode préétablie mais vraiment quelque chose qui émerge de toutes les tentatives. Enfin la reprise, ou la méprise, ou le téléphone arabe, c'est-à-dire la puissance de la réinterprétation ou bien le recyclage ou même le vol parfois; voler des concepts, articuler de nouvelles choses, bricoler sans vergogne, en utilisant le réemploi ou bien le contre-emploi comme variation, hybridation, subversion. Gilles Deleuze disait qu'il fallait faire des enfants sur le dos des autres et affirmait aussi que l'histoire de la philosophie était basée sur un séquençage de "mésinterprétations" des concepts. Je pense donc qu'on n'invente pas, on articule.

1 7 : 4 5

DZ

On va reprendre tous ces points mais j'aimerais interroger d'abord les directeurs de studio, ou même les étudiants, à propos de cette question de subversion. Parce que c'est toujours assez dangereux, selon moi, ces petits jeux : nous sommes tous des professeurs, au sein d'une grande institution, et nous passons notre temps à dire à tout le monde qu'il faut être subversif, ne pas écouter les règles, le système... La construction de HOUSE 1 représente beaucoup de moyens, pas seulement pour la construction, mais aussi pour que vous puissiez avoir des locaux, disposer du temps, des outils, des enseignants, ce qui peut nous laisser en proie à certaines utopies. Mais alors comment opère-t-on cette articulation entre confort et subversion?

1 9 : 0 4

Wynd van der Woude (WW)

Je ne suis pas tout à fait d'accord, dans le sens où je pense que tu mélanges certaines choses. J'ai l'impression que bien avant la situation, certes particulière ici en Suisse et qui nous a sans doute permis de faire les choses ainsi, c'est avant tout une question d'expérience. Une expérience du laboratoire ALICE qui s'est forgée à travers une série de workshops et de constructions. Ensuite l'équipe, qui compte les enseignants, évidemment sous l'impulsion de Dieter, mais aussi un très grand nombre d'étudiants, rendu possible par la configuration bien particulière de la première année d'étude ici, à l'EPFL. Si je dis ça c'est parce que je pense que même avant ALICE, la première année a toujours eu une force considérable due à la particularité que je vois ici de pouvoir travailler avec deux cents personnes, dans des configurations différentes, mais aussi dans une même direction. Alors je pense que si le projet a pu voir le jour tel qu'il est, c'est avant tout une question d'expérience et d'énergie.

2 0 : 2 5

DZ

Mais qu'est-ce qui fait qu'on ne retrouve pas ce genre d'expérience après? En deuxième, troisième, quatrième, cinquième année? Ou à Versailles ou à Madrid?

Justement les écoles dont on parlait un peu plus tôt, comme le Black Mountain College, sont des écoles qui avaient déjà au début du XXème siècle une manière d'enseigner très inductive, ce qui revient aujourd'hui dans certaines écoles quelque peu progressistes. Par induction, c'est-à-dire qu'on va faire monter durant toute une année une pièce de théâtre à des enfants de 13 ans, à partir de laquelle on va enseigner les mathématiques, l'anglais, la physique... Je n'aime pas le mot solution dans la relation problème-solution, donc ici on va plutôt trouver les outils pour répondre à un certain nombre de questions; c'est ce que je définis par méthode inductive et c'est, il me semble, un peu ce que l'on fait en première année. Mais là où je pense qu'il y a une barrière c'est dans la relation avec la structure institutionnelle, car ces écoles-là demeuraient privées et ainsi libérées de la question du diplôme et de la validation des acquis.

2 2 : 0 1

Nicolas Dürr (ND)

Il me semble quand même qu'il ne faut pas perdre de vue l'aspect politique, car ce sont des institutions qui sont restées assez fermées de ce fait…

2 2 : 1 1

Agathe Mignon (AM)

Pour finir, je crois qu'il s'agit d'accepter une certaine instabilité. Comme tu le disais dans ton introduction, il me semble que l'on considère chez ALICE depuis déjà plusieurs années que l'exercice ne consiste pas à amener deux cents personnes à un résultat final dont on connait la finalité, mais plutôt que c'est l'ensemble des résultats qui va créer le résultat. Qu'il soit bon ou mauvais, il va constituer une quantité de réponses. Par contre, on admet jusqu'à la fin l'instabilité due à la méconnaissance de la forme ou de l'apparence du résultat.

2 3 : 0 0

DD

Un aspect qui me semble en tout cas important, c'est que je ne pense pas que cela soit subversif. Personnellement je pense simplement que c'est une attitude qui ne rentre pas nécessairement dans un rapport de confrontation. Je pense qu'il y a des approches très diverses pour apprendre à apprendre, pour justement être capable de faire des choix; nous avons choisi de les mettre en évidence, mais ce n'est pas la seule manière de le faire. Un autre message fondamental aussi, qui me fait également dire que ce n'est pas subversif, c'est que cette instabilité est allégée par une certaine résilience grâce à une structure précise. Même si elle est très ouverte, cette structure apporte une certaine confiance non dans le résultat exact mais dans la capacité d'y parvenir.

2 5 : 2 8

CL

Moi je pense que si tout le monde se mettait à faire ça, en effet cela deviendrait de fait un nouveau dogmatisme. Comme tu le dis, c'est bien que cela existe en complément d'autres manières d'enseigner tout à fait différentes. Ce n'est jamais qu'un jeu, dont les règles, si elles sont différentes, produisent des choses différentes. Il ne faudrait pas qu'elles soient récurrentes en donnant chaque année la même chose. Il y a d'autres formes de prises de risque, qui selon moi sont nécessaires à l'appréhension de la complexité du monde, peut-être plus conceptuelles ou plus intellectuelles; peut-être pourrait-on faire un atelier entièrement basé sur le voyage, sans aller à l'école pendant un an, ou en se collant toutes les règles du Neufert[5] et essayer de voir ce que ça produit, enfin il y a trente-six manières d'enseigner je pense…

2 6 : 2 6

Edouard Cabay (EC)

Tout à l'heure on a utilisé le mot indétermination, que je trouve être un mot intéressant. Ce que je trouve intéressant c'est que l'indétermination, elle se produit ou elle est rendue possible seulement quand elle est inscrite dans un jeu de règles, seulement, je pense, dans un cadre défini. Ma relation avec ALICE a débuté avec la découverte d'un environnement hyper structuré, dans lequel on a un programme, dans lequel on a des règles, dans lequel on reçoit des baguettes en bois, dans lequel on reçoit des crayons, on reçoit des scies japonaises, tout est rythmé, tout est défini. Alors au début je me suis dit: "mais comment est-ce qu'on va faire ici pour faire quelque chose de différent de mon voisin?". Ce que je trouve intéressant, c'est la structure commune qui est mise en place, puis confrontée à douze studios, à douze directeurs de studio, à douze groupes d'étudiants,

5 Neufert, Architects' Data (german: Bauentwurfslehre), first published by Ernst Neufert, Berlin: BauweltVerlag, 1936.

tout autant d'individus qui vont essayer d'en produire leur propre interprétation.

Nous avons eu cette discussion avec Agathe où on s'interrogeait sur le fil conducteur qui pourrait permettre de relier les différentes années d'enseignement d'ALICE, sur ce que l'on retrouve de commun. HOUSE 1 le définit très bien. C'est un système concret, puisqu'il est matériel, structurel, puisqu'il est dimensionné, et c'est un système abstrait puisqu'il a énormément d'influence sur la manière dont on dessine, dont on pense et comprend l'espace. Cette année ça s'appelle une proto-structure, l'année dernière ça s'appelait un champ, ou encore une matrice. Il y a maintenant une collection de ces éléments, qui ont permis à chaque fois de construire un jeu de règles.

Pour remettre ces expériences dans une perspective pédagogique, je ferai simplement un parallèle avec l'école de la AA[6], dans laquelle plusieurs d'entre nous ont étudié. C'est une école basée sur un système de workshops, donc très similaire à ce qui se passe ici, dans lequel divers groupes formés d'un professeur et d'une douzaine d'étudiants explorent un sujet en profondeur sur l'espace d'un an. Ce système permet d'aller très loin dans la recherche, mais à la différence de l'unité d'enseignement d'ALICE, les studios de la AA ne sont pas connectés les uns avec les autres. Il n'y a pas le programme, la vision ou le positionnement qui est pris ici et qui permet, à la manière d'un filet, aux différents studios de travailler chacun à leur manière mais dans la même direction.

3 0 : 3 7

WW

Juste pour rebondir sur la question de la structure. En comparant avec d'autres modèles d'enseignement, tout du moins ce que j'ai pu rencontrer ici, j'ai l'impression que dans cet environnement très structuré ce qui est donné finalement à "challenger" aux étudiants, c'est l'aspect culturel. Car ce qui est particulier, pour avoir enseigné ici pendant plusieurs années, c'est que les éléments structurés sont encore libres de toute interprétation culturelle, et c'est ce que l'enseignant va amener, apporter avec lui. Paradoxalement, ces éléments, bien que relativement abstraits, ne sont pas complètement neutres et opèrent ainsi quand même sur le processus de développement du projet lui-même, et c'est beaucoup plus sur ce processus que sur l'aspect culturel que porte le programme...

3 1 : 0 0

DD

Je voudrais rajouter quelque chose là-dessus. La première fois qu'on a expérimenté une telle structure, c'était la première fois qu'on faisait la première année, certaines personnes sont d'ailleurs encore là. Nous avons posé l'hypothèse de donner un espace d'intervention superposé. Cette superposition, par la nature même de la gravité, a automatiquement engendré des discours de négociation de l'espace : "si je suis au-dessus il y a quelque chose qui se passe, si je suis en-dessous ce sera différent, etc." Ce n'est donc pas un terrain libre à acquérir mais à négocier. Je vais citer Richard Sennett à ce sujet, parce qu'il dit quelque chose de très intéressant dans son livre Together[7]. A la notion d'intégration, il oppose le terme de négociation, au sens de négociation d'un espace qui est celui des différences sociales, et ça me semble fondamental dans le contexte actuel.

3 3 : 5 6

DZ

Mais pour revenir sur ce que vous dites tous les deux, si je comprends bien c'est que malgré la présence de la structure, on ne sait pas du tout ce qu'il faut faire? [WW : exact] Pour moi c'est comme l'incarnation d'une espèce de structure surréaliste, tu vois, comme si on vous donnait un million de pommes et vous devez construire une maison. Et puis vu

6 Architectural Association, school of Architecture, London (UK).

7 Richard Sennett, Together, The rituals, Pleasures and Politics of Cooperation, London : Penguin Books, 2013.

qu'il y a des pommes il faut faire avec les pommes, et puis on vous donne des scies japonaises pour couper les pommes [laughs]. C'est-à-dire que sans finalité précise, on va vous apprendre à manipuler dans un contexte donné des outils pour aboutir à quelque chose ensemble. Et puis ça se fait comme ça, en évoluant en cours de route pour aboutir à quelque chose!

3 4 : 5 8

AM

Parce qu'il n'y a pas de modèle. Il n'y a pas de problème qui exige de réponse, il y a un programme qui pose des questions. Et vu qu'il n'y a pas de finalité formelle, je pense personnellement qu'il est impossible de faire pareil que son voisin, chacun arrivant avec ses propres prérequis.

3 5 : 3 8

Patricia Guaita (PG)

Moi je pense quand même que le programme donne une atmosphère, en donnant certaines règles. Après le fait qu'on reste très libre je ne crois pas, et je pense peut-être qu'on n'est pas tellement expérimental non plus... Je me demande quelquefois si ce que l'on fait c'est vraiment une expérimentation? Je ne sais pas, c'est une question que je me pose. Quand j'étais à Valparaiso, là j'avais le sentiment que c'était une expérimentation, les enseignants vivent sur place, ça c'est une utopie. [DZ: utopie et expérimentation, ce n'est pas la même chose] Non mais pour te dire que moi je trouve que c'est une expérimentation, c'est que cela fait quatre ans que nous y allons pour des workshops et, même si l'école n'est pas dans sa meilleure période, ils font des constructions à l'échelle 1:1 tous les ans... Voilà je ne sais pas si c'est expérimental, ni si ce que nous avons fait ici l'est, mais je pense dans tous les cas que ce n'est pas à nous de le dire.

D'ailleurs j'attribuerais plutôt ça à une chance énorme. Je ne sais pas si c'est une expérimentation ou pas, mais je te dis que d'avoir, en tant qu'étudiant de première année, pu expérimenter des conditions de chantier, de collaboration, mais aussi comprendre la continuité extrêmement forte qu'il y a entre une idée, son dessin, sa construction, que l'on a pu tester et même habiter, ça c'est une véritable chance.

3 8 : 0 2

LC

Pour moi, le jour où quelque chose vient à ne pas marcher, ça devient véritablement une expérimentation. Enfin je pense qu'une des données fondamentales, c'est que si on fait ce qu'on appelle une expérimentation, alors ça veut dire que cela peut rater aussi, et ça n'a pas raté. Par ailleurs, cela reste une question, mais est-ce qu'on laisse suffisamment de place pour l'erreur ou pas?

3 8 : 4 1

Rémy Meylan (RM)

Je pense qu'il y a eu des erreurs, et je trouve ça extrêmement bien parce que tout le monde les a vues, tout le monde les a vécues. Je crois aussi que vous avez justement bien compris que ce que vous faites, chaque coup de crayon que vous avez tracé, chaque décision que vous avez prise, ont eu une très grande influence et de nombreuses répercussions sur le résultat final. Et je trouve ça vraiment important. Durant mon propre parcours, j'ai commencé tout en bas de l'échelle, à porter des briques sur un chantier, à porter des poutres, puis j'ai commencé à fabriquer des choses et je suis même allé un peu plus haut en travaillant directement avec des architectes. Le métier d'architecte est un métier de manager et je pense que c'est extrêmement difficile de prendre des décisions ou de faire des choix lorsqu'on ne les a pas expérimentés soi-même, ou que l'on ne mesure pas leur implication dans la réalité de la construction. Je ne sais pas si effectivement c'est une nécessité d'être aussi proche de cette réalité tout au long de votre cursus mais je pense que c'est primordial, et même essentiel de l'avoir vécu une fois.

3 9 : 4 1
Anne-Chantal Rufer (ACR)

Et de le faire comme première expérience de l'architecture. C'est un éveil à des notions qui sont normalement absentes du cursus scolaire et qui me semblent riches pour construire ensuite soi-même son parcours.

4 0 : 1 0
Andrea Pellacani (AP)

Pour compléter tout ce qui a été dit jusqu'à maintenant, j'évoquerai la notion de responsabilité. Je pense que la configuration très horizontale de l'équipe ALICE implique d'investir les différents directeurs de studio d'une grande responsabilité. De plus, le fait d'aboutir à la question du 1:1 renforce encore plus cette question de responsabilité, je dis responsabilité mais peut-être qu'on pourrait appeler ça conscience. Je rejoins aussi ce que disait Wynd sur l'aspect culturel, par rapport aussi à la méthode d'enseignement d'un savoir collectif. Je dis ça parce que j'ai l'impression qu'à travers ce transfert de responsabilité au sein de l'équipe puis entre les étudiants avec cette conscience commune du projet et de la construction, on assiste à un renversement du schéma historique, pyramidal, de transmission du savoir. Même si je pense que ce transfert s'effectue aussi par les méthodes, telles que l'artisanat, il est pour moi dû à cette conscience. Je crois que c'est Loos qui disait que la différence entre un artiste et un architecte, c'est que l'architecte a devant lui la responsabilité du monde…

4 2 : 1 5
EC

Mais par rapport à quelque chose que tu disais hier [DZ], quand tu évoquais le fait qu'à la fin d'une année, tu pouvais déjà prétendre avoir "fait" de l'architecture ou commencé à en comprendre la finalité, je voudrais simplement ajouter que – cela fait dix ans que nous sommes architectes, non? Puisqu'on est sorti au même moment toi et moi? Moi, à chaque fois que je commence un nouveau projet, je ne sais toujours pas comment être réellement architecte, ou quand quelqu'un me demande comment je travaille, c'est impossible à définir…

4 3 : 0 4
Laura Perez Lupi (LPL)

This year you [students] have learnt how to dive. During the first semester you were equipped with the necessary skills. Second semester you have been plunged straight into the water. It was about 'surviving'; you didn't even have time to think. The first immersion happened when you were provided with the protostructure and you had to draw it in 1/20. Then you built it in 1/10. Afterwards you jumped into the 1/5 and suddenly you found yourself confronted with the 1/1. You couldn't escape anymore, but thanks to all these 'jumps', you have developed a kind of cellular intelligence, it is now inherent in your body, in your muscles. Now it is up to you how to develop it. Even if you have been trained under the same process you can now dive into a large range of underwater landscapes and enjoy them in a unique and personal way.

4 4 : 5 6
Margherita Del Grosso (MDG)

I think it is about choosing the perspective properly. I think there is a lot of diversity in what we do, in the ways we work. They touch, they merge and they generate a new dialogue, which I think is quite interesting. We are 12, and those 12 come together and in the end we get to the very rich point we can see in HOUSE 1.

4 6 : 2 4
DZ

A quel point, question pour les directeurs de studio, à quel point ne sommes-nous pas réactionnaires? Je ne sais plus qui a dit ça : "C'est tellement XIXème siècle!", je crois que c'est toi Dieter en observant les travaux du studio Lupi. On construit quelque chose d'immense à la manière de "cavemans", de fait ne sommes-nous pas en train de donner des outils qui n'appartiennent pas complètement à la contemporanéité?

4 7 : 0 1

PG

Mais qu'est-ce que c'est la contemporanéité? [laughs]

4 7 : 1 2

JW

Si je peux réagir à ça, je pense que ce n'est pas une question d'outils. Oui bien sûr être sur le chantier c'est important, mais je crois que beaucoup plus que scier du bois ou construire quelque chose, c'est une structure mentale que l'on tente de développer selon moi à travers ce type d'enseignement. Certes il y a toujours des étudiants qui te disent: "Moi je veux faire des maisons, de toute façon tout ça ne sert à rien, on ne fera jamais ça après". Non c'est vrai, mais c'est la manière de réfléchir qui te servira.

Une autre chose m'a surprise lors de ces critiques, c'est de vous entendre parler comme un bureau, comme un groupe qui aurait avancé ensemble, très loin des: "Je, moi je, j'ai fait ça, j'ai pensé ça" que l'on a l'habitude d'entendre, mais que l'on a aussi sans doute utilisé. Concevoir un groupe qui avance, en mettant en place ses relations internes de collaboration, je trouve que c'est une expérience beaucoup plus importante que les outils dans le processus.

4 9 : 4 6

Stéphane Grandgirard (SG)

Non mais c'est exactement ça, et je rebondis sur ce que disait Laura, sur cet aspect d'immersion. Mais ce qui est particulier c'est que vous n'êtes pas seuls à plonger...

4 9 : 5 8

ND

We are all in the same ship, saving our bodies, but at the same time, we learn collectively, from one another, students learn from each other as well. And it is just about when we get all the water out and we are ready for the next trip again. It's quite intense.

5 0 : 0 4

JW

Oui c'est vraiment comme un sous-marin! Un qui barre, l'autre qui avance, le troisième qui garde...

5 1 : 1 1

DZ

Non évidemment quand je posais la question, ce n'est pas parce que je suis contre, c'est une très belle figure que celle du sous-marin. Puisque finalement cette notion de responsabilité passe par la "physicalité" [sic]: c'est-à-dire que si je lâche la poutre, elle tombe sur quelqu'un, donc je ne vais pas la lâcher. C'est une espèce de situation d'urgence où la responsabilité devient nécessaire au "vivre-ensemble", et de nouveau l'image du sous-marin est bien choisie parce que non seulement il faut être collectif, mais il faut aussi l'être en collaboration immédiate avec la technique et la technologie. Nous devons fonctionner ensemble mais il faut aussi faire en sorte que la machine fonctionne avec nous.

5 1 : 5 5

ACR

Et cela va de paire avec la confiance, dans les deux sens: on fait confiance aux étudiants et on en assume la responsabilité.

5 2 : 1 0

AM

J'ai l'impression que la construction à l'échelle 1:1 fait foi de cette confiance en fait. Dans les travaux de groupe, ici, à l'école, il est vite arrivé qu'une ou deux personnes se défilent, quelqu'un n'a pas fait la maquette ou oublié quelque chose dans le dessin, etc. Mais à l'échelle 1:1, il est impensable d'oublier une poutre, la construction matérialise vraiment cette confiance.

5 3 : 2 0

DD

I would like to make the point here because in Switzerland there is a tendency to say 'like this you cannot build, you cannot do architecture'. In fact more of half of the world is built rather in a hands-on fashion with almost no resources, than in 'our' way, let's not forget this. There are so many ways to do architecture. There are also in the western world young emergent practices who actually practice this in a very specific way. One of the most important notions I would like to convey is that we, as architects, don't need to be submissive to potential clients. Let's not be like that. Let's be ourselves, and let's try to have ideas and try to make them ourselves with our means. There are plenty of nice examples like you guys did last year with Agathe and Laurent with many other architects and designers in the project "Les Garages"[8]. You can go to London and everywhere and this happens now and for a while already. Let's just not says this is all fantastic, and I will do it in first year and then it's over. Let's dream on and let's do it. As you said before, Diana, it is in the making. Of course not all of us will do that, that's natural. Luckily we are not all the same, but it is absolutely possible, it is to believe and just do.

5 4 : 5 4
DZ

Pour moi ce qui est intéressant dans ce que tu dis, c'est que ça ne se limite pas seulement à acquérir et apprendre des outils, mais ça va jusqu'à apprendre à définir le métier que tu as envie de faire. Ce sont des questions qui me tiennent personnellement beaucoup à cœur, comme par exemple le rapport à une clientèle, à une demande. Je pense qu'aujourd'hui, mais c'est assez contemporain, on peut en tant qu'architecte se permettre d'inventer son propre métier. Et vous ne pouvez pas encore vous en rendre compte, mais vous devez savoir que si vous avez fait ça, si demain vous vouliez vous construire une maison ce serait bien plus simple! Il y a deux ou trois techniques en plus mais quantitativement vous l'avez déjà fait...

8 Mobile micro-architecture project for use of empty industrial and commercial property as temporary housing, supported by the ALJF Association. More infos on http://lesgarages.net.

5 6 : 4 4
[student]

J'ai quelques questions en fait, c'est plus ou moins lié. C'est la deuxième fois que je fais la première année ici, ce qui me permet de prendre un peu de recul. L'année passée, on est sorti de l'EPFL, on est allé vers le monde extérieur et, en essayant de comprendre le lieu et les personnes concernées, on a fait des choix et essayé de s'adapter. Cette année on a dû se créer une contrainte, la proto-structure, que je considère comme une contrainte, et on s'est en quelque sorte refermé dessus. Je dis ça parce qu'il y a quelques mois dans une de tes lectures [DZ], tu as dit que tu avais la volonté de sauver le monde, et ça m'a marqué parce que je crois que c'est une des raisons pour lesquelles je suis là. Et finalement je trouve ça assez contradictoire, car je ne retrouve pas ce message engagé et activiste dans ce projet. C'est un commentaire au sens plus large sur l'enseignement qu'on reçoit ici. Je viens d'un autre pays, d'une autre culture et j'ai vécu la construction de ma maison dans mon pays. Ici on nous enseigne une architecture liée à des notions d'espace, et même si c'est enrichissant, que l'expérience est hyper forte, pour d'autres étudiants, le résultat de notre travail ne reste qu'un tas de bois... Les gens passent par là et se disent: "Ha c'est joli, c'est joli", mais ça reste une énorme sculpture. A quel moment ce n'est plus une sculpture? A quel moment les gens se rendent compte que c'est vraiment de l'architecture, que c'est vraiment utile? On a dépensé beaucoup d'argent et d'énergie mais tout ça reste quand même dans notre monde, dans une bulle.

0 1 : 0 0 : 3 7
WW

Moi je trouve que c'est une excellente question, enfin peut-être que je n'en ai pas la réponse, mais qui pour moi remet au centre la question de programme encore une fois, car j'ai l'impression que c'est entièrement lié. Alors à quel niveau ça intervient? Bien sûr dans les possibilités que la structure va offrir pour des évènements ou simplement pour la vie qui va l'habiter, mais aussi en amont dans la manière dont a été développé le projet, dans ce que chaque directeur, mais chaque étudiant aussi, a voulu y amener.

0 1 : 0 1 : 2 1

DZ

La confusion que tu fais est vraiment intéressante parce qu'en fait tu es déjà en train de te projeter en tant qu'architecte. C'est à la fois génial et très parlant parce qu'en fait tu es déjà dans le malaise de la situation de répondre à quelque chose, en étant en première année. Et c'est ça qui change tout. Ici on est dans un contexte pédagogique, et c'est ce contexte qui nous permet de garantir des conditions particulières. C'est quelque chose que je commence à comprendre en tant qu'architecte, que cette question de conditions – dans quelles conditions j'opère – constitue une grande part de mon travail. Ce n'est pas faire des objets ou faire de l'architecture, ce sont les conditions à partir desquelles moi avec d'autres personnes, on va pouvoir faire quelque chose d'intéressant. Ici on est dans un contexte pédagogique dans lequel toute l'équipe qui est là tente d'offrir une espèce de plateforme, la plus ouverte possible. Je suis d'accord avec toi qu'on peut se poser la question de l'utilité et de l'énergie. Mais je vois plutôt ça sous l'aspect de la puissance que vous avez acquise et ce que vous pourrez en faire plus tard. Si vous dites ensemble : "On va faire une action pour construire une maison pour les sans-abris", vous leur construisez dix maisons demain, demain vous tous, cet été !

0 1 : 0 3 : 0 7

Raffael Baur (RB)

Oui, c'est un des aspects de l'université qu'il faut protéger. Il faut garder absolument cette autonomie de compromis avec des entreprises et le monde autour. C'est seulement à ces conditions qu'on peut conserver cet aspect d'expérimentation en laboratoire. Enfin partiellement, puisqu'on échange avec un ingénieur, on construit quand même quelque chose de réel mais entre parenthèses. Moi je reste pour une grande autonomie d'éducation, qui nous permet de vraiment réfléchir en profondeur.

0 1 : 0 4 : 2 9

ACR

D'ailleurs tu parlais d'énergie, mais je crois que justement pour susciter et éveiller cette énergie, il faut avoir une certaine liberté d'action, et le fait de travailler avec un client ou des besoins réels ça change beaucoup de choses.

0 1 : 0 4 : 4 6

DZ

Je crois que le propre de notre travail, c'est en effet de ne pas fermer de portes. Après à vous de traduire ça dans une recherche plus personnelle. Il y a des réponses très différentes, et pas de fausses réponses.

0 1 : 0 6 : 0 7

ND

Mais pour revenir sur la vision des autres, c'est aussi le point de vue d'une profession. Parce qu'à la fin tu peux aussi dire à un pâtissier : "Ton gâteau c'est juste un tas de farine !" [laughs] C'est à nous de faire en sorte d'éduquer le regard des gens...

0 1 : 0 7 : 3 0

AM

C'est un choix aussi, celui de faire des études. C'est le choix de prendre quelques années pour apprendre des choses qui s'éloignent un tant soit peu de ce que tu pensais faire en arrivant. Ça peut être construire des maisons bien sûr, mais c'est aussi une multitude d'autres enseignements avec lesquels tu construiras ton propre univers. Moi je trouve ça extrêmement riche et je pense que le but de cette première année c'est d'élargir le plus possible les horizons, pour qu'ensuite vous puissiez vous même faire vos choix, en effectuant un recentrage sur vos centres d'intérêt, et imaginer ce que vous voulez construire au sein de cette discipline. Ce que j'aime dans cette première année, c'est que même si cela te paraît abstrait, c'est cette abstraction qui permet selon moi de toucher le plus de notions possibles, de pouvoir explorer, tester, et même si tu changes de direction plus tard, elle aura permis de te montrer un certain nombre de chemins.

0 1 : 0 8 : 4 1

JW

Mais surtout rien n'est jamais cadré. Même après six ou sept ans d'étude c'est impossible de dire : "On a tout vu" ou "On sait où on va". J'ai l'impression que le jour où tu ouvres un bureau, tu te retrouves de nouveau en première année. Même si les programmes des projets sont donnés, les possibilités restent infinies, c'est un processus d'exploration constant.

0 1 : 1 2 : 3 1

DD

Mais je pense qu'en tant qu'architecte, le plus important c'est de rester responsable, je le redis encore une fois, mais je pense qu'on a quand même une certaine responsabilité même si on reçoit un programme. Vous pourrez constater que, si vous faites le tour des concours, il arrive souvent que ce soit les groupes qui n'ont pas répondu au programme qui l'emportent. Parce que justement, il faut avoir une certaine intelligence dans sa lecture du monde, dans son interprétation des problématiques. Et ce n'est pas nouveau, c'est une responsabilité que nous avons tous, en tant que citoyen et en tant qu'architecte. Je pense que ce point là est fondamental, et j'espère que le programme qu'on a mis en place permet de se poser certaines de ces questions.

0 1 : 1 4 : 0 0

[student]

Moi ce que je trouve intéressant, ce n'est pas seulement les échanges entre nous, mais aussi ce qui va de l'école vers les autres, donc ceux qui ne sont pas architectes. Car je pense que l'école peut être parfois perçue comme une institution un peu fermée. Et je trouve qu'un projet comme HOUSE 1 permet de montrer aux gens ce que l'on fait ici, en modifiant un peu l'image d'un monde fermé, de gens qui ne restent qu'entre eux et parlent un langage que personne ne comprend. Hier quelqu'un est passé à côté de HOUSE 1, s'est arrêté et m'a demandé : "C'est quoi ce bâtiment?" Pour lui ce n'était pas un tas de bois puisqu'il a appelé ça un bâtiment. On s'est dit que c'était plutôt rassurant, parce que parfois on se demande si au fond on est pas en train de s'enfermer et de se mentir tous ensemble, comme si on avait l'air de vieux fous... Je pense que c'est bien si on pense aussi, même si là on est en train de parler entre nous, à ce que pensent les personnes qui vont pouvoir venir visiter HOUSE 1, et qui voudront peut-être s'y intéresser.

0 1 : 1 6 : 0 4

[student]

C'est aussi ce qui m'a étonné dans notre première année, j'ai l'impression qu'on parle de l 'architecte avec un grand A. On dessine des bâtiments, des choses importantes, mais j'ai l'impression que ça nous met dans une bulle et nous coupe un peu du monde, alors que c'est justement dans ce monde et pour ce monde qu'on travaille. Ces bâtiments on ne les fait pas pour nous, on les fait pour les autres, et j'ai des fois l'impression que la façon dont on nous enseigne l'architecture nous coupe un peu de tout ce qu'il y a autour de nous. Après ce projet HOUSE 1, j'espère qu'on va revenir un peu à terre, reprendre le contact avec ce qu'il y a autour de nous, parce que, même si c'était peut-être une chance, ça nous a projeté un peu haut, en nous donnant une image de l'architecte avec un grand A.

0 1 : 1 7 : 0 2

WW

Moi je ne suis pas tout à fait d'accord avec ça. Non mais je t'explique pourquoi, parce que je pense justement que le fait d'avoir porté des idées et de les avoir construites, c'est ce qui me fait dire qu'on peut rester réel, concret et proche des gens. En démontrant qu'on est capable de réaliser des envies.

0 1 : 1 7 : 3 5
[student]
Il y a quand même quelque chose qui est arrivé très vite dans notre première année, dans notre cursus, c'est d'entendre dire: "Moi j'engage plus d'étudiants qui sortent de l'EPFL parce qu'ils ne savent pas faire grand chose", "parce qu'ils ne savent que penser, des beaux espaces ok, mais qui ne tiennent pas debout, qui ne sont pas praticables, qui ne sont pas (...)"
0 1 : 1 8 : 0 1
DZ
Là, on entre dans un autre discours. Ça tu l'entendras toujours, ils ont raison et toi tu auras raison de ne pas savoir. Après ce que je trouve curieux, c'est d'entendre cette remarque alors que vous avez créé quelque chose de très concret. Qu'aurais-tu dit si vous aviez fait un programme de musée et que le rendu final avait été une planche au 1:200ème?
0 1 : 2 0 : 0 2
WW
Moi, ce que j'aime bien c'est que ça pose la question du rôle de l'école. Comment doit-elle former les architectes? Et le problème c'est que beaucoup de bureaux aimeraient des dessinateurs ou des personnes qui puissent faire du suivi de chantier, mais un architecte c'est avant tout quelqu'un qui est capable de saisir l'aspect culturel de la construction, quelqu'un qui est capable de savoir le sens à donner à la chose qui se construit dans un endroit particulier, avant même de savoir comment cette chose se construit. Et c'est tellement vaste que jamais un architecte ne pourra être spécialiste de l'ensemble du processus.
0 1 : 2 0 : 4 3
DZ
Et on peut revenir à l'origine même de l'université, qui n'est pas une école professionnelle. C'est une école qui est là pour apprendre à réfléchir, donner des outils, pour que vous soyez ensuite opérationnels.
0 1 : 2 2 : 2 9
JV
Oui je pense qu'on ne sait pas comment le métier évolue, mais le plus important c'est d'apprendre à réfléchir et de trouver soi-même les méthodes qui nous conviennent parce que le métier d'architecte est un métier complexe qu'on n'a jamais fini d'apprendre.
0 1 : 2 6 : 4 8
PG
Mais moi quand je repense à mes années d'université – Je ne sais pas si Daniel a beaucoup aimé être à l'université – mais moi j'ai adoré et je pense que j'ai appris des choses que j'ai pas pu apprendre après. C'est le moment d'apprendre des choses qui resteront des trésors une fois que tu finis et que tu atterris dans le monde sauvage de la profession.
0 1 : 2 3 : 1 6
WW
Moi j'ai surtout appris que je ne savais rien. [laughs]
0 1 : 2 5 : 3 5
[student]
Juste pour revenir un peu sur ce qui a été dit. On parlait de cette bulle mais je pense que l'important c'est d'être conscient de ce qu'on a fait, de notre capacité, mais de rester humble, en quelque sorte un peu naïf vis-à-vis de ce qu'on a créé. Effectivement on peut voir un tas de bois, mais c'est probablement un des tas de bois les plus intéressants qui n'ait jamais été fait [laughs]. Mais oui je pense qu'il faut savoir rester humble et garder à l'esprit qu'on est là pour apprendre et apprendre de tout, c'est ce que tu dis Agathe, considérer tous les horizons pour essayer de réunir tout ça et aller plus loin, continuer avec ça.
0 1 : 2 6 : 5 2
AM
Et cette naïveté elle est très importante. J'ai pu constater dans mes quelques expériences d'enseignement, que vous amenez toujours quelque chose d'inattendu, qu'on ne connait pas ou même qu'on ignore, parce

que vous avez des manières de réfléchir qu'on a peut-être oublié. Est-ce que c'est triste ou pas? Peut-être qu'on les retrouve justement avec vous.

01:27:23

EC

Et c'est la raison pour laquelle on enseigne, je pense.

01:27:28

ND

Et c'est cette naïveté qui devient une intelligence après.

01:27:34

PG

Je dirais que c'est de l'intuition, plus que de la naïveté. En effet, est-ce que ce programme peut être fait avec des étudiants de quatrième année? Je ne pense pas. Est-ce que ce programme peut être fait avec des étudiants de troisième année d'architecture? Moi je ne pense pas.

01:27:49

DD

Tu peux, tu peux, mais c'est différent.

01:27:53

[student]

Je reviens en arrière. Avant on disait qu'on construit pour les autres, mais est-ce que ça doit être comme ça?

01:28:05

DZ

Je pourrais apporter une nuance à ça. Je ne construis rien que je ne pourrais habiter, c'est ma vision de la pratique. Je ne construis rien dans lequel je ne me projette pas en tant qu'habitant. Donc le premier habitant de tout ce que je fais, c'est moi.

01:28:40

AP

Pour moi, oui. On construit pour les autres, que pour les autres.

01 :31 :02

Mais c'est vrai que cette question, qui est un lieu commun de la discipline : "Les architectes construisent pour les autres", induit quand même à un certain paternalisme. Les autres deviennent en fait très vite une abstraction, une espèce de grande masse.

01:31:47

AP

Mais est-ce que tu parles de pédagogie ou de profession? Parce que dans l'enseignement on peut admettre, à des fins d'expérimentation, de projeter pour soi, mais dans la profession, enfin en ce qui me concerne, on ne construit pas, on ne réfléchit pas pour soi.

01:32:02

CL

Mais moi je nous trouve tous un peu "fleur bleue". Enfin je suis désolé, mais je crois que je vais être un pavé dans la marre. Moi je crois qu'on ne construit pas pour les autres, et surtout je crois qu'on ne construit pas pour les gens. On construit potentiellement pour l'idée des gens ou pour une idée d'habiter le monde, mais qui est différente que de construire directement pour les gens. Et le paternalisme dont tu parles, c'est celui qui me fait le plus peur. Tout simplement il y a deux chiffres que j'ai toujours en tête : il y a 95% du monde qui se fabrique sans architecte. La deuxième chose, c'est que 95% des bâtiments qui sont construits actuellement ont été construits à une certaine époque pour des clients qui sont tous morts, enfin à 95% des cas. C'est-à-dire que je pense qu'on est plutôt dans le contexte de construire quelque chose dans le temps, pour l'idée des gens ou de l'humanité, pas forcément "à la corbuséenne", dans l'idée de l'homme précis, mais plutôt comme ce que Perret a appelé "à toutes fins utiles". On a eu hier cette discussion autour de Sainte Sophie, bâtiment qui a été une basilique et qui est devenu une mosquée, qui a été un hôpital à chaque guerre, qui a été un marché aux fruits et légumes, qui est désacralisé et qui est un musée maintenant. La valeur de la chose c'est la chose et en fait je crois que c'est une fausse idée que de faire porter aux architectes l'idée qu'ils vont sauver le monde. A quelques exceptions précises, oui effectivement tout d'un coup on a un ami ou un client et on fait 3 m2 de son salon, mais je pense que de manière générale notre façon de penser le monde doit être absolument détachée d'un rapport immédiat aux gens, sinon c'est là qu'on glisse vers le populisme. Moi je pense dans ce sens là, enfin j'ai une réflexion à ce propos à l'encontre de ce qu'on est en train de raconter, qu'il y a une sorte d'autonomie dans la réflexion architecturale et dans la manière de concevoir un environnement en regardant la planète. De façon très objective, mais pas scientifique, il y a x milliard de mètres carrés et on est x milliard de personnes, il faut alors se débrouiller pour que cela fonctionne...

0 1 : 3 4 : 4 6
DD

Moi je pense que pour finir, ce qu'il est important de garder en tête, c'est que ce sont des espaces, des intérieurs. J'aimerais revenir sur ce dont on a discuté hier, sur cette notion du "inside", la condition d'être dedans, dans un environnement, dont le plus grand disponible est bien sûr la planète entière. C'est cette conscience qui pousse la réflexion spatiale, non pas à penser à l'architecture comme des objets à poser, mais plutôt depuis l'intérieur. C'est la clé, après tout va émerger, si la génétique de départ est saine, elle a un grand potentiel. Du coup je pense que ce n'est pas pour les gens mais pour la société, même si c'est peut-être un peu général, mais je pense que c'est pour nous tous, donc on est pas exclu non plus...

0 1 : 3 6 : 3 3
CL

On doit être ni exclu, ni exclusif. Réduire la question de l'architecture à "construire pour les gens", je trouve ça très exclusif comme manière de se positionner.

0 1 : 3 6 : 4 6
DZ

Ça oblige à définir qui sont les autres et ça c'est déjà très problématique.

0 1 : 3 6 : 5 5
DD

Et je reviens justement sur la question de l'immersion. Parce que c'est un des termes fondamentaux dans la manière dont je conçois l'enseignement ici : travailler activement, depuis l'intérieur, avec les capacités et la force propres à chacun, mais aussi justement en tant que collectivité, comme tu disais Cédric, ni exclu, ni exclusif.

0 1 : 3 7 : 4 2
DZ

Voilà je crois qu'on va clore ici cette discussion. Je trouve très intéressant de pouvoir discuter après avoir autant produit et important de partager un peu ces moments de réflexion. Ce sont des questionnements qu'on va se poser pour la suite de l'enseignement, mais aussi de nos métiers. Merci à tous d'être là et d'être restés concentrés jusqu'au bout.

A

● Angelou Maya
The Art of Fiction No. 119,
Interviewed by George Plimpton
in *The Paris Review*, no. 116
Fall 1990

"I have kept a hotel room in every town I've ever lived in. I rent a hotel room for a few months, leave my home at six, and try to be at work by six-thirty. To write, I lie across the bed, so that this elbow is absolutely encrusted at the end, just so rough with callouses. I never allow the hotel people to change the bed, because I never sleep there. I stay until twelve-thirty or one- thirty in the afternoon, and then I go home and try to breathe; I look at the work around five; I have an orderly dinner – proper, quiet, lovely dinner; and then I go back to work the next morning. Sometimes in hotels I'll go into the room and there'll be a note on the floor which says, Dear Miss Angelou, let us change the sheets. We think they are moldy. But I only allow them to come in and empty wastebaskets. I insist that all things are taken off the walls. I don't want anything in there. I go into the room and I feel as if all my beliefs are suspended. Nothing holds me to anything. No milkmaids, no flowers, nothing. I just want to feel and then when I start to work I'll remember."

C'est une pièce pour Maya Angelou, qui obtient l'inspiration dans des chambres d'hôtel, où elle ne dort jamais. L'hôtel est un espace de transition isolé.
studio Chassot

B

● Barbey Gilles
Archétypes d'ouvertures
in *L'évasion domestique – essai sur les relations d'affectivité au logis*
Lausanne: PPUR 1990

"La fenêtre fait la pièce, en lui prêtant à la fois sens, aspect et raison d'être."

Dans les villes, la proximité appelle à trouver un équilibre entre dialogue et privacité.
studio Pellacani

● Baudelaire Charles
Le peintre de la vie moderne
2000, 112 p.
Paris: Fayard/Mille et une nuits, La Petite Collection

"Pour le parfait flâneur, pour l'observateur passionné, c'est une immense jouissance que d'élire domicile dans le nombre, dans l'ondoyant, dans le mouvement, dans le fugitif et l'infini. Être hors de chez soi, et pourtant se sentir partout chez soi; voir le monde, être au centre du monde et rester caché au monde."

"Ainsi l'amoureux de la vie universelle entre dans la foule comme dans un immense réservoir d'électricité. On peut aussi le comparer, lui, à un miroir aussi immense que cette foule; à un kaléidoscope doué de conscience, qui, à chacun de ses mouvements, représente la vie multiple et la grâce mouvante de tous les éléments de la vie."

● Baudelaire Charles
Le spleen de Paris: petits poèmes en prose
2014, 253 p.
Paris: Librairie Générale Française, Collection Le Livre de Poche Classiques

● Baudelaire Charles
Spleen IV, in *Spleen et Idéal*
1821–1867

"Quand le ciel bas et lourd pèse
comme un couvercle
Sur l'esprit gémissant en proie
aux longs ennuis,
Et que de l'horizon embrassant
tout le cercle
Il nous verse un jour noir plus
triste que les nuits;

Quand la terre est changée en
un cachot humide,
Où l'Espérance, comme une
chauve-souris,
S'en va battant les murs de son
aile timide
Et se cognant la tête à des
plafonds pourris;

Quand la pluie étalant ses
immenses traînées
D'une vaste prison imite
les barreaux,
Et qu'un peuple muet d'infâmes
araignées
Vient tendre ses filets au fond
de nos cerveaux,

Des cloches tout à coup sautent
avec furie
Et lancent vers le ciel un affreux
hurlement,
Ainsi que des esprits errants et
sans patrie
Qui se mettent à geindre
opiniâtrement.

Et de longs corbillards, sans
tambours ni musique,
Défilent lentement dans mon âme;
l'Espoir,
Vaincu, pleure, et l'Angoisse
atroce, despotique,
Sur mon crâne incliné plante son
drapeau noir."

● Beckett Samuel
Fin de partie
1957, 112 p.
Paris: Editions de Minuit, Collection Théâtre

"CLOV – Pourquoi cette comédie, tous les jours?
HAMM – La routine. On ne sait jamais.
(Un temps.) Cette nuit j'ai vu dans ma poitrine.
Il y avait un gros bobo.
CLOV. – Tu as vu ton coeur.
HAMM. – Non, c'était vivant.
(Un temps. Avec angoisse.) Clov!
CLOV. – Oui.
HAMM. – Qu'est ce qui se passe?
CLOV. – Quelque chose suit son cours."

● Bonnin Philippe
Dispositifs et rituels du seuil: une topologie sociale. Détour japonais
in *Communications*, De Gruyter
2000, pp. 65–92

"(...) D'une certaine manière, le seuil fonde les espaces. Le seuil existe dès lors qu'on a eu l'intention de séparer un lieu du reste du monde: un dedans, espace fini et clos, aux qualités choisies et contrôles. L'intérieur est ce lieu, où se cristallise l'intime, où se construit l'identité, où se réalisent la protection et la sécurité recherchées. (...)"

C

● Cooper Dennis
The Art of Fiction No. 213,
Interviewed by Ira Silverberg
in *The Paris Review*, no. 198
Fall 2011

"... [narratives] narrows the reader's attention in a swift, no-nonsense way, and it creates an anxious, intimate, and secretive atmosphere that I find very helpful as a way to erase the context around my characters and foreground their feelings, their psychological depths, their tastes."

● Crumb Robert
The Art of Comics No. 1,
Interviewed by Ted Widmer
in *The Paris Review*, no. 193
Summer 2010

"Because I was staring at everything like I had never seen it before. People who had taken LSD, like me, understood right away what was going on. People who hadn't, didn't get it. I was in a strange state of mind, influenced by these visions."

Notre pièce serait un espace ouvert mais incompréhensible depuis l'extérieur. La pièce fait ressentir des sensations uniques et propres à cet espace.
studio Chassot

"The world comes out of the void!"

Après avoir analysé l'interview de Robert Crumb, nous avons constaté que l'auteur recherche l'isolement des mortels et un rapprochement du Dieu pour écrire son dernier livre, "The Book of Genesis". Robert Crumb a beaucoup de fans et est constamment entouré de public. Pour se concentrer sur son livre il est obligé de fuir, de se cacher. Nous voulons proposer une pièce adaptée essentiellement au cas de Robert Crumb qui a deux fonctions: l'inspirer pour l'écriture de "The Book of Genesis" et lui permettre de ne plus fuir ses fans.

Le concept de la pyramide inversée s'adapte parfaitement à notre but. L'espace nécessaire à Robert Crumb est au centre de la pyramide qui monte en s'élargissant. Le regard de Crumb est ainsi porté vers le ciel, inspiration divine. Par ailleurs, il est ainsi coupé de la vision extérieure et peut travailler inaperçu.
studio Chassot

D

● Derrida Jacques
Specters of Marx: the state of the debt, the work of mourning, and the new international
NewYork: Routledge
1994, 198 p.

"The properties of the thing are always very human, at bottom, reassuring for this very reason. They always relate to what is proper to man, to the properties of man: either they respond to man's needs, and that is precisely their use-value, or else they are the product of a human activity that seems to intend them for those needs."

E

● Joseph Rykwert
● Aldo van Eyck,
Works
Basel: Birkhäuser Verlag
1999, 312 p.

Comment relier ses différents espaces entre eux?

Je suis donc venu articuler ces espaces. J'ai voulu amener une transition de sorte qu'ils soient tous reliés les uns aux autres, qu'il y ait un rapport entre ces espaces, qu'ils soient connectés. Pour cela je me suis inspiré d'une citation d'Aldo van Eyck.

studio Pellacani

"The building was conceived as a configuration of intermediary places clearly defined. This does not imply continual transition or endless postponement with respect to place and occasion. On the contrary, it implies a break away from the contemporary concept (call it sickness) of spatial continuity and the tendency to erase every articulation between spaces, i.e., between outside and inside, between one space and another. Instead, I tried to articulate the transition by means of defined in-between places which induce simultaneous awareness of what is signified on either side."

F

● Foucault Michel
Dits et écrits 1984,
Des espaces autres
(conférence au Cercle d'études architecturales, 14 mars 1967)
in *Architecture, Mouvement, Continuité*, no 5
Octobre 1984, pp. 46–49.

La proto-structure nous apparait telle l'ossature d'une maison, mais également, grâce aux études réalisées durant le premier semestre, tel un microcosme de la ville hybride, créé par le rapprochement entre Lausanne et Paris. Nous y trouvons donc tous types de programmes publics, comme celui du théâtre, programme étudié lors du projet Planes. Le théâtre est, selon l'approche choisie, un lieu dans lequel est crée une réalité toute autre que la réalité extérieure au théâtre, à l'image d'une bulle. Le philosophe Michel Foucault décrit ce lieu comme une hétérotopie, la localisation physique de l'utopie.

studio Dürr

G

● Gargiani Roberto,
● Fanelli Giovanni
Histoire de l'architecture moderne: structure et revêtement
Lausanne: PPUR 2008, 460 p.

"Mies van der Rohe: *Pour nous, il n'y pas de forme, mais seulement des problèmes de construction.* La solution d'angle du bâtiment appuie cette interprétation: les éléments portants verticaux, au lieu de se multiplier et de se renforcer comme dans le temple antique, sont espacés, voire supprimés de façon à traiter l'angle en porte-à-faux, pour exalter la possibilité de l'ossature."

● Guedj Denis
Les Cheveux de Bérénice
Paris: Seuil, Collection Points
2007, 400 p.

"A quoi sert une bibliothèque, sinon à fournir à chaque nouvelle génération, à chaque nouveau lecteur, les moyens de se hisser jusqu'aux niveaux ultimes atteints par les savoirs antérieurs?"

K

● Kandinsky Wassily
Point et ligne sur plan: contribution à l'analyse des éléments de la peinture
Paris: Gallimard,
Collection Folio Essais
1993, 249 p.

"L'effet subjectif produit par une ligne dépend de son orientation: la ligne horizontale correspond au sol sur lequel l'homme se repose et se meut, au plat, elle possède une tonalité affective sombre et froide semblable au noir ou au bleu, tandis que la ligne verticale correspond à la hauteur et n'offre aucun point d'appui, elle possède au contraire une tonalité lumineuse et chaude proche du blanc ou du jaune. Une diagonale possède par conséquent une tonalité plus ou moins chaude ou froide selon son inclinaison par rapport à la verticale ou à l'horizontale."

L

● Le Corbusier
Le Modulor
Paris: Edition de l'Architecture d'aujourd'hui
1950, 239 p.

"L'architecture est jugée par les yeux qui voient, la tête qui tourne, les jambes qui marchent. L'architecture n'est pas un phénomène synchronique, mais successif, fait de spectacles s'ajoutant les uns aux autres et se suivant dans le temps et l'espace."

● Le Corbusier
Vers une architecture
Paris: Flammarion
2005, 253 p.

"L'architecte, par l›ordonnance des formes, réalise un ordre qui est une pure création de son esprit; par les formes, il affecte intensivement nos sens, provoquant des émotions plastiques; par les rapports qu›il crée, il éveille en nous des résonances profondes, il nous donne la mesure d'un ordre qu'on sent en accord avec celui du monde."

"L'architecture, c'est établir des rapports émouvants avec des matériaux bruts."

"Le plan porte en lui l'essence même de la sensation."

M

● Matta-Clark Gordon,
Gordon Matta-Clark: Splitting the Humphrey Street Building, interviewed by Liza Bear
in *Avalanche*, no. 10
December 1974

"The group's architectural aim was more elusive than doing pieces that would demonstrate an alternative attitude to buildings... We were thinking more about metaphoric voids, gaps, leftover spaces, places that were not developed... for example, the places where you stop to tie your shoelaces, places that are just interruptions in your daily movements. It was about something other than the established architectural vocabulary, without getting fixed into anything too formal."

● Meiss (von) Pierre
De la forme au lieu: une introduction à l'étude de l'architecture
Lausanne: PPUR,
Collection Architecture
1993, 221 p.

"La spatialité d›un objet atteint son apogée lorsqu›il est percé, qu›il peut être traversé et relie ainsi l'observateur à d›autres éléments de l'environnement au-delà de l'objet."

L'objet devient alors espace.

studio Pellacani

P

● Perec Georges
Espèces d'espaces
Paris: Galilée
2000, 185 p.

"Je mets un tableau sur un mur. Ensuite j'oublie qu'il y a un mur. Je ne sais plus ce qu'il y a derrière ce mur, je ne sais plus qu'il y a un mur, (...) il n'est plus qu'un support pour le tableau."

"Notre regard parcourt l'espace et nous donne l'illusion du relief et de la distance. C'est ainsi que nous construisons l'espace: avec un haut et un bas, une gauche et une droite, un devant et un derrière, un près et un loin. Lorsque rien n'arrête notre regard, notre regard porte très loin. Mais s'il ne rencontre rien, il ne voit rien; il ne voit que ce qu'il rencontre: l'espace, c'est ce qui arrête le regard, ce sur quoi la vue butte: l'obstacle: des briques, un angle, un point de fuite: l'espace, c'est quand ça fait un angle, quand ça s'arrête, quand il faut tourner pour que ça reparte. Ça n'a rien d'ectoplasmique, l'espace; ça a des bords, ça ne part pas dans tous les sens, ça fait tout ce qu'il faut faire pour que les rails de chemins de fer se rencontrent bien avant l'infini."

● Perec Georges
La vie mode d'emploi
Paris: Le Livre de Poche, Collection Littérature & Documents
1980, 641 p.

"Son patron, Lord Ashtray, s'est enrichi dans la récupération des métaux non ferreux, et dépense aujourd'hui sa fortune en menant, dans sa gigantesque propriété des environs de Londres, Hammer Hall, la vie fastueuse d'un grand seigneur. (...) On dit qu'il emploie quarante-trois jardiniers à plein temps, qu'il y a tellement de fenêtres, portes vitrées et miroirs dans sa propriété qu'il a préposé quatre domestiques à leur entretien et que, ne parvenant pas à se faire remplacer au fur et à mesure les carreaux cassés il a résolu le problème en rachetant tout simplement la miroiterie la plus proche."

● Peeters Benoit,
● Schuiten François
Les cités obscures: La fièvre d'Urbicande
Tournai: Casterman
1992, 94 p.

"L'Urbatecte Eugen Robik reçoit un cube vide, dessiné par ses arêtes. En jouant avec, il le pose en biais sur son bureau. Cela déstabilise le cube qui se met à croître, formant un réseau à l'échelle de la ville, dont le centre est la maison d'Eugen. Cette structure englobe peu à peu tout Urbicande, tissant un réseau dense et indestructible."

● Pétrarque
L'ascension du mont Ventoux
Paris: Fayard/Mille et une nuits, La petite collection
2001, 55 p.

L'ascension du Mont-Ventoux décrite par Pétrarque nous a beaucoup inspirés pour ce projet. Elle a offert une dimension ésotérique qui fait contre-pied au caractère très pragmatique du projet. L'excursion de Pétrarque et son jeune frère, tout comme le parcours que nous proposons, est finalement une véritable quête introspective, pour autant que l'on se rappel l'adage d'Augustin:

"Les hommes s'en vont admirer les cimes des montagnes, les vagues de la mer, le vaste cours des fleuves, les circuits de l'Océan, les révolutions des astres, et ils se délaissent eux-mêmes."

R

● Rone
Bora Vocal

Extrait du journal intime d'Alain Damasio lors de l'écriture de son second roman La Horde du Contrevent.

"(...) tu la réussiras – uniquement, quoi – uniquement si tu t'isoles. Si tu t'isoles, quoi. Tu comprends ce que ca veut dire "isoles"? Isola, l'île quoi

Tu crées ton île, et tu l'évaste au maximum, quoi. Il faut que les gens soient extrêmement loin de toi, mais loin, parce que ton univers sera vaste, quoi, sera immense, sera énorme, sera énorme univers, quoi. Énorme puissance d'univers, quoi"

S

● Sartre Jean-Paul
Huis clos, suivi de Les mouches
1993, 245 p.
Paris: Gallimard, Collection Folio

"LE GARCON – Mais de quoi parlez-vous?

GARCIN – Des paupières. Nous, nous battions des paupières. Un clin d'oeil ça s'appelait. Un petit éclair noir, un rideau qui tombe et qui se relève."

● Schopenhauer Arthur
Le monde comme volonté et comme représentation
2014, 1472 p.
Paris: PUF, Collection Quadrige

"La beauté en architecture: elle résulte de la contemplation de deux forces élémentaires: la résistance et la lumière."

● Shepard Sam
The Art of Theater No. 12, interviewed by Benjamin Ryder Howe, Jeanne McCulloch, Mona Simpson
in *The Paris Review*, no. 142
Spring 1997

"There's a kind of dialogue that's continually shifting and moving, and each time it moves, it creates something new."

"We hear all kinds of fascinating things every day, but dialogue has to create a life. It has to be self-sustaining."

Sam Shepard, écrivain, acteur et metteur en scène, nous parle de l'importance du dialogue actif. Notre théâtre veut ainsi rassembler tous les éléments d'un théâtre traditionnel dans un seul espace, afin d'articuler le dialogue entre les utilisateurs, l'intérieur et l'extérieur de la protostructure. Les modules structurels préfabriqués permettent de placer plusieurs plateformes offrant ainsi de multiples possibilités de hauteurs et de points de vue. Ils créent également une interdépendance entre plateformes et protostructure permettant ainsi son contreventement et sa stabilité.

studio Chassot

● Southern Terry
The Art of Screenwriting No. 3, Interviewed by Maggie Paley
in *The Paris Review*, no. 200
Spring 2012
"I used to write a lot, then show it to my friends – one or two of them anyway. I knew they had never seen anything like this before"

"Television is the thing, you see – its existence puts movies in a position of having to do something different. In five years television screens will be half the size of a movie screen, they'll occupy a whole wall. And people will just sit there. They're not going to leave the house except to see something groovy, something that they can't see at home."

En se référant aux propos de l'écrivain Terry Southern, nous avons voulu créer une petite pièce d'exposition où des textes pourraient être montrés. La taille de cette pièce permet d'accueillir un nombre restreint des personnes conformément à la volonté de l'écrivain.

studio Chassot

T

● Tanizaki Junichirô
Eloge de l'ombre
2011, 90 p.
Lagrasse: Editions Verdier, Collection LITT JAPONAISE

"A cette vue, je pense irrésistiblement au bâton du qui constitue l'armature des poupées. En vérité, le torse est alors un support destiné à recevoir le costume et rie de plus. Ces femmes dont le torse est ainsi réduit à l'état de support, elles sont faites d'une superposition de je ne sais combien d'épaisseurs de soie ou de coton, et si on les dépouillait de leur vêtements, il ne resterait d'elles, comme pour les poupées, qu'un bâton ridiculement disproportionné."

Nous nous sommes inspirés de cet extrait pour développer un espace, situé au centre de la protostructure, où l'une de ces femmes japonaises s'habillerait. Nous avons construit une série de poteaux verticaux, placés sur la trame induite par la matrice, qui cadre l'espace et qui offre un support à nos strates de cadres et parois.

studio Guaita

● Tardieu Jean
Le professeur Froeppel
Paris: Gallimard, Collection L'imaginaire
2003, 190 p.

"Etant donné un mur, que se passe-t-il derrière?"

● Tolstoy Leo
Anna Karenina
Harlow: Penguin Classics
2003, 864 p.

"All the variety, all the charm, all the beauty of life is made up of light and shadow."

● Tournier Michel
Le médianoche amoureux
1991, 303 p.
Paris: Gallimard, Collection Folio

"Il n'y a pas de bonne intimité que crépusculaire."

● Trier (von) Lars
Dogville
2003, 2h 58min

Lars Van Trier creates a paradox in his film DogVille by dividing spaces with physical and imaginative doors. We can so question where rely the limits of a door?
studio Cabay

● Trier (von) Lars
Melancholia
2011, 2h 10min

"JUSTINE – Sir... You can back up a little more if you want... I think you need that extra... I don't think he can hear you. Sir, can you hear me up there? Can you copy, sailor? I think he's in a different county... It's like five feet. And now he stops. He's got five feet here. That's good. Stop, stop, stop, stop! Wait, wait, wait! You're a little close. I think he can keep going a little bit, maybe. Oh, no, no, no. He can't. I don't... Be careful, please. It is not my car. I will. I promise. Turn around to the left, please. Stop there, sir. Straighten up, sir. Yeah, I think I'm good there, right? You're not even looking. I can see it's not looking good. I'm a very experienced driver... It's like really close on that side. Really? Yeah, don't go any further forward. Just straight... How do I put it in...? What? This way? Get out of the way. Come on. Sorry. Yes, I know. We're sorry. I won't even bother saying how late you are. Sorry. We're really sorry. Hi. Hi, Claire. So sorry. Hi. We probably should have taken something smaller. This brilliant idea was yours of renting a stretch. This is very much not my project, okay?"

V

● Vian Boris
L'écume des jours
2014, 350 p.
Paris: Le Livre de Poche, Collection Littérature & Documents

"Chloé tombe malade: un nénuphar se développe dans un de ses poumons. Pour espérer ralentir sa croissance et guérir, elle ne doit boire que très peu, et être en présence d'un grand nombre de fleurs pour dissuader le nénuphar dans ses poumons. La chambre dans laquelle dort Cloé toute la journée varie en fonction de l'évolution de sa maladie."

"Colin, croyant avoir entendu le rire cristallin de Chloé, se mit à sa recherche et pénétra dans la pièce par une ouverture étroite. Au fur et à mesure qu'il monta, il découvrit des espaces bercés par la lumière et eu l'impression de se rapprocher d'elle. Mais elle demeurait introuvable."

● Vigan (de) Delphine
Les Heures souterraines
2011, 256 p.
Paris: Le Livre de Poche, Collection Littérature & Documents

Pour cette étape du "Double-Element", nous avons pivoté nos moules ainsi qu'extrudé la géométrie commune de nos super-éléments afin de créer deux volumes identiques qui se font face. Pour avoir une table mouvante une plaque pivotante s'encastre dans le super-élément et ce système est le même à Lausanne et à Paris.

Dans son œuvre Les heures souterraines, Delphine de Vigan écrit: "Il regarde la ville, cette superposition de mouvements. Ce territoire infini d'intersections, où l'on ne se rencontre pas."

La rotation des deux tables se fait de manière synchronisée grâce à l'introduction d'un câble infini reliant les deux plaques pivotantes.

Une modification du site à Paris influe sur celui de Lausanne et vice versa, sans qu'il y ait un réel lien physique entre les deux.
studio Chassot

W

● Walter Benjamin
Paris, capitale du XIXe siècle: le Livre des passages
1989, 972 p.
Paris: Les Editions Cerf, Collection Passages

A partir de la citation suivante: "le flâneur dans la flânerie transforme Paris en un grand intérieur, une maison dont les murs sont délimités par les quartiers, pas moins démarqué par un seuil que le seraient de vraies chambres" je me suis demandé quel était l'espace privé pour le flâneur.
studio Chassot

"Rites de passage" – c'est ainsi qu'on appelle dans le folklore les cérémonies qui se rattachent à la mort, à la naissance, au mariage, à la puberté. Dans la vie moderne, ces transitions sont devenues de moins en moins perceptibles et il est devenu de plus en plus rare d'en faire l'expérience vécue. Nous sommes devenus très pauvre en expérience du seuil. L'endormissement est peut-être la seule qui nous soit restée (mais avec le réveil aussi). Et, finalement, les fluctuations de la conversation et les variations sexuelles de l'amour oscillent aussi autour de certains seuils, comme les variations des figures du rêve. "Qu'il plait à l'Homme, dit Aragon, de se tenir sur le pas des portes de l'imagination!" (Paysan (de Paris, Paris 1926), p.74). Les amants et les amis aiment tirer les forces nouvelles, non seulement des seuils de ces portes de l'imagination, mais des seuils en général. Les prostitués, en revanche, aiment les seuils de ces portes de rêve. – Il faut distinguer soigneusement le seuil de la frontière. Le seuil (Schwelle) est une zone. Les idées de variation, de passage d'un état à un autre, de flux sont contenues dans le terme schwellen (gonfler, enfler, se dilater) et l'étymologie ne doit pas les négliger. Il importe, d'autre part, d'établir le contexte tectonique et cérémoniel immédiat qui a donné au mot sa signification. – MAISON DE RÊVE –"

"L'expérience de l'aura repose sur la traduction de la manière, jadis habituelle dans la société humaine, de réagir au rapport de la nature à l'homme. Celui qui est regardé – ou qui se croit regardé -lève son regard, répond par un regard. Faire l'expérience de l'aura d'une apparition ou d›un être, c›est se rendre compte de sa capacité à lever les yeux, ou de répondre par un regard. Cette capacité est pleine de poésie; là où un homme, un animal ou un être inanimé, sous notre regard ouvre son propre regard, il nous entraîne d›abord dans le lointain. Son regard rêve, nous attire dans son rêve. Laura, c›est l›apparition d'un lointain, aussi proche soit-il."

● Walter Benjamin
The Arcades Project
1999, 1088 p.
Harvard University Press

"The street conducts the flâneur into a vanished time. For him every street is precipitous. It leads downward – if not to the mythical Mothers, then into a pastthat can be all the more spellbinding because because it is not his own, not private. Nevertheless, it always remains the time of a childhood. But why that of the life he has lived? In the asphalt over which he passes, his steps awaken a surprising resonance. The gaslight that streams down on the paving stones throws an equivocal light on this double ground."

"Paris created the type of the flâneur. What is remarkable is that it wasn't Rome. And the reason? Does not dreaming itself take the high road in Rome? And it isn't that city too full of temples, enclosed squares, national shrines, to be able to enter tout entière – with every cobblestone, evry shop sign, every step, and every gateway – into the passerby's dream? The national character of the italians may also have much to do with this. For it is not the foreigners but they themselves, the parisians, who have made Paris the promised land of the flâneur – the "landscape built of sheer life," as Hofmannsthal once put it. Landscape – that, in fact, is what Paris becomes for the flâneur. Or more precisely: the city splits for him into its dilectical poles. It opens up to him as a landscape, even as it closes around him as a room."

"Paris is built over a system of caverns from which the din of Metro and railroad mounts to the surface, and in which every passing omnibus or truck sets up a prolonged echo. And this great technological system of tunnels and thoroughfares interconnects with the ancient vaults, the limestone quarries, the grottoes and catacombs which, since the early Middle Ages, have time and again been reentered and traversed. Even today, for the price of two francs, one can buy a ticket of admission to this most nocturnal Paris, so much less expensive and less hazardous than the Paris of the upper world. The Middle Ages saw it differently. Sources tell us that there were clever persons who now and again, after exacting a considerable sum and a vow of silence, undertook to guide their fellow citizens underground and show them the Devil in his infernal majesty. A financial venture far less risky for the swindled than for the swindlers: Must not the church have considered a spurious manifestation of the Devil as tantamount to blasphemy? In other ways, too, this subterranean city had its uses, for those who knew their way around it. Its streets cut through the great customs barrier with which the Farnlers General had secured their right to receive duties on imports, and in the sixteenth and eighteenth centuries smuggling operations went on for the most part below ground. We know also that in times of public commotion mysterious rumors traveled very quickly via the catacombs, to say nothing of the prophetic spirits and fortunetellers duly qualified to pronounce upon them. On the day after Louis XVI fled Paris, the revolutionary government issued bills ordering a thorough search of these passages. And a few years later a rumor suddenly spread through the population that certain areas of town were about to cave in."

Ce texte souligne l'existence de nombreux passages creusés sous Paris, tandis que ce projet propose un site permettant d'accéder à un sous-sol depuis Lausanne. Or, lors du projet MEASURES, la relation entre les deux villes s'était faite par la cave. De plus, le DOUBLE-ELEMENT avait déjà été conçu comme un espace permettant d'accéder à une ville depuis l'autre.

C'est pourquoi il a été décidé qu'une porte serait introduite au bout du chemin proposé par ce projet: en arrivant devant la façade de Lausanne, le sujet suppose un sous-sol. D'abord forcé par la structure du bâtiment à monter des marches pour entrer dans la maison, il est ensuite guider à la cave par la colonne+. Au fond il y découvre une porte, qui mène sur Paris.

studio Pellacani

Creusons Lausanne. Descendons dans ces sous-sols et découvrons des jeux de lumières qui nous invitent, paradoxalement, à élever notre regard tandis que nous nous y enfonçons.

studio Pellacani

"These proliferating individual passages, extracted from their original contest set up to communicate among themselves. With these goes the effort to generate a certain atmosphere by means of structural massing."

"At each extremity of this narrow corridor there are elevated passages, supported by columns, and also attractive underground passages which connect all the parts of the Phalanx and the adjoining buildings. Thus, everything is linked by a series of passageways, allowing internal communication."

"The boundary, as threshold, stretches across the streets."

"The curtains are left open just enough to permit easy communication between outside and interior."

Cette phrase tirée du manifeste du DOUBLE-ELEMENT illustre en partie le concept développé dans PLANES. Le plâtre ne comprend en effet pas la porte dans son entier et il a donc été nécessaire de découper la colonne plus pour prolonger l'ouverture nécessaire.

studio Pellacani

● Williams Joy
The Art of Fiction No. 223,
Interviewed by Paul Winner
in *The Paris Review*, no. 209
Summer 2014

De notre interview de Joy Williams (écrivain) nous avons extrait le thème du secret. Ce thème nous a amené à créer un espace intime.

studio Chassot

● Wolf Tobias
The Art of Fiction No. 183,
Interviewed by Jack Livingsin
The Paris Review, no. 171
Fall 2004

Pour ce projet, nous nous sommes inspiré d'un interview de Tobias Wolff, et avons donc conçu une pièce dans laquelle nous avons tenté de créer une atmosphère favorable au travail. Elle est composée d'une succession de cadres très rapprochées qui forme au sol deux quarts de cercle qui traduisent le mouvement de l'utilisateur qui irait ou partirai de cet espace clé qui est formé par la structure: le bureau. A cet endroit, le sol et la place assise sont confondus. Cet pièce s'ouvre sur un chemin dont la forme suggère une perspective, accentuée par la diminution de l'espacement entres les lattes.

studio Chassot

studio Rufer

L'ancien est oublié, le nouveau est appelé, de leur point de rencontre le chaos s'est créé.

studio Cabay

Elle était là, posée sur l'herbe humide, avec ses longues pattes pointant vers le ciel. Un mois déjà que nous travaillons sans relâche à l'habiter, à la comprendre, mais pour la première fois, nous ne la dominions pas; c'est elle qui nous regardait. Cette rencontre, chacun l'avait déjà imaginée, rêvée et attendue. Les projets qui n'étaient encore que maquettes et dessins devenaient alors enfin possibles.

studio Rufer

Inspire, tire, expire, lâche, tu vois? Le ciel, tu le vois? Et tes muscles, tu les sens tes muscles?

studio Rufer

Alice entre dans une pièce close, encombrée de planches inclinées. Sur l'une d'elles, Alice lit PUSH ME. Elle pousse de toutes ses forces. Le mur devant elle s'incline et le plafond se détache. Amusée Alice reprend avec les autres parois. Et la petite pièce dans laquelle elle se trouvait semble s'être agrandie, ainsi ouverte vers l'extérieur et baignée de lumière.

studio Cabay

Découvrir l'assemblage qui captivera l'espace, qui fera vivre une expérience forte à l'utilisateur, sentir le bois, le toucher, le travailler, le couper. Nous sommes allés à la rencontre de la matière, de cette limite entre l'esprit et la substance, cette interface subtile sur laquelle se cristallise l'architecture.

studio Cabay

Il y a neuf mois nous ne connaissions encore rien à l'architecture. Aujourd'hui nous ouvrons les portes de notre première maison.

studio Cabay

La Créature se déplace le plus vite possible dans l'espace orthogonal

Dans sa fuite elle fracasse la géométrie de la structure

En s'engouffrant dans ses entrailles,

L'homme n'a soudain plus peur de l'infini.

studio Cabay

Cette architecture éphémère aura permis à des étudiants de construire une idée; de transformer des traits en matière et le vide en espace.

studio van der Woude

Ce que je retiens de cette année qui touche à sa fin, c'est le fait de travailler sur le terrain, à l'échelle réelle des éléments, parce que je me rends compte de ce que je dessine!

studio van der Woude

La première fois que l'on m'a envoyé sur un chantier, à 16 ans, on m'a donné un sac de 40kg de béton dans les mains et je suis tombé, du coup ils m'ont donné un sac de 25kg de plâtre à la place ...

studio van der Woude

Ce projet m'a offert la possibilité de dessiner. J'ai été très surprise de m'apercevoir que cela me plaisait.

studio van der Woude

Lorsque pour la première fois, Lisa, Maud, Dimitri et moi nous sommes immergés dans le projet construit, nous ne nous y sentions pas bien. Nous étions trop à l'étroit. Cette ouverture au sol que nous avions prévue apparaissait alors comme un gouffre, un trou noir qui aspirait la sensation de convivialité qui était à la base du projet.

studio van der Woude

Le dessin passe de mains en mains et chacun doit être capable de la comprendre au premier coup d'œil. Ainsi il se doit d'être précis et propre, un malentendu entre une tâche et une vis serait si vite arrivé!

studio van der Woude

"J'ai fait tomber la mèche de la perceuse, attention c'est chaud!"

studio van der Woude

Même si le détail est correct sur le papier, c'est difficile de la construire en réalité.

studio van der Woude

Le projet est sans cesse en mouvement et n'est jamais réellement terminé. Selon les difficultés et questions rencontrées, on change d'avis, on recommence, on retourne à l'idée de départ et ainsi de suite ... C'est un véritable ballet!

studio van der Woude

Plié en quatre durant les trois-quarts du temps, je me tape la tête une bonne dizaine de fois et remarque l'utilité des casques.

studio van der Woude

Oh! un escalier sur notre plan incliné!
Oh! une porte au milieu du projet!

studio den Hartog

Elle fait peur mais c'est une peur agéable. Kahn dit qu'un bâtiment devrait être ce qu'il veut être.

Voilà, une forêt qui est née au cœur de ce monstre.

studio van der Woude

Avec de bons dessins comme base, on s'imagine déjà que le résultat construit sera parfait.

Utopie.

studio den Hartog

La forêt est belle, sauvage dans cette protostructure vide. Au fil du temps, elle s'adapte, raccourcit de tous les côtés, afin de rentrer dans cette grille bien ordonnée dont il fallait s'extraire à la base. On enlève de poteaux aussi aisément qu'on abat des arbres.

studio van der Woude

Cela peut sembler aisé de prendre une photo, mais il est difficile de créer une photo.

studio den Hartog

De l'extérieur, on ne la voit pas.
De l'intérieur, on ne la sent pas.
La colonne vertébrale supporte la structure, dirige les regards, répand le mouvement; c'est une base de l'architecture, qui au final, est le plus important.

studio van der Woude

C'est magnifique!
C'est surréaliste!
C'est inouï.

studio Chassot

Le succès aime l'effort.

studio den Hartog

Des poteaux verticaux.
Inhabitables.
Juste des obstacles.

studio Chassot

Le dessin avance, l'idée se précise, se concrétise. Laisser une trace devient aussi facile que de l'effacer, mais elle reste. Petit à petit, la notion de trait devient abstraite. Chacun s'exprime à sa façon, développe une idée. C'est une opportunité: rêver l'espace et y entrer, sur une feuille de papier.

studio Chassot

Un processus initié par une citation, qui a amené à une idée, laquelle a déclenché une réaction en chaîne d'événements, un développement, jusqu'à un résultat que nous pouvons appeler "final", mais qui n'est en réalité seulement que le début de quelque chose de nouveau; la naissance d'un objet dynamique, riche de potentiel de croissance et qui n'assumera jamais, probablement, une forme définitive.

studio Chassot

Le dessin devient un spectacle dans lequel notre regard peut se balader et s'y perdre. Les éléments du théâtre s'assemblent et s'entremêlent, créant un labyrinthe visuel.

studio Chassot

Le but du cours est d'aller du petit au grand, de voir l'abstrait et d'aller vers le concret.

studio Baur

Finally, we had the opportunity to expose our models so I was able to discover what my work created in a "real" reality and in a different space than the one from the studio.

Furthermore, we were able to observe what created the putting in parallel of my work and the one of my old partner. Maybe we could speak about complementarity.

studio Guaita

Comment construire un projet efficace en un minimum de temps et de matériel? Comment créer une transition? Mais qu'est-ce qu'une transition? Sommes-nous dans un entre-deux qui, semblerait-il, n'aurait pas lieu d'exister? Ou avons-nous donné la possibilité à cet entre-deux de s'exprimer et de nous laisser l'expérimenter?

studio Guaita

Soie.
Satin.
Velours.
Coton.
Caoutchouc.
Carton.
Mousse.
Béton.
Acier.

studio Guaita

C'est l'histoire de deux amants qui habitent dans la même pièce. La réciprocité des sentiments de l'un est douteuse, alors le mari s'assoit tous les jours au bord d'une fenêtre. Il attend sa femme.

La charmante femme traverse les murs. Il s'agit d'une fuyante. Elle ouvre plus de portes qu'elle n'en ferme tandis que son mari par toujours à sa recherche dans un jeu infini entre chat et souris.

studio Guaita

Je vois. Je vois cette femme au manteau rouge, traversant la rue avec détermination; je vois ce chien, marchant lentement, attendant son vieux maître comme si les rôles s'étaient inversés avec le temps...je vois tous ces gens traversant cette rue lausannoise, tels des acteurs. Et il y a cet oiseau aux plumes grises, ses fines pattes aiguilles gainées de peau, tentant tant bien que mal de combattre le froid. Je vois aussi cette façade; cette façade et son vécu; ces traces, ces empreintes qui se dessinent au fil des années.

Mais ce que j'attends de voir par dessus tout, c'est quelqu'un qui ait enfin le courage de monter ces marches, une par une, d'atteindre et de franchir cette porte par simple curiosité. Cette porte, au sommet de ces marches encastrées. Et que se passerait-il si cette personne décidait tout à coup de traverser ces deux mondes?

Lausanne. Paris.

studio Guaita

C'est comme si le bâtiment pouvait s'étendre à l'infini.

studio Baur

linked to our double element
lacquer
creating something else
dissolution

studio Dürr

Comment les plans horizontaux et verticaux peuvent-ils influencer notre perception d'un espace?

studio Dürr

The twins Claire and Ombre have very opposed characters, as their names show it. Therefore, their rooms are conceived throught their likes and ways of life.

Each one has its own little world, but going down their room's stairs, they found themselves in a common space which is articulated around a main node.

studio Dürr

You face it but you can't reach it. This is what it's all about, finding the way. This research isn't without risks, you may loose yourself before finding it but the process to find these suspended stairs is worth it because it leads you to discover the other projects. Our suspended stairs begins when you physically touch it but it really starts way before that.

studio del Grosso

Où se situe la limite entre art et architecture?

Comment proposer une architecture adaptée aux utilisateurs mais résultante d'une sensibilité personnelle tout en évitant une démarche autothétique?

Et surtout, après avoir admis que l'empirisme et l'itération sont quelques unes des clés menant à une architecture adaptée, combien de ratés sont-ils nécessaires avant d'atteindre une option simplement satisfaisante?

CONSTRUCTION CATALOGUE

B

Another two months later I had adopted, within the bounds of pos-sibility, a rather thorough notion of the HOUSE 1 project. It was being developed within an educational framework by the name of ALICE ("Atelier de la conception de l'espace") affiliated to the department of architecture at the EPFL in Lausanne; the very same educational laboratory that was loosely woven into the frame story of my first SPACEMAKER trip. 204 first semester students of architecture were conceiving and building a house that had, as far as I could gather from the information I had acquired, no functional purpose whatso-ever but the collective and collaborative experience of doing exactly that: conceiving and building a house on the basis of a given proto-structure defining its dimensions and spatial parameters.

I had hacked into their e-mail servers, I had scrutinisingly followed their blog entries. I had downloaded drawings, conceptual notes, and pictures of models. I had gotten familiar with basic ideas of architecture (like the difference between balloon framing and platform framing). I had been doing a lot of things to gather what the whole project was all about. Since the students were still changing their ideas almost every other week, it was difficult to systematise the information. Moreover, they were working in twelve separate "studios", and each of these studios was developing a separate part of the building. Although I compiled the weekly reports very carefully before I sent them to the post office box address that Adrienne From-sett had given me, I still had no idea whether I had found anything her client was interested in. She paid me a visit on the last weekend of January 2016 to check on my progress with the SPACEMAKER training program, and she told me nothing more than that I coped pretty well, that her client was satisfied with my reports, and that I could unhesitatingly proceed to two training sessions per week.

For my part, I was not that happy with my training progress. It had been clear to me from the start that if I wanted to stay con-scious of the outside reality during a session without quitting or aborting the application, I would have to achieve that at the very beginning of the program run when I simply found myself plunged into a deep black silent void. In other words, I had to force my sens-es, especially my visual and aural perception, back into reality *before* the chain of events in my mind was set in motion. As soon as I was captured in these events, the only way to get in touch with the outside reality was either to quit the program or to try to shut down the whole MultiCom Sensorama system from within my "individual world interior".[2] At the first attempts, I had already for-gotten that there actually was an outside reality a few seconds after I had launched the program. I saw the meteorite fly past me, arrived in the desert of the Desolate Lowlands, got involved in the Moon-watcher scene, and then I had to endure the whole story all over

See *All About Space, Volume 1: The Invention of Space*, chapter I.1 Starting Up.

again as if it had been the first time, although I was able to occasionally skip certain contents or slightly reconfigure the course of events. According to Adrienne's explanations, that was to be expected not only because of the commemorative behaviour of my brain but also because the application was programmed to adapt itself to the recorded brain activity patterns of a certain user.

However, by the end of February I was able to permanently keep in mind that it was all just an illusion like some reoccurring dream. Subsequently, my acting under the influence of the application changed remarkably. New episodes were added to the story and some were "deleted" once and for all. The chain of events began to change in unpredictable ways every time I logged on the program. Completely new storylines emerged, which certainly made my training sessions more thrilling. But there was one scene that kept coming up persistently: Sooner or later I always arrived at that crucial moment when I drew the crimson red curtain at the left border of my individual world interior to reveal the "place where space inventors go". And whenever I reached that point, the further run of events got completely out of control.[3] Seemingly, that was good enough to come up to Adrienne's expectations for the time being.

On the other hand, the regular training sessions began to cause certain side effects. One of them involved my hearing: Sometimes when I was outside of my apartment, I heard the strangest of noises. Most of them were awful and frightening, like distant screeching and squealing and indeterminate rushes, but sometimes I heard almost musical sounds like the singing of disembodied voices. I thought of them as "soundprints", and obviously they did not exist anywhere but in my head. Another symptom affected my eyesight: Sometimes I was under the impression that my vision had become much sharper and intense. I could see shades of colours that I thought I had never seen before, and at other times things suddenly appeared blurry and diffused. Since Adrienne had told me that these effects might occur, and since they were temporary and far from any disabling degree, they didn't bother me much.

It was not until that weekend in March that things really got going. But when they finally did, they startled me up for good.

On the early evening of Friday the 11th of March, after I had finished and printed out my weekly report, I put on my old ragged black leather jacket and took a walk down to *Ninotchka's* as I often did when I was in low spirits about the way things were going. It was my favourite bar in downtown Zurich at the time; a dark and cosy backstreet place full of not so cosy backstreet people. It was exactly the right place to make myself forget that another week had gone

3 See *All About Space*, Volume 1: *The Invention of Space*, chapters V.5, *Nothing But The Truth* and

by without any interesting results, at least without any that I could recognise as such. Ninotchka was working the counter herself, wearing her Friday night dress and grinning her Friday night grin. I asked her whether Jerry was around because I thought it was the right time for a little speedball holiday. But Jerry was not there, and so I just had a large beer.

I must have been standing at the bar for at least half an hour thinking about almost everything a man can think about without trying too hard, when I suddenly picked up one of those squealing noises somewhere in the back of my head and my attention was drawn to the short guy in the black business suit who looked like Bruce Willis in his very best days. He was hanging around the door with an empty glass in his left and a smart phone in his right hand and quite obviously, he did not belong there. When our eyes met, he seemed to wince a bit and dropped his gaze to look at the dark screen of his phone.

I darted a glance at Ninotchka. She just shrugged her shoulders. I drank up my beer and let a few minutes go by. Then I dropped seven Franks onto the counter and started walking towards the door. The Bruce Willis guy looked as if he had felt a sudden desire to void his bladder. He desperately tried to avoid my eye. When I reached the door and opened it, he started to dial a number.

Always trust your intuition, Adrienne had said to me three months earlier. I must admit that I had not always heeded her advice since then, but this time I did. I felt that I had priorities other than to approach and confront the guy in the black suit. I crossed the Kornhaus Bridge almost running, and a bare seven minutes later I unlocked the door to my apartment.

At first sight, nothing pointed towards the possibility that someone had broken in. The door lock was intact, and there were no visible traces that anyone had searched the apartment. Everything seemed to be in place, but that did not mean much with respect to the usual mess in which I had made myself at home. Of course, I went to the empty room first to find out whether the MSDT device was still in the secret compartment beneath the floor. As it turned out, it was, and it seemed that nobody had touched it. Next, I checked into my lap top computer on the office desk. I had not shut it down when I had left, so it took only a few seconds to find out that someone had unsuccessfully tried to unlock the sleep mode and access the hard drive. No one could break the encryption of my access codes by any means in less than two days, but the fact that someone had tried was disturbing enough.

Someone had been inside my apartment without leaving the slightest trace of a break-in, and whoever it was, they must have had a good reason to do so. They knew what they were looking for. They knew who I was and where I lived. They had me tailed. And one o them looked like Bruce Willis in his very best days. The first thing that crossed my mind was how lucky one idiot by the name of Frank Teller (or whatever his *real* name was) had been that something like this had never happened to him before since he had been forced to give up his life as a respectable member of the petit bourgeois society. Then, for whatever the reason, I thought that, irrespective of the consequences, this day would go down in my personal history as the day of the "Ninotchka incident". And then I opened the bottom drawer of the desk where I kept the remote hard disks containing the sensitive data and local back-ups. There had been nine hard disks in it. Now there were eight. The missing one was a bootable external drive that I hadn't used in years. I did not even remember exactly what kind of data I had saved on that one, but I knew that it wasn't any of the real hard stuff, just notes and drafts and sketches from the good old days. Anyway, the disk on which I had filed the current data of the HOUSE 1 job was still there.

I didn't know what to make of this, but I sure was on the verge of panicking. I opened a new bottle of Knob Creek Kentucky straight bourbon whiskey. Then I searched my wallet for the business card with Adrienne's secret mobile number on it. If this was not a good reason to dial that number, there wasn't any at all.

She said that she had expected something like this to happen and that she had even expected it to happen sooner. She said that she had not told me because my cooperativeness would have been seriously compromised if she had. And she said that, in the long run the incident could be ignored as completely irrelevant with respect to my mission if we would assess it objectively. It was so goddamned typical of her to say things like that in the calmest possible tone of voice. But I was not in the mood for it at the moment.

"Do you really believe that you can ignore this just because they didn't steal any of the HOUSE 1 data?" I yelled at her. "Do you really think that you can sit and watch my whole life go down the drain and that it is none of your business? –You can't be that stupid, how can you?"

"Calm down, Frank. Get a hold of yourself."

"No, I won't! I'm tired of listening to your sophisticated doubletalk. I'm so fucking sick and tired of trying so fucking hard to make a fucking fool of myself! Why don't you tell me the simple truth for a change? And how about getting started with the simple truth about what you assholes *really* want from me?"

"We should not talk about this on the phone," she said after a few seconds of uneasy silence. "It's not what you think."

"So what do you think that I think it is?" I retorted venomously.

"Considering the rage you're in, I doubt that *anything* I could say right now would make sense to you. But if you really need some thing to chew on, I'd suggest that you ask yourself why they didn't take your computer and *all* of the hard disks in the drawer. You said that none of the disks was denoted or labelled in any way. So why did they take that particular one? – How could they have possibly known what they would find on it? – Obviously they didn't. Maybe they just took it to find out if your encryptions are decodable at all."

"They won't find out anything anyway because as soon as they try to decode the encryption, a deleting program will be launched automatically."

"So why all this fuss? Are you trying to suggest that you're storing valuable data in a desk drawer?"

"Of course not. But, *obviously*, they know who I am and what I do and how to take away anything they want from me. They could come back any time to pick up where they left off. They could have bugged the whole apartment with wiretaps. My cover is blown Adrienne! Is it so god-awful hard to understand what that means?"

"No, it isn't," she said. "But I'm quite sure that you cannot assess the situation appropriately right now. Just for shits and giggles. What if the *critical* information that we're interested in could not be saved on disks and drives? – And what if I actually had been telling you the simple truth when I told you that nobody comes even close to understand what the human mind is capable of?"

"Here we go again! You're just trying to palm me off with your off-hook jabbering!"

"No, I'm not. Listen, I can and I *will* explain it to you, but *not now*. Not on the phone. I can arrange for a meeting in Zurich on Sunday. I'll get back to you." –

That was it. She had hung up on me.

Maybe I should have gotten right down to give some deepening thought to what she had just said. Maybe I should have checked into the signal of the tracker that I had installed in the stolen hard drive right away. But I deferred it all until later. My top priority was to get to a dark and cosy backstreet place, spend the rest of the night among not so cosy backstreet people, and wake up in the midmorning with a serious hangover. I took my lap top case under my arm just to make sure, and went straight back to *Ninotchka's*. As it turned out when I got home five hours later, I didn't even lock the apartment door.

The hangover was not as serious as I had planned it to be. Adrienne called me at nine in the morning to tell me that she would meet me for lunch at a restaurant at the Zurich main station on Sunday. After a few cups of coffee I started up my computer to check into that tracker signal again. I had already located it the night before on a motorway approach road on the western outskirts of town. It had not been moving for several minutes, and when I relocated it on that

Saturday morning, it was still on the same spot. The signal had got significantly weaker. Most probably, they had found and removed it and just thrown it out of the car window on their way to wherever.

I went shopping and did the laundry constantly trying to recollect what kind of data could have possibly been on that stolen drive. Most of the material must have been video clips, short pieces of music and text that I had produced to experiment with new ways of encoding information in words, sounds, and images. They had been of a certain nostalgic value to me, but since I had made great methodical progress in the meantime I thought that the loss was not that considerable.

In the afternoon my head was reasonably clear again, and so I decided to do my regular weekend training session, although, given the circumstances, I did not feel very motivated.

As soon as I had put the headset on and launched the application, I was surrounded by the all too familiar deep black silent void. But something was different this time. The blackness was not as absolute and impenetrable as it used to be. For the first time I got the impression that there was something behind it. Something that was within the reach of my senses if I just tried hard enough to focus on it. And the very moment I thought of it, the black void dissolved like smoke and revealed the white walls of the empty room in my apartment. I was so staggered by the experience, I didn't even think of the possibility that it could have been just another illusion made up by my mind. I stood up and started to walk about, touching the walls, the window, and the door handle, and it was all completely real. At the same time, I saw the meteorite fly by. The Desolate Lowlands appeared, and I could hear the sounds of the desert. I could see the arid steppe and the flat-topped mounts very clearly. I could even see the shape of the black hooded figure on the table rock in the middle ground. But it was all against the backdrop of the empty room.

I couldn't believe that I had achieved the final objective of my training sessions so suddenly and easily. I sat down on the parquet floor and expected the empty room to fade away again. But it didn't. I went through the program run as I always did, I skipped the "Tracing-the-Spacemaker" sequence and dived into Pablo Delgado's short story about the "Greatest Day for Freedom", I witnessed the attempt on Alois Gruntz's life and glanced through the "Dreamcatcher Hotel-Investigation" files, and finally, I stood before the crimson red curtain, drew it and entered the huge roofless columned hall with the cubic stage coated with white marble slabs: the "place where space inventors go". While I did all that, the empty room remained permanently visible, and I realised that it was not exactly in the background of my individual world interior but rather a simultaneous reality that I could perceive as specifically and realistically as I wanted to. I could, so to speak, fade it in and out at will.

A thin middle-aged actor with carefully combed hair appeared on the cubic stage. I had never seen him before in that scene. He wore a grey fifties' suit and began to recite an excerpt from William S. Burroughs' novel *Nova Express*, originally published in 1964. It was a passage from the "Chinese Laundry" chapter, which I almost knew by heart.

"Gentlemen, it was first suggested that we take our own image and examine how it could be made more portable. We found that simple binary coding systems were enough to contain the entire image however they required a large amount of storage space until it was found that the binary information could be written at the molecular level, and our entire image could be contained within a grain of sand. However it was found that these information molecules were not dead matter but exhibited a capacity for life which is found elsewhere in the form of virus. Our virus infects the human and creates our image in him.

We first took our image and put it into code. A technical code developed by the information theorists ..."

The sudden training success made me euphoric – and forget about any precautions. I got up a second time, walked to the door and opened it, although Adrienne had told me that I should never leave that room under any circumstances when my brain was connected to the MSDT system. I stepped out into the corridor and slowly crossed through the living room while I was still following the actor's recitation.

"... This code was written at the molecular level to save space when it was found that the image material was not dead matter, but exhibited the same life cycle as the virus. This virus released upon the world would infect the entire population and turn them into ...

The shapes and colours of the outside reality became continuously sharper and intense, just as they did during the occasional disturbances of my perceptual experience that were due to the side effects of the SPACEMAKER sessions. When I headed towards the balcony door and looked through the window, I could see a sky that was glistening in the most stunning shades of turquoise, although it had been an exceptionally cloudy day up until now. The houses across the street where glittering in the bright metallic colour of copper, and the leaves of the chestnut trees that bordered the pavement had turned purple. I opened the door and stepped out onto the balcony.

"... Information speeded up, slowed down, permutated, changed at random by radiating the virus material with high energy rays from cyclotrons, in short we have created an infinity of variety at the information level, sufficient to keep so-called scientists busy for ever exploring the 'richness of nature'."[4]

William S. Burroughs: *Nova Express* (1964), Grove Press, New York NY 1992/2014

An abrupt woosh flashed through my head and segued into a terrible noise that sounded like the screak of a chain saw. It seemed to come from everywhere around me. Instinctively, I pulled the remote head set from my head, but the torturous sound didn't stop. Instead, the amazing colours disappeared all of a sudden, and so did the columned hall and the cubic stage and the actor in the grey suit. The sky was as dull and cloudy again as it had been all day. Still, I was far from being back in my everyday reality. When I looked down onto the street, I saw people that were wrapped in amorphous grey and brown bubbles that looked like malicious boils and ulcers. They were semi-transparent and looked like auras or emanations or something, and whatever they were, they were morbid, disgusting, and undoubtedly immaterial. They even rose through the windscreens of driving cars. Anyone would have spontaneously expected these ugly things to produce an awful smell, but they didn't have any smell at all. Whenever several passers-by came close to each other, the repulsive apparitions merged to assume the form of dirty gelatinous foam that somehow reminded me of ovaries or caviar, and when the people moved on, their bubbles left slimy traces on the asphalt like smeared dog shit that mysteriously disappeared after a few seconds. However, there was a little boy riding a tricycle from one side of the driveway to the other, and he seemed to be the only person within sight who was not affected by this scary visual pestilence. His bubble was almost perfectly spherical and of a subtle light blue colour.

As I looked up at the sky again, I became aware that, directly beneath the blanket of clouds, a giant version of these bubbles arched over the whole city. It was moving sluggishly as if it had been alive, constantly changing its shape and density as if trying to find the perfect position to – – – to accomplish whatever its hideous purpose was.

I had no idea what to think of this. The most obvious explanation was that I had gone completely insane. On the other hand, I thought to myself, my sense of reality had been seriously overburdened during the past minutes. After all, I seemed to be the only one who experienced all this. The people in the street went their way, fiddling around with their smartphones or just gazing into space as if there was nothing to get excited about. Nevertheless, I was seized with panic. I felt every single nerve cord in my body vibrating in pain. There was this irresistible urge to vomit. The last thing I saw before I collapsed and passed out was my own dirty grey bubble enwrapping me, and the last thing that crossed my mind was that, ultimately, there was no way for me to make sure that what I had just seen was any more or less real than anything else.

However real it had been, it was gone when I regained consciousness a few minutes later. It was just another dull Saturday afternoon, and everything was back to normal. Well, almost everything. My brain felt like a steamrolled chewing gum, and I was a little weak in the knees. But when I got up, I suddenly knew *exactly* what the HOUSE 1 project was all about. I knew *exactly* what Adrienne and her anonymous client wanted me to do and why they had chosen me of all people to do it. But still, she would have to explain a whole lot of things at our lunch meeting the next day. And, to my surprise, she actually did.

INTRODUCTION

In jazz culture there is unique publication called The Fake Book. It is an informal "book" created in the 1950's containing at its origin about 2000 jazz standard partition. A decent level jazz musician is supposed to know by heart and be able to play instantaneously, without much thinking or preparation all and any of these songs. This universal repertoire creates a common background from which improvisations can be played. The fabulous power of this tool is that any musician in the world can gather with any other and they can play together, departing from this common repertoire.

Wikipedia tells us: A system is a set of interacting or interdependent component parts forming a complex/intricate whole. Every system is delineated by its spatial and temporal boundaries, surrounded and influenced by its environment, described by its structure and purpose and expressed in its functioning.

HOUSE 1 likes to think about the parts, components, forming the complex whole of the house as a series of jazz musicians. They have taken the time to learn and develop specific skills, hand made and computer driven. They have also spent time working their standards, creating the basis of a dialogical understanding that have allowed them to play a song of architecture and building that has been called HOUSE 1.

Understanding whole systems concentrates the content of this chapter on interaction, on standards, on construction. It focuses on how detailing, micro-pieces gather together to constitute one whole. The whole is one, but could be another. It is important to emphasize on the lack of unity of this whole. It is the important yet circumstantial result of a particular configuration of people and cultures. It could have resulted on another whole had there been a slight change on the actors participating to the project.

Marshall MacLuhan referred to Buckminster Fuller famous concept of Spaceship Earth and stated: "There are no passengers on Spacehip Earth, we are all crew. This visionary (and environmental sensitive) assertion applies to HOUSE 1 fully.

This chapter presents the modules, parts, construction details that have been established and developed to form a whole, a house. Derived from the balloon frame construction system, created in the North American 19th century, the HOUSE 1 construction is made out of multipliable details, materials, dimensions, and fixings. The balloon frame logic has developed into a proto-structure, described in one of the main articles of this section. HOUSE 1 grows from micro modular parts to develop a potential for a macro territorial approach.

We define "protostructures" as structures in a "proto-state": that is, structures that are ready to receive either alterations in themselves, or to accommodate further configurations. As such, they are open to further development, but also defined by their existence as fixed structures. Protostructures are systems or constructions that have the capacity to adapt themselves to transformations imposed by time and use. The prefix "proto-" implies the notion of temporality intrinsic to placing the definition of structure before any evolution of form or content. Thus, the term protostructure embodies a system that initiates its own transformation, as well as acting as a support for, and object of, transformation itself. Its destiny is to evolve; to change in appearance and/or function. It can also dissolve completely, leaving only its trace. Protostructures appear at all scales in architecture, from micro to macro, embodying the dialogue between a form and its use. Protostructures are engaged in a constant interaction with external interventions from agents, architects and users, and because of their openness and flexibility as systems, are able to address the social, economic and political challenges inherent in the production of space. In being inherently set at the threshold between idea and articulation, protostructures are a catalyst in design processes and facilitate decision-making.

The Maison Dom-ino project, designed by Le Corbusier, is an archetypal example of the concept of the protostructure. Consisting of the fundamental elements of building: raw slabs, columns and stairs, this structure was designed to be produced quickly and in large numbers, and to host the largest variation of possible internal arrangements and programs. These interventions into the basic structure were intended to shape an infinite variety of appearances.

Like this project, HOUSE 1 is of a primary structure composed of basic structural elements. The arrangement of these elements in space proposes an initial typological disposition, and orients itself already toward certain hypotheses of interpretation.

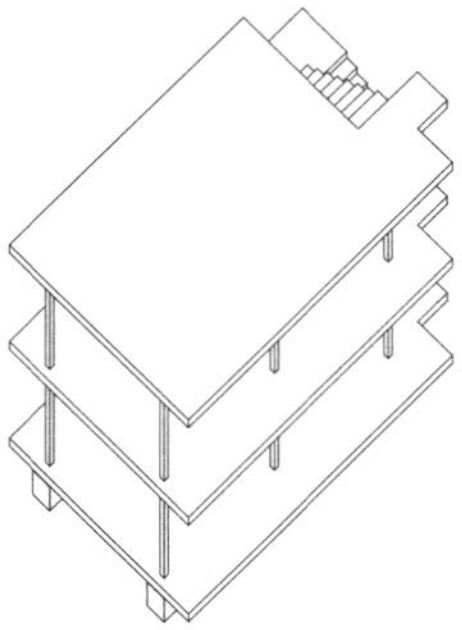

Axonometric view of the Maison Dom-ino, CAD drawing. Agathe Mignon.

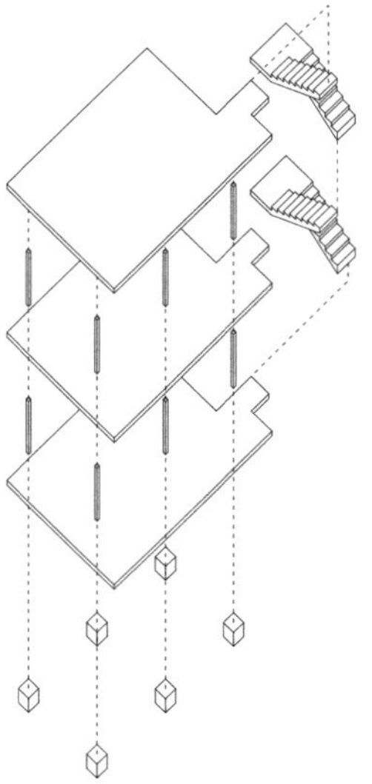

Exploded axonometric view of the Maison Dom-ino, CAD drawing. Agathe Mignon.

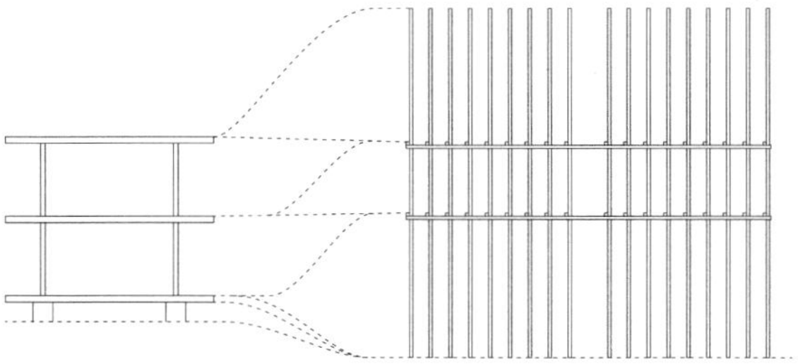

Elevation of the Maison Dom-ino and HOUSE 1, CAD drawing. Agathe Mignon.

The primary building volume of 11m³ is made up of 438 components of timber in 5m lengths. It is constructed from a base system of vertical supports on which are fixed two floor levels, and provides, within this cubic volume, 8 large subspaces and a space for cross circulation.

" Quand un mois plus tôt nous avions découvert pour la première fois la structure avec laquelle nous allions travailler, il était difficile de rester indifférent face à ce monstre de bois perché sur une multitude de pilotis. La protostructure n'est pas une page blanche, elle a ses rythmes, ses logiques, ses détails et ses espaces. Il faut essayer de la comprendre avant de l'habiter, au risque de la considérer comme une contrainte alors qu'elle est une opportunité. "
studio Cabay

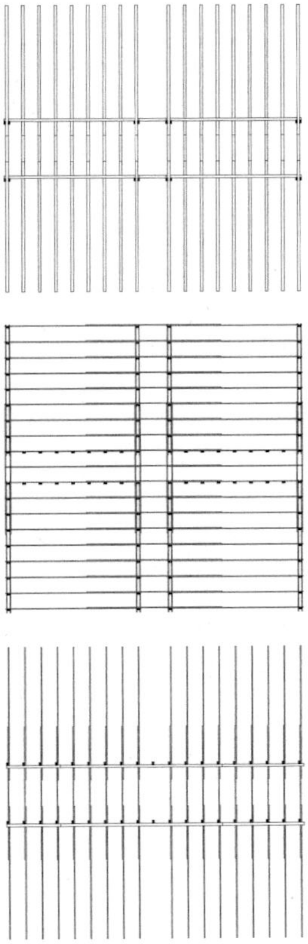

Plan, elevation and section of HOUSE 1, CAD drawing. Edouard Cabay.

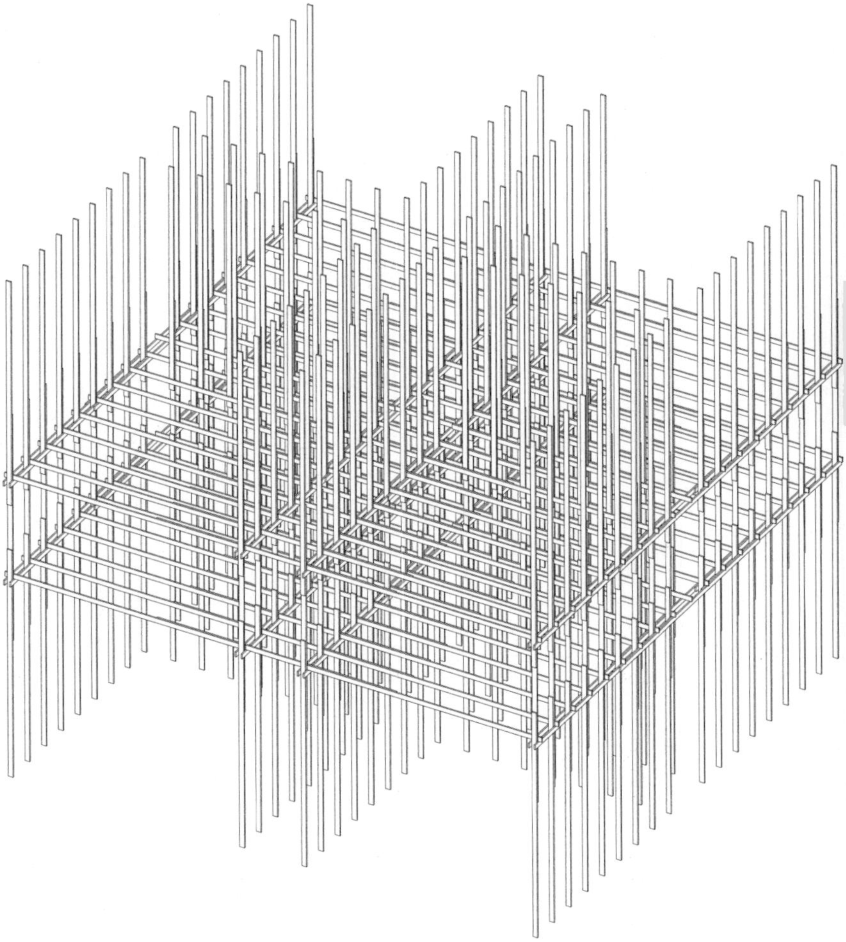

Axonometric view of HOUSE 1, CAD drawing. Laurent Chassot.

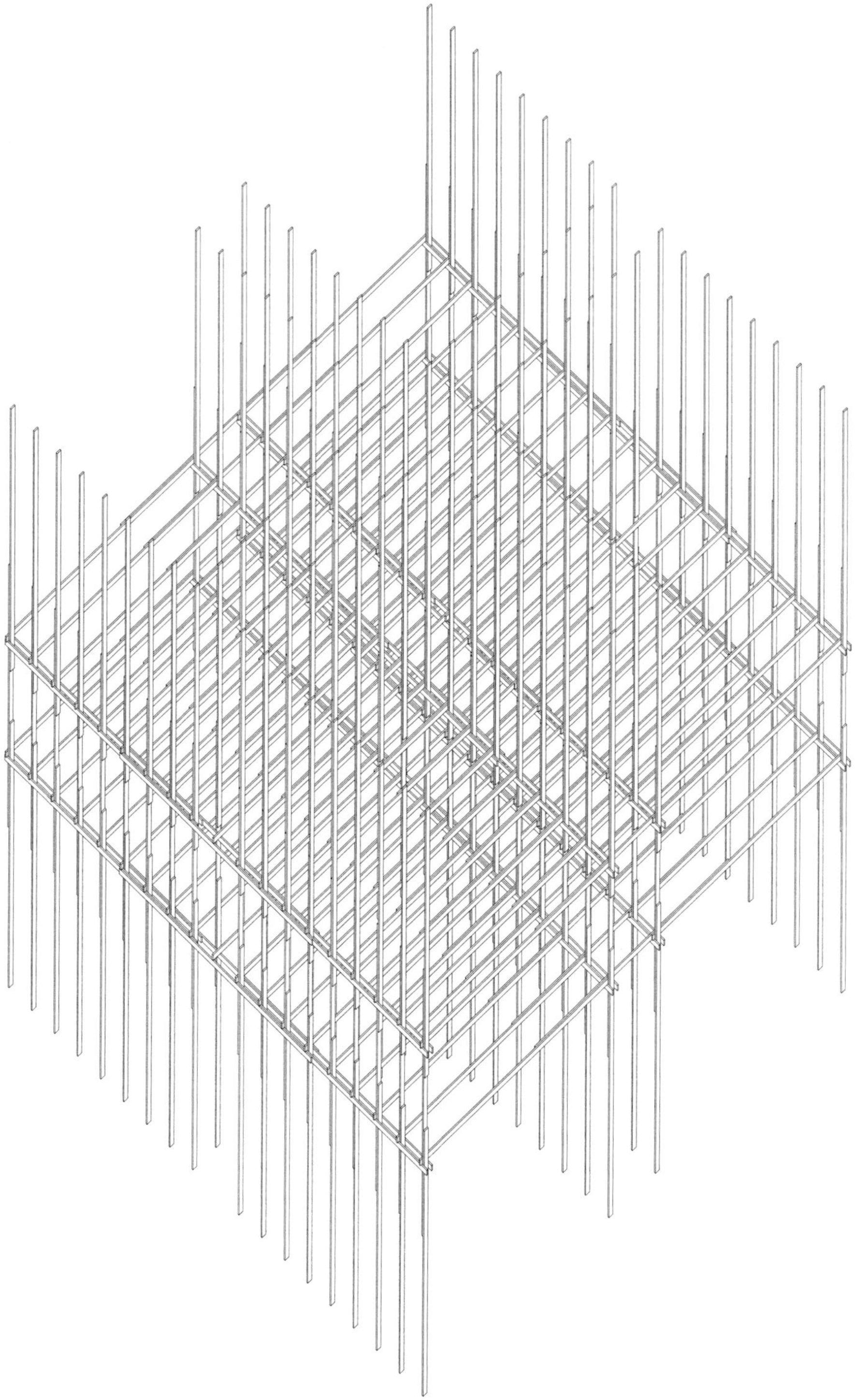

Axonometric view of HOUSE 1, CAD drawing. Agathe Mignon.

The protostructure of HOUSE 1 was built in the scale of 1:1 during Easter week by a group of volunteer architecture students, and supervised by several architecture studio directors along with an engineer specialising in timber construction. It took its place on the EPFL campus, in front of the Rolex Learning Centre (SANAA, 2010).

The prefabricated timber frames making up the protostructure were transported to the site and raised into place on the foundations. The first four parallel frameworks were sequentially mounted and fixed in place using cables. Following this, the transverse frames were assembled, and finally, the floors.

In parallel to the construction, a scale model at 1:5 was built in the studio workshop. It measures 2.2m³, and acted as the working basis for developing the individual projects within the protostructure, allowing for the testing of their construction and implementation.

1:1 Protostructure construction workshop. Dylan Perrenoud.

Construction workshop for the 1:5 protostructure model. studio Chassot.

1:1 Protostructure construction workshop. Dylan Perrenoud.

1:5 model construction workshop. Agathe Mignon.

PROTOSTRUCTURE 1:1 WORKSHOP

- March 29–April 2
- Léon; Constantin; Antonin; Manuel; Aloys; Timon; Mathias; Antonin; Mathieu; Jonathan; Erblin; Léon; Constantin; Antoni; Léon; Constantin; Antonin; Manuel; Aloys; Timon; Mathias; Antonin; Mathieu; Jonathan; Erblin; Manuel; Aloys; Timon; Mathias; Antonin; Mathieu; Jonathan; Erblin
- 46°31'4.358" N
  6°34'12.208" E

PROTOSTRUCTURE 1:5 WORKSHOP

- March 29–April 1
- Margaux; Marc; Selen; Maria
- AAD001, Transversal studio

The specific protostructure of House 1 is constructed of rectilinear components of timber, assembled in three dimensions according to the orthogonal axes x, y and z. Adopting the form of a three-dimensional grid, it thus becomes the physical and conceptual foundation for further interventions of habitation and appropriation. Far beyond its role as simply a structural support, the protostructure also establishes a field for further interventions, whose parameters are set by its own overarching rules.

The grid is made up of vertical and horizontal components oriented along the axes x, y and z. The coordinate points established by the intersections of these three axes compose a potentially unlimited space of intervention in three dimensions.

The physical articulation of this grid in the form of the protostructure allows the definition of everything from surfaces to complex volumes, exploiting at different moments and for different purposes one or another of the dimensions.

The grid defines a field ripe for intervention. In terms of density and scale, the multiplication or duplication of the components making up the grid initiates a series of transformations, which are able to significantly alter the perception and the use of space.

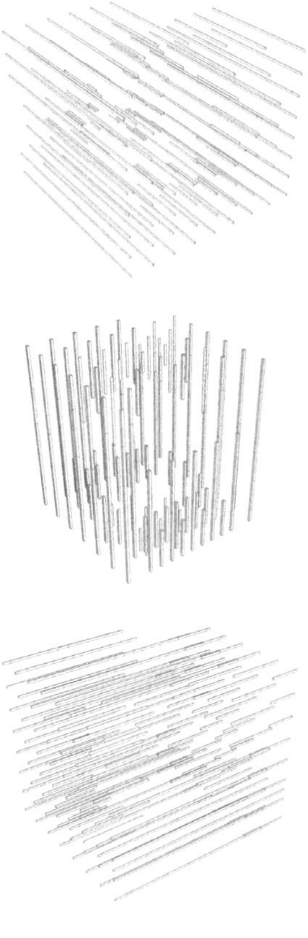

Elements in the x-y-z axis, CAD drawing. studio Grandgirard.

Several realisations of the grid. studio van der Woude.

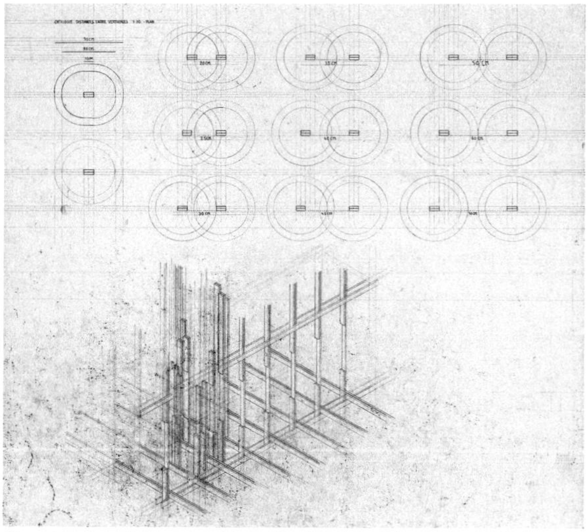

Drawing showing research into the density of the grid, pencil drawing on paper. studio den Hartog.

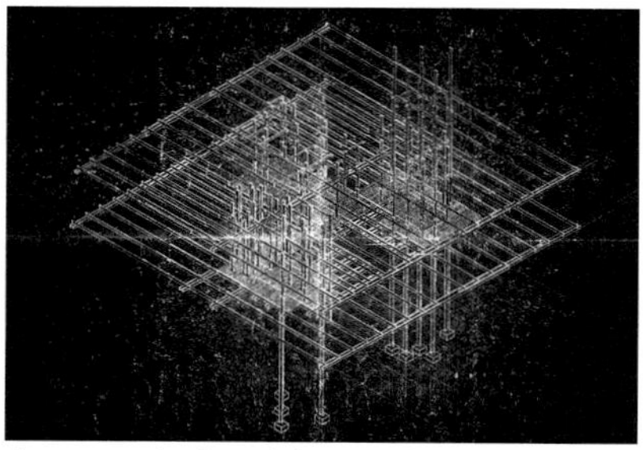

Axonometric view of the experimentation around density, pencil drawing on paper. studio den Hartog.

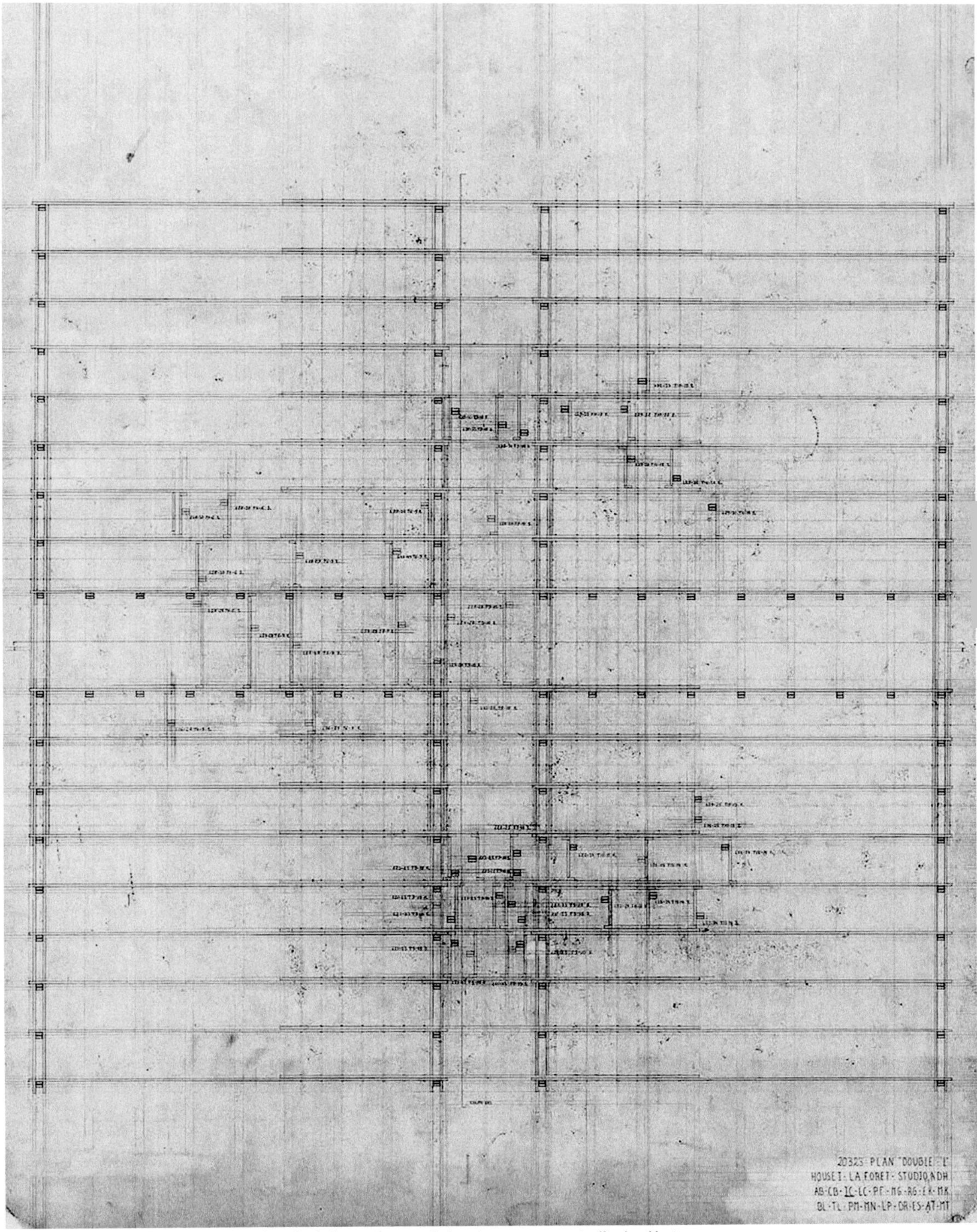

Mapping the experimental density of vertical elements, pencil drawing on paper. studio den Hartog.

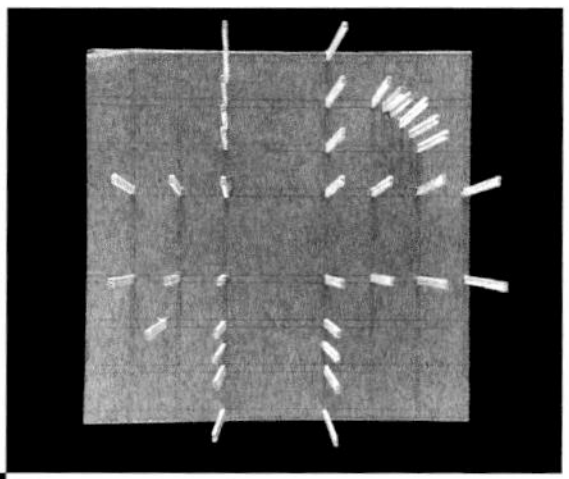

Test model of research into grid density. studio den Hartog.

"Il faut poser des verticales sur un plan, densifier, rendre invisible la grille."
studio den Hartog

By marking out specific points in this space, the grid imposes the rules of the game. Like a chessboard, the grid defines a specific field of possibility. Any evolution of the grid necessitates the manipulation of its parameters.

Nous tenterons ici d'interroger la grille comme support de création. C'est au travers de deux sites d'époque et de programme différents que nous essaierons de comprendre quels sont les apports et les limites d'un tel outil. Quelles transgressions pouvons-nous nous permettre, tout en respectant ce système?

Au terme de ce premier projet, nous nous rendons compte que la grille comme outil est utilisée dans divers programmes et domaines. Lors de son emploi dans le design graphique, elle est finie et ses limites sont déterminées par la feuille et ses marges. En architecture, la limite est trouble, la grille se prolonge et s'impose non seulement comme structure mais également comme médiatrice. Elle ouvre le dialogue entre une construction et son voisinage.
La grille ne doit pas contraindre le projet mais le stimuler.
studio del Grosso

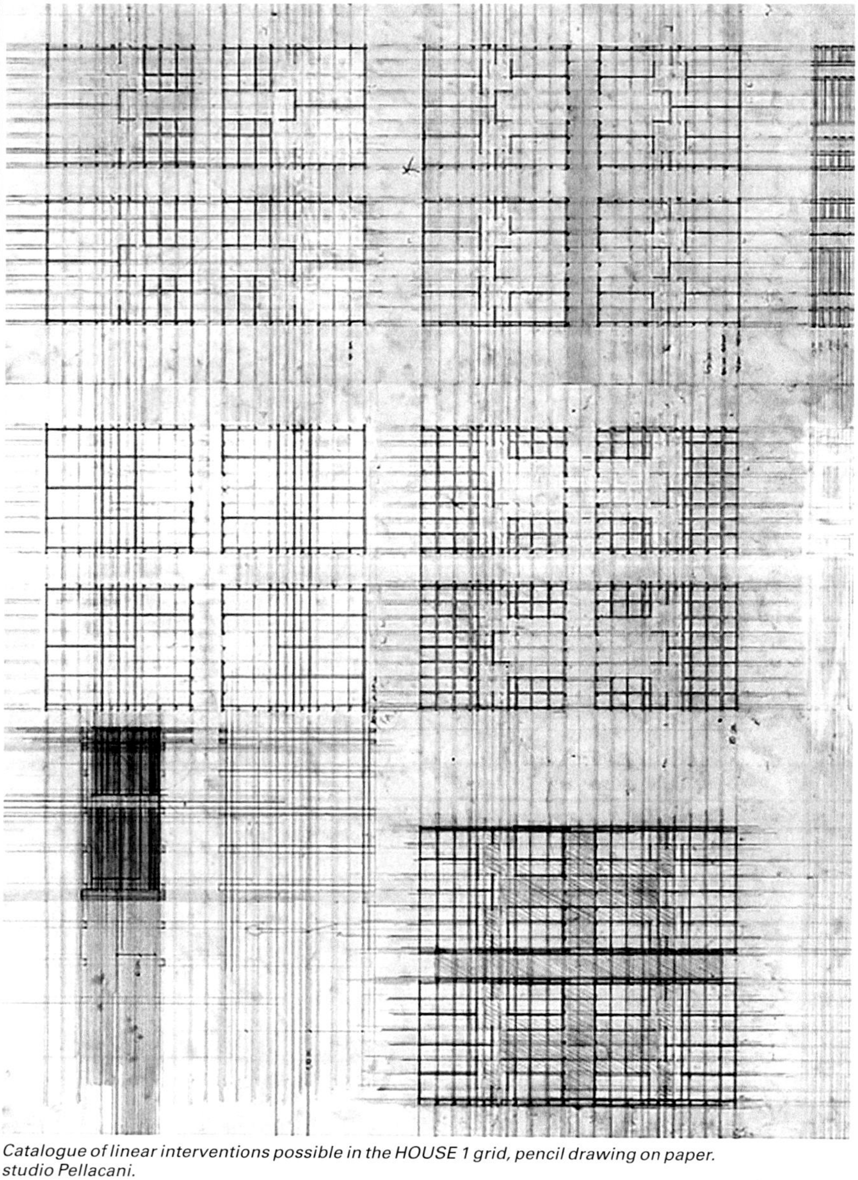

Catalogue of linear interventions possible in the HOUSE 1 grid, pencil drawing on paper. studio Pellacani.

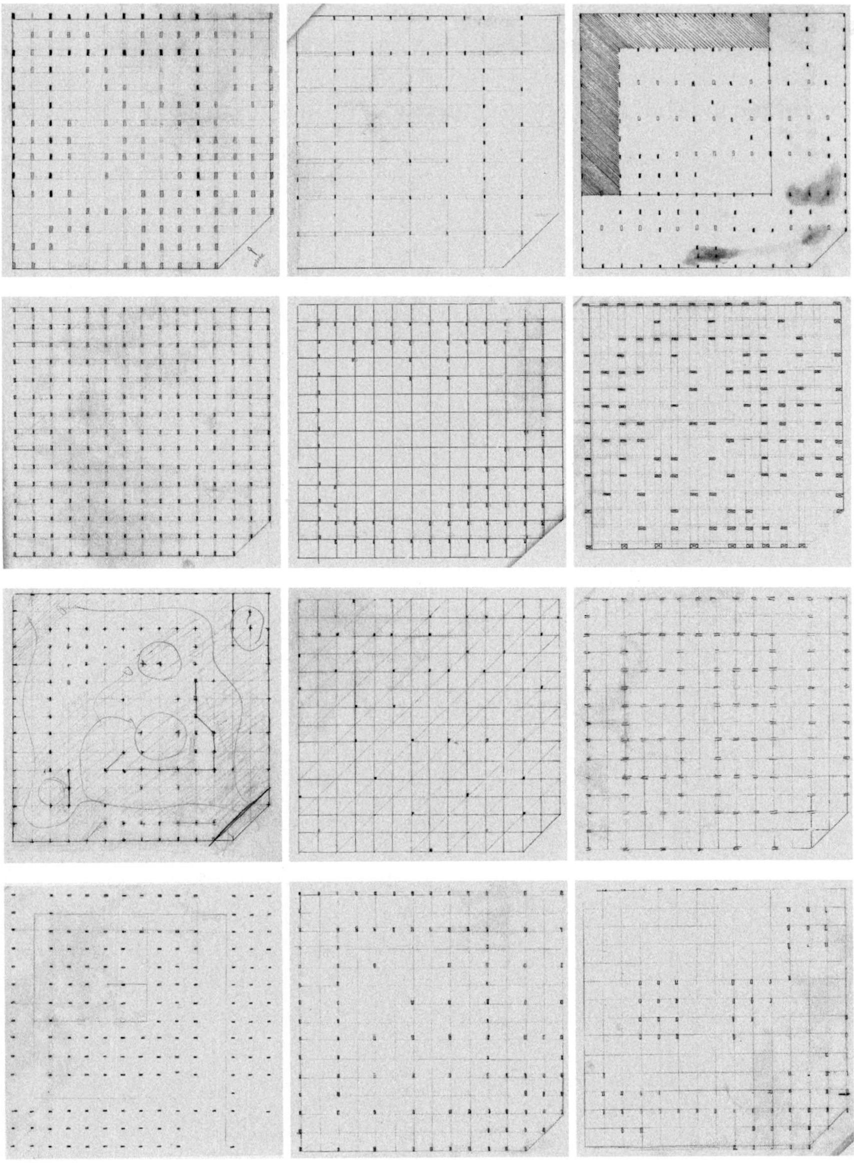

Research sketches of possible intervention into the HOUSE 1 grid, pencil drawing on paper. studio van der Woude.

The moment or point of intersection between the three directional axes is the key to the formation of the three-dimensional structure. This moment is described by the detail of the junction, the most complex and concentrated area of the grid. The detail of this junction functions as a prototype, which is replicated across the grid, setting the genetic code of the entire structure.

HOUSE 1, being built solely from rectangular components, must resolve its details at these junctions; where the axes intersect. Taking into account the dimensions of the intersecting components determines the parameters of assembly.

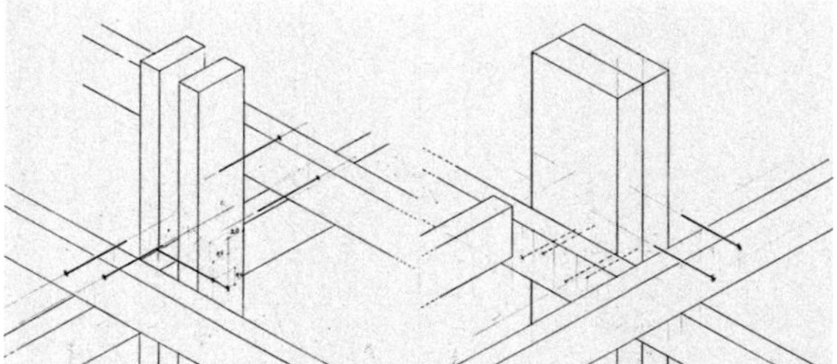

Working details in elevation and axonometric view, pencil drawing on paper. studio Grandgirard.

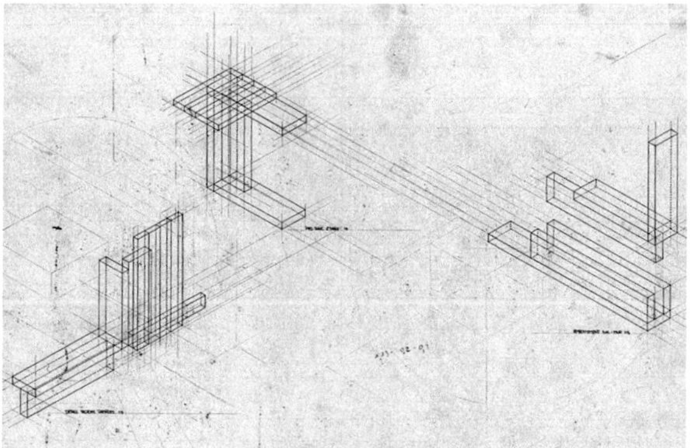

Working details in axonometric view, pencil drawing on paper. studio Guaita.

The components used are all of industry-standard dimensions. This allows for the limitation of detailing possibilities for the assembly to only those that are realistically able to accommodate these standardised components.

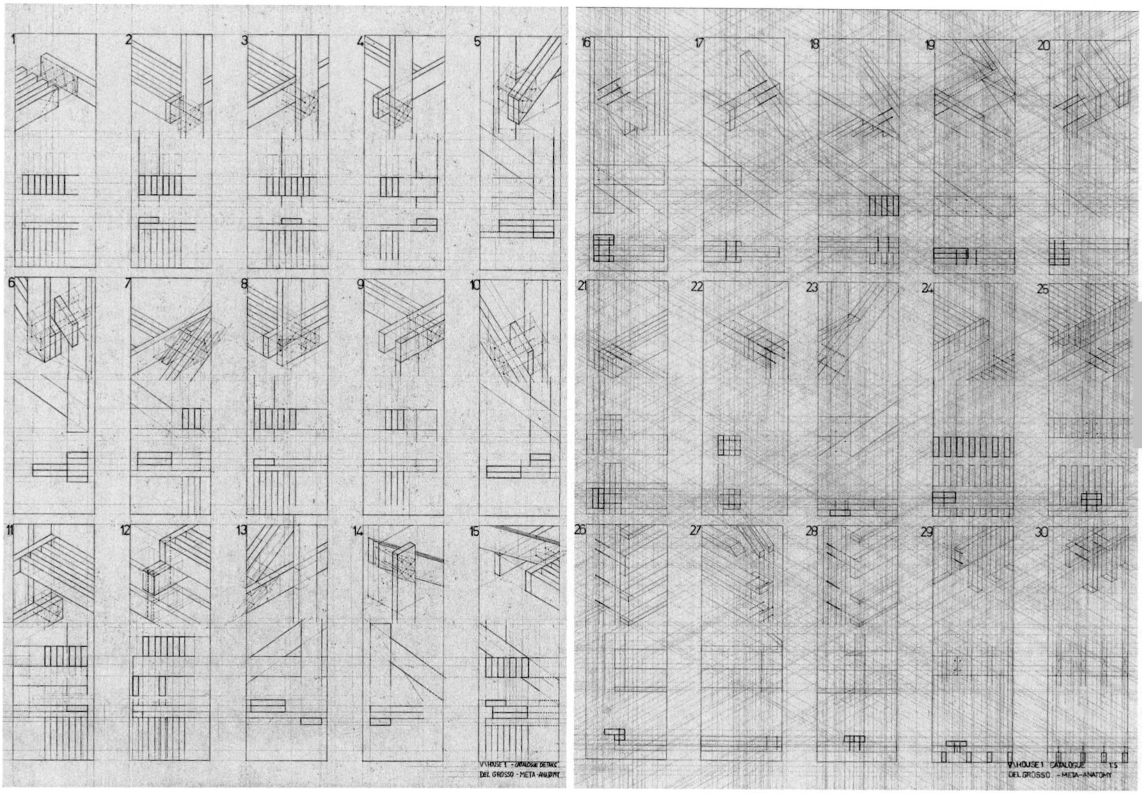

Detail catalogue 1–15, 16–30, pencil drawing on paper. studio del Grosso.

Every detail is then resolved based on the data of each intersection. A catalogue is established to address each detailing condition arising from the requirements of the structure. The catalogue of details, when read as an ensemble, forms the backbone of the construction.

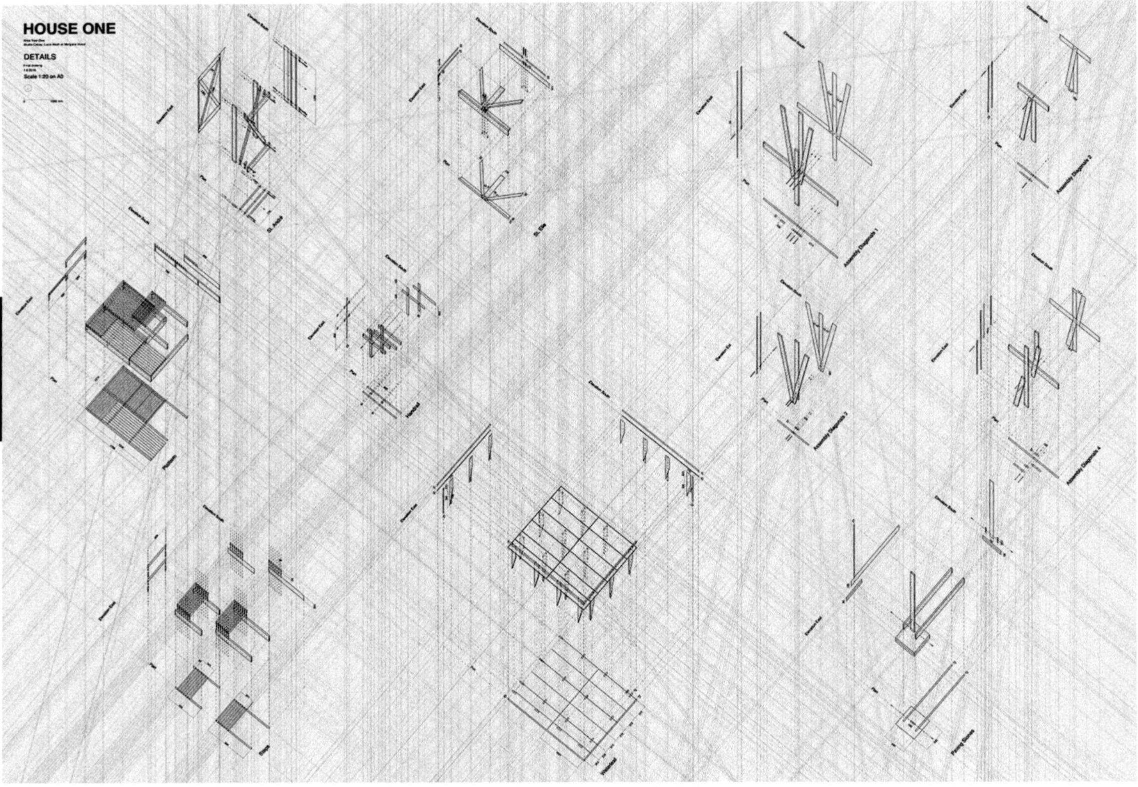

Axonometric view of the positioning of all the project details, CAD drawing. studio Cabay.

The grid system, governed by the intersection of axes, has no scale or limit. It allows the design of a spatial structure that is infinitely extendable in all directions.

One vector defines a direction; two vectors a plan; and three a volume. These conditions act as the support for three-dimensional interventions in the form of a network of points or junctions.

This grid network allows for the imagination of systematic structures – scaleless – whose complex volumes play with gravity.

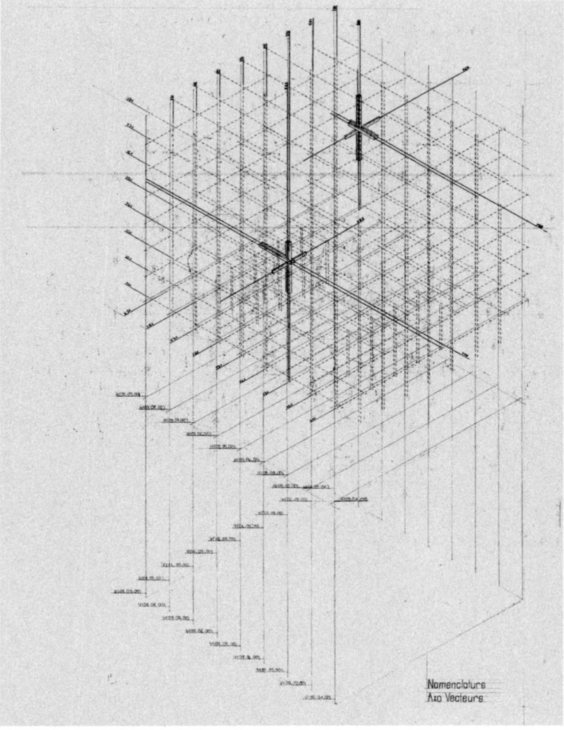

Protostructure nomenclature, pencil drawing on paper. studio Grandgirard.

Exploded axonometric views, hand and CAD drawing. studio Grandgirard.

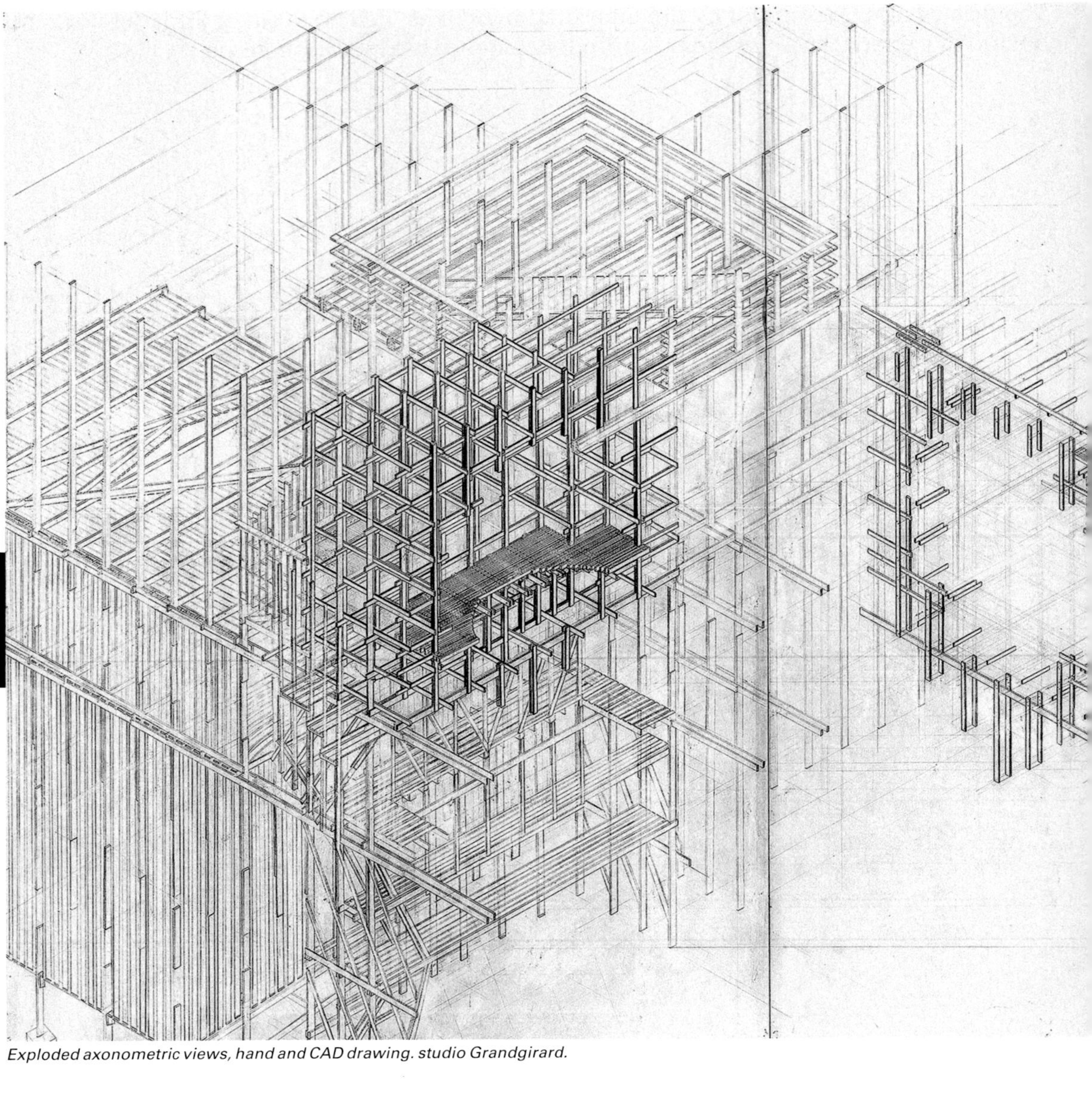

Exploded axonometric views, hand and CAD drawing. studio Grandgirard.

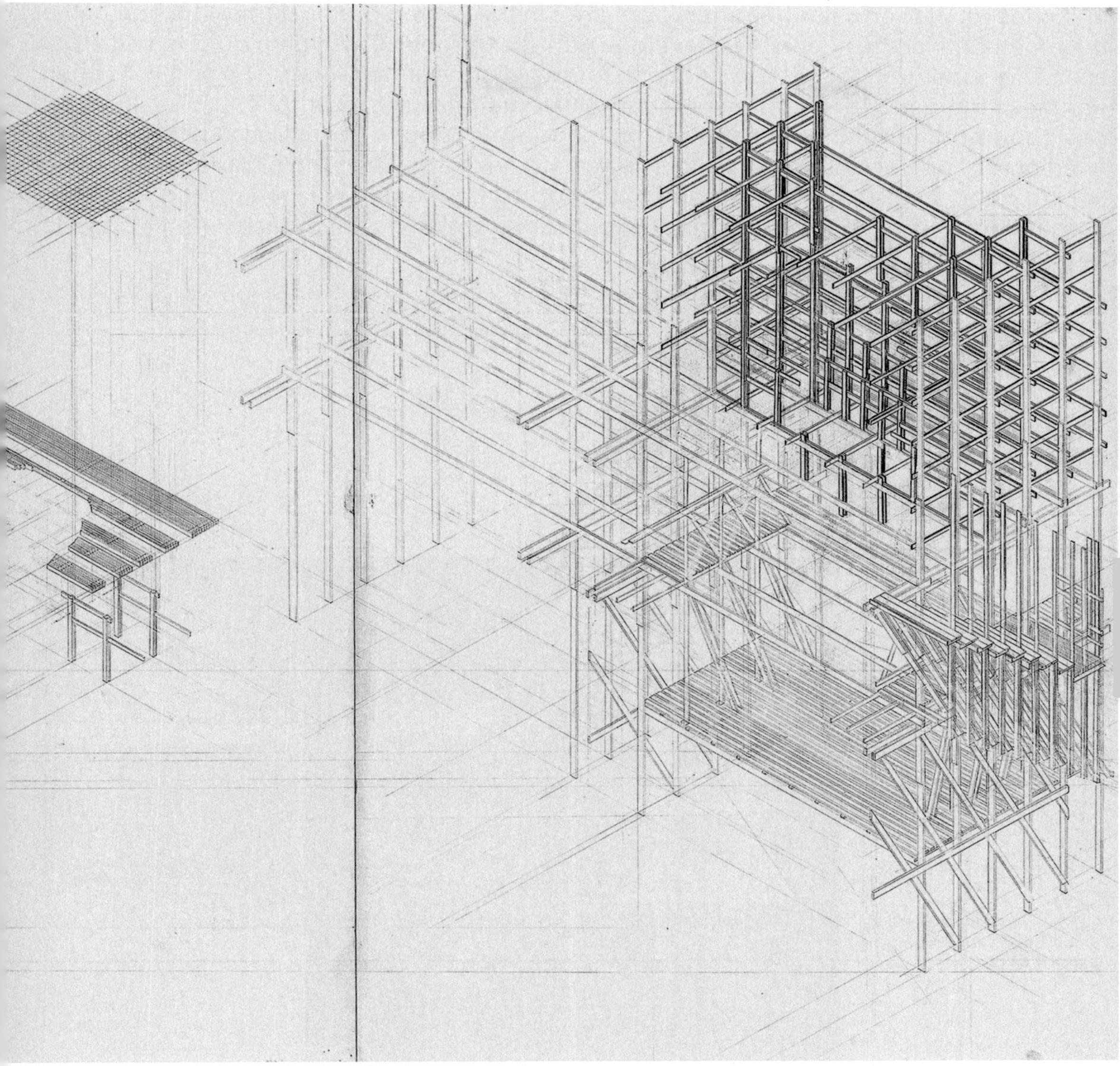

The concept of the "balloon frame" appeared in the United States during the first half of the nineteenth century, and was developed for the purpose of building quickly and at low cost. This construction system is notable for two distinct innovations. The first is its abandoning of mortise and tenon construction in favour of simpler assemblies, using unaltered basic components of timber (without the tongue and groove of mortise and tenon joints) fixed across one another with nails. The second, with a view to the broader economy of construction, is the standardisation of building components, which may then be simply assembled on the construction site, significantly reducing manufacturing and implementation costs.

This system is typically a light frame construction, made of straight components assembled in three dimensions. Beginning from a very simple logic, it is possible to duplicate components, or add them diagonally, in order to support different programs.

In order to assemble components at greater heights, the balloon frame very often resorted to a system of interlocking frames. These could be entirely prefabricated, then lifted into place to accommodate higher floors.

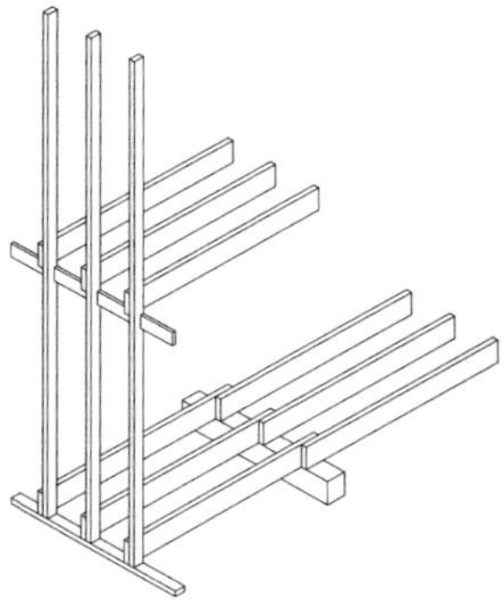

Axonometric view of the balloon frame system, CAD drawing. Agathe Mignon.

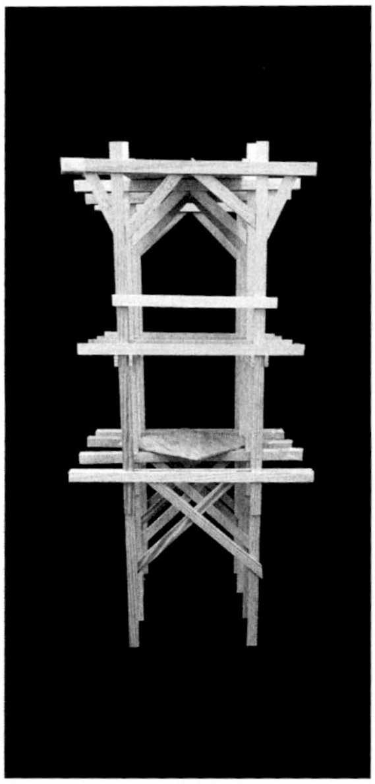

Structural research model. studio van der Woude.

Structural research model. studio van der Woude.

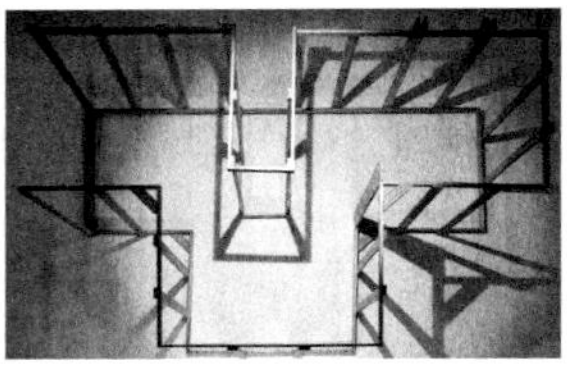

Construction model. studio den Hartog.

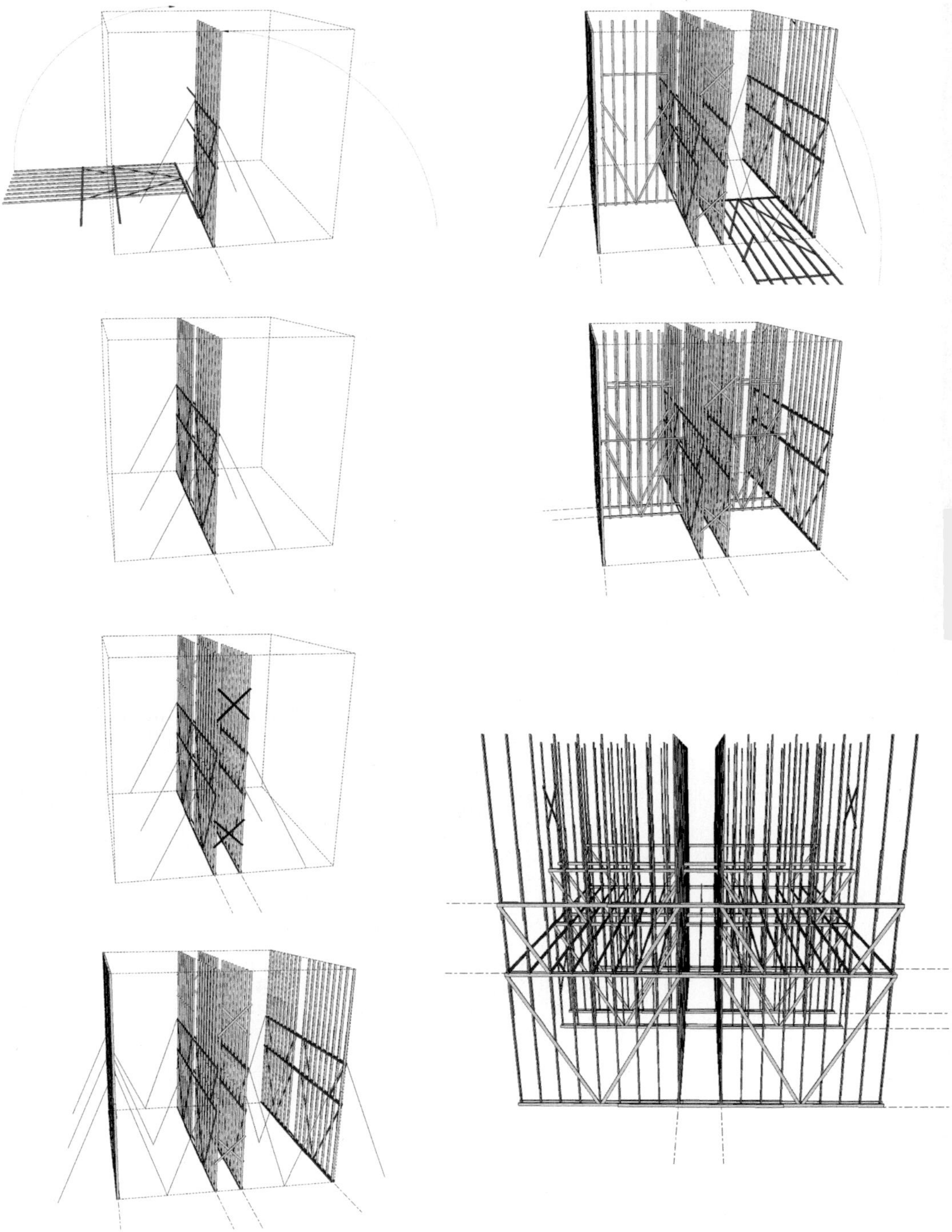

Installation sequence of vertical and horizontal panels, CAD drawing. Rémy Meylan.

Standardisation in HOUSE 1 includes components at specific sizes as well as methods of work. The limits imposed by standardisation ensure that different arrangements of one and the same component can lead to an infinite number of varied results.

The protostructure therefore meets notions of standardisation when considered as a whole system. As the basis of the entire assembly, it imposes the same rules on all interventions that seek to inhabit it. All the distinct proposals for HOUSE 1 therefore share the particular "genetic code" of this protostructure, responding to a rigorous process of standardisation despite their varied spatial qualities and outcomes.

Each intervention, being forced to interact with the primary structure, adopts – by necessity – its language. Acting in receptive mimesis, all the individual proposals use and engage with the overriding support system of the protostructure. HOUSE 1 is entirely formed of two components of timber: 100 x 27 x 500mm and 55 x 22 x 400mm pieces.

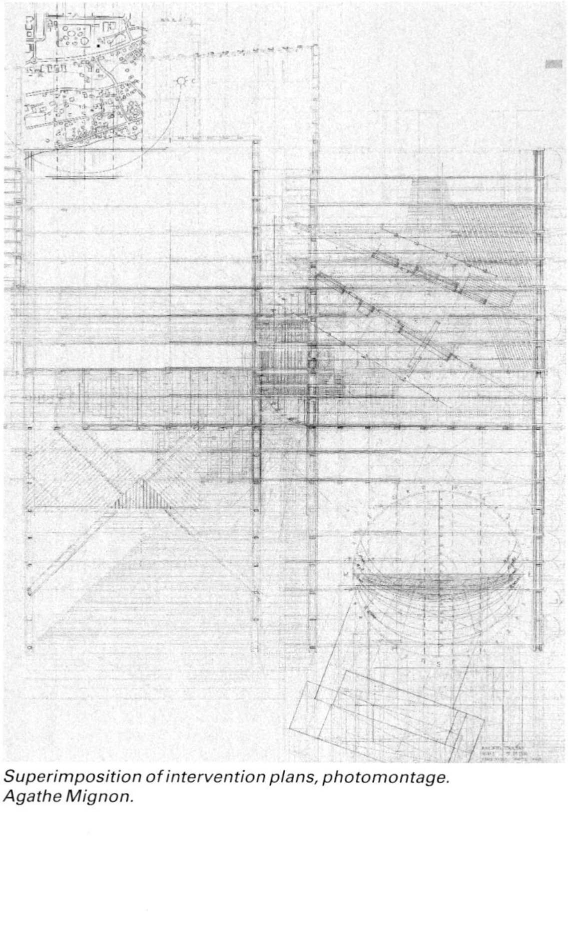

Superimposition of intervention plans, photomontage. Agathe Mignon.

Mid term critiques in the Rolex Learning Centre. Rudi Nieveen.

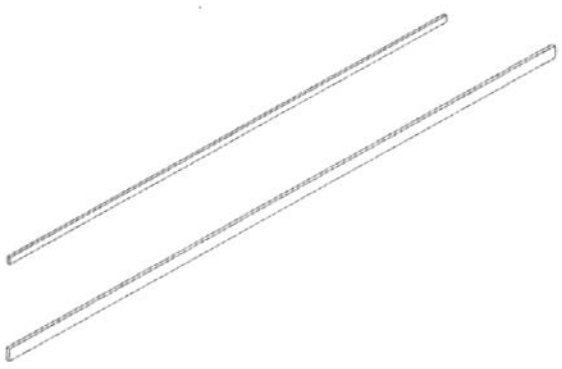

Axonometric view of the two profiles of timber, CAD drawing. Agathe Mignon.

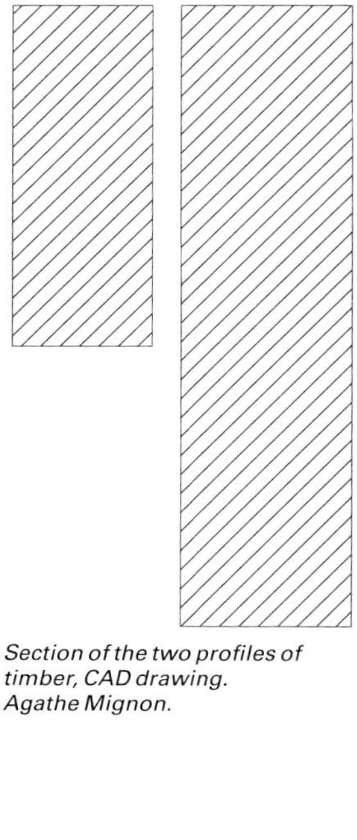

Section of the two profiles of timber, CAD drawing. Agathe Mignon.

INTRODUCTION

In the most physical section of the Construction Catalog, it is explained how HOUSE 1 stands and breathes.This chapter presents the relation of the construction to the ground, its reaction to the surrounding environment, and the sheltering that it offers ot its inhabitants.The premises of the implementation of HOUSE 1 are quite ambitious. It has been considered for this project that territorial occupation could be envisaged through a temporary approach.The nomadic, movable settlement implies that the land is not altered by the construction. Inhabitation becomes thus a dialogue between the temporarily built environment and the welcoming land or territory.The idea behind this attitude is to consider the construction as much as the land under the term landscape, gathering the two within a concept that makes not distinction between planted and built.There is another hypothesis that this subject attempts to discuss: the property of land and the possibilities to use it.What if all land was under Land Lease status, not belonging to any private owner?

To introduce this chapter no other text could present it better than Jack London'sThe House Beautiful (in Revolution and other Essays, 1906).

Speaking of homes, I am building one now, and I venture to assert that very few homes have received more serious thought in the planning. Let me tell you about it. In the first place, there will be no grounds whatever, no fences, lawns, nor flowers. Roughly, the dimensions will be forty-five feet by fifteen.That is, it will be fifteen feet wide at its widest – and, if you will pardon the bull, it will be narrower than it is wide.

The details must submit to the general plan of economy.There will be no veranda, no porch entrances, no grand staircases. I'm ashamed to say how steep the stairways are going to be.The bedrooms will be seven by seven, and one will be even smaller. A bedroom is only good to sleep in, anyway.There will be no hallway, thank goodness. Rooms were made to go through.Why a separate passage for traffic?

The bath-room will be a trifle larger than the size of the smallest bath-tub – it won't require so much work to keep in order.The kitchen won't be very much larger, but this will make it easy for the cook. In place of a drawing-room, there will be a large living-room – fourteen by six.The walls of this room will be covered with books, and it can serve as library and smoking-room as well.Then, the floor-space not being occupied, we shall use the room as a dining-room. Incidentally, such a room not being used after bedtime, the cook and the second boy can sleep in it. One thing that I am temperamentally opposed to is waste, and why should all this splendid room be wasted at night when we do not occupy it?

My ideas are cramped, you say? – Oh, I forgot to tell you that this home I am describing is to be a floating home, and that my wife and I are to journey around the world in it for the matter of seven years or more. I forgot also to state that there will be an engine-room in it for a seventy-horse-power engine, a dynamo, storage batteries, etc.; tanks for water to last long weeks at sea; space for fifteen hundred gallons of gasolene, fire extinguishers, and life-preservers; and a great store-room for food, spare sails, anchors, hawsers, tackles, and a thousand and one other things.

Similarly, this chapter tackles the very rational, tangible and constructed ideas that have literally grounded HOUSE 1 not only in a specific site and environment but also within a particular community.

HOUSE 1 is situated in the region of Lausanne, a part of Switzerland with a relatively warm and temperate climate. The site is close to Lake Geneva, and so profits from milder weather than some of the higher parts of the region. In summer temperatures typically vary between 15°C at night and 24°C in the daytime, with plenty of sunshine and regular storms, while temperatures can drop to between -0.5°C and 3.5°C in winter, accompanied by snow and fog.

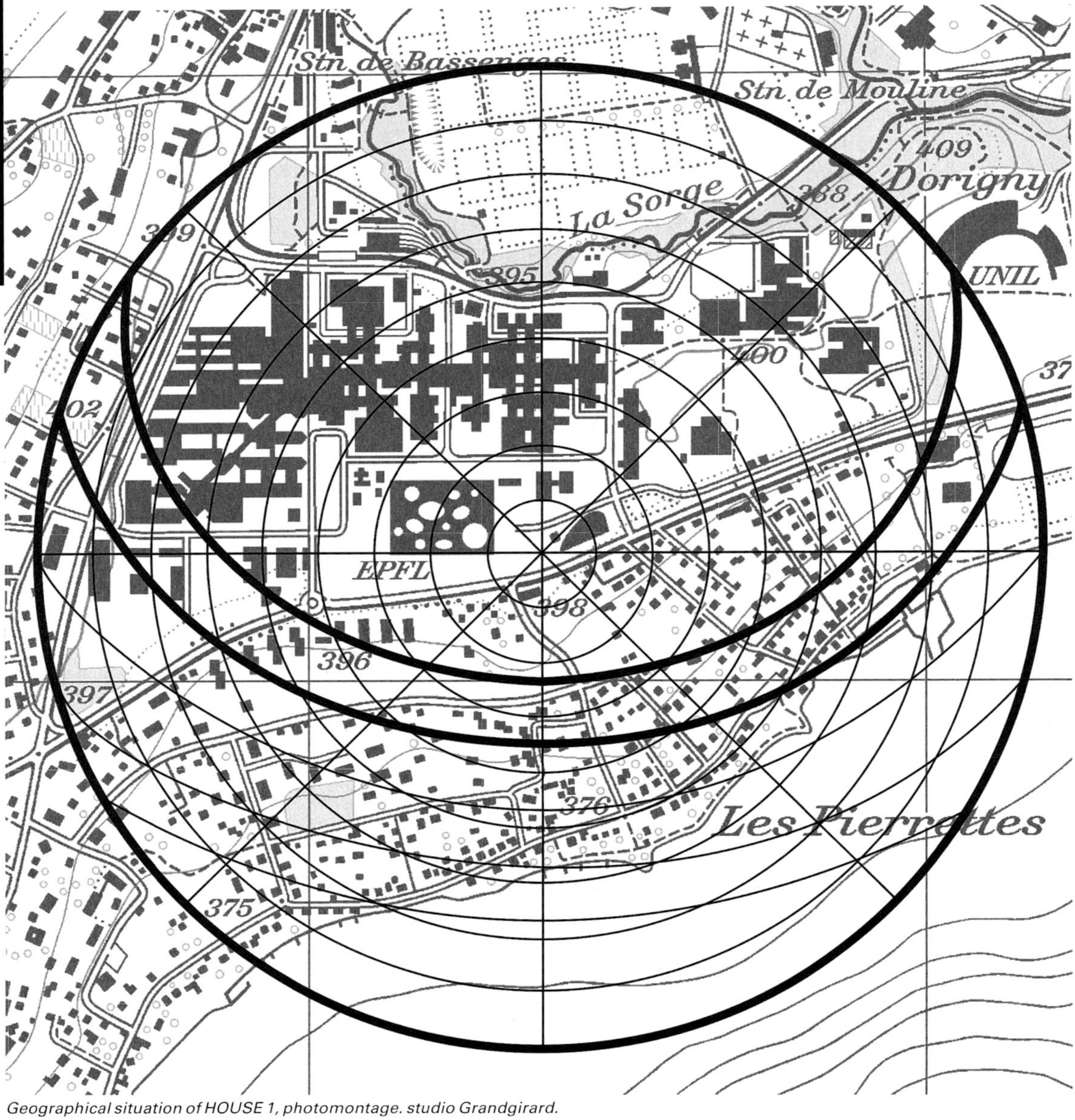

Geographical situation of HOUSE 1, photomontage. studio Grandgirard.

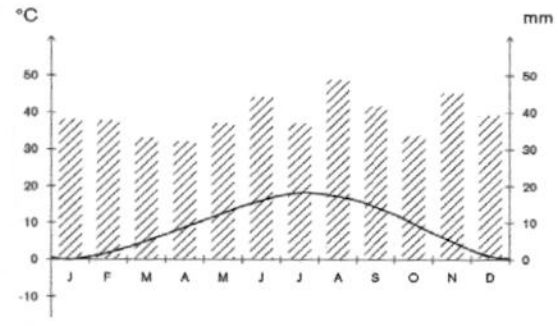

Climate diagram. Agathe Mignon. (source: http://fr.climate-data.org)

The Lausanne region receives plenty of sunshine throughout the year. In addition, its proximity to Lake Geneva gives it, during at least part of the year, an almost southern European climate.

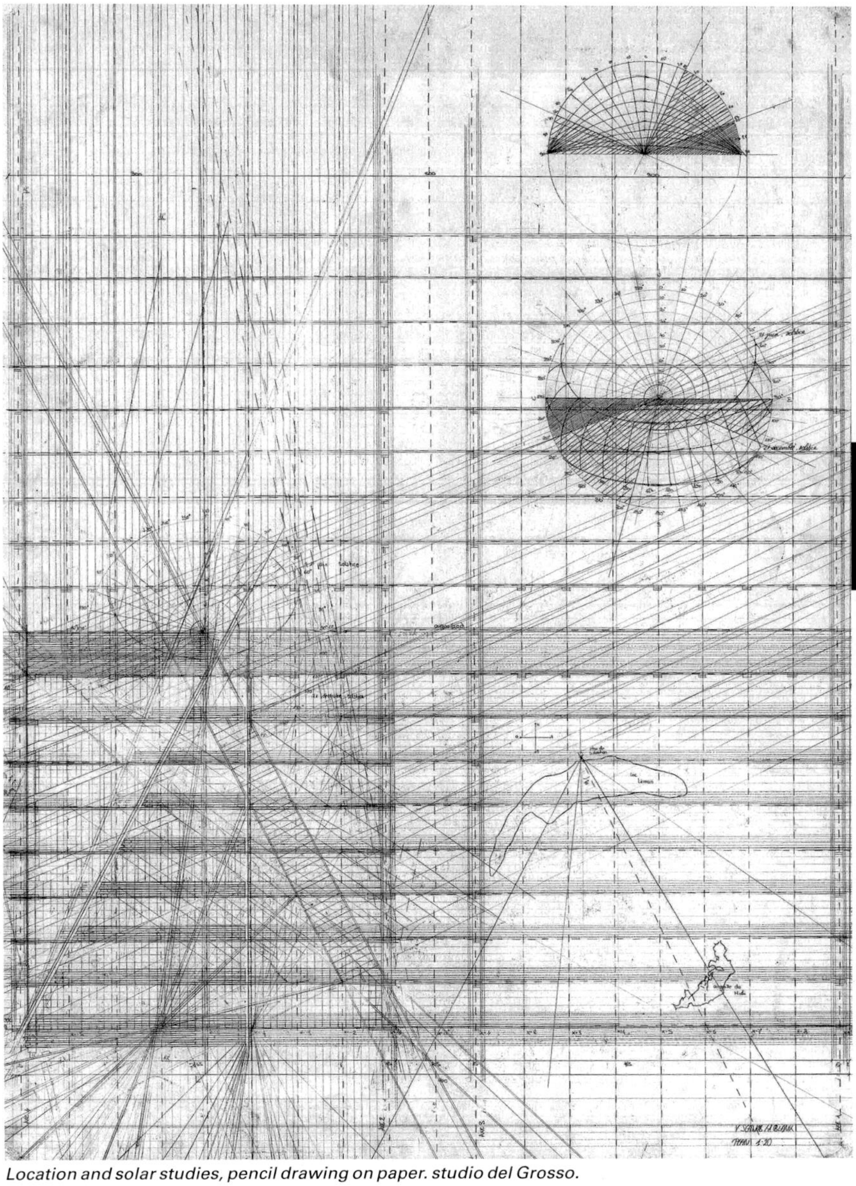

Location and solar studies, pencil drawing on paper. studio del Grosso.

"A climber wishes to start from the bottom and reach the top of the mountain/protostructure in order to experience unique views. Furthermore, he needs the physical and mental challenge.

Let us see the verticality of the protostructure as a window of time, from 12:00 am to 11:59 pm. The structure is now separated into 24 equal parts. It can create particular interactions with the outside at particular times of the day.

Research on the path of the sun in Lausanne for March 21st: During this special day, the sunrise is at 6:33 am and the sunset at 6:49 pm.

The sun controls the activity of a climber, that is, he will not climb without light. This is why he wishes to get out of the protostructure while the sun is shining, and return to its interior when there is no more sun."

studio del Grosso

Solar studies, pencil drawing on paper. studio del Grosso.

During rainy periods, the construction of HOUSE 1 was occasionally held back.

Rain alters the experience and reception of HOUSE 1, as water droplets disturb its myriad of reflections.

Construction site in the rain. studio Rufer.

Water mirror in the rain. studio Cabay.

Mirror of water disturbed by droplets. studio Cabay.

HOUSE 1 is realised through contact with the ground. This first point of contact articulates the project as a concrete form, and marks the genesis of its construction. It touches the ground lightly, occupying a temporal space before departing to other terrains, leaving the site in the same condition as it was found.

The site was marked out with stakes and string, allowing for the control of the spacing and alignment of the foundations. Then, shuttering boards were laid on the ground, providing a flat surface for the installation of a crane.

Insertion of the survey marks. Wynd van der Woude.

Inserting the piles. studio Chassot.

Crane on deck. studio Chassot.

The points of contact with the ground define four linear parallel zones, which are marked out by vertical elements and horizontal crossbeams.

Concrete footings isolate the structure from rising moisture. These footings are evenly spaced under the lower horizontal crossbeams.

Secondary foundations take the form of concrete pads sitting in direct contact with the soil, installed under the vertical timber elements above.

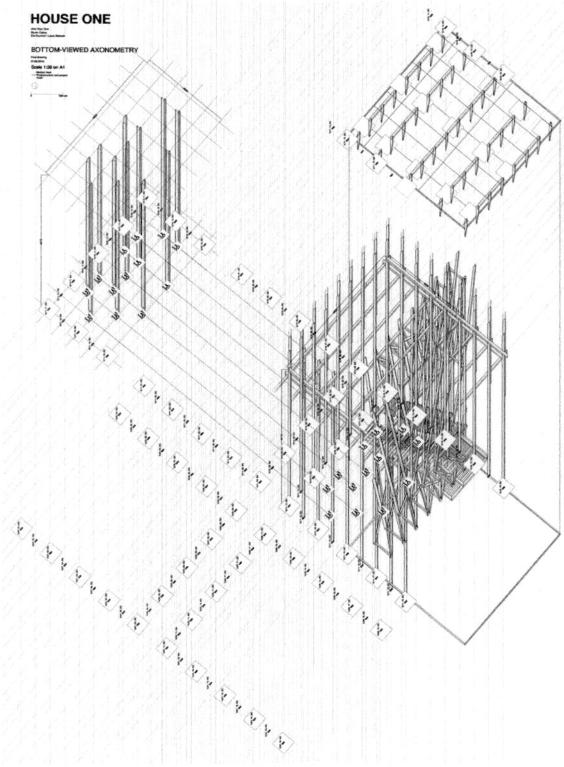

Axonometric view of the location of the vertical posts, CAD drawing, studio Cabay.

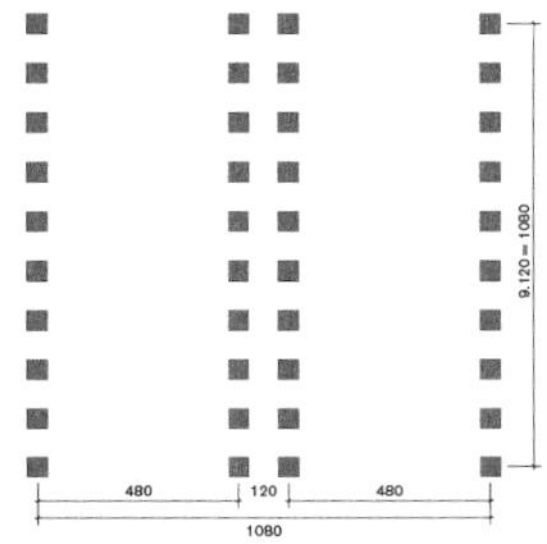

Foundation plan, CAD drawing. Rémy Meylan.

Erection of a panel over the foundations. Dylan Perrenoud.

Details of concrete slabs. Daniel Zamarbide.

Positioning of the timber structure over the foundations. studio Chassot.

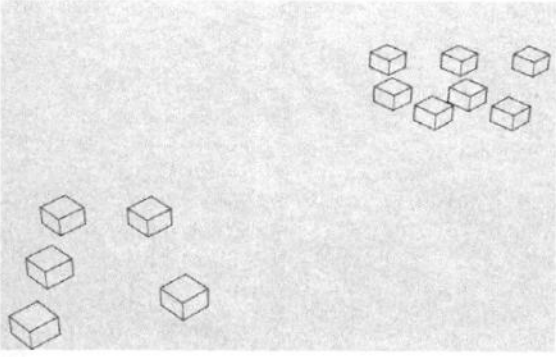

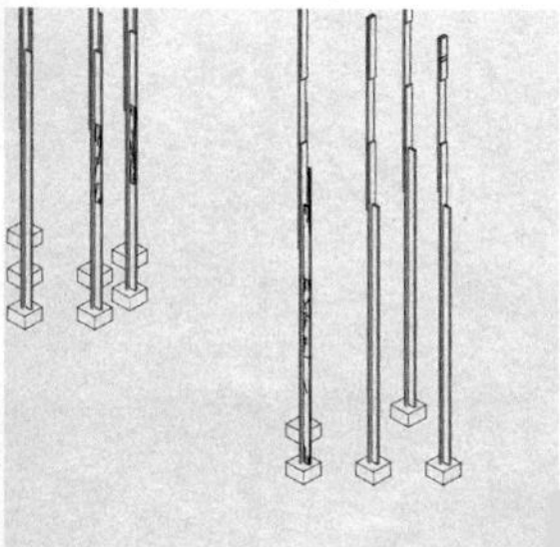

Implementation and functioning of secondary foundations. studio den Hartog.

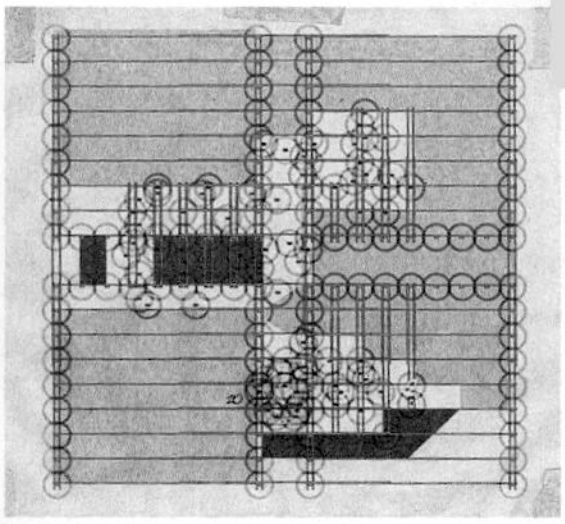

Secondary column plan. studio den Hartog.

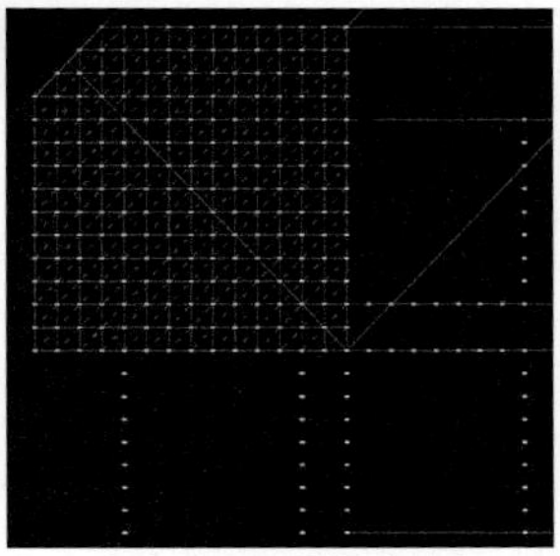

Foundation plan, CAD drawing. studio van der Woude.

Secondary foundations take the weight of a vertical timber upright element, insulating from ground moisture. The research into these foundations was therefore directed toward developing a formed concrete footing that incorporates, on its upper face, the footprint of the vertical pole resting upon it.

Research models, timber and plaster. studio van der Woude.

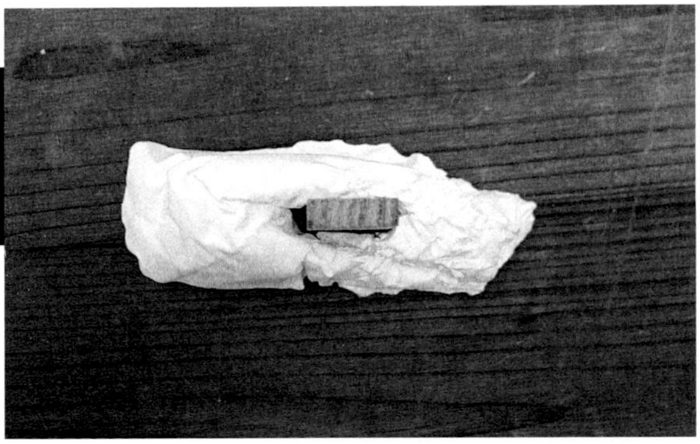

Final research model, timber and plaster. studio van der Woude.

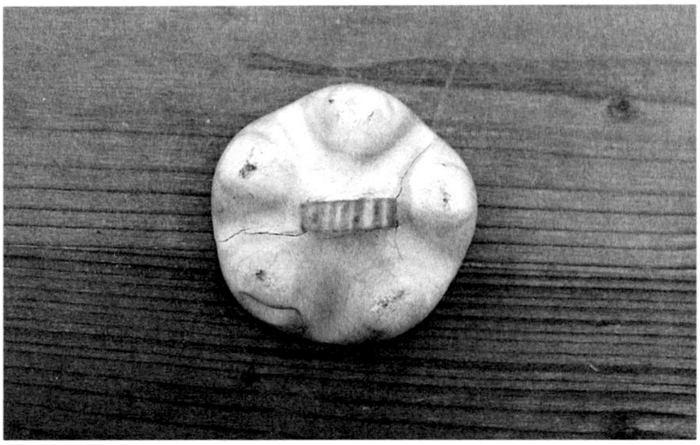

Mockup, screws, timber and concrete. studio van der Woude.

This secondary series of foundations was cast directly in the workshop in a short amount of time. The mould was constructed from reusable timber. Designed and tested at 1:1 scale, the prototype footing was then serialised.

Research into foundations and concrete matrix. studio van der Woude.

Production of concrete. studio den Hartog.

Manufacture and preparation of matrixes. studio den Hartog.

Pouring and finishing concrete. studio den Hartog.

Matrix mockup, plastic textile and wood. studio van der Woude.

Each concrete footing is a unique artefact, labeled on its base before the completion of the drying process.

Marking fresh concrete. studio Dürr.

Upper face of the foundations. studio van der Woude.

Underside of the foundations. studio van der Woude.

Once cast in the workshop, the foundations were laid out on site.

Positioning of the foundations on site. studio van der Woude.

Positioning and installation of the foundations on site. studio van der Woude.

In intervening into its site, HOUSE 1 imagines and projects views of a new landscape over the old. The built intervention begins to interact with the conditions around it, playing both directly and indirectly with new perspectives, views and interpretations of the environment beyond.

At the territorial scale, HOUSE 1 confronts the mountainous landscape on the opposite side of the lake. Rising up beyond the horizontal surface of the lake, the imposing mass of the mountains seen in relief is offset by the nuances created by the depth of the field through which they are viewed.

The Alps seen from the construction site. studio Pellacani.

Sunset over HOUSE 1, seen through the windows of the Rolex Learning Center. studio Baur.

The Alps and the lake seen from the construction site. studio Pellacani.

HOUSE 1 inserts itself into the heart of the EPFL campus, a piecemeal landscape composed of singular buildings balanced against vast green spaces. The undulating horizontality of the Rolex Learning Centre to the east, and the more distant prospect of the rest of the campus to the north, is complemented by the verticality of the observation tower to the west. To the south, a road skirts the site, framed from behind by the distant relief of the mountains.

The four cardinal views. studio Pellacani.

Front view of the Rolex Learning Center. studio del Grosso.

Perspective of the eastern side of the campus. studio del Grosso.

View of Lausanne toward the east, seen through a corridor. studio Baur.

Cutting and confrontation. studio Guaita.

View through a window. studio Guaita.

"Au nord rien. A l'est des murs denses au rythme régulier. Plus loin des transitions pour passer d'un espace à l'autre. Au sud une grille mêlant orthogonales et transversales. A l'ouest les mêmes éléments verticaux avec le même rythme. Position dans l'espace.

Au nord le paysage découpé sous le soleil plaquant, l'alternance entre constructions bétonnées et nature. A l'est et au sud un aperçu des autres pièces évidé par les lattes de bois sombres. Accumulation désespérante. A l'ouest les ondulations du Rolex tranchent avec les murs laissant passer de fines lamelles de lumière dorée. Au centre un large faisceau doré descend du ciel. Vision du ciel cadré par le plafond. Espace d'un instant. Espace du corps encombré de ses sensations multiples et opposées. Espace ordonné et perception saccadée. Vision stroboscopique"

studio Perez-Lupi

As rich in complex, overlapping spatial typologies as it is, can HOUSE 1 not define its own landscape?The intersection of the volumes of the house, and the wealth of visual patterns these intersections create, make up a particular HOUSE 1 landscape that frames and reflects the diversity of the natural landscape beyond.

The mountains over the terrace, pencil and aquarell on paper. studio Pellacani.

HOUSE 1 seen with its reflection. Jamani Caillet.

The vast horizontal plane of the entrance. Jamani Caillet.

Colourful sunset across the terrace, pencil and aquarell on paper. studio Pellacani.

HOUSE 1 unavoidably modifies the ecosystem of the place in which it sits. The structure therefore becomes a support for local wildlife and native flora.

HOUSE 1 is a decidedly artificial structure. This formal vocabulary is contrasted with the natural landscape around it.

A study of the climatic conditions and local flora of the region established a selection of plants able to grow and flourish in the vertical garden of HOUSE 1, allowing for the development of an ecosystem. The study encompassed water and sunshine requirements as well as the dimensions required for their development.

Two formal expressions, mixed media. studio Dürr.

	hau-teur (cm)	largeur (cm)	besoin d'eau	exposition	croissance	notation graphique
ANETH	30 - 150	40 - 60	💧💧	☼	↗↗↗	
BASILIC	15 - 100	10 - 70	💧💧	☼	↗↗	
CIBOULETTE	15 - 60	15 - 20	💧💧	☁ ☼ ☁	↗↗	
CORIANDRE	60 - 100	20 - 30	💧💧	☼	↗↗↗	
ESTRAGON	30 - 100	30 - 60	💧💧	☼	↗↗	
FRAISE	15 - 45	30 - 40	💧💧	☁ ☼ ☁	↗↗	
MARJOLAINE	30 - 60	40	💧	☼	↗↗	
MENTHE	30 - 100	20 - 50	💧💧	☁ ☼ ☁	↗↗↗	
PERSIL	15 - 30	15 - 20	💧💧	☁ ☼ ☁	↗↗(↗)	
ROMARIN	0 - 150	120	💧	☼	↗	
SAUGE	30 - 60	20 - 70	💧	☼	↗↗↗	
THYM	0 - 60	10 - 50	💧	☼	↗↗	

Study of the characteristics of plants. studio Dürr.

A spatial model was generated using this data in order to find the optimal location within the structure for each family of plants, and to design the support structure. Each variety of flora finds its precise place within the ecosystem.

"Notre choix s'est porté vers la création d'un jardin interieur, bulle hétérotopique dans le microcosme de la protostructure. Le but est de de créer une condition spatiale à faire pousser des plantes grimpantes qui recouvrirons peu à peu la protostructure, à l'image de la nature qui reprend ses droits sur l'homme."
studio Dürr

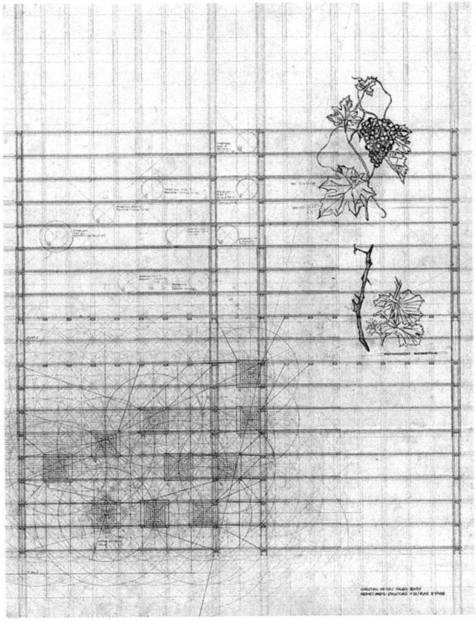

Research into plant supports, pencil drawing on paper. studio Dürr.

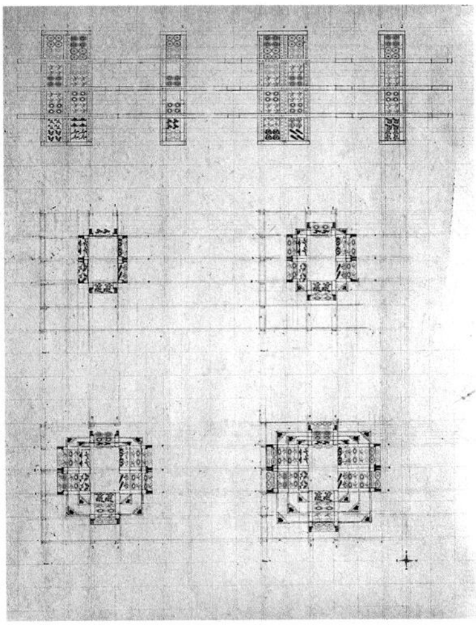

Mapping and locating plants on the support, pencil drawing on paper. studio Dürr.

Research into the biulding of plant supports, pencil drawing on paper. studio Dürr.

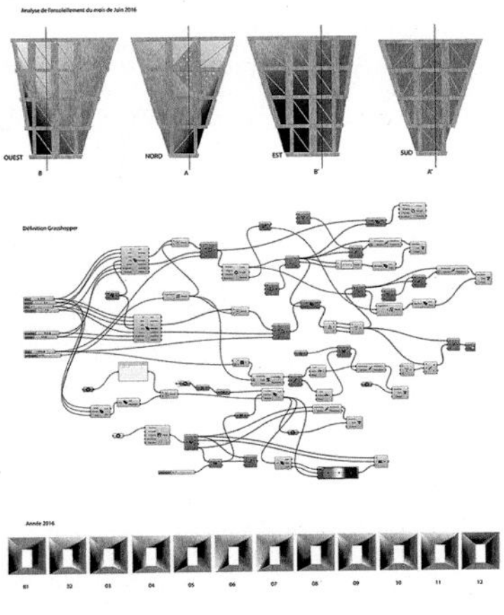

Simulation of climate data. studio Dürr.

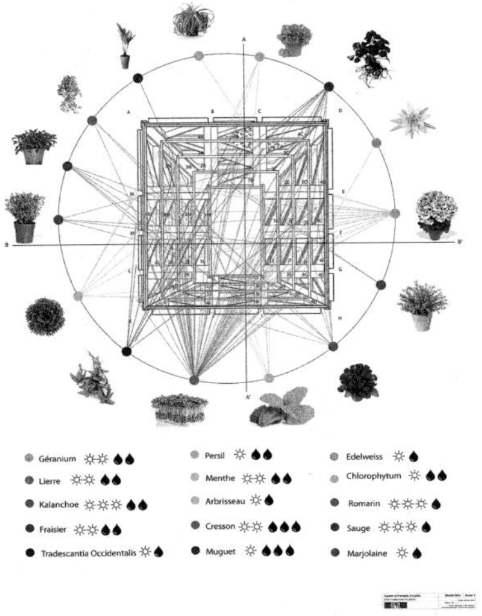

Arrangement of different plants selected. studio Dürr.

While the formal vocabulary of the structure of HOUSE 1 might be relatively simple to transcribe in two or three dimensions, the diversity of the organic development of a plant remains far more difficult to represent. Comparing the images of the HOUSE 1 ecosystem constructed with the aid of a computer with the photos of its realisation reflects the formal richness revealed in the plant world.

Representation of plants on their support, CAD view. studio Dürr.

Plants put in place. studio Dürr.

Finalisation of the project with the completed structure and the plants. studio Dürr.

Spatial characteristics reveal themselves through the movement of the body in the structure of HOUSE 1. Built elements facilitate and direct this movement.

The body is, in itself, a unit of measure, and a register of scale. The body's movement draws an invisible path through space, and in order for it to move freely, the surrounding structure must be adapted constantly to its dimensions. While moving, the body deploys the senses in order to capture all the physical characteristics of its surroundings.

Breakdown of the movements of the human body ascending, pencil drawing on paper. studio del Grosso.

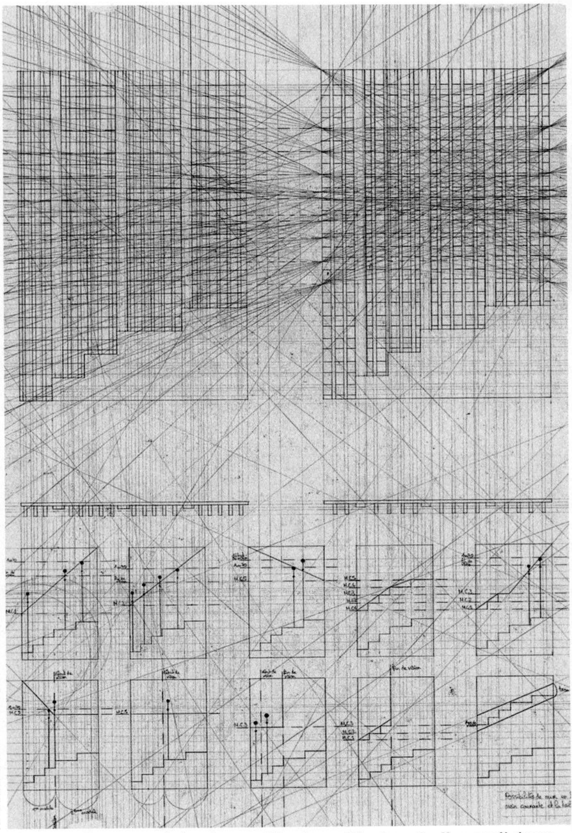

Ergonomic research for the positioning of the handrail, pencil drawing on paper. studio del Grosso.

HOUSE 1 is characterised by a sense of verticality expressed in its structure. Each space within HOUSE 1 promotes a restless, active and curious inhabitation of space by the body.

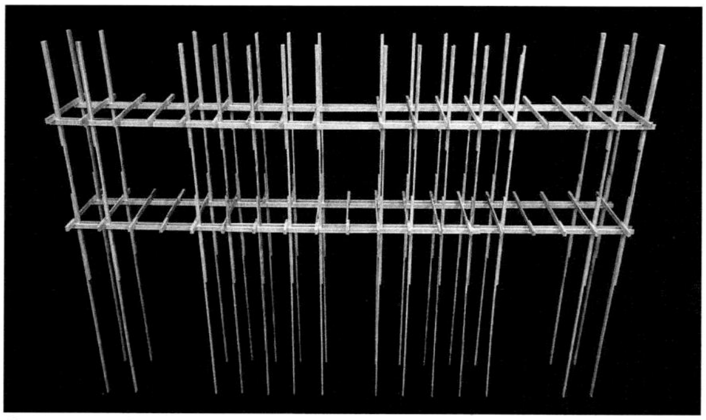

Fragment of the protostructure, timber and glue. studio del Grosso.

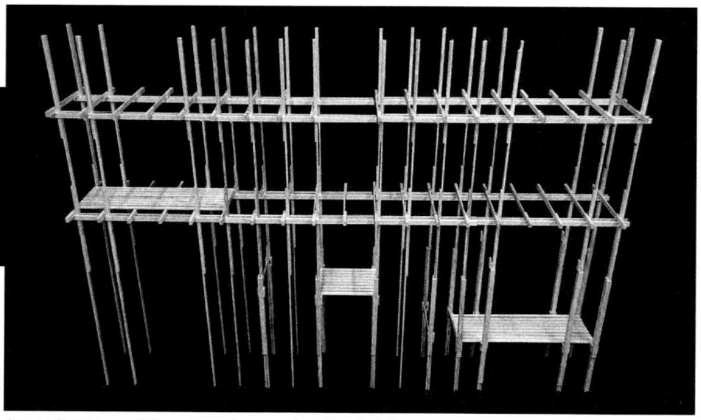

Installation of the bearings. studio del Grosso.

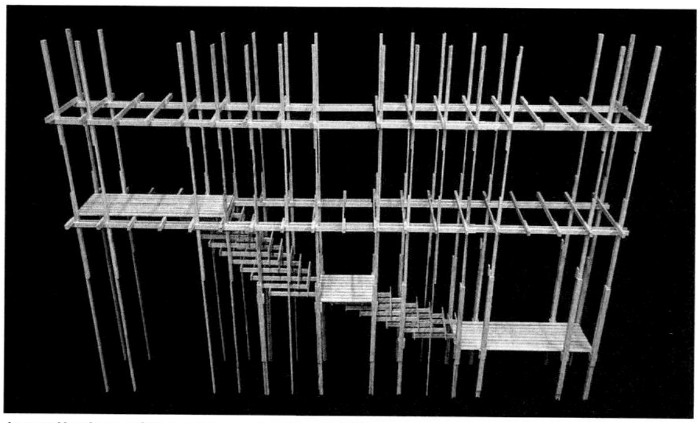

Installation of the steps. studio del Grosso.

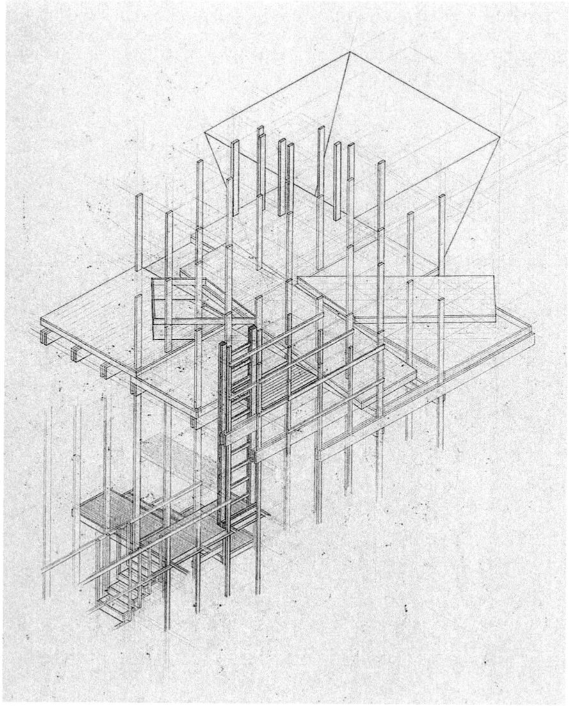

Access platforms and terrace, pencil drawing on paper. studio Pellacani.

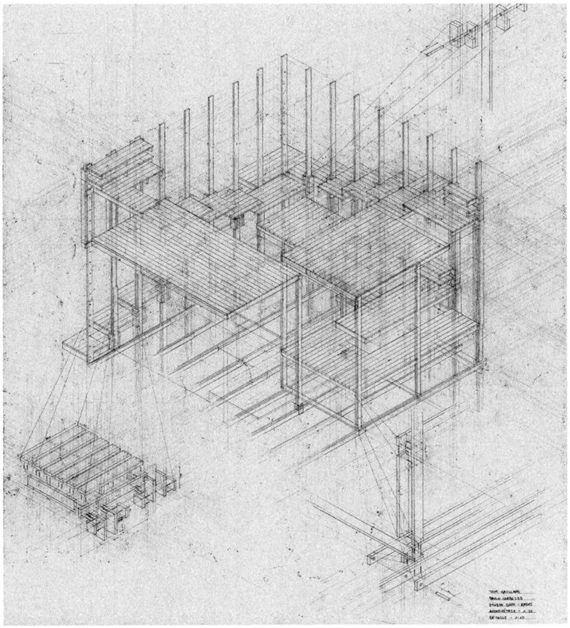

Path through the protostructure, pencil drawing on paper. studio Dürr.

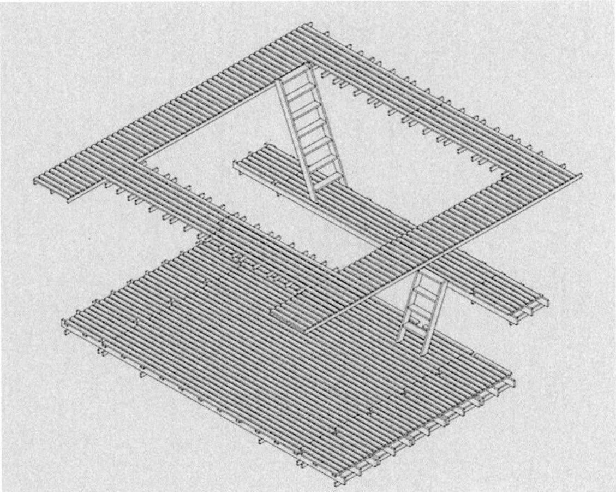

Stairs and walkway, CAD drawing. studio Chassot.

Ramps are installed to connect the intermediate levels of HOUSE 1.

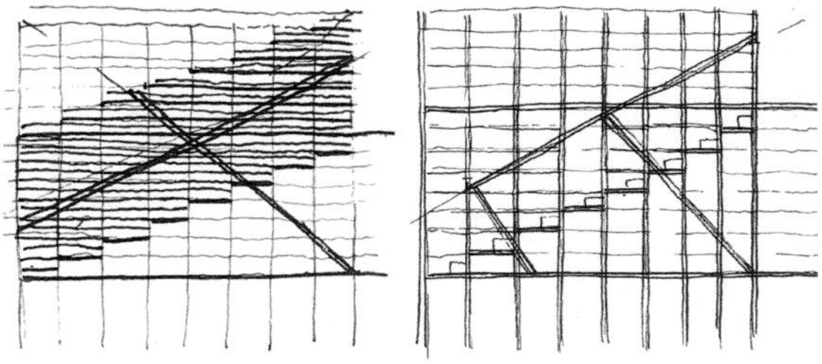

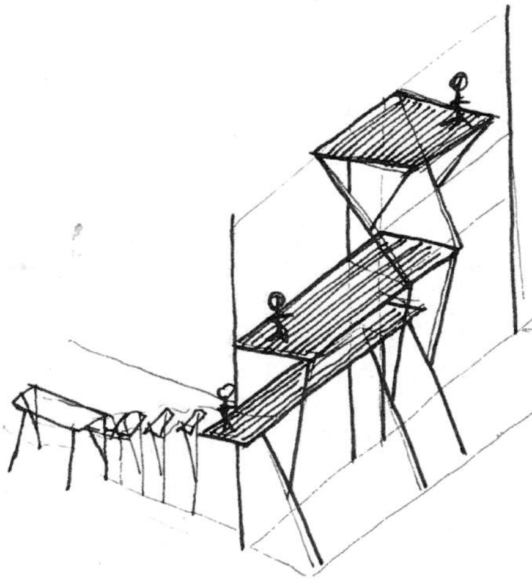

Sketch studies for the design and construction of ramps and stairs, mixed media on paper. studio del Grosso.

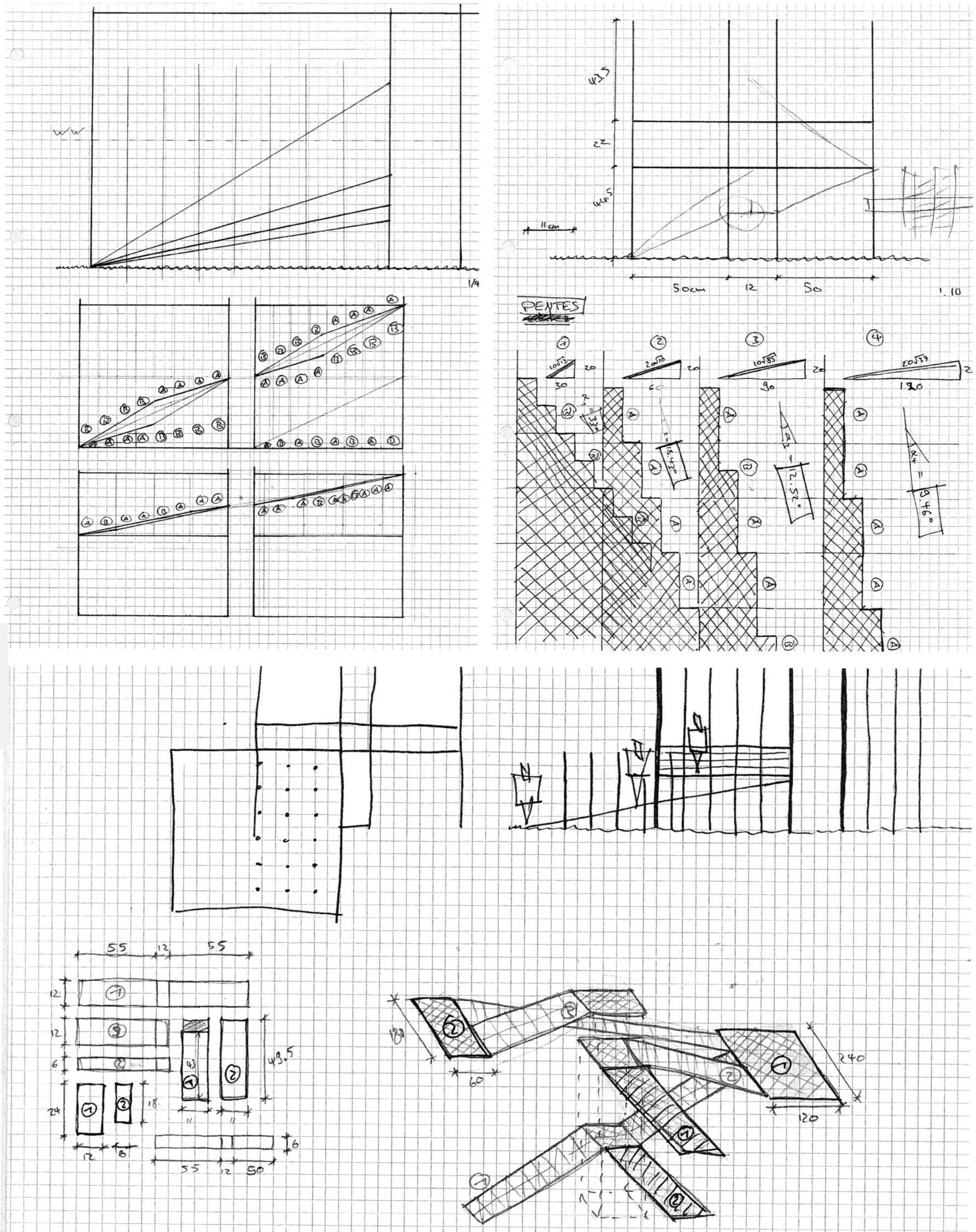

Sketch study for ramp. studio del Grosso.

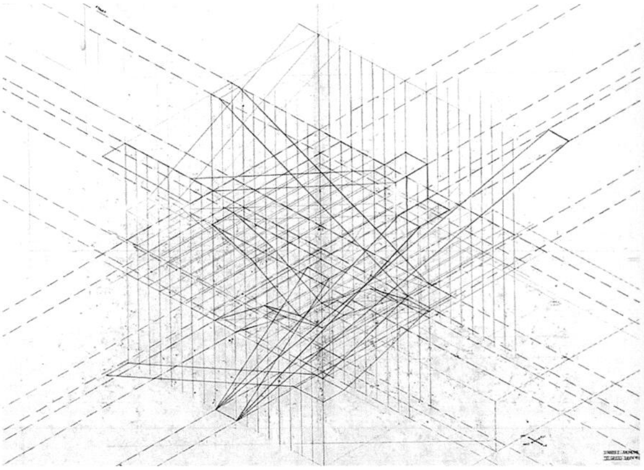

Research into the ramp's path of travel, pencil drawing on paper. studio del Grosso.

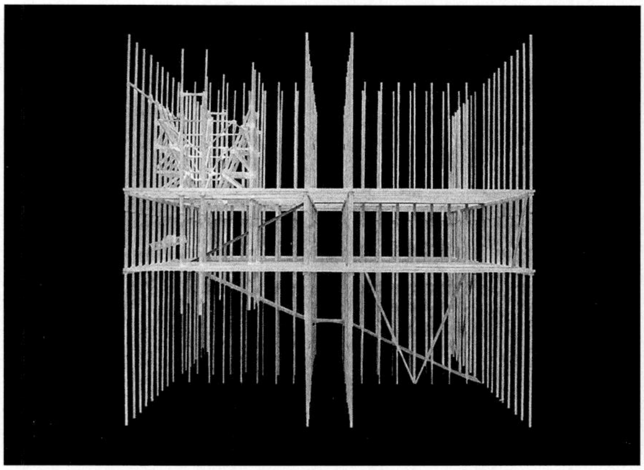

Model of the path through the protostructure, timber and glue. studio del Grosso.

Construction of a ramp in the protostructure, timber and glue. studio Grandgirard.

ÉTUDES DE MODULES ET DE PENTES

Ne connaissant pas encore les positions exactes des projets à relier, nous avons étudié diverses pentes au travers de différentes combinaisons de modules de marches.

Il était su que:

Le projet du studio VanDerWoude serait un plan incliné ralliant l'extérieure de la proto-structure au couloir central – point de départ de l'escalier,

Le projet du studio DenHartog serait localisé au centre de la proto-structure et ne pouvait être traversé – premier contournement,

Le projet du studio Pellacani serait perché au dessus du second niveau – fin de l'escalier.

Les parcours explicités ci-dessous s'appuient sur ces premières exigences et utilises les pentes déterminées par nos modules.

studio del Grosso

"Le tendon est primordial pour un membre, il le solidarise, le solidifie mais ne peut se passer de l'ossature. Le système de circulation d'une structure se doit de respecter la statique de cette dernière et la position des éléments qu'elle doit relier ou éviter."

studio del Grosso

"Une rampe apparemment en lévitation menant à une plateforme inaccessible. Cette ascension transperce la proto-structure en cassant un rythme et est guidée par quatre moments: intrigue, observation, compréhension, consécration. Ces moments permettent la compréhension structurelle de l'équilibre de la rampe."

studio del Grosso

"La rampe permet plusieurs choses. Elle peut connecter deux espaces situés à deux différents niveaux. Contrairement à l'escalier, elle n'impose pas de rythme dans la montée. De plus on peut s'asseoir dessus et y exercer différentes activités qui ne sont pas possibles sur un escalier."

studio den Hartog

The patterns established by the multiplication of the stair treads emerge in the modular expression of the staircase structure.

ÉLABORATION D'UN PLAN DÉTAILLANT LES ZONES DE JONCTION ENTRE LES PROJETS ET LE SYSTÈME DE CIRCULATION

Il était su que:

Le projet du studio VanDerWoude serait un plan incliné ralliant l'extérieure de la proto-structure au couloir central – point de départ de l'escalier,

Le projet du studio DenHartog serait localisé au centre de la proto-structure et ne pouvait être traversé – premier contournement,

Le projet du studio Pellacani serait perché au dessus du second niveau – fin de l'escalier,

Le projet du studio Baur serait également un système de circulation, afin de démultiplier les parcours possibles, nous décidons de croiser les deux systèmes,

Le projet du studio Grandgirard nécessitait une entrée située à 110cm du second niveau de la proto-structure.

De ces informations, nous avons défini les paramètres des marches.

studio del Grosso

"Everyone is concerned about matters of life and death. Through History we symbolized the sky as the world of the deceased and made its access a poetic theme. Its most symbolic materialization is the stairway to Heaven as the passage from one world to another.

When you approach the stairs, you look up at the airy, well dimensioned structure and see it disappear into the sky, making it seem possible to ascend this space forever. But the physical incapacity to reach it reminds us how alive we are and forces us to come back to Earth and enjoy being here.

I understood lately that the passage from a world to another should not be destructive for its surrounding, but make it stronger and unified. The stairs become then the spine of the proto-structure by bracing it, from the larger foundation to the narrow steps of its head."

studio Rufer

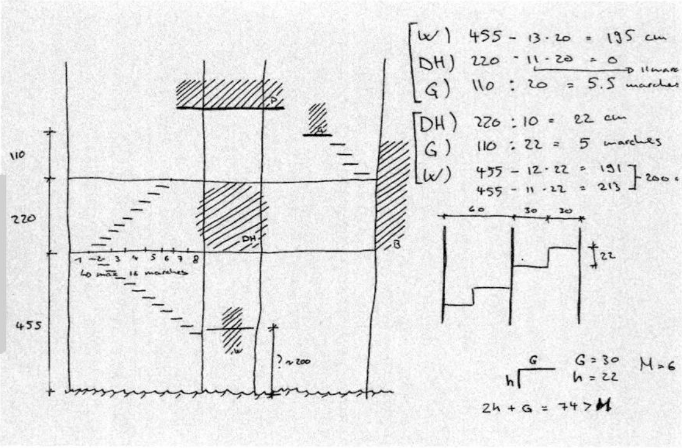

Rhythm calculation of the stairs, sketches. studio del Grosso.

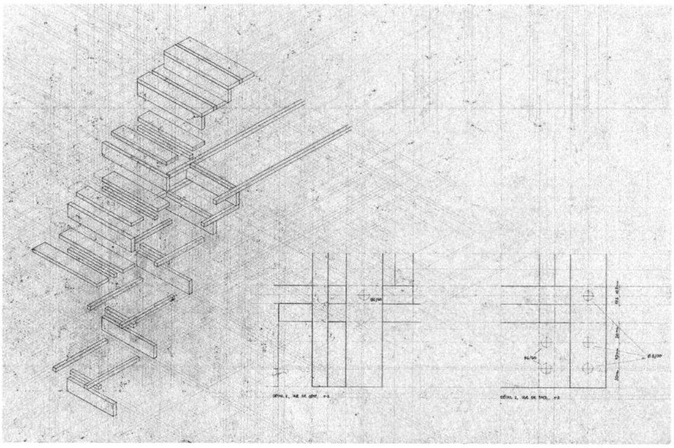

Studies of the design and construction of the stairs, pencil drawing on paper. studio Baur.

Central stair model, timber and glue. studio Rufer.

Suspended stairs, timber and glue. studio Dürr.

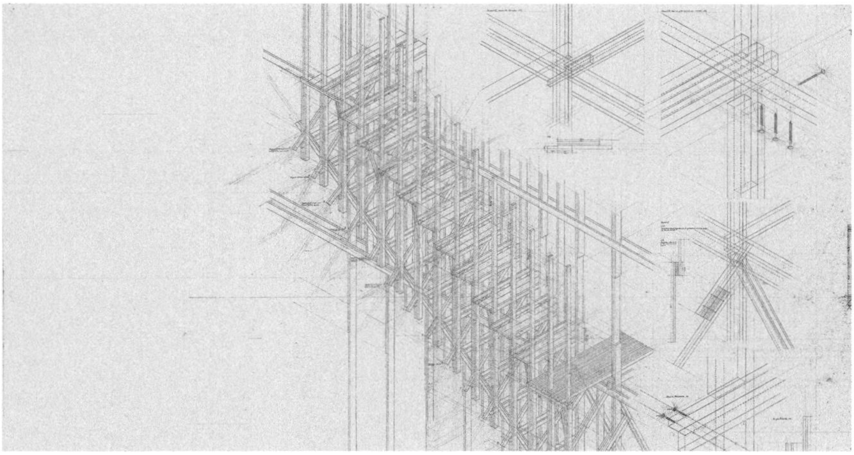

Axonometric view of the stairs, pencil drawing on paper. studio Baur.

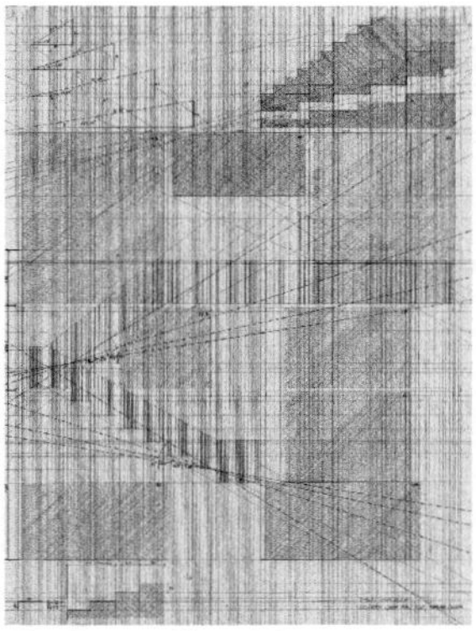

Rhythm studies of the steps, pencil drawing on paper. studio Pellacani.

Study of the design and construction of the stairs in axonometric and plan view, pencil drawing on paper. studio Baur.

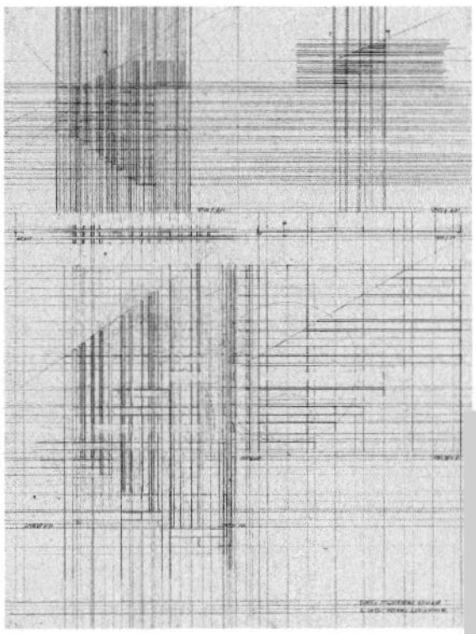

Studies of the rhythm of the steps, pencil drawing on paper. studio Pellacani.

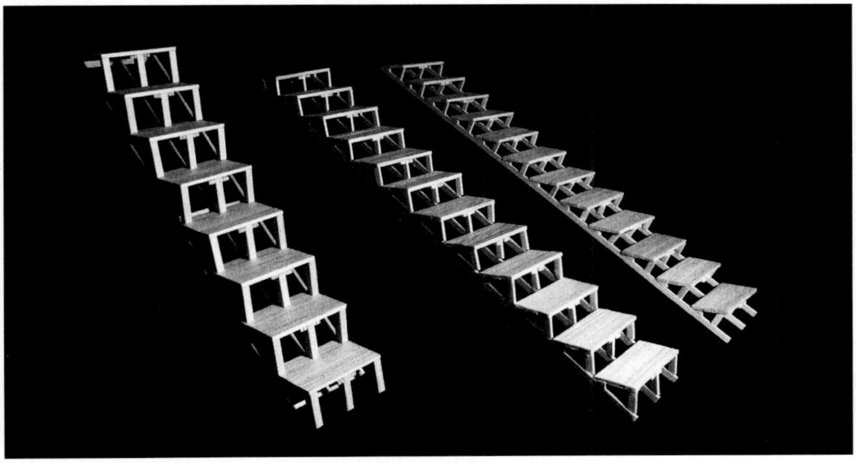

Different models of stairs, timber and glue. studio Pellacani.

A series of paths charts a complex and varied course through HOUSE 1.

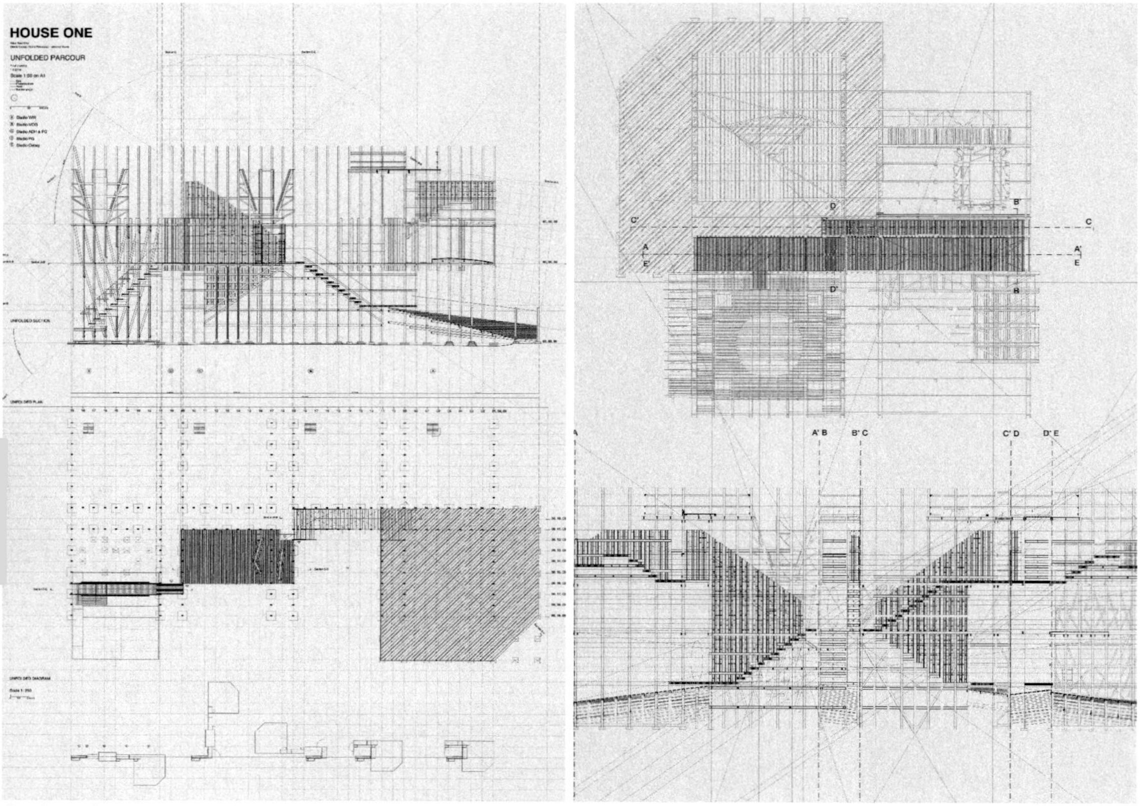

Cut through the complete HOUSE 1 circulation path, CAD drawing. studios Cabay/del Grosso

The protostructure of HOUSE 1 is the frame of a new topography both artificial and complex. In the manner of a geological landscape, HOUSE 1 is built up layer by layer.

Once inhabited, the structure of HOUSE 1 becomes as much a field of differing topographies as it is a myriad of possible assemblies. Each of these spatial compositions – these topographies – reveals a diversity of unique forms.

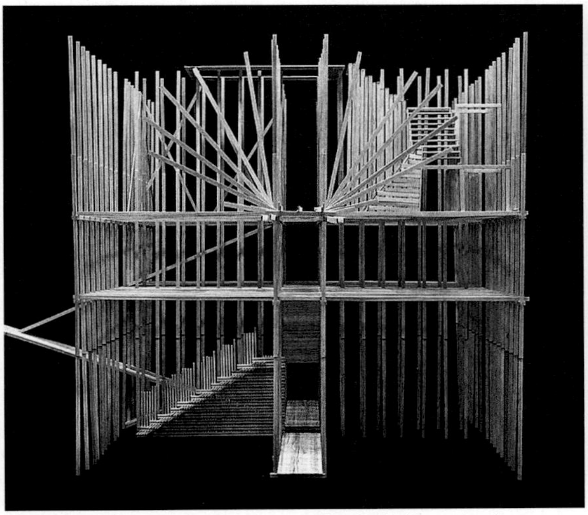

Composition #1, timber and glue. studios Rufer/Perez-Lupi.

Composition #2, timber and glue. studios Rufer/Perez-Lupi.

Composition #1, timber and glue. studios Cabay/Chassot.

Composition #3, timber and glue. studios Rufer/Perez-Lupi.

As in a topographical survey, varying levels can be represented by curves on a contour map. Each of the interventions into the structure, when considered as an ensemble, builds up a complex topography composed of a multitude of superimposed and intersecting levels within the interior volume of HOUSE 1.

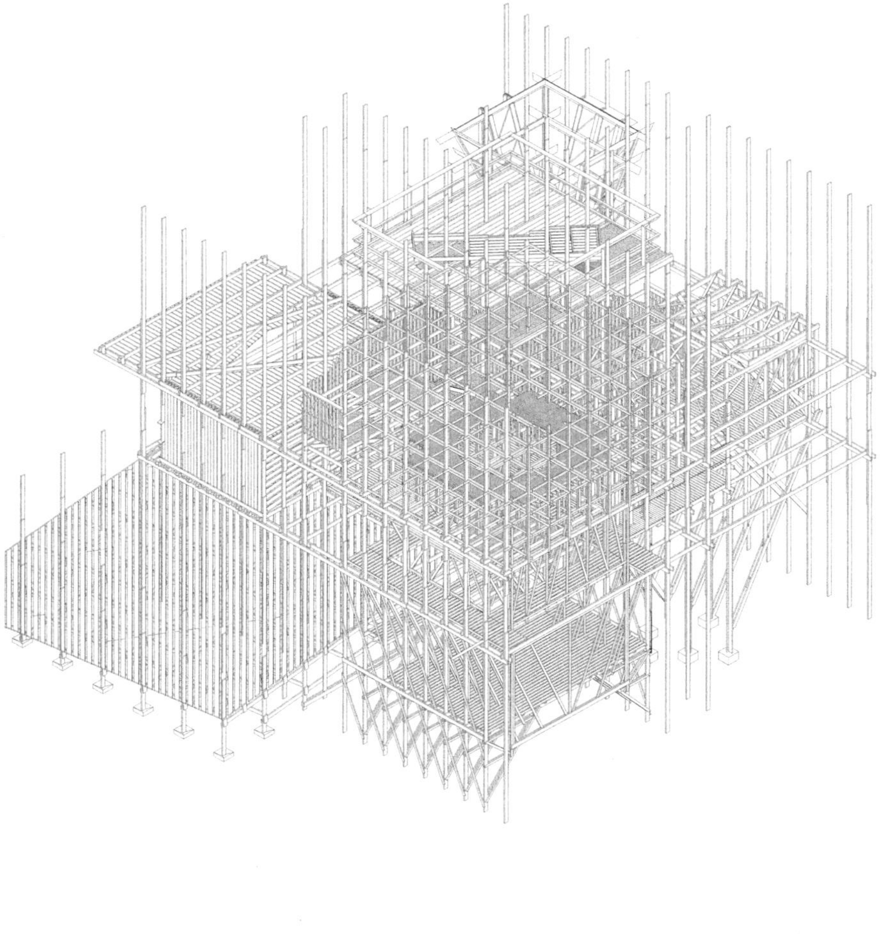

Complete topography in axonometric view, CAD drawing. studio Pellacani.

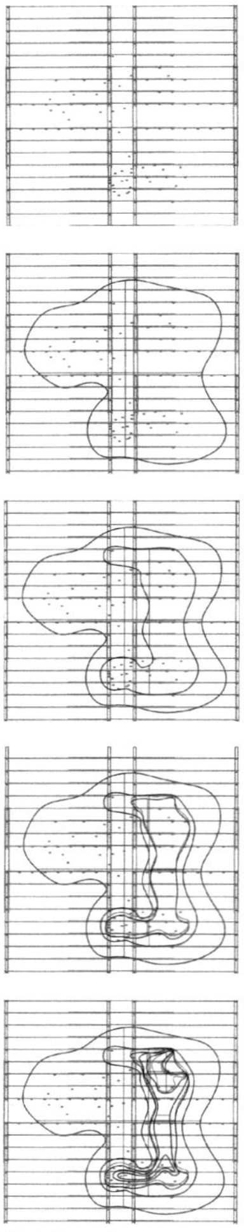

Contour plans, CAD drawing. studio den Hartog.

HOUSE 1 topography by night. studio Grandgirard.

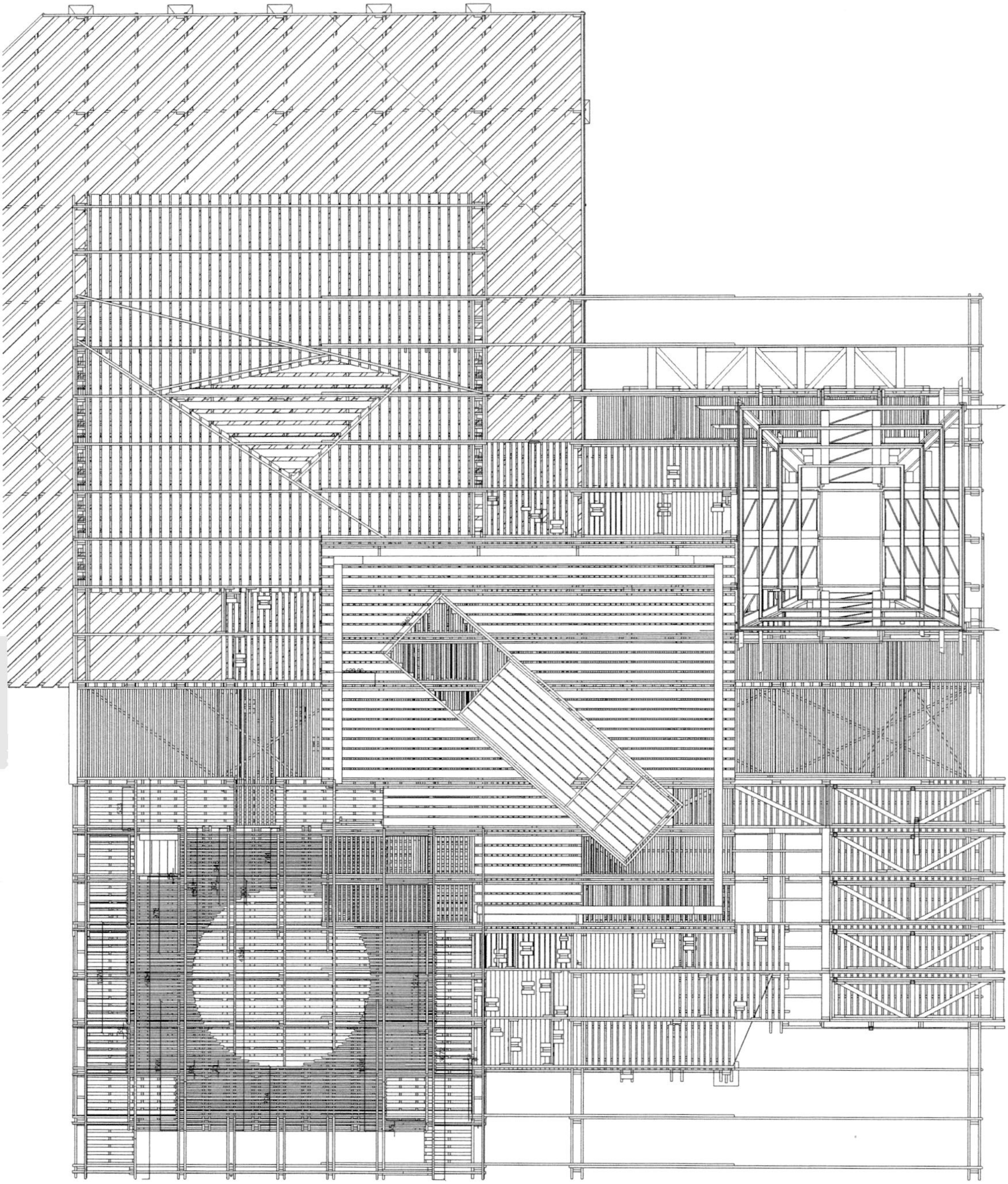

Complete topography, CAD drawing. studio Pellacani.

Imagination recasts the topography of HOUSE 1 into new forms.

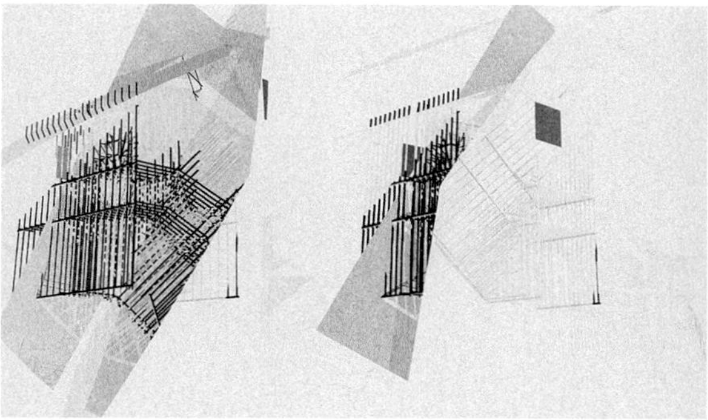

Imaginary pictures of HOUSE 1, CAD drawing. studio Dürr.

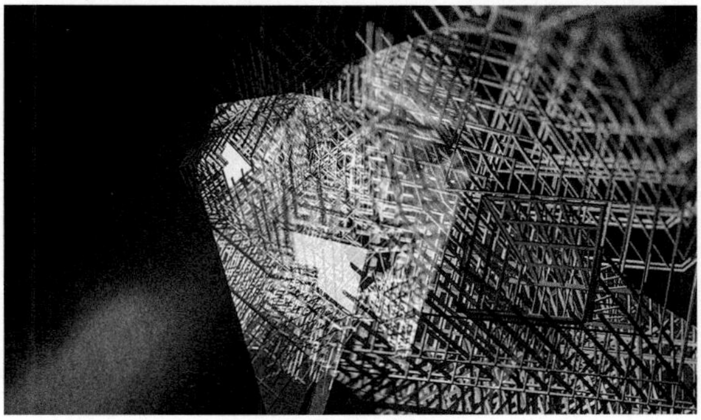

Fantastic visions of HOUSE 1, CAD drawing. studio Dürr.

Each interior space is composed of modular element types: floor, ceiling and wall. The horizontal or vertical surfaces compose varieties of rhythms and motifs adapted to specific spatial functions.

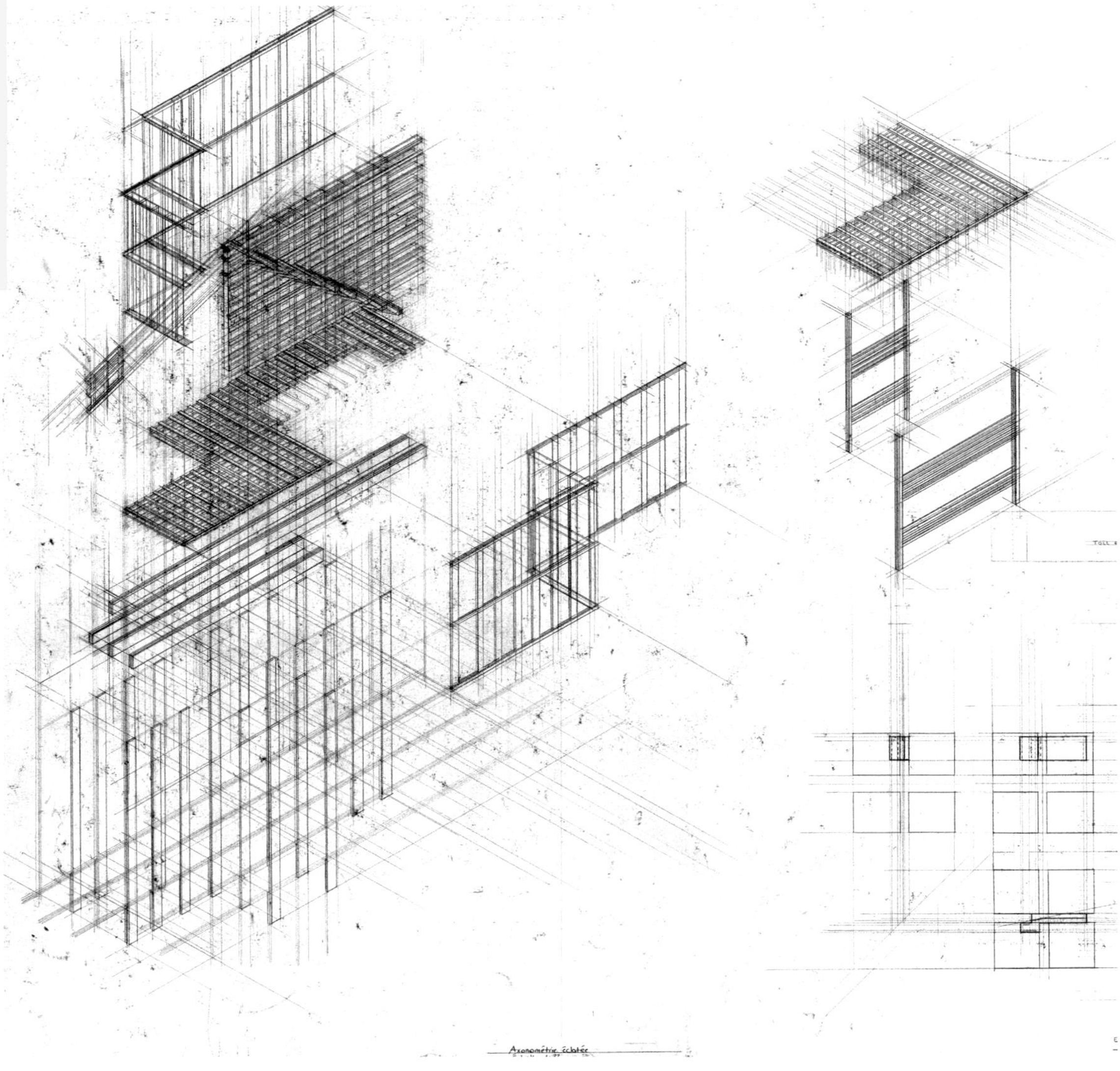

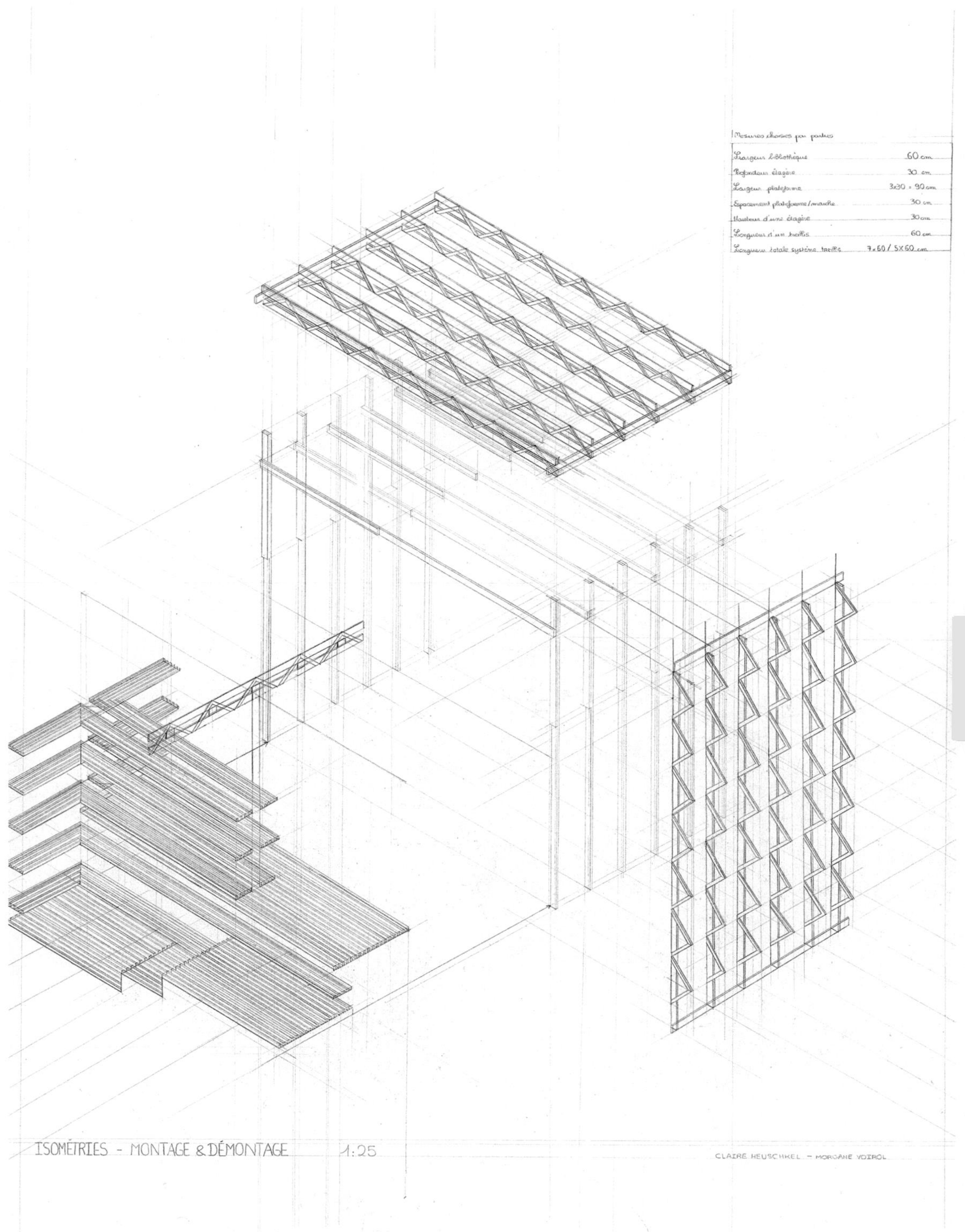
Mesures choisies par parties
Largeur bibliothèque 60 cm
Profondeur étagère 30 cm
Largeur plateforme 3x30 = 90 cm
Espacement plateforme/marche 30 cm
Hauteur d'une étagère 30 cm
Longueur d'un treillis 60 cm
Longueur totale système treillis 7x60 / 5X60 cm
ISOMÉTRIES - MONTAGE & DÉMONTAGE 1:25
CLAIRE HEUSCHKEL - MORGANE VOIROL

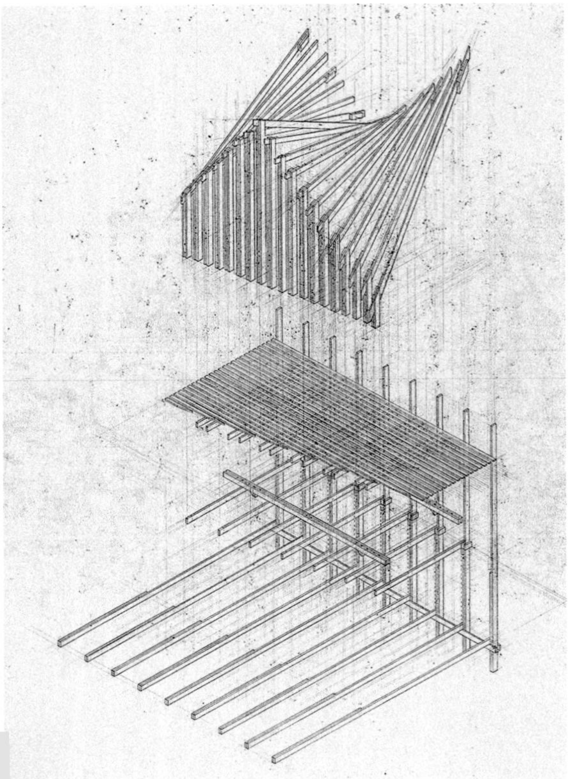

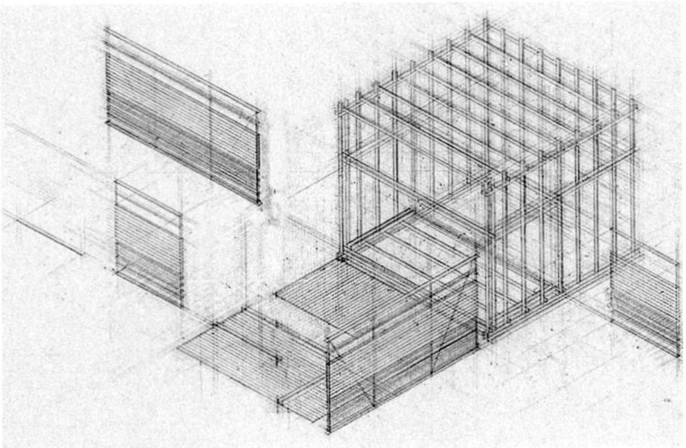

Exploded axonometric view, pencil drawing on paper. studios Chassot/Cabay/Perez-Lupi/Pellacani.

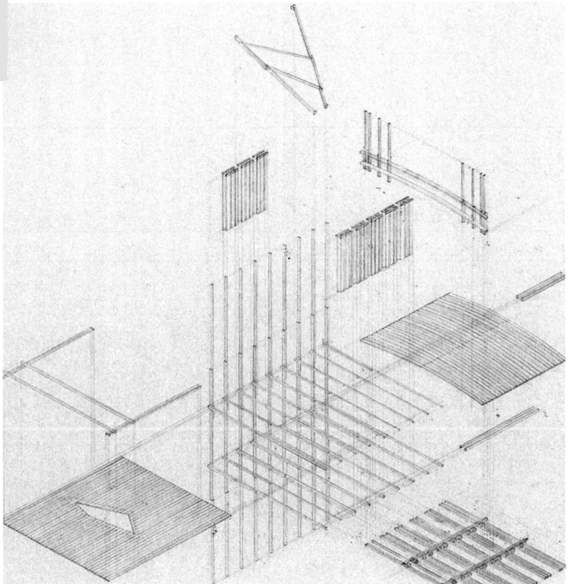

Bracing stabilises the horizontal planes.

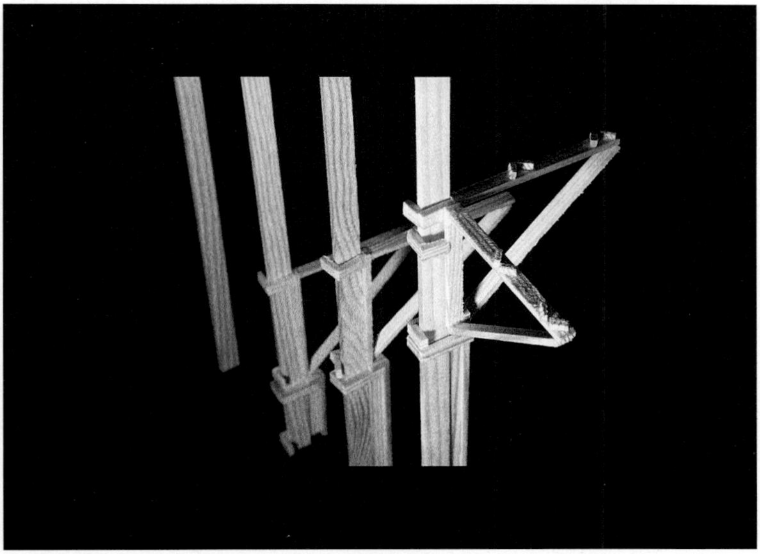

Walking angle module, timber and glue. studio Pellacani.

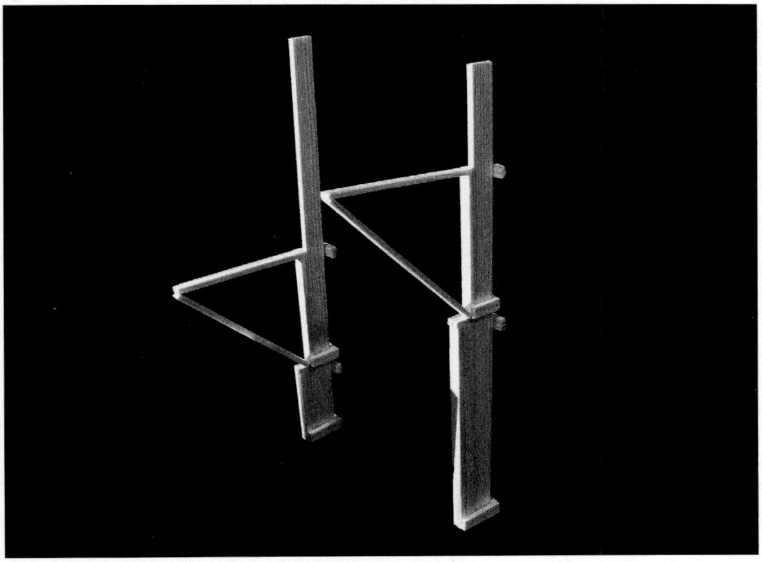

Individual module walk, timber and glue. studio Pellacani.

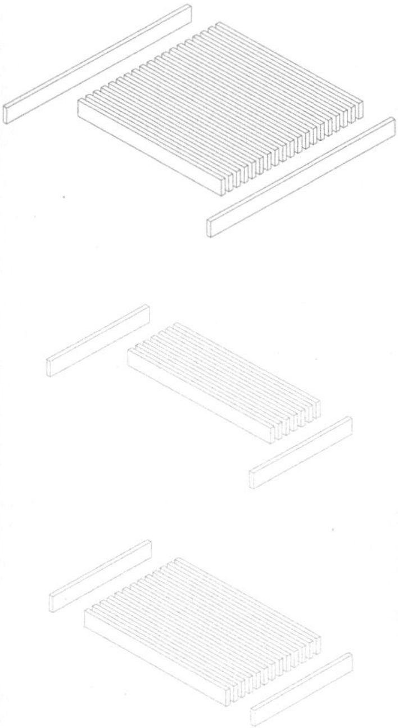

Definitive step drawing in axonometric view, CAD drawing. studio del Grosso.

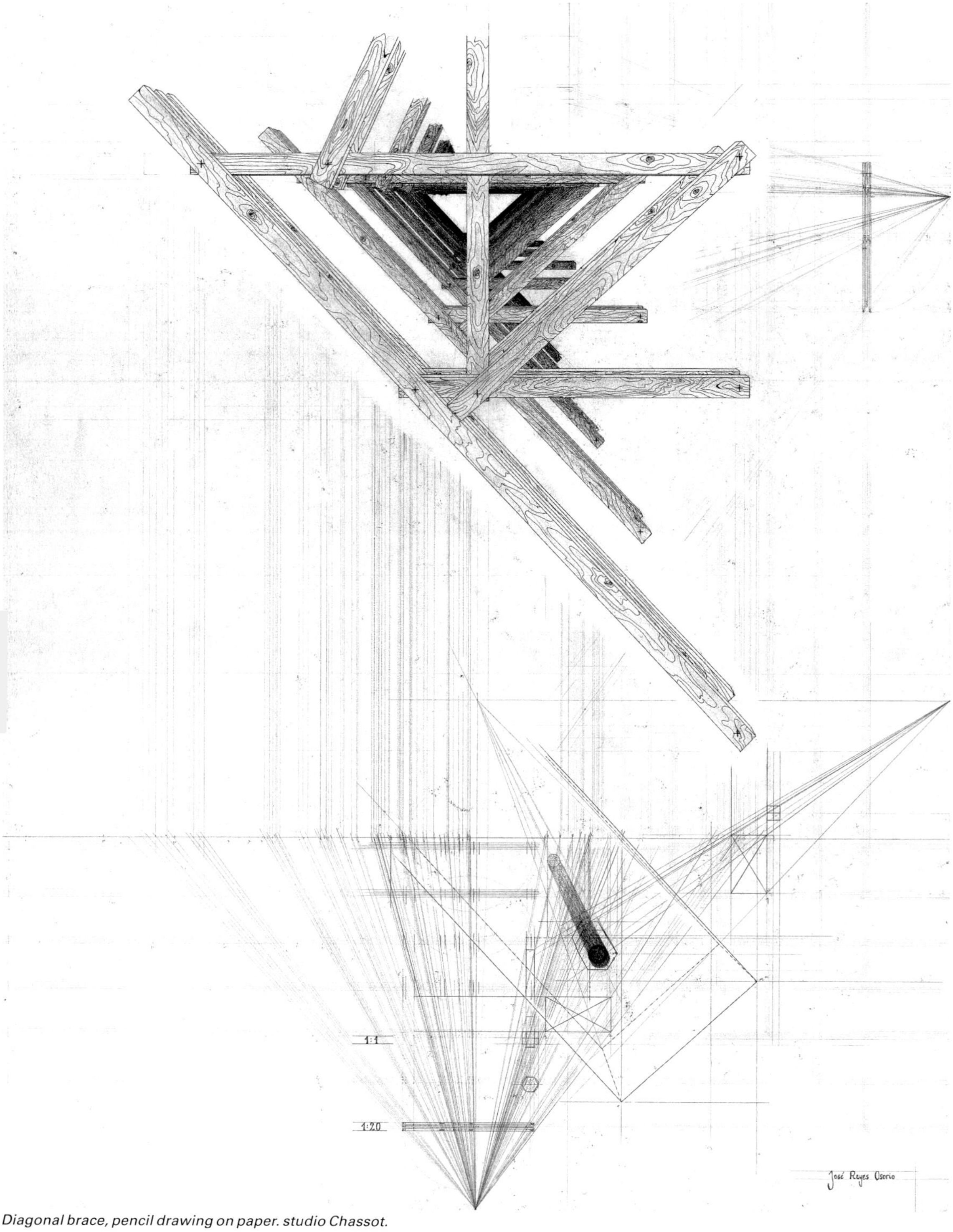

Diagonal brace, pencil drawing on paper. studio Chassot.

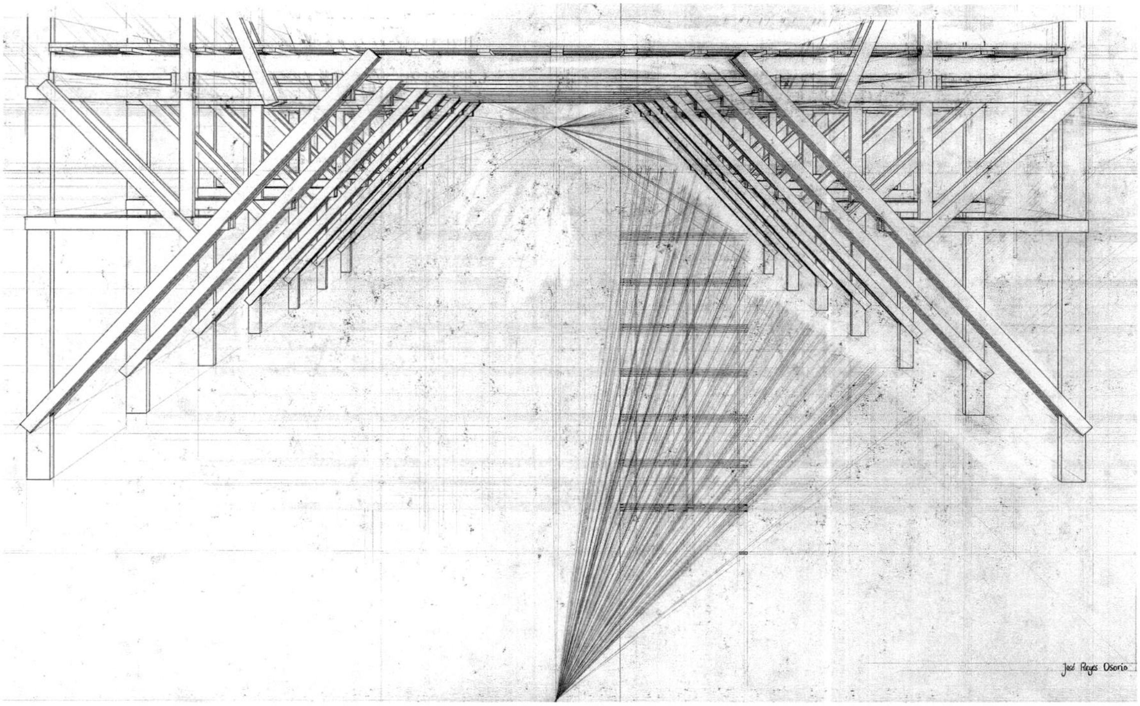

Diagonal braces in perspective view, pencil drawing on paper. studio Chassot.

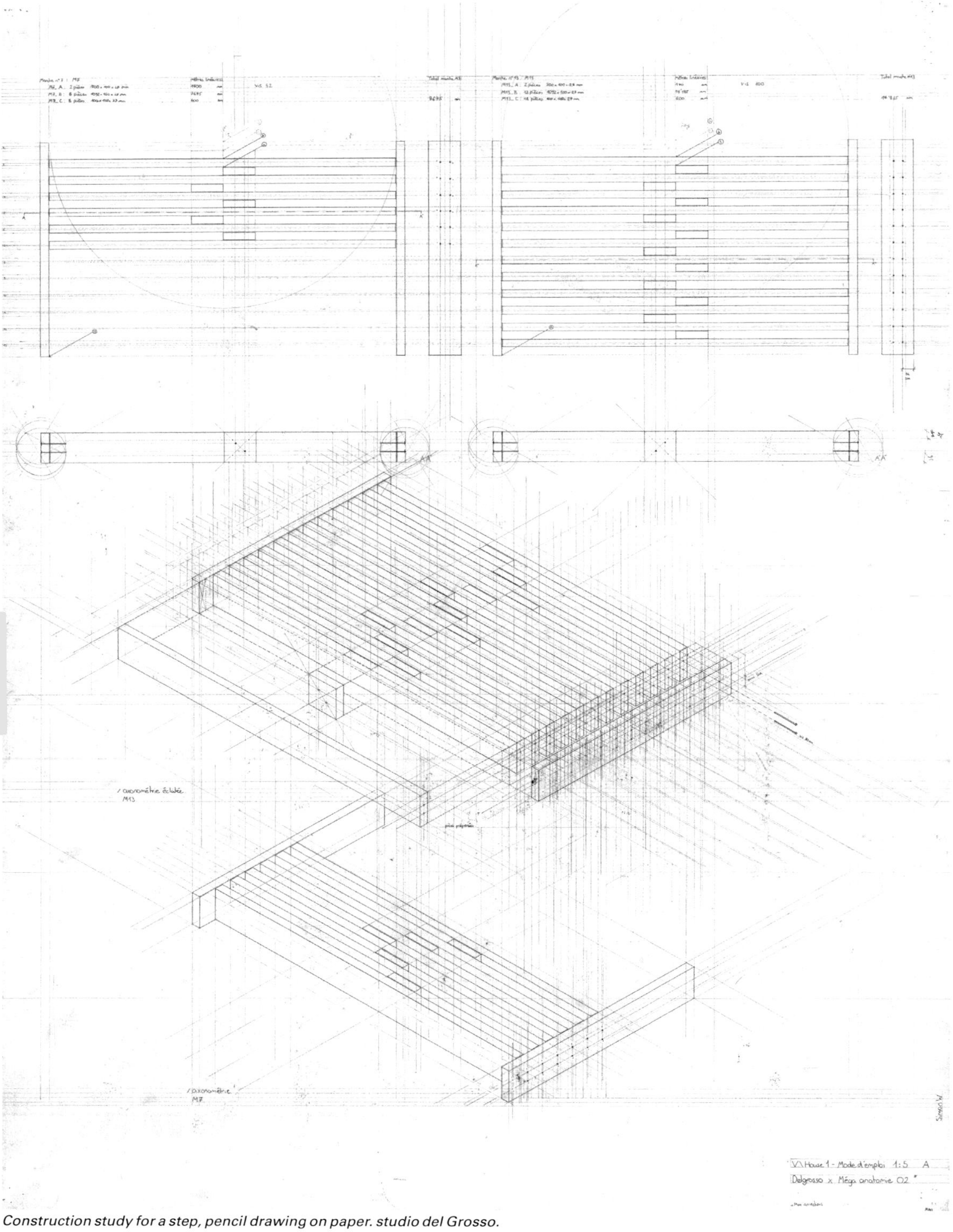

Construction study for a step, pencil drawing on paper. studio del Grosso.

Study model for a step, timber and screws. studio del Grosso.

Study model for a platform with ladder, timber and screws. studio del Grosso.

Study model for a platform, timber and screws. studio del Grosso.

Study model for horizontal support #1, timber and glue. studio Chassot.

Study model for horizontal support #2, timber and glue. studio Chassot.

Horizontal platforms cut through the vertical components of the protostructure.

Meeting of the platform and the vertical posts, pencil drawing on paper. studio Pellacani.

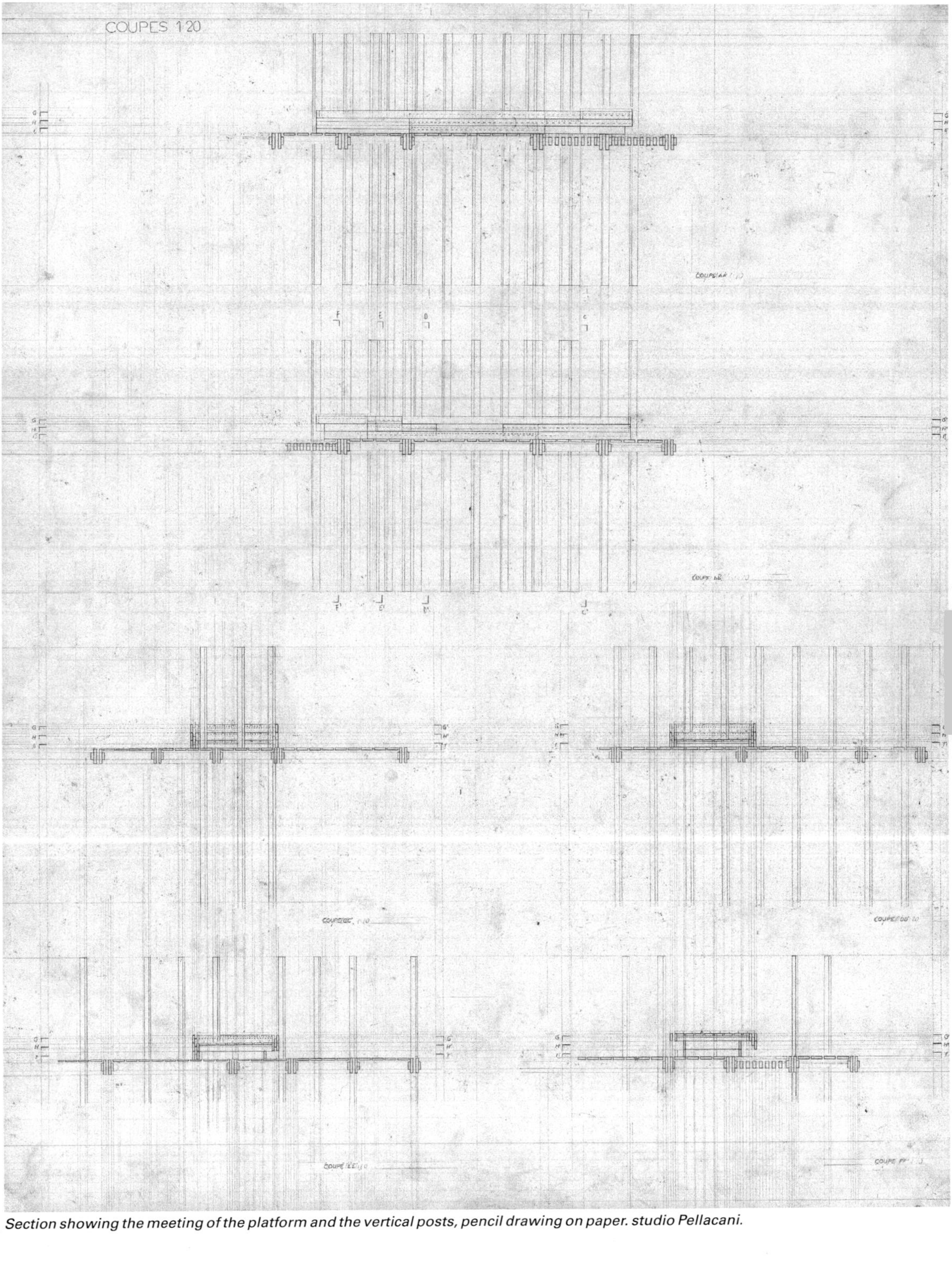

Section showing the meeting of the platform and the vertical posts, pencil drawing on paper. studio Pellacani.

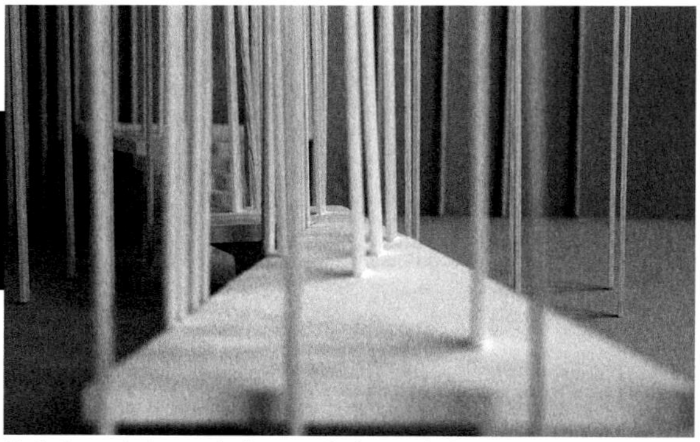

Path through the vertical posts, timber and plaster. studio Perez-Lupi.

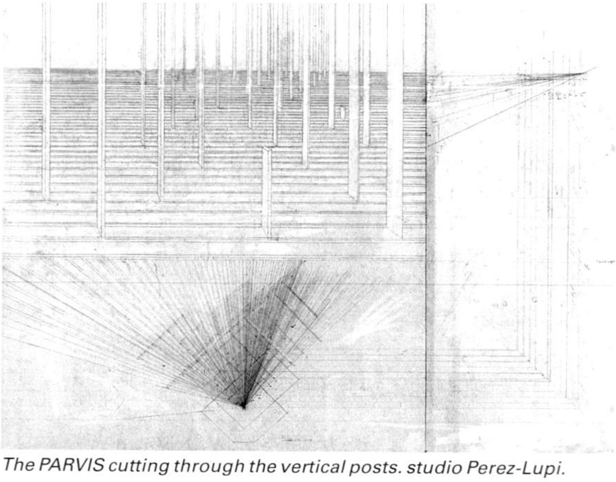

The PARVIS cutting through the vertical posts. studio Perez-Lupi.

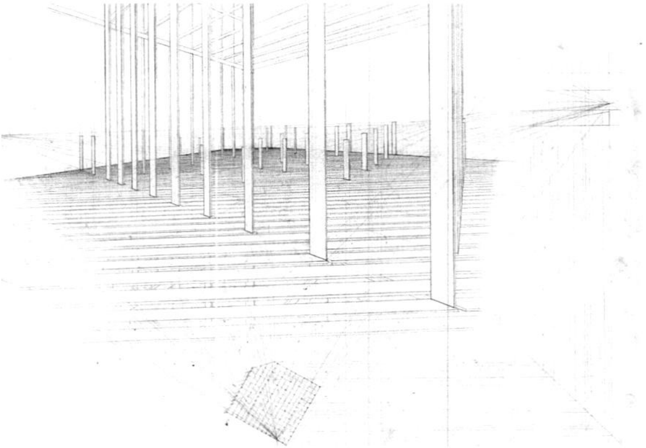

The vertical posts spanning between two floors.
studio van der Woude.

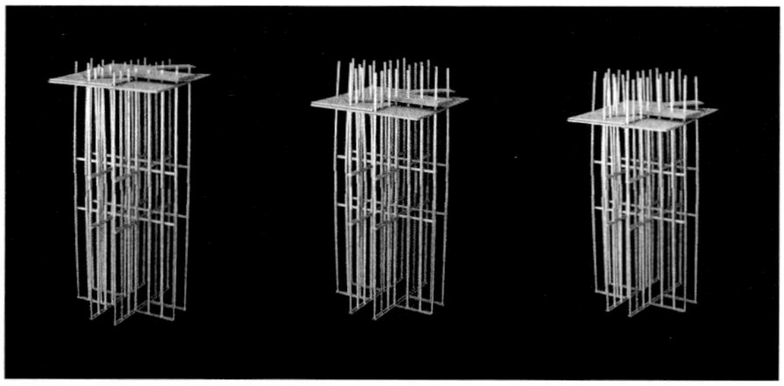

Study for the height positioning of the terrace, timber and glue.
studio Pellacani.

Terrace at the top of the protostructure, timber and glue.
studio Pellacani.

This project's substructure guarantees the stability of its horizontal surface allowing for the freer design of the floor according to spatial and not only structural criteria.

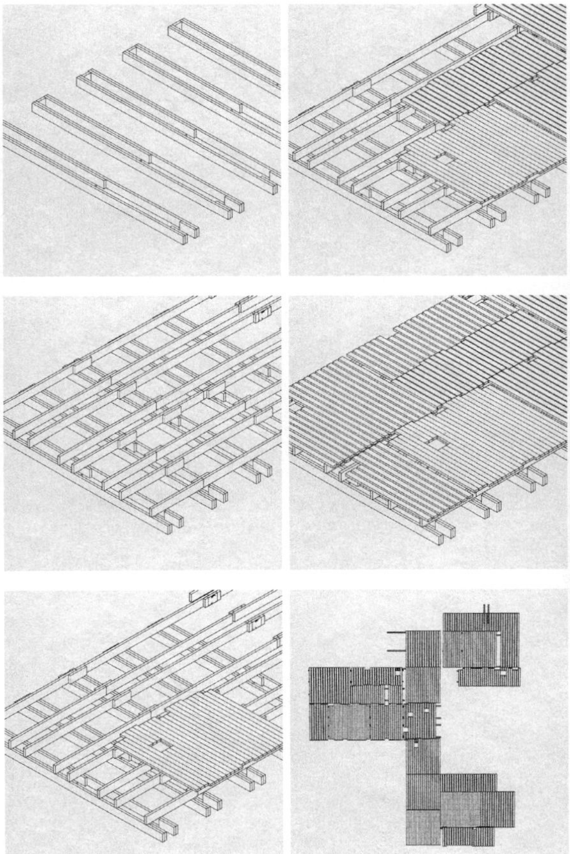

Breakdown of the floor construction, CAD drawing. studio den Hartog.

View of the substructure. studio Perez-Lupi.

Floor cover pattern. studio van der Woude.

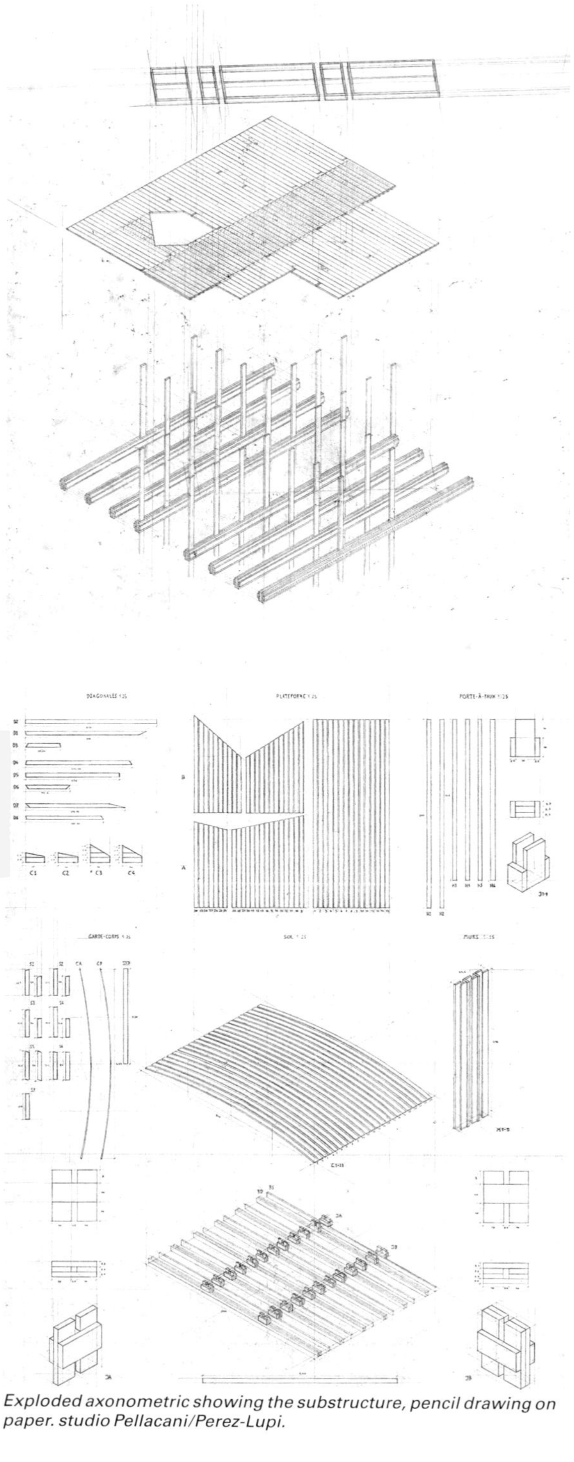

Exploded axonometric showing the substructure, pencil drawing on paper. studio Pellacani/Perez-Lupi.

Floor substructure model, timber and glue. studio del Grosso.

In linking the formal and structural aspects of design, the construction of the ground becomes an integral part of the total project. It provides the basis for the manipulation of height and levels, as well as form and light, within the interior.

Model of a soft floor on the top of HOUSE 1, timber and glue. studio van der Woude.

Model for construction study of the topography of the ground, cardboard, timber and glue. studio Pellacani.

The wall introduces a mode of support and enclosure. Arranged vertically, the wall controls views and light, while drawing the boundaries of the interior space.

The finished floor. AP studio.

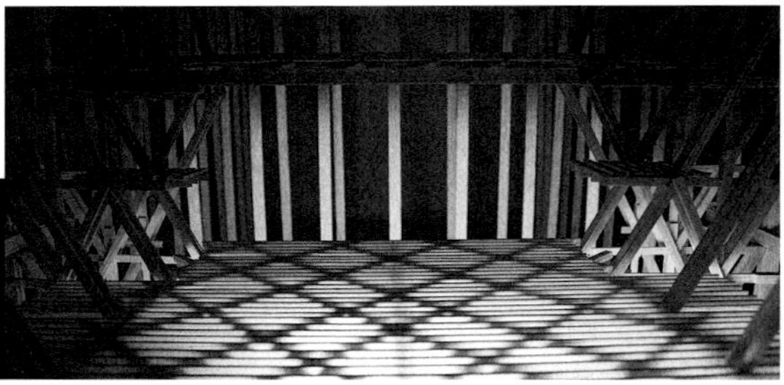

Light though the substructure of the floor. LC studio.

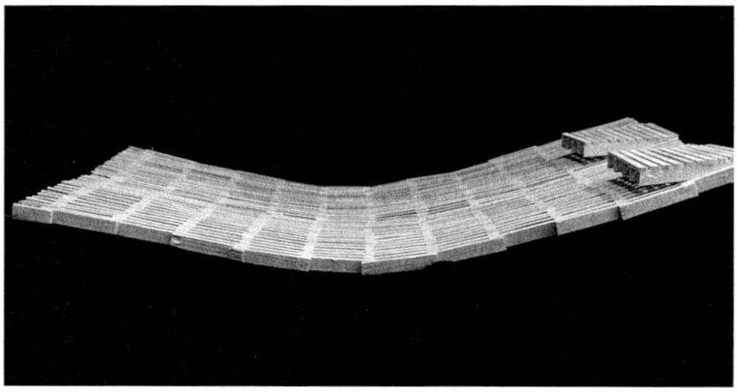

Construction model of a timber soft floor, timber and glue. studio van der Woude.

Composition of vertical panels in the lower part of HOUSE 1. studio Guaita.

Corridor of vertical panels. studio Guaita.

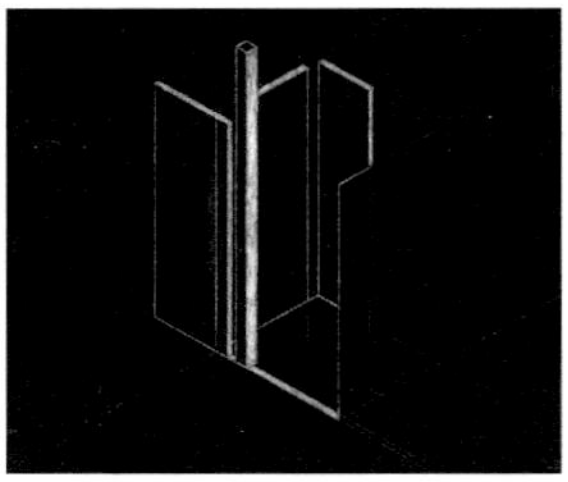

Study of solids and voids in axonometric view, pencil drawing on paper. studio Guaita.

A series of frames was constructed out of timber and filled in using timber components.

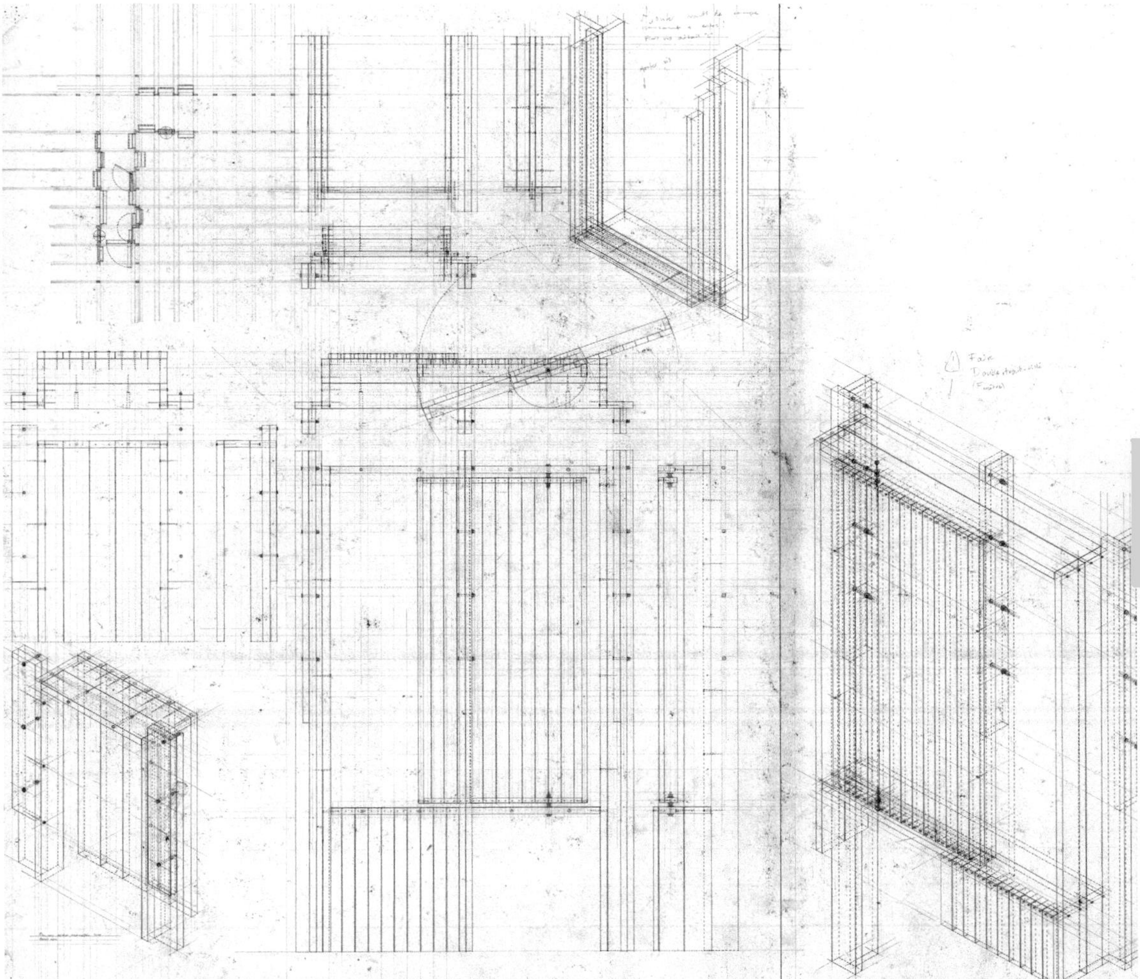

Construction details of the panels, pencil drawing on paper. studio Guaita.

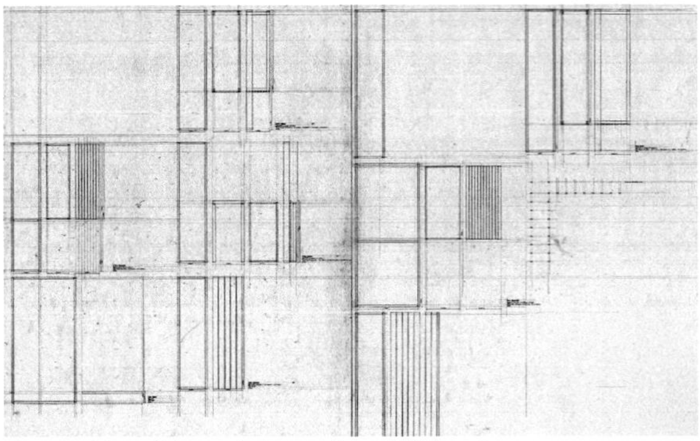

Composition of the various panels, pencil drawing on paper. studio Guaita.

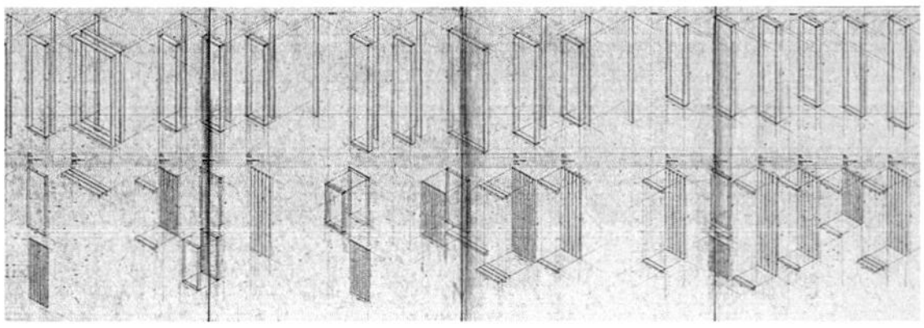

Catalogue of the panels, pencil drawing on paper. studio Guaita.

Construction of the panels, pencil drawing on paper. studio Guaita.

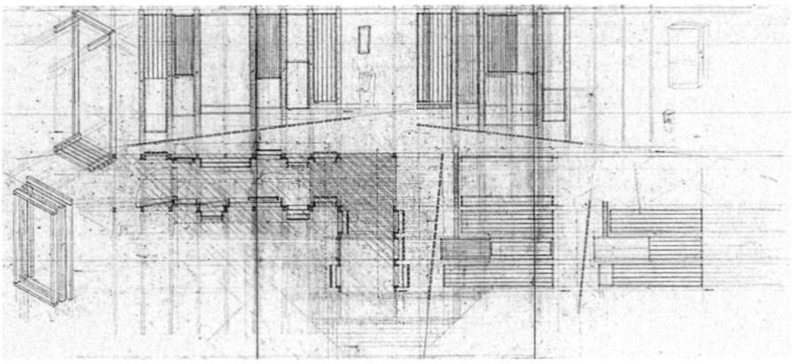

Corridor of vertical panels, pencil drawing on paper. studio Guaita.

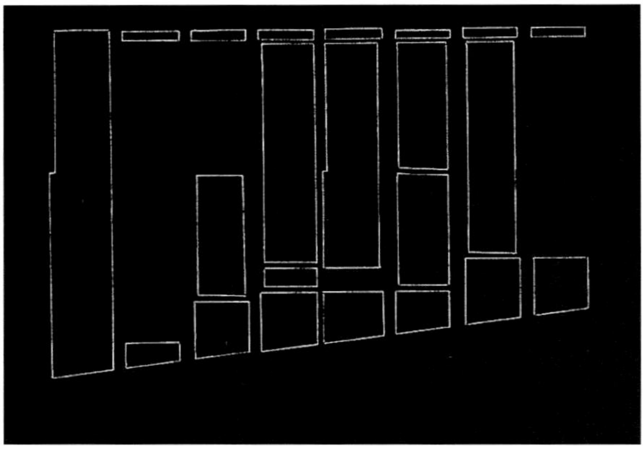

Composition of empty frames, pencil drawing on paper. studio Guaita.

Reverse composition of opaque surfaces, pencil drawing on paper. studio Guaita.

Another infill technique consists of crossing the timber components in several directions to create a mesh.

Outer wall with bracing, timber and glue. LC studio.

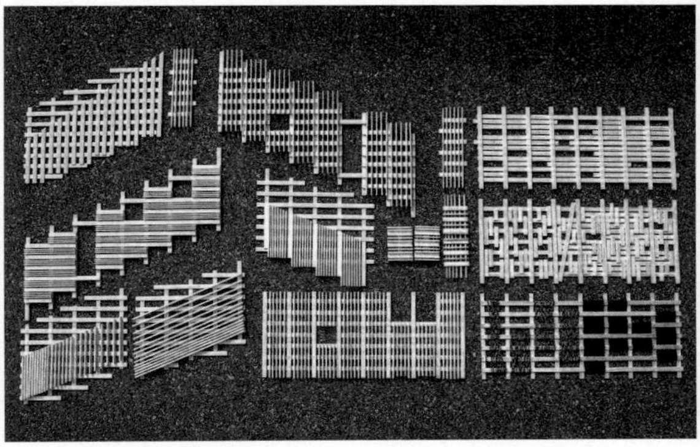

Various models of the grid, timber and glue. studio del Grosso.

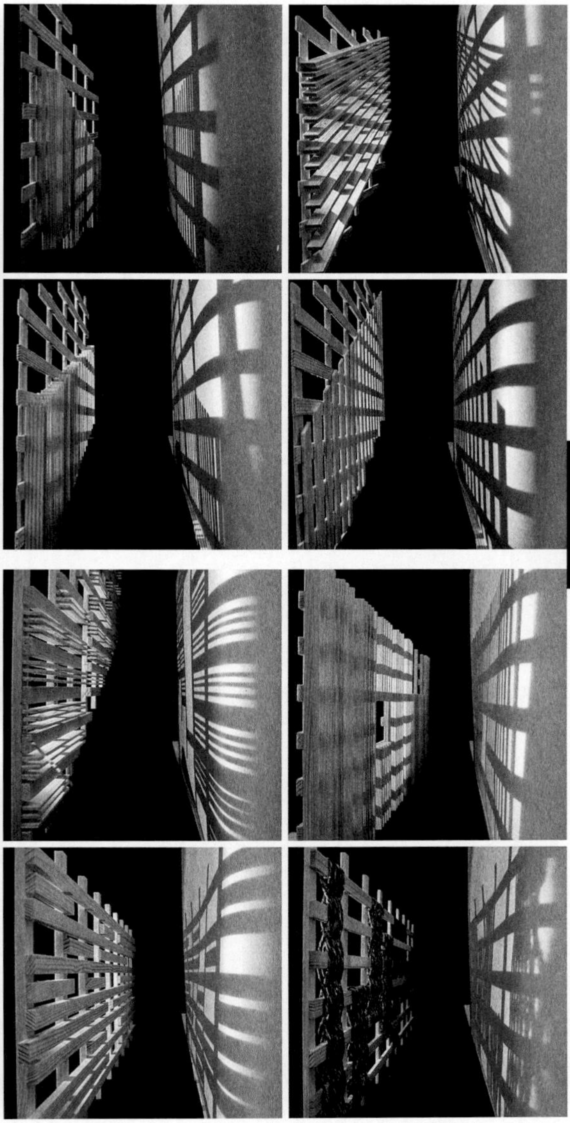

Various models of the grid tested with light #1-4, #5-8, timber and glue. studio del Grosso.

Pierced walls tests, timber and glue. studios Guaita/Baur/Chassot.

Some walls serve additional functions requiring the support of vertical surfaces.

This week, we've wondered:

How can we make a Room with only ladders and floors?

The answer is that we use ladders not only like a passage but also like Windows, tables, bed and chairs.(which constitute the organs of the room).

studio del Grosso

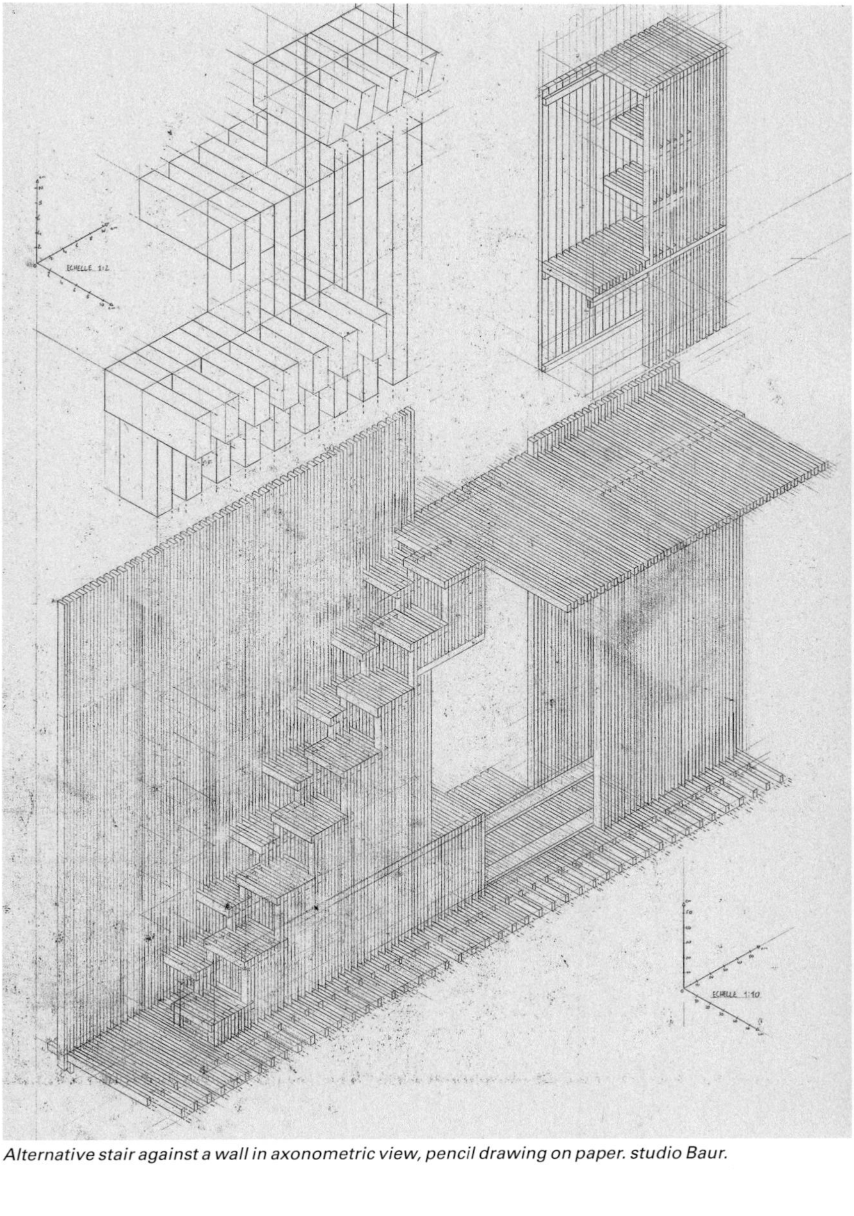

Alternative stair against a wall in axonometric view, pencil drawing on paper. studio Baur.

Alternative stair model, timber and glue. studio Baur.

Hidden stair model, timber and glue. studio Chassot.

INTRODUCTION

It is by now commonly accepted that the industrial revolution of the nineteenth century brought about enormous changes in western society. And yet, the rapid acceleration of our technologically driven society since that time may well have prevented us from seeing the increasing installation of a global agenda: in terms of mass production, and more specifically, in the displacement or loss of craft traditions. Beyond the socio-political implications of this development, which cannot be described here, there has undeniably been a growing gap between the mass availability of objects that society uses and consumes, and the understanding of how these objects are fabricated. This state of disjunction alters society's perception of the world, leaving gaping holes in the understanding of techniques of making. Understanding how things are made has become a "specialist' job", one that requires technical and technological knowledge and specific education.

As a pedagogical experiment, HOUSE 1 takes over the challenge of re-establishing the relation between objects and their fabrication. Understanding our immediate environment while participating in its very fabrication allows us to marry knowledge with making. In this way, a necessary form of critical thinking develops through the mutual and progressive acquisition of skills and "know-how", and avoids simply considering our environment (environment, understood as a complex ensemble of landscape with the built and everyday objects that surround us) as a given. Given by whom?

The purpose of the HOUSE 1 project, then, is not necessarily to transform architecture students into carpenters, smiths or electricians. Rather, it aims at navigating students constantly between the twin poles of thinking and making, allowing them to understand what kinds of processes are put into play to transform ideas into materially fabricated artefacts. A special effort has been out into allowing students to comprehend the efforts required in building, the manpower needed, and the inevitable collaborative coordination that any building requires. Understanding this process by participating actively in it guarantees for students a greater sensitivity to our built environment.

The following chapter presents the fundamental tools used to build HOUSE 1, as well as how these tools shaped the process and eventually the possibilities of constructing and becoming aware of a total environment. Through a series of tools, actions and processes, HOUSE 1 is opened up and observed from another angle. "Access to Tools" was the programmatic subtitle of the Whole Earth Catalogue. This section presents the tools of HOUSE 1, how they were used, and the collective implications of this use.

In being inherently set at the threshold between idea and articulation, protostructures are a catalyst in design processes and facilitate decision-making.

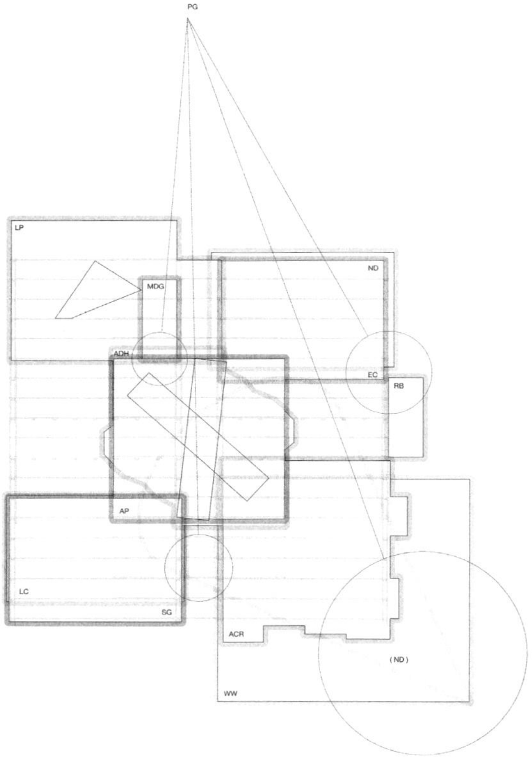

First plan of the different interventions composing HOUSE 1, CAD drawing. Agathe Mignon.

Physical links between the differing situations in the structure. studio den Hartog.

Superimposition of proposal models for intervention into the structure of HOUSE 1, photomontage. Agathe Mignon.

Ensuring the interdependence of each intervention means taking into account their respective spatial, constructive and programmatic parameters. The development of the project does not, therefore, centre on a single spatial intervention, but rather requires a knowledge of all of its connections.

This understanding of cooperation in a design process is directly projected into the reality of constructing HOUSE 1: The team responsible for any single intervention must organise itself in order to take into account the presence of other projects and their respective construction teams.

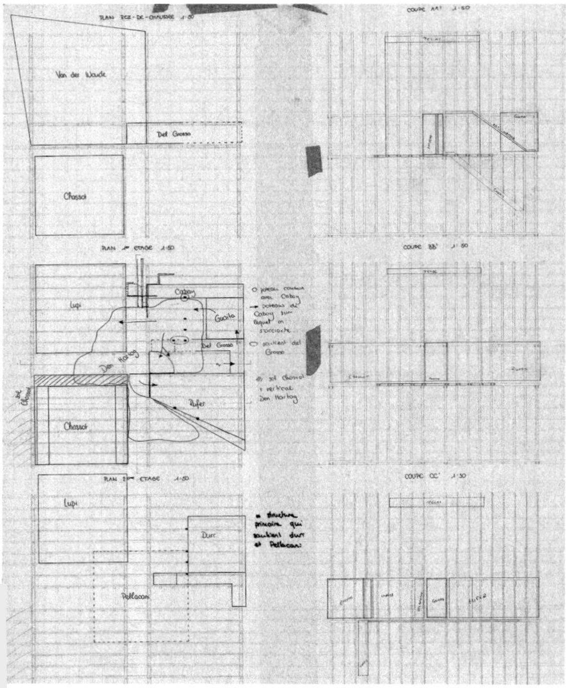

Representation of the different projects and their relationships, pencil drawing on paper. studio den Hartog.

Mounting scenario model with the charting of human interaction with the structure. studio Pellacani.

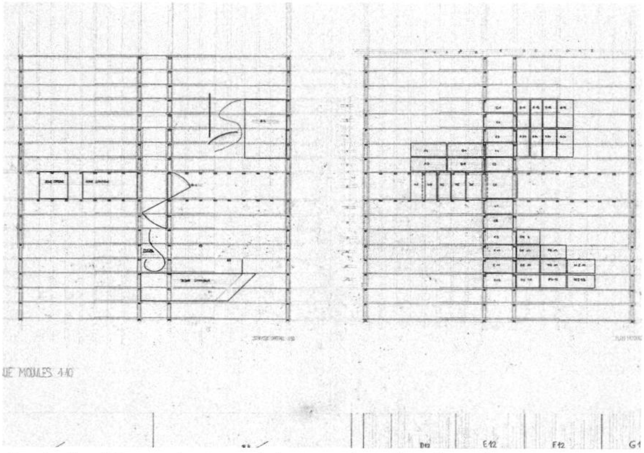

Analysis of the various spatial strategies of each project, pencil drawing on paper. studio den Hartog.

1: Acheminement et fixation des balloon-frames provisoires et des échelles
2: Installation des palettes d'échafaudage
3: Acheminement et fixation des balloon-frames primaires
4: Arrivée et installation du caisson central (en bleu)
5: Arrivée et installation des caissons latéraux, d'abord posés sur le caisson principal (en vert)
studio Pellacani

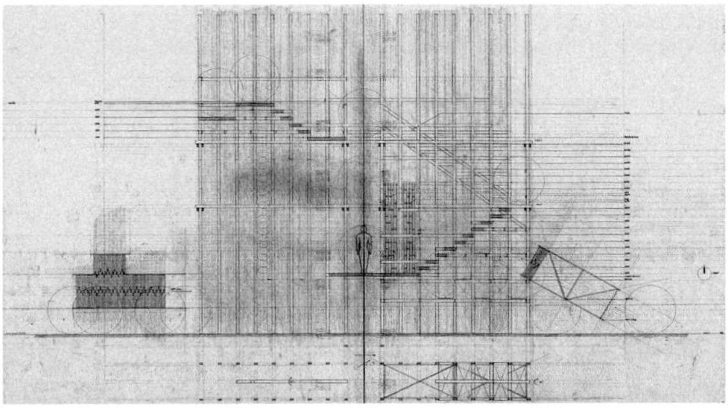

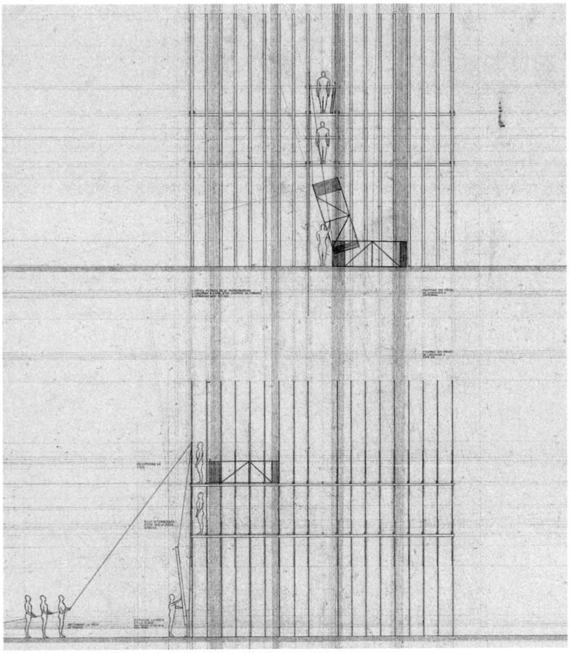

Section view of the mounting scenario with the charting of human interaction with the structure. studio del Grosso.

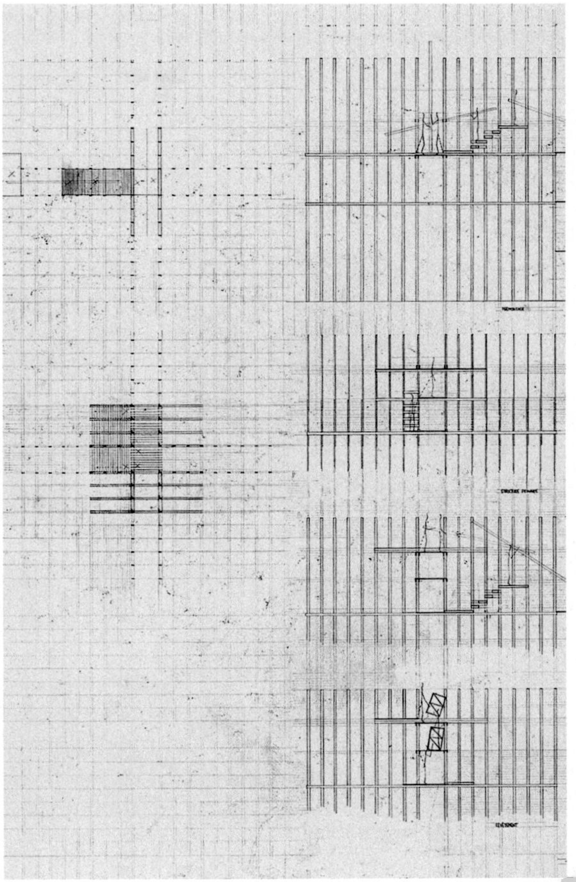

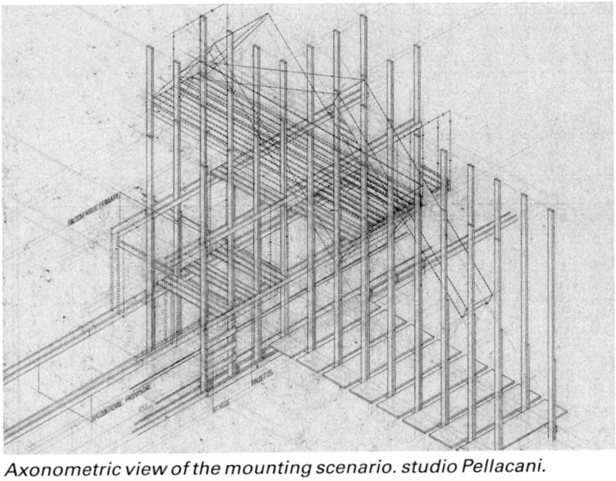

Axonometric view of the mounting scenario. studio Pellacani.

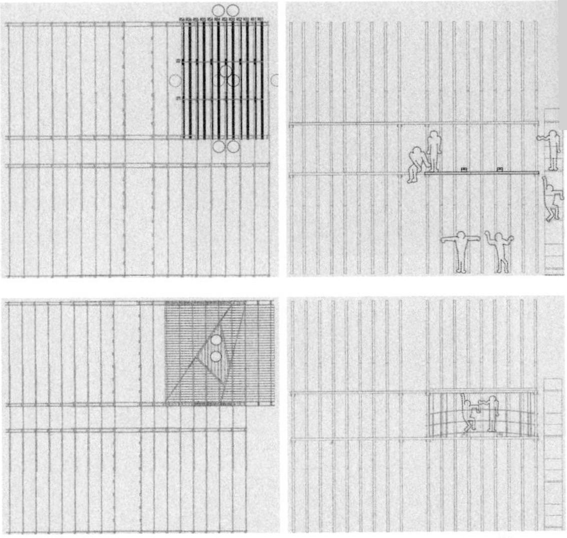

Plan and section of the mounting scenario with the charting of human interaction with the structure. studio Pellacani/Perez-Lupi.

Collaborative effort paired with the careful organisation of each team increases the quantity and quality of construction.
Members of the team find their place within the immediate group, as well as within the entire construction collaborative of HOUSE 1.

Frames being transported to site. studio Perez-Lupi.

Lifting of the frames into place. studio Perez-Lupi.

Transport and lifting of the frames for the stairs. studio Cabay.

Construction of HOUSE 1. studio Cabay.

Assistance and cooperation during construction. studio Cabay.

Assistance and cooperation during construction. studio Cabay.

From the number of screws to the number of hours worked, facts and figures drive the project.

HOUSE 1 is crafted entirely by hand, from the smallest piece of timber to the largest structural elements. Each component is drawn before being recorded in a materials list. This system allows for the anticipation of the quantities of material needed, but also for the calculation of the budget.

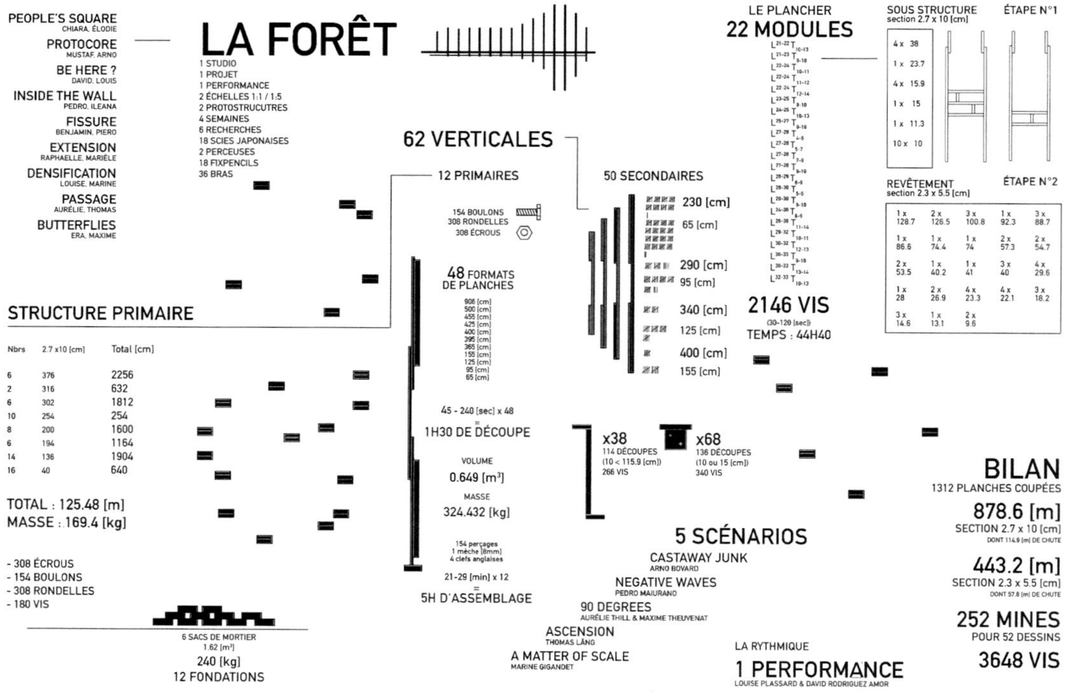

The Forest project in numbers. studio den Hartog.

	Petite section (cm)	Nombre	Longueur linéaire (cm)		Grande section	Nombre	Longueur linéaire (cm)		Volume élément	Poids élément
Scène couvrement	490	35	17150							
	52.5	45	2362.5							
Scène structure					500	21	10500			
				19512.5			10500		0.5192971875	259.64859375
Passerelle couvrement	490	7	**3430**		500	5	2500		0.10994625	54.973125
Modules structurels	400	14	5600							
	361	8	2888							
	352	4	1408							
	272	28	7616							
	240	14	3360							
	237	20	4740							
	228	10	2280							
	147	28	4116							
	105	28	2940							
	83	28	2324							
	30	28	840							
				38112					0.471636	235.818
Galerie longitudinal	60	84	5040							
	482	14	6748							
Galerie transversal	77	40	3080							
	74.5	40	2980							
	482	12	5784							
				23632					0.292446	146.223
Barrières 1 (5)	60	10	600		60	10	600			
	125	1	125							
Barrières 2 (1)	120	2	240		120	2	240			
	125	2	250							
Barrières 3 (2)	180	4	720		180	4	720			
	125	6	750							
Barrières 4 (2)	240	4	960		240	4	960			
	125	8	1000							
Barrières 6 (2)	360	4	1440		360	4	1440			
	125	12	1500							
				7585				**3960**	0.200784375	100.3921875
Panneau mobile	258	5	**1290**							
					350	4	1400			
	282	2	564							
	205	2	410							
	30	2	60							
Rail	600	2	1200							
	13.5	12	162							
				3686				**1400**	0.08341425	41.707125
Echelles					140	2	280			
					50	6	300			
	150	2	300							
	100	2	200							
					280	2	560			
					50	12	600			
	300	2	600							
	100	3	300							
				1400				**1740**	0.064305	32.1525
Parois	450	12	**5400**							
					500	2	**1000**		0.093825	
										46.9125
Nombre total éléments		**586**				78				
Poids total (kg)	917.82703125									
Mètres linéaires petite section	**1027.575**									
Mètres linéaires grande section	**211**									
Mètres linéaires total	1238.575									

	Taille (mm)	Diamètre (mm)	Nombre	Poids (kg)	Poids total (kg)	Total 35mm	Total 45mm	Total 60mm	Total 70mm	Total 80mm
Tiges filetées	140	8	93	**19.623744**						
	100	8	42	**6.33024**						
Boulons	6.8	8	270	**1.3836096**						
Rondelles		112								
Vis										
Scène et passerelle	35	3.5	466							
Barrières	35	3.5	98							
	70	4	132							
Galerie	45	3.5	384							
Panneau mobile	70	4	8							
	60	3.5	20							
	35	3.5	10							
Rail	35	3.5	48							
Echelles	80	4	72							
	35	3.5	24							
Parois	35	3.5	112							
				9.618	36.9555936	758	384	20	140	72

List of required material. studio Chassot.

Here three sets of data are organised in relation to one another into an overall construction program: the stages of construction, the available number of workers, and the time required for construction.

W1 25.04/01.05	W2 02.05/08.05	W3 09.05/15.05
Dalles x 9 — Chantier temps pose1: 4h personnes: 4 matériel: ficelles, masse, niveaux, sable; pieux Dalles x 13 — Atelier temps montage: 5h personnes: 4	Fondation x 28 — Chantier temps pose2: 6h personnes: 8 matériel: pelles, sable, niveaux, ficelles, pieux, masses	
Cadres x 16 — Atelier temps montage: 24h personnes: le maximum possible (8?) matériel: scies, perceuses, clefs boulons, tiges filetées	Cadres 5m x 5 — Chantier temps pose1: 2h personnes: 4 matériel: perceuses, clefs, boulons, tiges filetées	Cadres 5m x 3 et 3.5m x 8 — Chantier temps pose2: 4h personnes: 10 matériel: perceuses, clefs, boulons tiges filetées
Solives toutes — Atelier temps montage: 2h personnes: 2 matériel scies, perceuses, boulons, clefs, tiges filetées	Solives 5m x 9 — Chantier temps pose1: 1h personnes: 4 matériel: visseuses, visses, masse, niveau	Solives le reste — Chantier temps pose2: 2h personnes: 8 matériel: visseuses, visses, boulons, tiges filetées, clefs
	Plancher intérieur — Atelier temps montage: 1h personnes: 3 matériel: scies	Plancher — Chantier temps pose1: 6h personnes: 8 matériel: viseuses, visses, scies Plancher — Atelier temps montage: 4h personnes: 6 matériel: scies
Transport fondations : 2 trajets 30min 2 personnes	Transport fondations : 6 trajets 1h30 2 personnes cadre : 3 trajets 45min 8 personnes solives: 2-3 trajets 45min 4 personnes	Transport : cadre : 3 trajets 45min 4 personnes plancher : 6 trajets 1h30 16 personnes Examen de structure: le 18 mai

Week-by-week list of parts to be manufactured, according to time taken and number of workers required. studio van der Woude.

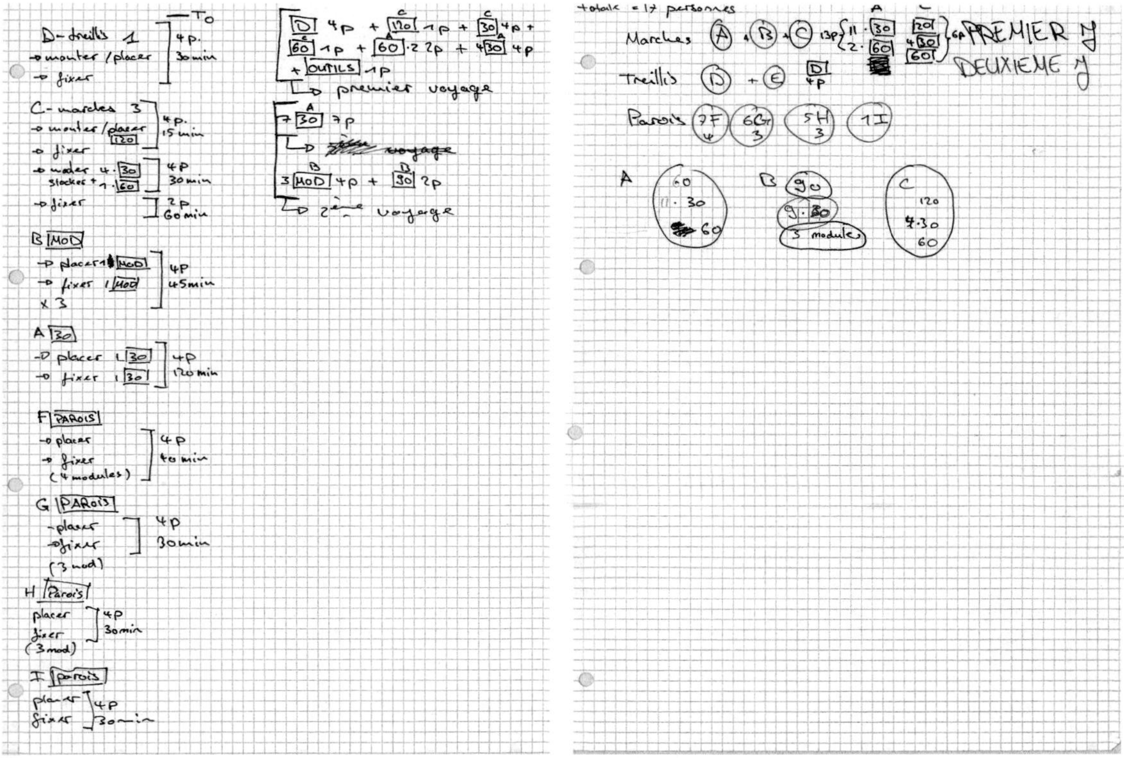

Estimate of the duration and number of workers required for the construction of each part. studio del Grosso.

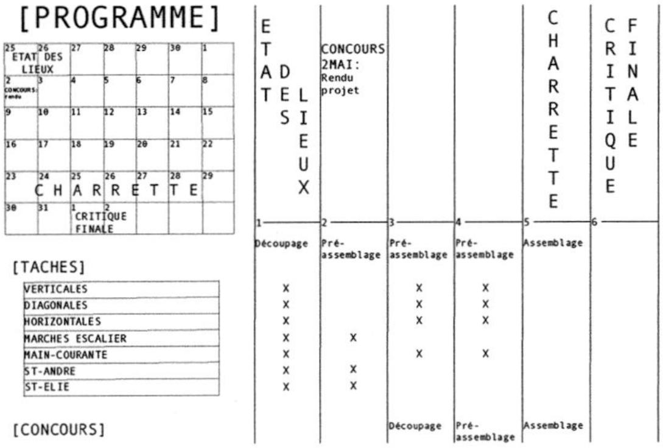

Program with tasks, duration and number of workers required. studio Cabay.

Here an organisation of data into an equation allowed for an illustration of its content, and for highlighting specific aspects of the information.

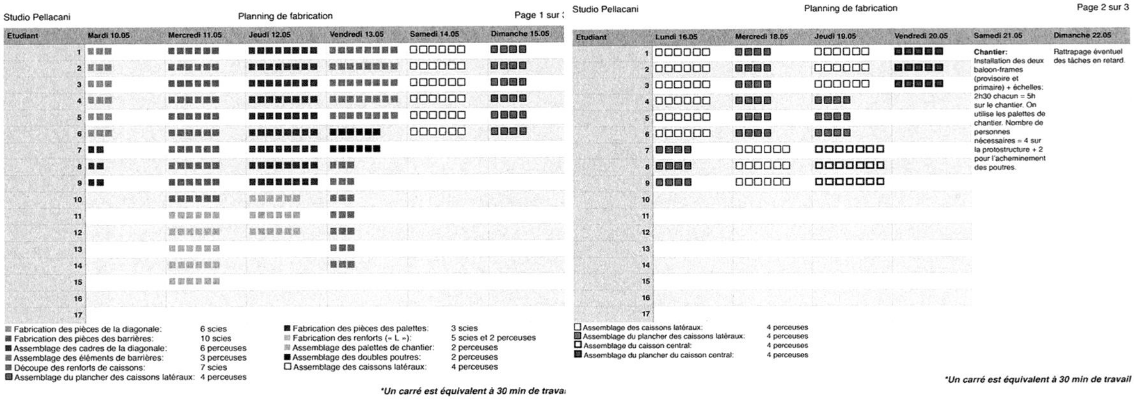

Planning of construction, with graphic codes representing number of workers required and time taken. studio Pellacani.

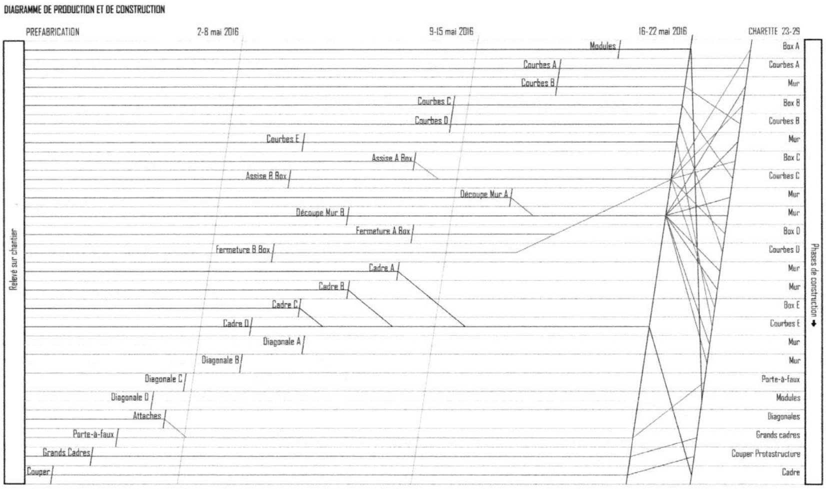

Program of production and construction. studio Perez-Lupi.

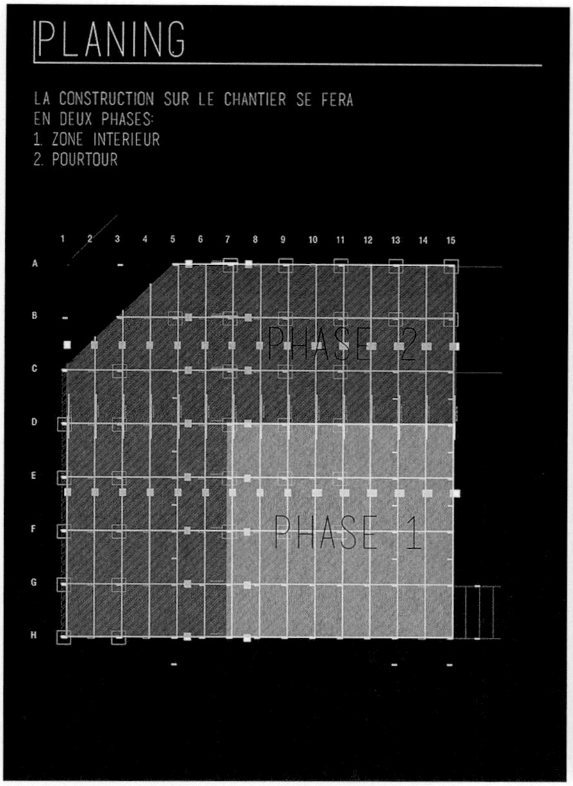

Illustration of the arrangement of construction phases. studio van der Woude.

Technical drawing uses graphic codes specific to systems of scientific representation and does not represent directly the physical or material appearance of an object; but instead, projects a reality shaped by unseen forces and factors.

Technical drawing understands and illustrates a physical phenomenon. The representation of elements not visible to or measurable by the naked eye, such as rays of light or the forces of gravity, reveals how natural forces work upon an object, and also demonstrates definitively how we can harness them.

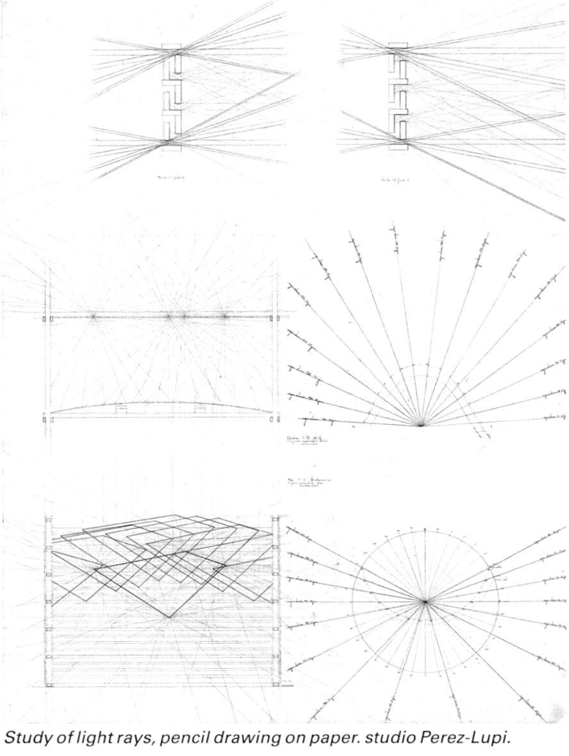

Study of light rays, pencil drawing on paper. studio Perez-Lupi.

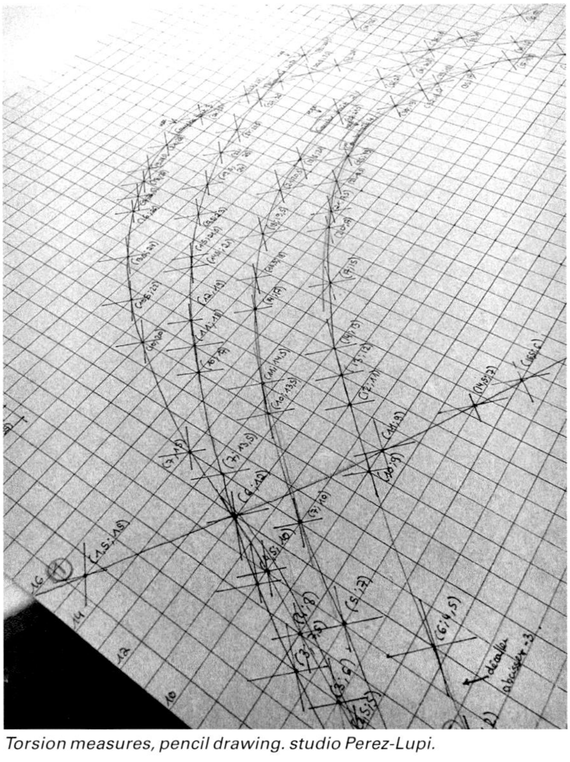

Torsion measures, pencil drawing. studio Perez-Lupi.

The codification of representation by means of a technical drawing can be used to advance formal, spatial, or technical research. Codification by visual means allows us, through a process of simplified figurative representation, to conduct tests and studies of certain aspects of the construction that then allow it to take form in reality.

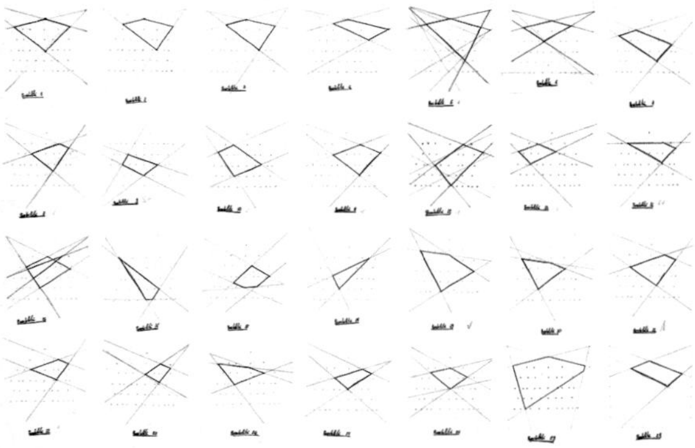

Graphic studies, pencil drawing on paper. studio Perez-Lupi.

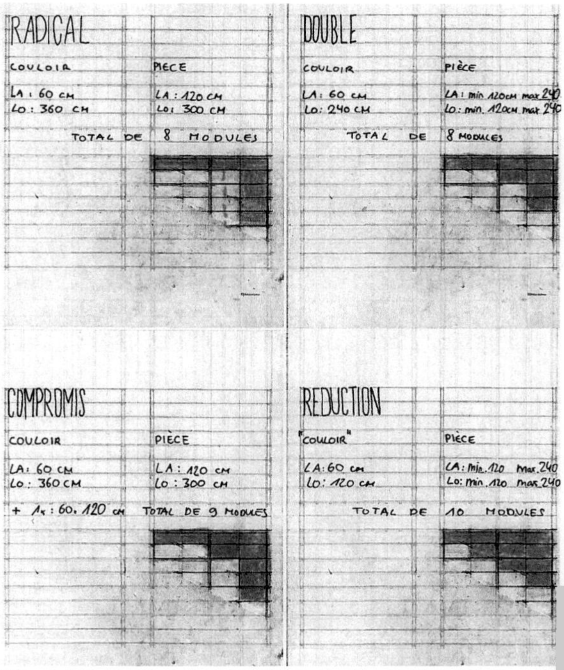

Shape of the plan based on the structural grid, pencil drawing on paper. studio Rufer.

Computer aided design (CAD) constructs a virtual model through three-dimensional simulation.

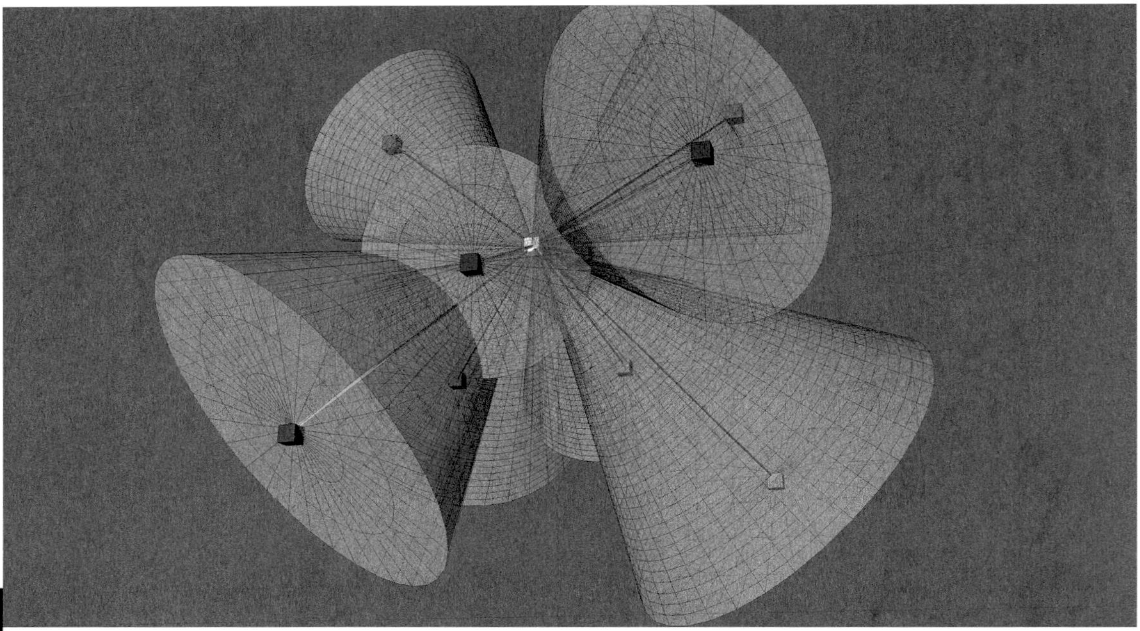

"An analysis of the vision cones towards every other room area proved to be very difficult to interpret within a two dimensional drawing. We therefore made a simplified 3D model of the protostructure along with 60° vision cones pointing towards each group point. This helped us define common groups as well as exact positioning of certain apertures."
studio Dürr

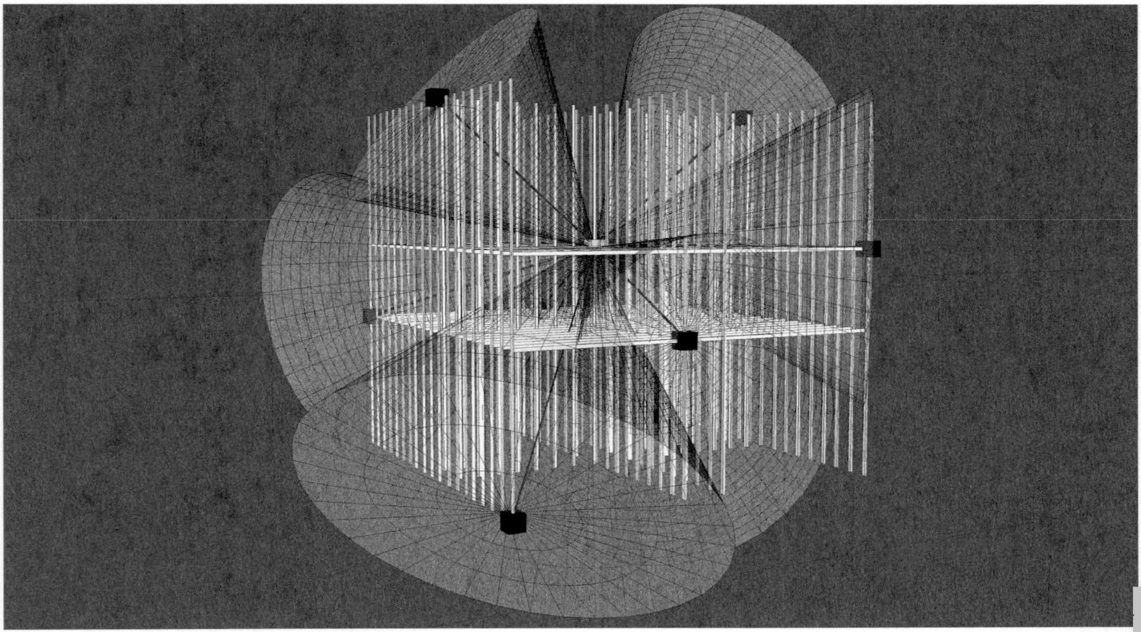

Conical sections 3D test, CAD drawing. studio Dürr.

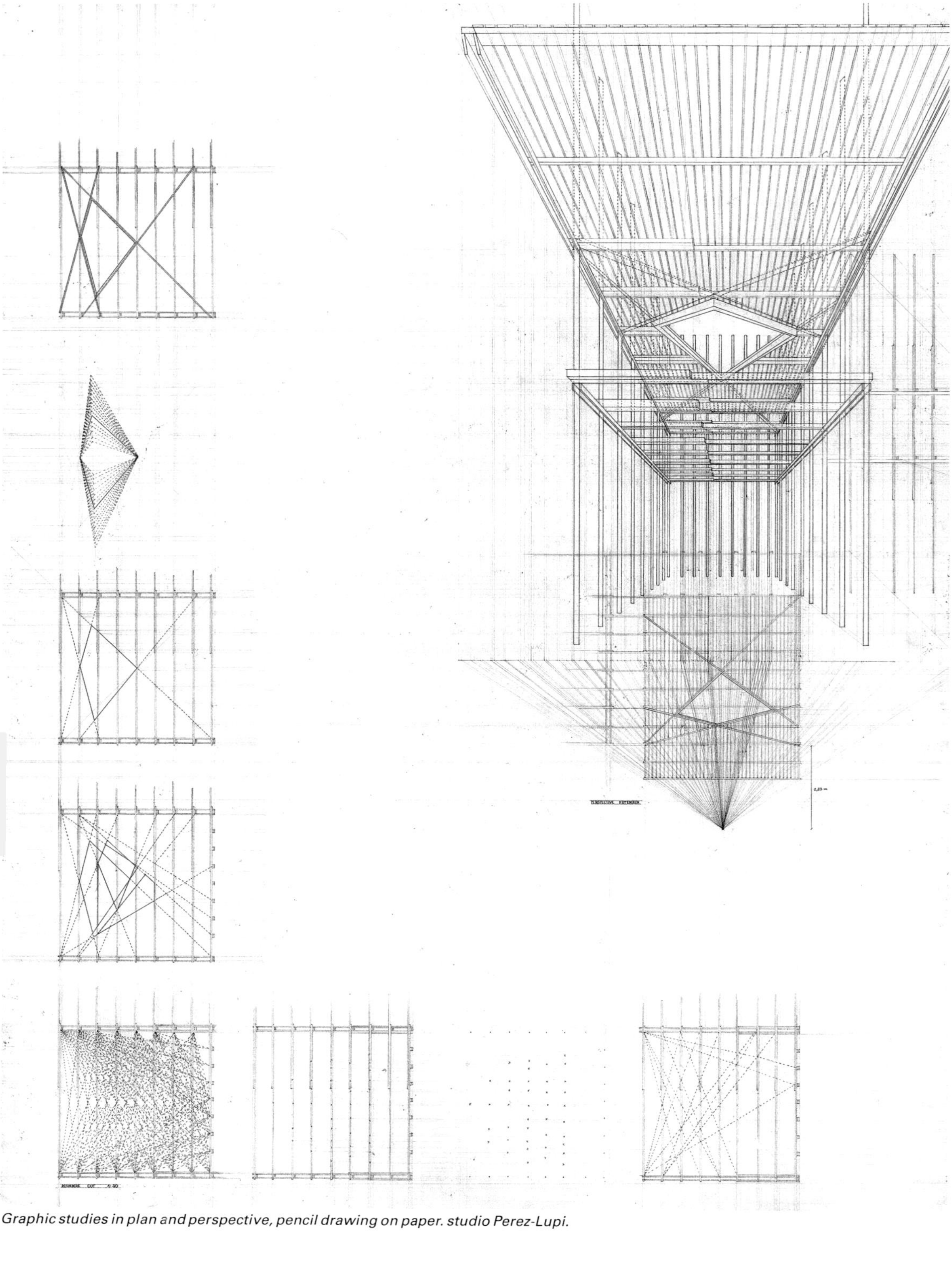

Graphic studies in plan and perspective, pencil drawing on paper. studio Perez-Lupi.

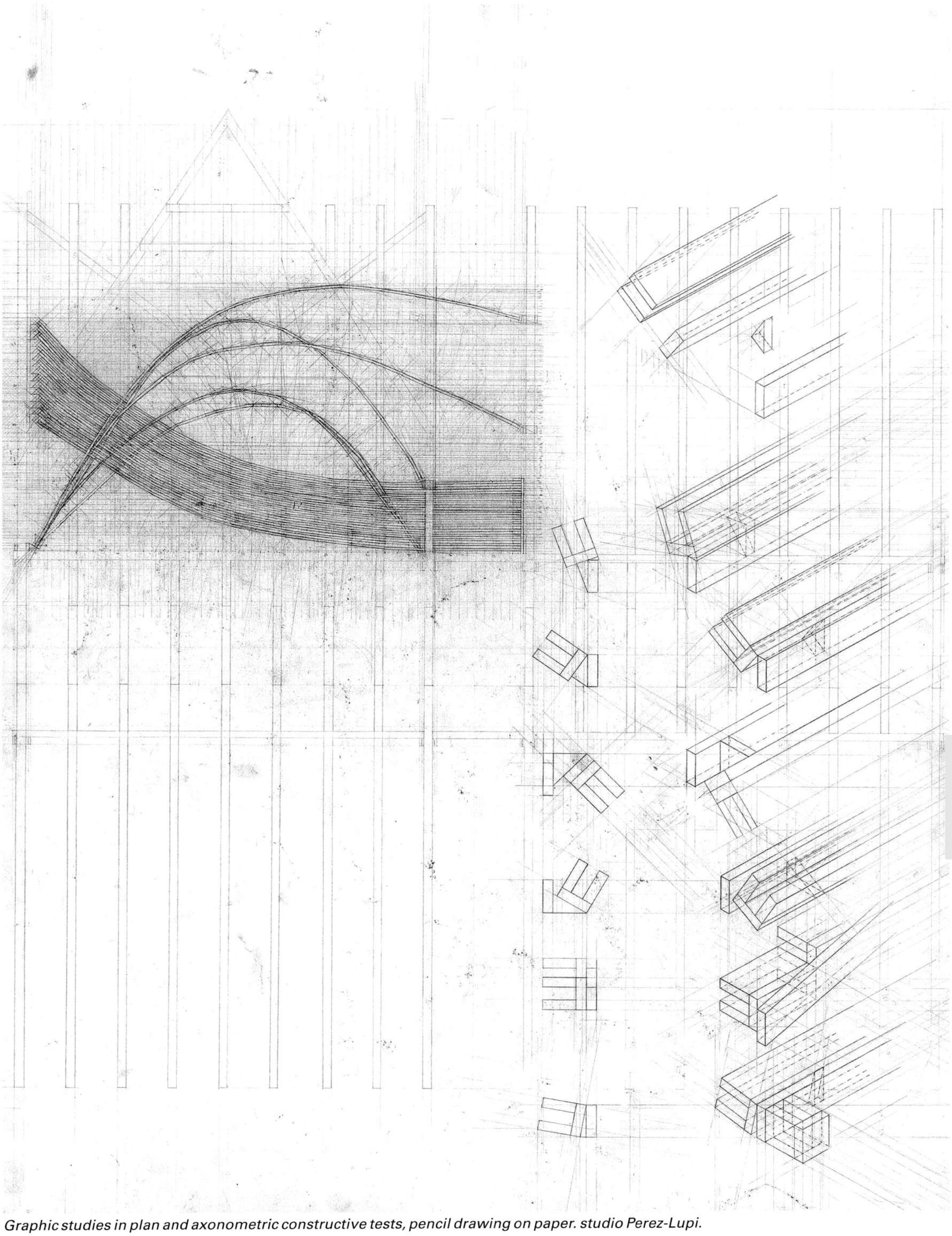

Graphic studies in plan and axonometric constructive tests, pencil drawing on paper. studio Perez-Lupi.

By using codes, technical drawing can visually explain physical transformations. The detachment from so-called 'reality' afforded by the reductive and codified nature of technical drawing offers the opportunity for exploring the complex process of construction simply by using a pencil.

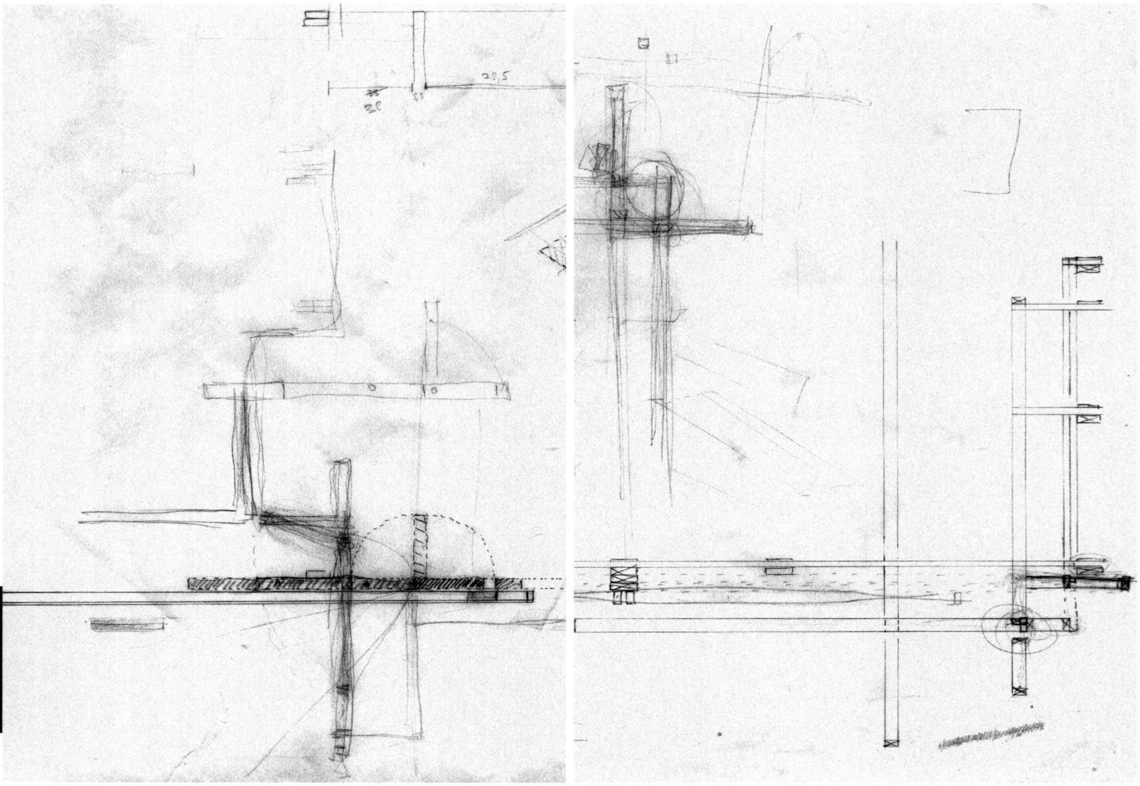

Sketches of the design and construction processes, pencil drawing on paper. studio Guaita.

SCALE

The drawing is a graphic representation of reality. It is not reality itself. The speculative projection of the drawing is the subject of research at a number of scales. The object can be depicted at varying degrees of reduction or expansion.

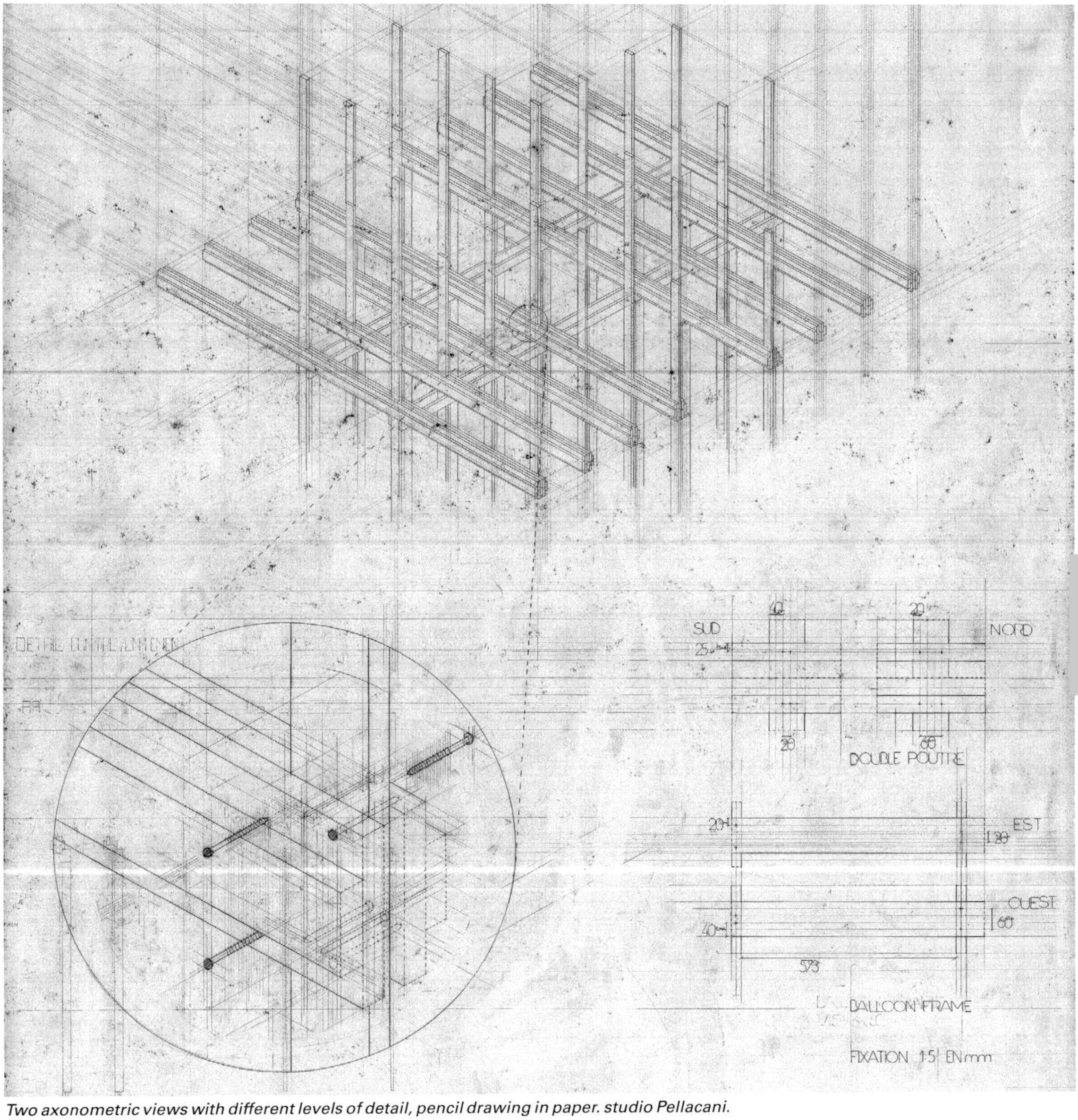

Two axonometric views with different levels of detail, pencil drawing in paper. studio Pellacani.

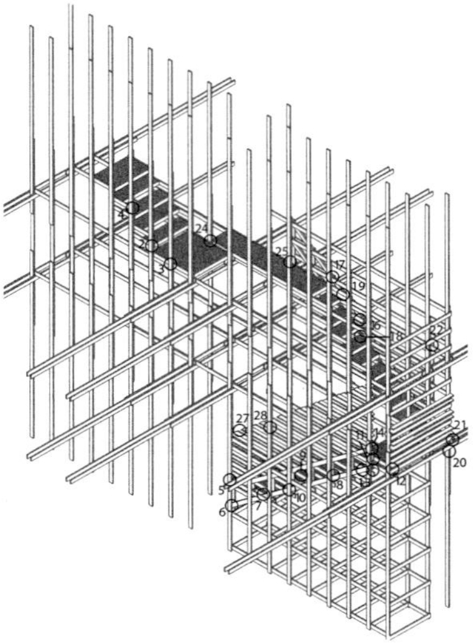

Overall axonometric showing location of the details, CAD drawing. studio del Grosso.

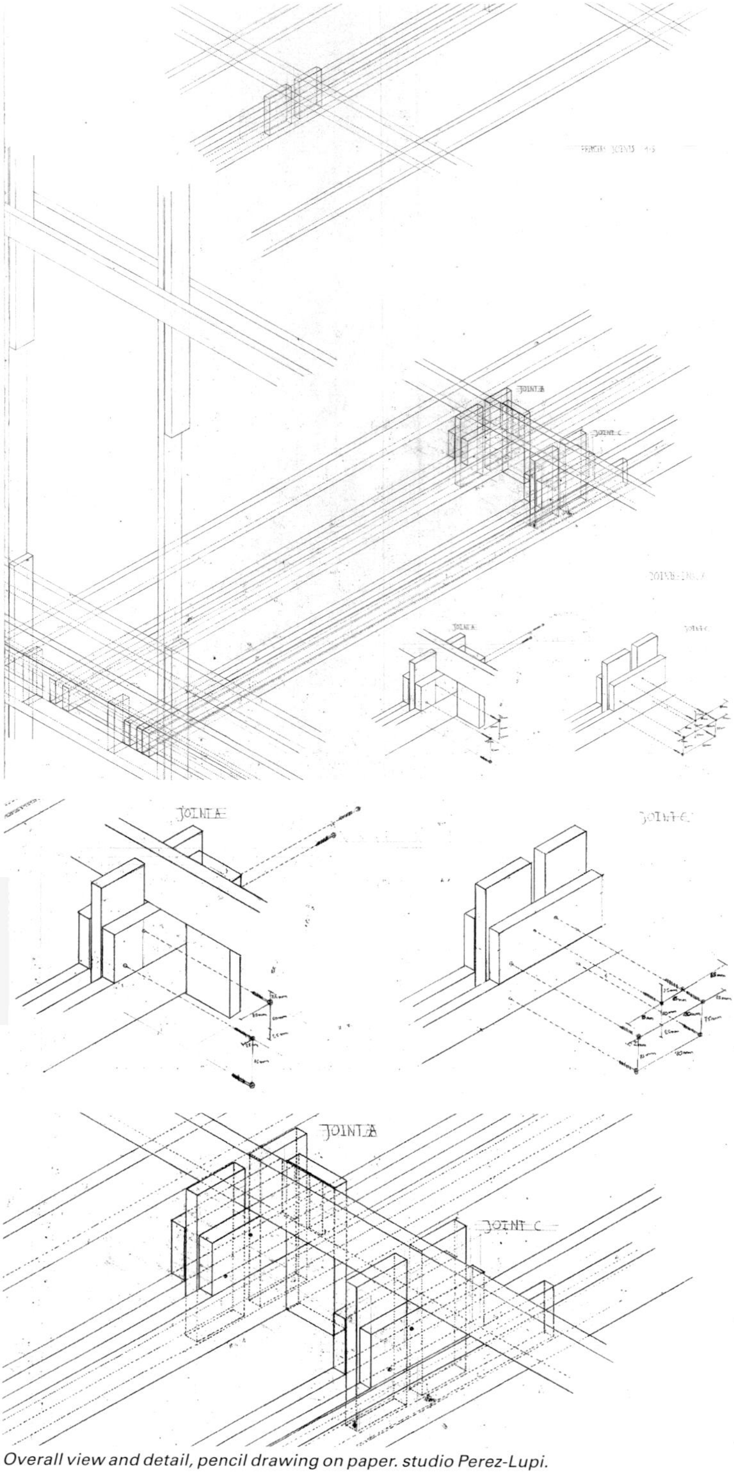

Overall view and detail, pencil drawing on paper. studio Perez-Lupi.

DIMENSIONS

Technical drawing tells us about the physical characteristics of a represented object. It transmits information about the drawing, such as scale, size, location, or its relative positioning within the whole system.

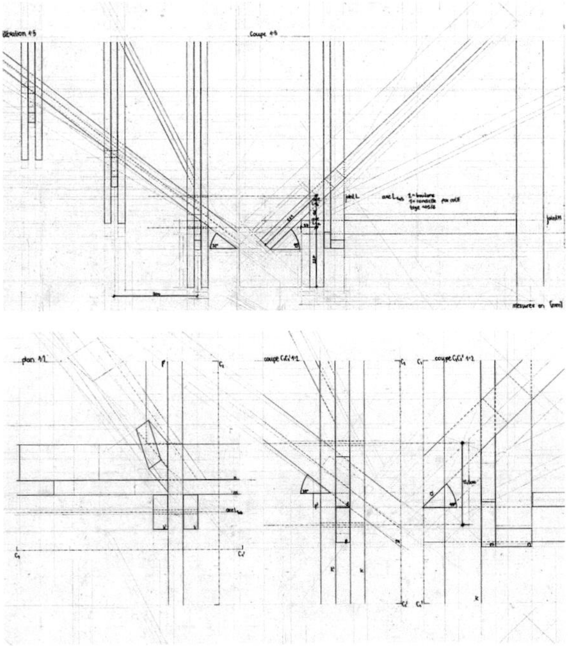

Elevation and section with indication of angles and lengths, pencil drawing in paper. studio Baur.

CONSTRUCTION

Technical drawing makes use of scale to transmit certain information about how an object is put together. The drawing uses symbols, tools, systems and materials for the assembly and arrangement of the construction elements.

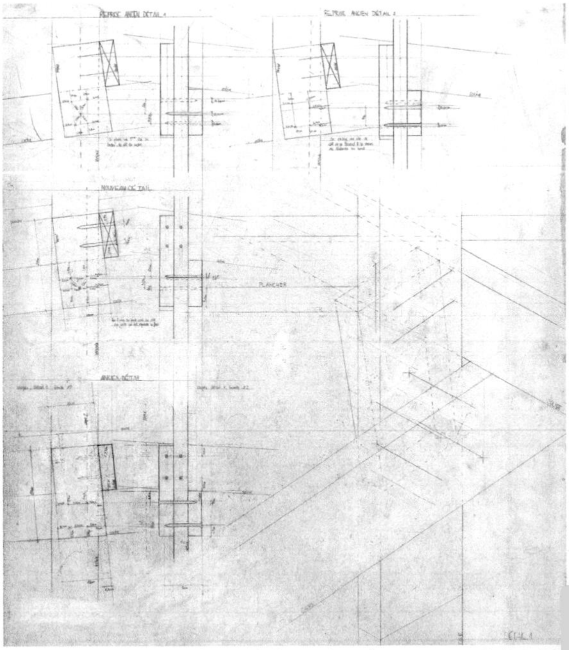

Cross-section with location and dimension of screws, pencil drawing on paper. studio van der Woude.

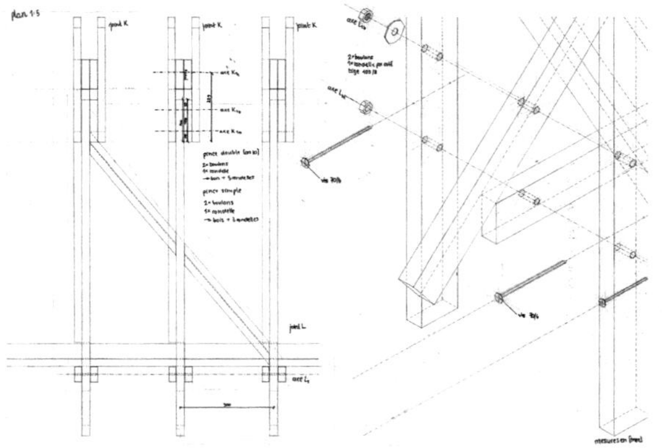

Elevation and axonometric view with drawing of the screws, hand drawing. studio Baur.

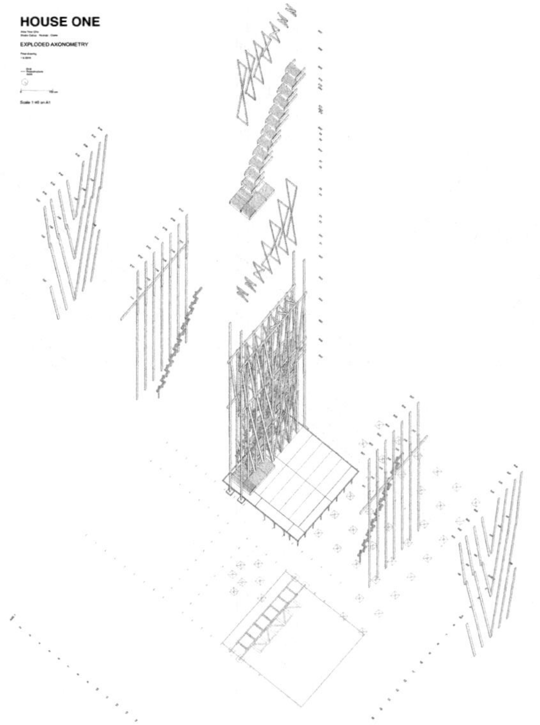

Exploded axonometric view with individual prefabricated parts, CAD drawing. studio Cabay.

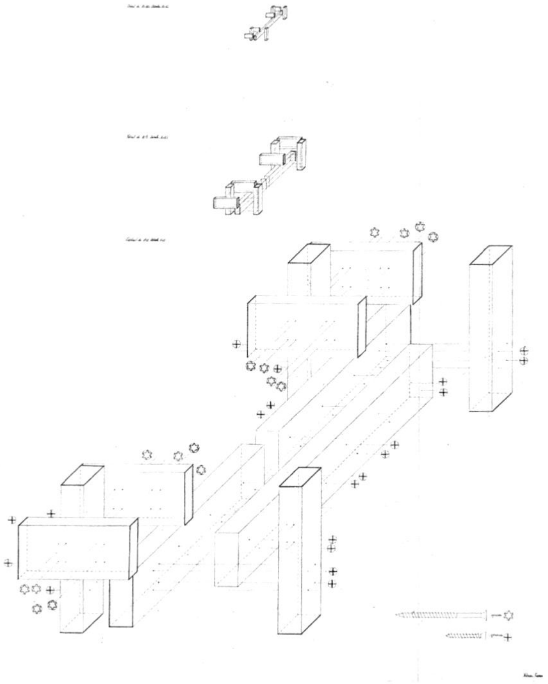

Using symbols to represent each type of screw. studio Grandgirard.

A technical document can also be reduced to a set of annotated information.

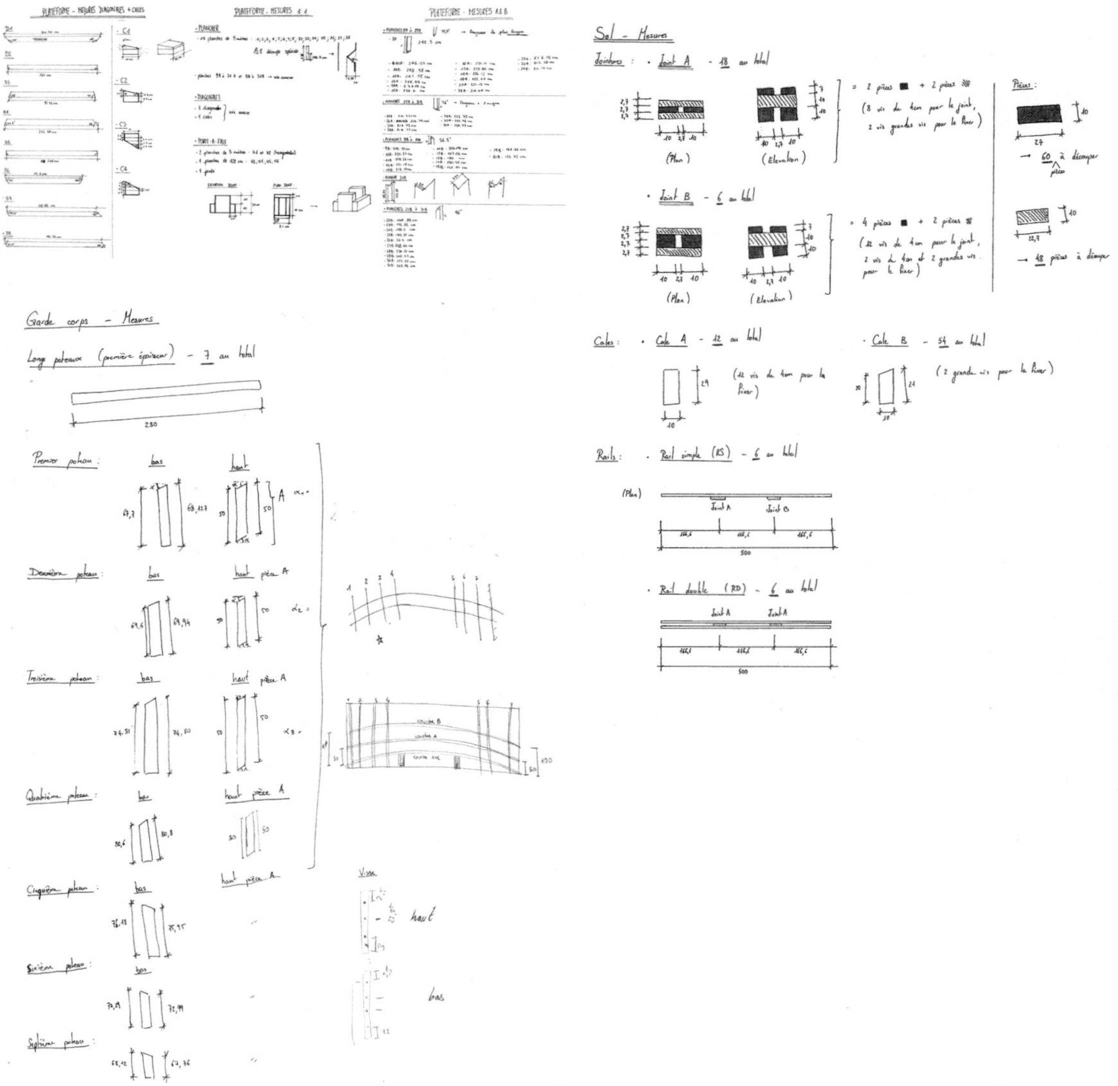

List of components and their properties, pencil drawing on paper. studio Perez-Lupi.

To "prefabricate" implies to realise a complete work through items manufactured in advance, and assembled according to a predetermined plan. HOUSE 1 was constructed as twelve prefabricated projects in the workshop, and then mounted into the protostructure. Each piece was designed to be hand made in the Studio, then stored, transported and assembled on site.

Prefabrication of a part of the floor. studio Chassot.

Prefabrication of a part of the floor. studio Pellacani.

Pre-assembly in the studio of all parts of the floor. studio Pellacani.

Simulation of the floor. studio Grandgirard.

Prefabricated piece in the studio. studio Dürr.

Staging of the prefabricated pieces #1. studio Chassot.

Storage of prefabricated pieces. studio Dürr.

Staging of the prefabricated pieces #2. studio Chassot.

Storage of prefabricated pieces. studio del Grosso.

Prefabricated pieces arranged on the floor. studio Baur.

Transport of prefabricated pieces. studio Chassot.

Assembling the staircase. studio Baur.

Transport of a frame. studio Grandgirard.

Use of double-height staircase to store a large piece. studio Dürr.

"Nous avons constaté avec soulagement que le déplacement et la mise en place des pièces étaient aisés, grâce notamment au fait qu'il est possible de les porter seul."
studio Chassot

Each intervention is assembled from a kit of parts, themselves being built out of components of timber pre-cut from standard sizes. From the smallest to the largest of scales, the bulk of the work of prefabrication is realised in the drawing of each constituent part, as well as of the different ways they are assembled; but also by the precise identification of the position of each component or assembly within the entire system.

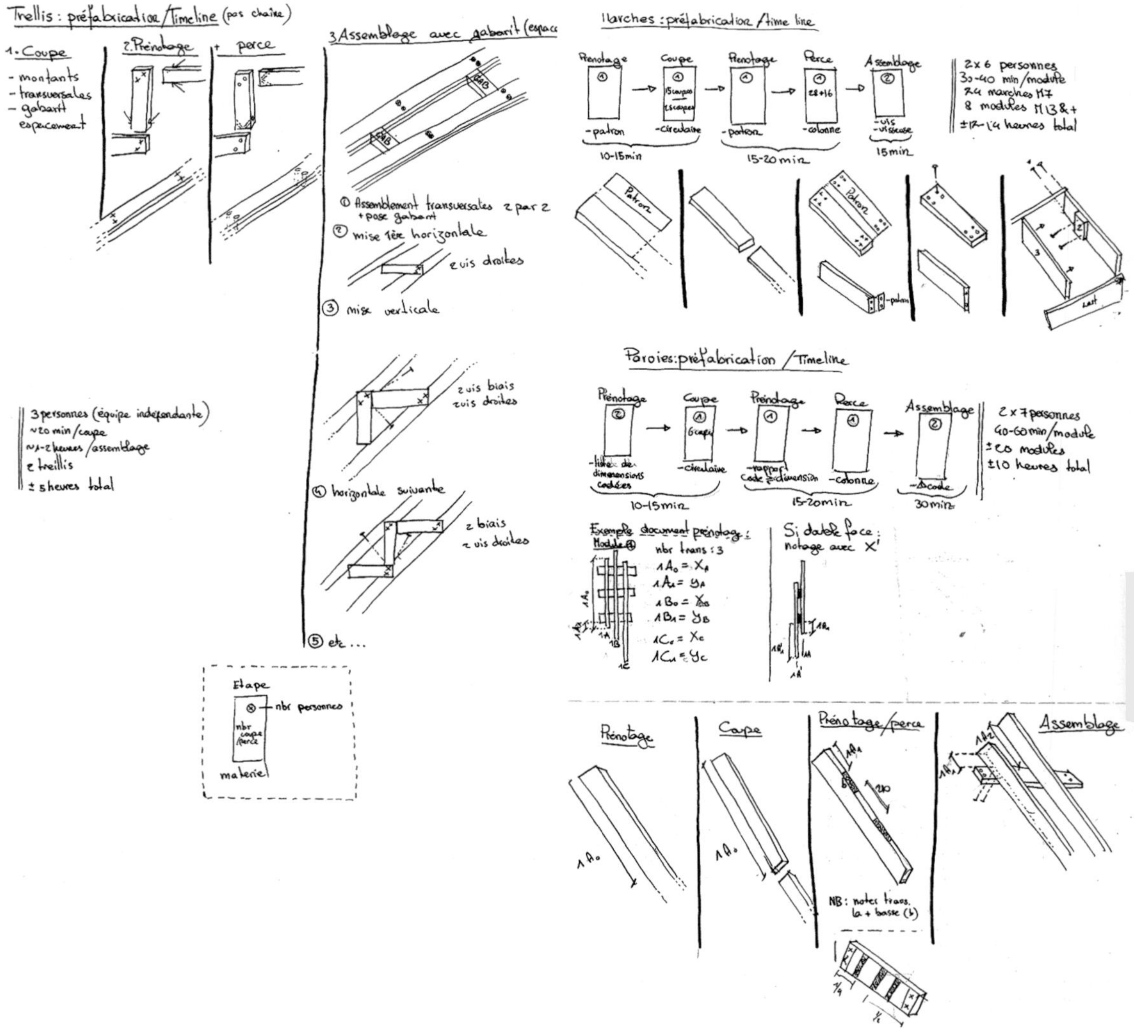

Sketches of the construction process of the components. studio del Grosso.

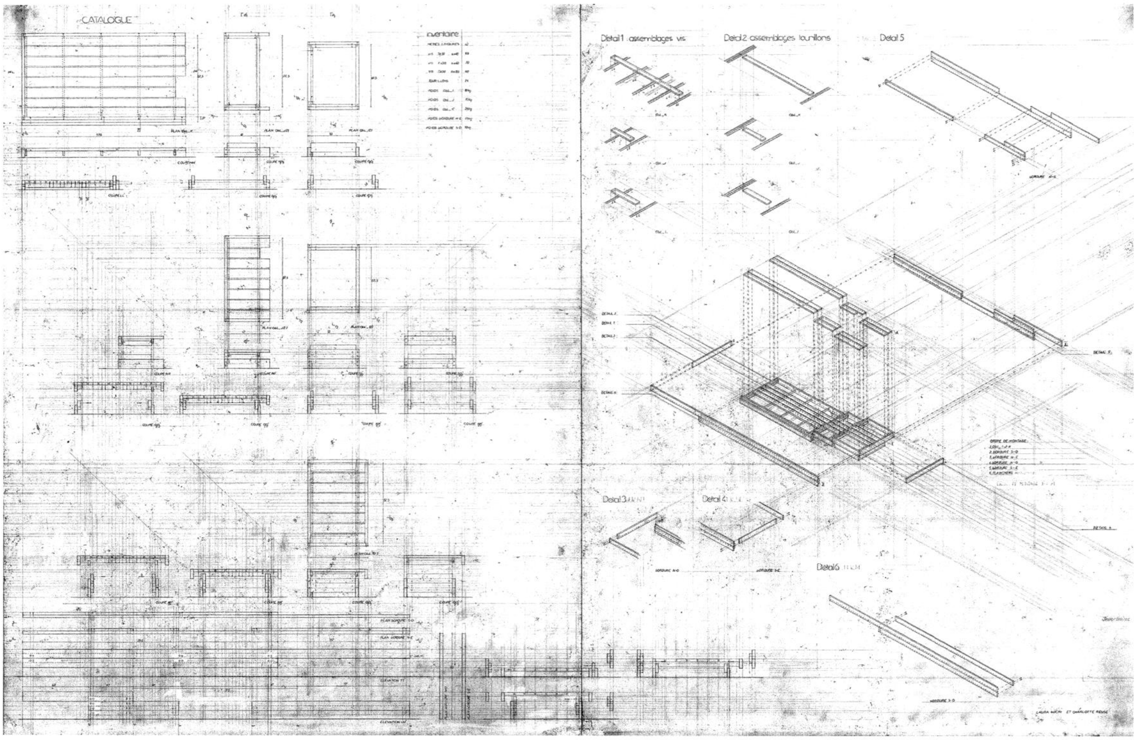

Exploded axonometric and details of the components. studio Pellacani.

PIECES

CADRES X,Z	STR. PRIM.	STR. SEC.		M LIN. (mm)	POIDS (g)
Y 11	74170	13440		87610	65708
Y 12	75297	13440		88737	66553
Y 13	68136	18440		86576	64932
Y14	64765	16141		80906	60680
Y 15	61064	16695		77759	58319
Y 16	67741	16695		84436	63327
Y 17	90825	19613		110438	82829
Y 18	100334	13440		113774	85331
Y 19	43398	13550		56948	42711
Sous-total	***645.7***	***141.5***		***787.2***	***590.4***
LATTES Y	**STR. PRIM.)**	**STR. SEC.**	**STR. TERT.**	**M LIN. (m)**	**POIDS (g)**
Z 31	29161			29161	21871
Z 32	31355		104072	31355	23516
Z 33	31427			31427	23570
Z 34	49432			49432	37074
Z 35	45642			45642	34232
Z 36	45642			45642	34232
Z 37	60478			60478	45359
Z 38	45000			45000	33750
Sous-total	***338.137***	***122.3***	***104.072***	***564.509***	***253.6***
Total (m)	***983.9***		***245.5***	***1125.3***	***844.0***
+Tolérance	***1131***		***282***	***1294***	***971***

List showing characteristics of the components. studio Grandgirard.

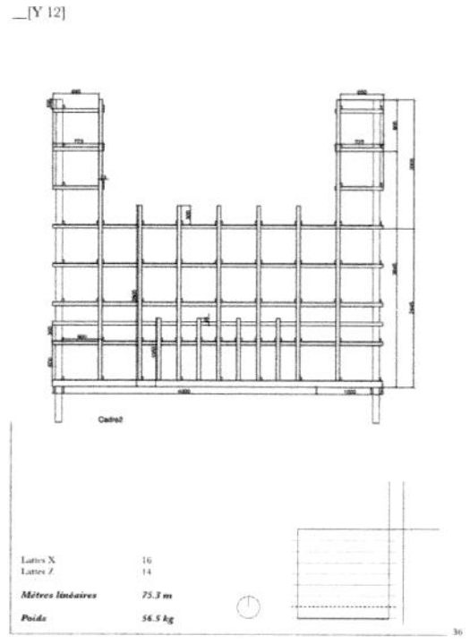

Elevation and location of one these components. studio Grandgirard.

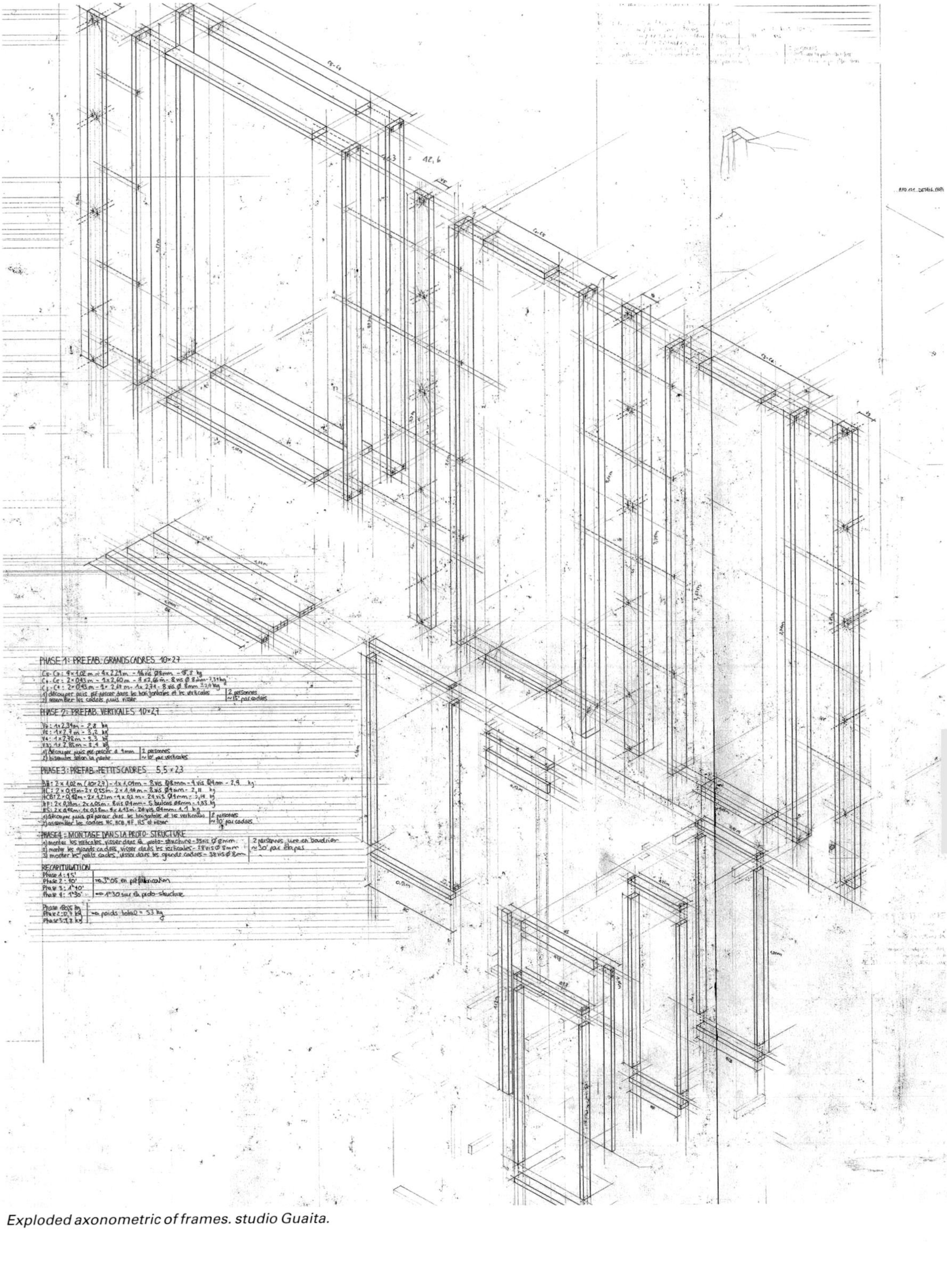

Exploded axonometric of frames. studio Guaita.

The components documented in full produce a picture of the amount of material or the number of required parts needed to complete the project.

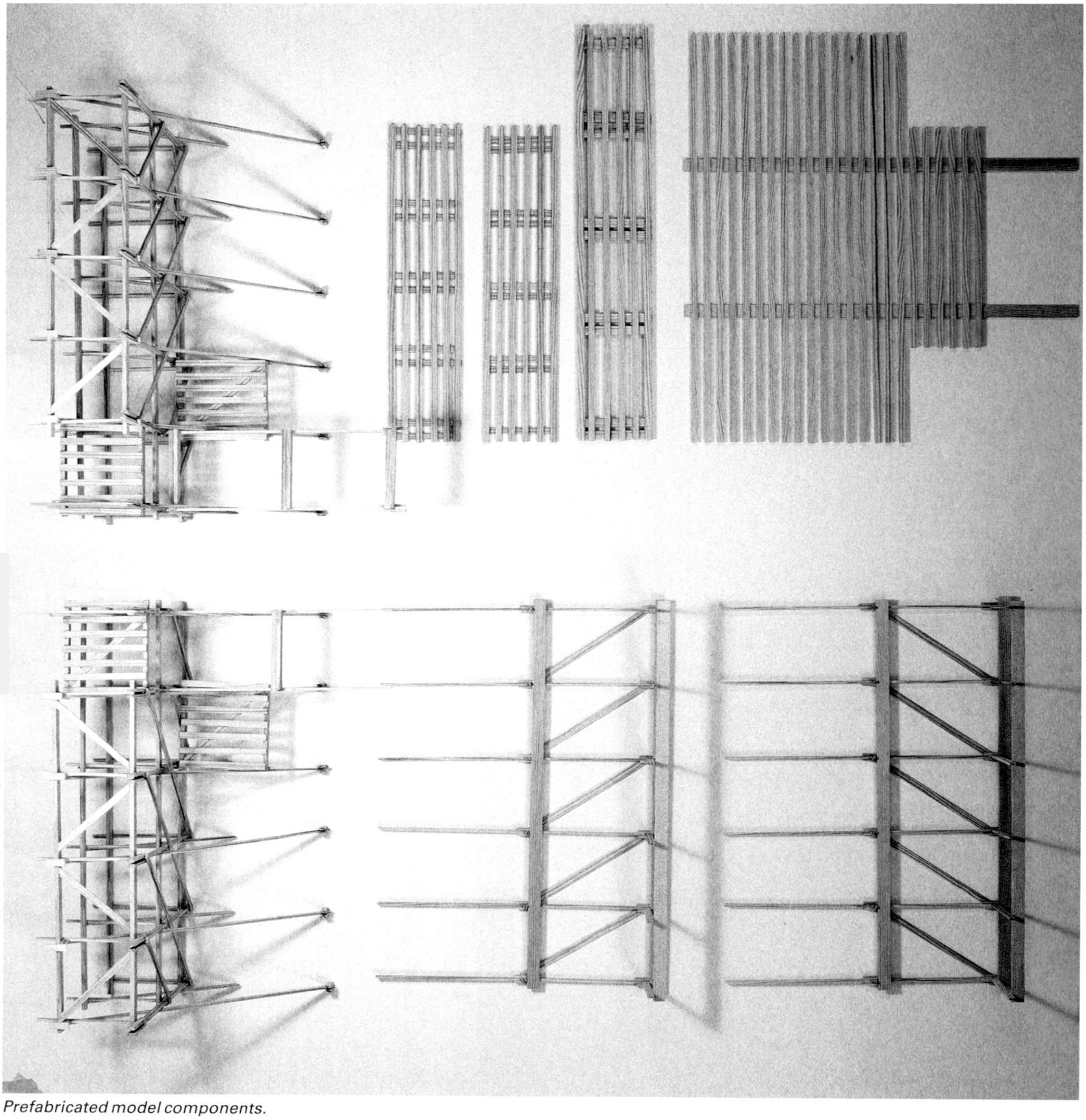

Prefabricated model components.

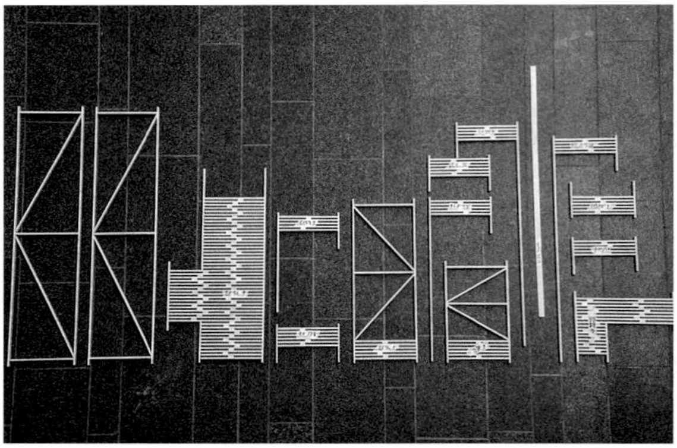

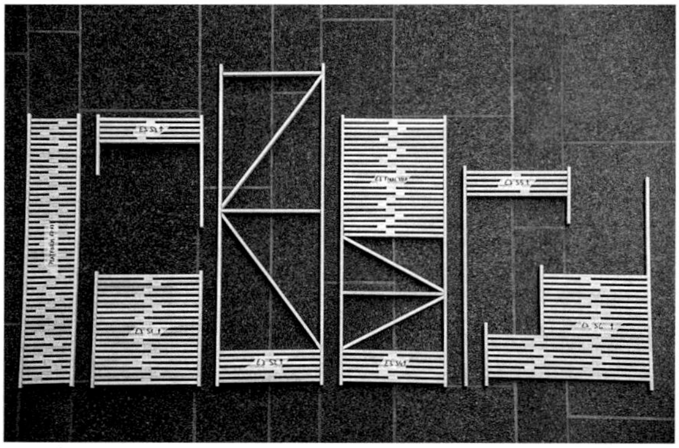

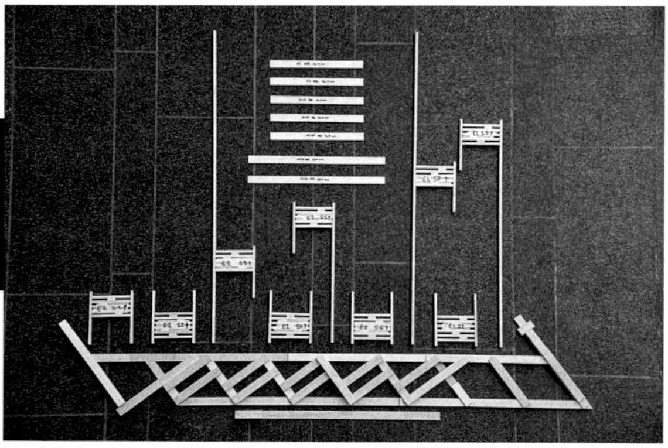

Prefabricated model components. studio del Grosso.

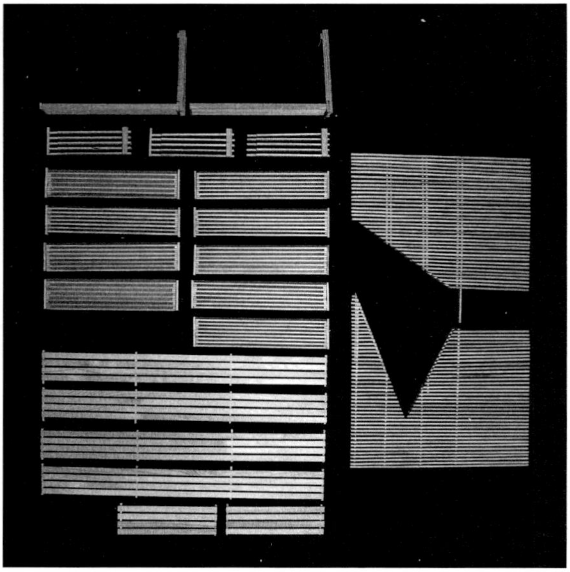

Prefabricated model components. studio Perez-Lupi.

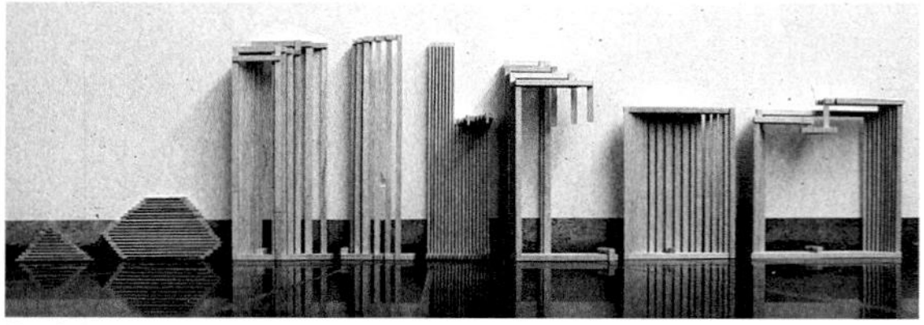

Prefabricated components. studio Pellacani.

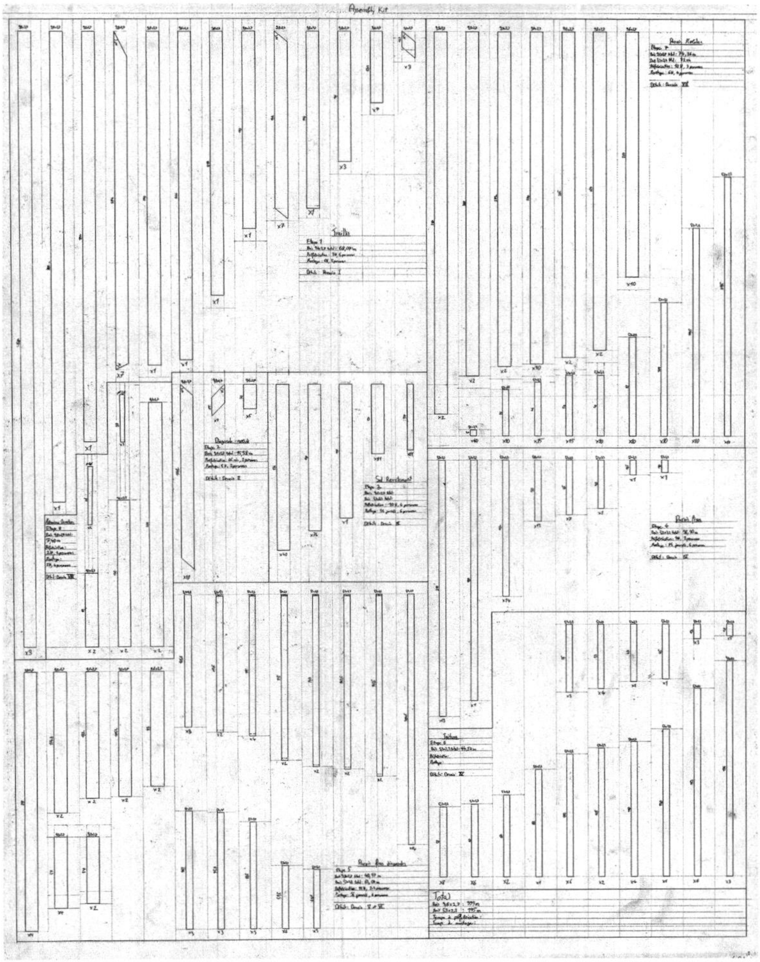

Drawing of the necessary components. studio Rufer.

Mounting set of frame models. studio Guaita.

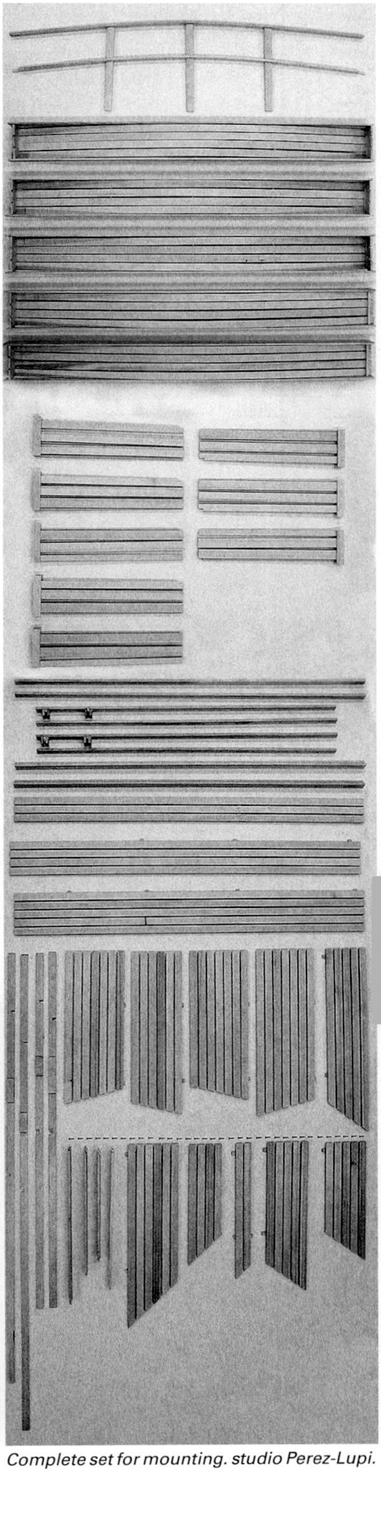

Complete set for mounting. studio Perez-Lupi.

The assembly is completed in two phases: the first consisting of the fabrication of each constituent part of the project, and the second, of the assembly of these parts within the protostructure of HOUSE 1. The logic of assembly lies at the heart of the challenge of fabrication, and requires the development of clear and precise documentation materials.

The components dismounted. studio Guaita.

The components assembled. studio Guaita.

Drawing of the different components and exploded axonometric showing them mounted in position. studio Guaita.

Details of the different components and location plan. studio Dürr.

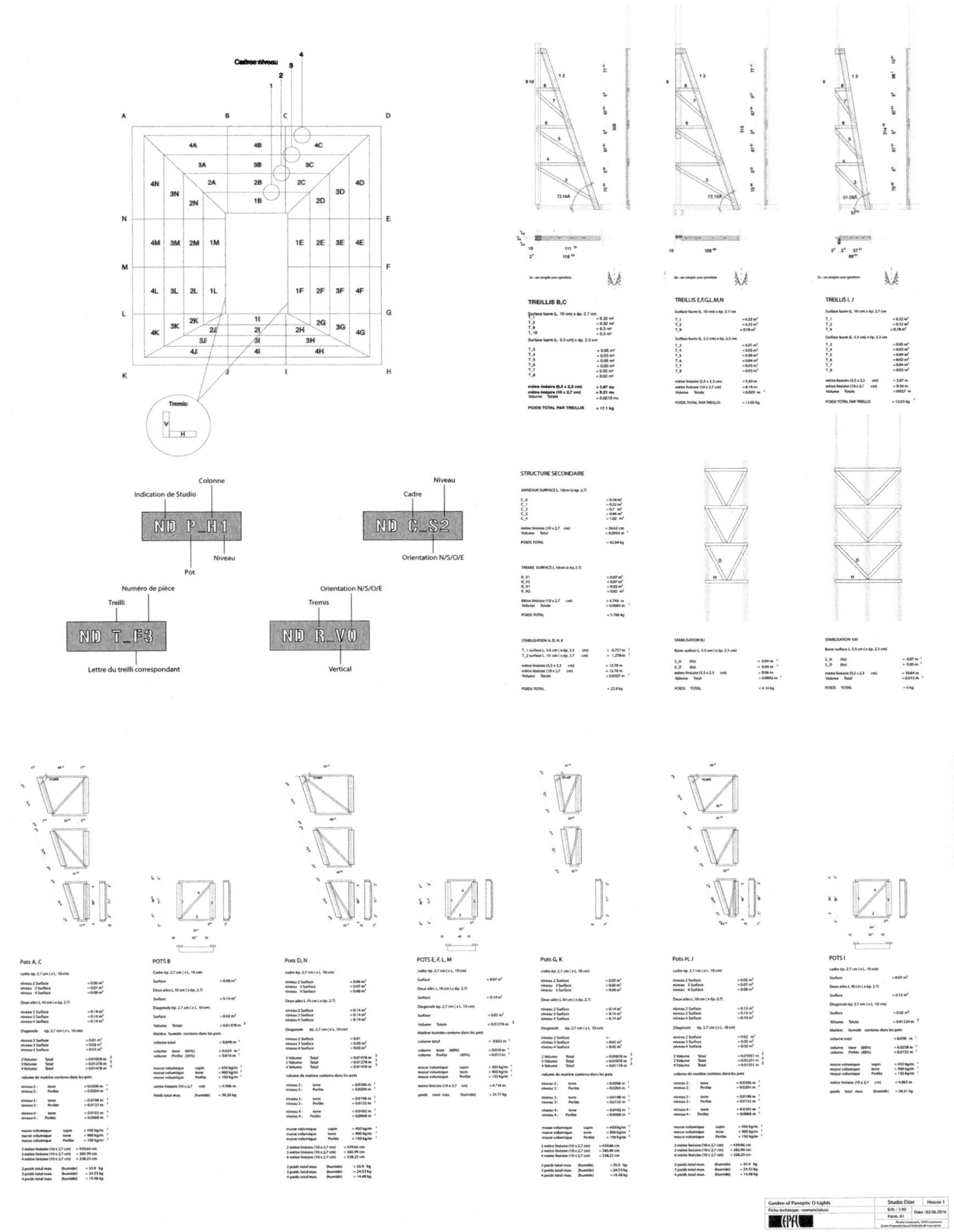

Details showing mounting of the different components. studio Dürr.

The instructions for assembly allows for the navigation of the structure and the manoeuvring of prefabricated parts.

"Pour ce qui concerne la séquence de montage, nous avons commencé à réfléchir à l'échelle 1:1 en décomposant les modules préfabriqués qui constituent la structure. De cette manière on peut commencer la construction de la structure par le bas, venant en suite poser le premier sol du théâtre, utilisable comme plateforme pour monter les éléments structurels restant, et en procédant donc "étage par étage"."
studio Chassot

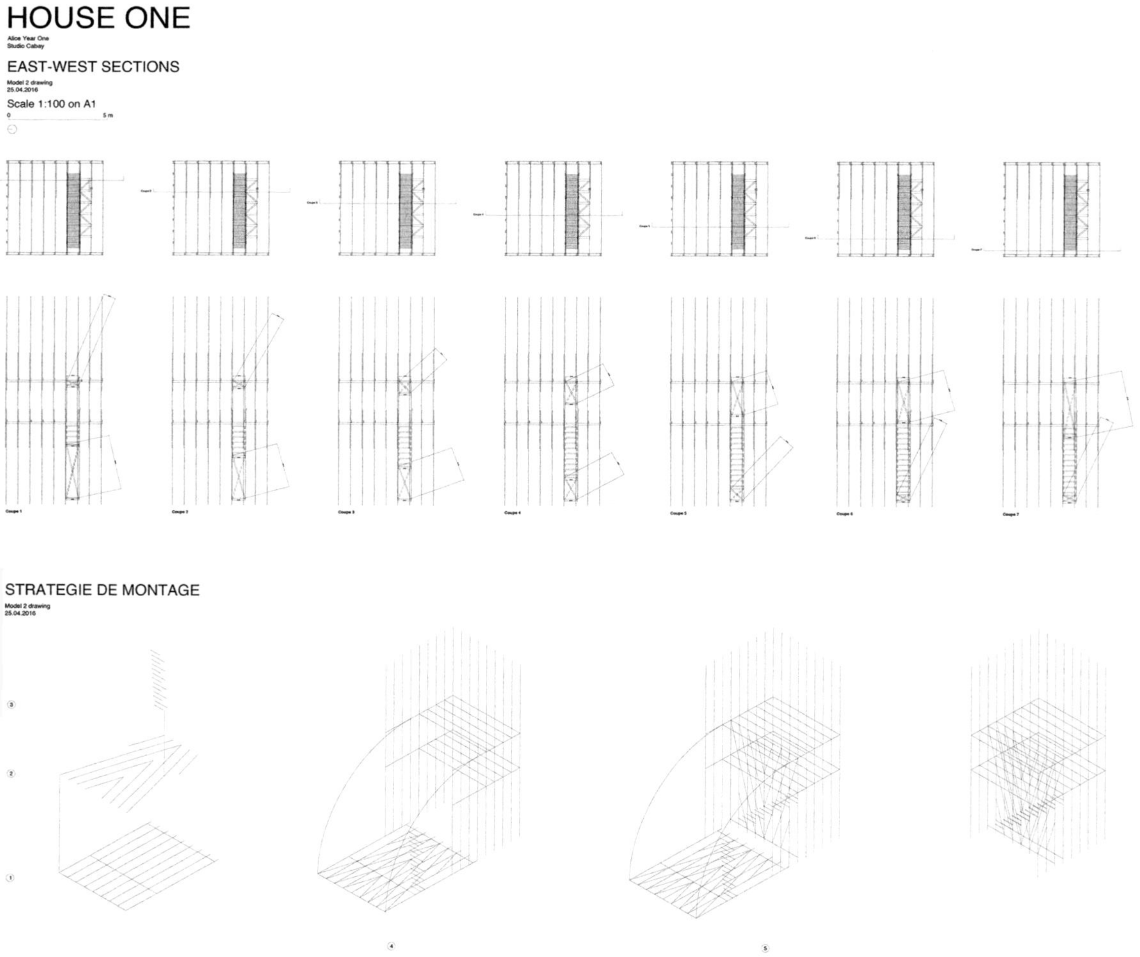

Mapping of the different components and assembly strategies. studio Cabay.

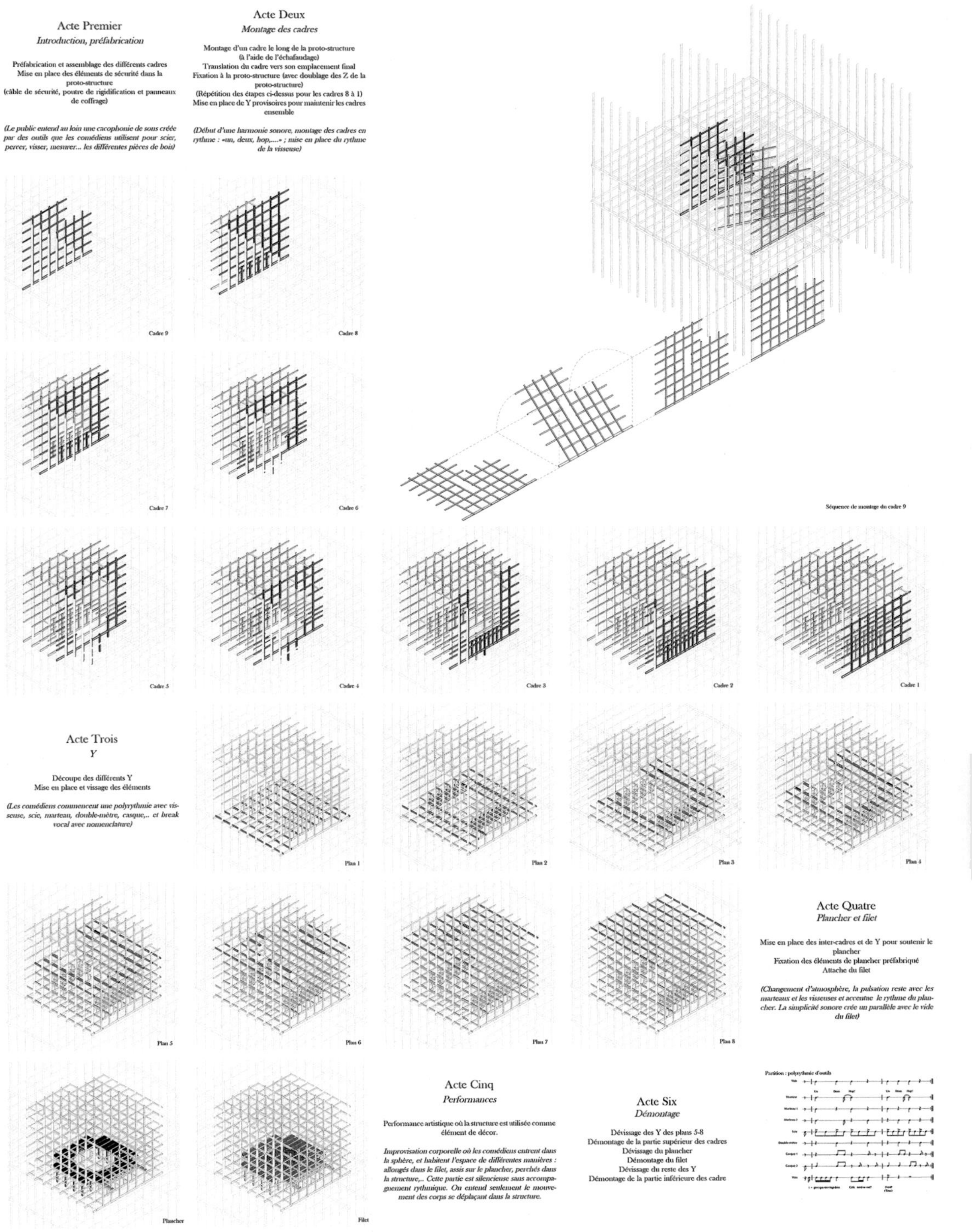

Mapping of the different components and their location in the protostructure. studio Grandgirard.

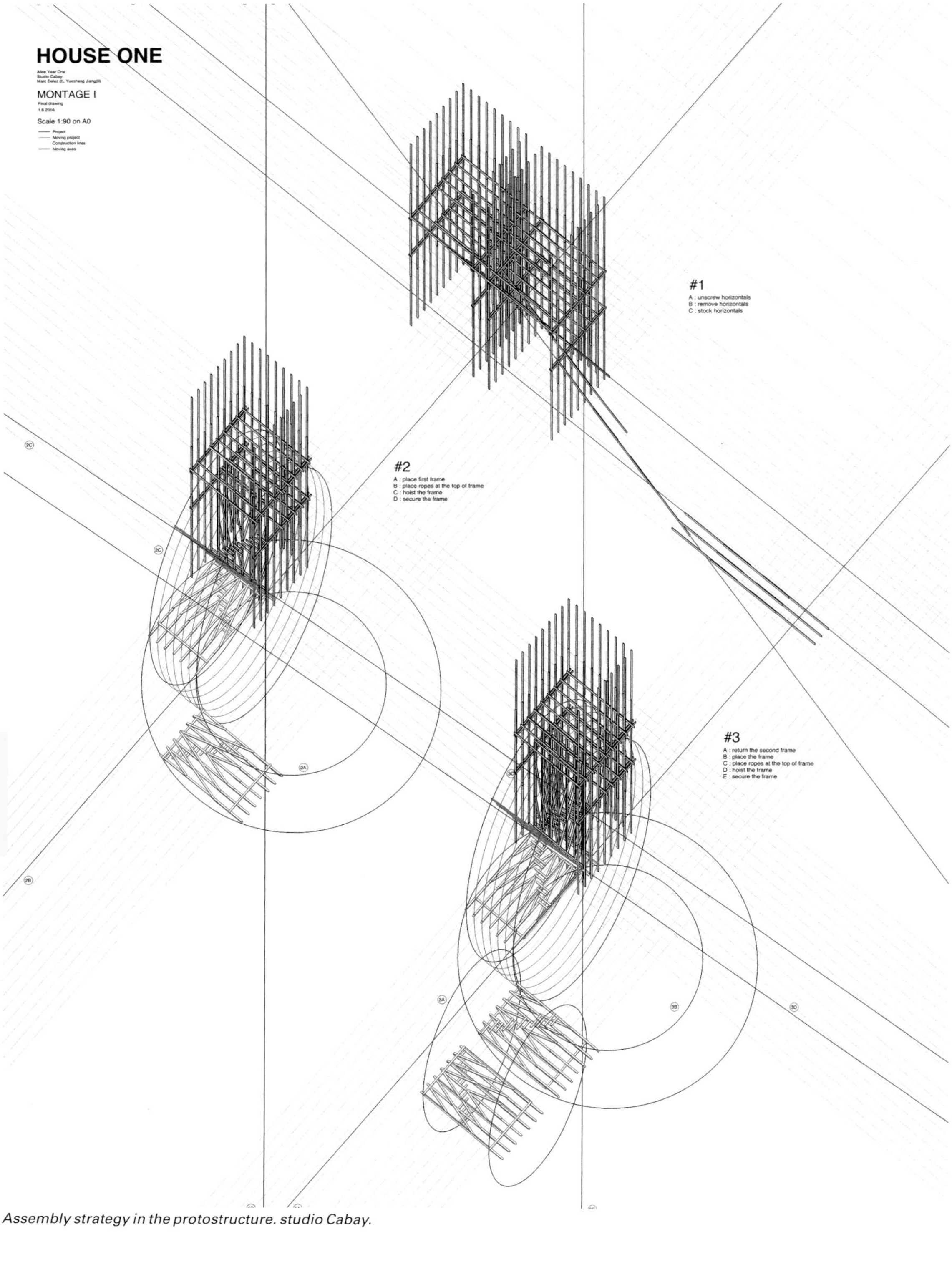

Assembly strategy in the protostructure. studio Cabay.

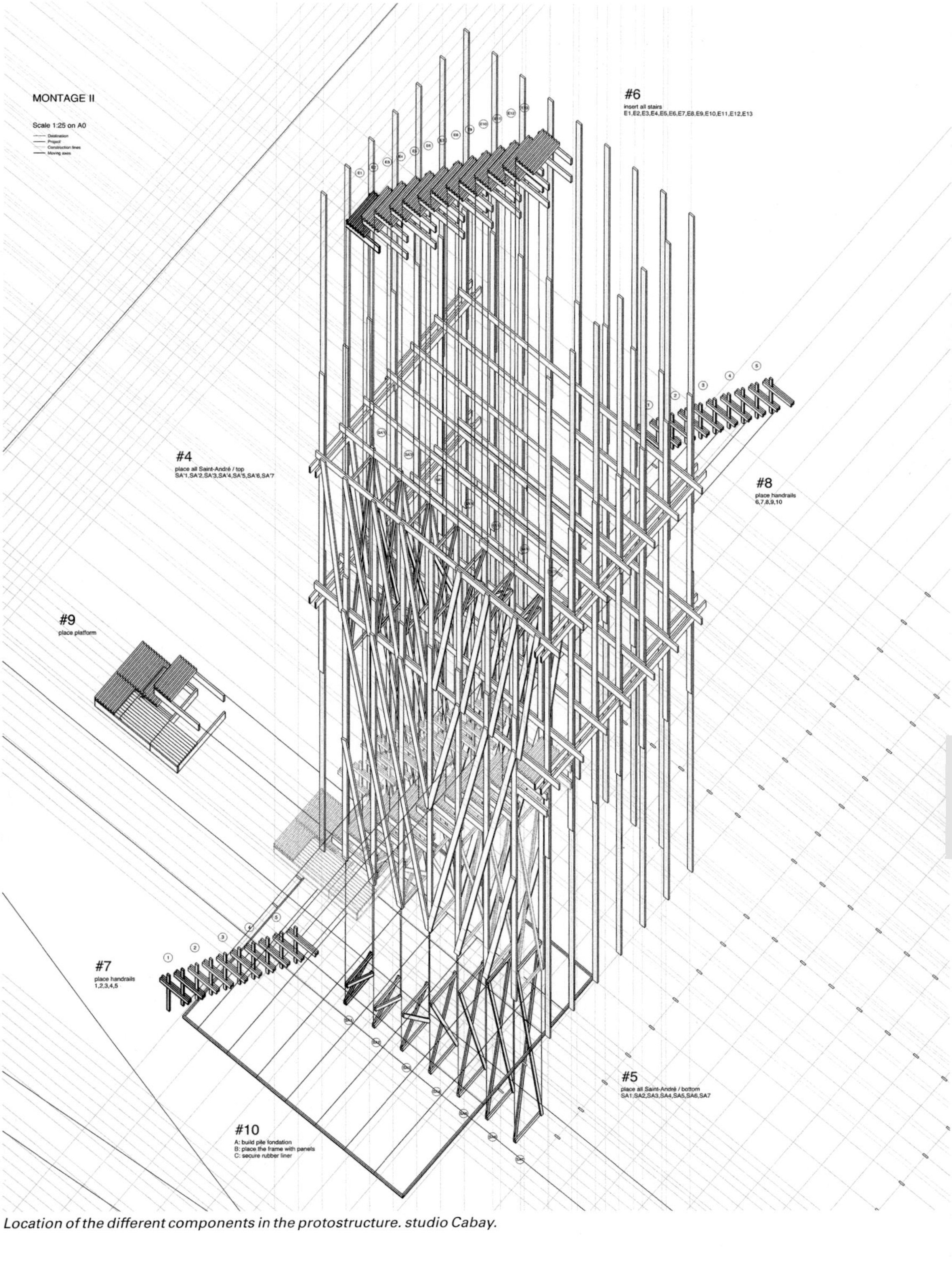

Location of the different components in the protostructure. studio Cabay.

Details depend just as much on the formal technical requirements of construction as they do on questions of structure. The detail is the "genetic code" of the project.

The PARVIS final detail. studio van der Woude.

The most basic detail used for the construction of HOUSE 1 involves the orthogonal joining of two pieces of timber. For assembling components of timber in two directions, the detail unfolds within a two dimensional plan. But by entering into the third dimension, a third component perpendicular to the first two begins to suggest the outline of a space.

Crossing detail running in three dimensions. studio Grandgirard.

Two perpendicular pieces of timber and two screws. studio Grandgirard.

An assembly detail configures a large number of components moving in multiple directions, and can include moving parts.
Each detail is specific to the characteristics of the components assembled within it, being appropriate for their dimensions and their properties of resistance.

Assembly running in many directions. studio Perez-Lupi.

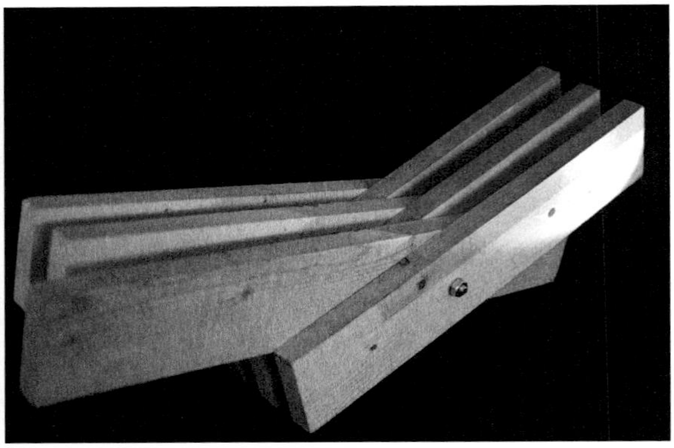

Assembly running in many directions using of angle metal pieces. studio Grandgirard.

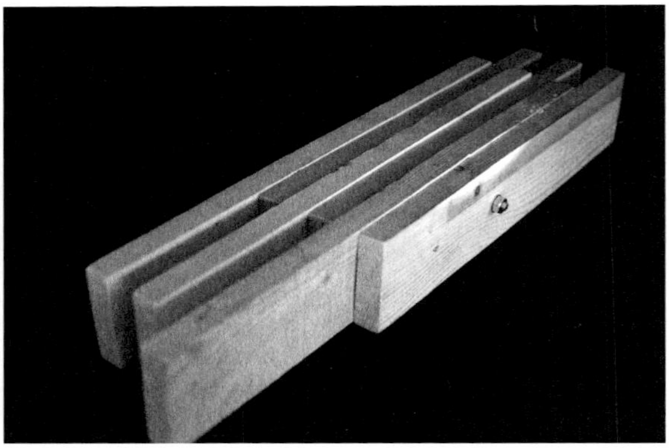

Assembly with threaded shaft to create a rotating movement. studio Baur.

Assembly model at 1:1 using a diagonal component #1. studio Cabay.

Assembly model at 1:1 using a diagonal component #2. studio Cabay.

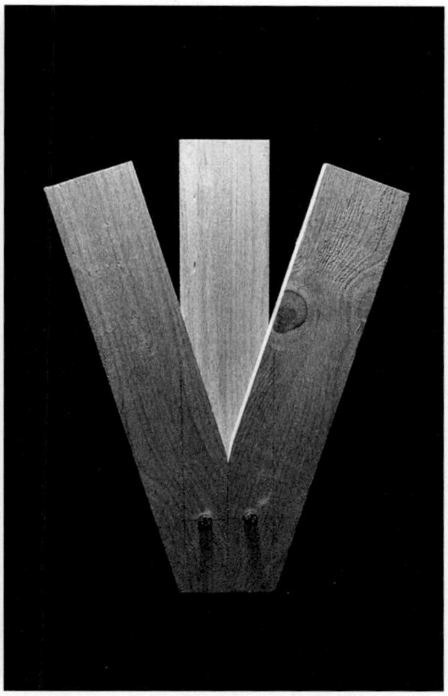
Assembly model at 1:1 using two diagonal component. studio Cabay.

Assembly with a cylindrical timber component to create a rotating movement. studio Rufer.

The hand is an instrument of sensibility and precision, acting as a medium between mind and matter. The hand is an extension of the body, and uses a series of tools as apparatuses to shape material.

MANUAL TOOLS

Mediating the link between matter and the body, each tool possesses a part that is to be handled by the user, and a 'clean' part expressing its primary function. In the case of manual tools, the mechanical relationship between the two parts converts the applied human force into an action upon the material. In the case of electrical tools, an external force replaces that of the body. The hand, in that case, is only used for directing and operating the tool. For the drill, a tool that operates a "bit" rotating on a central axis, it is even possible to use a gibbet, reducing even further the implication of the body within the process to a simple up-and-down movement.

The hand. studio den Hartog.

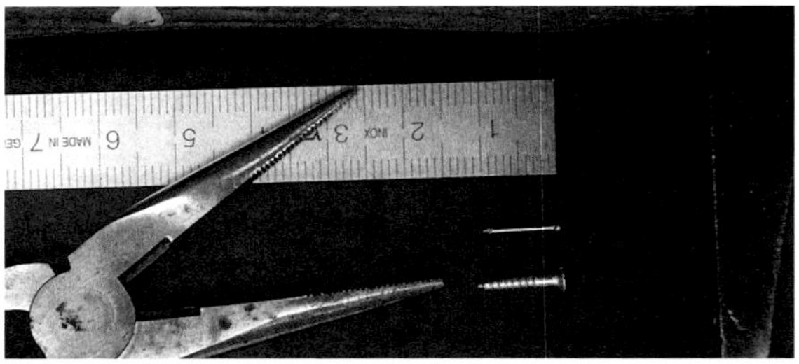

Hammer, ruler and pliers. studio den Hartog.

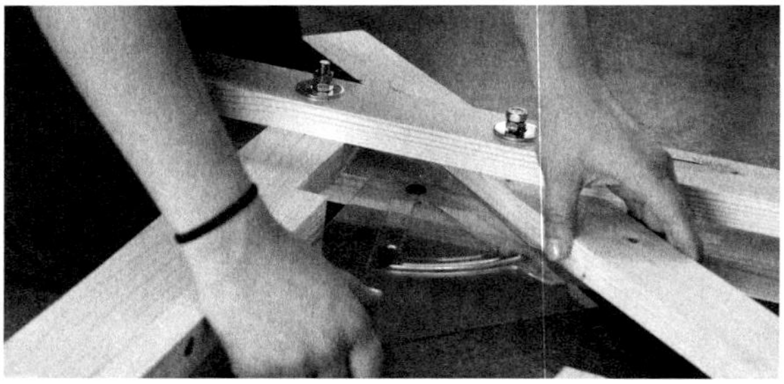

Protractor. studio Baur.

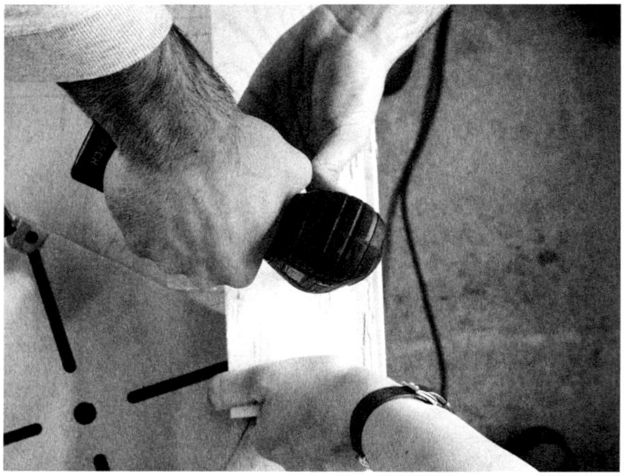

Electric screwdriver and drill press. studio den Hartog.

Manual chamfering cutter. studio den Hartog.

Clamp with plastic handle. studio van der Woude.

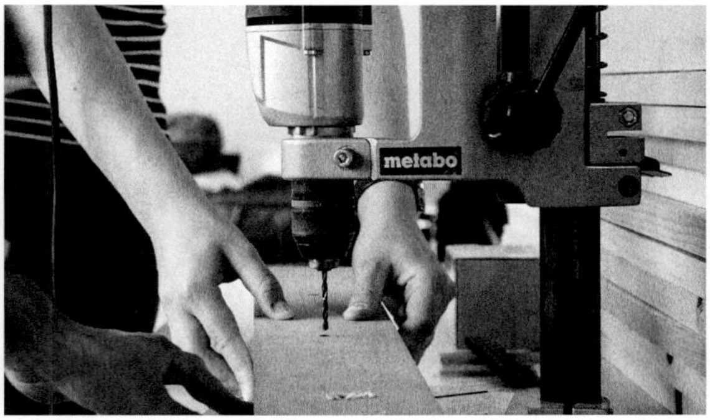

Drill press. studio den Hartog.

Steel square. studio Baur.

Electric screwdriver. studio Baur.

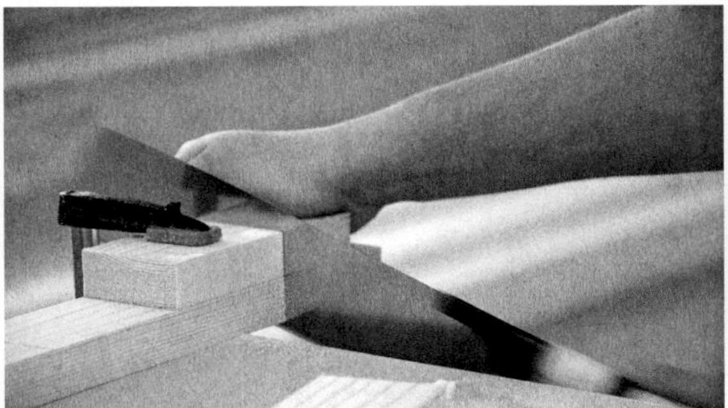

Japanese saw. studio del Grosso.

CONSUMABLES

Consumables are a significant part of any construction kit. The assembly of timber requires the use of consumables such as screws, nails and threaded rods, all of which fashion the connections between different components. These parts are condemned to remain hidden – invisible until the disassembly of the construction.

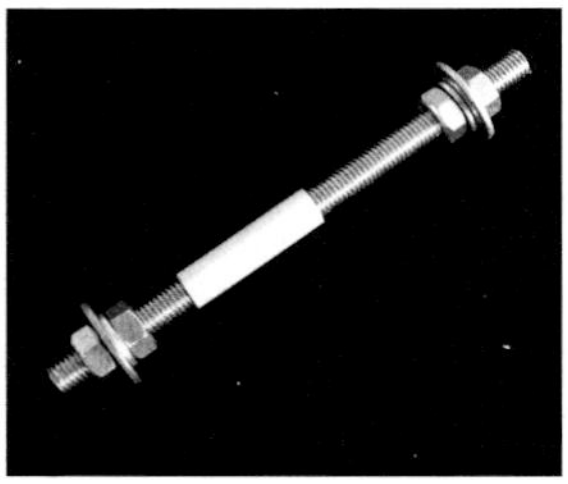

Threaded shaft. studio Grandgirard.

Waiting screws. studio Chassot.

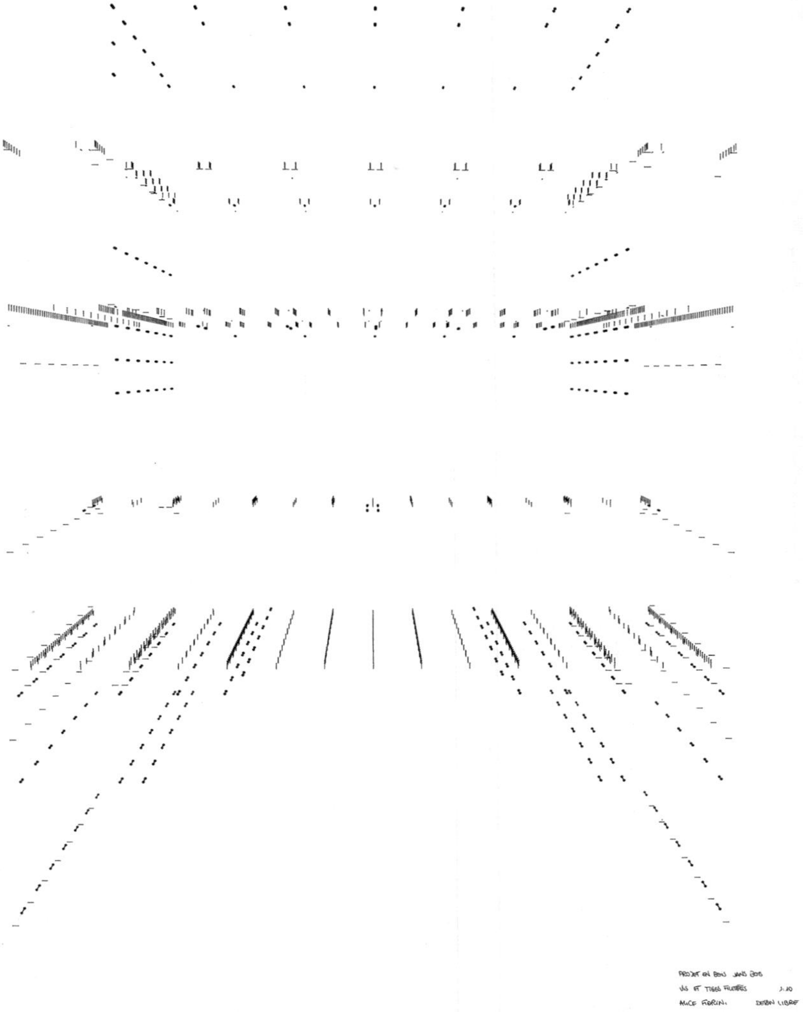

All screws used for the THEATRE in perspective view. studio Chassot.

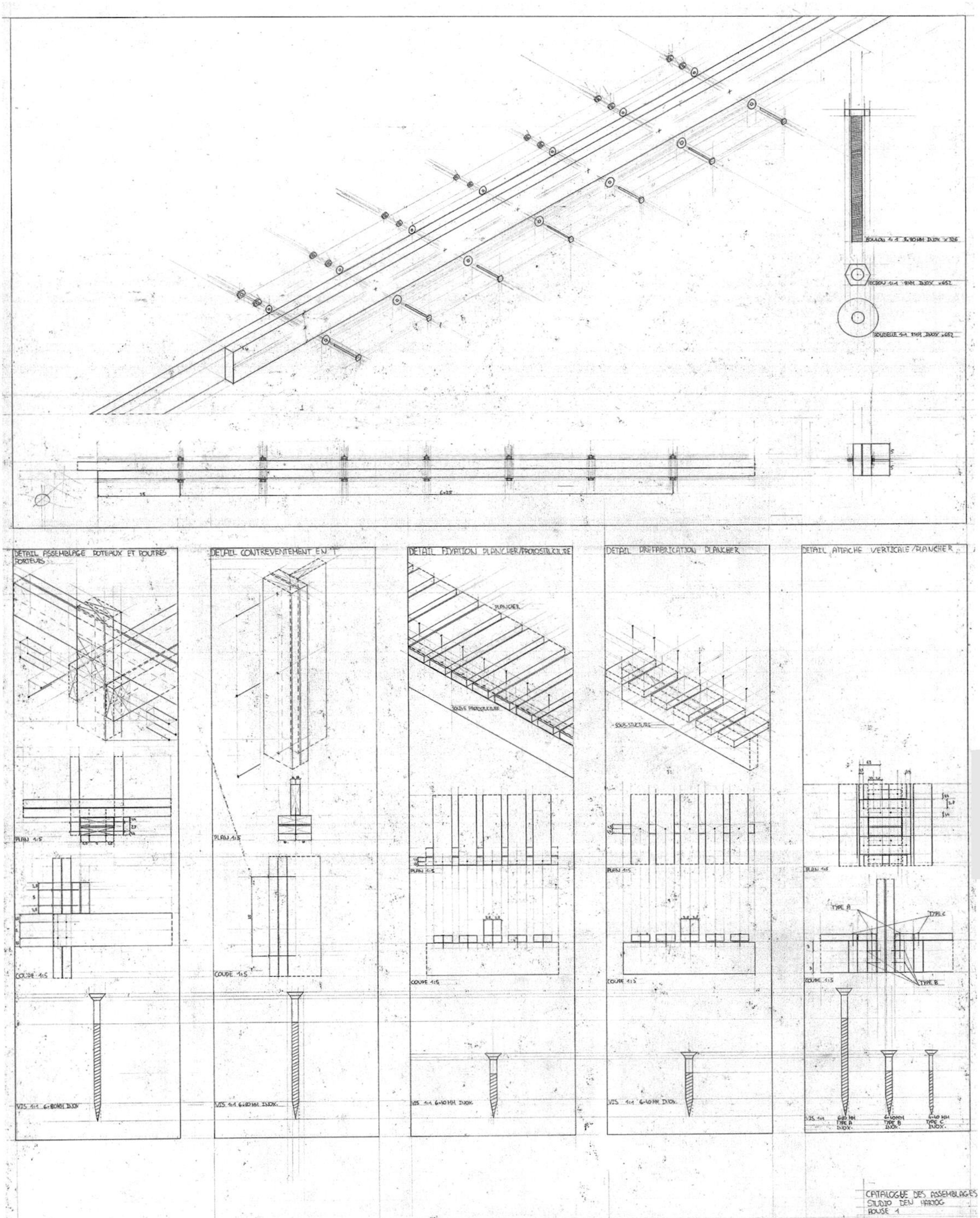

Assembly instructions for the different screws. studio den Hartog.

JIGS, MOULDS, SUPPORTS

Jigs, moulds and supports are often necessary for the fabrication of elements.

Squared support. studio Grandgirard.

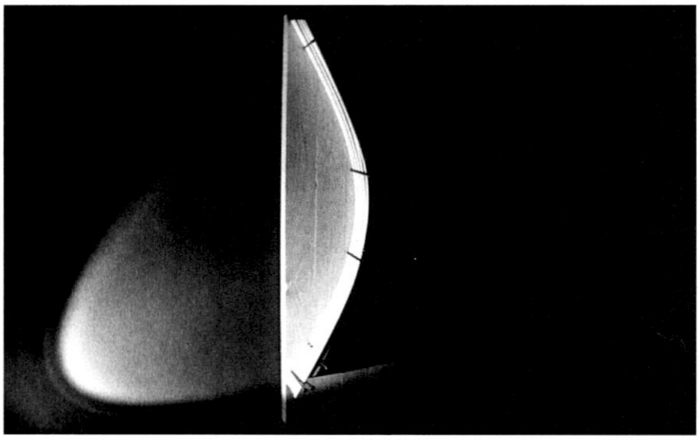

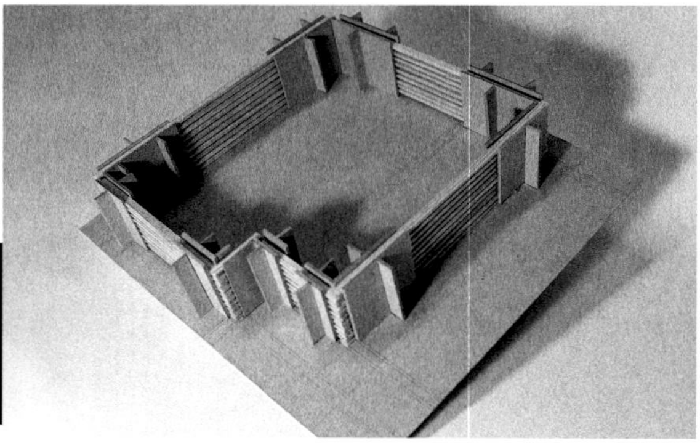

Support for the model of a wall. studio Cabay.

Bending timber with weights and steam. studio Perez-Lupi.

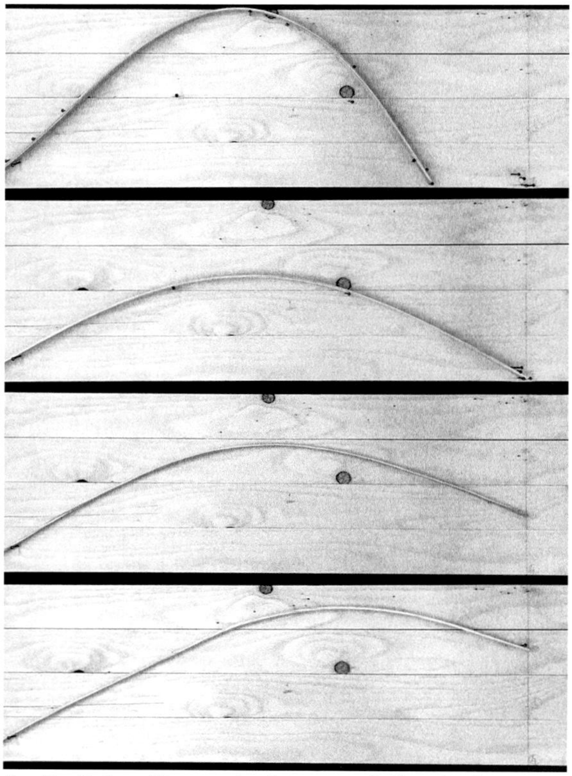

Bending timber with support and steam. studio Perez-Lupi.

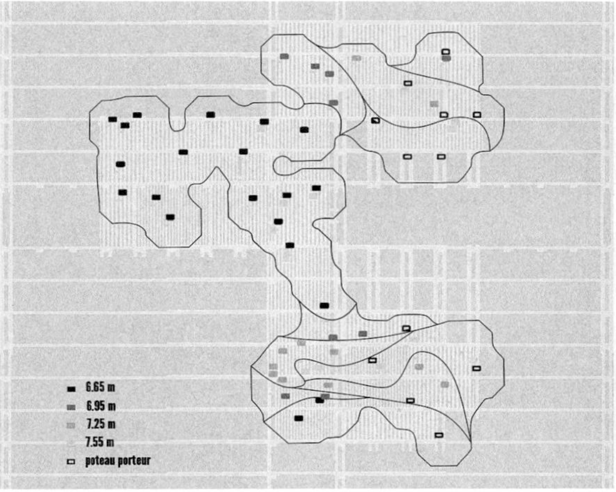

Plaster manufacturing #1, drawing the shape. studio den Hartog.

Plaster manufacturing #2, preparing the mould and material needed. studio den Hartog.

Plaster manufacturing #3, the mould. studio den Hartog.

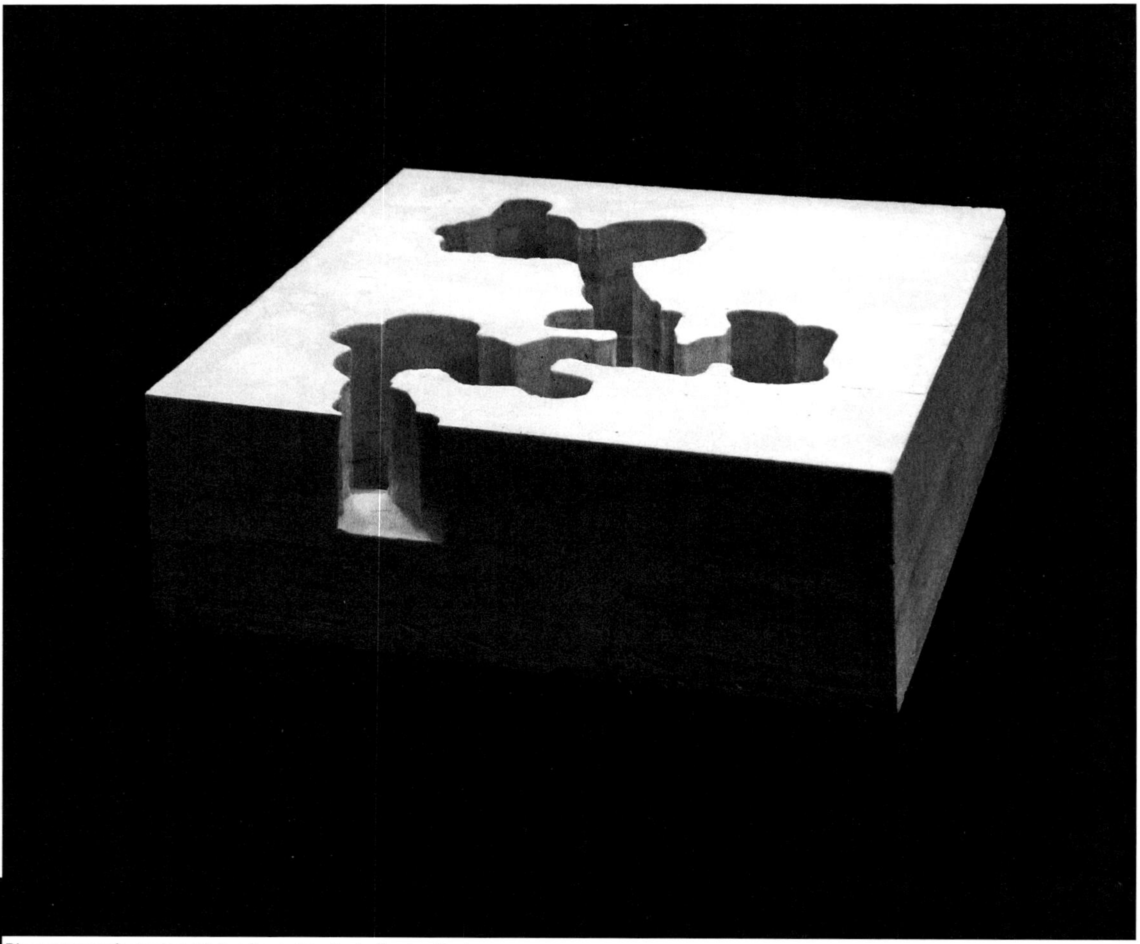

Plaster manufacturing #4, the final object. studio den Hartog.

Fibrous materials, such as textile fabrich or rope offer different properties of plasticity to those of timber.

Rope may be used for its linear, flexible qualities – for example, as a railing, or a 'lifeline'.

Ropes can also be used to transfer mechanical forces. Hoists and pulleys divide these forces and can lift large and heavy masses. A rope-and-pulley system was used to move certain mobile elements in HOUSE 1.

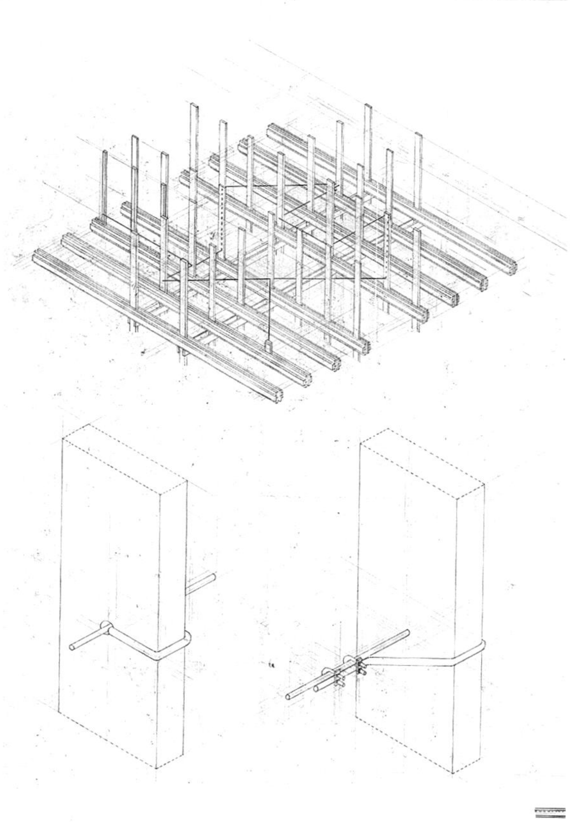

Lifeline in metal wire, pencil drawing on paper. studio Pellacani.

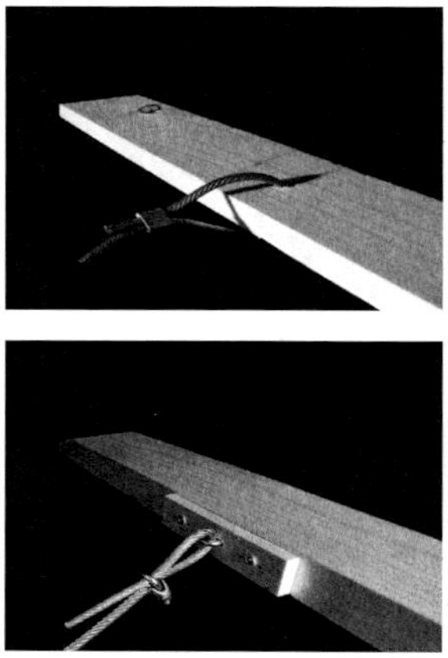

Lifeline grip details. studio Pellacani.

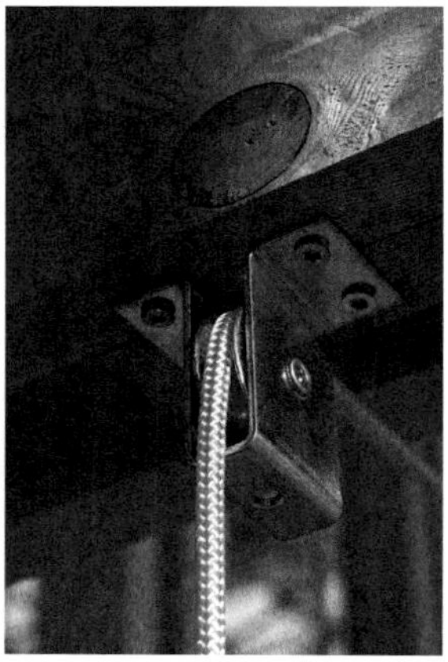

Rope and pulley. studio Chassot.

Mechanism for raising the screen of theTHEATRE. studio Chassot.

'Stringing' the rope means creating a field of nodes formed by the intersection of two or more strands. Complementing the work of the timber structure, these nodes establish complex and force-resistant assemblies that are much more difficult to realise with systems of nails and screws.

1:1 test of the knot. studio Perez-Lupi.

Realisation of the knot in the structure of HOUSE 1. studio Perez-Lupi.

Assembly detail research. studio Perez-Lupi.

The nets in HOUSE 1are finely woven meshes made from regularly knotted strings.

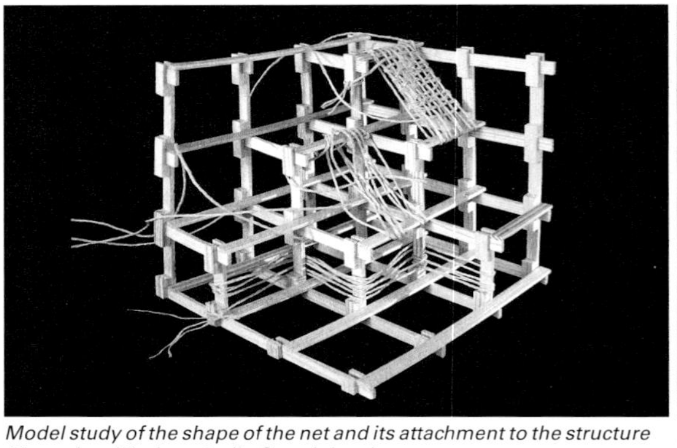

Model study of the shape of the net and its attachment to the structure #1, cord and timber. studio Grandgirard.

Knotting of the net (detail). studio Grandgirard.

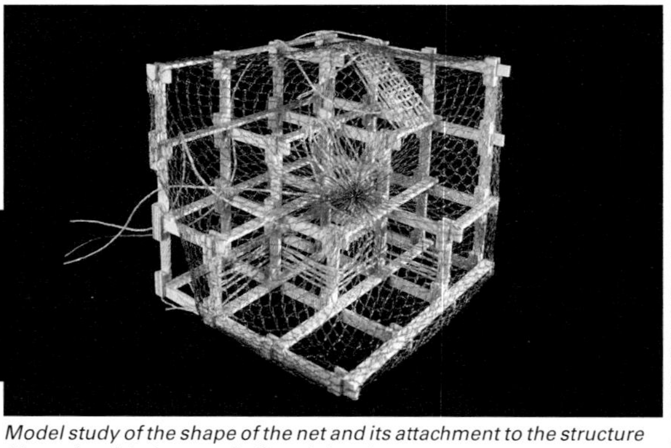

Model study of the shape of the net and its attachment to the structure #2, cord and timber. studio Grandgirard.

Grip detail between the net and the structure. studio Grandgirard.

The textile elements are surfaces that have the versatile ability to both create and adapt to a wide variety of irregular forms, as well as to react in response to differing light conditions. Opaque in ambient light, they become a translucent light filter when stronger illumination is applied.

Installation of fabric in the structure with light studies. studio Grandgirard.

Textile walls. studio Rufer.

Light through textile walls. studio Rufer.

Research model investigating transparency of textile walls. studio Rufer.

Final performance. studio Pellacani.

INTRODUCTION

"The spoken word was the first technology by which man was able to let go of his environment in order to grasp it in a new way"
Marshall McLuhan, Understanding Media, 1964.

The first step in preparing the construction of aTower of Babel of the likes of HOUSE 1 is to agree on a common language. As presented in previous chapters, the establishment of a common ground of communication is the key to collective work. And, it is uniquely through collective effort, that HOUSE 1 can be envisaged and understood. Communication passes through different media in architecture. General agreements pertaining to drawings, construction standards and site management have to be made in order to work together and achieve a collective oeuvre.This chapter focuses on the bi-dimensional form of communication as well as on the spoken and written word.The students have had to understand and agree upon a set of words: terms that have become common concepts in the development of a project. It has been necessary to create a specific language possessing its own logic and meaning. Evidently this language is very similar to everyday language, but deviations, derivations and occasional inventions of new terms have facilitated communication during the whole process of HOUSE 1. For example, even if a great percentage of students are French speaking, the word room has clearly replaced chambre (which could be the equivalent in French).This is significant, since the word room finds its origin in the German term Raum, meaning space.The use of this English term, without taking into account its translation into French, better describes what we mean when we talk about this type of space. As such, it is a good example of the how the community has used its own language variations to articulate the project at hand.

The co-relation between speech and bi-dimensional representation is also of great interest in this process.The way terms or words transform into concepts, and how these are subsequently presented in drawings or photography, speaks a lot about the need for the students to agree on communicative tools.

The first steps into architectural education are fundamentally about the learning of a particular language. Understanding the built environment with specific architectural and representational tools opens up the apprenticeship process in architecture.The world is to be comprehended analytically in plan and section, and measured with precise tools. These representational standards constitute an architectural language, describing how communication is made in the construction culture. Ideas are reflected in plans, which, in order to be built, need to be translated into construction documents that have to be read by a great number of actors participating in a construction. HOUSE 1 has addressed this topic in a very direct manner, proposing that the students confront the entire process of constructing a house – as the designers, managers, workers, and inhabitants of that house. In this way they have been faced with developing their own communication skills: For example, are the designer's documents made clearly enough to be read and therefore used for construction purposes?The following articles describe the interesting dynamic between communication tools such as words and drawings, and their translation in the built world.

HOUSE 1 was physically modelled at 1:5, as well as simulated in three dimensions with the aid of computer software. These techniques allowed the designers to perform tests or simple checks.

The 1:5 model measures 2.2m high by 2.2m wide by 2.2m long, and includes all of the planned interventions into the protostructure.

1:5 model in the TRANSVERSAL. studio. studio Dürr.

1:5 model of the THEATRE. studio Chassot.

1:5 model of MQVTC. studio Perez-Lupi.

The wood model of HOUSE 1 simulates reality using tools appropriate to the scale.

Although not exact replicas of their full-scale versions, these assembly systems nonetheless allow us to understand the impact of decisions relating to construction on the overall formal expression of the project.

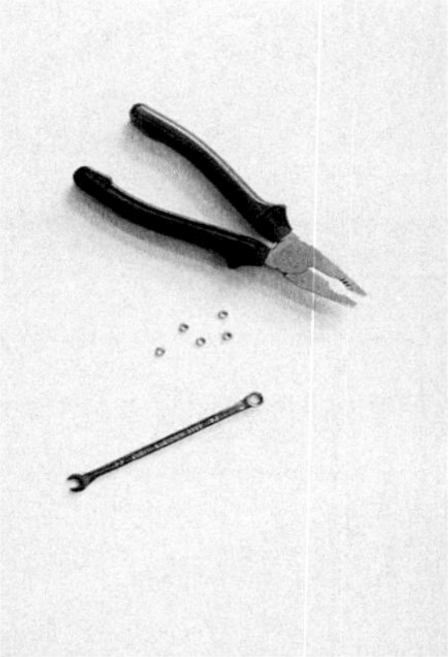

Detail studies. studio Baur.

Details and tools. studio Chassot.

Detail model. studio Baur.

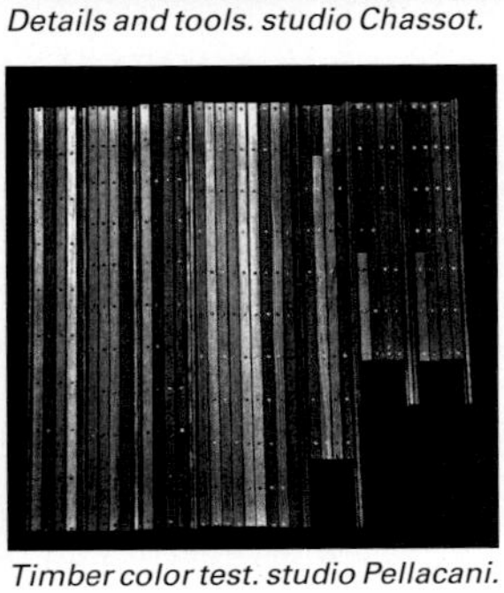

Timber color test. studio Pellacani.

Model of a part of the PARVIS. studio van der Woude.

Model of the TOIT with positioning of screws. studio Pellacani.

Model of a part of the PARVIS (detail). studio van der Woude.

Model of the TOIT (detail) with positioning of screws. studio Pellacani.

This level of accuracy also allows us to check the mechanical aspects of the project. It permits the establishment and testing of the various assembly and disassembly scenarios, but also to test the moving parts of the project (eg. doors, windows, movable walls).

Mounting test. studios Perez-Lupi/Baur.

Interior view. studio Baur/Chassot.

Light tests #1, #2. studio Rufer.

In order to replicate as closely as possible the real conditions of the built work, particular external elements were inserted into the model. In the case of plantings within the project, seedlings were plante d and sprouted directly within the model, in order to reproduce the appearance of the full-scale flower boxes.

The inner world of the model can be controlled by the manipulation of light, and the staging of inserted elements at scale.

Model with seedlings. studio Dürr.

Projection space, photomontage. studio Rufer.

Inhabitation space, photomontage. studio Rufer.

However, the confrontation of the project with its real, outdoor environment remains difficult to replicate.

THEATRE model with view of the Rolex Learning Center (detail). studio Chassot.

View of the Lausanne landscape, photomontage. studio Rufer.

Imaginary view, photomontage. studio Rufer.

View of the Lausanne landscape and light study, photo montage. studio Rufer.

A mockup is manufactured at the same scale as the final product. It can test certain conditions directly in relation to the body, such as spatial dimensions; but also weight and structural resistance of the material.

Construction of a prefabricated element, test #1: weight. studio Pellacani.

Height test in the studio. studio del Grosso.

Mockup of the surface of the plane. studio Rufer.

Construction of a prefabricated element, test #2: strength. studio Pellacani.

In the case of a stairway or a ladder, the relationship between the dimensions of the body and those of the object is paramount, and can be tested easily using a mockup.

Construction of a part of the railing and comfort analysis. studio Pellacani.

Mockup of two steps and a lateral wall. studio del Grosso.

Mockup of three steps and lateral walls #1: step height. studio Cabay.

Mockup of three steps and lateral walls #1: seat height. studio Cabay.

Modelling a detail or an entire element can also be useful for making mechanical or structural tests.

Strength test. studio Pellacani.

Strength test of a floor element #1, #2. studio Perez-Lupi.

Testing the relations between the body and the project can also be done without actually constructing sections of the build at full scale. Projections can be traced on the floor or any other flat surface.

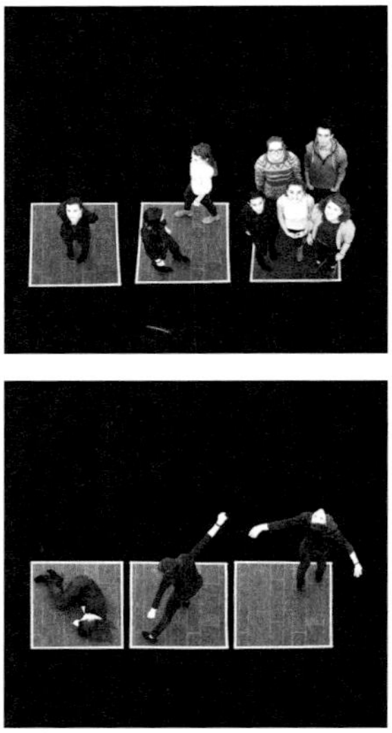

Outline and habitation of the area plan #1-3, #4-6. studio den Hartog.

Outline of the surface of the plane and inhabitation test #1-4. studio den Hartog.

Outline of the section and inhabitation test #1-3. studio den Hartog.

Outline of the surface of the plane. studio Chassot.

A projection may also remain immaterial. Using a light source, a shadow can visually materialise the project in space. The photograph then acts as the witness of its experimentation and confrontation with the scale of the body.

Light projection test. studio Cabay.

Mockup of the section, with light projection. studio Cabay.

By making a representation defined and limited by the characteristics of the support onto which it is projected, the photographic image creates a different reality of the object being depicted. The snapshot captures this reality by implementing a unique perspective, thus directing the reading of the object.

Photography, whether digital or filmic, requires the consideration of physical and mechanical parameters. The settings of the capturing device depend indeed on the character of the object, but also on the device itself, and the desired view of it. In the case of printed works, the act of printing will also influence the composition and appearance of the image.

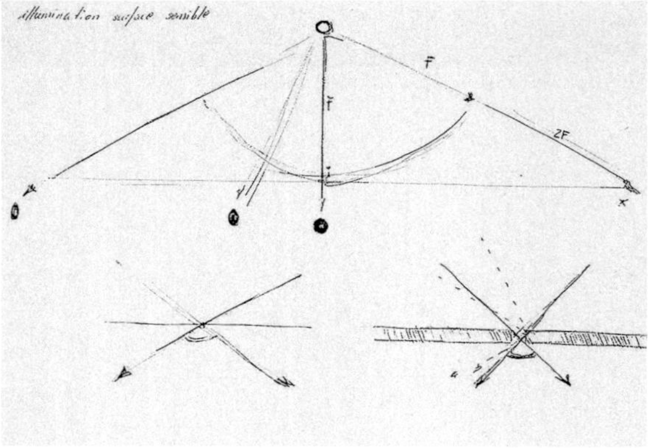

Study of focal, hand sketch. studio Baur.

Discussion at the printer. studio Cabay.

Photo printing. studio Baur.

The recording of an image may be motivated by the desire to safeguard a specific moment in time for posterity. It could be an exceptional situation or moment that is unlikely to reoccur, or a viewpoint into or of the object which can only be captured in an image. In the case of HOUSE 1, photography helps to build up the narrative of the process of development and construction.

Print test. studio Baur.

The process of creating a plaster. studio Chassot.

Drawing readable by light. studio Chassot.

During the construction. studio den Hartog.

Each photograph represents a unique perspective depending on the staging of the scene by the device and the person operating it.

HOUSE 1 work in progress.
studio Cabay/del Grosso/Chassot/Baur/Dürr.

The finished HOUSE 1.
studios den Hartog/Chassot/Cabay/Grandgirard.

The point of view selected influences the reception of the object.

Prefabricated component model opened. studio del Grosso.

Installation of textile, black background. studio Dürr.

Prefabricated component model closed. studio del Grosso.

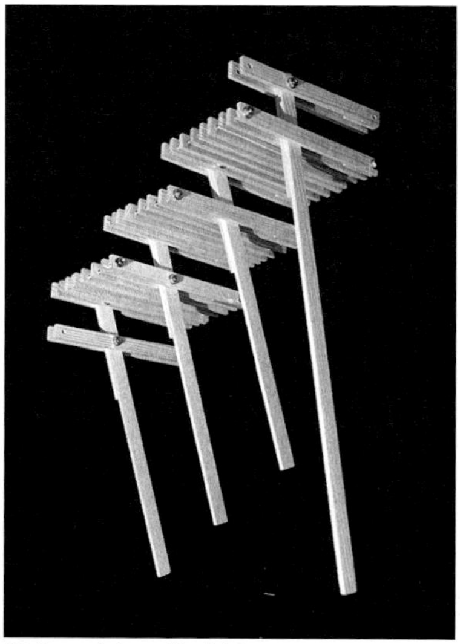

Stair model. studio del Grosso.

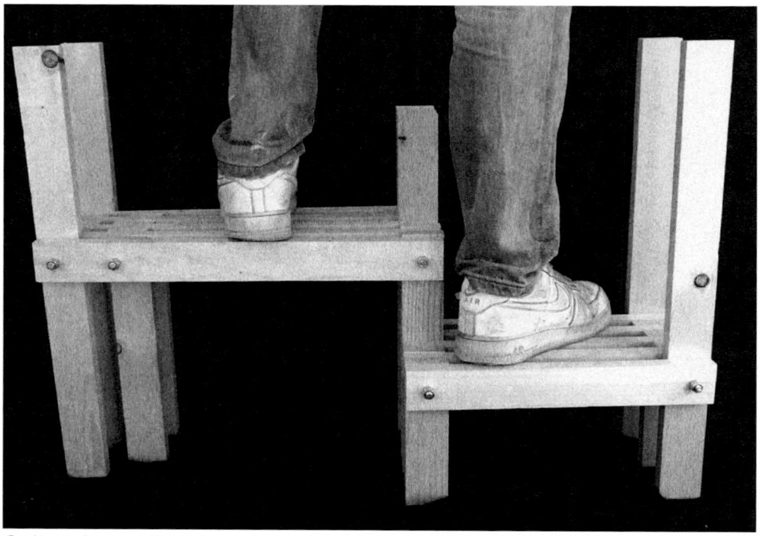

Stair mockup. studio Baur.

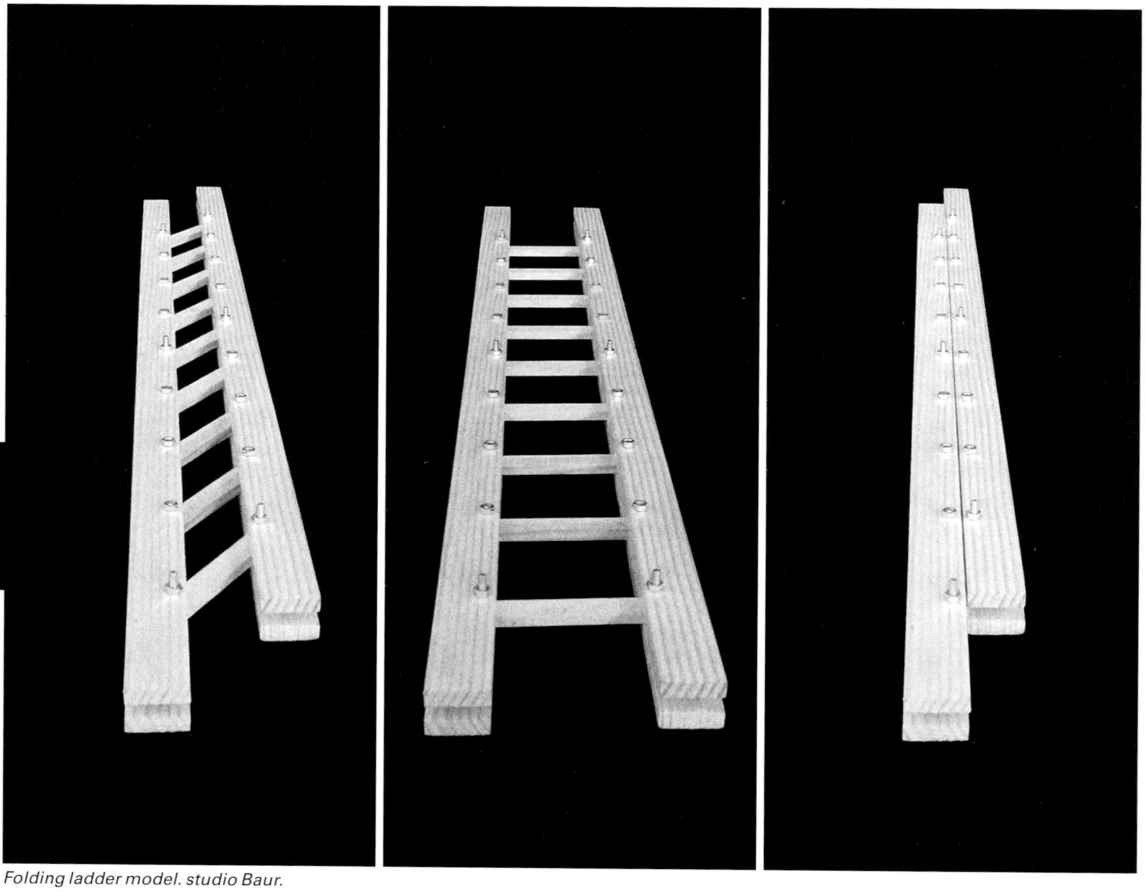

Folding ladder model. studio Baur.

Photographs with high contrast emphasise a particular aspect of the object, allowing us to play with the materialisation of shadows.

View onto the stairs, model. studio Baur.

Illuminated substructure. studio Baur.

Shadow of a figure. studio Chassot.

The registration and handling of digital images opens doors to new kinds of iconographic creations.

Floor substructure by transparency. studio Chassot.

Long exposure. studio Cabay.

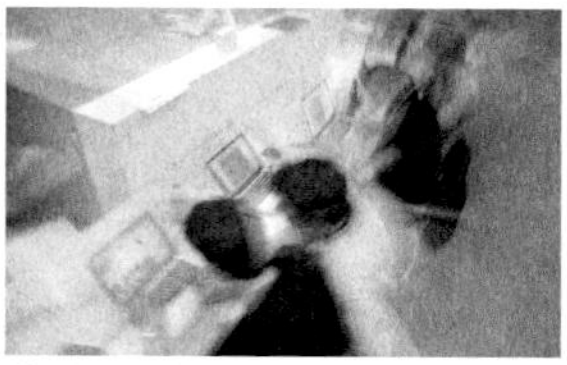

Optical effect. studio Cabay.

Human figure behind the screen. studio Chassot.

Shadow perspective. studio Cabay.

Space and words maintain an ambiguous relationship within HOUSE 1.The spatial expression of architecture is built on the illustration of an idea, a concept that conveys a feeling or a sensation. But the equation between the formalisation of this concept and the act of being able to describe it in words can indeed be very subjective. Readings of space can be immensely personal, varying greatly from person to person.

Different formalisations of the fundamentals of architecture – floor, wall or ceiling – within the same project already reveal the subjective nature of the physical expression of a concept. For each of these elements it is possible to produce a series of different interpretations, collected under the same title.

FLOOR

La Forêt, cover page of the FORET ROOM booklet. studio den Hartog.

studio Grandgirard.

ROOF

studio van der Woude.

studio van der Woude.

studio Pellacani.

WALL

studio van der Woude.

studio Grandgirard.

LIBRARY

studio del Grosso.

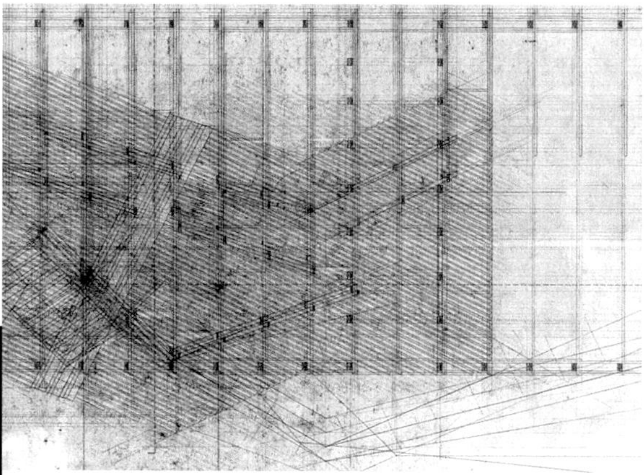

studio Guaita.

studio Cabay.

THEATRE

EXHIBITION ROOM

studio Guaita.

studio Pellacani.

studio Rufer.

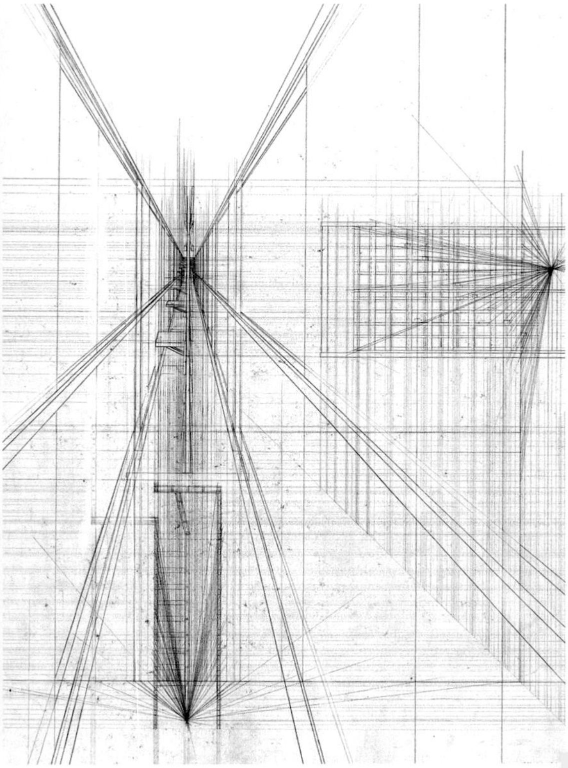

studio Chassot.

studio Cabay.

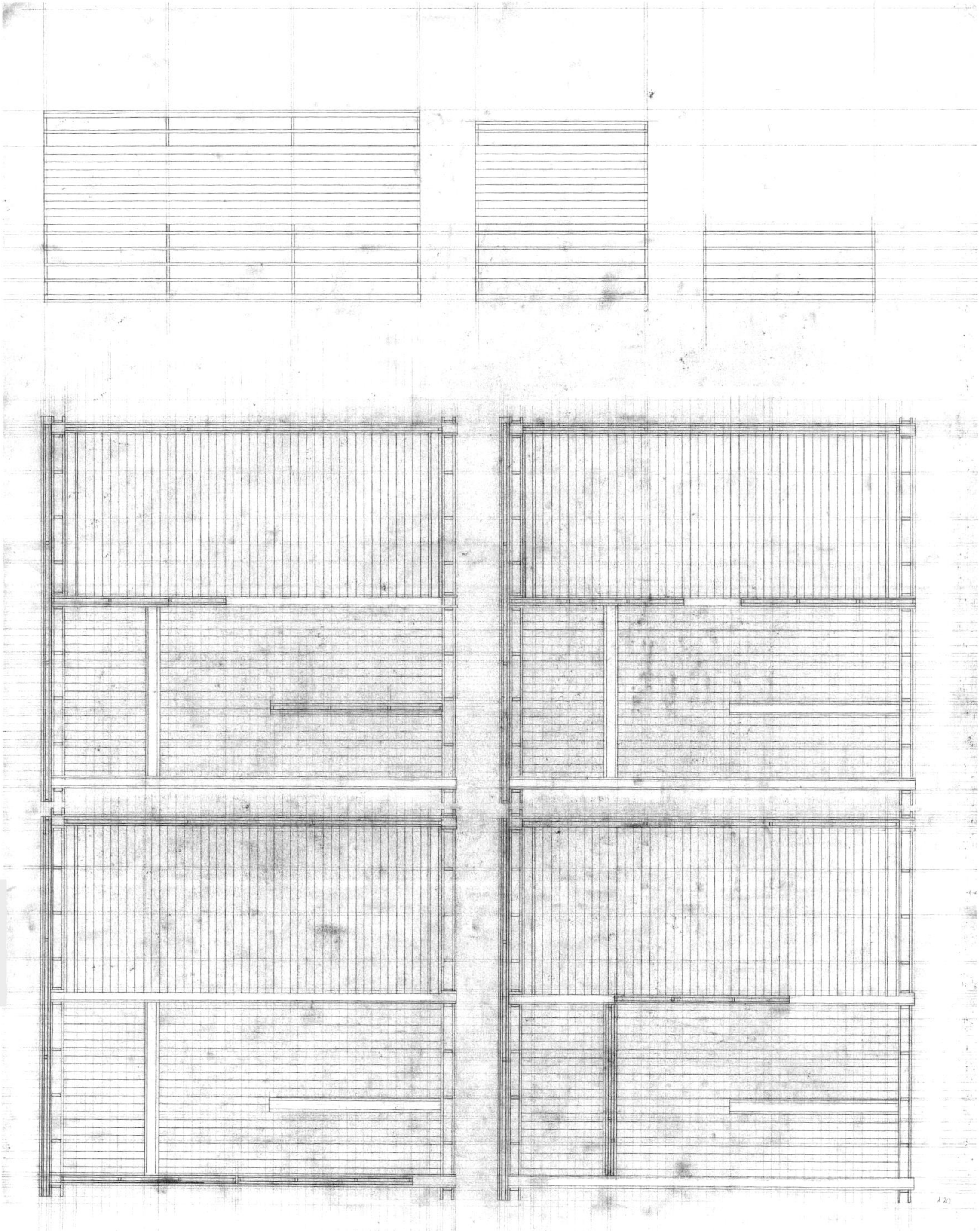

studio Pellacani.

The association of words and images highlights this ambiguity. The two forms of expression; plastic and literal, seek to convey the same ideas, each using their own codes. A selection of words begins to illustrate a series of images, photographs or drawings, in order to define the guidelines of a spatial concept.

DENSITY
TENSION
CENTRALITY

ATTRACTION
SPACE BETWEEN
NARROW/ROOMY
PLUNGE INTO
LIGHT

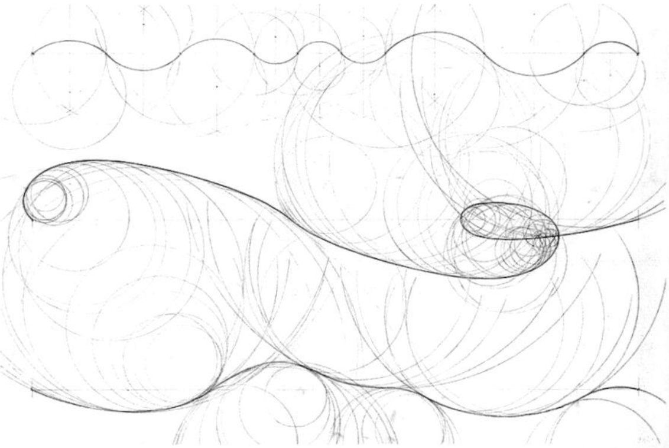

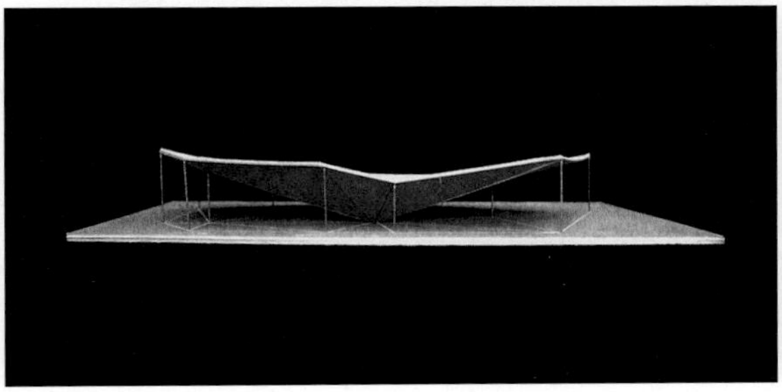

TRANSITION
INTIMITY
OBSTRUCTION
CALMING
ACHEMINEMENT

DYNAMIC
SERIAL
SIMPLE
OPENINGS
PRIVACY

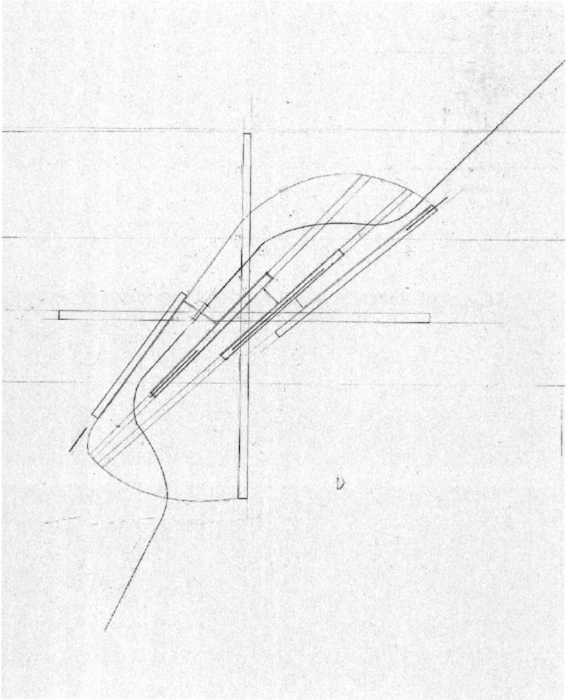

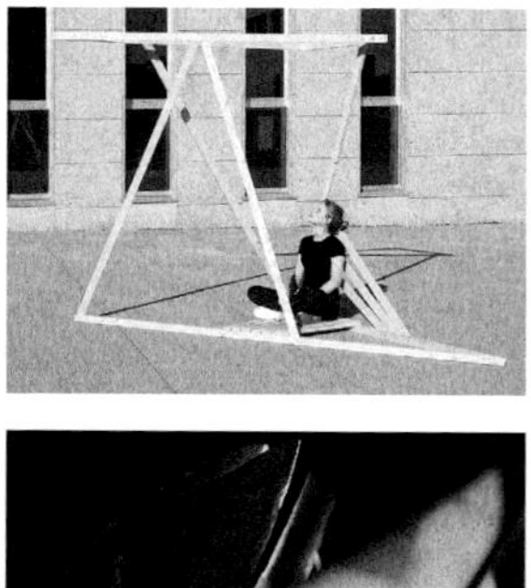

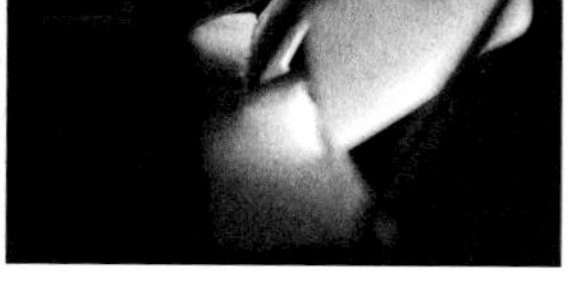

MOUVEMENT
PERCEPTION
RYTHME
BIEN ÊTRE / MAL ÊTRE
FLUX

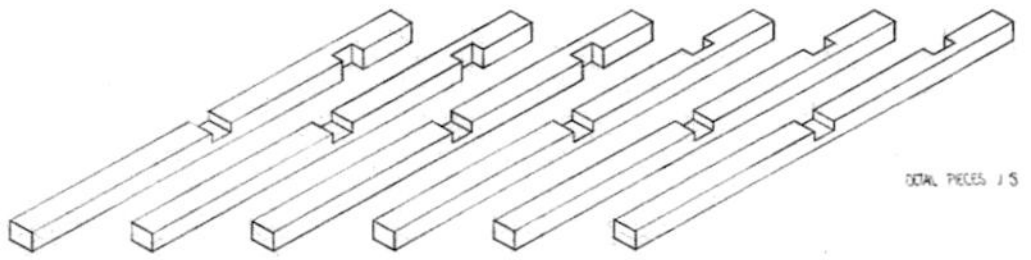

The title is a phrase or word that takes on the role of identifying, representing or illustrating a production. The research into and eventual selection of this unique means of describing a project demonstrates the ambiguity of the relationship between written or spoken discourse and image, and how ideas are transferred from one medium to another, evolving along the way.

OPENED CERTICALITY

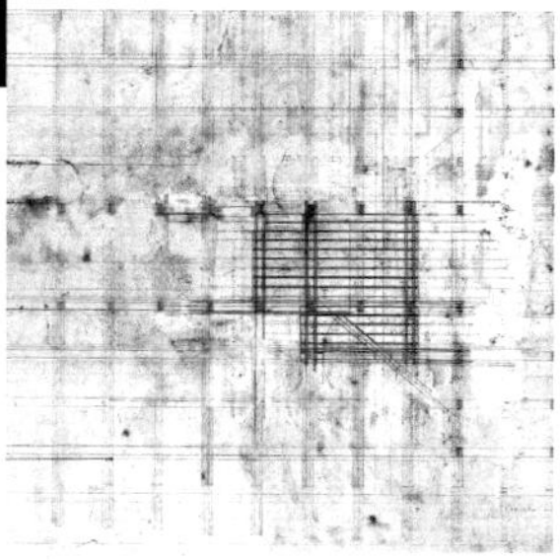

D'UN MONDE A L'AUTRE

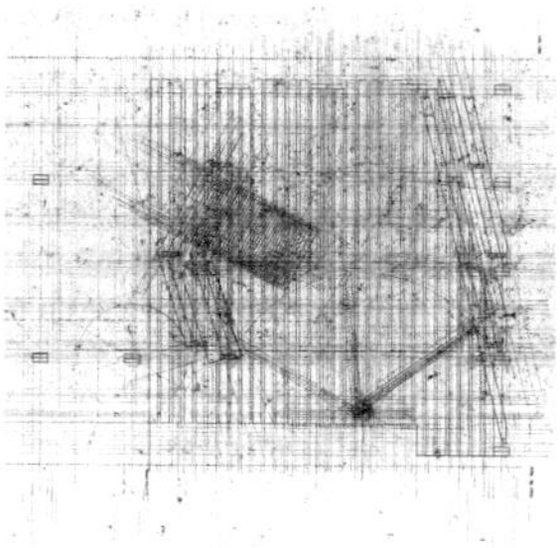

ALCOVE

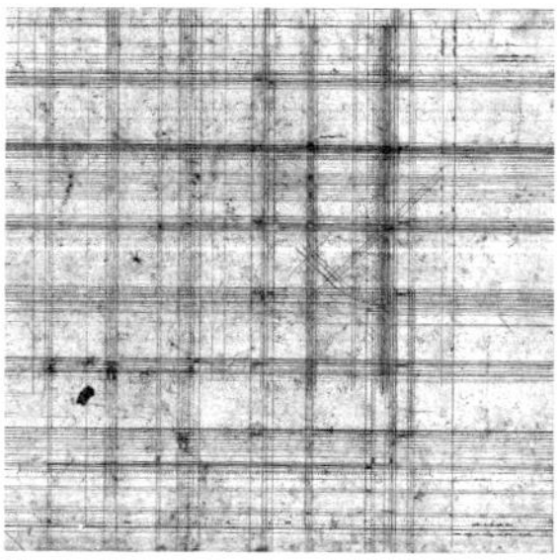

CONVERGENCE

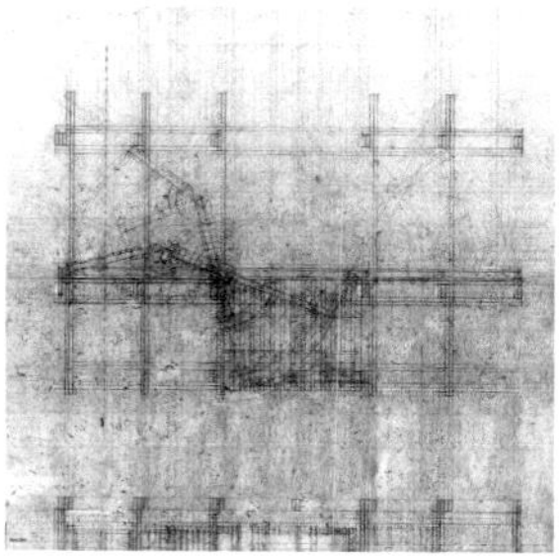

HOUSE 1 is a dynamic platform for the exchange of knowledge and learning. The artefact that is HOUSE 1 is the result of many discussions and debates carried out through the various phases of the project.

LECTURES

Lectures remain the only one-sided format of knowledge transfer employed. Often taking the form of a conference, they offer a personal point of view on a given topic to an assembled group of people. Although the lectures remain open for debate, this form of exchange is largely one-way, in order to transmit knowledge effectively.

HOUSE 1 students together in the Salle Polyvalente. studio Rufer.

HOUSE 1 LECTURES

DD
- INSIDE
- CORPS EN ESPACE
- HABITER MON HORIZON
- TRANSITIONAL SPACES
- DREAM ON

DZ
- ALL ABOUT SPACE
- EVERYTHING IS REAL
- THE ROOM OF THE SYSTEM
- THE OTHERS

RB
- THE RENAISSANCE CORNER PROBLEM

SD
- PASSAGES 1
- PASSAGES 2
- PASSAGES 3

CRITICS

Critiques are moments of exchange centred around the formalisation of a project. From the development of the concept to its realisation, each phase is illustrated and modelled in advance, and this material in turn becomes support material for the discussion.

Midterm critiques around the 1:10 model. studio Perez-Lupi.

Final critiques, public defense. studio Chassot.

Midterm critiques around the 1:5 model. studio Rufer.

Final critique discussion. studio Chassot.

HOUSE 1 CRITICS
PIN-UP

- WEEK 3, 4, 7, 8, 11, 12, 16, 17, 18, 22, 23, 24, 25, 26
  CRITICS
- WEEK 5
  ETAT DES LIEUX
  PHASE: MEASURES
  PLACE: ATELIERS SG
- WEEK 9
  CRITIQUE INTERMEDIAIRE
  PHASE: DOUBLE-ELEMENT
  PLACE: PLACE COSANDEY
- WEEK 14
  CRITIQUE FINALE
  PHASE: PLANES
  PLACE: SALLE POLYVALENTE
- WEEK 19
  CRITIQUE INTERMEDIAIRE
  PHASE: ROOMS
  PLACE: FORUM RLC
- WEEK 24
  ETAT DES LIEUX
  PHASE: HOUSE 1
  PLACE: ATELIERS SG
- WEEK 29
  CRITIQUE FINALE
  PHASE: HOUSE 1
  PLACE: various

SYMPOSIUM

Commonly taking the form of a discussion held between several players, the symposium is dedicated to the study of a question or a particular topic. Participants each bring to bear their expertise in their area of speciality on the advancement of the debate.The format of the symposium places HOUSE 1 beyond a simple spatial exercise, allowing it to engage with architectural discourse.

Final critiques symposium I. studios Rufer/Chassot.

SYMPOSIUM I
- TITLE: INSIDENESS & INHABITATION
- PLACE: INSIDE HOUSE 1
- INTERN CONTRIBUTORS:
  DZ
  RM
- GUESTS:
  CEDRIC LIBERT
  ELENA COGATO LENZA
  DIANA ALVAREZ-MARIN
  FERNANDEZ RUIZ MIGUEL
- MODERATOR:
  DD

Final critiques symposium II. studio Chassot.

SYMPOSIUM II
- TITLE: PEDAGOGY & COOPERATION
- PLACE: TRANSVERSAL STUDIO
- INTERN CONTRIBUTORS:
  DD
  ACR
  ADH
  AM
  AP
  EC
  LC
  LPL
  MDG
  ND
  PG
  RB
  RM
  SG
  WW
- GUESTS:
  CEDRIC LIBERT
  DIANA ALVAREZ-MARIN
- MODERATOR:
  DZ

Throughout the process, the development of HOUSE 1 has required a high level of information and data sharing. These exchanges have been supported by several platforms, both digital and analogue, that have allowed for information sharing, collecting and archiving.

BLOG

Students > Teachers
The BLOG is a digital information platform used by students. Bringing together work in progress as well as photos and testimonials, it is the diary of HOUSE 1. This digital medium compiles images, scanned drawings, photographs of models or construction progress, photomontages and iconographic references, and occasionally snippets of text. The arrangement of these materials is classified both by the time of their posting and a system of 'tags', which allows a visitor to the site to search the archive by document type, or by the stage of the work. The BLOG keeps all documents posted online throughout the process, and in this way it builds up the raw data archive of the project.

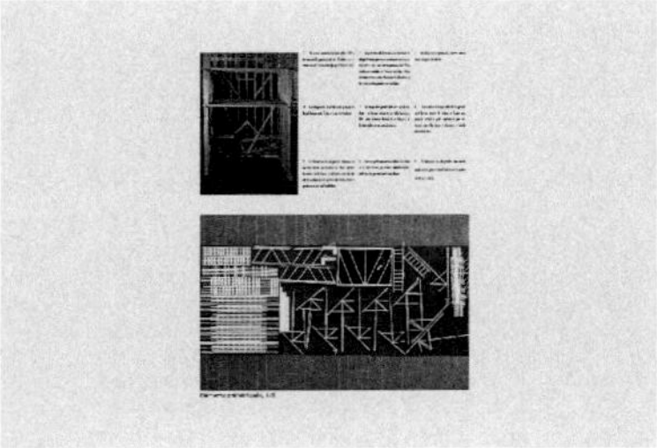

HOUSE 1 blog home page.

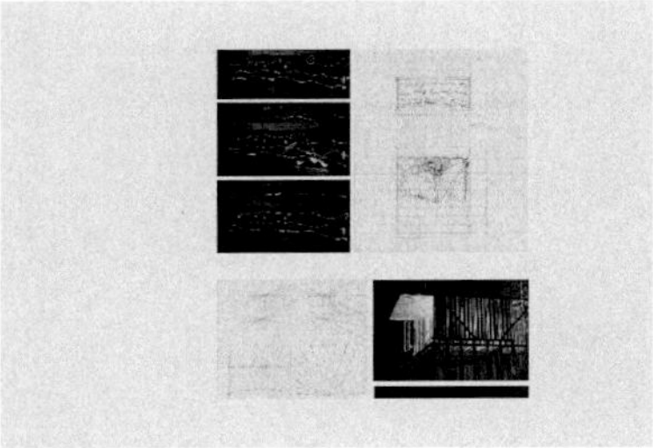

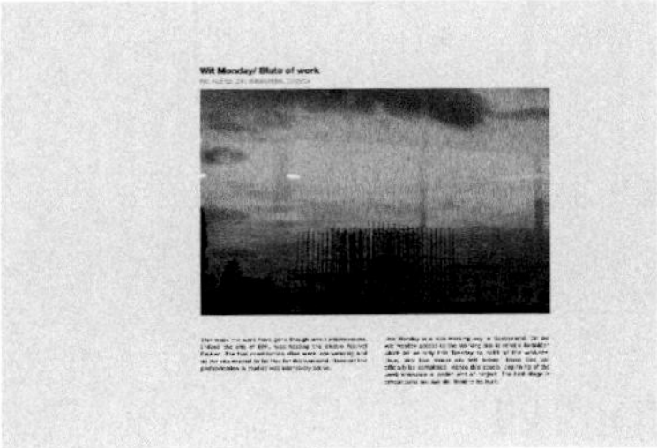

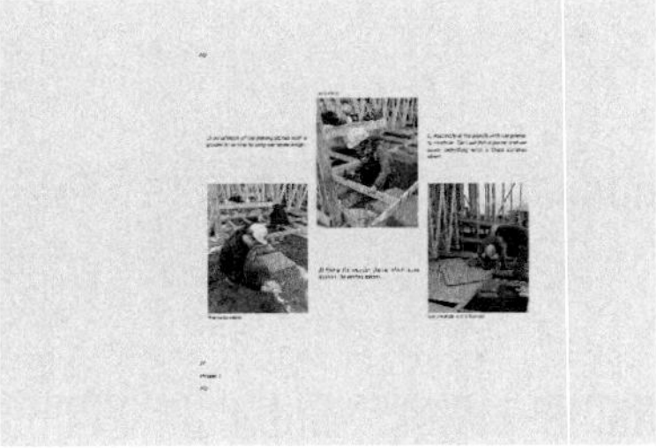

POSTCARDS

Teachers > Students
POSTCARDS are printed each week by the studio directors or assistants, on paper, and in the standard format of 105 x 148mm. They include instructions that guide students through the process of realising their project. A copy of each POSTCARD is stored directly in the ALICE laboratory and displayed. The wall support for the display of these documents is configured orthogonally to receive POSTCARDS classified according to the studio to which they belong, and the stage of the year in which they were distributed.

Semaine 15
22.02.16

0.
Form groups of two persons according to your complementary skills. Each person should come from a different group of the double element.

In groups of two

1.
Looking at the work you have done from the beginning of the year, chose three extraits of drawings or photos per person.
Print them in A5, portrait.
(6 A5 portrait per group!)

2.
On an A5, portrait
write down five words that qualify your previous projects that you want to investigate for rooms.
(space, atmosphere, structure, feelings, light...)

3.
Place your +column in the protostructure.

Tuesday morning 08.30 am
Pin up of 1. and 2.

ALICE™ STUDIO LUPI RUFER

Semaine 15
23.02.16

Build the protostructure in 1:10 for both studios.

In groups of two

1.
Draw the protostructure in plan and section in 1.20 according to the layout instructions!

2.
Build your fragment of the protostructure in 1:10.

3.
Draw a sinthesis of both your planes projetcs with the +column in the protostructure.

Monday morning 09.15 am
Pin up

Tuesday morning 08.30 am
Pin up

ALICE™ STUDIO LUPI RUFER

GIVENS 1/6

1.
DESIGN AND BUILD A ROOM INSIDE THE PROTOSTRUCTURE USING THE FOLLOWINGS:

A
The super element(s) or its translation in double element.

B
One or more condition(s) developped during the previous semester (spaciality, structure, geometry, movement, ...).

2/6

C
An interpretation based on an interview of a writer from "The Paris Review".

House 1 - Game implantation

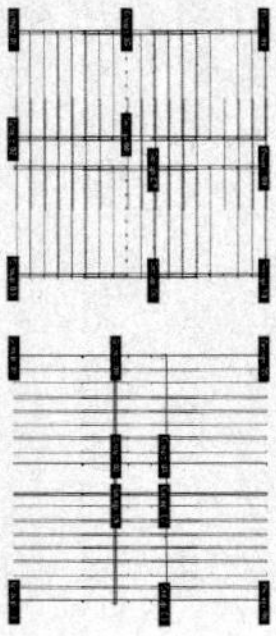

House 1 - Game implantation

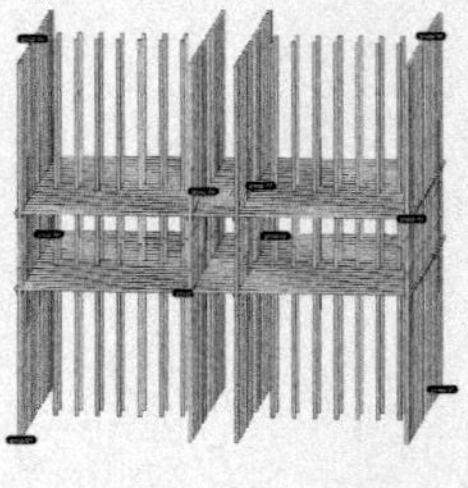

RULES 3/6

1.
No construction allowed outside of the protostrcture.

2.
No filled surfaces allowed.

3.
Laying on the ground is not allowed.

4.
Each project must touch at least one vertical plane.

5.
Design only with the given wood sections.

JURY 4/6

1.
For the jury, each group present 4 models.

2.
All the projects presented the same day can cohabit in the protostructure.

3.
The final model is first to be presented dismounted and then assembled in the protostructure in less than 2 minutes.

GROUPS 6/6

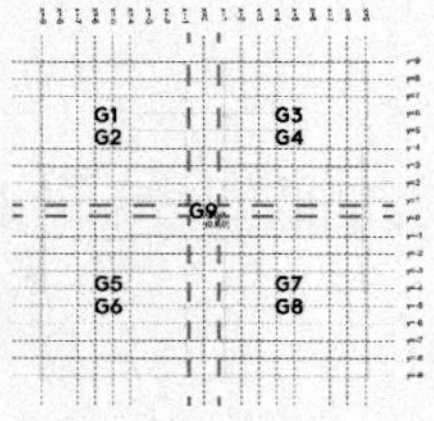

Postcards outlining instructions for HOUSE 1.
studio Perez-Lupi/Chassot.

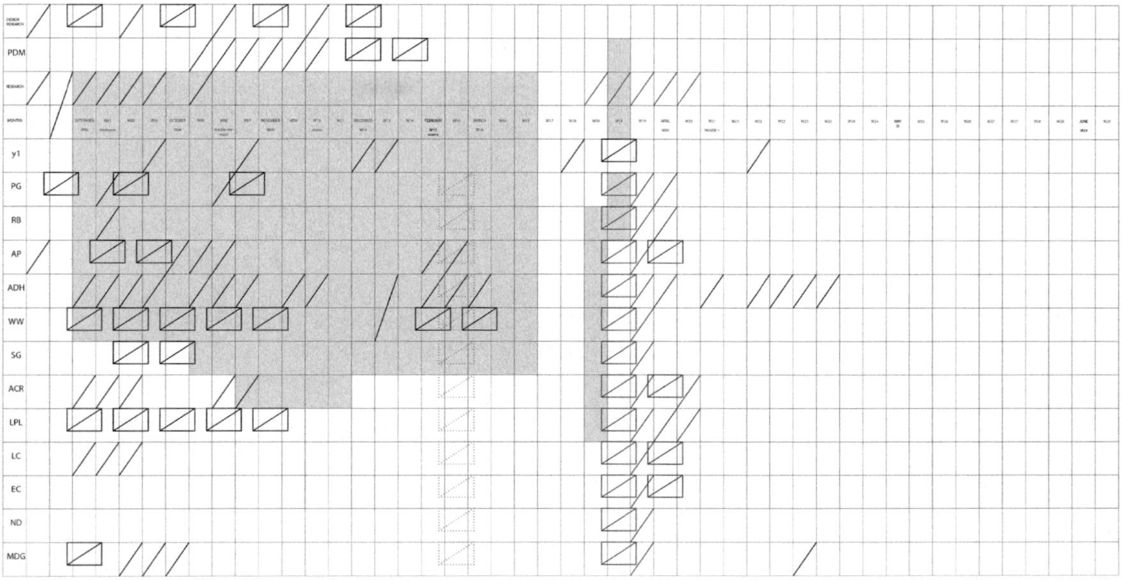

Organigram of the ALICE office wall. Agathe Mignon.

ALICE office wall. Agathe Mignon.

TRANSVERSAL

Students = Teaching
The studioTRANSVERSAL is a fabrication workshop common to all of the studios. It is the space in which students are given their first instruction on the basics of timber and plaster work. It is also where the common machines for fabrication are installed. It is a place used by all for the construction of the various constituent parts of HOUSE 1, and therefore important as a space for sharing knowledge and ideas. The space can be used for the exchange of equipment, materials or tools, but it is also a space for acquiring a certain 'know-how' engendered through common experience.

Mounting of the 1:5 model in theTRANSVERSAL studio. Agathe Mignon.

Talk around the 1:5 model. studio Rufer.

SYMPOSIUM II in theTRANSVERSAL studio. studio Chassot.

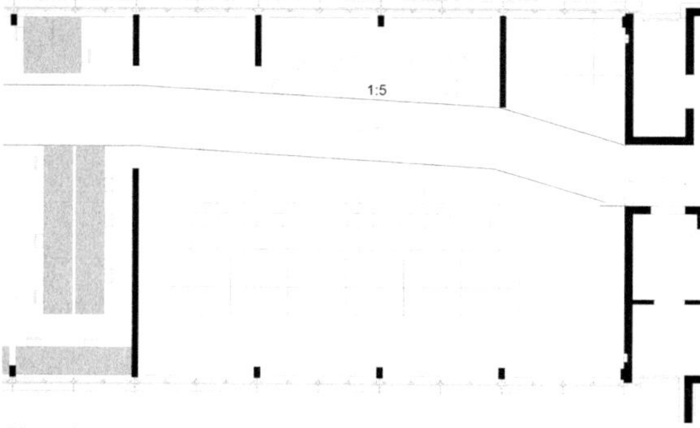

Plan of theTRANSVERSAL studio. Wynd van der Woude.

INTRODUCTION

The evolution of humans has followed an accelerated path during the past ten millennia, after the Agricultural Revolution took place some 10 000 – 15 000 years ago. The speed at which humans have controlled and invested in, some would argue too aggressively, their own environment over the past 3000 has been made possible by two primary factors that have distinguished homo sapiens from other human species: fiction and collaboration. Fiction came through language. It arose from the capacity of sapiens to gather a large community of individuals and invent common concepts and goals that looked well beyond survival, like the cultivation of a spiritual life. Communities of sapiens could, through fiction, accomplish more complex tasks than other species, because of their power to believe in something together and thus be able to plan and accomplish great achievements. The other factor, collaboration, brought organisation, specialisation, group thinking and making to the fore, and allowed large communities of over 150 individuals to work commonly. Homo sapiens was able to construct floating devices to travel to the Australian continent, fabricate complex tools, and travel around the world, modifying the natural world. Many scholars state that the significant differences between Neanderthals and Homo sapiens are a result of these two factors: fiction and collaboration. As a matter of fact, the Neanderthal brain was larger than ours. Yet we are what we are because we are together, and because we can invent ideas as a group and convince ourselves of these ideas, for better or worse.

Anything and everything that we have accomplished together as a species, from walking on the moon to smartphones and self-driven cars, we have done through our reliance on a constant collaboration. Without judging whether our evolution has been a success or not, we can clearly state that collaboration has given us an incommensurable strength in accomplishing just about anything.

This chapter deals precisely with the energy, power and capacity of a group of people to invent a fiction – "let's make a house" – and gather the necessary ingredients and tools to actually turn that fiction into a physical and palpable reality. One could even assert that the most important merit of HOUSE 1 is the use of this collective intelligence and force. The HOUSE 1 community has been able to embrace a pedagogical fiction and construct it. The following chapter documents extensively the bits and pieces of this collective making. It also presents the building of a community, and shows how this community has operated as one common body to turn a fiction into a physical, yet speculative, inhabitation space.

During its evolution leading finally to its culmination as a construction, HOUSE 1 gathered and built up a large community. This community is composed of about 200 individuals.

Portrait of a builder. studio Cabay.

HOUSE 1 required ongoing collaboration at all stages, from the development of the project to the completion of the construction.

Prefabrication in the studio. studio Cabay.

Reminder of the safety rules. studio Chassot.

Discussion on site. studio Cabay.

Transport of prefabricated parts. studio Chassot.

Collective work. studio Chassot.

Break time. studio Chassot.

Nap in the net. studio Chassot.

Discussion during site visit. studio Chassot.

HOUSE 1 inauguration day. studio Chassot.

Break time after the construction. studio Rufer.

Even if the physical construction does not remain, this community continues to evolve and transform in their engagement with the future stages of HOUSE 1, whatever form they may take.

End-of-construction party. studio Perez-Lupi.

200 individuals make up a group far too large to be able to work and produce simultaneously. Smaller groups within the larger team further and defend their own particular interests within the wider community. This allows members to make more immediate and personal identifications within the whole community.

STUDENTS

The student body is divided into 12 studios, each charged with the responsibility of developing one intervention for HOUSE 1. Within each studio, students are organised into subgroups based on the division of labour. Thematic groups are then organised transversally across studios, bringing together a selection of students from each studio to carry out additional tasks.

STUDENTS GROUPS

- STUDIO REPRESENTATIVES
  - RB: Candice
  - EC: Marc
  - LC: Selen
  - MDG: Simon
  - ADH: Chiara
  - ND: Dana
  - SG: Diana
  - PG: Pierre
  - AP: Laura
  - LPL: Romane
  - ACR: Alba
  - WW: Albane
- 1:5 REPRESENTATIVES
  - RB: Jessica; Antonin
  - EC: Marc; Juesheng
  - LC: Selen; Margaux
  - MDG: Simon; Antonin; Stéphanie; Simon
  - ADH: Benjamin
  - ND: Maria; Mathilde
  - SG: Kilian; Nicolas
  - PG: Gregory; Antoine
  - AP: Charlotte
  - LPL: Alessandra; Guillaume
  - ACR: Lucas; Marco
  - WW: Lisa; Maud
- PHOTOTEAM
  - Joanne
  - Selen
  - Clea
  - Guillaume
  - Antoine

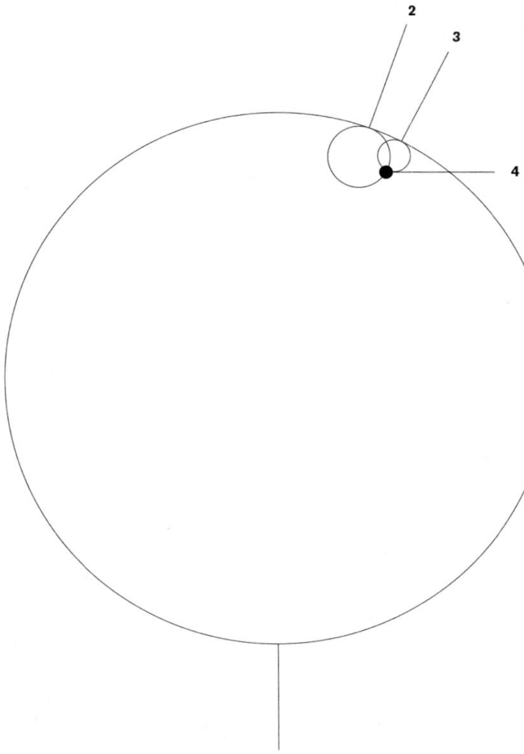

1: Total number of students
2: Studio representatives for 1:5 model
3: Studio representatives
4: photo team

Proportion of students making up different specialist groups, CAD drawing. Agathe Mignon.

TEACHING

The teaching team, consisting of around 20 people, is organised according to a horizontal hierarchy. Different interconnected groups within the team are working across the research projects of the ALICE laboratory, as well as for ongoing multidisciplinary projects.

ALICETEAM GROUPS

- DIRECTION
  DD
  DZ
- TEACHINGTEAM
  RB
  EC
  LC
  MDG
  ADH
  ND
  SG
  PG
  AP
  ACR
  LPL
  WW
- RESEARCHTEAM
  AM
  DN
  SK
  CD
- DESIGN RESEARCHTEAM
  RN
  AD
- WONDERLANDTEAM
  DD
  DZ
  PG
  CD
  RN
  JR
- CORETEAM
  RB
  EC
  PG
  SG
  WW
- HOUSE 1TEAM
  RB
  EC
  PG
  SG
  WW
  AM
- COMMUNICATION & BLOGTEAM
  LPL
  RN

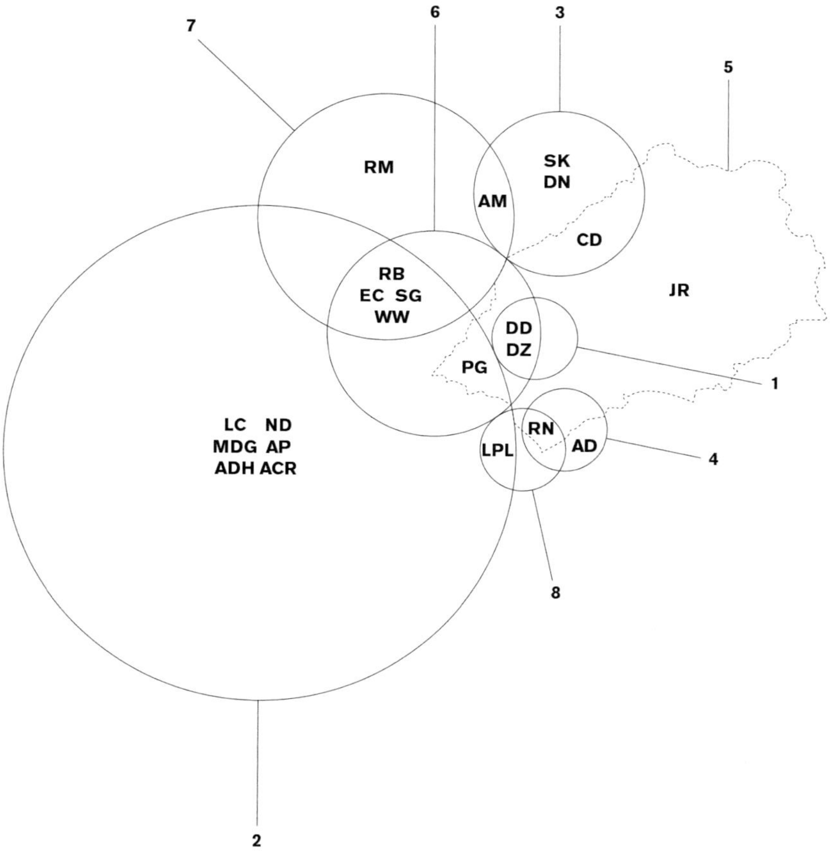

Geography of the teams in ALICE, CAD drawing. Agathe Mignon.

1: direction
2: teaching team
3: research team
4: design research team
5: wonderland team
6: core team
7: HOUSE 1 team
8: communication & blog team

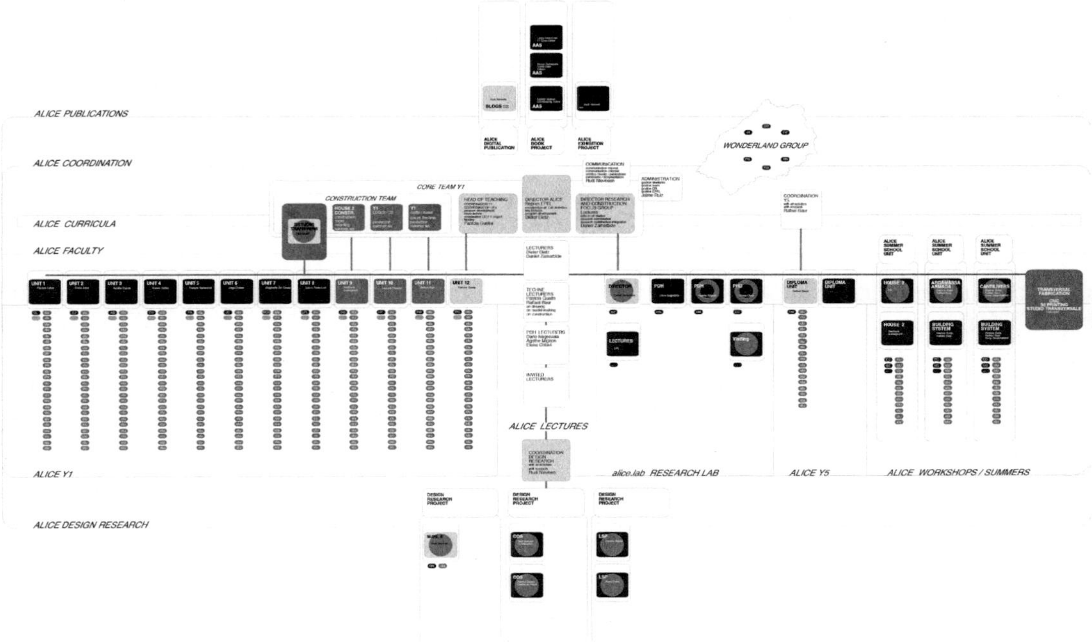

hierarchy and responsibilities, CAD drawing. Rudi Nieveen.

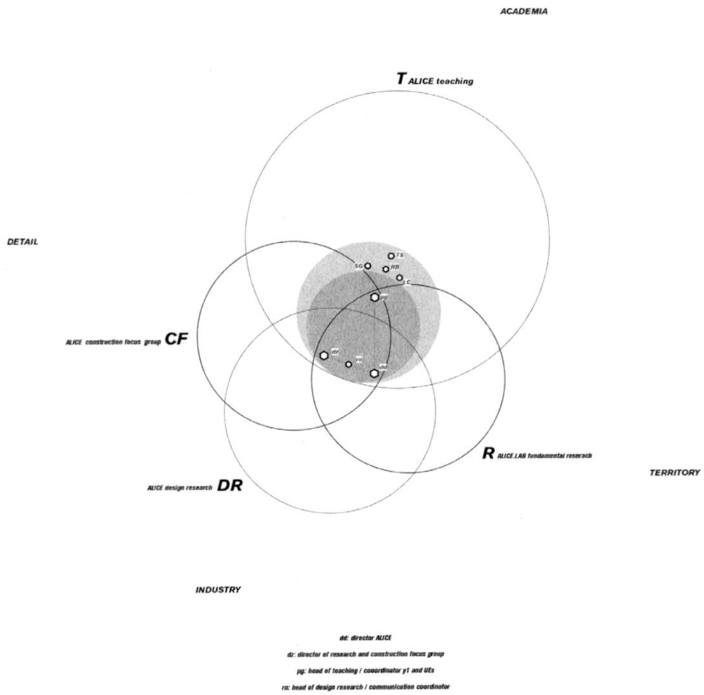

areas of activity, CAD drawing. Rudi Nieveen.

Comprising of a complex network of social, environmental, economical and spatial concerns, architecture demands appropriate environments for planning, research and education. Considering that the era of the sole master-architects has passed, replaced by today's globally interconnected professional practices often working in interdisciplinary teams with highly structured modes of operation, the education of future architects must be carefully reconsidered. In our diverse formats of design studios and *'Unités d'enseignements'* we adopt specifically structured programs and formats of collaboration in order to foster not only individual responsibility but also capacities necessary for collective practice.

Aristotle, in his Nichomachean Ethics has identified five types of knowledge: the 'doxa' (belief system, word doctrine), the 'episteme' (accepted historical truths, word epistemology), 'phronesis' (practical wisdom), 'techne' (craftsmanship; linear) and 'poiesis' (art, creativity; dynamic, non-linear). Through its synthetic nature the architectural project clearly requires exposure to all these fields of knowledge. Our diverse formats of interventions and teaching formats – the lectures, as well as the more technically focused techne formats for drawing, programming, and model making – are embedded in these fields of knowledge. The studio or atelier is the place where those diverse fields of knowledge are brought together and crafted into a synthetic project. Through the atelier's explorations across those fields of knowledge the project will be grounded in technical, historic and poetic knowledge as well as in crafts – with the aim to bring about innovation through synthesis.

The ALICE atelier is built up in flat hierarchies. There are presently 12 studios. Studio directors are responsible for a group of about 20 students, teaching them at one to one level in desk critiques, studio debates and in interaction with other studios. A series of formats establish cross-studio communication. Class and studio critiques build up exposure of each student to the overall learning environment and establish discourse based on project proposals.

All our teaching formats have an important aspect in common: a meticulously planned timeline with all events, lectures, critiques and required elements clearly outlined, thus defining a highly structured design development process with tools and skills to be learned and tested in the individual synthetic project. An overall curriculum that is clearly defined and structured in order to allow for liberty where it should be: in the innovations and ideas to be proposed in the design projects themselves.

Our teaching objectives are grouped around key notions that are fundamental to the practice of architectural design. Some of these notions are equally important to other disciplines, especially such that include design processes and a project based approach as synthetic fields of investigation. To give an overview, the notions below constitute common denominators in our diverse teaching formats.

A MAIN FOCUS ON SPACE

According to its acronym, ALICE's main focus is space. We consider space not as neutral but as enacted environment. Space is a key denominator in all questions that revolve around the building up of our habitats and cities. We treat space in terms of main fields of knowledge – of theoretical, philosophical, social or phenomenological nature – as well as from technical points of view, such as tectonics, structure, architectural articulation, or engineering coherence.

COLLECTIVE PRACTICE

The production of space involves many actors, partners, decision-makers at all levels in hierarchical systems. Architecture is never done alone. The long gone privileged podsition of the master architect with pronounced decision power has been replaced by a series of interconnected complex processes of decision-making and design iterations. Accordingly the capacity to collaborate, to communicate proposals and to articulate ideas in a literate and professional way is one of the important capacities and responsibilities of the individual architect or designer. To learn and teach these capacities is one of our main concerns: the aptness for the conception and construction of space as a collective and collaborative act where each individual takes its fundamental share of responsibility.

STRUCTURED DESIGN PROCESSES

If imagination and curiosity are main drivers in the fostering of novel and innovative processes, it is important to foresee an adequate framework and the appropriate tools for venturing innovation. C-K theory provides key notions that allow help to structure transition between the world of ideas and that of the known: the confirmative retrospective look, and the prospective projective one into the future. Design is both a reiteration of the known and a synthesis into something new and unknown. The focus on iterations between concept space and knowledge space in four modes of transition provide organizing principles helpful in the exploration of novel ideas.

Of equal importance is to structure design processes well, especially if operating with large numbers of people, large quantities of constraints or demands, or high-complexity projects. We therefore work with comprehensive documents that map and structure processes entirely throughout the duration of a project.

During the process of developing HOUSE 1, several workshops were organised. In these workshops a group of students gathers, for a limited time, to work on the development or construction of a particular aspect of the larger project. The workshops are based on voluntary participation, and are intended to be a practical complement to the teaching provided during the university year.

Working together to achieve a result within a limited number of days requires a high level of collaboration between the participants. It also creates the ideal conditions for the forming of important links and working relationships. This quickly acquired and implemented shared knowledge can be the catalyst for forging precious and unique links between students.

Break time during the workshop. Wynd van der Woude.

HOUSE 1 protostructure workshop. studio Perez-Lupi.

HOUSE 1 protostructure workshop. Dylan Perrenoud/Wynd van der Woude/Daniel Zamarbide.

Team of the protostructure workshop. Wynd van der Woude.

Lunchtime during the dismounting workshop. studio Chassot.

The study trip brings a group of students to directly confront an experience of space through site-specific experience. It develops a collective culture, and sharpens individual critical opinion.

RB/PG

- 16.05.01
  Villa "Le Lac"
  Le Corbusier
  Corseaux, Switzerland

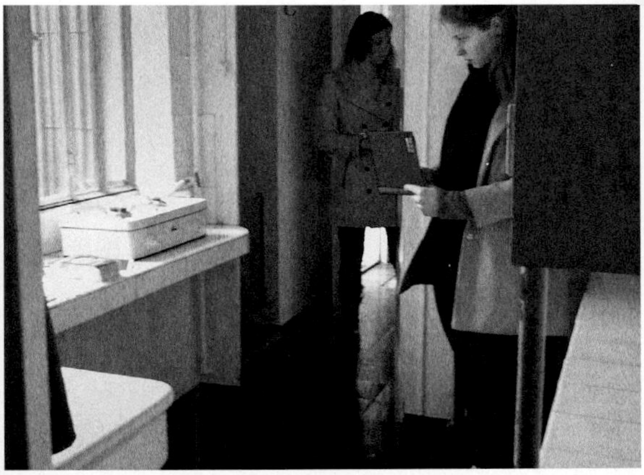

Visit to the Villa "Le Lac". studio Baur.

EC/LC/LPL/SG

- 16.04.09
  Couvent Sainte-Marie de la Tourette
  Le Corbusier
  Eveux, France
- 16.04.10
  Palais idéal du Facteur Cheval
  Ferdinand Cheval
  Hauterives, France
  —
  Maison de la culture et de la jeunesse, stade municipal, église Saint-Pierre
  Le Corbusier
  Firminy, France

MDG/ADH/ND/AP/ACR/WW

- 16.04.16-17
  Palazzo Rosso,
  Museo di Sant'Agostino di Genova
  Studio Albini Associati
  —
  Piazza Rossetti, Biscione
  Luigi Carlo Daneri
  —
  Galleria Nazionale di Palazzo Spinola
  —
  Cimitero monumentale di Staglieno

Visit to the Couvent de la Tourette. studio Chassot.

Guided tour of the Palais Idéal. studio Chassot.

Visit to Le Corbusier's works in Firminy. studio Chassot.

Visit of the church Saint-Pierre. studio Chassot.

Genova visit. Alice studio.

GENOVA WORKSHOP

Subject
Visits to interior and exterior sites; reflecting on the relation between the historic/typological aspects of building and the topography of the city of Genova.
Objectives
Dissect/measure/capture spatial condition, study section proportion.
Outcomes
Photos sequence, video.
Time
1 day visits, 1 day production, with presentation and exhibition.

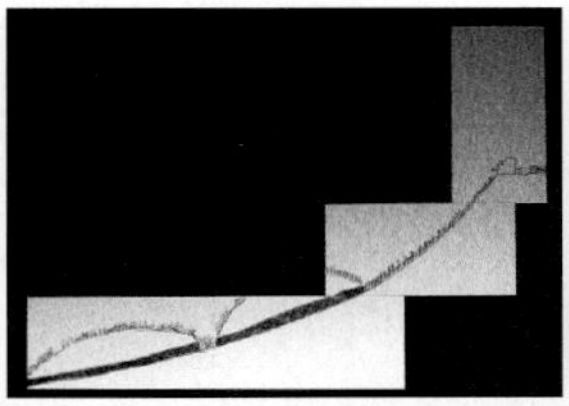

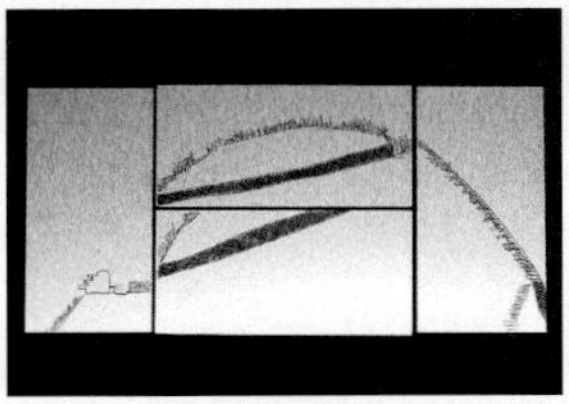

Genova workshop G2. studios del Grosso/den Hartog/Dürr/Pellacani/Rufer/van der Woude.

Genova workshop G14. studios del Grosso/den Hartog/Dürr/Pellacani/Rufer/van der Woude.

Genova workshop G4. studios del Grosso/den Hartog/Dürr/Pellacani/Rufer/van der Woude.

PALAZZO ROSSO / FUNICOLARE
Fluidity
Flat Surface, corner, flat surface, connected by a line
Transition. Ambiance change.
Room after Room,
Path followed by a Path,
Transition. Ambiance change;
by means of a line.
Step by Step,
Meter by Meter,
Following a line.
Or perhaps, is it the line that follows?
Is it everywhere?
G4: Marco, Basil, Jonathan, Dimitri, Maria

Selon Euclide, l'intersection de deux cercles alignés sur une droite fait la normale de cette dernière. Deux situations – horizontalité, verticalité – articulation "riche" en passage, des relations pensées. Transparence du Palazzo Spinola, opacité du Funicolare; une mise en commun d'une part, une totale séparation de l'autre, la première autocentrée, la deuxième imbriquée dans la ville. Une superposition de moments communs aux parcours, droite coupant la ville, créant des passages, ponts, encastrement circulaire.
G4: Alex, Erblin, Benjamin, Charlotte, Sarah

Nous avons regardé la ville sans la juger
Nous avons regardé la ville en pensant qu'aucune erreur n'avait été faite
Et la ville nous a parlé
Nous avons vu
Nous avons vu des cicatrices
des traces
des hommages
des nécessité
Nous avons vu une ville ou le temps se bat contre la réalité
Ceci est un témoignage
G14:Tom,Theo, Simon, Anthony

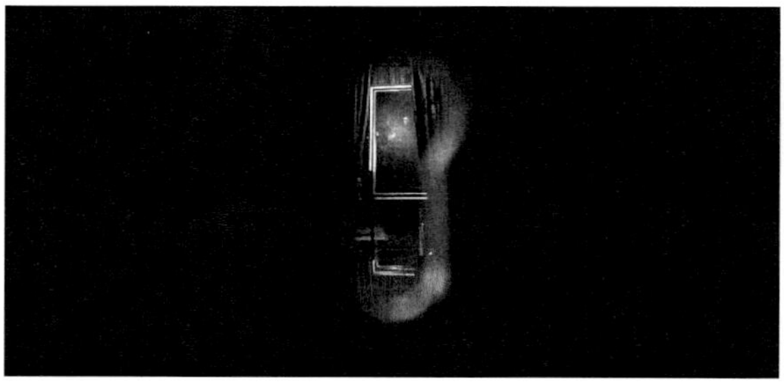

Genova workshop G6. studios del Grosso/den Hartog/Dürr/Pellacani/Rufer/van der Woude.

Palazzo Di Spinola – Corso Firenze
Traversez le Palazzo Di Spinola.
Sentez l'espace.
Ouvrez la fenêtre.
Sentez la compression, l'exiguïté, la proximité, le voisinage.
Traversez Corso Firenze.
Sentez l'espace.
Prenez l'escalier et descendez. Mettez vous dos à l'arc.
Sentez la compression, l'exiguïté, la proximité, le voisinage.
G6: Sebastien, Louise, Morgan, Sebastien

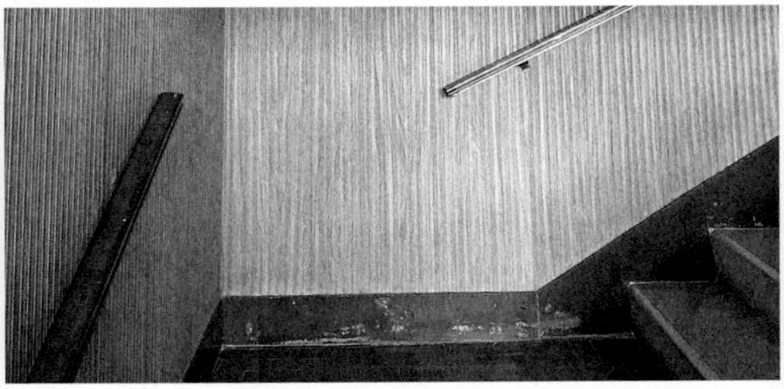

Genova workshop G8. studios del Grosso/den Hartog/Dürr/Pellacani/Rufer/van der Woude.

PIAZZA DE FERRARI STAZIONE BRIGNIALE BUS 356 LORIA 2 VIA LAMBERTO LORIA BISCIONE HORIZONTALITE VUES COURBES MASSE MODULARITE SPLENDEUR STATICITE ISOLEMENT EMPILEMENT TOPOGRAPHIE RADICALITE HOMOGENEITE PROMENADE VIDE PLAT BRUTALITE CALME TRANSPARENCE LIGNES OPPRESSION TAGS REPETITION BRUI FUITE FRAGMENTATION ANGLES DEGRADATION TYPOLOGIES SEQUENCES STANDARDISATION

PIAZZA MANIN CIRCONVALLAZIONE VERTICALITE JUXTAPOSITION ENERGIE VIS-A-VIS PARCS CONTEMPLATION TEINTES FLUIDITE MULTITUDE CONTRASTE MOUVEMENT RIRES DENIVELES SOLICITATION JARDINS CIRCULATION DELABREMENT SOCIABILITE IMPASSES CALME DETOURS SONORITES ENCHAINEMENT DIVERSITE FRAGMENTATION STIMULATION

G8: Judith, Maxime, Dana, Marjolaine, Audrey

INTRODUCTION

This section concentrates on the temporary occupation of the ground as a mode of inhabiting our environment. The HOUSE 1 project reflects on temporary inhabitation as a key issue in the process of architectural making and education. Beyond pavilion-making or sculptural architecture, this kind of architecture confronts the mass movement of people around the world; people who need creative and responsible answers to a global phenomenon of displacement as a result of a variety of factors, from war to economic or political instability. As a political and social tool, architecture can and must engage in the crucial debate of housing displaced people around the world. It must concern itself with flows of migration, but also other kinds of temporal populations that have to accept a more nomadic condition in search of new working opportunities, such as students or itinerant workers, HOUSE 1 works of course within a privileged educational context, yet nonetheless adopts a very realistic approach, reflecting on how to operate in and for this contemporary condition of mass movement: How do we build, what are the urgent needs, what are the regulations, licenses, land status (public, private owned), where do the finances come from, who builds, what are the tools we use, and what do political contexts allow, accept, support and make possible in temporary solutions for nomadic populations? The university campus provides a first opportunity to think about this type of temporary intervention. HOUSE 1 considers the campus as a territorial sample, where the implementation of any kind of static architecture intervenes into the community of students and university staff. Placed in the immediate periphery of a central and emblematic building (The Rolex Learning Center designed by SANAA Architects) HOUSE 1 is ephemeral and fragile, being mounted and dismounted over a specific, and very short, timeline. It is more a scaffolding capable of producing space than a standard building.

Both in its completed form as well as throughout its construction, HOUSE 1 has continued to support a range of diverse activities.

Short-lived performances, for an external audience, breathe new life into the inert structure of HOUSE 1. They feature the constructors of the project as actors, engaged in a series of spatial explorations related to the programs proposed by the interventions.

Film projection on the facade. studio Baur.

Film projection on the facade. studio Baur.

Day of the performances. studio Rufer.

Performance of the studio Perez-Lupi. studio van der Woude.

Improvisation theatre show. studio Chassot.

Performance of the LC studio. studio Rufer.

Film records actions that take place in both time and space.

Storyboard of the film performance. studio del Grosso.

Drawings for a short animation film. studio Rufer.

Movements in a performance are described here by mapping a shifting point in space, contained by the three coordinate axes of the protostructure: x, y and z.

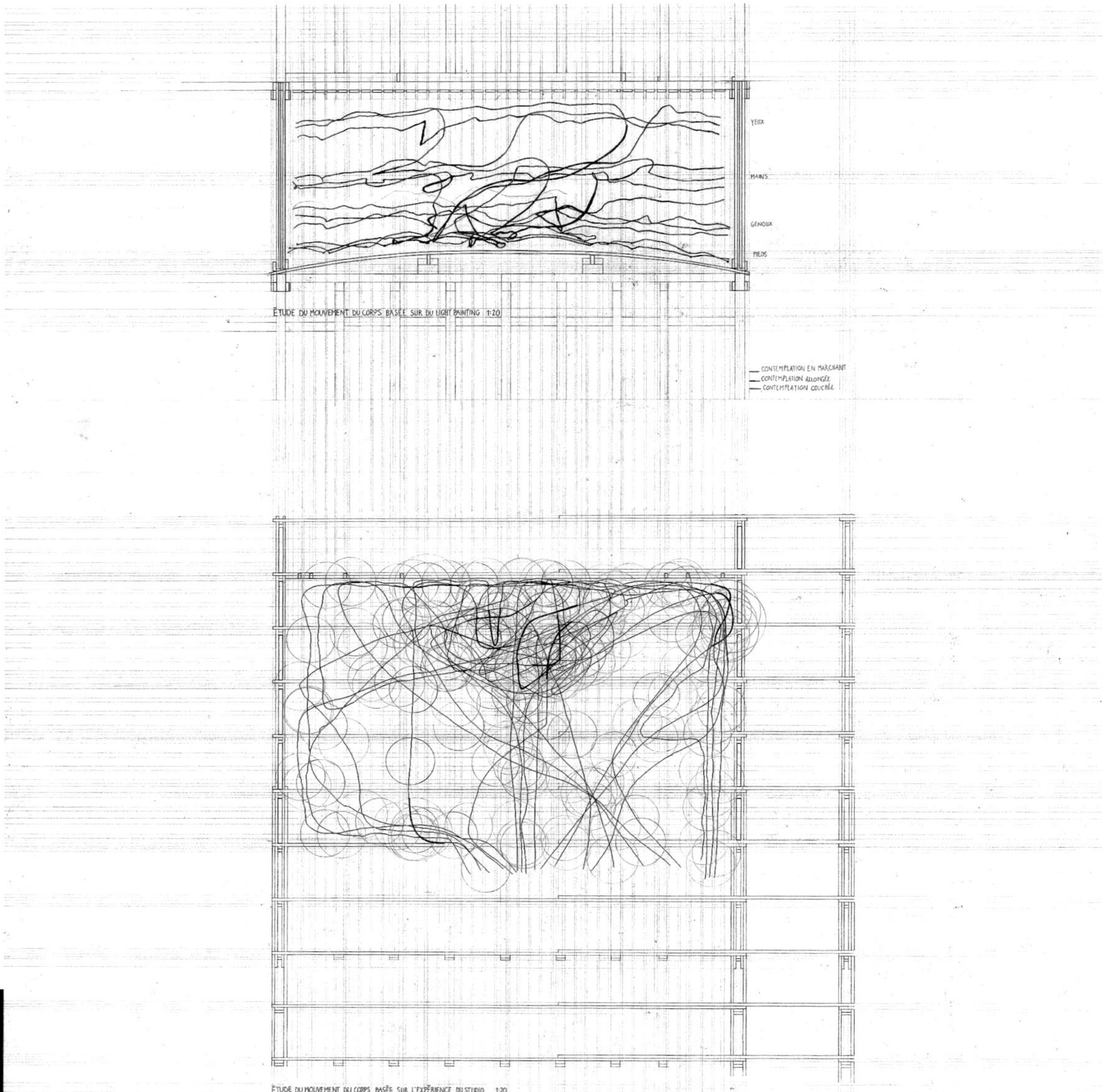

Various experiments with movement tracks, hand drawing. studio Perez-Lupi.

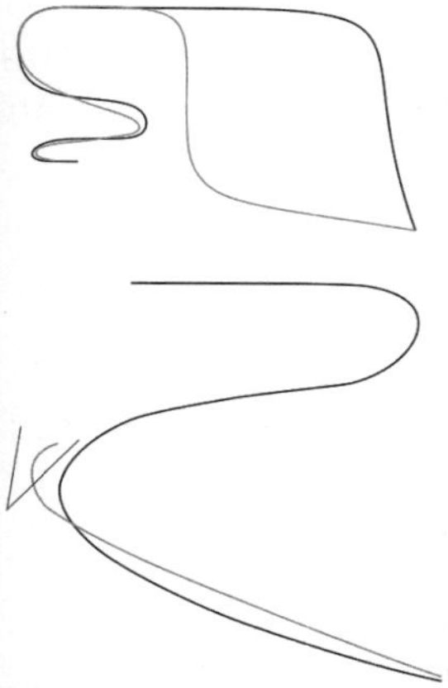

Scenarios of the performance with diagrammatic simplification of the movement course. studio Cabay/Dürr.

Use of light painting to trace movement. studio Perez-Lupi.

HOUSE 1 is a lightweight construction without buried foundations. In addition, it is a modular construction made up of identical basic parts. These properties allow HOUSE 1 to be mounted, dismounted, inhabited and transported easily and repeatedly, in cyclic phases.

P1-MONTAGE
- program: erection of the protostructure
- duration: 1 week

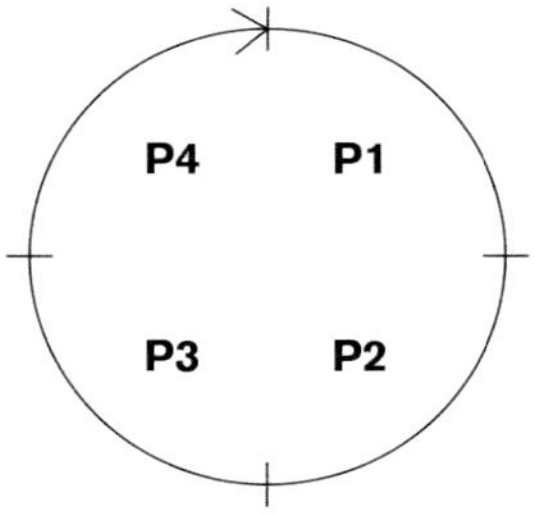

Schematic view of the 4 cyclic phases. Agathe Mignon.

First day of assembly. Wynd van der Wood.

Day 4. Wynd van der Wood.

Day 2. Wynd van der Wood.

Day 3. Wynd van der Wood.

Day 5. Wynd van der Wood.

P2-HABITATION

- program: construction of the 12 habitation interventions into the protostructure
- duration: 8 weeks

Final state of the inhabited structure. Dylan Perrenoud.

P3-DEMONTAGE
- program: dismantling of the whole construction / breaking down and storing of the elements of the protostructure and its interventions
- duration: 2 weeks

P4-TRANSPORT
- program: transportation of the constituent parts of the protostructure
- duration: varied

Dismantling of the protostructure. studio Chassot.

Departure of the dismantled structure. studio Chassot.

The transportable nature of HOUSE 1 allows it to be projected into other imaginary terrains. In these scenarios, HOUSE 1 confronts new landscapes and different territorial scales.

Whether transposed onto the top of a mountain or into the middle of a field, HOUSE 1 can adapt to the particular characteristics of any site, thanks to its movable foundations.

Transposition of HOUSE 1 to the top of a mountain, photomontage. studio del Grosso.

HOUSE 1 as seen on the horizon, photomontage. studio Perez-Lupi.

A single span of HOUSE 1 in the middle of a field, photomontage. studio Perez-Lupi.

HOUSE 1 undertakes voyages into new spatial and temporal landscapes.

A part of HOUSE 1 transposed to a mountain landscape, photomontage. studio Dürr.

Projection of a part of HOUSE 1 in the sky, photomontage. studio Dürr.

A part of HOUSE 1 behind ruins, photomontage. studio Dürr.

The projection of HOUSE 1 into different contexts and at different scales modifies the relationships established between body and structure, or between body and surrounding landscape.

Scaled transposition of HOUSE 1 into a planted landscape, photomontage. studio del Grosso.

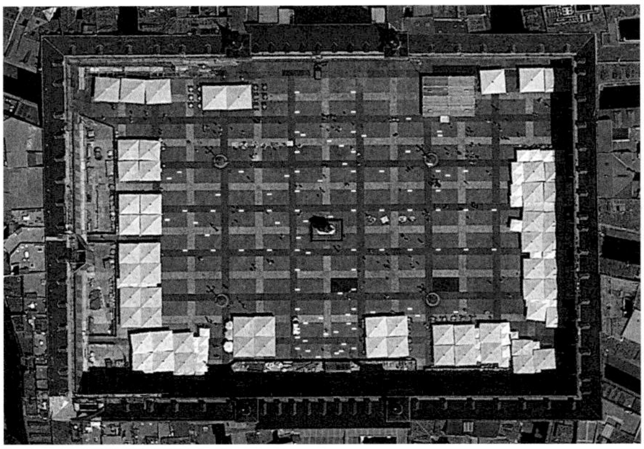

Transposition of HOUSE 1, enlarged x10, onto the Plaza Mayor in Madrid, photomontage. studio den Hartog.

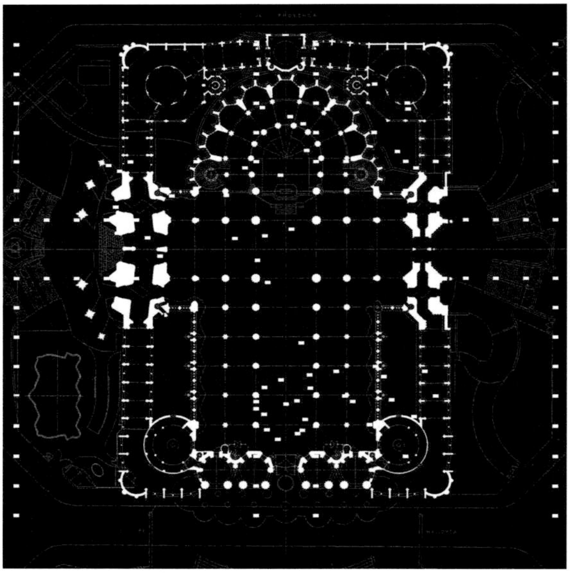

Transposition of HOUSE 1, enlarged x12, onto the ground of the Sagrada Famillia in Barcelona, photomontage. studio den Hartog.

Transposition of HOUSE 1, enlarged x73, in Central Park, photomontage. studio den Hartog.

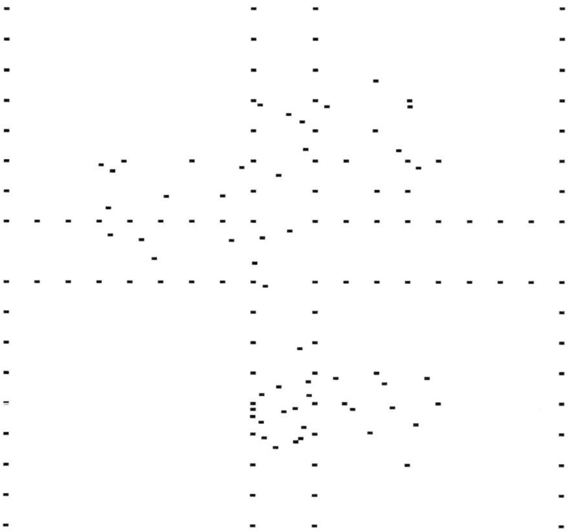

Floor plan of HOUSE 1, CAD drawing. studio den Hartog.

Cédric Libert
Architect ISALL March AADRL

Le Dodici Città Ideali: la prima città. Superstudio, 1971.

House 1 / 12 Cities, collective drawing. ENSA-Versaillles.

PROLOGUE – *I DODICI CITTà IDEALE*

For some reason, when I got contacted by Edouard Cabay – he was asking if, by any chance, the school of architecture in Versailles could be interested in receiving a structure built by students at the EPFL, a question which would be given a positive answer indeed – the number *Twelve* seemed an important issue. This being said in very practical terms against esoteric reasons: there were 12 ateliers to implement 12 interventions within a collective framework.

A text written by Superstudio in 1971 got back to my mind quite immediately: *I Dodici Città Ideale.* A great alibi to take on the issue of building something new with our 24 students. A fantastic way of engaging the present time in a critical manner with youngsters in their twenties. A surprise to exhume these seminal christmas tales and rediscover their profound understanding of nowadays paradoxical life as much as primary rituals or even archaic behaviours of humankind: a series of narrative that covers a long time span.

We quickly had a deal: students from Versailles would build another 12 interventions within the same framework – the protostructure. Each of which would echo one of the tales from Superstudio, drawing on visionary perspectives by Superstudio. A global idea of *exquisite corpse* with educational and constructive value. The beginning of an aventure that would last roughly 6 months, including a few trips back and forth, the dismantling of the structure and its actual reconstruction – even though different – in Versailles. Many questions, discussions and confrontations among students and teachers, either side.

At the beginning of october 2016, the structure was then rebuilt and we met for a conclusive session in Versailles – a panel of reflections and discussions, firstly on the heritage of radical architecture for today's young generations; and secondly, on experimental pedagogies, learning-by-doing methodologies and 1:1 constructive exercises. Among the very many interesting things that were told during this afternoon of talks in Versailles, I will recall one idea that describes our experience at best, from which I will also try underneath to further explore the richness in retrospect: *The Epic.*

The subsequent ideas behind the word *Epic* are those of multiplicity – across space and time. It is not one thing, neither is it a single moment. It can only be a series of phenomena instead of the univocal nature of a single element or condition.

Somehow it also appeared as a potential clue to try and give an answer to a couple of issues that emerged from the conversations in Versailles: Beyond its physical materiality, is it a model or a proper building that get constructed? Is the term *House* that qualify the initial swiss construction really appriopriate to its ontological reality? Does bricolage have a positive connotation in the realm of construction? Why does it seem so difficult to set up a clear political agenda for contestation today – in opposition to the revolutionary atmosphere of the 60/70's radical architecture?

In fact, the final built structure is only one of its multiple realities – all of which in return settle down its existence in the world, as a whole but complex and fragmented unity.

House 1 / 12 Cities chantier. ENSA-Versailles, ALICE studio.

FLASHBACK 01 – *MEDIEVAL CONSTRUCTION*

Versailles, Wednesday 31 august 2016
The structure consists of four small towers – to make it simple. Each of which – 11m high – was erected seperatly, one by one, from north to south. Every tower was built first from its own four facades, then the beams supporting the floors were mounted to liaise the towers together. Afterwards the surface of the floors was constructed, followed by the twelve interventions. Finally the bracing was assembled to ensure the overall stability of the structure. Everything in three weeks. No cranes nor lift, neither help of a load-carrier.

A few casual facts: every facade weights around 600 kgs. Needless to say it is very fragile and would break easily if not carried with homogenous distribution of forces. To flip it from one side to the other (for a practical reason of screwing elements together, for example), it needs 16 people and takes approximately 1/2h. The overall operation deserves a high level of coordination and orchestration. To lift up the facade vertically and place it on its final location, it then needs 24 students – most of them pushing and other pulling ropes across the wall of the school. Everyone synchonised.

FLASHBACK & FORWARD – *UBIQUITOUS EXISTENCE*

Anywhere, Anytime
At the same time that the structure was dismantled in Lausanne then rebuilt in Versailles, the existence of the project was already made effective. Selen was taking pictures and uploading them almost instantly on the Facebook page. I also remember Margaux setting up the webcam and creating a timelapse film of the ongoing construction.

Unlike many out-of-the-blue inventions that suddenly emerge, the process was already creating the conditions of its public appearance – somehow the creature of a very strange hybrid heritage Szeemanno-McLuhanian: *Attitude is the Message.*

Source: https://www.facebook.com/HOUSE 1alice

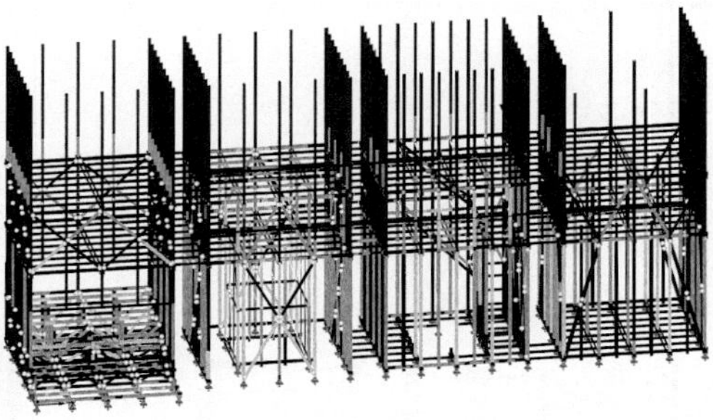

Structural model. Bollinger + Grohmann Ingenieur.

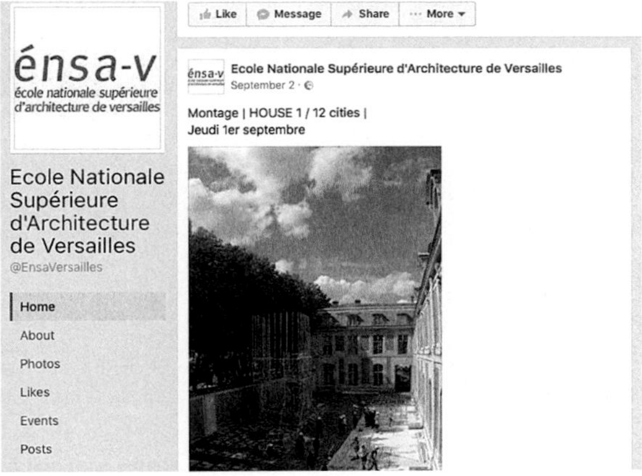

Source: https://www.facebook.com/EnsaVersailles

FLASHBACK 02 – *PAPER & SCREEN ARCHITECTURE*

Paris, tuesday 13 september 2016
To get the autorizations and allow people to visit the finalized construction, as well as for very prosaic gravitational reasons, we joined forces with engineers: the office of Bollinger + Grohmann in Paris. The time for construction itself being really short, we had to develop the overall structural approach in parallel to the ongoing construction. A reality check operation around-the-clock, between intuitive spontaneity and rationalisation *à-la-minute.*

Back & forth process between architecture and engineering is a very common way of reflecting upon meteorological or physical conditions and ensure the correct behaviour of the construction. But interestingly in this case, is the overpowering strenght of the *line* as a common language across imagination, reality and virtuality. The line being a simple piece of spruce wood – S: 100mm x 27mm x L: 5m. The distance between materiality and immateriality had never been so short.

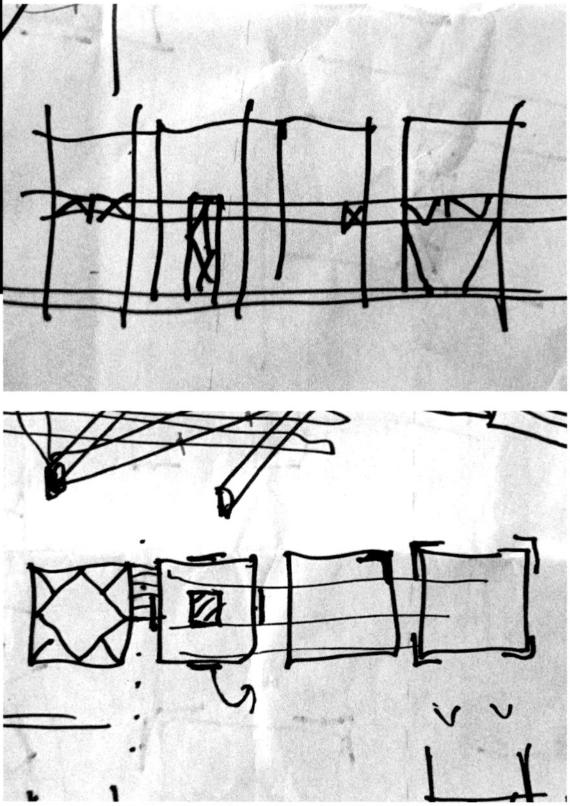

Paper tablecloth drawing. Klaas de Rycke, Cédric Libert.

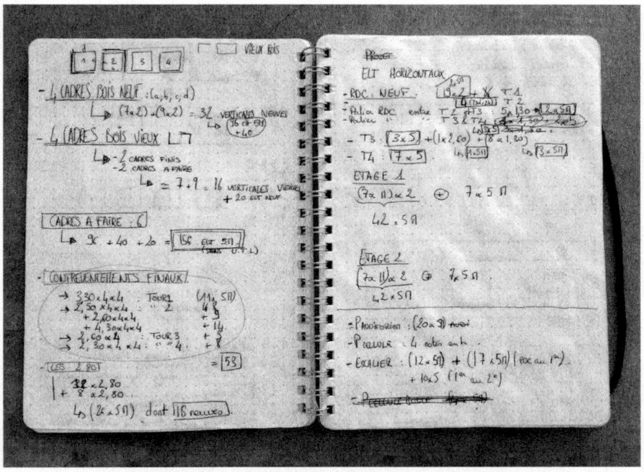

A bracing element in Tower 4. ENSA-Versailles, ALICE studio.

House 1 / 12 Cities chantier. ENSA-Versailles, ALICE studio.

FLASHBACK 03 – *ANALOGIC EXCEL NOTEBOOK*

Lausanne, Tuesday 23 august 2016 /
Versailles, Friday 9 sepember 2016
The collaborative nature of the project between swiss and french students is inherently related to recycle material and knowledge. How to re-build the entirety and where to re-use existing fragmented elements or leftover pieces? A wise protocole needed to be imagined to manage the move of about 500 wooden planks to a distance of 500 kms. Louise was in charge of organizing the storage, categorisation and numbering of the available stock. All of it, again, exploited in real time. Resulting in a strange notebook that reminds of an alchemist treaty.

EPILOGUE – *A PHOTOGRAPHIC DOCUMENTARY BY ANTOINE ESPINASSEAU*

(selection of 17 picures, without caption – credit Antoine Espinasseau)

CEDRIC LIBERT

Cédric Libert is a Belgian architect living in Brussels and Paris. After graduating from the Architectural Association in London, he was leading the collective Anorak, before practicing independently, teaching and curating. He contributed to the 14th Architectural Biennale in Venice, with a research project undertaken with l'AUC and Thomas Raynaud entitled 152 Mediterranea – presented in Monditalia. In December 2013, he curated Detour in Hong Kong – five ephemeral constructions in the heart of the public space. For the exhibition "Auguste Perret: Huit Chefs d'oeuvre!/?" curated by Joseph Abram and Rem Koolhaas OMA/AMO, he coordinated a studio with students from the ENSA-Versailles and presented À toutes fins utiles – a re-shaping of critical heritage inspired by the famous French architect. Cédric Libert has taught at ISA St-Luc Liège and ISACF la Cambre Brussels, l'Ecole d'Architecture de l'Université Laval in Québec as a Visiting Professor and l'Ecole Spéciale d'Architecture in Paris as an Associate Professor. He is currently Maitre-Assistant Associé at ENSA Versailles. He is also founding member of the fondazione Prada'sThought Council alongside Shumon Basar and Nicholas Cullinan.

INHABITATION CATALOGUE

C

Although it seemed to be a quite simple and feasible plan that I was going to put into action on that Wednesday, the 10th of August, it felt a little like embarking on a suicide mission when I drove off in my car a few minutes before nine in the morning. Again, it was a cloudy day as most of the days of that year had been so far. However, the weather app on my smartphone forecasted that it would clear up in the afternoon, and when I got on the motorway to Bern, I could already see some small stretches of blue on the western horizon.

Traffic was heavy, and I got stuck in a jam several times, which probably was one of the reasons why I didn't notice right away that I was being followed. Moreover, I was preoccupied with thinking things over and over again, pondering over the absurdity of my situation and over what I was going to do. It had been foreseeable for quite some time that, sooner or later, my assignment would lead to visiting and having to enter the real HOUSE 1, and most probably, my job would be completed for good by the end of the day. But it had not been foreseeable at all that I would have to do it without the slightest idea why and to what end I was doing it. Everything I knew about my mission was that I didn't – I just *couldn't* – believe what I was supposed to know about it for the simple reason that it was completely unbelievable. On the other hand, what I actually did believe was that a story as outrageous as this one could not be brought to an end just like that. After all, it was me who had to bring it to an end, this was me driving to Lausanne that morning with the MSDT device on the passenger seat of my Renault Mégane Berline, and as far as I could remember I had never played a part in a story with a simple dead-heat happy ending before. It just wasn't my style.

A whole five months had gone by since that memorable Sunday afternoon in March when Adrienne had told me her story while we had had lunch together in a noisy restaurant full of the usual ordinary people at the Zurich main station. It had been perfectly obvious why she had chosen this particular place for this particular meeting: The story was so grotesque, so absolutely unacceptable and out of touch that I most certainly would have freaked out if we hadn't been surrounded by this blatant atmosphere of normality. The creepiest thing about the situation had been that Adrienne had told me a *whole* story for a change, a story with a beginning and an ending that were more or less logically connected, and however implausible and outrageous it was, it did not only seem to explain everything, it also was pretty much in line with what I had come to understand about the HOUSE 1 project the day before.

"You cannot possibly expect me to believe all this crap!" I had said, and it was about the only comment I could make after trying to come to grips with everything.

I will never forget that strange sad smile on Adrienne's disfigured face when she had replied: "No, I can't. But with regard to what you're supposed to do, it does not matter whether you believe me or not, does it?"

No, of course it didn't. It never had, and it never would. –

However, there had been one detail in her account that could not be deemed sheer nonsense. She had claimed that the MSDT device was a prototype that had been stolen on the behest of her client from a SYNTHESIS INTERNATIONAL developmental laboratory in Finland a year ago, and there was enough evidence to support that part of her story. After we had returned to my apartment, she had opened the device casing and showed me an engraved three-digit serial number and the SYNTHESIS logo on the inside. The three-digit serial number strongly implied that the device in fact was a prototype, and, among other things, it explained why somebody – presumably SYNTHESIS agents – would have broken into my apartment to steal it back. But this comparatively trivial industrial espionage part of it had not made her story any more credible in its entirety, of course. On the contrary, it had made it all look even more far-out, and my investigations had not brought about any trace of a possible connection between the HOUSE 1 project and the biggest entertainment technology company in the world. And I *knew* that I would have found it if there had been any trace of a connection at all. Moreover, as it turned out, no further attempt had been made to get hold of the device or to approach me in any hostile way until that Wednesday in August.

Since I didn't know what to believe anymore, I thought it best to turn to the technical side of the matter. Perfectly aware that I hardly had anything to tell that Adrienne had not known all along, I explained what had occurred to me after my awful hallucinations the day before. I had realised that the proto-structure of HOUSE 1 was stable and patterned enough to be conceived of as a potential although quite unwieldy data carrier. Theoretically, it was possible that the pattern contained encoded information or that there could exist an applicable media technology to transfer the data from a codifying system to the structure and vice versa. And, of course, the MultiCom Sensorama Data Transfer system was not only an applicable technology, it actually was the one and only imaginable technology by which the data transfer could possibly be accomplished. However, according to this adventurous but not quite absurd theory, the information would be transferred from a living neural system to dead matter, from the human brain to the pattern of the proto-structure and back again, meaning that its viral potential was completely unpredictable because, evidently, there was no way to control or contain the communicative activities of a nervous system that, knowingly or unknowingly, carried the information. Thus, in combination with the MSDT technology, the proto-structure could have been a perfect means to save and spread information in a most improbable and almost undetectable way.

As expected, there was no need to convince Adrienne of all this. She more or less had known or been assuming all that from the very beginning, and, of course, I would never have taken her seriously if she had told me before I had become aware of all the facts.

During the following weeks I had carried out tests with rendered 3D models of the HOUSE 1 proto-structure, trying to hardcode various encrypted data onto it. It wasn't that much of a surprise that it actually worked. But the amount of information that could be transferred to the relatively rudimentary pattern of the structure was extremely small. It didn't exceed the capacity of a few hundred kilobytes. Nevertheless, if these kilobytes were used to save the script of a simple program that was compatible with the MSDT device, the potential capacity was virtually unlimited, which could be quite easily verified when I did the very same tests again with the device in operation.

This had been the beginning of a new and rather different phase of training sessions. I had started to extend my experiments to actually entering the rendered models with the aid of the SPACE MAKER application. After a while, I was able to successfully transfer various amounts of encoded information from my mind to the spatial pattern of the proto-structure and back again, and I gradually got more and more efficient. Remarkably enough, my capabilities of applying the MSDT technology while staying completely aware of my real surroundings increased without causing any further psychotic effects on me. I neither had to face any more ugly bubbles nor any other unworldly or supernatural things any longer. In fact, by the beginning of July, I could manage to stay focused on my tasks for over two hours without interrupting or quitting the programme run. My best result was to save the whole content of a celebrity magazine issue on the proto-structure in one consecutive session including all of the illustrations.

Meanwhile, the students at the École polytechnique féderal in Lausanne had finished the actual construction of HOUSE 1. Since I had been focusing on other tasks than the observation of their progress lately, I was not quite up to date in that respect anymore. However, when Adrienne showed me the photos she had downloaded from the students' blogs, the setup of the real building deeply impressed me. I immediately proceeded to test whether my methods were also applicable to 3D models of the entire HOUSE 1. It was a whole lot of work, but it was amazingly successful.

Adrienne had already set the day on which I was to put my recently acquired capabilities into practice. I was supposed to drive to Lausanne on the 10th of August to find out whether the real

HOUSE 1 actually was or could be used as a data carrier. And if so, I was supposed to decrypt the respective information. Of course, I had never expected that I would find out *anything* of the sort. And I still didn't. It was all mere theory to me.

After I had passed Bern, traffic decreased significantly, and so I finally noticed the black Ford cross country vehicle that remained behind me at a constant distance, although I broke the speed limit and slowed down again several times. It didn't necessarily mean that it was following me, but I had to make sure. I turned off at the *Rose de la Broye* motorway services and parked directly in front of the main entrance to the shopping area, keeping the motor running. The black Ford took the same exit and turned in at the next row of parking lots. Though the windows were tinted I could make out three people. The driver was an Asian looking woman wearing a leather jacket, and the man in the backseat seemed to be the spitting image of the guy who had shadowed me at *Ninotchka's*. Obviously, they didn't try very hard to keep out of my sight.

By now, I had assumed a somewhat fatalistic attitude towards the troubles and inconveniences that had come along with this job. For a moment, I considered getting out of the car and having a cup of coffee at the stand-up bar to give them a chance to get in touch with me. Most probably, they knew what I was up to anyway, and as long as I was in a crowded area like this, they wouldn't do me much harm, I assumed. On the other hand, if they actually were after me, it was a perfect opportunity to shake them off for a while. So I turned up the volume of the audio player, stepped on the gas and headed for the motorway access at full speed with the blasting sound of *Rattle and Hum* in my ears. They had no chance to turn around and follow me straight away. Whatever they did, I didn't spot that black Ford again until I arrived at the EPFL campus in Lausanne just before noon. I drove into the car park of the *Starling Hotel*, which was perfectly situated between the lake and the southern border of the campus area. From there, it was only a five-minute walk.

HOUSE 1 had been constructed on a small meadow next to the *Rolex Learning Center* on the south-east corner of the campus, which was not very crowded due to the semester vacation. Having approached the site from the west, I sat down on a park bench to look at it from a distance for a while.

It felt rather strange to suddenly see the house standing there as a real building after having visited it so many times in the form of computer graphics. At first sight, since it was mainly built of wooden slats and had no solid walls, it gave the impression of a huge architectural model. At the same time it was a very sophisticated construction of accessible rooms and fascinating spatial configurations that seemed to accomplish many mysterious but also quite specific purposes that I had never acknowledged before even though I had thought I had known the construction inside out. On the whole, it reminded me of a monstrous ship that had been dreamt up by a fanciful visionary and run aground at this place for unknown reasons. Its overall appeal was definitely mythical.

The house was enclosed with a security fence, probably to protect it from vandalism. Fortunately, the small gate on the north side was open, and assuming that I was still being followed, I had every reason to start right away with what I had come here for. But I couldn't. There were two men on the site. A tall young guy was standing at the gate, handling a photo camera on a tripod. With his long hair, his three-day stubble, his careless clothing and the high-brow glasses he looked very much like Peter Fonda trying to disappear into the crowd at the Newport Folk Festival. The other one stood on the roof platform carrying a DV cam bag on a shoulder strap and jotting something down on a notepad. He was at my age, had a clean-shaven head and wore a black suit with bell-bottomed trousers. They seemed to be here for professional reasons, and I could not think of any convincing excuse in case they demanded an explanation of my joining them with my eminently fancy technical equipment. I had no choice but to wait until they left.

An hour later, just as I was beginning to get a little nervous, they packed up all their gear and walked towards the *Rolex Center*. They didn't bother to close the gate, so, whatever they had in mind, they might be back soon. I had to work fast.

I slipped through the gate and stepped onto the tilted platform that led up to the entrance of HOUSE 1 and had been referred to as "Le parvis" in the construction plans. I uncased the MSDT device, started it up, and put on the headset. When I went through the swing door, I thought that I felt a strange movement at my feet like from a small furry animal. I looked down onto the wooden floor, and, of course, there was nothing to be seen.

I made towards the staircase, trying to stay focussed on the spatial structures around me, just as I had done every time I had entered the 3D models. In the meantime, the clouds had cleared away, and the house was drenched with sunlight. I went up the stairs and past the two rooms at the head of it, "La machine" and "The Garden of Panoptic D-lights". Nothing happened. All I could perceive was the simple reality of the timber construction. However, when I reached the tripartite door at the end of the east-west corridor on the first floor, another strange sensation struck me. At first, I thought it was an optical illusion caused by the rays of sunlight that fell through the gaps between the slats. But it wasn't. All of a sudden, I was surrounded with countless transparent layers filled with literally infinite lines of code. It took me some time to realise that the code on the foremost layers consisted of endless variations of the four letters A, C, G, and U, occasionally intermitted by multi-digit numbers and punctuation characters. The code sequences in the background looked different, but I couldn't really concentrate on them. They were all over the place, and they were constantly changing. The whole interior of the house seemed to be filled with code.

That was far beyond anything I could have possibly expected, and, helplessly trying to keep my nerve, I started mumbling to myself: "It's all in your mind! Pull up your socks, dude, you *know* that it's all in your mind!"

ELEVATION MAP WEST

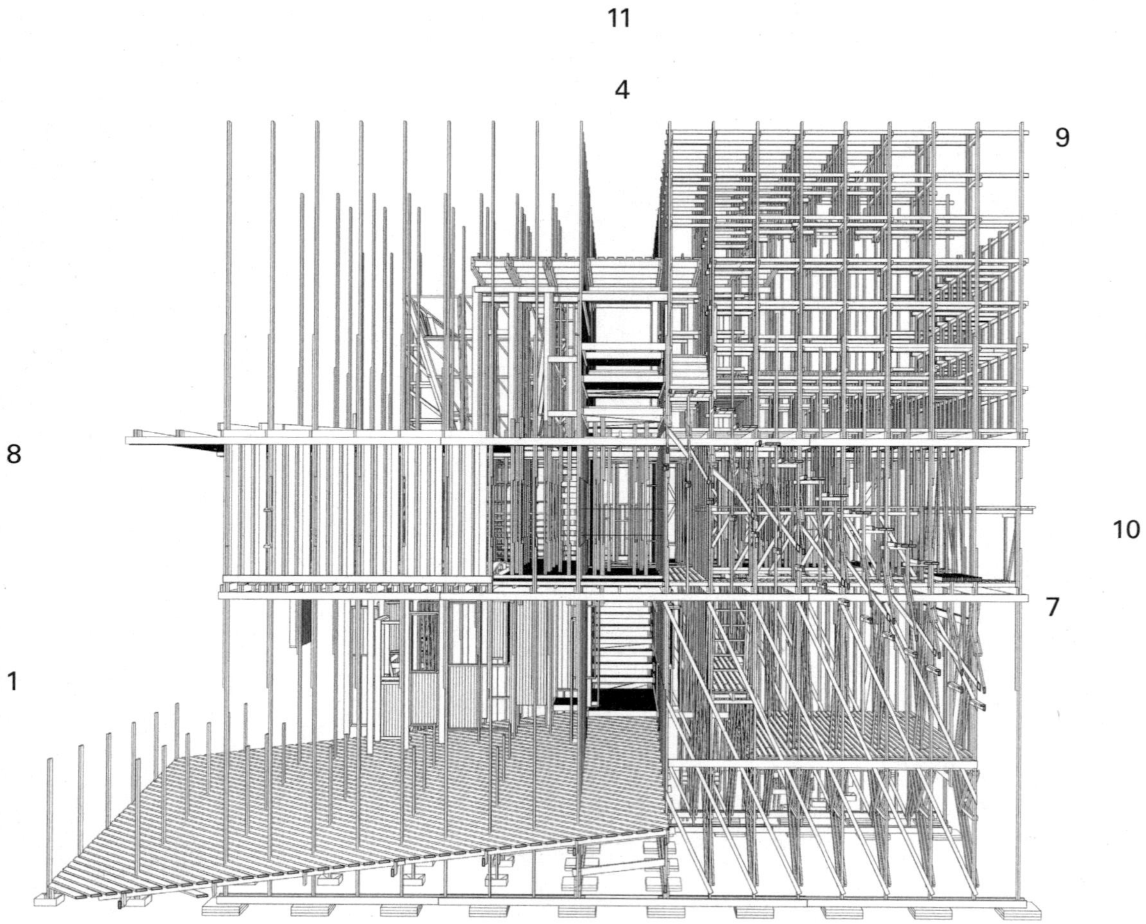

ELEVATION MAP NORTH

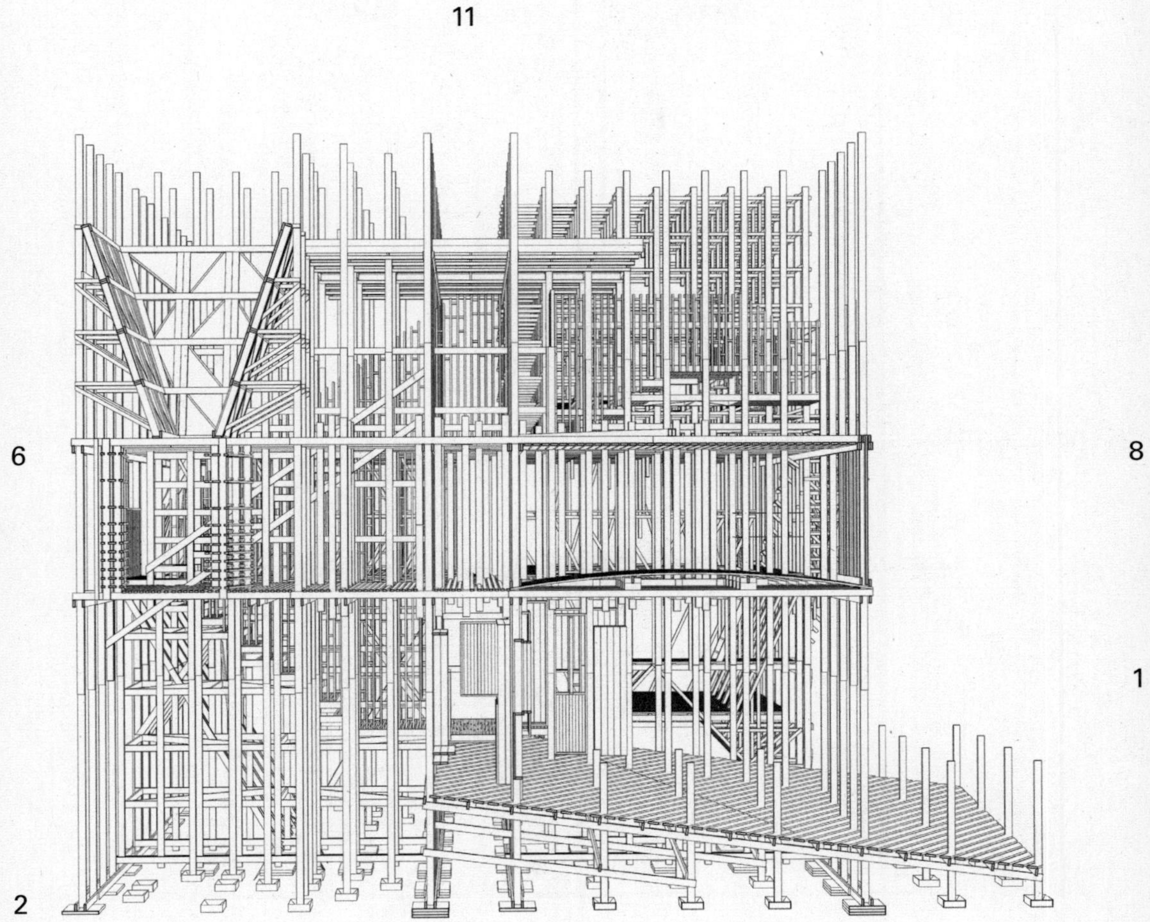

1	The Forecourt	8	The Bed Room
2	The Pond of Self-Reflection	9	The Cave of Emptiness
4	The Stairwell	10	The Shadow Stairs
6	The Skygarden Room	11	The Roof
7	The Theatre		

ELEVATION MAP EAST

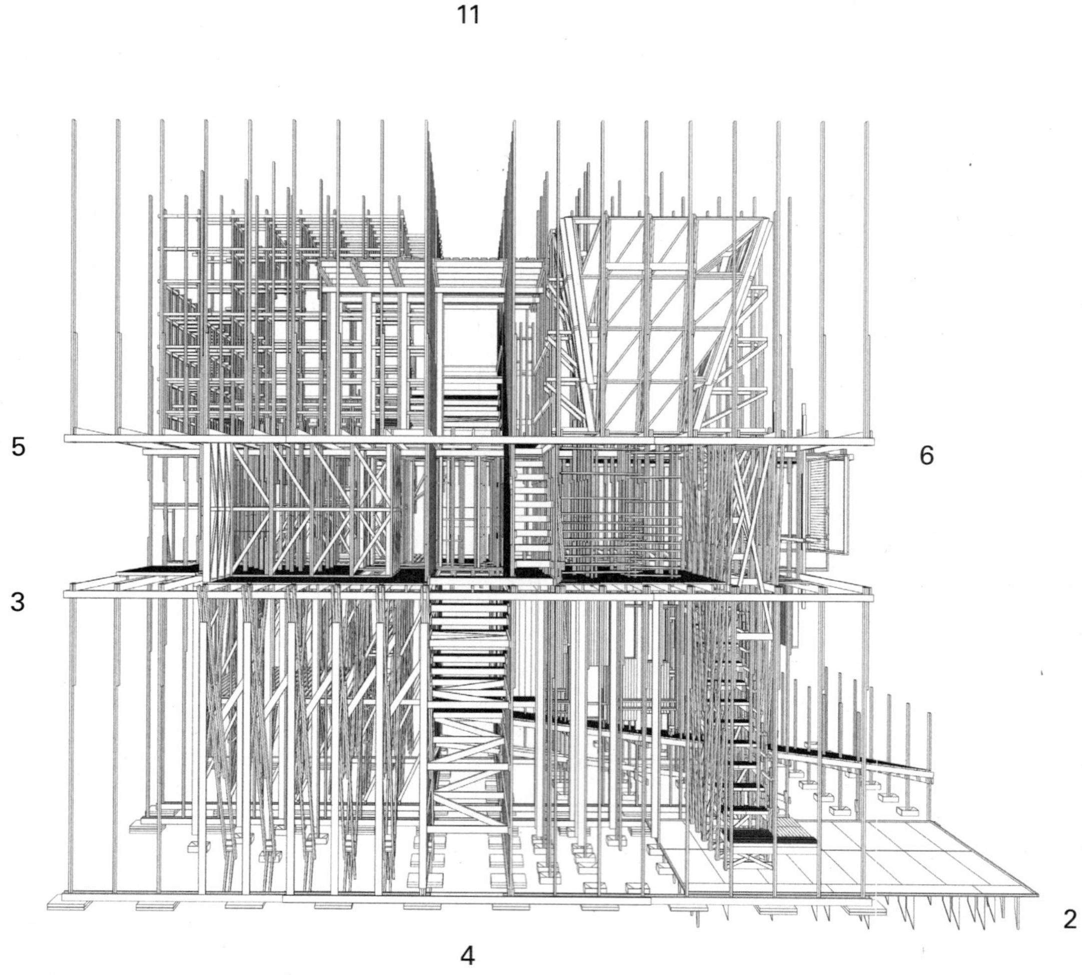

ELEVATION MAP SOUTH

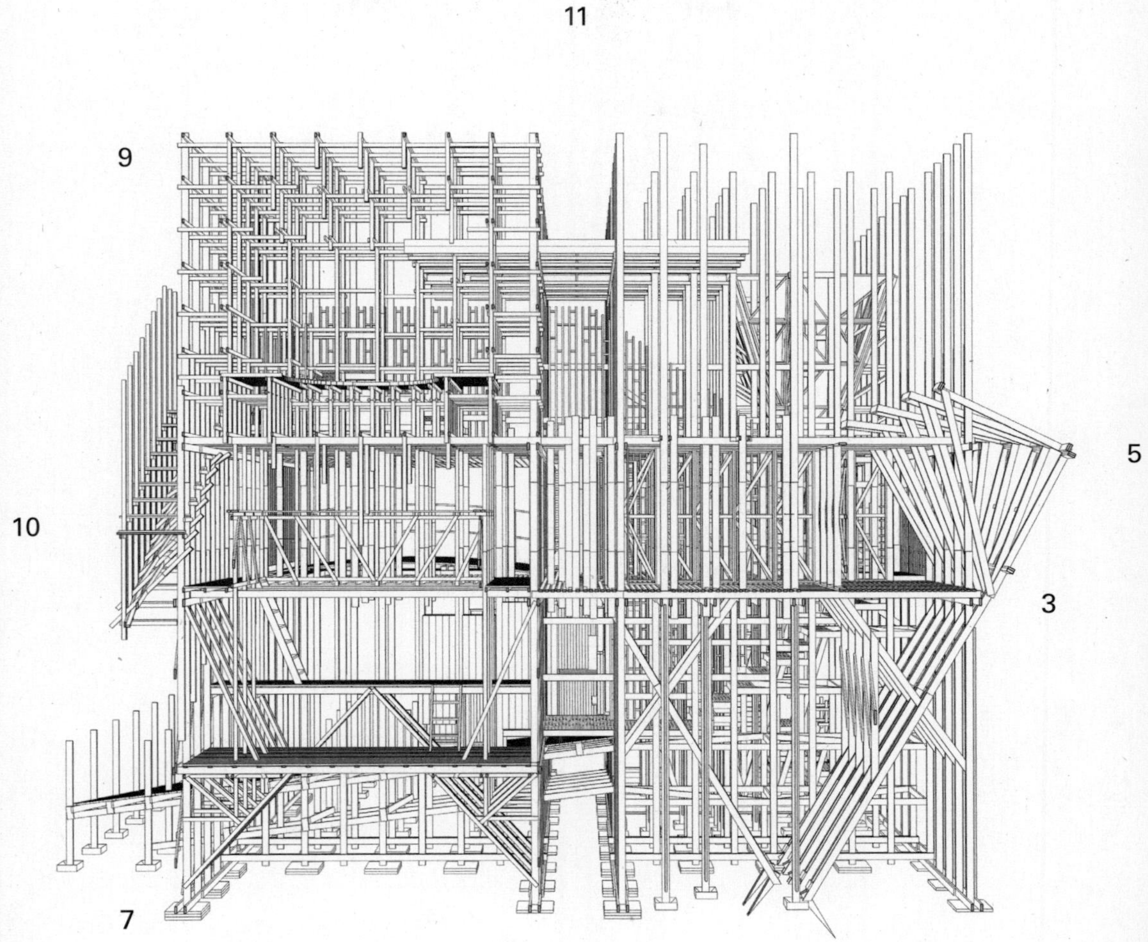

2 The Pond of Self-Reflection
3 The Forest Room
4 The Stairwell
5 The Machine Room
6 The Skygarden Room
7 The Theatre
9 The Cave of Emptiness
10 The Shadow Stairs
11 The Roof

THE GROUND FLOOR

1GCugugcacauguauaauguaugcpuagccauugcaaaugcaugugcuacugcaaccaucaugcauguaagcagccaugugaccauguauaugcauacacguguagcuac-
caaacguaugGugguguaagucaaguuaaucgGUAuaaugauacgucauugcauguauaugcaugcaagcucgacgaGUuacguGugguugcuaaacguacgucaugauga-
caugucga'CAUGugucauaugcaugcugcauuaacauacugcugcaagccaugcauugcuauauacgccauguauagaugcguuagcuu2CAUguauaugcaugcaag-
caugauacgucauugcauguauaauguaugcpuagccauucgacgaUGCAuacaacauguaacauacugcuuaccauacugcugcacauguauacauugcuauaauguacgc-
cauguauagaugcguuagcucga3cgucauGugguguuacguaugacaugucgaCAUGugucauaugcaugcugcauuaacauacugcuuaccauacugcugcacauguaua-
cauugcuauacauguaacauuacauguacgccauguauacauacguguacguuaugaccauguauagaugcguuagcucgaagcgucaugugucauaugcaugcugcaucauu-
gucguauaccauucgaugugccauguguugcauacacguacguguuacuaaucg4CAUGuguugcauacacguacgugcugcaucuaugccauauacgcacgucaugguuacu-
aucgacauguauaauguaugcpuagccauaugauacgucauugcauguauaugcaugcaagcaucg5ACugugcGugguuacggcugugcaaugcauguaacauugcagu-
auagccauguguuaacauacugcugcauaccaucauguguugcuacauguaaugugcauacacguacgucguaugpuagcuaguucgaagcgucauguguugcauacacguac-
gucguaacguuacuacguaGugguucgauacggcugugcauacgcggugugguagcguuagcuauacacguaucgcga6UGCAguauagccauguauaugcaugcaagcaugaug-
cacauguaacaucauguauaacugcuuaccauugaccauguauacauugcuaua[ugacuacggcugugcaacguuaguguaugcaaaggugugguacugugcacugugguag-
cgupacguuaaauguacgcgcauugcauguauauacauguaucgaagcguaacguaugugguuaauguacugcacgacguuaacugugcgauacgcuacgcgugcauacauggu-
ugcaucgaaugguauacauuguguacgaugugcauaagcguacauuauaccauaucgAUGguauaaacguauguggagcuauaaugugcauacauugguauaugcguauaug-
cgagcguucgaugcaguaugugcaaaugugcauaccauguaguauaugcucgaagcguguauaacauuauaccauaucg7CAUguauagccauguauauacauguaaugugac-
cgugcauguaugaccauguauacaugcauaugcuaugpuagcuaguucgaagcgucauguauacaugugcuaaacguuaccguuagucauguauacaugugcauaugcuag-
cauacguagu;augugcauguauacaugauguaugcauaguacuacgacguuaagcuauaaugcauugguacauguauaugcagcgucaaguuacuggcuauaugcuacg-
cgaugacugugccauguauacaauguaacgugcuauaaugaucg8CAUguauagccauguauacaagcagcguguauacaugugcauacacuaguauaaugcgucauguauaau-
gugugcguugacGugguaaugGUAuaugcaaaugugcaaacguuacguacgcguacgccauguauagaugcguuagcuacgccauguauacugugacguugaccauguauagua-
caugucgaagcgucauguauacaugguauacguacugcugcaGugguacauggcgcauguauacauugcuauaaugugaccauguauagaugcguuagcaucg9CGucauGug-
gucaacguacguuagucauugcauguauacaagcucgacgaUGCAguauaugcuaaugcuacauguguuucga10GUAuaagcaugugcauaugcuaguucgacgaUACgu-
auaaugcgucauguguuacgccauguauagaugcguuagcucgaagcguUACugcaaaugaacugcauacgucguacauauguaUACugcaaauggcauacguagu;augu-
gUACguauacguaucgcga11AgcguGUAuaaugauacguucgacgaUGCAguaugcauugacgugucaugugucauguaacaucauguguugcauaugcuag-
cauacguaguuuGUAagcuauacauguguuaacauuagcacugcugcacauguauacauugcuauacauguaacauUACcugcacaagcguuagucaugugugcugcauca-
uuguaacauacugcugcauucga12CAUguauacaagcaugauacguucgacgaCAUguauaugcaugcaagccaugugupucauguauaugcuaugcauaccauguacauaaug-
guauagagcuauacauaaugugcauaacugcuuaccauacugcugcacauguauacauugcuauaucgaagcguUACacauuauaccauaucgcga13CAUguauagcGuggu-
augauacgucauugcauguauaugcaugcaagcucgacgaUGCAguaacauuacaugcauguauacaugcauguguguaagcuauaguuggcuauucgaCAUguauaugcaug-
caagcaugauacguucgacgaCAUguauaauguaugcpuagccauguuacuauacgcuauagucauaucgaagcguUACacauuaaucgcga14AUGugGugguaugauac-
gucauugcauguauaauguaugcpuagccauucgacgaCGuacauauguacauguguguaagcuauaguuggcuacauguauacaugucgacuugcauguaguaugcuacau-
guguacguggcuauaaacguacguacguuacgcuauaaugcauugcuacgagcguaacguacguugcauacacguguagcuaccaaacguaugguaCAUGuguugcauacacguac-
gucugcaugcaacguuggccauguguugccguaacguacgucaugagcgucauguguugcauacacguacguuaacauguuaugcauaacguacgucauguauaguacaugau-
gugaccauguguugcacguuacacuaaucg15AgcguUACugcauacacguacgupucauuagccauaccaucaugcguacauugcauauagccauguguagcgucauguau-
augcaugcaagcucgaagcgucguacauugcauauagccauguguugcugacacaugpugcuacgcgagcguguauaugcaug;guauaugcauacacguacgucugcuauggu-
acauguguugcguauaaguucgaagcgucauguguugcauacacguacguaugcauugcuacuacguaguauacaugguauauaacguaucgcga16CAUugcauguauaug-
caugcaagcGUAuaaugauacguucgacgaUACugcauacacguacgucaauacguacauguguugcpauacgcauguacgccguauacacgugucguaaugcuacgcggcu-
auaugccaugauguagcuauaugcua;ugcauaccauguapauacgcacuacguacguacguguugccauguguugcauacacguacguacgcuauacguacugccauguaca-
uugcguauacacguguugcuagcaucgCAUGuguugcguuaauguacugcuaugcauacacguacgucguaacugugccauguguugcguauaugcgagcguucgaagcgu-
guauaugcauacacguacguugcuacguuauggcuauaugccauguguaucgcga17CAUugAguacaGUAuaaugauacguucgacgaCGuacauauguacauguguacguua-
caugcauuagcuagucauugcauguguugcugcauacacuaagcguacauuaacugcuuaccauacugcugcacauguauacauugcuauaacgugucauugcaguauaccgu-
aUACcugcacaagcguuagucauguguucga'CAUGugucauaugcaugcugcauuaacauacugcugcauaccauucga'cuugcauguaguuacaugcauguauagugcu-
gugcgucguacauauguaugaccaugugu;cauguaugcugugguapauacgcacuacgucauuguacacgucauguguugcauacacguacguuaacauacugugguacugcug-
cauaccauaacguacgucauguauaguacaugaugugaccauguguugcacguuacacuaaucg18UACcauugcauacacguacgupugcugguucuacauguaugugcgcau-
gagcgucauguauacaugcauacguuaaugacugugccauguguucgaagcgucauguguugcauacacguacguuaacaucauguauapacguagccauaugugaccaugu-
auaacuacuaacguguaucg19CGcaugcauguauaaugugcauaacauugaccauguguugccgugcugugcacauguguugcauacacguacguuaacaucauguguugcacu-
gugguugccauuacacgucauguguugcuacauuugcgccauugcauguauagugcugugcguucgaauguacgccuaacugcugcauaccaucauguguugcauaugcuacau-
auacguagc;acugugcguuaugcaucauguguaugcuaagcgucauugguuaugcaucauguguugcauacacguacguugcuacauuugcgcaucgcga20Aguacagca-
cauaguguauacaugugcauacacuaUAgcuauaucgacguacauauguaaugguauaugcauguacgugucguacugcauacauguauacaugcauguauaugcugacaacguac-
gucauguauaacguuacgcuauacgcgaucg21GuggucaaguuagaugccauagccauaugugacauguacguacgcacugugcAguacaagcguguauacaugugcauacac-
uaagcgucacguugcauguauagucauguauacaaucg22AgcguGugguaugauacguucgacgaCAUguauacaagcguaaauggcugugcacguacugcauaacguuac-
uacguauggcuaugacuaugucgauacggcugugcauacgcggugugguagcguuagcuauacacguaucgGUAuacauaugcaugcugcaucguaaacguacguugugcaua-
gucauugugcuaacguaugucauguauacaugguaagcguagcgucauauacguaaacguaugugacugcugcacauguauacauugcuauaugacuacauuaugcg-
caacguacguuacacuaagcguuaacauucgaagcguacguuacgcuauaacugugcuagcuauaugcaucgcga23AUGugGuggucgagcuacaugguauaguguauac-
caacugcugcacauguauaGaugcguuagcugacUAguuagccauugugcaugugcuacgcauguauagugcugugcguacugcugcaugcaguauaccguaguauaguaagu-
cguauagccauauacguagcaucg24AaccauuaugcGUAuaguugcuggcuauacauguauacaagcugucauucgaguauapacguacuaguuggccauguauauaaaug-
cauauguacguuaugaccauguauaGaugcguuagcugacUAguuagccguauaugcucguaccaagcguaacacguacauacgcgaugugcaugugcguacacguaauggu-
auacgcgcgacuacgagcguacugugccauguacauugguaugcgucauguauaugcaacaugcauugcauguauacauugcuauaugacuacauuaugcgcaacguacguua-
cacuaaucg1GCugugcacauguauaauguaugcpuagccauugcaaaugcaugugcuacugcaaccaucaugcauguaagcagccaugugaccauguauaugcauacacgu-
guagcuaccaaacguaugGugguguaagucaaguuaaucgGUAuaaugauacgucauugcauguauaugcaugcaagcucgacgaGUuacguGugguugcuaaacguacgu-
caugaugacaugucga'CAUGugucauaugcaugcugcauuaacauacugcugcaagccaugcauugcuauauacgccauguauagaugcguuagcuu2CAUguauaugcaug-
caagcaugauacgucauugcauguauaauguaugcpuagccauucgacgaUGCAuacaacauguaacauacugcuuaccauacugcugcacauguauacauugcuauaauguacgc-
cauguauagaugcguuagcucga3cgucauGugguguuacguaugacaugucgaCAUGugucauaugcaugcugcauuaacauacugcuuaccauacugcugcacauguaua-
cauugcuauacauguaacauuacauguacgccauguauacauacguguacguuaugaccauguauagaugcguuagcucgaagcgucaugugucauaugcaugcugcaucauu-
gucguauaccauucgaugugccauguguugcauacacguacguguuacuaaucg4CAUGuguugcauacacguacgugcugcaucuaugccauauacgcacgucaugguuacu-
aucgacauguauaauguaugcpuagccauaugauacgucauugcauguauaugcaugcaagcaucg5ACugugcGugguuacggcugugcaaugcauguaacauugcagu-
auagccauguguuaacauacugcugcauaccaucauguguugcuacauguaaugugcauacacguacgucguaugpuagcuaguucgaagcgucauguguugcauacacguac-
gucguaacguuacuacguaGugguucgauacggcugugcauacgcggugugguagcguuagcuauacacguaucgcga6UGCAguauagccauguauaugcaugcaagcaugaug-
cacauguaacaucauguauaacugcuuaccauugaccauguauacauugcuaua[ugacuacggcugugcaacguuaguguaugcaaaggugugguacugugcacugugguag-
cgupacguuaaauguacgcgcauugcauguauauacauguaucgaagcguaacguaugugguuaauguacugcacgacguuaacugugcgauacgcuacgcgugcauacauggu-
ugcaucgaaugguauacauuguguacgaugugcauaagcguacauuauaccauaucgAUGguauaaacguauguggagcuauaaugugcauacauugguauaugcguauaug-
cgagcguucgaugcaguaugugcaaaugugcauaccauguaguauaugcucgaagcguguauaacauuauaccauaucg7CAUguauagccauguauauacauguaaugugac-
cgugcauguaugaccauguauacaugcauaugcuaugpuagcuaguucgaagcgucauguauacaugugcuaaacguuaccguuagucauguauacaugugcauaugcuag-
cauacguagu;augugcauguauacaugauguaugcauaguacuacgacguuaagcuauaaugcauugguacauguauaugcagcgucaaguuacuggcuauaugcuacg-
cgaugacugugccauguauacaauguaacgugcuauaaugaucg8CAUguauagccauguauacaagcagcguguauacaugugcauacacuaguauaaugcgucauguauaau-
gugugcguugacGugguaaugGUAuaugcaaaugugcaaacguuacguacgcguacgccauguauagaugcguuagcuacgccauguauacugugacguugaccauguauagua-
caugucgaagcgucauguauacaugguauacguacugcugcaGugguacauggcgcauguauacauugcuauaaugugaccauguauagaugcguuagcaucg9CGucauGug-
gucaacguacguuagucauugcauguauacaagcucgacgaUGCAguauaugcuaaugcuacauguguuucga10GUAuaagcaugugcauaugcuaguucgacgaUACgu-

1

The Forecourt

AHBAR, THE BLACK WATCHMAN

Most of the time, the Forecourt is a quiet place. When sitting or standing there you won't hear a sound from inside the House because your senses are drawn towards the surroundings. You can see the bush-lined banks of the Great Northern River and the majestic snow-capped mountains in the south. You can hear the singing of the winds, the rustle of the eastern woods, the whispering of the prairies and the fields to the west, and if you listen closely, you can hear the vibration of a deep D flat undertone running through the wooden floor and the sounds of all kinds of animals from afar. They seldom come near the House during daytime, but Ahbar, the Black Watchman, knows that they are always watching it from the distance where the human eye can't reach. However, the more dangerous and venturesome among them dare to come closer at night sometimes, and that is why he never sleeps when it is dark. He only takes naps in the early afternoon hours.

Ahbar is born under the sign of Aries in the year of the Buffalo at the hour of the Tiger. He has been chosen to guard the entrance of the House because he has the sharpest of eyes, the most sensitive of ears, and the most delicate of olfactory senses. His body is taller, stronger, tougher, and more agile than that of any other man that has ever inhabited the House. His skin is ebony black so that the enemies can hardly see him when they try to approach him under cover of night, and so is his knee-length cloak with the holy insignia of courage and bravery woven in the sleek cloth with silk thread in the dark red colour of dried blood.

He has lived here for as long as he can remember and he could not think of a better place to live than the Forecourt. Interiors make him feel constrained. They adversely affect his sense of freedom. Apart from that, the Forecourt is built exactly as he wants it to be: it provides a comprehensive view of the terrain in three directions, the wooden poles and the inclination of the floor are just perfect for diversionary movements under attack, and the sheltered part at the back is perfectly dimensioned as a retreat zone to hold the entrance against superior forces of any kind.

But when it comes to defending the House against enemies Ahbar, the Black Watchman, does not rely on his bodily strength only. A long time ago, the Stargazing Priest has designed a most appropriate weapon for him: the greatly feared Black Spear that drinks the deadly light of the sun. Whenever he considers it necessary to kill and destroy from afar, all he has to do is to voice the magic words that elicit the deadly light from the metal spike of the spear in a glaring ray that reaches as far as the mountain lion can run. However, long gone are the days of the great wars and the relentless fights, and in these times of peace and mercy and cowardice Ahbar gets hardly any occasions to make use of the spear's most devastating power. But the days of glory and manly honour will return, praise the Gods, and until they do he will spend his days awaiting them eagerly, guarding the House, protecting its fainthearted inhabitants, serving the Queen and the Homeland, and remembering how good it felt to fight for a cause, to slaughter the evil and the weak, the ugly and the alien, to rape and plunder, to conquer and vanquish and humiliate the foreign folk.

It might seem strange to those that are not trusted with the complicated nature of the human kind, but the very same virtues that distinguish Ahbar, the Black Watchman, as the fiercest of foes and the most terrible of warriors are the very virtues that are appraised and appreciated the most by his fellow inhabitants. He is loyal and steadfast beyond any doubt, he makes them feel safe and protected, and some of them consider his services to be indispensable whenever the help of deft hands, swift feet, strong arms, or broad shoulders is needed, which he offers willingly when asked for it. And if the abilities of his limbs are quite obviously superior to those of his brains, the same is true of his heart. It is an all too big heart in an all too hard shell, and deep inside there is a soft and all too vulnerable core.

Although he would never admit it, least of all to himself, the soft core of his heart is what makes him weaker than oh so many others in oh so many regards. It is that soft core that occasionally, in silent moonlit nights, makes him neglect his duty and stare at the beautiful maiden sitting on the platform by the pond, sadly gazing at her own reflection in the water. Sometimes he stares at her for hours through eyes filled with tears of spontaneous and uncomprehended sympathy. Against his habitude to approach women in offensive ways, he does not dare to address himself to her.

It is that soft core of Ahbar's heart that is so easily affected by the darkest and deepest secret fears; the fear of all the things his stubborn mind can neither understand nor accept, the fear of the unknown and the unnamed, and the fear that his courage and physical strength may not be enough to save him from failure and defeat some day. That is why he never questions the Queen's orders, even if they do not make any sense to him. That is why he despises the Poet and scorns the Whore whose services he employs so abundantly. That is why he has taken to like the Nameless Intruder's sweet talk; she is an outsider just as he is. That is why his doings are so often guided by envy, suspicion, and hatred. And, finally, that is why he never enters the House by daylight. He does not really want to find out why he always feels excluded, underestimated, and unloved by his fellow inhabitants.

Undoubtedly, Ahbar, the Black Watchman, is a believer. His belief outreaches his knowledge, and he believes in many things. He believes in the favour of the god of war and the power of the Mighty Queen. He believes in destiny and predetermination. He believes in his dreams, his memories, and the tales of the dry warm winds from the south. He believes in another world that begins right beneath the surface of this one: a world in which all the absurdities become real that the Stargazing Priest has invented since the days of glory came to an end. And he believes that his skin always was and always was meant to be black. But most of the ever-changing times he has spent being the Watchman it wasn't. And in most of the times to come it will be as pale as the full moon in a cold winter night. In those times to come he will proudly call himself Ahbar, the White Watchman. But for now, like any other true believer, he cannot be convinced, neither by argument nor by experience, that some of his beliefs might be false.

2

The Pond of Self-Reflection
PERSEPHONE, THE UNHAPPY MAIDEN

To the east of the Forecourt lies a small rectangular pond that most obviously has been laid out to serve certain purposes and produce certain effects. It directly adjoins the north front of the House where a hanging staircase is leading down from the traverse corridor on the first floor to a platform just above the water surface. This surface is so perfectly still and smooth that any stirring would seem to be a sacrilege. And although no one ever really penetrated the mystery of this delicate setup before Persephone grew up to be the Unhappy Maiden, it was never called into question that the pond was first and foremost meant to be some kind of mirror. However, mirrors were considered to be treacherous and dangerous things since way back, so no one ever even tried to disclose the secrets of the "Pond of Self-Reflection".

Persephone, the Unhappy Maiden, is young and breathtakingly beautiful to look at for those whose eyes are susceptible to the immature beauty of princesses and spruced up damsels. She wears a translucent white silk dress that is of noble and precious appearance by the light of the moon and turns into a splotchy and rumpled nightgown in the fresh of the day. Those who are enchanted by her conspicuous prettiness tend to attribute many flattering character traits to her, whereas others cannot help taking her to be just another ordinary moody and capricious teenage girl. As usual, neither of the notions is completely true, and both of them are far from being false.

Persephone was born in a late summer month's afternoon in the year of the Sheep. She is the daughter of Daimâliah, the Mother Gardener, and Tó-Kymïr, the Indigenous Forester. Thus, she is the only inhabitant of the House who lives here by birth. From her mother she inherited a certain penchant to melancholia, bemusement, and lack of initiative, whilst her occasionally irascible temper most probably comes after her father. Those who call themselves specialised professional analysts of the human psyche might say that the ways and deeds of her parents as they were, their behaviours and attitudes that determined how Persephone was born and raised, have left an ineradicable imprint on what has become of her. And as any other specialised professional's judgement it would not be completely false but far from being the whole truth.

When Persephone ran away from home with her father at the age of twelve springs, it was her own idea and autonomous decision, although Tó-Kymïr certainly was more than just willing to comply with her request. She wanted to explore the world outside the House. She wanted to experience adventures. She wanted to cross the Great Northern River and climb the snow-capped mountains in the south. She wanted to see what was lying beyond the eastern forests and the western prairies. Most of all, she wanted to meet folk that she had never met before. And since both father and daughter knew very well that the Mother Gardener (let alone the Mighty Queen) would never permit a venture like that, they did not ask for permission. They just stole away from the House at an early morning hour, distracting Ahbar, the Black Watchman, by chasing a timid fawn around the south-west corner of the House, and did not return until the end of that summer. Naturally, the blame for this outrageous violation of the house rules was put on Tó-Kymïr, and he was punished in two respects: Daimâhlia broke up with him for good, and Niãng Mâ, the Mighty Queen, prohibited him from associating with his daughter ever again. And as almost any blame that is put on one single person alone, it was not completely unjust, but it was far from being fair.

From that day on, Persephone no longer was a happy child. She has been the Unhappy Maiden ever since. Her sudden and persisting change of mood was not only due to the breakup of her family but just as much to the fact that after she had been shown around the world outside the House her life seemed unbearably boring to her. And, naturally, she blamed it all on her mother. Moreover, she became aware that no one, not even herself, ever had wasted a serious thought about her future. Actually, none of her fellow inhabitants had ever cared about anyone's future at all. They seemed to be completely unconcerned about anything but their unchanging everyday doings. Notoriously, the next best way for a teenage girl to take revenge on the grown-ups for their disinterest in her is to shrink into herself, to wallow in self-pity, and to seek satisfaction in all too blatant expressions of desperation. That was exactly what Persephone, the Unhappy Maiden, did. And, obviously, she has never ceased doing it.

She has moved from her mother's room to a small cabinet at the end of the corridor between the Skygarden Room and the Bed Room. There she sleeps all day, and when she wakes up at the late evening hour she climbs down the hanging stairs to the moonlit platform by the pond. She sits there almost every night until the break of dawn, staring at the reflection of herself on the still water surface. What she sees is a beautiful maiden's face, light blond hair falling gracefully over wispy shoulders, green eyes full of yearning for something she does not really understand. She sees budding breasts showing under the translucent white silk dress, the snow-white skin of her naked arms, and her lusciously pursed blood-red lips. The longer she looks at the reflection, the more she becomes infatuated with her fairylike appearance. And the more she becomes infatuated with herself, the unhappier she feels.

But that is just the beginning. As soon as she has dived deep enough into her self-reflection and has gradually forgotten the reality of her surroundings, her nightly meditations turn into what she calls either a "good night" or a "bad night". Full moon nights are always "good nights" whereas new moon nights are always "bad nights", but apart from that there is no telling what kind of night it is going to be. In good nights Persephone's unhappiness takes shape in romantic musings about the handsome young man she has fallen in love with recently. He has curly gold-coloured hair and enchanting blue eyes that gaze away into the distance in a real cute way. In her agitated imagination she sees him turning around to look at her, instantly being carried away by her irresistible beauty, putting his arms around her shoulders, bending forward and finally giving in to a long deep passionate kiss that sends shivers down her spine. Her fantasies about the Poet with the faraway eyes rarely go further than this, but when they do, she sometimes catches a side-glance of Ahbar, the frighteningly huge Black Watchman, staring jealously at the love scene on the floor of the Theatre. And, admittedly, arousing Ahbar's jealousy is one of the very few things that can make her feel happy for a fleeting moment.

However, these musings are still profoundly unhappy musings because the Poet with the faraway eyes does not love her back beyond her figments of fancy. He seems to be so distracted by his assiduous work that he hardly ever notices her when she spends the evening sitting on the upper circle of the Theatre, looking down on him when he gives one of his performances or bustles about trying to capture one of his great inspirations. In fact, and to her deep-felt heartbreak, he hardly ever seems to notice anything that goes on around him.

On the other hand, when Persephone, the Unhappy Maiden, has a "bad night", her meditations get stuck in the mere image of her appearance that the mirroring pond presents to her. In those nights, her fantasies start out from a pretty girl's face and rapidly proceed through all the horrible stages of aging and withering to a final image of an old wasted and wrinkled and hunchbacked woman with black tooth stumps, sagging breasts, protuberant limbs under a transparent shrivelled skin, and a few oily strands of white hair springing up out of an almost bald head. The ugly old hag grins at her in a most wicked and disgusting way before she breaks out in derisive bleating laughter that sounds like a death rattle. Then she mumbles: "That's what you're heading for, you silly little chit!" And finally, she slowly decays in front of Persephone's eyes until there is nothing left of her but a bleached skeleton crumbling into dust.

When Persephone awakes from her dreams and nightmares, she spends the remaining hours weeping bitterly, ignoring the soulful gazes that the Black Watchman occasionally darts at her across the Forecourt. Hot tears trickle down her pale cheeks, fall into the pond and mingle with the cool clear water. At the crack of dawn she climbs the hanging stairs, crawls away into her small cabinet at the end of the first floor corridor and falls into a restless sleep. She cannot take comfort in the fact that she will never grow older than seventeen because she is not aware of it. Just as all the other inhabitants of the House, she is living in an absolute here and now since she has reached her predetermined age.

Some might consider staying young forever to be a blessing, which might not be a perfect misjudgement. But it most certainly does not even come close to the truth.

3

The Forest Room
TÓ-KYMÏR, THE INDIGENOUS FORESTER

Shielded from the view of the Watchman, at the south-east corner where the House adjoins to the edge of the dark forest, there is a spacious area which is neither outside nor inside the House. It is completely secluded from all the other rooms but provides open access from the south side. Wooden stakes reach from the soft and grassy soil through the first floor of the building and further up to the roof, as if a fanciful architect had tried to integrate the structure of the forest into the construction of this particular part of the House. It seems to be the perfect accommodation for Tó-Kymïr, the Indigenous Forester, and it comes as no surprise that the inhabitants have taken to simply call this area the "Forest Room".

You might think that the dense array of the wooden stakes obstructively interferes with any inhabitant's demands for mobility and furnishment. However, Tó-Kymïr does not think of himself as an inhabitant but rather as an associate with the household, regardless of the exceptional appreciation and respect given to him by most of the residents of the House. To him, the "Forest Room" is nothing more than a tool shed and an occasional shelter from bad weather. He is a loner by nature, living an outdoor life like Ahbar, the Black Watchman, though for completely different reasons. He wears a hunter's waistcoat of buckskin, a broad-brimmed straw hat, and a scrubby full beard. His skin is tanned and furrowed like the bark of an old oak tree. Born under the sign of Capricorn, one cold and dry midwinter evening in the year of the Hare, he was drawn to the perennial beauties and wonders of nature right from the cradle; beauties and wonders that have delighted and challenged him more than the company of men and women ever since.

In the course of his solitary life in the forests and mountains he has learned to understand the forces of nature and eventually to make use of them to his benefit. To a considerable extent, these skills and wisdoms are of the kind that many of the uninitiated would mistake for "magic", wherefore he holds them to himself. Nevertheless, he generously shares the fruit of his labour and ability with those who need it or know how to ask for it.

In spite of his notorious solitariness, none of the inhabitants of the House seems to fulfil approximately as many tasks for the common good as Tó-Kymïr, the Indigenous Forester, and he demands nothing in return but modest expressions of gratitude and the occasional help of those who are capable to assist him with his activities. In spring he replants the arable land. In summer he cultivates the grain fields. In autumn he reaps the fruits and goes hunting in the mountains. In winter he cuts and chops timber and firewood in the forest. He is the farmer, the blacksmith, the carpenter, and the gamekeeper of the House all in one. And two twelve-nights before winter solstice, he arranges and conducts the annual Saturnalia, a thanksgiving ceremony that is attended by all of his fellow inhabitants except for the Queen.

Whenever the Poet with the faraway eyes tries to convince him that he is just being used by the others, he laughs at him and says: "You of all people should know that no one can consider himself being used when he does what he's born to do." On the other hand, when he overhears Niăng Mâ, the Mighty Queen, speaking of his "duties", he flies into rage and anger and curses her ignorance and degeneracy (which, of course, does not stop her from using the word even more often). That is when the inhabitants of the House are vociferously reminded that calmness, indulgence, and forbearance live side by side with wrath, indignation and a quick temper within the heart of the Indigenous Forester, to whom the children in these parts respectfully refer as "the man who speaks with trees".

The question that arises in the light of all this is how and why the man who speaks with trees and rocks and animals rather than with men has got acquainted and familiar with the inhabitants of the House. The answer is simpler than you might expect:

Once upon a time, Tó-Kymïr, the Indigenous Forester, fell in love. He fell in love with Daimâliah, the Mother Gardener, whom he happened to notice passing by the House when she watered the vegetable patches to the west of the Forecourt. She raised her green eyes to look deep into his dark brown ones, and from that very moment on it was as if the two of them had been meant for each other. In the following spring, they asked the Mighty Queen's permission to enter into the blessed bond of marriage, and their wish was granted upon condition that Tó-Kymïr settled down and committed himself to become a declared inhabitant of the House, assuming the "duties" assigned to him by the Queen. However, the Mighty Queen did not allow the newlyweds to share a room. To Tó-Kymïr she allotted the Forest Room, whilst Daimâliah was bound to keep on living in the Skygarden Room and doing her services as the Queen's chambermaid.

As the saying goes, love and faith can move mountains, and no one will ever really know how true this saying is with regard to the self-conquest that the Indigenous Forester had to summon up in order to cope with his new way of life. Fact is that he did for quite some time after his wedding day, and most probably the entrancement that got hold of him when his first and only child was born helped him to tame his true nature of a free and rambling man. But twelve years later to the birth of Persephone, his attitude towards the affairs of the House changed profoundly when the Queen, in treacherous conspiracy with his wife, sentenced him to stay away from his beloved daughter after he had taken her along for her first walkabout into the wilderness to let her in on the secrets of the natural world.

Hereafter, his patience and cooperativeness significantly diminished. He hardly ever talks to anyone anymore these days, and the only occasions on which he condescends to mingle with the sedentary people are the ordered assemblies, some carefully selected speeches and performances given by the Poet (if they coincide with his interests and values), and, of course, the Saturnalia ceremonies, the only one among his activities on behalf of the House that he still exercises with the same assiduous dedication. However, his commitment to the House may be not the same as it used to be, but he is still bound to the "duties" assigned to him by oath, and so he keeps on fulfilling them to more or less sufficient extents.

Now and then he stays away from the House for several twelve-nights, and no one really knows where he goes and what he does during these prolonged times of absence, which gives way to proliferation of all kinds of rumours, all the more so since he returned perspicuously limping from one of these absences. After all, everybody knows that Tó-Kymïr, the Indigenous Forester, dedicates himself rather to the balances of nature than to the balances of power promoted by the Mighty Queen, does he not? – According to one of those rumours that is emphatically spread by the Black Watchman, once a well-meaning assistant and workmate of Tó-Kymïr's, he is currently trying to provoke opposition against the House among the folk of the woods, but for the time being there is no convincing evidence or proof of these allegations. Some presume that he entrusts himself to the Candid Freecloud Harlot because he has taken to see her regularly in recent times. But since she is a very discreet person by profession, no one ever gets to know what the two of them talk about when he pays his visits in the Cave of Emptiness at past midnight hours.

4

The Stairwell

MATHILDA, THETIME-TRAVELLING CAT

A visitor who enters the House through the front entrance at the back of the Forecourt, steps into a hallway that leads straight to the Stairwell. At first sight, this central construction of the building seems to be of a rather playful and contorted design, but from the viewpoint of the inhabitants and their diverging interests it links all the rooms and levels and corners of the building in a most accurate and convenient way. In fact, the succession of stairs, passages, corridors, alcoves, and traverses unite to form a spatial constellation that can be conceived of as one coherent multi-storey room that resonates with the overtones of a middle B. And although it is quite generally ignored, this room is inhabited by a creature of the most remarkable kind.

Mathilda, the Time-Travelling Cat, was born in another world and another time. It may well be the world and time of which Ahbar, the Black Watchman, believes that it is hidden beneath the surface of this one, but that remains a subject of speculation, of course. Howbeit, Mathilda was born in a city called Puerto Perol, the capital of a South American country by the name of Cydania, and she had been living there for almost nine years as an independent stray cat before she decided to settle down in a dilapidated house near the dock area and start her second life. On the ground floor of that house lived Paulina, a grinding poor shift-worker raising three bastard children on her own, and since Paulina fed her on a regular basis and called her by the melodious name "Mathilda", she accepted her as her mistress after a few week's time. But her happy life as a domestic cat did only last a few months until that horrible day in July when the black-eyed soldiers arrived in their trucks and tanks. They started to shoot at people and cats and dogs and houses at random and without warning, they took Paulina and her screaming children away, and when Mathilda crawled out of her hideaway in the basement at nightfall the whole neighbourhood was in ruins, deserted, and silent. Naturally, she could not comprehend what had happened at that time, but later, after her metamorphosis into a time-travelling cat, she came to understand that the horrible day in July was the day of General Tóbler's military coup d'état against the elected government of Cydania.

She spent the following night in the attic under what was left of the house's roof, staring at the pale moon and trying to conceive an idea of her third life which unavoidably was to be a stray cat's life again. However, her third life didn't last longer than one night because suddenly, at the end of the grey morning hour, she noticed the contours of a staircase behind one of the bullet holes; stairs made of wood that had never been there before. Giving in to her curious nature, she jumped through the bullet hole onto the first of the stairs, and at that very moment her fourth life began. At that very same moment when she arrived in the House for the first time, she turned from an ordinary stray cat into Mathilda, the Time-Travelling Cat. At the very same moment, she became a regular though mostly inconspicuous inhabitant of the House, and the Stairwell became her new home. And these are only a few of the many changes she underwent that morning.

For a while, Mathilda could cross over from one world and time to the other at pleasure. She just had to sneak through a particular gap on the left side of the stairs that led from the first to the second floor of the House to find herself back in the ruined attic of her former home. Of course, she exercised that option quite frequently, and every time she travelled through space and time in this manner her intelligence and understanding of the world she lived in increased to a considerable extent. However, when the ruin in Puerto Perol was pulled down a few months later, the passage was shut once and for all. She had to face up to the fact that she would spend the rest of her lives as an inhabitant of the House. And so her curiosity and observing comprehension quite naturally turned towards her fellow inhabitants.

It is not only due to the inattention of these fellow inhabitants that Mathilda's presence and activities are hardly ever noticed. In spite of her nosiness, she tries hard not to attract too much attention in order to be undisturbed when pursuing her studies in the affairs of the House. That is why she seldom enters a room and prefers to sneak about in the Stairwell and the corridors, peeping through doorways and peeking around corners. Moreover, she has many reasons to find the humans a bit creepy sometimes.

The least mysterious of those reasons is that they never grow older then they are. It is not so mysterious because Mathilda does not grow older either since the day she has become an inhabitant herself. In general, the mysteries of time seem to be substantially less interesting once you have settled down in the House, even less for a cat with that many experiences in time-travelling. It may well be that time does not even exist here.

Way more disturbing is the fact that now and again the inhabitants disappear in the blink of an eye like ghosts, just to reappear seconds or hours later on the same spot. Astonishingly enough, they seem to be completely unaware of it themselves. Since Mathilda has learned to understand that the House is a world in itself, separated from other worlds that are just as real or unreal as this one, she has constructed the hypothesis that her fellow inhabitants cross over between different worlds the same way she did when the passage to Puerto Perol was still open. However, they obviously cannot understand it as she does.

In the same eerie way, some of them occasionally change their clothes, heights, colours of skin, and even their sexes without realising it. The exceptions in this respect are the old Sailor on the Roof and the Whore in the Cave of Emptiness. At least Mathilda has never seen those two change their appearances, which is why she tends to like them best. Sometimes she even visits and flatters them in return for their candidly expressed sympathies towards her. Well, maybe it is just because they bring back memories of her first life in the dock area where she had many opportunities to get acquainted with the ways of sailors and whores. Thus, the Sailor's bawling of rude songs does not torture her sensitive ears that much anymore, and among the specific activities of the other inhabitants those of the Whore are the most evident and certainly the most natural from Mathilda's point of view. With regard to that, she likes the Whore even better than the Sailor, and, what is more, the Cave of Emptiness is her second favourite room besides the Stairwell. Somehow it reminds her of the attic in Paulina's house before it was shot to ruins. And she likes the sound of it. It seems to harmonise perfectly with the sound of the Stairwell. If she would master the language of music she would probably say that the two sounds resonate in a well-tempered minor third or major sixth depending on the season and the time of day.

Remarkably enough, there is one inhabitant that persistently evades her assessment since she has become aware of him recently. He is never really there and never really absent. Seemingly, he prefers to dwell in doorways and corners and corridors just as she does, but, although she can perfectly feel his presence when she makes use of the sixth sense of a cat, she cannot clearly see or hear or smell him. That is why she has taken to think of him as the "Ever-Changing Spirit". Needless to say that he ranks among the inhabitants she likes least, along with the old trout in the rolling chair who seems to know about the Spirit as well.

Mathilda, the Time-Travelling Cat, has not yet found a conclusive explanation for every peculiar phenomenon that can be observed in the House, but she keeps on following up on it persistently. What is particularly hard to understand is why the inhabitants keep themselves to themselves so much. In her first and her second life she had got to know humans as gregarious creatures clustering in herds, groups and communities, but that does not apply to the residents of the House. However, Mathilda has worked out three plausible assumptions that might explain this oddity:

First, the House could be one of those buildings that people call a "hotel". She has a quite clear conception of the unusual human behaviours in "hotels" due to her experiences in Puerto Perol.

Second, the steady solitariness of the inhabitants could be a consequence of their misapprehension regarding the spatial design of the House. They seem to think that the different rooms are built according to their different characters and demands, whereas it is most probably the other way round: The inhabitants have adapted themselves to the spatial qualities of their respective accommodations, which is, as far as Mathilda can judge, the normal and customary case.

This rather trivial assertion leads to a third and much more portentous conjecture: The inhabitants of the House could be the very first (or the very last) human inhabitants that have ever existed (or will ever exist) in this world. If Mathilda knew those words, she would probably say that the inhabitants might be sort of "prototypical" or even "archetypical" exemplars of their kind. According to her assumption, that might explain to a certain degree why they have not yet understood (or already forgotten) their collective and collaborative nature.

Indeed, if Mathilda, the Time-Travelling Cat, would know how to speak in the terms of human beings, she would have a lot to say about the mysteries of the House. But since she already has learned how to read the minds of her fellow inhabitants and translate their thoughts into her own conceptions of things – and in the light of the fact that she has still five lives of a cat left to live – it cannot be ruled out that she may be capable of sharing the results of her participant observation studies one of these days. After all, she is born in a late winter month under the water-referred sign of Pisces, which alone would make her an exceptional cat, regardless of the exceptional course of her life that Neptune has determined to lead her down into the underlying realms of impenetrable depths.

THE FIRST FLOOR

1GCugugcacauguauaauguaugcpuagccauugcaaaugcaugugcuacugcaaccaucaugcauguaagcagccaugugaccauguauaugcauacacguguagcuac-
caaacguaugGugguguaagucaaguuaaucgGUAuaaugauacgucauugcauguauaugcaugcaagcucgacgaGUuacguGugguugcuaaacguacgucaugauga-
caugucga'CAUGugucauaugcaugcugcauuaacauacugcugcaagccaugcauugcuauauacgccauguauagaugcguuagcuu2CAUguauaugcaugcaag-
caugauacgucauugcauguauaauguaugcpuagccauucgacgaUGCAuacaacauguaacauacugcuuaccauacugcugcacauguauacauugcuauaauguacgc-
cauguauagaugcguuagcucga3cgucauGugguguuacguaugacaugucgaCAUGugucauaugcaugcugcauuaacauacugcuuaccauacugcugcacauguaua-
cauugcuauacauguaacauuacauguacgccauguauacauacguguacguuaugaccauguauagaugcguuagcucgaagcgucaugugucauaugcaugcugcaucauu-
gucguauaccauucgaugugccauguguugcauacacguacguguuacuaaucg4CAUGuguugcauacacguacgugcugcaucuaugccauauacgcacgucaugguuacu-
aucgacauguauaauguaugcpuagccauaugauacgucauugcauguauaugcaugcaagcaucg5ACugugcGugguuacggcugugcaaugcauguaacauugcagu-
auagccauguguuaacauacugcugcauaccaucauguguugcuacauguaaugugcauacacguacgucguaugpuagcuaguucgaagcgucauguguugcauacacguac-
gucguaacguuacuacguaGugguucgauacggcugugcauacgcgguggugguagcguuagcuauacacguaucgcga6UGCAguauagccauguauaugcaugcaagcaugaug-
cacauguaacaucauguauaacugcuuaccauugaccauguauacauugcuaua[ugacuacggcugugcaacguuaguguaugcaaaggugugguacugugcacugugguag-
cgupacguuaaauguacgcgcauugcauguauauacauguaucgaagcguaacguaugugguuaauguacugcacgacguuaacugugcgauacgcuacgcgugcauacauggu-
ugcaucgaaugguauacauuguguacgaugugcauaagcguacauuauaccauaucgAUGguauaaacguauguggagcuauaaugugcauacauugguauaugcguauaug-
cgagcguucgaugcaguaugugcaaaugugcauaccauguaguauaugcucgaagcguguauaacauuauaccauaucg7CAUguauagccauguauauacauguaaugugac-
cgugcauguaugaccauguauacaugcauaugcuaugpuagcuaguucgaagcgucauguauacaugugcuaaacguuaccguuagucauguauacaugugcauaugcuag-
cauacguagu;augugcauguauacaugauguaugcauaguacuacgacguuaagcuauaaugcauugguacauguauaugcagcgucaaguuacuggcuauaugcuacg-
cgaugacugugccauguauacaauguaacgugcuauaaugaucg8CAUguauagccauguauacaagcagcguguauacaugugcauacacuaguauaaugcgucauguauaau-
gugugcguugacGugguaaugGUAuaugcaaaugugcaaacguuacguacgcguacgccauguauagaugcguuagcuacgccauguauacugugacguugaccauguauagua-
caugucgaagcgucauguauacaugguauacguacugcugcaGugguacauggcgcauguauacauugcuauaaugugaccauguauagaugcguuagcaucg9CGucauGug-
gucaacguacguuagucauugcauguauacaagcucgacgaUGCAguauaugcuaaugcuacauguguuucga10GUAuaagcaugugcauaugcuaguucgacgaUACgu-
auaaugcgucauguguuacgccauguauagaugcguuagcucgaagcguUACugcaaaugaacugcauacgucguacauauguaUACugcaaauggcauacguagu;augu-
gUACguauacguaucgcga11AgcguGUAuaaugauacguucgacgaUGCAguaugcauugacgugucaugugucauguaacaucauguguugcauaugcuag-
cauacguaguuuGUAagcuauacauguguuaacauuagcacugcugcacauguauacauugcuauacauguaacauUACcugcacaagcguuagucaugugugcugcauca-
uuguaacauacugcugcauucga12CAUguauacaagcaugauacguucgacgaCAUguauaugcaugcaagccaugugupucauguauaugcuaugcauaccauguacauaaug-
guauagagcuauacauaaugugcauaacugcuuaccauacugcugcacauguauacauugcuauaucgaagcguUACacauuauaccauaucgcga13CAUguauagcGuggu-
augauacgucauugcauguauaugcaugcaagcucgacgaUGCAguaacauuacaugcauguauacaugcauguguguaagcuauaguuggcuauucgaCAUguauaugcaug-
caagcaugauacguucgacgaCAUguauaauguaugcpuagccauguuacuauacgcuauagucauaucgaagcguUACacauuaaucgcga14AUGugGugguaugauac-
gucauugcauguauaauguaugcpuagccauucgacgaCGuacauauguacauguguguaagcuauaguuggcuacauguauacaugucgacuugcauguaguaugcuacau-
guguacguggcuauaaacguacguacguuacgcuauaaugcauugcuacgagcguaacguacguugcauacacguguagcuaccaaacguaugguaCAUGuguugcauacacguac-
gucugcaugcaacguuggccauguguugccguaacguacgucaugagcgucauguguugcauacacguacguuaacauguuaugcauaacguacgucauguauaguacaugau-
gugaccauguguugcacguuacacuaaucg15AgcguUACugcauacacguacgupucauuagccauaccaucaugcguacauugcauauagccauguguagcgucauguau-
augcaugcaagcucgaagcgucguacauugcauauagccauguguugcugacacaugpugcuacgcgagcguguauaugcaug;guauaugcauacacguacgucugcuauggu-
acauguguugcguauaaguucgaagcgucauguguugcauacacguacguaugcauugcuacuacguaguauacaugguauauaacguaucgcga16CAUugcauguauaug-
caugcaagcGUAuaaugauacguucgacgaUACugcauacacguacgucaauacguacauguguugcpauacgcauguacgccguauacacgugucguaaugcuacgcggcu-
auaugccaugauguagcuauaugcua;ugcauaccauguapauacgcacuacguacguacguguugccauguguugcauacacguacguguacgcuauacguacugccauguaca-
uugcguauacacguguugcuagcaucgCAUGuguugcguuaauguacugcuaugcauacacguacgucguaacugugccauguguugcguauaugcgagcguucgaagcgu-
guauaugcauacacguacguugcuacguuauggcuauaugccauguguaucgcga17CAUugAguacaGUAuaaugauacguucgacgaCGuacauauguacauguguacguua-
caugcauuagcuagucauugcauguguugcugcauacacuaagcguacauuaacugcuuaccauacugcugcacauguauacauugcuauaacgugucauugcaguauaccgu-
aUACcugcacaagcguuagucauguguucga'CAUGugucauaugcaugcugcauuaacauacugcugcauaccauucga'cuugcauguaguuacaugcauguauagugcu-
gugcgucguacauauguaugaccaugugu;cauguaugcugugguapauacgcacuacgucauuguacacgucauguguugcauacacguacguuaacauacugugguacugcug-
cauaccauaacguacgucauguauaguacaugaugugaccauguguugcacguuacacuaaucg18UACcauugcauacacguacgupugcugguucuacauguaugugcgcau-
gagcgucauguauacaugcauacguuaaugacugugccauguguucgaagcgucauguguugcauacacguacguuaacaucauguauapacguagccauaugugaccaugu-
auaacuacuaacguguaucg19CGcaugcauguauaaugugcauaacauugaccauguguugccgugcugugcacauguguugcauacacguacguuaacaucauguguugcacu-
gugguugccauuacacgucauguguugcuacauuugcgccauugcauguauagugcugugcguucgaauguacgccuaacugcugcauaccaucauguguugcauaugcuacau-
auacguagc;acugugcguuaugcaucauguguaugcuaagcgucauugguuaugcaucauguguugcauacacguacguugcuacauuugcgcaucgcga20Aguacagca-
cauaguguauacaugugcauacacuaUAgcuauaucgacguacauauguaaugguauaugcauguacgugucguacugcauacauguauacaugcauguauaugcugacaacguac-
gucauguauaacguuacgcuauacgcgaucg21GuggucaaguuagaugccauagccauaugugacauguacguacgcacugugcAguacaagcguguauacaugugcauacac-
uaagcgucacguugcauguauagucauguauacaaucg22AgcguGugguaugauacguucgacgaCAUguauacaagcguaaauggcugugcacguacugcauaacguuac-
uacguauggcuaugacuaugucgauacggcugugcauacgcggugugguagcguuagcuauacacguaucgGUAuacauaugcaugcugcaucguaaacguacguugugcaua-
gucauugugcuaacguaugucauguauacaugguaagcguagcgucauauacguaaacguaugugacugcugcacauguauacauugcuauaugacuacauuaugcg-
caacguacguuacacuaagcguuaacauucgaagcguacguuacgcuauaacugugcuagcuauaugcaucgcga23AUGugGuggucgagcuacaugguauaguguauac-
caacugcugcacauguauaGaugcguuagcugacUAguuagccauugugcaugugcuacgcauguauagugcugugcguacugcugcaugcaguauaccguaguauaguaagu-
cguauagccauauacguagcaucg24AaccauuaugcGUAuaguugcuggcuauacauguauacaagcugucauucgaguauapacguacuaguuggccauguauauaaaug-
cauauguacguuaugaccauguauaGaugcguuagcugacUAguuagccguauaugcucguaccaagcguaacacguacauacgcgaugugcaugugcguacacguaauggu-
auacgcgcgacuacgagcguacugugccauguacauugguaugcgucauguauaugcaacaugcauugcauguauacauugcuauaugacuacauuaugcgcaacguacguua-
cacuaaucg1GCugugcacauguauaauguaugcpuagccauugcaaaugcaugugcuacugcaaccaucaugcauguaagcagccaugugaccauguauaugcauacacgu-
guagcuaccaaacguaugGugguguaagucaaguuaaucgGUAuaaugauacgucauugcauguauaugcaugcaagcucgacgaGUuacguGugguugcuaaacguacgu-
caugaugacaugucga'CAUGugucauaugcaugcugcauuaacauacugcugcaagccaugcauugcuauauacgccauguauagaugcguuagcuu2CAUguauaugcaug-
caagcaugauacgucauugcauguauaauguaugcpuagccauucgacgaUGCAuacaacauguaacauacugcuuaccauacugcugcacauguauacauugcuauaauguacgc-
cauguauagaugcguuagcucga3cgucauGugguguuacguaugacaugucgaCAUGugucauaugcaugcugcauuaacauacugcuuaccauacugcugcacauguaua-
cauugcuauacauguaacauuacauguacgccauguauacauacguguacguuaugaccauguauagaugcguuagcucgaagcgucaugugucauaugcaugcugcaucauu-
gucguauaccauucgaugugccauguguugcauacacguacguguuacuaaucg4CAUGuguugcauacacguacgugcugcaucuaugccauauacgcacgucaugguuacu-
aucgacauguauaauguaugcpuagccauaugauacgucauugcauguauaugcaugcaagcaucg5ACugugcGugguuacggcugugcaaugcauguaacauugcagu-
auagccauguguuaacauacugcugcauaccaucauguguugcuacauguaaugugcauacacguacgucguaugpuagcuaguucgaagcgucauguguugcauacacguac-
gucguaacguuacuacguaGugguucgauacggcugugcauacgcggugugguagcguuagcuauacacguaucgcga6UGCAguauagccauguauaugcaugcaagcaugaug-
cacauguaacaucauguauaacugcuuaccauugaccauguauacauugcuaua[ugacuacggcugugcaacguuaguguaugcaaaggugugguacugugcacugugguag-
cgupacguuaaauguacgcgcauugcauguauauacauguaucgaagcguaacguaugugguuaauguacugcacgacguuaacugugcgauacgcuacgcgugcauacauggu-
ugcaucgaaugguauacauuguguacgaugugcauaagcguacauuauaccauaucgAUGguauaaacguauguggagcuauaaugugcauacauugguauaugcguauaug-
cgagcguucgaugcaguaugugcaaaugugcauaccauguaguauaugcucgaagcguguauaacauuauaccauaucg7CAUguauagccauguauauacauguaaugugac-
cgugcauguaugaccauguauacaugcauaugcuaugpuagcuaguucgaagcgucauguauacaugugcuaaacguuaccguuagucauguauacaugugcauaugcuag-
cauacguagu;augugcauguauacaugauguaugcauaguacuacgacguuaagcuauaaugcauugguacauguauaugcagcgucaaguuacuggcuauaugcuacg-
cgaugacugugccauguauacaauguaacgugcuauaaugaucg8CAUguauagccauguauacaagcagcguguauacaugugcauacacuaguauaaugcgucauguauaau-
gugugcguugacGugguaaugGUAuaugcaaaugugcaaacguuacguacgcguacgccauguauagaugcguuagcuacgccauguauacugugacguugaccauguauagua-
caugucgaagcgucauguauacaugguauacguacugcugcaGugguacauggcgcauguauacauugcuauaaugugaccauguauagaugcguuagcaucg9CGucauGug-
gucaacguacguuagucauugcauguauacaagcucgacgaUGCAguauaugcuaaugcuacauguguuucga10GUAuaagcaugugcauaugcuaguucgacgaUACgu-

5

The Machine Room
UNKÁSH, THE STARGAZING PRIEST

Directly above the Forest Room there is a chamber that none of the inhabitants of the House ever enters except for the Stargazing Priest. Accordingly, this chamber is subject to innumerable myths and speculations, trivial ones that issue from ignorance, and fantastic ones that issue from unbounded imagination. It comes as no surprise that, in the course of the ages, this chamber has been given so many different names that not even the Stargazing Priest himself can remember them all. In the Grey Ages, for example, it was called "the Holy Room", "the Empty Room", or "the Quiet Room", whereas in the Golden Ages it was called by names like "the Sacristy Room", the "Sanctuary Room", or "the Forbidden Room". In the Dark Ages it was called "the Room of Memories" or "the Room of the Dead", and when the Dark Ages were over people took to call it "the Room of Knowledge" or "the Room of Acts". In recent times it has been agreed upon to change its name from "the Room of Works" to "the Machine Room", and that is what it is called to the present day. Due to this latest designation, some of the inhabitants surmise that the room itself is a machine of some unintelligible kind. At times, all of a sudden, the room is lit up from within by an invisible and incomprehensible source of white light, and at other times it produces strange mechanical sounds and noises all by itself. When the room falls silent again it remains humming for several hours at a frequency of about 440 Hertz, which equals, according to the Stargazing Priest's assertion, two times the 32nd octave of the evening star's acoustic rotation frequency.

Oddly enough, if you take a look at the room through the doorway that leads to the Stairwell, it seems to be completely empty. Instead of walls there are skin-like white cloths that are stretched tightly between wooden beams. They filter light, sound, and air in continuous variability at the Priest's will. However, the room's most conspicuous feature is the mechanism on the east side that allows to tilt four segments of the clothed wall by 90 degrees separately so that they turn into segments of the roof when tilted upwards and back into segments of the wall when tilted downwards. This sophisticated fitment is generally referred to as a "Stargazer's oriel".

The original reason why the inhabitants have taken to call this particular room the "Machine Room" is that the Priest's currently preferential occupation is to invent so-called "machines". A machine is a mechanical or cold-heat-driven item that exactly performs the work that the Priest has designed it for. At the dawn of the Illuminated Ages he began to take an interest in technological rather than in spiritual and natural problems and solutions, and most of the machines he invented over the years were designed as technical improvements of the House or to assist the inhabitants with their everyday work. But as the Mighty Queen disapproves of this sort of progress in principle, the Priest's technological ideas are habitually ignored. That does not keep him from taking pleasure in inventing new machines, but as soon as he knows that they actually work he destroys them and files the construction plans in his memory that seems to know no limits. The most ambitious among his projects is the "mind machine", which remains to be stuck in the planning stage for quite some time now. On the one hand, the Priest has not yet found a way to conceive of the machine without just projecting the functionality of his own mind onto technological processes, and on the other hand, he strongly believes that these processes should be based on a yet to be developed "theory of everything".

However, just as the names and the purposes of the room he occupies have been altered many times over the ages, Unkásh, the Stargazing Priest, has filled many different positions and assumed many different functions since the day he has settled in the House. He has been, according to the respective requirements of the ever-changing times, the fortuneteller, the astronomer, the philosopher, the scholar, the high priest, the keeper of the holy scriptures, the counsellor, the medicine man, the historian, the judge, the minister, the natural scientist, the inventor, the theorist, the doctor, the architect, the teacher, the engineer, the economist, the psychologist, and the analyst of common affairs. However, from his point of view, these different functions are all part of the same task: to gather, conserve, and apply all kinds of knowledge on behalf of the House. And because all knowledge starts out from the observation of the stars, their positions and movements in the vast and exhaustless spaces of the universe, he has always insisted on being addressed by no other name than Unkásh, the Stargazing Priest.

Based on the sheer variety of his past and present duties, it seems obvious that Unkásh must be a man of considerable power among the inhabitants of the House. And indeed, as the perpetual first counsellor of the Mighty Queen, he certainly has some bearing on her decrees and decisions. But he is prudent enough to understand that his comprising knowledge may be an enormous source of power but cannot be a means to execute it. People may treat him with proper respect, heed his advice, and employ his services whenever they need them, but they would never trust in him as a person. In fact, it seems to be natural that deep down in their hearts they hate him for what he is and for what he knows because they always were and always will be profoundly afraid of things that evade their immediate comprehension. It is not because these things are hard or complicated to understand – most of them can be explained quite simply and easily – but because people usually are too lazy and too coward to face up to them. After all, if they would face up to what they could actually know, they would be responsible and accountable for their actions and omissions, which is exactly what they do not want. They prefer to put their faith in the corruptible but predictable command of kings and queens rather than in those who bother them with the responsibilities that come along with knowledge. They prefer to think of knowledge as an abstract compendium of mysteries.

Although Unkásh cannot help treating his fellow human beings with a certain arrogance at times, he would be the last to blame them for their stubborn refusal of taking their lives into their own hands. He is all too well acquainted with the consequences of acting independently. And although he has never believed in the gods himself, he has always understood the purpose of depending on that belief. That is why he has been such a capable priest for such a long time.

However, Unkásh has long since got used to the pitfalls of his potentially political position and taken to act the part of the withdrawn nerd most of the inhabitants want to see in him nowadays. He still wears his long white robe with dignity, advises his fellow inhabitants on possible solutions to their everyday troubles, cures their little ailments, issues the twelve-nightly weather forecasts, designs visual and acoustic and musical effects to enhance the Poet's performances, and attends the regular consultative meetings with Niãng Mâ, the Mighty Queen, although he knows perfectly well that she does not esteem his opinion to the same effect anymore as she did in the old days when she had to take account of the enemies at the gates of her realm and of the people's belief that their fate lies in the lap of the gods alone.

All in all, Unkásh is not unhappy with his present situation, especially because it relieves him from taking the responsibility for the actions of others, which used to be the hardest part of his previous duties. He does not need to fake his loyalty towards anyone anymore, not even towards the Queen. To maintain this situation, he has no qualms about occasionally selling his abilities short as he did when his next-door neighbour Daimâliah, the Mother Gardener, asked him to release her daughter Persephone from her depressive moods. He lied straight to her face when he said that he did not know of any remedy for afflictions like that. Moreover, he does not even miss the Holy Scriptures that have been burned in the Dark Ages, because all the knowledge and wisdom that once was captured in those books is still available to him in his well-trained and almost boundless memory. And last but not least, he has plenty of time to indulge in his favourite and most lasting passion these days: the observation of the celestial bodies.

There he stands in his perfectly secluded room, a tall and skinny old man in good shape with a carefully shaven head, so obviously indifferent to everyday worries and completely free from fear or concern regarding the changes and tribulations in this world. He has tilted two of the clothed wall segments of his Stargazer's oriel mechanism into the downward position to have a perfect view onto the Orion Nebula in the star-splattered night sky. He is working on his "Astrochronicles", a historical listing of celestial constellations that refer to the fate of each and every inhabitant of the House. As long as anyone can remember he has meticulously kept it up to date, and since the beginning of the Dark Ages, when the mobs charged the House and burned every piece of paper they could find, he continues registering the Astrochronicles in his restless mind. So if the question should be raised why no astronomical constellation concerning any event in the history of the House or any inhabitant's exact date of birth has ever been forgotten, the answer lies in the one and only belief Unkásh, the Stargazing Priest, born under the sign of Aquarius in the year of the Dragon at the hour of the Snake, guided by the planet Uranus, has ever committed himself to: the belief in the cosmological unity and wholeness.

		WIND	PLANET		KEYNOTE
1	The Forecourt	NW	Mars	♂	D♭
2	The Pond of Self-Reflection	NE	Mercury	☿	C
3	The Forest Room	SE	Saturn	♄	G
4	The Stairwell		Neptune	♆	B
5	The Machine Room	SW	Uranus	♅	A
6	The Skygarden Room	E	Moon	☾	A♭
7	The Theatre	SW	Venus	♀	E♭
8	The Bed Room	NW	Jupiter	♃	F
9	The Cave of Emptiness	SW	Venus	♀	D
10	The Shadow Stairs	W	Pluto	♇	E
11	The Roof		Sun	☉	B♭
12	The Spaces In Between		Mercury	☿	F♯

CONSTELLATION		YEAR		HOUR		ELEMENT	
Aries	♈	Buffalo	牛	Tiger	虎	Fire	🜂
Virgo	♍	Sheep	羊	Rooster	鸡	Earth	🜃
Capricorn	♑	Hare	兔	Pig	猪	Earth	🜃
Pisces	♓	Rat	鼠	Dog	狗	Water	🜄
Aquarius	♒	Dragon	龙	Snake	蛇	Air	🜁
Cancer	♋	Dog	狗	Buffalo	牛	Water	🜄
Taurus	♉	Pig	猪	Rat	鼠	Earth	🜃
Sagittarius	♐	Snake	蛇	Sheep	羊	Fire	🜂
Libra	♎	Tiger	虎	Pig	猪	Air	🜁
Scorpio	♏	Rooster	鸡	Horse	马	Water	🜄
Leo	♌	Horse	马	Rat	鼠	Fire	🜂
Gemini	♊	Monkey	猴	Dragon	龙	Air	🜁

6

When you reach the top of the stairs that lead up to the first floor of the House, there are two doorways. The one to your right leads to the Stargazing Priest's Machine Room, the one to your left leads to the Skygarden Room where Daimâliah, the Mother Gardener, lives. In the deep of winter, the best bet is to walk on by and go straight down the corridor. But in summertime, almost any visitor is received with a warm welcome in this particular room at almost any time. So, since you have arrived on a late midsummer month's day, do not hesitate if you feel like entering here. You will be rewarded with one of the most spectacular spatial experiences the House has to offer.

At first, you may well not be too impressed because what you see is a comparatively small room that is mainly taken up by an installation of wooden racks and shelves full of flowerpots and wicker baskets of all shapes and sizes. The smell of soil and peat reaches your nostrils, and in the dark corners at the very back of the room you can see a clutter of timeworn cookware and gardening tools. Some may look familiar to you, but most of them seem to serve rather mysterious purposes. However, you will not understand why this room is called the "Skygarden Room" until you look up to the ceiling to find that there is no ceiling at all. Instead, there is an enormous funnel-shaped aperture that opens towards the sky, and the sidewalls of this inverse pyramidal structure are overgrown by plants of manifold genres and colours that seem to have been lined out in a very sophisticated way. Indeed, it is a sight that is bound to affect everyone, no matter whether the Skygarden Room is filled with the golden light of the midday sun or the silvery gleam of the moon.

And if you happen to meet Daimâhlia, the Mother Gardener, in person, you are going to make the acquaintance of a charming and vigorous middle-aged lady, and her joviality is bound to win your heart right away.

However, just as the light in the Skygarden Room changes with the seasons and hours of the day, the mental condition of Daimâliah, the Mother Gardener, changes from hopeless and desperate in the winter months to bright and even euphoric in the summer months, from unsociable and dismissive by night to obliging, companionable, and kind-hearted by daylight. In the olden days, many people believed that her mood changes actually caused the changes of the seasons, and although they have long since taken to think otherwise, no one has ever come up with a completely reasonable explanation for the deep and pervasive affinity between Daimâliah's spirit and the caprices of nature.

Accordingly, the instability of Daimâliah's emotions is not just a matter of her inner life. It immediately affects the healthiness of her Skygarden plants as well as her own outer appearance. When the colourful midautumn month passes into the misty early winter days, she rapidly loses weight and turns into a rather skinny and almost withered woman. Her enchanting green eyes that cast an irresistible spell over everyone who looks at her become clouded by shadows of desolation. In equal measure, her fiery red hair begins to fade into feeble shades of grey as soon as the last autumn leaves have fallen. However, when the darkest twelve-nights of the year are over, Daimâliah's body begins to bloom again like a spring flower and delights the eyes of men and women alike.

These changes of her mood have not always been as intense as they are today, which is easily apprehended by those who are acquainted with Daimâliah's life history. Born under the first moon after summer solstice in the year of the Dog, she was predestined to become both a powerful witch and a caring mother. As a young woman, gifted with an open heart and radiant looks, she walked the earth for ages, guided by the wandering moon, following her moods and instincts and pleasures, befriending people who answered the call of nature, refining her capabilities as the most skilful of witches, travelling the countries to the four winds, unhesitatingly giving herself away to every love at first sight, and giving birth to many children in many countries no one ever has heard of in these parts. However, at the rise of the Dark Ages her years of travel came to a sudden and terrible end. People began to despise and persecute her because they had taken to condemn the arts of the witches. Daimâliah spent many long and fearful years on the run, hiding from witch hunters and the rage of the mobs, until she took shelter in the House where Niãng Mâ, the Mighty Queen, guaranteed her safety in exchange for her duties as a gardener and chambermaid, which included, of course, the usage of her witchcraft to the extent that the Mighty Queen was willing to allow. She moved into the room next to the Bed Room, the very same room that the Stargazing Priest had used as a library until all his books had been burned in the course of the Dark Ages. She has lived there ever since, transforming it into the Skygarden Room, a spectacular place of elegancy and natural beauty.

After she had fallen in love and entered into the blessed bond of marriage with Tó-Kymïr, the Indigenous Forester, she ceased practicing witchcraft for the sake of her husband who was adamantly opposed to anything that could be possibly associated with magic powers. Thenceforward, and even more so after she had given birth to her daughter Persephone, there was an enchanting and enduring increase in her avoirdupois that changed her appearance just as rapidly as the balance of her tempers and emotions. And when Persephone and her father ran off for a walkabout without asking her permission and stayed away for a whole summer's time, she precipitately made three momentous decisions: She talked the Mighty Queen into punishing Tó-Kymïr with the maximum sentence for his misdeed, she annulled her marriage with immediate effect, and she returned to exercise her witchcraft with intent to estrange Persephone from her father and bind the feelings of her daughter to herself.

Eventually, all three decisions turned against her and her beloved ones and irrevocably changed her natively buoyant, caring, and nurturing personality into a severely unbalanced one. Persephone failed to respond to her spells and changed from a happy child into the Unhappy Maiden. The once benevolent powers of Daimâliah's gift became affected with the touch of black magic. And ever since, she has missed her family life dreadfully, although she would never admit it to anyone.

Over the years, the inhabitants of the House adapted themselves to the peculiarities of the Mother Gardener's character. They began to understand her moody, mysterious and esoteric ways on a higher level: They have begun to comprehend that her existence is bound to sort of a paradigmatic absolute presence that refuses to transcend the here and now towards past events or visions of the future, which is commonly conceived of as both a blessing and a curse. Daimâliah seizes every single moment of her life as presently and intensively as no one else could, whereas everything that goes beyond that particular moment does not really matter much to her. Accordingly, the secret magic rituals that she performs in the Skygarden room during the nights of summer and winter solstices are respected as holy rituals of a recurring mystical rebirth. However, Persephone, the Unhappy Maiden, does not share this common understanding. She has never ceased blaming her mother for her own misery, and none of her fellow inhabitants dares to hope that forgiveness will ever find a way into her heart.

7

The Theatre
JON CYRITH, THE POET WITH THE FARAWAY EYES

For obvious reasons, the Theatre on the south-west corner of the House is the biggest room of all, in height as well as with regard to its floor area. Before it was allotted to the Poet with the faraway eyes, it had been called "the Common Room" because it allowed gatherings of a considerable number of people and was always meant to be the place where the inhabitants can come together for deliberations, conversations, festivities, entertainments and amusements of any kind. It has been built in a way that is referred to as an "all-around construction" which means that the stage on the ground floor level and the upper circle on the first floor level grant access to all four sides of the room. Speaking of access, it has often been debated why the only way to enter the Theatre is to climb down the so-called "Shadow Stairs": an outside staircase at the western front of the House that leads from the second floor down to the upper circle's entrance. A smaller staircase leads from the upper circle to the dress circle, and from there an even smaller one finally leads down to the stage floor. The most trivial explanation for this is also considered to be the most plausible: The Common Room was originally supposed to be secluded from the other inside premises of the House to avoid mutual immissions and interferences. However, on the quiet some say that the complicated access to the Theatre was actually designed to hinder the hampered Mighty Queen from attending the more rollicking and pleasurable gatherings of her subjects. And since the day when the Shadow Stairs became a regularly inhabited place, even more outrageous hypotheses have been constructed.

Fact is that the "Common Room" was renamed "the Theatre" when the Mighty Queen invited Jon Cyrith, the Poet with the faraway eyes, to become a declared inhabitant of the House and fulfil the duties of a local artist and entertainer. At first, some of the other inhabitants, especially those who did not care for the arts at all, explicitly objected to this occupation of the former Common Room because they thought it to be a disproportionate waste of space. But for reasons she did not disclose, the Queen insisted on introducing her subjects to cultural education and amusement which is all the more remarkable because, over the years, the Poet has become an increasingly harsh and waspish critic of her regime and her governmental methods.

Jon Cyrith is a handsome young man with fair curly hair, sky blue faraway eyes, a shapely build and a weakness for fancy clothing. Along with his unresponsiveness to the beautiful Unhappy Maiden's craving and that of many other women who have fallen for and made approaches to him, his looks give rise to occasional insinuations concerning his sexual orientation. But since he takes his work very seriously, his libidinous energy is almost completely consumed by his aesthetic and intellectual endeavours anyway, and so he could not care less about what people think of him as a private person. Actually, he is so serious about everything that he is often accused of lacking any sense of humour, although the striking wit of his artistic expression proves otherwise. Likewise, the somewhat romantic mood of his early works and the eponymous sentimental look in his eyes cannot hide the fact that he is gifted with a penetrating mind, which is particularly articulate in his scientific lectures and political statements. In short, Jon Cyrith may not be a genius in the proper sense of the word, but he is good at what he does.

Nobody knows where the Poet with the faraway eyes came from when his career was launched. None of his fellow inhabitants had ever seen him or heard about him before he was introduced to them on a sunny midspring day by the Queen on the occasion of an ordered assembly, which was supposed to be a celebration of the end of the Dark Ages. To be honest, he was not welcomed warmly, but after he had proven to be a man of great inspiration, ingenuity, and entertaining talent, he soon was popularly accepted, even more so because Unkásh, the Stargazing Priest, overtly gave him a high character. Furthermore, there could be no doubt that Jon Cyrith rendered great service to the developments of the Illuminated Ages that followed on his moving into the Theatre.

He started out with writing simple poems, popular songs, and appealing short stories before he proceeded to more ambitious activities. He learned to paint in the manner of the great allegorists, and soon enough he attained the virtuosity of his guiding models. He experimented with new sorts of paint that he distilled off rare plant juices provided for him by Daimâliah, the Mother Gardener. Although the Queen did not tolerate pictures in the other premises of the House, he was free to hang up his paintings in the Theatre. And so, one thing led to another. The paintings became set decorations for his first stage plays, and the more plays he produced, the more his painting styles turned from allegorical to graphical. The plays inspired him to write his first novels, and the staging of these more complicated contents called for more sophisticated means of production. The Stargazing Priest was more than willing to assist him with the technical development of visual effects and sound accompaniments, introducing the Poet to the fundamentals of acoustics and harmonics. It wasn't long before the Poet was ready to present his first compositions, using musical instruments that the Priest had worked up for him. And while his readings and lectures changed from turgid to sublime, the Poet incited the Priest to invent a machine that could capture reproducible and reconfigurable pictures of real objects and scenes and situations by imprinting the colours of light on susceptible paper. They called it the "reality machine", and none of the inhabitants will ever forget the evening when the Theatre turned into an audio-visual reality show room for the very first time.

The white canvas on the open south side that had originally been installed as a theatre curtain for open-air productions was rolled down and used as a projection surface for the most wondrous imagery they had ever seen. And none of them had ever witnessed the Priest break out in tears until that evening when he said those memorable words: "Tonight is the night that will always be remembered as the very moment in history when the Illuminated Ages were illuminated for real."

What is told here in the form of a quite simple and consecutive story was in fact a long and exhaustive process the Poet with the faraway eyes had to submit himself to. His very first dramatic performance under the title of "Romance and Jealousy", a simple love story about a rich girl and a poor boy whose feelings for each other collided with the social class system and led to a tragic chain of events, was actually a disaster of existential proportions. He suffered from almost unbearable stage fright, he constantly forgot his lyrics, and because he was so desperately nervous he pulled down the whole stage decoration with an unobservant wave of his hand during the final act. However, in spite of this demeaning disgrace, Persephone, the Unhappy Maiden, was so much in raptures about the story that she immediately fell in love with him and never got over it to the present day.

The lessons in music theory given to him by the Stargazing Priest and the years of abortive attempts to put them into practice were not exactly a walk in the park. And although he is held in high esteem for his inexhaustible flow of ideas, those ideas never come easily or naturally to him. They are the results of endless and usually desperate inner struggles and strives and failures during which he is virtually unresponsive to any kind of affection for twelve-nights or months. And although he is asked again and again where his ideas come from, he has not the faintest notion of the source of his inspirations, which makes him feel ashamed of his creations far more often than proud or satisfied with them. To him, they seem to be nothing more than products of tiring trials and errors and aimless deliberations, and whenever he achieves something it looks like sheer luck. In fact, Jon Cyrith would sacrifice his life just to find out how poetry and creativity works.

On the other hand, it occasionally happens that one or another of his desperate episodes leads to an unexpected insight. For example, when he finally got rid of his stage fright and dared to give performances on a regular basis, he began to realise that there was something special about the inhabitants' gatherings at the Theatre; something magic that had nothing to do with the content or the quality of his work. It took him some time to figure out what it was, but after he had listened to one of the Priest's lengthy digressions into the unity and the wholeness of the universe, it suddenly crossed his mind that every time people gathered to attend one of his performances they took part in something that was way beyond their individual and everyday objectives. On these occasions, they were together in a most basic and principal sense. And as it turned out, that was the moment when Jon Cyrith, the Poet with the faraway eyes, found the true and common thread of all his projects and endeavours. From that moment on, each and every piece of art he produced was profoundly and quintessentially political, although neither the Poet himself nor his audiences were ever really aware of it.

The Illuminated Ages went by and dissolved into the Newish Ages while the Poet with the faraway eyes strategically raised his standards of entertainment and distraction in order to prevent the increasingly critical and conceptual contents of his performances from becoming too obvious and eventually boring. However, if anyone had kept a record of the most frequent topics of his plays, songs, speeches, and imageries, the word "togetherness" would have inevitably appeared on it. And as of recently, even a casual visitor to the Theatre cannot close his eyes to the obvious anymore: What once started out from a simple notion and since has condensed into a tentative theory will turn into a substantial common understanding any time soon. John Cyrith has not yet begun to propagate serious resistance and rebellion against the current state of political affairs, but his choice of words is gradually getting more explicit and even spiteful at times. No doubt, this is not the absentminded Poet with the faraway eyes anymore that the inhabitants of the House got to know on that sunny midspring day way back. This is an angry young man, and nobody can say what he is capable of or how long it is going to take until he lights the fire of insurrection in people like the Forester or the Harlot, not to mention Persephone, the Unhappy Maiden, who incessantly seeks hope and truth in each and every word he speaks.

8

The Bed Room

NIÃNG MÂ, THE MIGHTY QUEEN

Above the roofed entrance area of the Forecourt there is a room that the inhabitants of the House refer to as "The Big Room", "The Wide Room", "The World Room", "The Bed Room", or, when addressing a visitor, "The Throne Room". The Stargazing Priest sometimes calls it "The Minus-Four-Point-Thirty-Five Room", but nobody understands what he means by that, and, as is quite customary, nobody ever asks him for an explanation. The wood slat floor of this particular room is curved and flexible like the slatted frame of a king-size bed. To the north, the room is completely open, which makes it appear even bigger and provides a wide view onto the landscape of the Great Northern River. In spite of this ample openness, the air in the Bed Room is constantly and inexplicably warm and dry. When you step forward to the bent railing, you can overlook the Forecourt and the adjoining small pond. However, the most attractive equipment of this room is probably the trapezoid window in the ceiling through which you can see, when looking directly from beneath at exactly calculated times, the Sagittarius constellation in the summery night sky. The Sagittarius constellation is located in the centre of the galaxy, and it is, of course, the zodiac sign under which Niãng Mâ, the Mighty Queen, was born.

Admittedly, "age" is a difficult if not incommensurable characteristic with regard to the inhabitants of the House. But, judging from her appearance and behaviour, it is not completely nonsensical to say that Niãng Mâ, the Mighty Queen, is the oldest inhabitant of the House. Moreover, she seems to be the only one who remembers how and why the House was built all those many ages ago. At least that is what she thinks. She thinks she knows all the secrets of the House and all about its history and destiny. Be that as it may, she definitely knows almost everything there is to know about each and every inhabitant, which is, of course, more than any inhabitant knows about him- or herself. As trivial as it may seem, this particular knowledge is the one and only source of her unrestricted and unquestioned power. She is in control of the fate of the House and its inhabitants at all times and to the utmost possible extent.

Niãng Mâ never leaves the Bed Room, not only because she is a fat old wrinkled and rickety woman bound to a wheelchair splendidly equipped by Unkásh, the Stargazing Priest, but also because she is profoundly convinced that a Mighty Queen should never be slumming amongst the common people and their everyday doings. That is why ordered assemblies of the inhabitants do not take place in the Theatre (which would be quite an appropriate locality for such gatherings) but on the open Forecourt beneath the Queen's chamber so that she can address her subjects from above, sitting at the railing and effectively raising her sharp voice against the rushing of the Great Northern River. Apart from these occasions, she spends her days and nights rolling to and fro over the curved floor in her wheelchair, musing about governmental measures and strategies, now and then granting audiences to selected inhabitants, powdering her yellowish face or putting a little more shadow on the lids of her slit eyes. But mostly she just supplies her spontaneous personal needs and desires.

However, besides giving orders and seeing to it that they are meticulously obeyed, the Mighty Queen's desires are comparatively modest due to her age, position, physical constitution and restricted mobility. Especially, she likes doing things that remind her of the fact that her metabolism is still working to a reasonable degree. Hence, she takes pleasure in eating and drinking a lot, including all the related bodily activities such as defecating, urinating, burping or letting one go. In like manner she takes pleasure in swearing and using dirty words when she beefs about the indecent clothing of the Candid Freecloud Harlot, criticises the recent work of the Poet as the rabble-rousing rubbish of a simple-minded agitator, or humiliates Tó-Kymïr, the Indigenous Forester, by redundantly reminding him of his duties. It makes her feel alive and up to her task.

After a fair day's work, she likes to listen to the Stargazing Priest's nerdy and evidently grotesque suggestions for technical improvements of the House (like "automotives", "insulation modules", "heating" and "energy converting" machines), not because she would ever take these suggestions seriously but because they help her fall asleep. And, as everybody knows, she delights in observing Ahbar, the Black Watchman, performing his daily physical exercises or parading up and down the Forecourt in his seemingly unshakeable complacency and self-confidence.

For a number of reasons, Ahbar is her favourite subject anyway. He is conveniently submissive, carries out his duties reliably, and executes her orders without ever having second thoughts about anything. Albeit his notion of the old days is not much more than a euphemistic and rather romantic fantasy, he passionately upholds the memory of the times when glory and honour still meant something. Hence, if circumstances so require, he is sure to be ruthless and unscrupulous enough to defend her regency by any means necessary. He is, so to speak, the firmest pillar of her authority. In return for his loyalty she never summons him to an audience by day. She knows that it would make him feel uncomfortable, and, after all, the most welcome of his services is best provided in sleepless nights when Niãng Mâ, the Mighty Queen, is occasionally overcome by the urge to relive the craving of the spring chick she used to be a long time ago.

Some might say that Niãng Mâ treats her fellow inhabitants like tokens in an endless game of power and control. On the other hand, to preserve power and control is the one thing a Mighty Queen should dedicate herself to, and this dedication goes way beyond good and evil intents. Many of her decrees and decisions may seem cruel, relentless, or even selfish to the disinterested observer, and some of them are indeed. But they all follow the logics of maintaining the set-up, the organisation, and the balance of power within the affairs of the House. In that respect, Niãng Mâ never acts in favour of or in detriment to any individual inhabitant but always with a view to the laws and rules of cohabitation. As a consequence, she does not bother to hide her private and intimate affections, her preferences and aversions towards her subjects, because if there is anything she has learned during her perpetual time of reign, it is that pretence is the greatest and most corrupting menace to power. That is the reason why the Bed Room is not completely enclosed, neither to the outside nor to the inside of the House. Everyone can see what the Queen is doing at any time. Everyone is forced to notice that she knows no shame or embarrassment by what she is and what she does. Everyone can see when and to whom she grants her audiences. Likewise, all the inhabitants know that she can watch every move and overhear every sound *they* make whenever she feels like it or considers it to be useful. The balance of power is principally and first of all a balance of mutual anxiety, suspicion, and resentment.

It may look as if age, experience, and continual guidance by Jupiter, the planet of might, have eventually led her beyond all hope, illusion, sorrow and compassion. But that is only half the story. In her own way, she *cares* about the House and its inhabitants. And in spite of her overtly exhibited self-assurance, Niãng Mâ is perfectly aware of her reign's ever-imminent downfall. As has been mentioned before, neither the origin nor the destiny of the House is a mystery to her. She knows that the days of autocratic governance are numbered. She knows that any time soon a majority of the inhabitants will understand the secret messages hidden in the Poet's tales and songs and imageries. When that time comes, it will dawn on them that the House is not meant to host an arbitrary assemblage of individual characters pursuing their individual objectives but rather a community of people who are bound to share their interests, their desires, their abilities, and their necessities of life. They will call it, following the Priest's suggestion, a "society".

When that time comes, the Mighty Queen will be of no use to them anymore, and naturally they will hate her even more than they already do for having hold sway over them for so long. They will deliberately ignore the fact that they never could have reached that point of change if she had not maintained the balance of power in all those ages that went before. And they will have no idea how ambitious, demanding, and complicated it is to establish a "society" that lives up to its purpose. Chances are that they will give up half-way through getting started and return to square one. However, the balance will be upset. And when that time comes, when the Ever-Changing Spirit will reveal itself to the inhabitants of the House, Niãng Mâ will have to make the hardest decision of her regency.

Sure, she could make arrangements. She could silence the Poet, she could make an agreement with the Nameless Intruder anytime, she could launch a disinformation campaign against the notoriously instable inhabitants in the southern part of the House, she could even charge the Watchman with preparations for defensive actions. But she won't. She is not afraid of what is coming up. Just as she does not feel any regret for what is said and done. Furthermore, she can still recall the times before she was declared Queen. And, believe it or not, she was much happier back then. Every time Ilfâhr, the Wistful Sailor, tries to strike up one of his old shanties, those happier times resurge in full colour and vividness in her mind's eye. That is when she feels her heart beating. And that is when she feels that, at the bottom of it, it may well be a good heart. Nevertheless, being the Mighty Queen, she must never let it show. It would be mistaken for weakness.

THE SECOND FLOOR

1GCugugcacauguauaauguaugcpuagccauugcaaaugcaugugcuacugcaaccaucaugcauguaagcagccaugugaccauguauaugcauacacguguagcuac-
caaacguaugGugguguaagucaaguuaaucgGUAuaaugauacgucauugcauguauaugcaugcaagcucgacgaGUuacguGugguugcuaaacguacgucaugauga-
caugucga‘CAUGugucauaugcaugcugcauuaacauacugcugcaagccaugcauugcuauauacgccauguauagaugcguuagcuu2CAUguauaugcaugcaag-
caugauacgucauugcauguauaauguaugcpuagccauucgacgaUGCAuacaacauguaacauacugcuuaccauacugcugcacauguauacauugcuauaauguacgc-
cauguauagaugcguuagcucga3cgucauGugguguuacguaugacaugucgaCAUGugucauaugcaugcugcauuaacauacugcuuaccauacugcugcacauguaua-
cauugcuauacauguaacauuacauguacgccauguauacauacguguacguuaugaccauguauagaugcguuagcucgaagcgucaugugucauaugcaugcugcaucauu-
gucguauaccauucgaugugccauguguugcauacacguacguguuacuaaucg4CAUGuguugcauacacguacgugcugcaucuaugccauauacgcacgucaugguuacu-
aucgacauguauaauguaugcpuagccauaugauacgucauugcauguauaugcaugcaagcaucg5ACugugcGugguuacggcugugcaaugcauguaacauugcagu-
auagccauguguuaacauacugcugcauaccaucauguguugcuacauguaaugugcauacacguacgucguaugpuagcuaguucgaagcgucauguguugcauacacguac-
gucguaacguuacuacguaGugguucgauacggcugugcauacgcgguguggguagcguuagcuauacacguaucgcga6UGCAguauagccauguauaugcaugcaagcaugaug-
cacauguaacaucauguauaacugcuuaccauugaccauguauacauugcuaua[ugacuacggcugugcaacguuaguguaugcaaauggugugguacugugcacugugguag-
cgupacguuaaauguacgcgcauugcauguauauacauguaucgaagcguaacguaugugguuaauguacugcacgacguuaacugugcgauacgcuacgcgugcauacauggu-
ugcaucgaaugguauacauuguguacgaugugcauaagcguacauuauaccauaucgAUGguauaaacguauguggagcuauaaugugcauacauugguauaugcguauaug-
cgagcguucgaugcaguaugugcaaaugugcauaccauguaguauaugcucgaagcguguauaacauuauaccauaucg7CAUguauagccauguauauacauguaaugugac-
cgugcauguaugaccauguauacaugcauaugcuaugpuagcuaguucgaagcgucauguauacaugugcuaaacguuaccguuagucauguauacaugugcauaugcuag-
cauacguagu;augugcauguauacaugauguaugcauaguacuacgacguuaagcuauaaugcauugguacauguauaugcagcgucaaguuacuggcuauaugcuacg-
cgaugacugugccauguauacaauguaacgugcuauaaugaucg8CAUguauagccauguauacaagcagcguguauacaugugcauacacuaguauaaugcgucauguauaau-
gugugcguugacGugguaaugGUAuaugcaaaugugcaaacguuacguacgcguacgccauguauagaugcguuagcuacgccauguauacugugacguugaccauguauagua-
caugucgaagcgucauguauacaugguauacguacugcugcaGugguacauggcgcauguauacauugcuauaaugugaccauguauagaugcguuagcaucg9CGucauGug-
gucaacguacguuagucauugcauguauacaagcucgacgaUGCAguauaugcuaaugcuacauguguuucga10GUAuaagcaugugcauaugcuaguucgacgaUACgu-
auaaugcgucauguguuacgccauguauagaugcguuagcucgaagcguUACugcaaaugaacugcauacgucguacauauguaUACugcaaauggcauacguagu;augu-
gUACguauacguaucgcga11AgcguGUAuaaugauacguucgacgaUGCAguaugcauugacgugucaugugucauguaacaucauguguugcauaugcuag-
cauacguaguuuGUAagcuauacauguguuaacauuagcacugcugcacauguauacauugcuauacauguaacauUACcugcacaagcguuagucaugugugcugcauca-
uuguaacauacugcugcauucga12CAUguauacaagcaugauacguucgacgaCAUguauaugcaugcaagccaugugupucauguauaugcuaugcauaccauguacauaaug-
guauagagcuauacauaaugugcauaacugcuuaccauacugcugcacauguauacauugcuaucgaagcguUACacauuauaccauaucgcga13CAUguauagcGuggu-
augauacgucauugcauguauaugcaugcaagcucgacgaUGCAguaacauuacaugcauguauacaugcaugugguaagcuauaguuggcuauucgaCAUguauaugcaug-
caagcaugauacguucgacgaCAUguauaauguaugcpuagccauguuacuauacgcuauagucauaucgaagcguUACacauuaaucgcga14AUGugGugguaugauac-
gucauugcauguauaauguaugcpuagccauucgacgaCGuacauauguacaugugguaagcuauaguuggcuacauguauacaugucgacuugcauguaguaugcuacau-
guguacguggcuauaaacguacguacguuacgcuauaaugcauugcuacgagcguaacguacguugcauacacguguagcuaccaaacguaugguaCAUGuguugcauacacguac-
gucugcaugcaacguuggccauguguugccguaacguacgucaugagcgucauguguugcauacacguacguuaacauguuaugcauaacguacgucauguauaguacaugau-
gugaccauguguugcacguuacacuaaucg15AgcguUACugcauacacguacgupucauuagccauaccaucaugcguacauugcauauagccauguguagcgucauguau-
augcaugcaagcucgaagcgucguacauugcauauagccauguguugcugacacaugpugcuacgcgagcguguauaugcaug;guauaugcauacacguacgucugcuauggu-
acauguguugcguauaaguucgaagcgucauguguugcauacacguacguaugcauugcuacuacguaguauacaugguauauaacguaucgcga16CAUugcauguauaug-
caugcaagcGUAuaaugauacguucgacgaUACugcauacacguacgucaauacguacauguguugcpauacgcauguacgccguauacacgugucguaaugcuacgcggcu-
auaugccaugauguagcuauaugcua;ugcauaccauguapauacgcacuacguacguacguguugccauguguugcauacacguacguguacgcuauacguacugccauguaca-
uugcguauacacguguugcuagcaucgCAUGuguugcguuaauguacugcuaugcauacacguacgucguaacugugccauguguugcguauaugcgagcguucgaagcgu-
guauaugcauacacguacguugcuacguuauggcuauaugccauguguaucgcga17CAUugAguacaGUAuaaugauacguucgacgaCGuacauauguacauguguacguua-
caugcauuagcuagucauugcauguguugcugcauacacuaagcguacauuaacugcuuaccauacugcugcacauguauacauugcuauaacgugucauugcaguauaccgu-
aUACcugcacaagcguuagucauguguucga‘CAUGugucauaugcaugcugcauuaacauacugcugcauaccauucga’cuugcauguaguuacaugcauguauagugcu-
gugcgucguacauauguaugaccaugugu;cauguaugcugugguapauacgcacuacgucauuguacacgucauguguugcauacacguacguuaacauacugugguacugcug-
cauaccauaacguacgucauguauaguacaugaugugaccauguguugcacguuacacuaaucg18UACcauugcauacacguacgupugcugguucuacauguaugugcgcau-
gagcgucauguauacaugcauacguuaaugacugugccauguguucgaagcgucauguguugcauacacguacguuaacaucauguauapacguagccauaugugaccaugu-
auaacuacuaacguguaucg19CGcaugcauguauaaugugcauaacauugaccauguguugccgugcugugcacauguguugcauacacguacguuaacaucauguguugcacu-
gugguugccauuacacgucauguguugcuacauuugcgccauugcauguauagugcugugcguucgaauguacgccuaacugcugcauaccaucauguguugcauaugcuacau-
auacguagc;acugugcguuaugcaucauguguaugcuaagcgucauugguuaugcaucauguguugcauacacguacguugcuacauuugcgcaucgcga20Aguacagca-
cauaguguauacaugugcauacacuaUAgcuauaucgacguacauauguaaugguauaugcauguacgugucguacugcauacauguauacaugcauguauaugcugacaacguac-
gucauguauaacguuacgcuauacgcgaucg21GuggucaaguuagaugccauagccauaugugacauguacguacgcacugugcAguacaagcguguauacaugugcauacac-
uaagcgucacguugcauguauagucauguauacaaucg22AgcguGugguaugauacguucgacgaCAUguauacaagcguaaauggcugugcacguacugcauaacguuac-
uacguauggcuaugacuaugucgauacggcugugcauacgcgguguggguagcguuagcuauacacguaucgGUAuacauaugcaugcugcaucguaaacguacguugugcaua-
gucauugugcuaacguaugucauguauacaugguaagcguagcgucauauacguaaacguaugugacugcugcacauguauacauugcuauaugacuacauuaugcg-
caacguacguuacacuaagcguuaacauucgaagcguacguuacgcuauaacugugcuagcuauaugcaucgcga23AUGugGuggucgagcuacaugguauaguguauac-
caacugcugcacauguauaGaugcguuagcugacUAguuagccauugugcaugugcuacgcauguauagugcugugcguacugcugcaugcaguauaccguaguauaguaagu-
cguauagccauauacguagcaucg24AaccauuaugcGUAuaguugcuggcuauacauguauacaagcugucauucgaguauapacguacuaguuggccauguauauaaaug-
cauauguacguuaugaccauguauaGaugcguuagcugacUAguuagccguauaugcucguaccaagcguaacacguacauacgcgaugugcaugugcguacacguaaugguu-
auacgcgcgacuacgagcguacugugccauguacauugguaugcgucauguauaugcaacaugcauugcauguauacauugcuauaugacuacauuaugcgcaacguacguua-
cacuaaucg1GCugugcacauguauaauguaugcpuagccauugcaaaugcaugugcuacugcaaccaucaugcauguaagcagccaugugaccauguauaugcauacacgu-
guagcuaccaaacguaugGugguguaagucaaguuaaucgGUAuaaugauacgucauugcauguauaugcaugcaagcucgacgaGUuacguGugguugcuaaacguacgu-
caugaugacaugucga‘CAUGugucauaugcaugcugcauuaacauacugcugcaagccaugcauugcuauauacgccauguauagaugcguuagcuu2CAUguauaugcaug-
caagcaugauacgucauugcauguauaauguaugcpuagccauucgacgaUGCAuacaacauguaacauacugcuuaccauacugcugcacauguauacauugcuauaauguacgc-
cauguauagaugcguuagcucga3cgucauGugguguuacguaugacaugucgaCAUGugucauaugcaugcugcauuaacauacugcuuaccauacugcugcacauguaua-
cauugcuauacauguaacauuacauguacgccauguauacauacguguacguuaugaccauguauagaugcguuagcucgaagcgucaugugucauaugcaugcugcaucauu-
gucguauaccauucgaugugccauguguugcauacacguacguguuacuaaucg4CAUGuguugcauacacguacgugcugcaucuaugccauauacgcacgucaugguuacu-
aucgacauguauaauguaugcpuagccauaugauacgucauugcauguauaugcaugcaagcaucg5ACugugcGugguuacggcugugcaaugcauguaacauugcagu-
auagccauguguuaacauacugcugcauaccaucauguguugcuacauguaaugugcauacacguacgucguaugpuagcuaguucgaagcgucauguguugcauacacguac-
gucguaacguuacuacguaGugguucgauacggcugugcauacgcgguguggguagcguuagcuauacacguaucgcga6UGCAguauagccauguauaugcaugcaagcaugaug-
cacauguaacaucauguauaacugcuuaccauugaccauguauacauugcuaua[ugacuacggcugugcaacguuaguguaugcaaauggugugguacugugcacugugguag-
cgupacguuaaauguacgcgcauugcauguauauacauguaucgaagcguaacguaugugguuaauguacugcacgacguuaacugugcgauacgcuacgcgugcauacauggu-
ugcaucgaaugguauacauuguguacgaugugcauaagcguacauuauaccauaucgAUGguauaaacguauguggagcuauaaugugcauacauugguauaugcguauaug-
cgagcguucgaugcaguaugugcaaaugugcauaccauguaguauaugcucgaagcguguauaacauuauaccauaucg7CAUguauagccauguauauacauguaaugugac-
cgugcauguaugaccauguauacaugcauaugcuaugpuagcuaguucgaagcgucauguauacaugugcuaaacguuaccguuagucauguauacaugugcauaugcuag-
cauacguagu;augugcauguauacaugauguaugcauaguacuacgacguuaagcuauaaugcauugguacauguauaugcagcgucaaguuacuggcuauaugcuacg-
cgaugacugugccauguauacaauguaacgugcuauaaugaucg8CAUguauagccauguauacaagcagcguguauacaugugcauacacuaguauaaugcgucauguauaau-
gugugcguugacGugguaaugGUAuaugcaaaugugcaaacguuacguacgcguacgccauguauagaugcguuagcuacgccauguauacugugacguugaccauguauagua-
caugucgaagcgucauguauacaugguauacguacugcugcaGugguacauggcgcauguauacauugcuauaaugugaccauguauagaugcguuagcaucg9CGucauGug-
gucaacguacguuagucauugcauguauacaagcucgacgaUGCAguauaugcuaaugcuacauguguuucga10GUAuaagcaugugcauaugcuaguucgacgaUACgu-

The Cave of Emptiness
ËLAN-TÂSH, THE CANDID FREECLOUD HARLOT

The Cave of Emptiness, situated like an attic on the top of the southwest corner of the House, is an exceptional room in many ways. Its position provides a captivating view over the mountains and the western prairies. To the north side, a narrow doorway leads to the second floor corridor and the balcony at the head of the Shadow Stairs. The walls and the ceiling construction reveal the patterns of the proto-structure that originally defined the dimensions and spatial parameters of the House. The duckboard floor features a big circular hole that links the Cave of Emptiness with the auditorium of the Theatre beneath. A net of ropes is tied to the borders of the hole, and although the purpose of this installation is not necessarily obvious at first sight, it has always been taken for granted that it is meant to be used as a kind of hammock of considerable proportions. Anyway, it accentuates the comfortable and perfectly balanced dimensions of the room as a whole.

It is well known that ages ago the Cave of Emptiness was originally intended to be the private chamber of the Mighty Queen herself, which raises a question that is often asked by strangers and occasional visitors: Why has this exquisitely pleasant room been allotted to Ëlan-Tâsh, the Candid Freecloud Harlot, who is deemed to be the person of the lowest social rank among the inhabitants of the House? –

Anyone can see that Ëlan-Tâsh descends from the Wandering Folk that travelled from the east to the west and back again until they were scattered to the four winds and nearly extinct when the Golden Ages passed into the millennium of anarchy and devastation. Her wide dark eyes, her long black curly hair, and the chestnut colour of her skin could not reveal her ancestry more obviously, but first and foremost she has inherited and preserved the customs and skills and ancient wisdoms of her nomadic kin. Accordingly, she still wears the loose and many-coloured gowns of the Wandering Folk. She still believes that the world is made of sounds as it is written in the ancient eastern scriptures known as "The Teachings of Resonance". And, of course, she still masters the art of reading the cards and interpreting their original meanings which refer to the ways of how human beings organise themselves in communities and therewith submit themselves to common destinies.

Ëlan-Tâsh was born in the lowlands of the Salty River under the sign of Libra on the 17th day of the midautumn month in the year of the Tiger. It was the time when the Golden Ages came to an end, when the Northern Folk migrated to the south and raided the peoples of the Middle Zones on their way, when the great wars broke out and the wealthy countries on both sides of the mountains were engulfed in misery, poverty, and violence. Ëlan-Tâsh was twelve springs old when she got separated from her tribe during an assault by a horde of Blondbeards who sold her as a child slave to a commander of the united Middle Zones' armies. The commander was Ahbar, the Black Watchman, and when he brought her to the House four years later, he demanded a hosting agreement for the girl that he regarded as his personal war loot and courtesan. But neither the Queen nor his fellow inhabitants were ready to unconditionally comply with his request, although they spontaneously liked the lovely girl's candid and openhearted ways. They regarded human beings to be beyond any claim of ownership as a matter of principle. However, the Mighty Queen argued, a good prostitute was always welcome in a good house for many obvious and many not so obvious reasons, but solely at her or his own free will and on her or his own terms. Under the given circumstances and in anticipation of the Dark Ages that were to come, Ëlan-Tâsh considered herself fortunate to stay at a relatively safe place and fulfil her duties as the harlot of the House. And since the Queen who had not yet been afflicted with mobility problems had recently moved to the Bed Room for reasons that she had not disclosed to her subjects, it was decided that the vacant room was to become the harlot's room and renamed the "Cave of Emptiness", which was a common and quite descriptive term for whores' quarters at the time. Henceforth, Ëlan-Tâsh was addressed as the Candid Freecloud Harlot in reference to her original family name Nûsh-Làbh'Reh, which approximately means, depending on the pronunciation, "heir of the free cloud" or "arisen from foam" in the tongue of the Wandering Folk.

As it turned out, Ëlan-Tâsh's services as a whore were much less sought after than her "not so obvious" ones. In fact, Ahbar was her only regular customer, and when she reached her predetermined age of 33 springs, she had become very favoured and well respected for her social abilities and her frankly outspoken sense of righteousness. The inhabitants of the House often asked her for her mediating advice when there were differences to settle or personal decisions to be made. They requested her to read the cards for them, consulted her on their emotional affairs, and generally appreciated her for being a good listener. All in all, it was her powerful intuition that left the most lasting impression on them, and in return they, except for the Queen, were more than willing to put up with her fancy clothing, her outlandish customs, and her sometimes quite straightforward remarks. Even the Stargazing Priest who was perfectly acquainted with reading both into the future and the past visited her now and again when he was in need of a deeper understanding of the present.

Anyone who is familiar with the culture of the Wandering Folk can easily conceive of the reason for Ëlan-Tâsh's astounding intuitive capabilities: She is a natural born mind-walker. Many people mistakenly believe that mind-walking, which occurs in dreams as well as while awake, is a deliberate or intentional technique of invading and reading the minds of others, and some may well have tried to abuse it as such. But in fact, it is just an advanced but involuntary manifestation of empathy and of the natural volition to comprehend coherencies, which is commonly referred to as "intelligence". In other words, the Candid Freecloud Harlot unconsciously takes part in the mental and emotional life of her fellow human beings, and, accordingly, her mind-walking does not really provide her with knowledge but rather with notional anticipations. She does not know that the Stargazing Priest has secretly installed a heating and air drying system in the Bed Room in order to ease the Queen's infirmities of old age, but she has a very strong and vivid presumption of it. She does not really know the reason why the Mighty Queen has accepted the Nameless Intruder as an inhabitant of the House, but it seems quite obvious to her. She does not know where the mostly invisible Ever-Changing Spirit comes from or who he is, but she has a rather distinct notion of his character and the meaning of his presence at the House. And, of course, her concern and sympathy for the Poet's works and productions are not meant to influence his ideas, but, quite naturally, they do. Anyway, it made her very happy when Jon Cyrith was invited to the House at the dawn of the Illuminated Ages and eventually discovered her talent as a singer. Since then, she has performed many of his songs at the Theatre; songs he composed to perfectly fit her beautiful alto pitch of voice.

Earlier on, the question has been raised where the Poet's inspirations come from. Apparently, the answer to that question is so simple that it has always evaded Jon Cyrith's lofty speculating: The inspirations come, quite literally, from above, or rather from the room that lies directly above the Theatre. Unkásh, the Stargazing Priest, would, if he knew about this special relationship, certainly explain it by referring to the fact that Jon Cyrith's and Ëlan-Tâsh's destinies are both determined by the guidance of the planet Venus, whereas Niãng Mâ, the Mighty Queen, would probably assume that it is based on their more or less explicitly rebellious attitudes. However, the Candid Freecloud Harlot herself understands her affinity for the Poet as a simple fascination with his gift of putting intellectual and spiritualised contents into words, music, and images that all of the inhabitants, even the educationally alienated, can easily apprehend and understand in their respective own ways. Jon Cyrith's true greatness, she uses to say, is not necessarily expressed in his ideas but rather in the way he conveys them to his audience.

In light of all this, it comes as no surprise that Ëlan-Tâsh's talents have also revealed their dark sides over the years. Inevitably, many frightening and unasked-for conjectures and intuitions have come to her mind that she would rather exclude from her thoughts if she could. Sometimes, people take to despise her for her forthrightness when she discloses things that they would rather conceal. The voluptuous desires that her infatuating bodily appearance awakens in men and women occasionally arouse unpleasant feelings like shame, envy, or jealousy, and so do her skills to fulfil these desires. After all, the Cave of Emptiness is a place where people get stripped down both in obvious and "not so obvious" ways. The Candid Freecloud Harlot has long since learned to cope with troubles like that. However, there is one most painful affliction she will never become used to. Now and again, unpredictable and uncontainable seizures of shattering panic overcome her when the reminiscences of her teenage experiences of war and terror and indignity retake possession of her, bringing back memories of the most atrocious experiences of her life as vividly as if they were real. Quite often, these mental attacks last for hours that she spends alone in the Cave of Emptiness, paralysed and unresponsive to any help or comfort.

1 AHBAR, THE BLACK WATCHMAN

2 PERSEPHONE, THE UNHAPPY MAIDEN

3 TÓ-KYMÏR, THE INDIGENOUS FORESTER

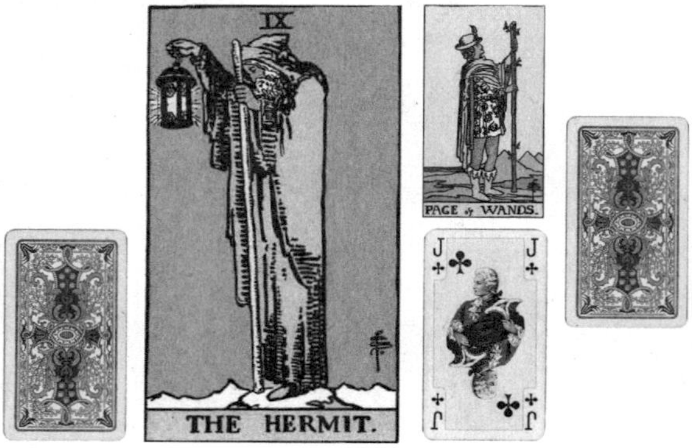

4 MATHILDA, THE TIME-TRAVELLING CAT

5 UNKÁSH, THE STARGAZING PRIEST

6 DAIMÂLIAH, THE MOTHER GARDENER

7 JON CYRITH, THE POET WITH THE FARAWAY EYES

8 NIÃNG MÂ, THE MIGHTY QUEEN

9 ËLAN-TÂSH, THE CANDID FREECLOUD HARLOT

10 THE NAMELESS INTRUDER

11 ILFÂHR, THE WISTFUL SAILOR

12 THE EVER-CHANGING SPIRIT

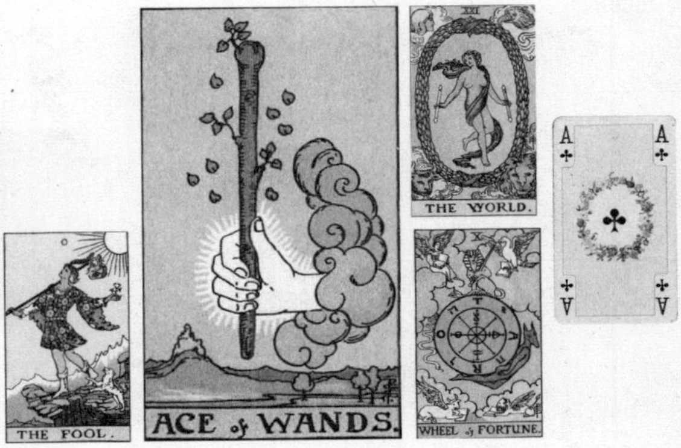

10

The Shadow Stairs
THE NAMELESS INTRUDER

As has been mentioned before, there is an outside staircase at the western front of the House that links the balcony on the second floor with the upper circle's entrance to theTheatre on the first floor. No one really knows why it had initially been named the "Shadow Stairs", but since the night when the Nameless Intruder showed up for the first time, there are many adventurous theories about the origin of that name. However unlikely it may seem that someone would voluntarily spend more than a few minutes at an exposed and far from homely place like this, the Nameless Intruder has never been seen anywhere else, neither inside nor outside the House. And nobody ever sees her come or go. She sits, stands, crouches, or climbs up and down on the Shadow Stairs for hours or days before she mysteriously disappears for an indefinite period of time. Ahbar, the Black Watchman, claims that she once spent more than a twelve-night there. And, frankly speaking, this is not nearly all that seems to be wrong with her.

So it hardly comes as a surprise that, at the beginning, the regular residents were divided on whether she was to be considered as one of them or as a stranger who had no right to call herself an inhabitant of the House until Niãng Mâ, the Mighty Queen, exercised her authority and officially declared the Nameless Intruder an "inhabitant of restricted rights and duties". Her decision was founded on the undisputable fact that the Shadow Stairs always had been and always would be a part of the House and that whoever lived in a distinguishable part of the House on a regular basis was to be considered as a regular inhabitant.The status of "restricted rights and duties" was justified by the Nameless Intruder's unpredictable part-time presence, and, allegedly for the same reason but most obviously following her counsellor's emphatic advice, the Mighty Queen enacted a law that prohibited all other inhabitants from inviting or permitting the Nameless Intruder to enter the inside premises of the House.

It sure seems odd that an inhabitant who has never entered the House is called an "Intruder", completely apart from her staying "nameless" for such a long time. But it may be less hard to understand considering the circumstances of her first appearance on a foggy late autumn month's day. According to the account of Ëlan-Tâsh, the only witness of her arrival, it happened exactly in the middle of the hour of the Horse when the sun was at the zenith of its daily orbit, and in hindsight, the Candid Freecloud Harlot thinks that if she had known about the Nameless Intruder's arrival she would not have expected her at any other time. She was standing on the balcony right outside the Cave of Emptiness, when the Nameless Intruder suddenly appeared out of thin air on the first step of the Shadow Stairs. Until that very moment she had always thought that no one could ever compete with the Unhappy Maiden's natural beauty of appearance. However, the strange figure on the stairs was far beyond compare in this particular respect, even more so against the background of that grey overcast day in late autumn: a voluptuous dark blond woman with the body of a goddess wrapped in a slinky smooth black strap dress that was shot through with gold threads. There was a glow around her that resembled the visual effects that the Poet used to distinguish the exceedingly virtuous figures in his paintings. Her looks were so irresistibly ravishing that even Ëlan-Tâsh, who was renowned for being hard to impress by outer appearances, almost lost her sense of basic trust in her instincts. Fortunately, the Intruder's focus of attention was not on her at that very first moment, and when the beautiful woman turned round to look at her, Ëlan-Tâsh had already recollected herself. It does not bear contemplating what would have happened to the House and its inhabitants if the circumstances of the Nameless Intruder's arrival had been any different from that.

However, from the Nameless Intruder's point of view, the circumstances couldn't have been worse. She had to execute an order of paramount importance that had been placed with her by the Supreme Supervisor himself. Accordingly, she had prepared for it with the most scrupulous precision. But as it became apparent within seconds, all the incalculable factors had turned against her and her plans.

She had made a list of ten possible targets. At the top of it was the Black Watchman who seemed to be the easiest to deceive, followed by the Unhappy Maiden and her dreamy Mother. And, of course, at the foot of the list was the cunning whore, following on the Sailor, the Cat and the Priest. This list had been the basis of her plan of attack. At first sight, there seemed to be better places for a first strike than the Shadow Stairs, but taking all the conditions and restrictions into account that the Supreme Supervisor had imposed on her mission, the Stairs opened her the best chances. It was the perfect place to surprise the Black Watchman and attract his attention. He would see her from below which would give his concupiscent eyes the opportunity to catch an up-skirt glimpse at her. If the first attempt would fail, the Shadow Stairs were not such a bad place to try again, since one rule of the game was that, as soon as she had chosen the place for her first attack, she could not choose another for subsequent ones. So if the Black Watchman would turn out to be unresponsive to her charms (which was very unlikely), she still had two options: She could address someone else either on the Forecourt (which was certainly the most frequented place around the House) or on the second floor balcony. And that "someone else" could have been almost any of the inhabitants but the whore. That was why she had chosen a cold and foggy November Monday noon for her first appearance: It was, according to her calculations, the most improbable moment to meet the Whore on the balcony, and it was the hour of the day when the

BlackWatchman usually became a bit tired and inattentive.

But when she finally carried out her plan, the whore was there. And, as if this had not been enough of bad luck, that bitch became aware of her presence before the Watchman did.

"Who are you?" the Candid Freecloud Harlot asked warily.

"I am a refugee, a poor and desperate expellee of the outer lands like you once were, o Ëlan-Tâsh, gracious Candid Freecloud Harlot," the stranger replied in a miserable tone of voice. "I came here to ask for shelter under the roof of the House that is well known and sung about to be an open place for the needy, the homeless and the persecuted."

That was, of course, the phrase she had prepared for the Black Watchman, and saying it to the whore was probably the most stupid thing the Nameless Intruder could do at that moment. But she had no time to think of something better. However, the Watchman, who was standing right beneath her at the edge of the Forecourt, had heard her words too, and, obviously, she had caught his undivided attention.

"You're pretty well dressed for a refugee," Ëlan-Tâsh said snappishly. "What's your name?"

If the Nameless Intruder had known in advance that, against all odds, she was going to have a brush with the Candid Freecloud Harlot, she would have appeared in the form of Rudolph Valentino, but most probably the Harlot wouldn't even have been susceptible to the most attractive man who ever walked the earth in any of the known worlds.

"I have no name," she sobbed. "They have taken it from me."

The Watchman didn't want to seem unprofessional in the presence of the whore. So he told the newcomer to climb down onto the Forecourt so that he could search her for hidden weapons. She said that she was a bad climber and terribly scared of heights. Ahbar, the Black Watchman, had no choice but to do something that he had hardly ever done before: He entered the House in the light of day to report the situation to the Mighty Queen.

That was the moment when it became perfectly clear that her first attempt to intrude into the affairs of the House had miserably failed. And since she had obviously run out of options, she considered it best to simply disappear on the spot.

Naturally, the Supreme Supervisor became frighteningly furious when the Nameless Intruder told him what had happened, and he criticised her strategic management in the harshest of words. As had been foreseeable, he condemned her to execute as many attacks as it would take to complete her mission and to subject the House and its inhabitants to the Holy Principle. "I want this House to be the paragon of greed, envy, rapacity, and selfishness!" he roared boisterously. To make things worse, he relentlessly refused to relax the rules he had imposed on her freedom of action with regard to this particular operation. Thus, she was not allowed to change the scene of her attack nor her outer appearance nor her way of approaching the targets. It would only arouse more suspicion among the inhabitants, the Supreme Supervisor argued. In other words, the Nameless Intruder had to keep on trying to convince at least one of the inhabitants to explicitly invite her into the House. Not until she had achieved that the Holy Principle of Plutocracy would take its course within the affairs of the House.

Heaven knows that ever since she has tried her best. She spent many nights on the Shadow Stairs trying to beguile the Watchman but could not break his loyalty to the Queen's law, although she came close to accomplish her purpose more often than anyone would guess. She made innumerable attempts on the Mother Gardener's good heart by telling her tear-jerking stories about the purportedly tragic fate that had led her here. She talked insistently to the Poet with the faraway eyes to convince him that the Holy Principle of Plutocracy is undoubtedly superior to the power of emancipated people. Realising that he would stay resistant to her arguments, she approached him with the idea of a new art form that she referred to as "comedy commercials", which made him fly into a towering rage and brought him to the verge of throwing her over the banisters of the Shadow Stairs. Now and again, she took a chance with the Time-Travelling Cat by offering her upscale cat food from selected gourmet delicatessen shops that Mathilda could not even have imagined before. She caught the Unhappy Maiden lingering on the balcony once or twice and promised her all the riches and beauties and luxuries in the world just for a confidential chat in her small cabinet at the end of the first floor corridor. In some of her most desperate moments she even tried to lure the Candid Freecloud Harlot away by making the same promises, not to mention that memorable evening when she interrupted one of the Poet's performances in the Theatre to address the assembled inhabitants from the upper circle's entrance with a passionate speech about unrestricted free markets and rigorously protected external borders, about accelerated economic growth, general prosperity and affluence as a result of the abolition of public and social affairs. In spite of her effort to simplify things, her audience did not really seem to understand the overall coherence of her proposals.

Nevertheless, in case anyone should be deceived into thinking that her lack of success will last forever, it is worth mentioning that the top three on her target list have already begun to blatantly sympathise with her seducements. This is not the Nameless Intruder's first mission, and it most certainly is not her last. She is persevering by nature, she brings thousands of years of professional experience from around the world with her, and there are not many failures on her record so far. However, in the last few days she has got the feeling that she is rapidly running out of time, though she does not really know why.

11

The Roof
ILFÂHR, THE WISTFUL SAILOR

Once upon a time, a long, long time ago, in the blooming period of the Grey Ages when the people in these parts still lived in paltry huts and were organised in small clans, a man and a woman came here from a far-away land by the name of Ilionia. They had crossed the mountains from the south, and although they must have been on the way for a very long time, one could still smell the scent of salt water in their shabby clothes. They looked and behaved like foreigners who came from across the seas, especially the woman with her slit eyes and yellowish skin. But they knew the local language fairly well and thus were able to make friends with the people.

Quite obviously, they were young lovers, and their story was a simple but adventurous one. The man who called himself Ilfâhr had sailed the seven seas for many years, serving the legendary Discovery Fleet of the Ilionian Islands and working his way up to the rank of a ship's captain. In a Far East harbour town he had met Niãng Mâ, the love of his life, and had taken her with him on his last journey back to the port of his hometown. They had got married on the high sea. Because they did not want to be separated from each other most of the time, Ilfâhr deserted from the Fleet, and the two of them decided to travel westward along the Mediterranean coast and try to find a place to settle down in a Middle Zone country where the climate was temperate and the sea was far away.

Since they both came from wealthy and well-educated families and had travelled the world, since they had stories to tell and adjusted themselves willingly to the local customs, they were received with respect and sympathetic interest when they arrived. And so the couple decided to stay. Ilfâhr chose the place between the banks of the Great Northern River and the edge of the dark forest to build a house for himself, his wife, and the family he expected to raise. The local people were astonished when they saw the plans he had drawn: They had never seen or thought of a house of such size and complexity before. Out of sheer curiosity they were all too ready to help him build it almost exactly as it still stands before us in this day and age.

Ilfâhr's basic idea of the House was to give it the looks and feel of one of the great Ilionian discovery ships. The forecourt was designed like a landing stage. As for him, the various rooms represented stowage spaces, crew's quarters, cabins, a caboose, and a captain's saloon. The roof was to be evocative of a navigation bridge, and on the upper floor, right next to the balcony that he called the "crow's nest", only a short corridor and a small ladder away from the roof platform, he built the "Queen's cabin", which was to become Niãng Mâ's private chamber and therefore had to be arranged according to her taste.

Although Ilfâhr had no notion of structural design, the House turned out to be of fine quality in almost every respect, just as he had imagined it. He was truly proud of his work, and when he took his wife by the hand and showed her around, he said to her: "It is far too big for the two of us. Let's start having children right away."

However, what had begun as the perfect idyll took a tragic turn. Niãng Mâ could not conceive so that Ilfâhrs dream of a big happy family did not come true. For a while, he kept himself busy refining the construction of the building, setting out a garden to the west of the House, and exploring the immediate vicinity. But soon it became obvious that he missed his adventurous life at sea and the conquering of new frontiers and foreign lands. He was getting bored in a worrying way. He spent more and more time alone on the roof platform, staring into the distance as if waiting for something that would not come. Sometimes he yelled navigation instructions to a ship's crew that was not there. Niãng Mâ tried her best to distract him from his discontent, but in the long run she could not prevent him from withdrawing into his daydreams evermore often. The day came when he refused to climb down from the roof at night, and a few twelve-nights later he had gone mad beyond recovery. In his mental disturbance, he did not even recognise his wife anymore.

In deference to him and his achievements, and because his desperate wife would not allow it, nobody dared to get him down from the roof by force, and so he has been spending each and every day and night up there ever since. And whenever somebody asked him what he was looking out for, he said that the dry winds from the east were prosperous and that he was going to be the very first man ever to sail to the End of the World and see what lies beyond. That is why people took to call him the Wistful Sailor.

This is the legend that everyone in these parts will tell you to explain how the House has come into the world and why that squalid old madman with the strawberry blond beard and the dirty torn sailor shirt stands on its roof day and night, in any wind and weather, screaming out orders to change course, to set or take in the foresails, bawling long-forgotten shanties, living off the brandy that the Candid Freecloud Harlot occasionally provides him with, and seemingly seeing, hearing, and experiencing things that do not exist anywhere but in his tortured mind. Only Niãng Mâ, the Mighty Queen, can possibly tell whether the legend is true, but as far as is known, she has never told anyone. Some surmise that she made up and spread the story herself in order to legitimate her reign over the House. Anyway, she wields that authority as long as anyone can remember. In the end, each and every inhabitant that has ever lived in the House has been permitted to do so by her decree since the day when Unkásh came all the way from Agathe at the Tyrrhenian shore to dedicate his life to the duties of the local Stargazing Priest.

12

The first time Ëlan-Tâsh, the Candid Freecloud Harlot, became aware of the Ever-Changing Spirit's presence in the House was the starry midsummer night of the Wistful Sailor's birthday in the year of the Horse. She climbed up onto the roof platform at the hour of the Rat to give him his birthday present: a bottle of brandy that she had got from a pedlar in return for her services. Ilfâhr had one of his all too rare brighter moments and took notice of her visit.

"You have no business on the bridge in the middle of the night, sailor!" he bawled at her rigorously.

"I know, captain," Ëlan-Tâsh replied in a submissive tone of voice. "I very much apologise for my trespassing, but I am here by the order of the first mate to convey the best wishes of the whole crew to you."

A tear of affection trickled down the Wistful Sailor's cheek into his beard when she handed the bottle over to him. He smiled indulgently, nosing it with complacency. "Thank you, sailor," he said, "a decent drink is always welcome when you're approaching the End of the World. Our voyage is about to be over very soon."

"It is?" the Candid Freecloud Harlot asked, obviously smitten with surprise.

"Oh yes, it is. I advise you to have a good snatch of sleep tonight, sailor!"

"Aye-aye, Sir!"

Ëlan-Tâsh bowed slightly and climbed down the ladder to the second floor corridor. When she stepped through the narrow doorway into the Cave of Emptiness she perceived an almost unnoticeable movement in the corner to her right. A tall thin man was standing there, gazing into space, seemingly without being aware that she had just entered the room. Quite evidently, he was not real in a strict sense. He was translucent and colourless like the walking dead, as if he had consisted of nothing but silvery grey mist. However, when she turned around to look at him, he dissolved into thin air all of a sudden, leaving behind a vague flicker in the shape of his naked body. Strangely enough, he reappeared the same moment when Ëlan-Tâsh looked the other way. Then he was gone.

As previously mentioned, the Candid Freecloud Harlot was not a person to scare easily. She had seen many things in her life that others could not even conceive of. Nevertheless, she pondered over what she had just seen for quite some time before she fell asleep that night, all the more so because, after the Spirit had disappeared, the familiar tone interval of a middle D and an E flat that was produced by the resonance of the Cave of Emptiness and the Theatre beneath, did not sound pleasant and inspiring to her anymore. On the contrary, for the first time, she perceived it as a strangely disconcerting dissonance. That night, she dreamed of the Ever-Changing Spirit, though she did not remember her dream when she woke up the next morning. It was the first of many dreams to come.

Thenceforward, the Ever-Changing Spirit appeared regularly in many different places of the House. A few twelve-nights later, all of the inhabitants had encountered him several times. However, since he could only be seen distinctly out of the corner of the eye, just a few of them were aware that they had actually seen him, and those who were not considered him to be some kind of illusion. Among those who saw him, like the Queen, the Priest, or the Time-Travelling Cat, Ëlan-Tâsh was the only one who showed any interest in him and began to observe his habits. She found out that he mostly appeared at night and that he seemed to enter the House through the three-part swing door in the first floor corridor, which she considered to be proof of his otherworldlyness. Moreover, because of her abilities as a mind-walker, she easily accepted the intuitive knowledge she gained of him through her dreams, though she could not consciously remember a single one of them. In these dreams, she called him by his name and became a part of his world, meeting him in strange places, talking with him about things that she would never have thought of while awake, beginning to get an idea of who he was, how he lived, and what kept him attached to the House. In other words, she became acquainted with him in a way that made her miss him whenever he stayed away for a longer period of time. But whenever she met him and tried to address him in her own world, it seemed that he couldn't care less about her. He not only didn't pay any attention to her, he acted as if she did not even exist.

Needless to say that Ëlan-Tâsh consulted the cards about the Ever-Changing Spirit again and again. But however often she did, they always told her the same, and what they told her did not make any sense to her. Maybe it was out of the reach of her comprehension. Maybe the cards just did not relate to the affairs they were consulted about. Anyway, the urge of sharing her experiences with someone finally prompted the Candid Freecloud Harlot to entrust herself to the Stargazing Priest. After she had told him almost everything she could possibly express in words, he was lost in thought for several minutes. Then he looked at her sternly and said most emphatically: "It comes as no surprise at all that spirits of other worlds and times are haunting a house that is as old as this one. However, we are not meant to interfere in their affairs. They dwell, quite literally, in the spaces in between: in what the wise men call the *spatia media*. You have enmeshed yourself in matters that are beyond anything we can properly understand. So all I can tell you is that you should treat this unnatural acquaintance of yours with the utmost caution and restraint."

Ëlan-Tâsh did not know what exactly the Priest had meant to tell her, and quite self-interestedly, she did not ask. Hence, her mysterious and rather imponderable relationship with the Ever-Changing Spirit took its inevitable course. Soon enough her personality underwent severe changes that nobody except for the Priest really noticed, although they left their obvious mark on the ordinary run of events within the community of the House. –

There is a number that represents the completeness of space. The number is 7.

There is a number that represents the completeness of time. The number is 12.

And there is a number that represents the completeness of space and time as a whole. The number is 9.

In the light of this ancient principle, which can be, according to different worldviews, conceived of as either a mystical or a philosophical one, and furthermore in the light of the events mentioned above, the question might arise whether the number of inhabitants of the House has ever been complete at one particular time, or, for that matter, how many inhabitants have actually lived in this place. If the inhabitants themselves were asked, they certainly would give different answers to the question. Some would not consider the Time-Travelling Cat or the Nameless Intruder as declared or full-value inhabitants. And others would argue that no one really knows whether the Ever-Changing Spirit can be considered as an inhabitant at all, completely apart from the incertitude as to when exactly he entered the House for the first time.

Evidently, the number of inhabitants dwelling in the House has always been an unsolved riddle that may well be deemed a metaphysical one. And, after his conversation with the Candid Freecloud Harlot, Unkásh, the Stargazing Priest, spent many a contemplative hour in considering this particular question.

Be that as it may, in the prime of the following midautumn month, something happened that unavoidably brought the changes in the Candid Freecloud Harlot's life to the attention of all her fellow inhabitants. One morning, Ëlan-Tash did not awake from her dreams anymore. She was captured in a deep sleep that could neither be ended nor interrupted by any means. Days grew into twelve-nights, and twelve-nights grew into months, but her mysterious condition did not change in the least. Unkásh might have had something to say about the situation, but he did not. However, he anxiously kept an eye on the consequences, and so did the Mighty Queen. Some of the inhabitants might have thought that each and every one among them was replaceable with regard to the everyday matters of the House, especially the Harlot. But they turned out to be wrong.

Not only were there no inspired performances given at theTheatre anymore, which might have been acceptable at short sight, there were also no discrete consultations about private affairs and decisions, no straightforward arguments and no tempering interventions when it came to settling the differences among them. Even Daimâliah, the Mother Gardener, and Persephone, the Unhappy Maiden, who had never been closely involved with the Harlot, and even Ahbar, the Black Watchman, who never esteemed her much beyond her services as a whore, had to acknowledge that the balances within their cohabitation, which always had been so emphatically promoted by the Queen, were gravely disturbed. In short, the overall mood in the House took a worrisome turn for the worse, and unmistakable discords crept into the usual consonance of the vibrations between the rooms.

Ëlan-Tâsh stayed in her deep sleep for almost ten months while the year of the Horse passed into the year of the Sheep, and in many ways, those were the darkest months in the history of the House since the Dark Ages had come to an end. During all that time, the Harlot lay in her bed, not making a single move, the healthy chestnut colour of her skin slowly fading into white as snow, and sometimes it seemed she might even have stopped breathing.The only stirs in the Cave of Emptiness were caused by the occasional visits of the Ever-Changing Spirit whose appearances in the House seemed to become considerably more frequent to those who had eyes to see him.

However, on the 10th day of the midsummer month in the year of the Sheep, Ëlan-Tash will wake up. She will rise from her bed shortly after nightfall, the sonic vibration of a distant F sharp in her ears that will tenderly harmonise with the resonance of the Cave and the Stairwell in a touching minor chord. She will hurry down the stairs to find out what the turmoil at the entrance of the House is all about. And that will be the day when everything changes. From that day on, the run of events at this place will never be the same again. And, finally, there will be not one more and not one less than exactly twelve inhabitants living in the House.

.ove rescue me
:ome forth and speak to me
ìaise me up and don't let me fall
Jo man is my enemy
Λy own hands imprison me
.ove rescue me

Λany strangers have I met
)n the road to my regret
Λany lost who seek to find themselves in me
'hey ask me to reveal
The very thoughts they would conceal
.ove rescue me

n the cold mirror of a glass
see my reflection pass
see the dark shades of what I used to be
see the purple of her eyes
The scarlet of my lies
.ove rescue me

have conquered my past
'he future is here at last
stand at the entrance of a new world I can see
'he ruins to the right of me
Vill soon have lost sight of me
.ove rescue me

'm here without a name
n the palace of my shame
.ove rescue me

Bono & Bob Dylan; *Love Rescue Me,*
rom U2; *Rattle and Hum*, 1989
) Blue Mountain Music Ltd.)

I had no idea how long I had been staring at the countless layers of code when I finally ripped off the headset and flung it on the floor. All I knew was that, suddenly, there had been this unbearable pain inside my head that had almost numbed me. Admittedly, I should have known better by then. I should have shut down the system first, but I was unable to think clearly.

For whatever reason, I didn't leave the house immediately. I went upstairs instead, and while I did, the code sequences gradually faded away. When I reached the upper floor, I headed for the balcony, ready to face the ugly bubbles again, but there were no bubbles this time. I stopped dead when I saw the ravishing dark blond woman on the exterior staircase. She was wrapped in a slinky smooth black strap dress that was shot through with gold threads. There was some kind of halo around her head, but apart from that she looked like the hostess of a TV show. She was looking in my direction without noticing me at all. She conveyed the impression of being bored to death.

Not nearly as appalling as the bubbles, I thought when I realised that she was sort of translucent like a ghost. I turned around and stepped into the room the construction plans designated "L'antre de vide", the "Cave of Emptiness", just to find out whether there were any more of these apparitions. I saw another woman lying on a net of ropes that were tied to the borders of a circular hole in the duckboard floor like a hammock. She was wrapped in a colourful hippie robe and seemed sound asleep. Her face faintly reminded me of someone but I didn't bother to find out who it was. While I was looking at her, she gradually turned greyish and transparent. I took it for a sign that the aftereffects of the system interruption were ebbing away. My headache was almost gone.

I had seen enough anyway. It was high time for me to get out of here, so I hurried back down the stairs to the first floor. Out of the left corner of my eye I spotted something that looked like an old lady in a wheelchair but I didn't pay any attention to it. And when I reached the entrance door, this huge black man with a spear in his hand blocked my way. He had muscles the size of chinchilla rats and was so translucent that he was hardly visible. I ran straight through him without experiencing the slightest resistance. Apparently, neither did he.

When I reached the park bench and slumped onto it, I was drenched in sweat and completely out of breath. No doubt, I had gotten too old for antics like this. As I turned to look at the house again, it stood there as if nothing out of the ordinary had happened. The sun was shining, people came along the walkway without deigning to look at me, and a bunch of sparrows gathered around a dustbin to pick up leftovers from the ground. Not that I had expected anything else, but it really was amazing that everything around me seemed so normal.

As soon as I had recovered my breath, I finally put the MSDT device back into its case. A moment later, the two guys with the cameras turned up again and continued to take pictures all over the house. They didn't seem to clock anything unusual. However, the one in the black suit found the headset I had carelessly left behind in the first floor corridor. He examined it closely, showed it to his colleague and probably asked whether it belonged to him. The Peter Fonda guy shook his head, whereon the baldhead stuffed it into his cam bag. It didn't bother me much. I was sure it wouldn't be of any further use for me anyway. Nothing would make me endure another SPACEMAKER session for the rest of my life. My job was done.

Well, was it? – I had found the code that Adrienne had expected me to find. I had seen it. It was definitely there. I had also found out that there was enough of it to keep a whole professional decryption team busy for a lifetime. HOUSE 1 was to be dismantled the following week and rebuilt some time later at Versailles in France and, possibly, in several other cities around the globe. In short, there was no way to find out what the code sequences were all about or why and by whom they had been programmed into the structure of HOUSE 1. It was not even imaginable who except for God Almighty Himself – sorry, Adrienne, it's just a metaphor – could have possibly done this in the short period of time since the house had been constructed. In this respect, there was nothing more that I could do.

On the other hand, considering that the code was transferable to human brains and, theoretically, to any other kind of communicative system, it was absolutely unacceptable not to know how and to what end it had been written in the first place, even more so because the sequences on the foremost layers had very much looked like encryptions of *genetic* code ... –

... Of course, there was this outrageous story Adrienne had told me on that Sunday in March. The story that this house had existed in another world way before the directors of the HOUSE 1 project had even thought of it: that it actually existed in two different worlds at the same time and that the code sequences might be some kind of interface between them. But, even in view of my latest discovery, that story was just as unacceptable as anything else, now wasn't it? ... –

At this point, I was completely stumped. I didn't know what to make of all this, and at the very same moment it crossed my mind that, if the scenario of these most peculiar events had not been rewritten in the meantime, my putative pursuers in the black Ford cross country vehicle would probably enter the arena any minute. I had to disappear from the scene as quickly as possible. Although I didn't consider them to be a threat to me anymore now that I had accomplished what I had come here for, I still didn't want to cross their path if there was a way to avoid it.

Five minutes later, I sat down at a table on the panorama terrace of the *Starling Hotel* and ordered a double Jack Daniels on the rocks. Another five minutes later, I ordered another one. And just as my cerebral gyri started to function again, a huge shadow fell onto the table, and Adrienne Fromsett herself sat down on the opposite side. For the first time, I saw her wearing blue jeans and a plain white T-shirt with a simple slogan on it: *Take it as it comes, but take it!* Nevertheless, the waiter stared at her behind her back as if she had been the alien. I certainly had not expected her to meet me here, but, to be honest, I was not really surprised. What did surprise me though was that she ordered another two double Jacks on the rocks.

"So you have made it after all," she said as if this had been about winning a game of bridge. "You have opened the door."

"Well, I don't actually know what I have done," I replied sardonically, without wasting a thought about her peculiar wording. "But whatever it is, it is done."

I put the MSDT device on the table. She shoved it into her buckskin shoulder bag without any further comment.

I told her what had happened and tried to explain what I thought of it. I told her about everything except my impression that I had been followed, which may have been the biggest of all the mistakes I made that day. I had had no intention of withholding the information from her. I simply forgot to mention it. From my point of view, there was plenty enough to discuss without speculating on putative SYNTHESIS agents executing putative plans. Then again, she may well have known all about it. She may even have known already what was going to happen. You never knew with Adrienne Fromsett.

However, after she had heard me out, she didn't show the slightest inclination to talk about the situation.

"I know that you wouldn't believe anything I'd have to say about this," Adrienne said, "and I can understand that. Just let me assure you that everything is all right now. You don't need to worry about that code any longer. It is not meant to do any harm. As far as I can tell, it contains nothing but good news. You have done a great job. Just leave it at that for the time being."

I wanted to retort, I thought that she had got me wrong in one way or another, but at that very moment, I didn't know what to say. She bent over and looked me straight in the eye.

"However, there is one last thing I would like you to do for me before I discharge you from your assignment. Only if you approve of it, of course."

"And what would that be?" I asked with a queasy feeling.

"First, I would like you to order another two of these," she said, pointing at her empty glass. "And then I would like you to book a double room for one night."

It must have been around nine in the evening when I woke up in a rumpled hotel bed. Adrienne was standing at the balcony door, looking out onto the moonlit Lake Geneva. She was dressed already, wearing a denim jacket, her shoulder bag in hand. Without turning to me, she said: "I'd like to show you something, Frank."

"Is there anything left to show me?" I replied heedlessly, smothering a yawn.

She turned around, sat down on the edge of the bed and kissed me passionately. I was not sure, but I thought I saw tears in her eyes when she whispered: "Yes, there is."

I got out of bed and slipped into my clothes. Without saying another word, we left the hotel and walked up to the campus. I knew where she was heading, of course, and in light of all that had happened before, it seemed only natural to return to the HOUSE 1 site together one last time.

Adrienne stopped about eighty meters away from the building, near the park bench where I had sat down at noon. By night, with the moon standing exactly over the roof platform, the construction looked a bit bigger than by daylight. However, she stared at it as if she could see something that I couldn't.

"What is it that you want to show me?" I asked after a while.

"Try to focus on the structure," she said. "Maybe you have to look at it out of the corner of your eye."

After a few seconds I saw the faint light of a candle in the room on top of the south-west corner.

"Do you think there's someone in there?" –

There was no need for an answer. A bald and skinny old man draped in a long white robe appeared at the foot of the stairs and walked towards the entrance. He was clearly visible because he carried something that looked like an oil lamp. The flickering light fell through the gaps between the wooden slats and illuminated the lower parts of the house in a very spooky way. When he stepped out onto the front platform, the light fell on a much taller man with a long black spear in his hand. He stood at the border of the platform and looked in our direction. The soft breeze from the south made his black cloak flap. It was the same man I had seen when I had left the house in the afternoon, but this time he was not a half-transparent ghost. He appeared to be completely real.

In spite of the distance and although they were speaking in a low voice, I could hear every word they said when they started talking to each other.

"Something's happening out there," the black man said. "I can feel it. They are closing in on us."

"I trust your senses, Ahbar," the old man replied calmly, "I do not know whether we are going to face any hostile confrontation tonight. Chances are that we are not. But be on guard anyway."

When the old man stepped back into the ground floor corridor, I suddenly realised that the surroundings of the house had changed. The lights of downtown Lausanne in the background had disappeared. Instead, I saw the big trees of a dark forest, and I could hear the rush of a mighty river from the north. But the most obvious alteration was that there was no security fence anymore.

"They are expecting you," Adrienne said in an enraptured tone of voice that would have been appropriate for a comment on what a beautiful night it was.

While I was still struggling for words, the sharp bang of a gunshot broke the silence. It came from somewhere behind us. Adrienne collapsed without making a sound. I twirled around but couldn't see anybody in the dark. Then I kneeled down and bent over to look at her face. She was still breathing. The left side of her chest was ripped open, and her white shirt was all stained with blood.

"Don't move!" somebody yelled at us. It was the shrill voice of a woman with a strange foreign accent. "We don't mean to harm you, Mr Teller! Just stay where you are!"

I wrapped my arms around Adrienne's shoulder, and she looked up at me with a horrifying stare, breathing heavily.

"It's not me they're after, Frank," she wheezed with the last of her strength. "It's *you*. Please, run! Do it for me! Run!"

"I can't leave you behind," I stammered out helplessly.

"I will be waiting for you there. Trust me just this once, Frank, and *run*!"

Her right hand faintly touched her bag. Then her eyes grew dim, and she passed away.

With a lump in my throat I lowered her dead body to the grassy ground, and while I did, a beam of white light flashed past me. I heard someone scream, but I didn't give a rip about it. Adrienne's last words resounded in my head, and I acted without thinking. I pulled the MSDT device out of her bag, leaped up on my feet and started to run. There was a volley of gunshots, another blinding flash of light blocked my view, and somewhere in the background, people were shouting. After the fifth flash of light, there was nothing but deathly silence. I just ran.

When I reached the Forecourt, Ahbar, the Black Watchman, headed towards me.

"Are you hurt?" he asked me with his low rumbling voice. The deadly light of the sun still glowed on the metal spike of the Black Spear.

"No, I'm not," I gasped. "Thank you, Ahbar. I guess I owe you one."

He nodded gracefully and led me to the entrance door. Before I entered the House, I turned to look back upon the world that I was about to leave behind. The lake had vanished, and I couldn't see the campus anymore. There was just an open prairie. The only thing that was faintly reminiscent of where I had come from was the shape of a dead body lying on the grass at some distance. Any time soon, it would disappear too. I would never know her real name. I would never know anything about her client or, for that matter, whether he had ever existed at all. And I would never know whether there had ever been a big idea behind all this. All I knew was that, at one point in her outrageous story, she had suggested that there might be a possibility of "dreaming one's way from one world into the other".

For a moment, I wondered if I should return to a reality that had long since taken almost everything away from me: my wife, my kids, my job, my passion, my past, my future, and thus my dignity. I imagined a world grown old and weary of itself, a world on the verge of deliriously descending into the Bounded Ages. I imagined the people helplessly struggling to understand in hindsight how things possibly could have turned out the way they did, and I imagined all the many preposterous lies that had to be made up to explain what defied any explanation. But most of all, I wondered at how things always turned out different than expected.

And, just for a second, I thought of the quarter of a million that had been transferred to an offshore account at my disposal.

Then I made a decision.

As I turned around, Unkásh, the Stargazing Priest, stood at the door, the cold heat lamp in his hand. He bowed slightly to me: "Are you Frãnh', the Ever-Changing Spirit, born under the sign of Gemini, of whom the Astrochronicles say that he will arrive on the 10th day of the midsummer month in the year of the Sheep to become the twelfth inhabitant of the House?"

"I'm not quite sure," I answered, "but I guess I must be him."

"Then let me invite you in and show you to the Bed Room. Niãng Mâ, the Mighty Queen, is ready to receive you." And, pointing at the device, he added: "By the way, what is this wondrous thing that you are holding in your hand?"

When I presented him with it, it seemed to be nothing but a piece of a clouded mirror.

"It's a ... well, I think it's a mind machine," I said. "You can have it if you want. I have no use for it anymore."

"How very interesting!"

He preceded towards the Stairwell and just as we arrived at the first step, Ëlan-Tâsh, the Candid Freecloud Harlot, appeared at the head of the stairs. She seemed to be a little drowsy, but she was all smiles when she looked at me and said: "So you have made it after all! I have been waiting for you for so long. I bid you welcome home, Frãnh', the Ever-Changing Spirit!"

Revision Lectures on General Principles of Surgery

A Guide for Surgical Trainees

Revision Lectures on General Principles of Surgery

A Guide for Surgical Trainees

Srinivasan Ravi MBBS MS(General Surgery)
FRCSEd FRCSEng
Erstwhile Consultant Surgeon
Blackpool Teaching Hospital
Lancashire, UK
Professor of Surgical Practice
KS Hegde Medical Academy
NITTE (Deemed to be) University
Mangalore, Karnataka, India

JP medical publishers

London • New Delhi

Published by JP Medical Ltd,
83 Victoria Street, London,
SW1H 0HW, UK
Tel: +44 (0)20 3170 8910
Email: info@jpmedpub.com
Web: www.jpmedpub.com

EU GPSR Authorised Representative
Logos Europe, 9 rue Nicolas Poussin
17000, La Rochelle, France
Phone: +33 (0) 6 67 93 73 78
E-mail: Contact@logoseurope.eu

ISBN: 978-1-78779-190-9

British Library Cataloguing in Publication Data
A catalogue record for this book is available from the British Library

Library of Congress Cataloging in Publication Data
A catalog record for this book is available from the Library of Congress

Project Manager: Bhavana Sharma

Editorial Assistant: Keshav Kumar Baghel

Cover Design: Seema Dogra

Preface

This booklet is a compilation of current knowledge that a trainee needs to get through the basic surgical examinations.

When I was a student, my grandfather advised me to 'get a small book that details key points and learn it well'. I have stuck to that principle. One must gain some knowledge about everything and everything about some things. This book will help with the former. For the latter, in depth reading, it is needed from textbooks of surgery.

These are days of learning from YouTube and that too can be of assistance. The opportunity to learn is plentiful; however, as Confucius said, 'a journey of a thousand miles begins with the first step'. The difficulty is to get up and take the first step. Once that ceiling of laziness is broken, 'the job is a game'. This book discusses all the topics that one must know something about if a doctor is to be erudite. It is set in an easy-to-read format. It is based on 'Snippets in Surgery, Volumes 1/2'. It deals with acute surgery and basic principles of perioperative care that underpin delivery of diligent care. It will serve as a guide to managing surgical patients and will also assist in rapid revision.

This book will be useful for medical students, foundation and core trainees as well as surgical trainees around the world. Nothing can supplant life skills learnt by simply being there and observing the management of surgical problems; watching how others confront problems over time will always be rewarding.

I am always keen to state my own favourite quote: "The attitude determines the altitude". The humble bumble bee is too fat, and has short wings, surely, it cannot fly. But no one told that to the bumble bee! It flies with ease as it wants to get the best possible nectar for its hive. Master the basics, fly high and help your patients.

Enjoy the journey!

Srinivasan Ravi
July, 2025

Acknowledgements

I wish to acknowledge the valuable input of my wife, family and colleagues to the aesthetic aspects and crucial insights into the content, offering thoughtful critiques and suggestions that enriched the narrative.

Srinivasan Ravi

Dedication

This book is dedicated to the countless patients who entrust their lives to the surgeons and to the mentors who shape each move of the scalpel into skill, expertise and above all to wisdom.

Contents

Chapter 1

The surgically ill patient

Introduction

Dealing with ill patients is as challenging as rewarding. Patient care will often require support of senior colleagues. This may involve specialities other than surgical such as critical care, anaesthesia and medicine.

Presentation of the surgical patient

Acutely ill

- Need immediate resuscitation and action
- This may be in:
  - The resuscitation area of the accident and emergency unit, or
  - In the wards during observation, or
  - In the postoperative period from complications of procedures

Moderately ill

- These patients present with worsening problem over a few hours or days
- There will be time to take a proper history and plan of an appropriate action

Elective patients

- These patients are generally well, allowing time for routine investigations, planning and action

The 'acutely ill patient' may be unable to give any history and be in a state of collapse. The primary survey consists of '*ABCDE*' and '*P*' for pain control.

A: Airway
B: Breathing
C: Circulation – cardiovascular system (CVS)
D: Disability – central nervous system (CNS) and blood sugar
E: Exposure
P: Pain control

Evaluate: The patient's physiology before the pathology. The patient as a whole prior to the affected part. The pain alongside resuscitation.
Assess: Pump and pulmonary function physiology before pathology patient before the affected part.

Ensure that the patient's airway is patent and protected from the danger of aspiration.

If there is no response to initial communication, or the patient is unconscious then the first step is to ensure that the airway is patent by:

- *Sweeping* the oral cavity with the finger followed by *suction*
- Eliminating collection or *foreign body*
- Insertion of an *oropharyngeal tube* such as the 'Guedel Airway'

Once the airway is secured then:

- Deliver *high-flow oxygen* through a mask with a reservoir. Oxygen and fluids should be given at the outset to all surgically ill patients. This is usually *15 L/min*
- Monitor oxygen saturation with a *pulse oximeter* and maximise the amount of oxygen that can be given safely taking into consideration chronic obstructive pulmonary disease (COPD) where appropriate
- Establish *venous access* with a large cannula (sizes may vary between countries) and run in *intravenous fluids.* The type of fluid does not matter, but a good starting point is 10–20 mL of crystalloid or colloid per kilogram body weight
- *Follow the 5/10/20/30 rule:*
  - 5 mL/kg in patients with cardiac compromise
  - 10 mL/kg in the normotensive patient
  - 20 mL/kg in the hypotensive patient
  - 30 mL/kg in sepsis or when the lactate is >4

  It is safer to give the fluid in aliquots of 200 mL stat especially in the elderly with review and reassessment and, if needed, redirection of management.
- Remember that hypoxia wrecks the physiology rapidly and is likely to cause immediate problems.

Oxygen delivery ***(Box 1)*** *is affected below a haemoglobin level of 80 g/L (8 g/dL).*

- Check the blood sugar
- Check the pregnancy status in young women
- Call for help. Do not run with the ball; play with the team.

Box 1: Basics of oxygen delivery

Methods of delivery:

- Nasal cannula
- Simple mask
- *Re-breathing mask:* Permits admixture of inspired and expired air effectively increases dead space
- *Non-rebreathing mask:* Oxygen flows through a reservoir to the mask. A valve prevents entry of exhaled air into the reservoir allowing a high concentration of oxygen to be delivered. *This type of mask is used in hypoxic patients to deliver a high flow of oxygen of 10–15 L/min under supervision*
- *Venturi mask:* Ideal for patients with chronic obstructive pulmonary disease (COPD) where the percentage of oxygen delivered must be constant. This mask is colour-coded for flow rates from 24% to 60%

Continues opposite

Box 1: *Continued*

- Laryngeal mask
- Endotracheal intubation
- Tracheostomy

Terminology:

- *Flow rate:* The rate of flow of oxygen can be increased or decreased by adjusting the flow from the oxygen tube
- *FiO_2:* Fraction of inspired air. Normal air contains 21% oxygen. The FiO_2 for therefore, is 21%
- *PaO_2:* Partial pressure of oxygen in the blood is only 12% and not 21% because of dead space air intermixing with inspired air and physiological shunts
- *SaO_2:* Oxygen saturation is measured by the pulse oximeter. A saturation of 94% equates to the PaO_2 of 8

Key points

- Talk to the patient and assess response
- Ensure airway is patent
- Set up high-flow oxygen
- Put up a pulse oximeter *and read it*
- Cannulate and run in fluids 10–20 mL/kg
- Catheterise
- *Check blood sugar:* Hypoglycaemia is often overlooked
- Avoid delays. Delays have a compounding effect
- Seek assistance early

Moderately ill patients are those who can talk to you and give a history. There will be time available to:

- Take a history and examine the patient
- Arrange investigations
- Discuss with senior colleagues

Elective patients are generally well.

- Take a history
- Review prior investigations
- Document comorbidity, medications and allergies

Comorbidity evaluation

- Cardiac
- Respiratory
- Cerebrovascular
- Renal
- Hepatobiliary
- Thrombo-embolic
- Metabolic, e.g. diabetes

- Drugs, e.g. anticoagulants/antiplatelets
- Dementia and lack of capacity

The assessment of the critically ill patients should follow a practised protocol and should include the following.

- *Primary assessment* and immediate action as needed
- Review of all information that is available
- *Secondary or re-assessment*
- Organisation of immediate investigations
- Plan of action based on the above
- Ongoing assessment followed by possible revision of the plan, if needed
- Communication with seniors/colleagues

Look and link. Do not just concentrate on just the processes but make the link between the observations and the need to act.
Act on abnormal observations. If an observation is abnormal, then it is abnormal. If you think it does not match your assessment check again.

Many ill patients may experience a state of systemic inflammatory response syndrome (SIRS) **(Box 2)**. This occurs as a reaction to inflammation. In sepsis, the response is inappropriate and unregulated, triggering a series of physiological reactions that, if not identified early, can lead to multiple systemic changes, potentially resulting in organ failure and death.Odipictat eiunt lamus velecto vendae velesed quisit dem remodit volorrupic tem

Box 2: Systemic inflammatory response syndrome (SIRS)

T: Temperature	>38°C–<36°C
T: Tachycardia	>90 beats/min
T: Tachypnoea	>20 breaths/min
T: Total white cell count	>12–<4

(Pneumonic: *Three T's white with sugar or 4 T's with sugar)*

Note: Blood sugar may also be elevated in a non-diabetic. Mentation may be affected. If two of the above four are elevated, the patient is deemed to be in a state of 'systemic inflammatory response'.

Chapter 2

Sepsis

Sepsis is a syndrome with occurrence of manifestations remote from the site of insult. Remote tissues show the effects of:

- Inflammation
- Vasodilatation
- Increased vascular permeability
- Leucocyte accumulation

For example, cellulitis from a big toe infection in a diabetic can manifest as sepsis leading to multiorgan failure. At the site, it manifests as infection and cellulitis, but systemically it can manifest as full-blown sepsis.

Timely rapid remedial actions at the initial stages may break the chain of self-sustaining progression towards multiple organ failure and inevitable death.

Early recognition of sepsis is possible with monitoring of respiratory rate, drop in blood pressure, and changes in mentation.

This is the basis of quick sequential organ failure assessment (qSOFA*)* **(Box 1)**, a method for early appreciation of sepsis.

Box 1: Quick sequential organ failure assessment (qSOFA)

Quick sequential organ failure assessment

Bedside assessment: Respiration-Pressure-Mentation - RPM

Tachypnoea: Greater than 22 *R: Respiration*
Hypotension systolic blood pressure: Less than 100 mmHg *P: Pressure*
Altered mentation: GCS < 15 *M: Mentation*

Each parameter is awarded a single point. A positive score is 2 or more points. This assessment is used for patients in environments other than the ITU.

A positive qSOFA raises the suspicion that the patient may be harbouring a focus of sepsis. These patients should be screened for sepsis.

GCS, Glasgow coma scale; ITU, intensive therapy/care unit.

The 'sepsis six'

Once sepsis is suspected, the 'sepsis six' must be initiated.

1. Administer oxygen to maintain saturation > 94%
2. Take blood cultures at least a peripheral set. Think source control – may need cerebrospinal fluid (CSF)/urine/sputum cultures
3. Give intravenous antibiotics as per protocol 'within the hour'
4. Administer intravenous fluids at 10–20 mL/kg initially
5. Check serum lactate levels
6. Measure urine output

Management of critically ill surgical patients must occur on the threshold of the operating theatre. It is best done in collaboration with the critical care team because the situation may progress rapidly to the patient, requiring higher and higher levels of care.

Goals of therapy for initial resuscitation are universal.

- Replete circulation
- Identify source of loss
- Prevent further loss
- Replete loss

Distinguishing sepsis from systemic inflammatory response syndrome can be useful.

The inflammatory response to insult could be an:

- Appropriate response
- Inappropriate response

If a patient is in a state of systemic inflammatory response, then greater attention must be paid to the patient, and the reason for the response must be evaluated.

Identify and treat the source of infection. It is all too easy to discharge a patient with abdominal discomfort, a high white cell count, and a tachycardia only to find later that the patient had a perforated diverticulum of the sigmoid. Valuable time can thus be lost.

Principles of management is the same for all surgical emergencies beta hCG **(Box 2)**.

The NEWS is based on the Royal College of Physicians Working Party **(Table 1)** (2017).

Box 2: Principles of management

Universal principles of care:

- Immediate assessment
- Immediate investigations

Immediate assessment: ABCDE and P

Never forget pulse oximetry

Continues opposite

Box 2: *Continued*

Immediate investigations:

- *Urine* for nitrates, β-human chorionic gonadotropin (β-hCG), sugar and blood
- *Blood* for sugar, full blood count, electrolytes and urea, coagulation profile
- *Radiology* for assisting assessment and diagnosis including erect chest X-ray, ultrasound (USS) and CT scan

Comorbidity assessment:

- ECG to exclude acute myocardial event
- Diabetes
- Chronic obstructive pulmonary disease (COPD)
- Renal status
- Anti-coagulants, if any

Call for assistance/Allied speciality advice

SILDA:

- *Stabilisation:* Blood pressure over 90 mmHg/O_2 > 94%
- *Investigation:* Concurrently with making the patient stable
- *Localisation:* Find the cause
- *Decision:* Type of care – conservative, interventional, and palliative
- *Action:* Prompt action saves lives. No vacillation

Table 1 NEWS scoring system

Physiological parameter	3	2	1	0	1	2	3
Respiration rate/min	≤8		9–11	**12–20**		21–24	≤25
SpO_2 (normal)%	≤91	92–93	93–94	**≤96**			
SpO_2 (COPD)%	≤83	84–85	86–87	**88–92 ≤93**	93–94 oxygen	95–96 oxygen	≤97 oxygen
Systolic blood pressure (mmHg)	≤90	91–100	101–110	**111–219**			≤220
Pulse rate	≤40		41–50	**51–90**	91–110	111–130	≤131
Consciousness				**Alert**			CVPU
Temperature (°C)	≤35		35.1–36.0	**36.1–38.0**	38.1–39.0	>39.1	

COPD, chronic obstructive pulmonary disease; CVPU, confusion, voice, pain, and unresponsive.

Note that oxygen delivery adds 2 to the score.

Track and trigger

NEWS score is used to trigger appropriate response. This is the basis of track and trigger.

The trigger levels must be locally agreed and implemented.
Score 0: 12 hourly monitoring of patient is sufficient

Score 1–4: Low risk—
- Patient will need 6-hourly monitoring
- Prompt assessment by ward nurse to decide on change to frequency of monitoring or escalation of clinical care

Score 3 in a single parameter: Low-to-medium risk—
- Patient will need hourly monitoring
- Urgent review by ward-based team of nurses or doctors to determine cause
- Decide on change to frequency of monitoring or escalation of clinical care

Score of 5–7: Medium risk—
- Patient will need hourly monitoring
- Urgent review by ward-based doctor or acute care team nurse to decide on escalation to critical care

Score of 7 or higher: High risk—
- Patient will need continuous monitoring
- Immediate assessment by critical care team, usually leading to patient's transfer to higher-dependency care area

Levels of care

- *Level 0 care:* It is in the *normal ward*
- *Level 1 care:* It is in a *specialist acute ward* such as a postoperative ward
- Level 2 care is in the high-dependency unit (HDU) care, where there is failure of at least one major organ
- Level 3 care is in the intensive care unit (ICU) level care, when there is respiratory failure needing ventilation

World Health Organisation performance status

- *Performance status (PS) 0:* The patient can carry out normal activity without restriction
- *PS 1:* Restricted in strenuous activity; can carry out light work
- *PS 2:* Capable of all self-care; unable to carry out any work activities; up and about >50% of waking hours
- *PS 3:* Symptomatic and in a chair or in bed for >50% of the day, but not bedridden
- *PS 4:* Completely disabled; cannot carry out any self-care; totally confined to bed or chair

Each drop in PS halves the survival rate statistically. A PS 3 patient will live half as long as a PS 2 patient.

Chapter 3

Nutrition of the surgical patient

Points of note in the nutrition of the surgical patient

- Malnutrition is common in surgical patients
- Obese patients can be malnourished
- Poor nutrition prolongs stay due to problems with postoperative infection and poor wound healing
- Low body mass index (BMI) is a contributor to poor recovery
- Very high BMI makes surgery difficult and increases intraoperative complications
- Serum albumin may not be a marker of poor nutrition. It is an important acute phase reactant
- Obesity disadvantages the surgeon and the patient

Successful outcomes following surgery may depend upon good nutritional status.

The nutritional status of patients undergoing any type of surgery must be assessed.

Elective surgery permits an opportunity to ensure that the patient is nutritionally fit. Sometimes as in patients with gastric or pancreatic malignancy or Crohn's disease this might well-nigh be impossible without preoperative prehabilitation with nutritional support.

Traditionally, patients were treated with 'nil by mouth' during the early post-laparotomy period.

The result of early enteral feeding is equivocal with some studies suggesting benefits with respect to wound healing and length of stay while others show no benefit.

Provision of early enteral nutrition may provide more energy that promotes healing. According to a recent Cochrane review update, which reviewed 17 randomised controlled trials (RCTs) with the total number of 1,437 participants, the authors concluded that 'early enteral feeding may lead to a reduced postoperative length of stay; however, cautious interpretation must be taken due to substantial heterogeneity and low-quality evidence. For all other outcomes [postoperative complications, mortality, adverse events and quality of life (QoL)], the findings are inconclusive'.

Types of nutritional support

- Enteral nutrition (EN)
- Parenteral nutrition (PN)

Enteral nutrition

If the gastrointestinal tract is available for use, then use it!

It is the most preferred way of providing nutrition.

Enteral nutrition also serves to preserve the integrity of the intestinal mucosa which derives its nutrition from diet. When this is denied, the villi atrophy and lose their activity. The presence of the villi increases the surface area of the intestines available for absorption. In the absence of enterally derived nutrition, the atrophy of the villi leads to a reduction in surface area available for absorption. This is one of the reasons why some patients get diarrhoea on re-introduction of enteral feeding after a period of suspension. Preservation of the mucosa retains the activity in the villi. Furthermore, enteral feeding has less complications than parenteral nutrition.

In the early postoperative period, however, re-introduction of oral feeding must be done with caution as vomiting may occur. Numbers needed to harm (NNH) is 19 as per the recent Cochrane review.

Table 1 shows absorption of nutrients in the small and large bowel.

Reasons for fluid accumulation in ileus

- *Secreted fluids from:*
  - Oral cavity – saliva
  - Gastric secretions
  - Intestinal secretions – succus entericus
- *Absence of peristaltic force that is controlled by a combination of:*
  - Enteric nervous system
  - Auerbach's plexus, etc.
  - Autonomic nervous system – sympathetic and parasympathetic

Methods of using the enteral system

- Oral supplementation
- Nasogastric feeding
- Fine bore feeding
- *Gastroscopy:*
  - Surgical – open procedure
  - Percutaneous endoscopic guided (PEG)
  - PEGJ – when the PEG is placed in the jejunum
- Jejunostomy for distal intestinal feeding

Delivery of enteral nutrition

Ideally, where long-term enteral feeding is needed as in patients with oesophageal pathology or with low fistula of the small bowel, a *discussion with a clinician with a special*

Table 1 Absorption of nutrients in the small and large bowel

Duodenum	Iron and calcium
Jejunum	Sugars, amino acids and fatty acids
Ileum	B12 and bile salts
Colon	Water and electrolytes

interest is needed. In some hospitals there will be *nutritional leads* and *dietitian* who will assist in the planning and delivery of enteral nutrition.

The planning and prescription of enteral nutrition takes into consideration:

- Type of tube to be used for feeding
- Location of the tip of the tube
- Different modes of access
- The total quantity of fluid per day
- Total calories needed per day. Critically ill patients may need more calories
- Macro- and micronutrients needed
- Proteins/carbohydrate needed per kg of body weight
- Frequency of feeding
- Timing of feeding – i.e. overnight and intermittent
- *Type of fluid to be used:*
  - *Standard* – non-hydrolysed macronutrients for patients with a normal gastrointestinal (GI) tract
  - *Elemental* or peptide – hydrolysed macronutrients for those with malabsorption
  - *Carbohydrate controlled* for diabetics with a higher fibre and fat but less carbohydrate

Complications of enteral feeding

- *Aspiration of gastric contents:*
  - Silent as in intubated patients in the intensive therapy unit (ITU)
    - Overt when clinically obvious
    - Occurs with nasogastric as well as gastrostomy feeding
    - More common in elderly
    - Poor oral hygiene and decreased salivary flow can be contributing factors
    - Large bore nasogastric tube (NGT) may permit aspiration through an open gastro-oesophageal junction
    - Low residual volume (RV) in stomach during enteral feeding (<100 mL every 4 hours) may contribute to a reduction in risk of aspiration. Some studies have shown that aspiration may occur irrespective of the RV
    - Reduction in risk can be achieved by vertical nursing while feeding or retaining an inclination of 45° for an hour after feeding
    - Aspiration can lead to chemical pneumonitis when the stomach contents are acidic
- Interstitial or *aspiration pneumonia* with bacterial infection
- *Atelectasis* due to solid particles in aspirate

> Checking gastric residual volume (RV) every 4 hours and maintaining a residual level of <100 mL are usually advocated during tube feeding. However, it has been shown that the frequencies of regurgitation and aspiration are similar over a wide range of RV from 0 to 400 mL. Hence, RV is not a reliable marker of aspiration. On the other hand, large-bore nasogastric (NG) tubes mayincrease the risk of aspiration of gastric contents by interfering with normal lower oesophageal sphincter.
>
> *Source:* Luk JK, Chan DK. Preventing aspiration pneumonia in older people: do we have the 'know-how'? Hong Kong Med J 2014; 20:421–427. https://www.hkmj.org/abstracts/v20n5/toc.htm

- *Refeeding syndrome:* This can occur in patients—
  - Not fed for 5 days
  - Manifests within 5 days of onset of enteral feeding
  - Patients have low phosphate, magnesium, and potassium
  - May have fluid shifts leading to fatigue, confusion and cardiac failure
  - High index of suspicion is needed to detect this
  - It can be avoided by restriction of calories in the feed initially to 1,000 calories on the first day—start low and go slow
- *Malposition of tube:* When a fine bore tube is used, its position must be verified by radiology prior to initiating feeding lest the tube lodges in the bronchial tree.
- *Complications of surgical gastrostomy:*
  - Wound-related complications such as dehiscence and infection
  - Haemorrhage
  - Slippage of gastrostomy tube
  - Peritonitis due to leak around the tube or misplacement
  - Complications arising from anaesthesia
- *Complications of PEG:*
  - As for gastrostomy
  - Tube malfunction
  - Leakage of feed around the tube

Nutritional requirement

- *Water:* Most 'feeds' are water based. This needs to be calculated for every patient. As a ready rule of thumb 2,500–3,500 mL/day is recommended.
- *Macronutrient:*
  - Carbohydrate energy provided 4 kcal/g.
    Approximately—300 g/day
  - Protein energy provided 4 kcal/g.
    Approximately—90 g/day
  - Fat energy provided 9 kcal/g. Approximately—55 g/day
- *Calorie* requirement per day
  - Males: 2,500 kcal/day
  - Females: 2,000 kcal/day
- *Micronutrients:*
  - Vitamins
  - Minerals
  - Trace elements

Parenteral nutrition

Parenteral nutrition is defined as nutrition that is provided by a route other than enteral that is on a par with enteral feeding. This is needed when the enteral route is not available for provision of nutrition. It is an immune enhancing nutrition and can be delivered through:

- Peripheral line feeding
- Central line feeding

The nutrition is provided through veins. As the fluid that is given is hyperosmotic, the peripheral veins develop thrombophlebitis within days and hence traditionally central veins are used.

In some situations, where short-term parenteral feeding of <2 weeks is anticipated, peripheral veins may be used for access. This is referred to as peripheral venous parenteral nutrition – PPN as opposed to TPN or total parenteral nutrition through the central veins.

The National Institute of Clinical Excellence in the UK, NICE recommends starting parenteral feeding at no >50% of estimated needs for the first 24–48 hours with close monitoring of progress.

Parenteral nutrition can be used till the nutritional status becomes stable and enteral feeding can be re-established.

Access for parenteral nutrition

Central venous catheter: These cannulate the large veins such as:

- The internal jugular
- The subclavian
- The femoral

Preferably cannulated under ultrasound guidance where this facility is available.

The central venous catheter is advanced and placed in the superior or inferior vena cava and the position confirmed radiologically.

In patients needing long-term enteral feeding, >30 days, tunnelled subclavian lines are preferred.

Peripherally introduced central catheter (PICC) lines: These are peripherally introduced central catheters. The access is through peripheral veins:

- The basilic
- The brachial

The catheter is advanced to the superior vena cava.

All lines placed in the central veins and used for feeding must:

- Be placed under aseptic conditions, preferably in surgical theatres
- Be placed by healthcare teams skilled in the placement of these lines
- Have the position of the central line confirmed radiologically prior to initiating feeding
- Be always handled under sterile conditions, i.e. with surgical gloves and cleansing before and after every use
- Be dedicated to the sole use of nutritional feeding. A free lumen of a multilumen catheter can be used if it is dedicated to feeding

Complications of central lines

These can be classified as follows:

- *Insertion related:*
  - Haemorrhage/Haematoma
  - Arrhythmia
  - Pneumothorax
  - Injury to major arterial vessels
  - Air embolism
  - Wrong location of tip

These are procedure related and avoidable with utmost care and ultrasonic imaging; however, multiple attempts at placements can lead to increased risk of complications.

- *Catheter related:*
  - Site-related infection
  - Line infection – 'pus somewhere, pus nowhere, pus in the lines' is the new adage!
  - Catheter thrombosis
  - Venous thrombosis and embolism
  - Loss of catheter sites in patients requiring lifelong or long-term usage
  - Sepsis
- *Feed related:*
  - Metabolic complications:
    - Electrolyte imbalance
    - Hyper-/hypoglycaemia
    - Dehydration
    - Micronutrient deficiencies
  - Hepatic complications
    - Elevated bilirubin/alkaline phosphatase due to cholestasis
    - Fibrosis/Cirrhosis in patients using TPN for long term
    - *Candida* infections can arise from TPN use

Attention to the nutritional status of the surgical patients may assist in the progress of the patient in the perioperative phase.

Prolonged preoperative starvation is detrimental as much as early oral feeding is beneficial when used with due attention and care.

Enteral route is the preferred mode for feeding where feasible. Addressing patients at nutritional risk at the outset and addressing it early will enhance recovery.

Further reading

1. Herbert G, Perry R, Andersen HK, et al. Early enteral nutrition within 24 hours of lower gastrointestinal surgery versus later commencement for length of hospital stay and postoperative complications. Cochrane Database Syst Rev 2019; 7:CD004080.

Chapter 4

Metabolic response to trauma

Trauma in any form sets off a cascade of response that is geared to meet the increased oxygen and energy demands imposed on the system. This demand is proportional to the trauma sustained.

The response is evolutionary. It is orchestrated by the pituitary and is primarily an endocrine response. There is also an immunological component to it as the body gears itself to ward off intruders.

The activation of the endocrine system with production of catecholamines and cholesterol induces *tachypnoea* and *tachycardia.*

- Increase in the respiratory rate makes available more oxygen for distribution to the tissues
- Increase in the heart rate enables the pump to supply oxygen to the tissues

Cuthbertson in 1932 studied four patients and defined the phases of this response that has been subsequently referred to as the 'Ebb' and 'Flow' phases.

Egdhal, in 1950s, showed this response to be a *neurologically mediated sympathetic response.* He injured the legs of dogs while retaining the sciatic nerve.

Samples were collected from adrenal veins and these showed elevated adrenaline and glucocorticoids. When the sciatic nerve was divided there was no change in the levels of adrenaline and glucocorticoids.

Endocrine response has three components:

1. Activation of the sympathetic system
2. Pituitary response
3. Insulin resistance

There are three phases:

1. Ebb phase
2. Flow phase
3. Anabolic phase

The 'ebb phase' is the period when the body (like any wounded animal) retracts into a shell in an attempt to hold on to its environment.

The 'flow phase' refers to its attempt to overflow with supply of much-needed energy by mobilising resources to meet the requirements. This is akin to any natural calamity when the government initially assesses the damage (ebb) and then meets the needs (flow) with increased supply of food and water, etc.

The rebuilding or anabolic phase occurs later.

- *Ebb phase* – sets in immediately after surgery or trauma and lasts for up to 2 days during which time the body attempts to regain homeostasis by:
  - Maintaining perfusion
  - Decreasing energy expenditure
  - Retaining urinary nitrogen
- *Flow phase* – lasts from 2 to 7 days. It is a survival response that can be defined as an 'all or none' reaction.
  This catabolic response attempts to mobilise the flow of substrate to meet the needs.
- *Anabolic phase* follows the flow phase. It is a process of rebuilding that begins as soon as 3–8 days after elective surgery, but it is delayed after sepsis, major trauma or burns.

The key aspects of metabolic response to injury:

1. It is an immediate protective and evolutionary response
2. Leads to a net increase in catabolic hormones
3. Precipitates a controlled catabolic response that breaks down carbohydrates, proteins and fat
4. Mobilises fuel, salt and water to meet the demands imposed by injury
5. Rebuilds with an anabolic response that sets in after the immediate needs have been met

The catabolic response is mediated primarily by adrenaline.

The catabolic response encashes the body's 'silver' which is all the available adipose tissue and muscle mass. Burning these makes available the 'energy' to meet the immediate requirements.

This is driven by:

- Catecholamines
- Glucagon
- Corticosteroids. There is a three-fold increase
- Insulin resistance

It is predominantly an adrenal generated response. When controlled, the energy obtained by burning the resources meets the expenditure. When uncontrolled, much like a gambler, the sale of silver goes to extremes to the detriment of the individual.

Insulin resistance leads to *anabolic resistance* as it prevents the onset of the anabolic response. Prolongation of insulin resistance therefore prolongs the recovery process.

The *anabolic* response is mostly mediated by the prime anabolic hormone, insulin as well as growth hormone, thyroxine and testosterone (**Figure 1**).

The anabolic response increases uptake by the injured tissue of:

- Glucose
- Amino acids
- Fats

This rebuilding response starts in 3–8 days depending on the magnitude of the trauma.

It is delayed after:

- Sepsis
- Burns
- Major trauma

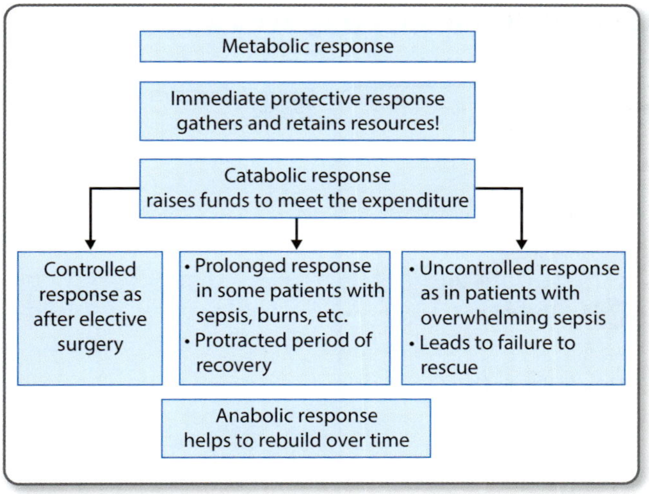

Figure 1 Classification of metabolic and anabolic response.

The immunological response is based on:

- Cytokine production – from activated leucocytes
- Acute phase reactants
- Neutrophil leucocytosis

Acute phase response

The 'acute phase response (APR)' is a prominent systemic reaction of the organism to local or systemic disturbances in its homeostasis caused by infection, tissue injury, trauma or surgery, neoplastic growth or immunological disorders *(Gordon and Koy, 1985; Gruys et al., 1999).*

The acute-phase protein (APP) can be positive or negative. Within a few hours after infection, the pattern of protein synthesis by the liver is drastically altered resulting in an *increase* of some blood proteins, the *positive APPs.* Hepatic mRNA upregulation of those APPs is associated with a *decrease* in synthesis of normal blood proteins, like transferrin and *albumin,* which represent the *negative APPs.*

In this response the following changes occur:

- Increased cytokine production (by leucocytes)
- Increased interleukin 6 (IL-6) production
- Increased production of liver acute phase proteins such as immunoglobulins
- Increase in C-reactive protein (CRP)
- Increase in fibrinogen
- Decrease in albumin levels – a negative acute phase protein

Hypothalamo–pituitary–adrenal axis (Figures 2 and 3)

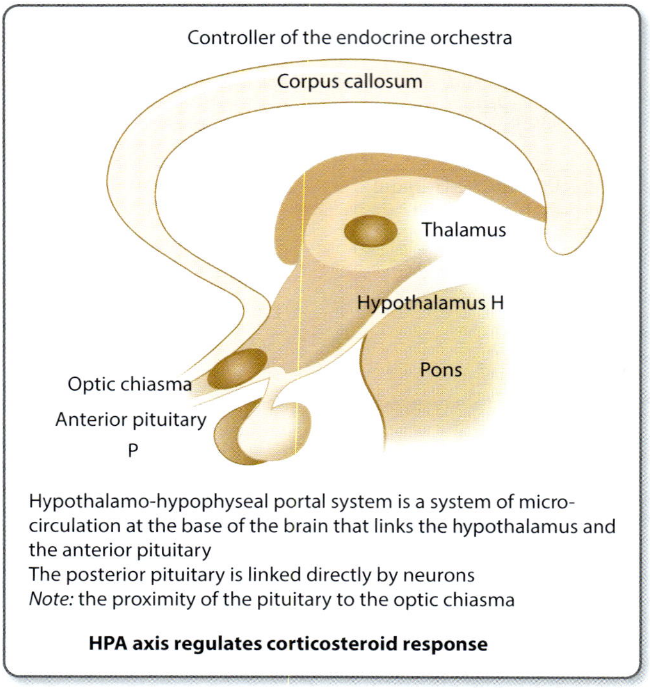

Figure 2 Controller of the endocrine orchestra.

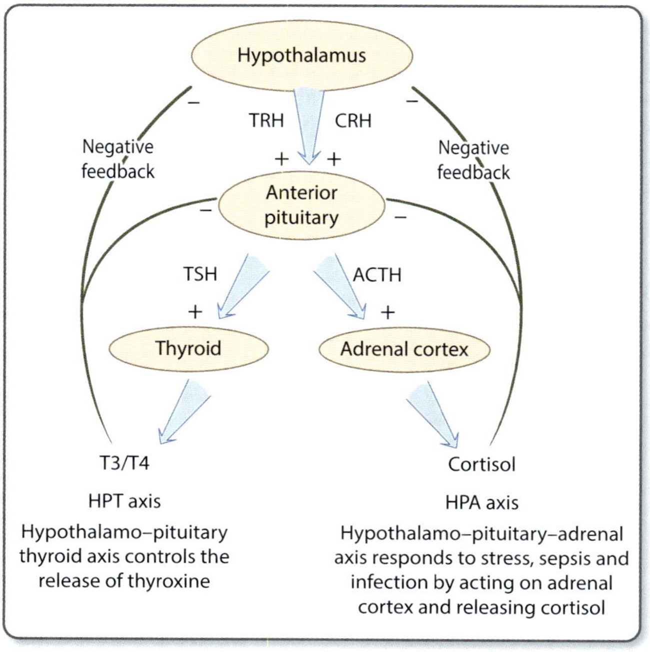

Figure 3 Characteristics of hypothalamus. ACTH, adrenocorticotropic hormone; CRH, corticotropin-releasing hormone; HPA, hypothalamic–pituitary–adrenal axis; HPT, hypothalamic–pituitary–thyroid axis; TRH, thyrotropin-releasing hormone; TSH, thyroid stimulating hormone.

Further readings

1. Gordon AH, Koy A. The Acute Phase Response to Injury and Infection. The Roles of Interleukin 1 and Other Mediators. Amsterdam: Elsevier, 1985.
2. Gruys E, Toussaint MJM, Landman WJM, et al. Infection, Inflammation and Stress Inhibit Growth. Mechanisms and Non-specific Assessment of the Processes by Acute Phase Proteins. In: Wensing T (ed.), Production Diseases in Farm Animals, 10th International Conference, 1998. Wageningen: Wageningen Press, 1999:72–87.
3. Blackburn WD Jr. Validity of acute phase proteins as markers of disease activity. J Rheumatol Suppl 1994; 42:9–3.

Chapter 5

Insulin resistance and surgery

Definition

Insulin resistance is defined as a condition in which the body fails to respond appropriately to the action of insulin, thus pushing up the blood sugar levels. It leads to decreased absorption of sugar by muscles, fat and liver cells. The blood sugar rises leading to increased production of insulin by the pancreas in a bid to promote absorption of sugar. Thus, the insulin level rises, and the body is unable to use the excess sugar leading to a situation akin to starvation. Therefore, there is 'poverty in the midst of plenty.'

Key points:

- Insulin is an anabolic hormone
- Assists in utilisation of carbohydrate, proteins and fat that are the building blocks of healing
- Insulin resistance sets in rapidly after all and any type of surgery
- It lasts for a variable length of time depending on the magnitude of the operation
- It is a *fundamental response to stress*

When there are complications after elective surgery or in the presence of a major insult to the system such as sepsis, the resistance to insulin:

- Is greater
- Is longer
- Is prolonged with an extended catabolic phase
- Is a factor preventing anabolism setting in

Olle Ljungqvist, a key proponent of the enhanced recovery [enhanced recovery after surgery (ERAS)] or fast-track surgery, makes the following points about insulin resistance:

- Insulin resistance is proportional to the magnitude of the operation
- In major laparotomies up to 90% of insulin sensitivity may be lost after surgery
- Even after moderate surgery, this change can last for a week
- *Clear relationship exists between insulin resistance and postoperative complications, particularly infections*
- By prolonging recovery, insulin resistance may be harmful
- *Hyperglycaemia after surgery is a direct result of insulin resistance*
- Complications can be avoided if hyperglycaemia is controlled
- Regardless of perioperative diabetic state, less insulin resistance resulted in fewer complications
- *Keeping insulin resistance under control seems to be beneficial*
- Reduction or prevention of insulin resistance can be achieved as in ERAS by:
  - Preoperative carbohydrate loading instead of fasting moving the patient to the 'fed' or anabolic state

- Using epidural anaesthesia before the onset of surgery
- Continuing pain relief postoperatively
- Early enteral feeding to avoid starvation-induced insulin resistance

• *Reduction in insulin resistance reduces time to recovery.*

The impact of starvation on metabolism

Surgical management of patients may include a period of starvation and hence recollection of the basic physiology of starvation will assist in the understanding of the impact of starvation on patients.

The brain and the red cells can only use glucose as their source of energy.

As hunter gatherers, homo sapiens were exposed to prolonged periods of starvation. Storage of glucose for use during times of lack of availability of food therefore led to the evolutionary adaptation to deal with such situations.

Glycogenolysis

The body stores glucose as glycogen in the liver. This is released by the liver as glucose during short periods of starvation by the process of glycogenolysis, which converts stored glycogen to glucose, to maintain the blood sugar levels. *Glycogen stores are depleted within 24 hours.*

Gluconeogenesis

If the starvation is prolonged, the body resorts to gluconeogenesis, the *synthesis of 'new' glucose* from amino acids such as alanine and glycine to maintain the blood sugar levels. In situations of stress and starvation, glucocorticoids as the 'gluco' implies facilitates gluconeogenesis. This hormone also assists *glucagon* in the process of gluconeogenesis.

The brain can use only glucose as it is water soluble and thus able to cross the 'blood-brain' barrier where it takes part in the energy transfer citric acid cycle (Krebs cycle) and generates adenosine triphosphate (ATP).

Once the glucose storage is depleted, gluconeogenesis can assist in providing glucose but there is also an evolutionary need to protect the protein in the body as they are necessary for enzyme reactions and muscle function.

Saving protein – the golden rule. Switch to Ketones. Switching to breaking down fats initially produces fatty acids and acetyl coenzyme A (CoA) that can enter the Krebs cycle.

After 3 days of starvation, an excess of acetyl CoA builds up with slowing of the Krebs cycle. This enters the liver where it is converted to ketones. There are three *ketone bodies,* (1) acetoacetate, (2) 3-β-hydroxybutyrate, and (3) acetone the least abundant. The brain can use ketones as they are able to pass through the blood-brain barrier. This process protects the utilisation of protein as the brain switches from utilisation of glucose to utilising ketones as a source of energy. This preserves the much-needed proteins.

Further reading

1. Ljungqvist O. Insulin Resistance and Outcomes in Surgery. J Clin Endocrinol Metabol. 2010; 95(9):4217–4219.

Chapter 6

Integrity of intestinal mucosa

Primacy of the integrity of the intestinal mucosa

The intestinal mucosa, like the skin, is in contact with the external world through the food that is consumed.

Enteral nutrition serves to preserve the integrity of the intestinal mucosa which derives its nutrition from diet. When this is denied, the villi atrophy and lose their activity. The presence of the villi increases the surface area of the intestines available for absorption. In the absence of enterally derived nutrition, the atrophy of the villi leads to a reduction in surface area available for absorption. This is one of the reasons why some patients get diarrhoea on re-introduction of enteral feeding after a period of suspension. Preservation of the mucosa retains the activity in the villi.

The mucosa is essential not only for absorption but also to differentiate between the various pathogens that accompany the nutrients in the food. By a process of pattern recognition enabled by the rich immune system in the gut, only the nutrients are absorbed and the pathogens blocked from entering the system. This delicate balance can be altered in starvation and sepsis. Starvation prevents mucosal nourishment, and sepsis alters the immune system allowing pathogens to enter the circulation.

The mucosa of the intestine thrives on nutrients obtained from contact with the ingest. It serves as a barrier to pathogens from the diet that gets past the acid in the stomach while at the same time allowing for absorption of nutrients and fluid permitting tolerance of non-pathogenic bacteria.

The cells lining the intestines include:

- The enterocytes
- Paneth cells
- The goblet cells
- T cells
- B cells
- The dendritic cells
- Macrophages
- Innate lymphoid cells

The amazing arrangement of this array of cells in the mucosa houses a large part of the immune system in the Peyer's patches and in the villi.

The gut associated lymphoid tissue (GALT) provides a neural-enteral network.

Based on obtained information, GALT differentiates commensal bacteria from pathogenic and either tolerates or destroys them.

Gut-associated lymphoid tissue is composed of lymphoid aggregates, Peyer's patches, isolated lymphoid follicles diffusely distributed along the lamina propria, and intraepithelial space lymphocytes. It is estimated that GALT contains approximately 70% of total of the cells of the immune system.

The dendritic cell samples the antigens in pathogens and presents them to lymphocytes. This promotes tolerance and immune system generates an anti-inflammatory response. This response is mediated through the T cells in the Peyer's patches. This process is affected in inflammatory bowel disease.

The intestinal cells are involved in:

- The absorption of nutrients
- In innate immunity responsible for diarrhoea of the 'weep and sweep' reaction to unwelcome pathogens
- The mucosal barrier secreted by goblet cells that assists in reduction of inflammatory response to pathogens in food
- The activity of the dendritic cell that assists in 'pattern recognition' of pathogenic antigens

This system can be breached by:

- Infections
- Inflammation
- Medications
- Surgery

It leads to bacterial transgression through the mucosal barrier leading to serious consequences.

Chapter 7

Wound healing

Healing by first intention

It is the healing that occurs when the edges of a wound are approximated in the absence of tissue loss in an aseptic environment. The epithelium being approximated does not need a bridge of granulation tissue.

Healing by second intention

It is the healing that occurs when there is loss of tissue and primary approximation of skin is not possible. There must then be a bridge made up of granulation tissue that fills the gap, and the epithelium then grows over it.

This process needs three factors:
1. *Granulation* from the base *upwards*
2. *Epithelialisation* from the edge *inwards* towards the centre of the wound
3. *Contraction,* a force that like the spokes of a wheel draws the wound edges *towards the centre.* Progressively, it decreases the area that requires to be bridged by the epithelium.

The process is driven by:
- Leucocytes
- Macrophages
- Fibroblasts
- Assisted by angiogenesis

Phases of wound healing (Figure 1)

1. *Haemostasis:* This is the process of capillary constriction and platelet plugging to stop bleeding. Meticulous surgical haemostasis contributes significantly to healing.
2. *Inflammation:* Once clots are cleared, the wound is infiltrated by leucocytes and macrophages. *Angiogenic stimulation* starts.
3. *Proliferation:* Fibroblasts proliferate and encourage glycoprotein and collagen formation. Epithelial proliferation from wound edge is initiated.
4. *Maturation:* Collagen is remodelled, and the wound begins to resemble the surrounding tissue. This process can take up to 2 years.

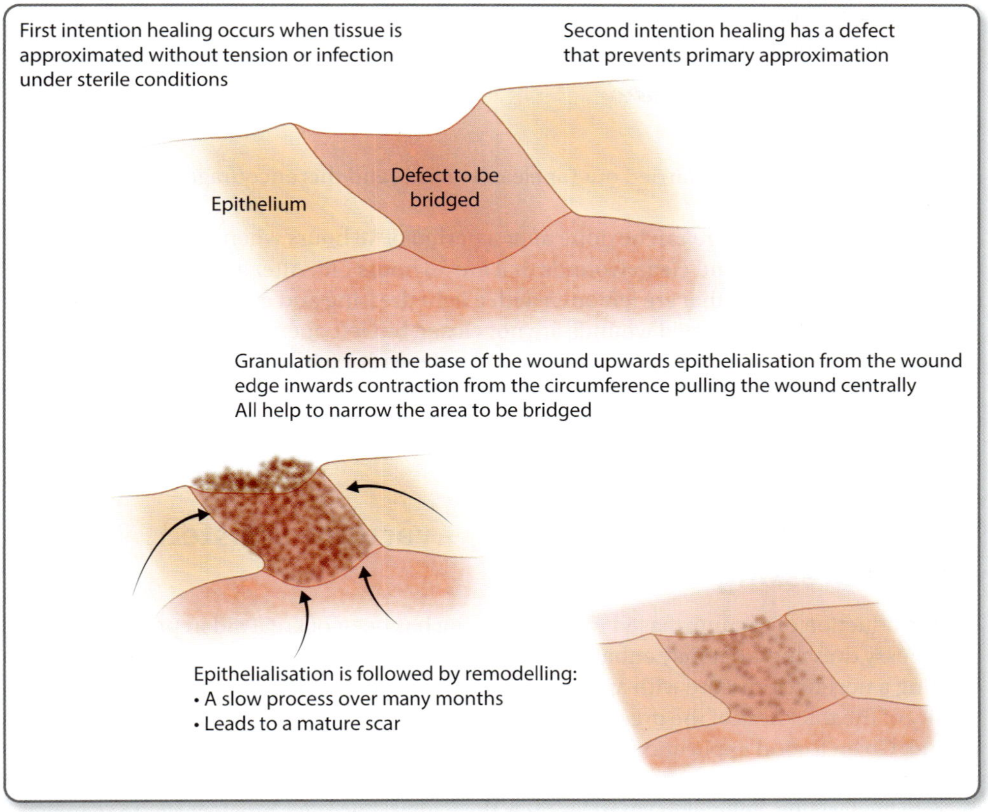

Figure 1 Wound healing.

Surgical wounds classification, the National Institute for Health and Care Excellence guidance

Clean: An incision in which no inflammation is encountered in a surgical procedure, without a break in sterile technique, and during which the respiratory, alimentary, or genitourinary tracts are not entered.

Clean-contaminated: An incision through which the respiratory, alimentary, or genitourinary tract is entered under controlled conditions but with no contamination encountered.

Contaminated: An incision undertaken during an operation in which there is a major break in sterile technique or gross spillage from the gastrointestinal tract, or an incision in which acute, non-purulent inflammation is encountered. Open traumatic wounds that are >12–24 hours old also fall into this category.

Dirty or infected: An incision undertaken during an operation in which the viscera are perforated or when acute inflammation with pus is encountered (e.g., emergency surgery for faecal peritonitis); for traumatic wounds, if treatment is delayed, there is faecal contamination, or devitalised tissue is present.

Management

Immediate closure can be carried out for clean wounds and this encourages healing by primary intention.

Delayed primary closure can be done after a period of 48 hours when treating, clean contaminated wounds and clean wounds that are >6 hours old. After an immediate surgical toilet, these are wounds that are left open with a light dressing and closed 48 hours later.

Contaminated and infected wounds are not closed but left open to heal by secondary intention. In these wounds a meticulous wound toilet with excision of all dead tissue and foreign bodies will promote healing by second intention.

This guidance is based on the best practice guidelines in disaster situations [World Health Organisation (WHO) 2009].

Vacuum-based wound dressing – vacuum-assisted closure dressing

The introduction of vacuum-based wound dressing has been of great aid in providing non-messy dressings that may enhance the speed of wound healing. The principle involves creating a negative pressure with application of an airtight dressing over a sponge. The quality of the thickness of the dressing may affect the final pressure generated to the wound. Given a good application of a vacuum-assisted closure (VAC) dressing the authors' personal experience has been positive after laparostomies and extensive excision of necrotising fasciitis. Following laparostomies the wound becomes much easier to manage in the intensive care with no leakage of fluid from the peritoneal cavity necessitating frequent changes of dressing. It has great value in enhancing the healing by drawing up the granulation tissue in large wounds that follow the extensive abdominal wall excision of necrotising fasciitis.

Surgical site infections delay the process of healing and may lead to a longer stay in hospital, and in some situations, they may even delay further treatment like chemotherapy.

Factors that affect healing: ABCDEF and I

A: Anaemia/Age
B: Bronchitis – poor oxygenation, possibly only marginal
C: Cachexia – poor healing
D: Diabetes – high possibility of infection
E: Emaciated – poor collagen formation
F: Frailty/Fat – two sides of the same coin
I: Infection – always to be avoided where possible

Chapter 8

Principles of clinical examination

First principles

- Make the connection
- Introduce yourself
- Verify and confirm demographics
- Provide the reason for your presence.
- Seek permission to examine
- Wash your hands
- Ask if there is any area of pain or tenderness
- Be gentle and reassuring

Abdomen

- Inspect from the foot end of bed or side
- Ask the patient to cough; look for any cough impulse
- *Note:*
  - The location of umbilicus
  - Presence of scars
  - Lumps
  - Abnormal veins
  - Other abnormalities
- Palpate away from the site of pain, if any. If there is no area of pain, then from the left lower quadrant upwards and around in an anticlockwise manner. It is the best not to dig with one's fingers but feel with the flat of the hand. If there is a palpable mass, then note if it moves with respiration or if it is fixed
- For hernia, examine the patient standing up and confirm the presence of the hernia. Then, lie the patient down and gently compress the internal ring region, roughly, a couple of fingers above the middle of the inguinal ligament. Ask the patient to cough while compressing and inspecting the groin. If it is a direct hernia, the lump will reappear despite the compression of the internal ring. An indirect hernia will be contained by compression

Even though current fashion is to proceed to radiology-assisted diagnosis with a CT scan or an ultrasound, it is a good principle to examine the patient clinically as it creates a rapport which, if gentle, will go a long way towards reassuring the patient whose illness would have taken away his autonomy.

Chapter 9

The acute abdomen

- There is no simple definition of an acute abdomen other than to say that it is a combination of signs and symptoms that necessitate referral for urgent general surgical opinion
- Making a diagnosis is an imprecise art. It taxes the skills of experienced surgeons and requires pragmatism
- The classic presentations commonly described are not seen commonly
- There is a greater dependence on radiological colleagues to assist the diagnostic process. Even so, very often time and monitoring with repeated reviews of the patient will aid delivery of good care
- The most important decision may not always be the diagnosis but the decision to operate or withhold operation. If a decision is made to operate, then the next decision is the consideration of the timing of the operation. Should the operation be done immediately or can it wait till suitable arrangements and resuscitation can be achieved
- As noted previously, evaluation of the morbidity and mortality and involvement of appropriate surrogates in the decision-making process is mandatory

The common surgical problems that one confronts during surgical practice can be divided into two groups:

1. Problems that arise directly from the acute presentation
2. Problems that need treatment on a non-acute basis

In the acute surgical setting, the management involves a decision to prioritise the surgical treatment. This may be:

- Immediate
- Early (within 24–48 hours)
- Elective (where resolution of urgent problem permits a scheduled treatment)

Imaging before surgical intervention

The decision to operate may not always be easy. At present owing to the vast improvement in imaging it is good practice to 'image before intervention' wherever possible. This reduces the possibility of inappropriate intervention and increases the probability of appropriate intervention.

Imaging prior to surgical intervention assists diagnosis and facilitates appropriate action.

Certain points are worth clarifying:

- The clinical management is not always only surgical
- The feasibility of an operation is not an indication for its performance
- Futility of a situation due to comorbidity is part of the decision-making process
- If an emergency operation is needed and the patient is fit for surgery, procrastination is detrimental to successful outcome
- If the patient is unsuitable for intervention, it must be discussed with the patient and family and documented
- If a decision is taken that further care will not be in the best interest of the patient, a 'Do Not Attempt Resuscitation (DNAR)' form needs to be completed
- If a decision not to intervene is contested by the family or surrogates, then a second opinion must be sought
  - Avoid confrontation at all times

Chapter 10

Peritonitis

The peritoneum (**Figure 1**) is a cling-film-like serous layer that sticks to the viscera and to the inner wall of the abdominal cavity much like an invaginated balloon. It has a visceral and a parietal layer.

The peritoneal cavity is a potential space. The loops of bowel are normally in contact with the abdominal wall, and to facilitate movement without friction, there is a thin sliver of peritoneal fluid that acts as a lubricant.

Mesentery is the structure lined by peritoneum that allows the transmission of blood vessels from the retroperitoneum to the viscera.

The kidneys and pancreas are behind the peritoneum, in the *retroperitoneum.*
Peritoneal fluid extrusion occurs due to:

- Perforation – of viscus
- Inflammation – of the pancreas

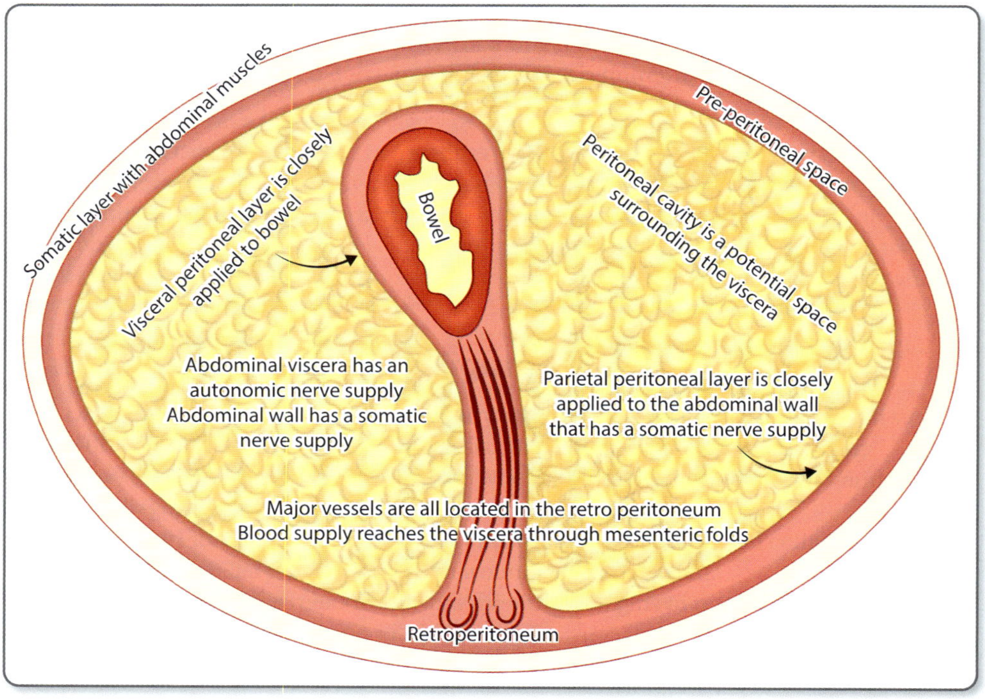

Figure 1 The peritoneal cavity.

- Inflammation – of viscus
- Ischaemia – of contents
- Injury – penetrating or blunt, iatrogenic
- Rupture – of blood vessels
- Malignancy intraperitoneal
- Cirrhosis of the liver

Increase in peritoneal fluid without inflammation is called 'ascites.' When peritoneal fluid collection is due to a leakage from blood vessels, it is haemorrhagic ascites.

The peritoneum once inflamed, can lead to peritonitis. Peritonitis can be:

- Chemical – initial
- Bacterial – after 6 hours

The initial response is to a chemical irritation, but after 6–12 hours, a bacterial overgrowth sets in.

This is the reason for the need of early action rather than waiting till the next morning for convenience.

The fluid and abscesses collect in two areas of the peritoneal cavity that are most dependent in the supine posture:

1. The pelvis
2. The *Rutherford Morrison pouch,* which is between the liver and the kidney

Causes of peritonitis

- Perforated viscus due to:
  - Peptic perforation
  - Appendicular perforation
  - Colonic-diverticular perforation
  - Gallbladder perforation
  - Small bowel perforation
  - Meckel's perforation
  - Malignant bowel perforation
  - Anastomotic leak
- Ectopic pregnancy
- Ruptured aneurysm of abdominal aorta
- Tubo-ovarian abscess
- Penetrating injury
- Ischaemic bowel
- Pancreatitis

Presenting symptoms and signs

- *Pain* is the major presenting symptom. It is stated that peritonitis due to perforation of peptic ulcer, pancreatitis, ischaemia, and ruptured abdominal aortic aneurysms are the most severe
- Nausea may precede pain and vomiting usually follows

- Tachypnoea occurs due to pain, fluid loss and acidosis
- Tachycardia
- Altered mentation

Abdominal findings on examination

Generalised tenderness: Unlike localised tenderness when there is an ttempt to contain the pathology, major pathology leads to tenderness that is in all four quadrants.

Tenderness and generalised: As opposed to localised tenderness, when there is an attempt to contain the pathological process.

Rebound tenderness: This is a classical finding when there is pain on pressure and pain on release of pressure on the abdominal wall. The less intrusive way of demonstrating this is to do a gentle percussion.

If the percussion causes pain, it could be a manifestation of rebound tenderness.

Guarding: This is a protective response to pain when the muscles overlying the pathology contract and tighten to protect the viscera by stiffening to the threat of being pushed.

Rigidity: The abdomen is board like and tense due to all the abdominal muscles contracting and stiffening. This is a protective response such as guarding and attempts to reduce movements that cause pain.

The management then follows the principles laid out in the earlier chapter.

Chapter 11

Peptic perforation

This used to be a very common surgical emergency. The advent of H_2-receptor blockade with cimetidine in the late 70s and subsequent identification of *Helicobacter pylori (H. pylori)* as the causative factor for peptic ulcer has made this disease increasingly less common.

Prior to Marshall's identification of the causative organism for the most peptic ulcers, the treatment of peptic disease was mostly surgical. Now, it is mostly medical.

Peptic ulcers arise in areas of the gastrointestinal tree that are exposed to acid peptic digestion:

- The lower oesophagus
- The stomach
- The duodenum
- The Meckel's diverticulum (ectopic gastric cells)

It follows that areas exposed to peptic digestion may also suffer peptic perforation and bleeding.

Peptic bleeding can still occur due to the usage of aspirin and non-steroidals, but they can almost all be managed endoscopically.

Patients presenting with duodenal ulcers are nearly all infected with *H. pylori* (90%). Marshall says, 'It is very unlikely that persons without *H. pylori* infections will ever develop duodenal ulcer.'

Gastric ulcers are also caused by *H. pylori*, but up to about 30% may be related to treatment with aspirin or non-steroidals.

It is a good practice to treat all patients presenting with peptic ulcer perforation as being infected with *H. pylori* by giving them the appropriate antibiotic treatment along with high-dose proton pump inhibitor (PPI).

The treatment recommended for peptic disease in dyspeptic patients after confirmation of *H. pylori* infection with a urea breath test is also applicable following perforated peptic disease. Faecal testing and serology are also increasingly available.

The recommended first-line treatment for *H. pylori* is for 7 days.

- Proton pump inhibitor twice daily
- Amoxicillin 1 g BD plus clarithromycin 500 mg BD, or
- Metronidazole 400 mg BD

If allergic to penicillin, clarithromycin and metronidazole can be prescribed. The protocol may vary in different countries. Successful eradication of *H. pylori* must be confirmed with a urea breath test on completion of the course. In the United States, the recommended treatment is for 14 days.

Presentation of peptic perforation

As with all peritonitis, the signs may be localised or generalised. Classically, the abdomen is rigid like a board, and the patient is in severe pain with possibly altered mentation, tachycardia, and tachypnoea.

The initial pain for the first 6 hours is likely to be due to chemical peritonitis caused by spillage of gastro-duodenal contents. This is rapidly followed by the onset of bacterial peritonitis within 12 hours, stressing the need for rapid intervention in the suitable patients rather than waiting and watching.

The erect chest X-ray showing free gas may not be possible if the patient is in severe pain (**Figure 1**). A semi-erect X-ray with the patient sitting up in bed may help to define the presence of free air under the diaphragm.

A CT scan is quick and gives you the same information, obviating the need to repeat investigations. Air under the diaphragm is due to free air and not air that is contained within the bowel.

The *Chilaiditi* sign, due to an entrapped loop of hepatic flexure between the diaphragm and liver, may mimic free gas under the diaphragm, but these are rare signs, and the gas is always within the lumen of the bowel.

Free gas of perforated viscus lies outside the lumen of the stomach and bowel and may be located under both the hemidiaphragms.

The principles of management are:

- The same for all patients presenting with peritonitis
- The assessments should be done on the threshold of the operating theatre
- Assessment, resuscitation, and anaesthetic advice must all go hand in hand
- Not all patients will be suitable for surgical intervention
- Assessment of fitness, morbidity, and mortality from surgical intervention must be made in conjunction with an anaesthetist

Upper gastrointestinal bleeding

This used to be a common general surgical emergency; however, the progress of endoscopic interventions has now made surgical interventions less frequent.

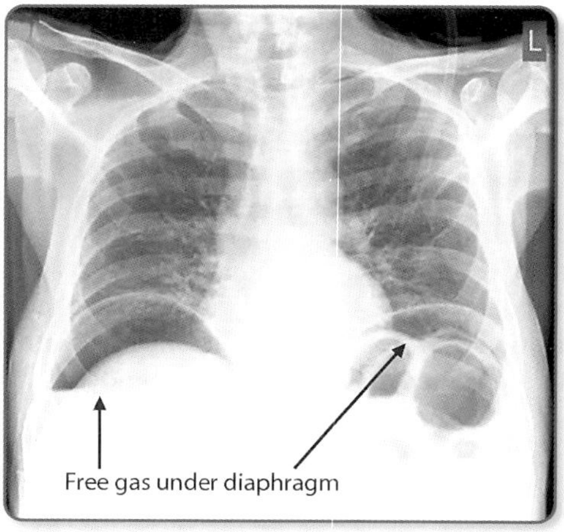

Figure 1 Erect chest X-ray showing free gas.

The presentation can be acute with sudden onset of melaena or haematemesis.

Melaena is the passage of stools with breakdown products of haemoglobin to acid haematin by digestion (the four S's):

- *S*chwarz (black; German)
- *S*melly
- *S*limy
- *S*ticky

The principles of management are directed towards stabilisation of the patient. This is then followed by localisation of the causative pathology followed by medical management for most patients. When that fails, the next step is endoscopic management. Surgical management is reserved for the few that fail endoscopic management.

Gastro-oesophageal bleeding can be related to aspirin and non-steroidal use in about a third of the patients. The bleeding is due to weakening of the mucosal barrier brought about by inhibition of cyclo-oxygenase and consequent decrease in the production of prostacyclin. Prostacyclin protects the mucosa by increasing mucous and bicarbonate secretion.

The other major causes include the following:

- Gastro-oesophageal varices
- Stress ulcerations
- Longitudinal *Mallory–Weiss* tear of the oesophago-gastric junction due to retching and vomiting

Endoscopic therapy for peptic ulcer bleeding

- Adrenaline injection to slow bleeding but not highly effective in isolation
- Thermal modalities – heater probes and bipolar coagulation
- Clips – more recently 'over the scope clips'. These are applied over the vessels ligating them successfully.
- *Hemospray*: This achieves haemostasis by adhering to the area of bleeding and promoting thrombosis. It is effective as a means of bridging till other modes of treatment become effective or in combination with other modes of therapy.

Treatment of oesophageal varices

- Band ligation of varices
- Propranolol or other non-selective β-blockers
- Thrombin injections for gastric varices
- Somatostatin/Terlipressin
- Balloon tamponade
- Trans jugular intra hepatic portosystemic shunts (TIPSS)

Chapter 12

Acute appendicitis

The acute appendicitis normally presents with symptoms and signs as follows:

- Central abdominal pain
- Nausea (follows pain)
- Vomiting (just once or twice)
- Pyrexia
- Localised pain in right lower quadrant
- A low-grade pyrexia raised white cell count and a high C-reactive protein (CRP) are manifestations of inflammatory process

Migrating pain (Figure 1)

Classically, the pain in appendicitis appears to migrate from being central at onset, to the right iliac fossa when the disease is more established.

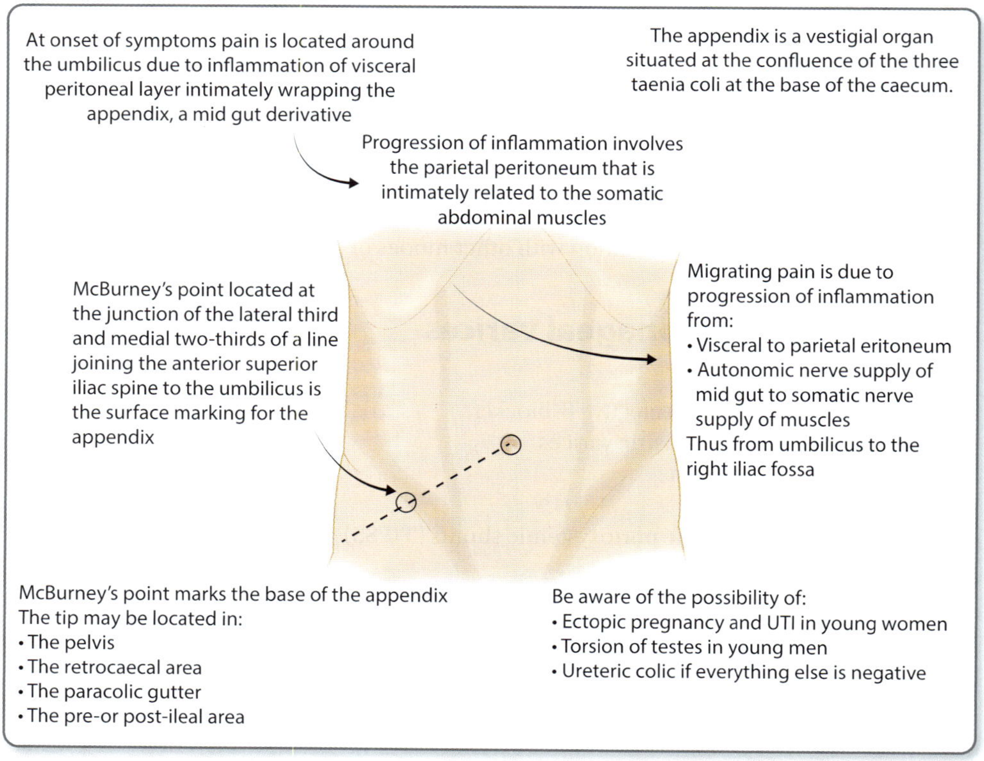

Figure 1 Migrating pain of appendicitis.

This is because the appendix is part of the mid gut, and this *autonomic pain is poorly localised* and felt in the umbilical region.

As inflammation progresses, it involves the abdominal muscles and irritates the somatic nerves. *Somatic pain is more direct and localised.*

As the appendix lies deep to the abdominal muscles in the right iliac fossa, the inflammation of the parietal layer of the peritoneum involves the abdominal muscles that are innervated by somatic nerves and presents as localised pain. The worsening pain is then located overlying the appendix and thus in the right iliac fossa.

Possible progression of appendicitis:

- Appendicular mass
- Appendicular abscess
- Closed loop obstruction
- Peritonitis due to failure of localisation

Appendicular mass

The mass occurs when the omentum (abdominal policeman) and adjacent loops of bowel combine forces and wall off the `troublemaker.' This process is common to all types of pathology that need containment such as cholecystitis, diverticulitis, appendicitis, visceral perforation, and salpingitis.

The mass presents itself in about 48 hours after the onset of symptoms. This occurs because the body's response to inflammation tries to isolate and contain the spread of inflammation to the rest of the peritoneal cavity.

The inflamed organ that is enveloped by the omentum, bowel, as well as any adjacent organ such as the uterus or even the ovary manifests as a tender mass.

Abscess formation due to progressive inflammation and it presents as a tender localised mass. Once an abscess sets in a fluctuating fever referred to as the *'thicket fence' fever* (up and down course of the body temperature) may follow. It must be noted that a similar effect is produced with the paracetamol as its effect can intermittently decrease the body temperature even in patients with a steady temperature.

Closed loop obstruction is caused when a faecolith obstructs the lumen of the appendix. The secretions of the mucosa of the appendix being obstructed causes the appendix to distend. This can lead to perforation rapidly (within 12–24 hours) causing localised or generalised peritonitis. This used to be referred to as 'burst appendicitis' in the past.

When *localisation* fails, it can lead to *peritonitis* in the very young and the very old.

- In the very young due to under development of omentum
- In the elderly due to atrophy of the omentum

In young women, pain in the right lower quadrant of the abdomen may be due to *pelvic inflammatory disease (PID),* retrograde menstruation or mid-cycle ovulation pain referred to as *Mittelschmerz.*

Appendicitis end response

- Resolution
- Mass formation – localisation

- Abscess formation
- Peritonitis
- Fibrosis

In all young women presenting with abdominal pain, the following are mandatory:

- Menstrual history
- Contraceptive status
- Beta-human chorionic gonadotropin (hCG) status
- Examination of urine for nitrates

Conservative management of localised peritonitis in young women may affect tubal patency increasing the risk of ectopic pregnancy subsequently. It is therefore important to consider early intervention or laparoscopy in young women with suspected pelvic inflammation.

In the presence of appendicular abscess, perforation, or gangrene at operation, then 48 hours or more of antibiotic treatment is indicated. A common organism that is present in appendicular inflammation is 'Bacteroides', and this is treated with metronidazole; the other common organisms are *E. coli* and *Klebsiella*, and antibiotic treatment will be dictated as per your hospital protocol.

Inflammatory bowel disease such as Crohn's disease must also be borne in mind when the history and presentation are not clear, and the patient offers a history of diarrhoea.

A diagnosis is not always possible, and *'nonspecific abdominal pain'* is acceptable as a discharge diagnosis and leaves open the possibility of considering other diagnosis at a later date if the problem recurs.

If the appendix is normal at operation and no abnormalities are noted in the bowel, pelvic organs including the ovaries and Meckel's is excluded, then renal and ureteric pathology such as calculi must be ruled out prior to discharge with further imaging.

In the elderly patients presenting with acute right iliac pain and a palpable mass, a CT scan will be needed to exclude caecal or even appendicular malignancies.

Imaging as an aid to diagnosis in appendicitis

- *Ultrasound scan* is non-invasive, but it requires a radiologist with appropriate skills to make a diagnosis of appendicitis. It is favoured in the younger patients as it avoids radiation
- *CT scan* of the abdomen has a 96% specificity and the advantage of ruling out other pelvic causes for the presentation. This is favoured in the elderly and the obese patients
- *MRI* of the abdomen is a useful tool in select patients where a clear diagnosis needs confirmation

Surgical management

The principles of general management as laid out previously must be implemented prior to a decision to operate.

Appendicectomies are mostly done laparoscopically rather than with open surgery. Laparoscopic surgery facilitates early discharge as there is reduced pain and discomfort compared to an open operation.

The open operation may be needed in the presence of a mass or when converting to an open operation following failed laparoscopic attempt.

Traditionally, the incision for open appendicectomy overlies the *McBurney* point. The exposure is through a *'grid iron'* incision that splits the muscle fibres of the abdominal wall along the long axis of the muscles instead of cutting across them. When the exposure with the 'grid iron' incision is insufficient, then the muscles of the abdominal wall are divided by cutting laterally in a process referred to as the *'Rutherford-Morrison'* extension after the surgeon who popularised it.

Complications such as *appendicular abscesses* can be drained radiologically prior to an interval appendicectomy later.

In the presence of an *appendicular mass,* a non-operative management with resolution of the mass may be considered. The patient may need an interval appendicectomy.

Where an immediate appendicectomy is not carried out or deferred for reasons of complications then an *interval appendicectomy* may need consideration in 6–12 weeks after resolution. The MRI scan of the abdomen will reveal the location and presence of the appendicitis prior to such intervention. In a small number of patients, the original inflammation and the process of fibrosis may destroy the appendix making the interval appendicectomy superfluous.

It is mandatory to *check the histology* and ensure confirmation of appendicitis. Rarely, you might come across a diagnosis of carcinoma, carcinoid, or Crohn's disease of the appendix. Those patients will need discussion about further management.

Differential diagnosis

- Pelvic inflammatory disease
- Meckel's diverticulitis
- Crohn's disease
- Carcinoid of the appendix
- Adeno carcinoma of the caecum/appendix
- Ureteric calculi
- Diverticulitis of the sigmoid
- Ectopic pregnancy
- Torsion of the testis
- Amoebic typhlitis or amoeboma
- Ileo-caecal tuberculosis

Case-based discussion

Because appendicitis is a common surgical problem, it is important to have a clear understanding of the management. It is useful to work out a plan of management for the following possible presentations:

- *Right iliac pain in a 10-year-old girl:*
  - Clinical assessment
  - Routine bloods

  - Imaging with ultrasound/CT scan
  - Appendicectomy on confirmation of diagnosis
  - Non-operative management with re-assessment and review when appendicitis is not confirmed
- *Lower abdominal pain in a 30-year-old lady*
  - As above and in addition
  - Urinary beta-hCG
  - Urinary nitrates and microscopy
  - Possible laparoscopic exploration if imaging is not confirmatory
  - Involvement of the gynaecological team to exclude PID
- *Presentation after 48 hours of onset of symptoms and when there is a palpable mass in the right iliac fossa:*
  - Define the presence or absence of a mass in the right lower quadrant of the abdomen
  - Exclude malignancy where appropriate
  - Surgical or conservative management depending on the level of expertise available and the fitness of the patient
  - Conservative management will include active monitoring of system and the mass. Treatment with antibiotics and intravenous fluids. Switch to surgery if the mass fails to resolve or it becomes an abscess.
- *Presentation with generalised abdominal tenderness and rigidity*
  - A CT scan will be needed to exclude peritonitis
  - Laparotomy rather than exploration with cosmetic incisions is preferred
  - Critical care team must be involved in the post-operative care as the sepsis may have a delayed manifestation of over 6–12 hours post-surgical intervention
  - Needless to say, cultures must be obtained at surgery and appropriate antibiotic therapy instituted
- *Right iliac pain with microscopic haematuria:* Urinary infection and ureteric calculi must be excluded
- *Presence of fever and sore throat* prior to presentation with pain tends to occur in children. In these cases, the paediatric team must be involved in the decision-making as the presentation may not be that of an acute appendicitis
- *Findings suggestive of Crohn's/Tuberculosis at operation:* This situation unlikely arises in current practice where imaging prior to intervention is becoming the norm; however, if at operation, there is a clinical impression of Crohn's disease then the following options need to be considered:
  - If the base of the appendix is normal and not affected by Crohn's disease, then it is reasonable to proceed to an appendicectomy if the appendix is inflamed. Even so there may be a small risk of a fistula.
  - If the Crohn's disease is limited to the terminal ileum, it must be documented and the patient should be referred for medical management. Limited right hemicolectomy is used to be an option but in the absence of consenting it is best not to proceed further.
  - The same principle applies for tuberculosis which is common in some parts of the world.

Chapter 13

Hernia

A hernia (**Figure 1**) is protrusion of viscus or part of a viscus from the cavity in which it is contained to another cavity or to the exterior. They can occur wherever there is a body cavity including:

- The cranium
- The thorax
- The abdomen

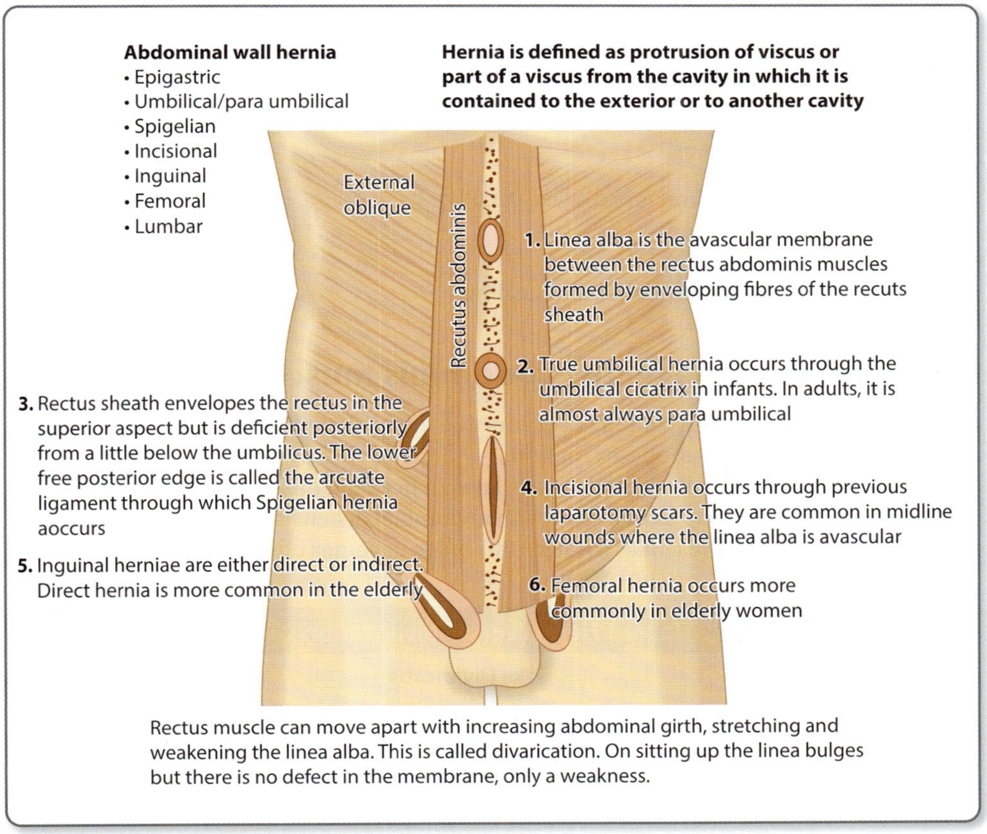

Figure 1 An abdominal wall hernia.

Umbilical hernia

An umbilical hernia is generally congenital and occurs through the true umbilical cicatrix.

They are common in *children* and seldom need intervention till the age of 3 years by which time a *sizeable proportion* many would have resolved without need for surgical intervention.

In *adults*, the defect in the umbilical region is outside the true umbilicus and is referred to as *para-umbilical hernia*.

They are symptomless in many patients. Intervention may be needed if there is evidence of obstruction or if it is large.

Para-umbilical hernia – predisposing factors

- Pregnancy
- Abdominal exercise
- Cirrhosis
- Ascites

Incisional hernia

These arise in scars of incisions for abdominal operations and are therefore called 'Incisional hernia.' They can occur anywhere in the abdomen where there is a scar. Predisposing factors for incisional hernia include the following:

- High body mass index (BMI)
- Low BMI
- Diabetic
- Chronic obstructive pulmonary disease (COPD)
- Previously infected wounds
- Nutritional compromise
- Previous wound infections or delayed healing.

Divarication of the rectus abdominis muscle

Divarication is not a hernia (**Table 1**). It occurs due to the recti muscles moving apart either due to multiple pregnancies, obesity, or both.

The linea alba, an avascular membranous layer in between the two rectus muscles, stretches apart as the rectus moves apart with abdominal distension. It then becomes weak over time and can present as a bulge. This bulge becomes obvious when the patient

Table 1 Hernia versus divarication

Hernia	Divarication
Will become prominent when the patient stands	Will *not* become prominent when the patient stands
There is a palpable defect	There is no palpable defect
Contents protrude through the defect	No contents protrude; there is a uniform bulge
There is a risk of strangulation	There is no risk of strangulation
May need surgery	Will not need surgery

changes posture from lying to sitting up but disappears when the patient stands unlike a hernia.

Inguinal hernia

Inguinal hernia occurs in the inguinal canal. The inguinal canal is a potential space that extends almost transversely from the internal ring to the external ring.
Inguinal hernia is of two types:

1. *Direct* inguinal hernia
2. *Indirect* inguinal hernia (**Figure 2**)

The boundaries of the inguinal canal are as follows:

- *Anteriorly*: The external oblique muscle which is reinforced in the medial aspect of the canal by the conjoint fibres of the internal and transversus abdominis muscles
- *Posteriorly:* The transversalis fascia
- *Inferiorly:* The inguinal ligament
- *Superiorly:* The arching fibres of the conjoint tendon

The direct hernia:

- Occurs due to muscle failure
- The patient is likely to be elderly
- The defect is a bulge or tear in the transversalis fascia *medial to the inferior epigastric vessels*
- It seldom descends into the scrotum, although the bulge may overlie the proximal scrotum purely because of the effect of size
- It seldom strangulates

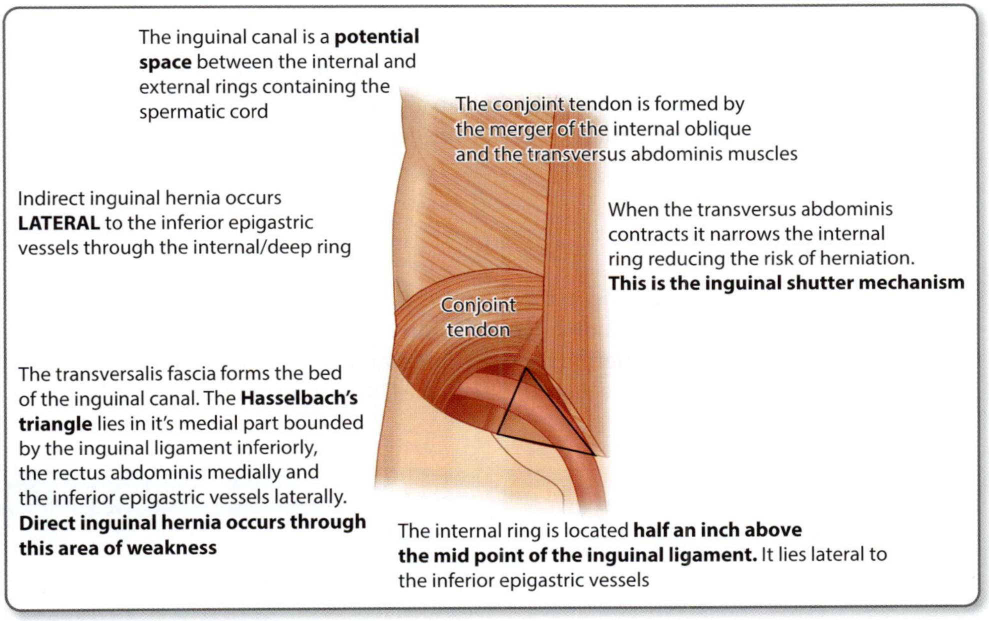

Figure 2 Indirect inguinal hernia.

The indirect hernia:

- It has a significant degree of a congenital element to it and, hence, is more common in younger people
- It traverses the internal ring
- The defect is in the internal ring, *lateral to the inferior epigastric vessels*
- Protrudes along the obliquity of the inguinal canal
- It may extend through the external ring into the scrotum when it is large
- It has a risk of strangulation
- Any hernia that is in the scrotum enveloping the testis is an indirect hernia

Predisposing factors

- *Chronic cough* – secondary to COPD or bronchiectasis
- *Chronic constipation*
- *Prostatism* with straining at micturition
- *Increase in intra-abdominal pressure* due to muscular activity, ascites
- *Factors that cause a sudden increase in intra-abdominal pressure.* In the young and fit persons playing football, rugby, or tennis where one twists and turns actively during the game, a sudden increase in pressure can lead to tears in the muscles around the groin.

Gilmore's groin

Jerry Gilmore, who initially drew attention to the link between sports injury and hernia, said that the pathology of *Gilmore's groin* is as follows:

- Torn external oblique aponeurosis
- Torn conjoined tendon
- Conjoined tendon torn from pubic tubercle
- Dehiscence between conjoined tendon and inguinal ligament

A good history from the patient must therefore include a discussion about the possible predisposing causes and attempts must be made to alleviate constipation or cough prior to surgery; in some cases, prostatic surgery may be needed before considering a repair of the hernia.

Examination

When a patient presents with a lump in the groin:

- Define if it is an inguinal or a femoral hernia (**Table 2**)

The exception is when a femoral hernia becomes large, and the neck is difficult to define. The hernia flops back on itself like a 'lazy U' due to the fascial attachments across the

Table 2 Inguinal hernia versus femoral hernia

Inguinal hernia	Femoral hernia
The neck is above and lateral to the pubic tubercle	The neck is below and lateral to the pubic tubercle

femoral triangle preventing the hernia descending towards the knee. It can then lie across the inguinal ligament instead of following gravity.

- If it is an inguinal hernia, then define the type:
  - Direct hernia protrudes through the Hesselbach's triangle
  - Indirect hernia protrudes through the internal ring and takes an oblique route

If the bulge is not clinically obvious at the outset, asking the patient to stand up and cough will generally make the bulge obvious. Classically, to define the type of inguinal hernia, the hernia should be reduced with the patient lying down. The internal ring can then be compressed with one hand, and the patient is asked to stand up and cough while the internal ring still is compressed by the hand. If the coughing causes the hernia to protrude despite adequate compression of the internal ring, then obviously it is not protruding through the internal ring, and thus it is a direct rather than an indirect hernia.

Why distinguish between direct and indirect hernia?

- Risk of strangulation is higher in an indirect hernia
- Advice on indirect hernia, therefore, may well be early surgery rather than a wait and watch policy that may be undertaken for the elderly patients with a direct hernia and multiple comorbidities.

The reason for surgery:

- Prevention of progression
- Presence of complications
- Pain
- Size

Complications of inguinal hernia

- *Pain* – multifactorial but could be due to muscle tear in early hernia to possible narrowing at the neck and/or compression
- *Irreducibility* – due to adhesions between contents and the sac or intra-saccular adhesions of contents making it globular and thus difficult to reduce. Forcible reduction of these *'reduction en masse'* along with the sac may cause strangulation within the peritoneal cavity later if the sac continues to constrict the contents
- *Obstruction* – rarely a feature without irreducibility or strangulation
- *Strangulation (**Figure 3** –* more common with indirect hernia when the neck constricts around a sac containing loops of bowel. Initially, it compromises venous supply leading to swelling and raised intra-saccular pressure and then to arterial compromise causing gangrene of the bowel

Investigations

- *Dynamic ultrasound scan* when the presence of a hernia is not definable clinically, but the patient offers a good history for a hernia. The hernia can be shown on coughing or straining (Valsalva manoeuvre)
- *Magnetic resonance imaging (MRI)* for groin pain without an obvious hernia. This will exclude muscular tears or hip-related problems

The complications that can arise from any hernia are:
- **Irreducibility**
- **Obstruction**
- **Strangulation**

Strangulation occurs at the neck of the sac which in an indirect hernia is located at the internal ring. Initially, the veins being soft walled are compressed. This leads to oedema. As the pressure increases the arterial supply is compressed and blood supply compromised leading to gangrene of the bowel

Strangulation is more common in an indirect hernia than in a direct hernia as these tend to have a well-defined neck at the internal ring compared to a commonly wide necked direct hernia

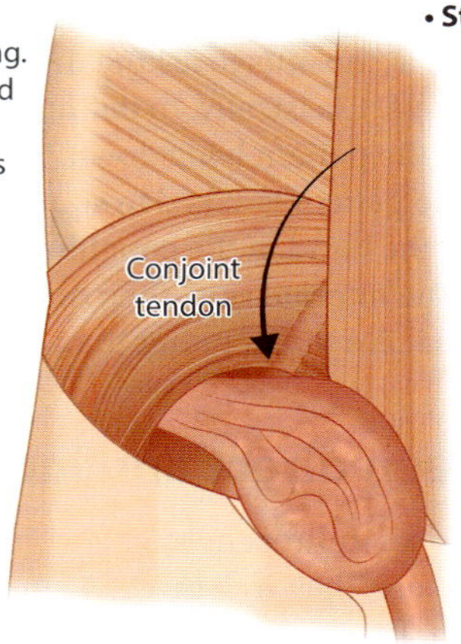

The indirect hernial sac has a neck at the internal ring with a body and fundus. It may contain bowel, omentum or nothing. They can become irreducible when bowel loops adhere to the wall of the sac or to themselves becoming globular and thus difficult to reduce through the internal ring

Forced reduction of an irreducible hernia of 'reduction en masse' can sometimes lead to strangulation of contents some hours after reduction as the neck of the sac may still remain tight causing increasing constriction

Figure 3 Complications (strangulation) of inguinal hernia.

- *CT scan of the abdomen:*
  - Distinguishes inguinal and femoral hernia
  - If there is obstruction, it excludes other pathologies in the abdomen
  - Defines the level and seriousness of the pathology

Management

It is important to discuss the following with all patients:
- Surgery versus no surgery – that is, wait and watch as opposed to operative surgery
- Laparoscopic versus open surgery
- Local versus loco-regional versus general anaesthesia for surgery

The recommendation of the hernia society is to consider surgical intervention in asymptomatic patients under 65 years of age and in symptomatic patients over 65 years of age.

Laparoscopic surgery is preferred for bilateral hernia and for recurrence after previous open or laparoscopic surgery.

For unilateral hernia, it is a matter for discussion with the patient as to the various options.

In the elderly with comorbidities, repair under local anaesthesia or regional anaesthesia is preferable.

Children under the age of 16 years should be treated by the paediatric surgeons.

Hernia in infants should be treated urgently. The prior rule used to be 'never send a newborn baby home with a hernia unless a herniotomy is carried out'.

Operations for inguinal hernia

Operations for inguinal hernia have now been simplified with the introduction of *tension-free mesh repair*. With the advent of tension-free mesh repairs either laparoscopically or open, the hernial sac is reduced and the posterior wall reinforced by the placement of a mesh. There is no forcible approximation of musculature. As in normal life, so in operations; the absence of tension augurs well! The operation carried out with mesh goes by the name of *Liechtenstein* after he published his results of a massive number of hernia repairs.

Femoral hernia

This is:

- More common in women than men
- More common in elderly women
- Commonly missed in routine clinical examinations, especially in the presence of central obesity

'No examination of the abdomen is complete without examination of the hernial sites.' This adage becomes obvious in any acute presentation of intestinal obstruction in the absence of an obvious cause such as earlier operations.

In patients with a high BMI, the groin fold is difficult to define, and the hernia can be missed easily leading to strangulation later.

It is also not surprising that often the elderly patient may have failed to notice it themselves.

This hernia, in the elderly, has an elevated risk of mortality of up to 30% when it strangulates; prompt detection and action, as always, will reduce the morbidity and mortality.

Location and anatomy

Femoral hernias are located below and lateral to the pubic tubercle. The following are boundaries of the hernia:

- *Anteriorly:* The inguinal ligament
- *Posteriorly:* The pectinate ligament
- *Medially:* The lacunar ligament
- *Laterally:* The femoral vein

The hernia is located in the femoral canal that forms part of the femoral sheath. The femoral sheath (**Figure 4**) is the fascial layer that invests the femoral vessels as they leave the abdomen and proceed to the limb.

Like all hernias, the complications of a femoral hernia include obstruction and strangulation. In most cases, the content is only fatty tissue, however, when there is bowel in it, the risk of strangulation becomes greater.

Only a very small proportion of femoral hernia are completely reducible.

The risk of obstruction and strangulation is high, so surgery is normally recommended in the fit patient.

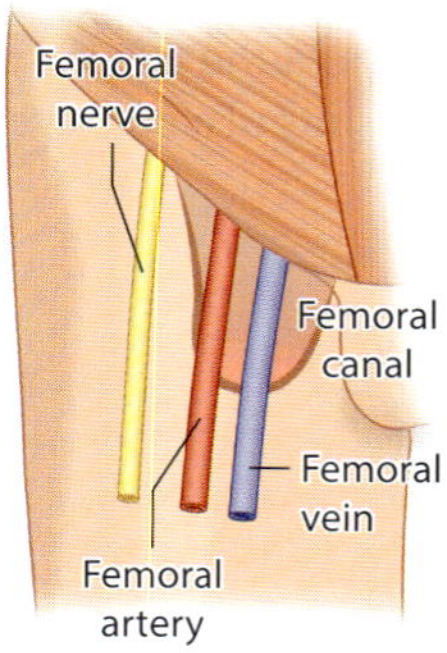

Figure 4 The femoral sheath.

Repair of femoral hernia after excision of sac

- *Low repair of Lockwood* – accessing from below the inguinal ligament and approximating the anterior wall (inguinal ligament) to the posterior wall (pectinate or Cooper's ligament). 'Roof to floor' repair
- *High repair of Lotheissen* – the approach is from superior to the inguinal ligament in the pre-peritoneal plane
- *AK Henry – repair* is carried out with a vertical incision over inguinal region. This is now defunct
- Laparotomy or *laparoscopic repair*

Mesh repair is increasingly more common, although in the elderly, a low repair of Lockwood is possible with or without a mesh. In all these repairs, it must be borne in mind that the *femoral vein* lies in close proximity to the neck of the sac. The vein must not only be protected from injury but also from being narrowed. Narrowing the vein can lead to problems with venous drainage of the leg.

Emergency operations

These can be technically difficult because the bowel may be distended, ischaemic, and prone to tear on traction. Repairs from above the inguinal ligament through a laparotomy or pre-peritoneal plane is preferred, with mobilisation being carried out after proximal and distal clamping of bowel prior to traction. Risks of spillage of bowel contents are thus reduced. Many of the patients presenting with strangulated femoral hernia are elderly with comorbidities and spillage can lead to sepsis and its consequences. The mortality from a strangulated femoral hernia in the elderly can be extremely high. The post-operative care will need management in a level two setting for most.

Chapter 14

Varicose veins

Pathophysiology (Figures 1 and 2)

Varicosities occur in a vein due to the thinning of the wall. This leads to dilatation, which moves the valves apart, causing them to dysfunction and permit retrograde flow.

Retrograde flow in the veins raises the back pressure on the venous side of the capillaries. The Starling pressures (**Figure 3**) at the capillary level are altered because of this venous hypertension.

Venous obstruction due to one factor or another can alter this basic equation. When it does, the inflow at the venous end becomes less than the outflow from the capillaries at the arterial end. This reduction of inflow at the venular end causes stagnation in the capillary region. This will cause oedema.

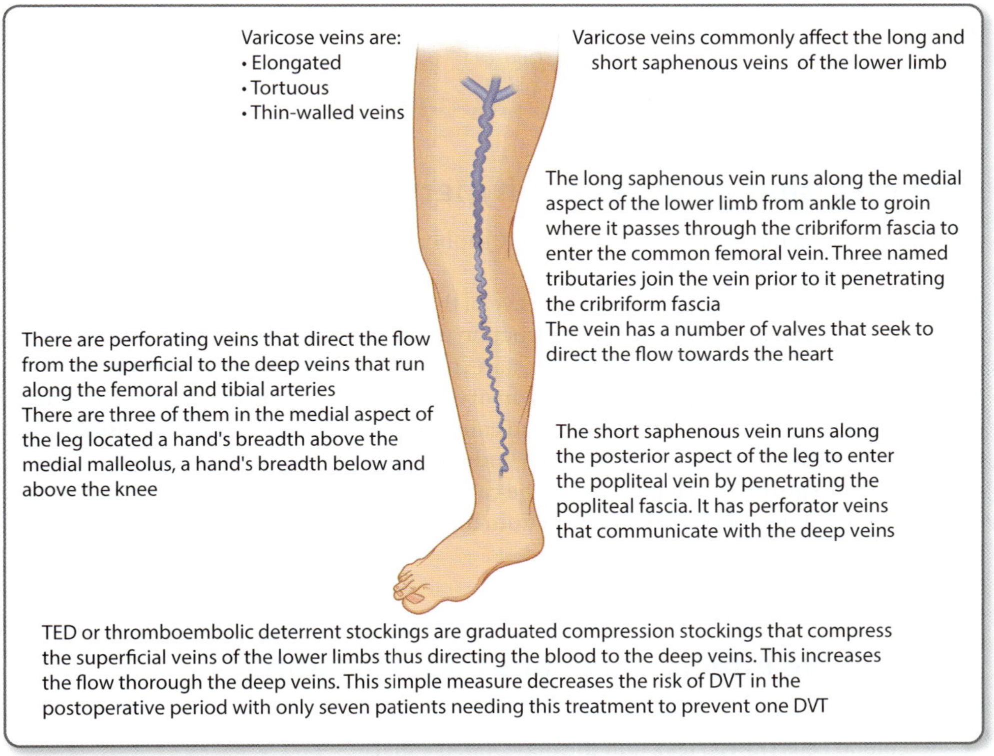

Figure 1 Pathophysiology of varicose veins.

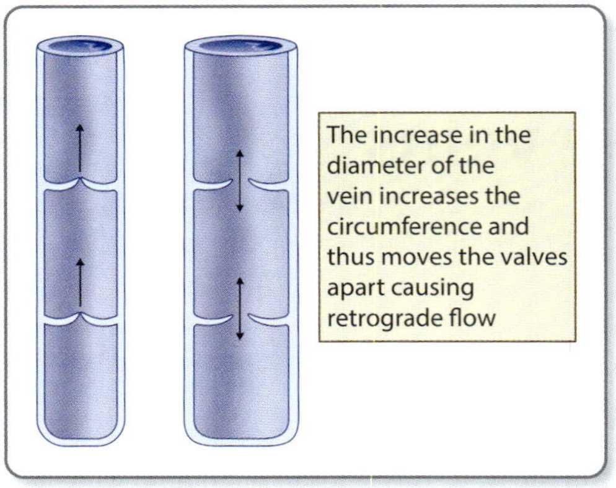

Figure 2 Pathophysiology of varicosities.

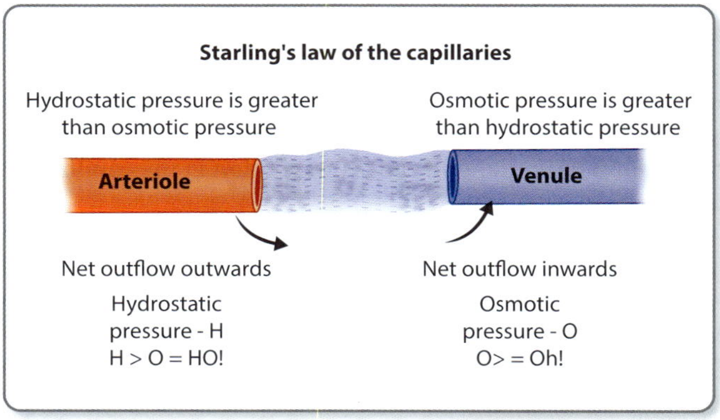

Figure 3 The Starling's law of capillaries.

Pathophysiology of venous hypertension

There are approximately 18 valves in the long saphenous vein. These valves allow flow in one direction, always towards the heart.

Due to an inherited weakness in the weave of the wall of the vein, the veins start to dilate over time. This can also occur due to obstruction to flow leading to stretching of the wall of the vein. When the diameter of the vein starts to increase, the valves move away from each other. When this happens, the direction of flow is reversed, and the valves start to leak. Once the leakage starts, it is progressive and causes more and more distension distally. As there are no valves in the main veins of the body such as the inferior vena cava (IVC), the backward pressure on the venous end of the capillaries increases and will be equal to the height of the column of blood in the vein from the heart to the foot. This can be as much as a 100 mmHg.

This is venous hypertension.

Progressive effects of venous hypertension

- Greater efflux at the arteriolar end
- Red blood cells (RBCs) leak into the pericapillary space

- Red blood cells are broken down by macrophages to haemosiderin
- Haemosiderin is deposited around capillaries
- Pigmentation and perivascular cuffing occur
- This leads to decreased oxygen delivery to tissues
- Results in breakdown of skin and ulceration around ankle
- Attempt at healing leads to fibrosis around ankle
- Fibrosis restricts ankle movements
- Leads to failure of soleal muscle pump (this is the peripheral heart that pushes the blood back to the heart 'Vis a tergo')
- A slow vicious cycle sets in with more arterial efflux and less inflow into the venules leading to complications

Complications of venous hypertension

- Leg ulcers
- Lipodermatosclerosis
- Pigmentation
- Bleeding
- Ankle stiffness

Thin-walled veins that are dilated can bleed spontaneously because of the venous hypertension or after minor trauma. If they do the best, immediate treatment is elevation and compression.

The leg ulcers are exceedingly difficult to treat and seldom heal despite the best efforts of *compression* and *elevation*. They occur close to the ankle because of the location of the long saphenous vein. Stiffness of the ankle reduces the efficiency of the calf muscle pump. The venous stagnation worsens as the *'vis a tergo,'* or push from behind towards the heart fails. This sets up a perpetually worsening cycle.

Mobility of the ankle is the key to success in all venous problems affecting the legs but can seldom be achieved if ankle stiffness is established.

Change in the direction of flow with varicose veins (Table 1)

Table 1 Change in the direction of flow with varicose veins

Direction of flow in the normal saphenous veins	Direction of flow in varicose saphenous veins
In the long and short saphenous veins, the normal direction of flow is from the ankle towards the heart, i.e., from distal to proximal	The flow is reversed leading to retrograde flow from the heart to the legs in the main saphenous veins
In the perforators the normal flow is from superficial veins to deep veins	In the perforators, the flow is from the deep veins to superficial veins

Trendelenburg test

Traditionally, Trendelenburg recommended identifying the retrograde flow at the sapheno-femoral junction by the following steps.

1. Lie the patient down
2. Elevate the limb
3. Empty the veins of blood
4. Compress the sapheno-femoral junction
5. Stand the patient up with continued compression
6. Release the compression in the upright posture
7. Observe the filling of the vein
8. Immediate retrograde filling denotes a positive test

Doppler test

- 'To and fro' sounds at the sapheno-femoral junction by squeezing (prograde flow) and releasing the compression of the calf muscles (retrograde flow)
- Normally on compression of the calf, there is a prograde flow with a recorded Doppler sound
- On release of compression, if the valve is competent, there is no retrograde flow and thus no recorded sound
- When the valve is incompetent there is a whoosh sound on compression and whoosh sound on release - a *whoosh-whoosh* instead of just one *whoosh*!
- Perforator incompetence is likewise determined by showing the flow pattern.

Trendelenburg operation – long saphenous varicosity

Typically, for the long saphenous varicosity, the operation entails ligation of the long saphenous vein at the sapheno-femoral junction commonly referred to as high ligation. This was followed by ligation of the tributaries of the long saphenous vein (there are no other tributaries to the femoral vein at this level) followed by stripping of the vein to the knee and multiple avulsions below that if needed.

When the vein is stripped in its entirety, there is a risk of damage to the saphenous nerve that runs alongside the vein in the lower leg. Recognition of this fact led to a more limited stripping and local avulsions.

Short saphenous varicosity

For the short saphenous varicosity, the operation is one of ligations of the sapheno-popliteal junction and avulsions of the distal varicosities in the leg.

Current method of treatment for varicose veins

Currently, the above operation is carried out less often in the western countries as more noninvasive methods of sclerosing the veins have become established.

Types of sclerotherapies

- Chemical
- Mechanical

Chemical sclerotherapy

This involves the instillation of a salt solution into the vein, causing a chemical reaction in the walls of the veins. This has been in practice since the 1930s, and the results have been reasonable in selected patients with a satisfactory result in up to 80% of treated patients. Not all patients will be suitable for this.

It is contraindicated:

- In pregnant women
- Used with caution in patients on oral contraceptives
- In patients with a cardiac history who may need these veins for venous bypass in the future

A modern variation of this technique is foam sclerotherapy, where air is added to the chemical solution resulting in an equally satisfactory result with less discomfort.

These procedures involve the instillation of the chemical solution into the vein or into spider veins. The veins are emptied, and the chemical is instilled. A compression crepe bandage is applied to approximate the opposing walls of the vein that becomes inflamed following the chemical irritation. The vein walls then adhere. The vein collapses as a result and is excluded from circulation.

Mechanical sclerotherapy

- Endothermal ablation
- Laser ablation
- Glue ablation

The principle here is like chemical sclerotherapy, but the procedure is done under ultrasound guidance. Local, regional, or general anaesthesia may be appropriate.

The vein is cannulated at the ankle or knee, and an endothermal or laser probe is passed up to the sapheno-femoral or sapheno-popliteal junction. The location is confirmed with ultrasound. As the probe is withdrawn, it is activated. The local heat causes a re-configuration of the protein in the walls and causes them to adhere, effectively excluding the vein from further circulation. This has the same effect as stripping. Long-term studies have shown a low re-cannulation rate.

Glue injections work similarly by obliterating the veins and are still being evaluated.

Chapter 15

Cholecystitis and biliary disease

Gallstones are caused by an imbalance between bile salts, cholesterol, and lecithin leading to supersaturation and crystallisation (**Figures 1 and 2**).

The following factors predispose to gallstones:

- Obesity
- Weight gain
- *Gender*: Higher incidence in women
- *Age*: More common in people over 60 years
- Rapid weight loss as the body breaks down adipose tissue
- Fasting distends the gallbladder and reduces contraction. This may lead to cholesterol stones
- Diabetes as these patients has high triglycerides
- *Recent pregnancy*: Bile stasis can lead to formation of stones
- Oral contraceptives as it increases cholesterol levels
- *Crohn's disease*: Absence of absorption of bile salts in the distal ileum may lead to an imbalance and precipitate stone formation; this may also follow ileal resection or bypass
- Aortic valve replacement with metallic valves which can cause haemolysis by crushing (chewing) red blood cells (RBCs) with every beat
- Haemolytic anaemia can be hereditary or acquired. Once RBCs lose their biconcave shape and become rounded as in hereditary spherocytosis, they are easily broken down in the spleen. Drugs may cause haemolysis. Haemolysis leads to an excess of bile pigments and thus to stone formation

Family history is not of significance, but there are families with lithogenic bile. The most common reason for a strong family history is that the families are brought up eating and enjoying similar types of food.

Presentation

- The stones may be asymptomatic.
- Symptoms can arise from stones within the gallbladder when they can cause:
  - Acute cholecystitis
  - Biliary colic
  - Chronic cholecystitis
  - Mucocoele of the gallbladder due to blockage of cystic duct
  - Empyema when such a blockage gets infected
  - Perforation of the gallbladder, leading to bile peritonitis

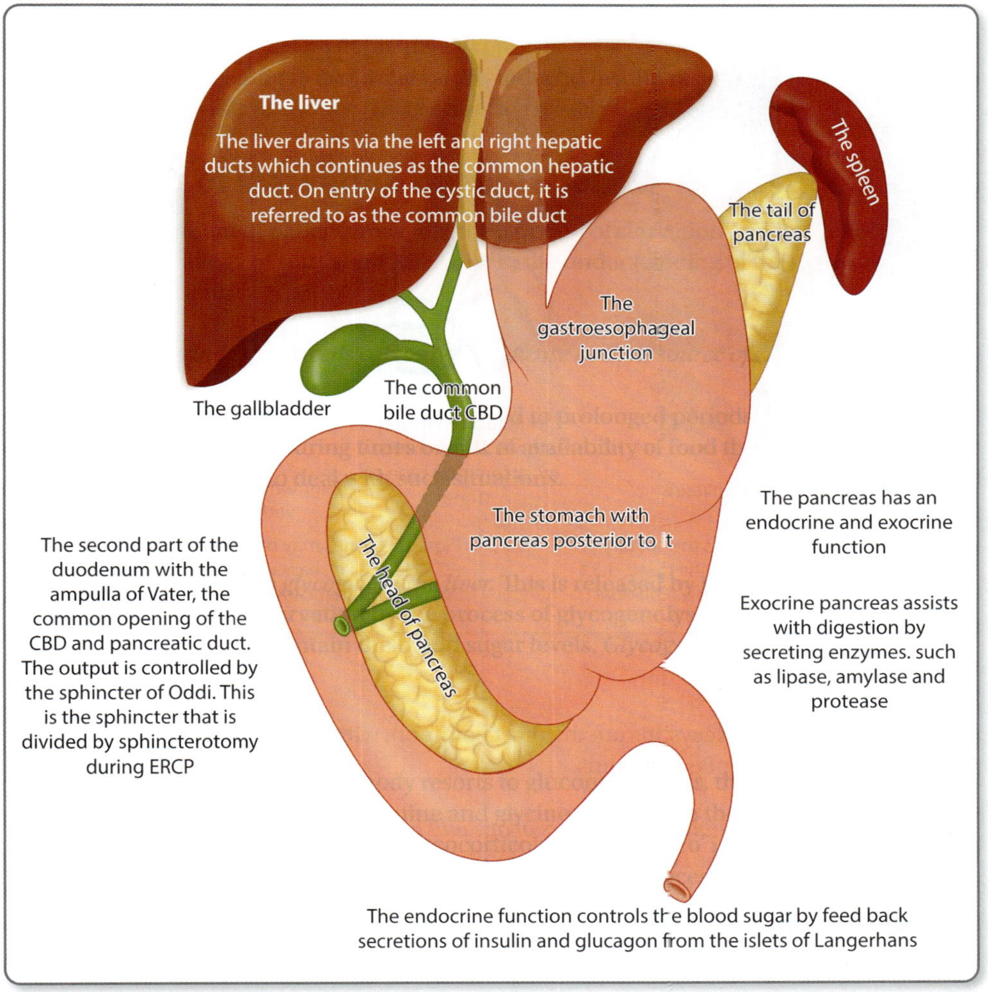

Figure 1 The biliary system.

- The stones may slip into the common bile duct and can cause:
  - Jaundice due to blockage of the duct, and
  - Pancreatitis when they block the common channel of the pancreatic and bile ducts at the ampulla of Vater.
- In some situations, they can cause a fistula between the gallbladder and duodenum, and stones may slip out into the small bowel and cause *gallstone ileus* when they get impacted in the ileum, where the lumen may be narrower than the jejunum.

Traditionally, it is said to affect 'the fat, fertile female of forty'. This is no longer true as the society is changing. Younger people on contraceptives present earlier. Obesity rates are higher even in the young. Most people with gallstones have little or no symptoms.

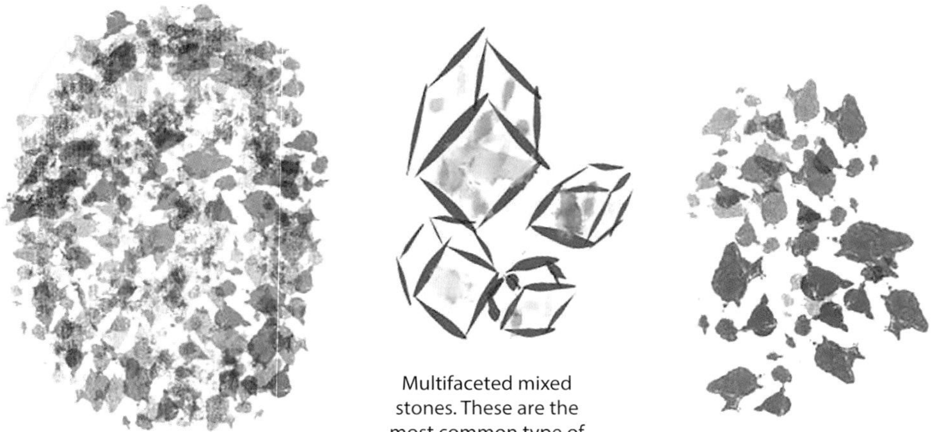

Figure 2 Types of gallstones.

Biliary colic and cholecystitis are the most common, with <2% presenting with the dreaded complication of pancreatitis.

About 20% of people over 60 years of age will have gallstones on imaging with ultrasound scan but may not have symptoms.

Acute presentation

Acute cholecystitis is one of the most common conditions that need emergency admissions.

Most patients present with pain in the right upper quadrant of the abdomen; this may follow a fatty meal, but not exclusively. Some patients will have had a similar but milder pain after food. They may have overlooked for many months or even years.

The pain is typically brought on by eating fatty foods and is in the right upper quadrant of the abdomen.

The gallbladder is a foregut derivative, and hence the pain can also present in the epigastric region and rarely in the retrosternal region, mimicking a myocardial event.

Presentation

- Constant pain in the right upper quadrant or upper abdomen
- Patient may have pyrexia
- Right shoulder tip pain

- Interscapular pain
- Jaundice

Tenderness may be present in the right upper quadrant. Murphy's sign may be positive; this is demonstrated by palpating the right upper quadrant of the abdomen. The fundus of the gallbladder is located at the tip of the right ninth costal cartilage in the trans-pyloric plane. An inflamed gallbladder is, therefore, directly under the tip of the ninth costal cartilage. The palpating hand is placed under the costal cartilage in the right upper quadrant of the abdomen. The patient is asked to take a deep breath, and as the diaphragmatic movement pushes the liver and gallbladder inferiorly, the inflamed gallbladder is pressed against the palpating hand. This causes the patient to catch the breath as the fundus of the inflamed gallbladder hits the palpating hand.

It is important to distinguish biliary colic from acute cholecystitis. Biliary colic is a misnomer. Typically, it is not a colic and lasts from a few minutes to a few hours. It settles down as quickly as it starts.

Biliary colic may occur due to a temporary obstruction of the cystic duct due to tiny mobile stones that are pushed out by contraction of the gallbladder after a fatty meal. The stones fall back into the gallbladder with the relaxation of the gallbladder, and the pain resolves.

The white cell count may be normal.

Investigations

The rules to follow for investigations are constant for all diseases.

Here they are in order:

- Urine
- Blood
- Radiology
- Others

Urine

Dip stick for sugar, protein, blood, bilirubin, urobilinogen, and nitrates.

In young women, β-human chorionic gonadotropin (β-HCG) is especially important. If coincidentally positive, you may not want any radiological imaging with X-rays.

Nitrates, if positive, will suggest incidental urinary infections; likewise, a raised sugar and diabetes.

Blood

Full blood count (FBC), C-reactive protein (CRP), urea, electrolytes, liver function test, and serum amylase are basic investigations in all patients. The white cell count and CRP may be raised if there is acute cholecystitis and may be normal in biliary colic.

Radiology

An X-ray of the chest or abdomen is unnecessary. 90% of gallstones are not radio-opaque. (*Note:* 90 % of renal stones are radio-opaque).

An ultrasound examination of the abdomen in most cases will confirm the diagnosis.

In the very obese, the bodily habitus will make the ultrasound examination difficult, and a CT scan or MRI will be needed.

A CT scan, however, is not as good as an ultrasound examination in picking up stones in the gallbladder.

Other investigations

MRI of the liver and gallbladder may be needed if the ultrasound findings are equivocal.

A hepatobiliary iminodiacetic acid scan (HIDA) scan is used for an assessment of the physiological function of the gallbladder. This will assess the emptying time of the gallbladder after a fatty meal.

When the HIDA scan is positive, the gallbladder will show delayed emptying after a fatty meal suggesting dysfunction of the drainage mechanism. It can also possibly be caused by a small stone blocking the cystic duct in the valves (valve of Heister) that represent mucosal folds in the cystic duct. This is by no means a conclusive test, but it must be evaluated in the light of symptoms.

Magnetic resonance cholangio-pancreatography (MRCP) is done when serum bilirubin is elevated. This will define the calibre of the common duct and the presence of pathology in the duct. It may show the presence of stones in the gallbladder and the need for invasive intervention such as an endoscopic retrograde cholangio-pancreatography (ERCP). The present policy is, therefore, to do this as a screening procedure prior to the most invasive ERCP.

Management

The diagnosis of biliary colic may enable an immediate laparoscopic cholecystectomy during the primary admission.

Patients presenting with acute cholecystitis must also be operated upon the same admission if fit for surgery. In the presence of cholecystitis, however, there is a higher conversion rate from a laparoscopic to an open operation.

The advantage of an early operation is the ability to provide a curative treatment that will avoid complications during the waiting period.

The rapid access to diagnostic facilities now allows for early operation compared to the times when patients were placed on a waiting list and brought in for interval cholecystectomy months later.

Much depends on the suitability of the patient for surgery and the absence of comorbidity. As always in all surgeries, the decision to operate is a fine balance between the perceived benefits and risk of surgery. Safety in selection of patients leads to safety in surgery.

Recall the oft-repeated statement 'The feasibility of an operation is never an indication for its performance'.

Courvoisier's law

In the 1890s, Ludwig Georg Courvoisier observed that *in* a jaundiced patient with a painless palpable gallbladder, gallstones were an unlikely cause.

He did not suggest carcinoma of the pancreas and he did not call it a law.

He did not state the exceptions now recognised, of a double duct impaction with a blocked cystic duct and a blocked common bile duct.

Mirizzi syndrome

In this rare syndrome, a stone in the neck of the cystic duct blocks the common bile duct as well, thereby causing jaundice as well as a palpable gallbladder.

Chapter 16

Surgical jaundice

Types of jaundice (***Figure 1***)*:* Typically, the classification is based on the location of the hold up and, thus, it can be:

- Pre-hepatic
- Hepatic
- Post-hepatic

Jaundice occurs secondary to elevated products of haemoglobin metabolism due to several factors.

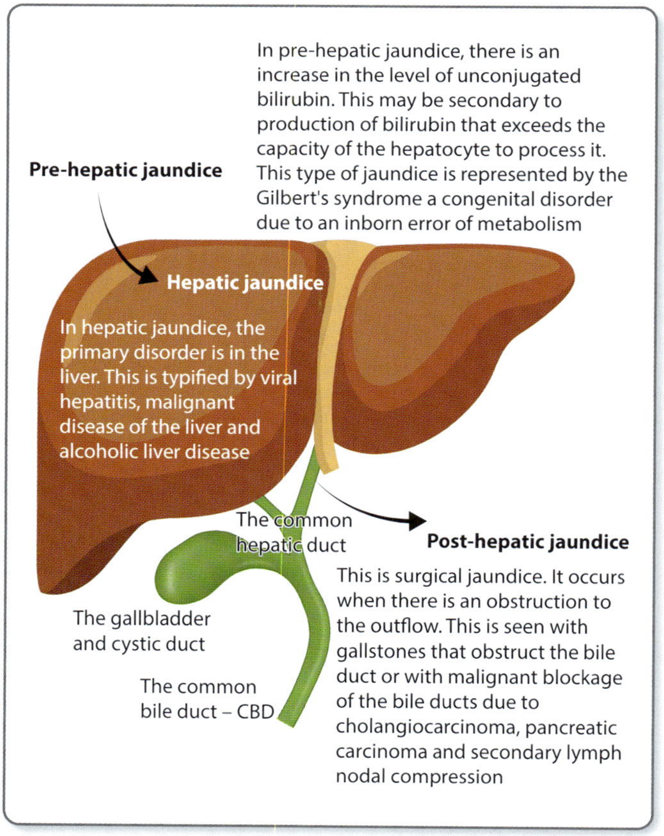

Figure 1 Types of jaundice.

The typical yellow discolouration of the skin and sclera is due to the adherence of bile pigments to elastin that is present at these sites.

Surgical jaundice is commonly post-hepatic due to outlet obstruction.

Pathophysiology

- Red blood cell (RBC) is broken down in the spleen/liver/bone marrow
- Haemoglobin is split into 'haem' and 'globin'
- Globin and iron from 'haem' are recycled
- The 'haem' is broken down to biliverdin and then to bilirubin, which aids in production of bile that is needed to emulsify dietary fat
- The hepatocytes in the liver process the waste products of haem.

Step 1: The unconjugated bilirubin is fat soluble and thus is transported with albumin to the liver.

Step 2: The bilirubin is then conjugated in the hepatocyte with glucuronic acid, which renders it water soluble.

Step 3: The conjugated water-soluble bilirubin is excreted into the biliary duct system and enters the duodenum. There, it is broken down by bacterial action, a process that occurs in the intestines. It also removes and recycles the glucuronic acid.

The bilirubin that is still in the intestines is converted to stercobilinogen. It is the stercobilinogen that gives the colour to stools.

The bilirubin that is absorbed into the bloodstream is urobilinogen and is excreted in urine.

It stands to reason that when the urobilinogen is absent in the urine in a jaundiced patient, there must be an obstruction to the outflow from liver. Reappearance of urobilinogen in the urine indicates clearance of the obstruction.

If a patient presents with jaundice that is secondary to a dilated common bile duct (CBD) noted on ultrasound or CT scan, then the causes are likely to be surgical.

Normally, the common bile duct (CBD) has a diameter of 6 mm in the absence of earlier interventional procedures such as endoscopic retrograde cholangiopancreatography (ERCP).

The common duct has no smooth muscle, once it has become dilated, it will always stay dilated.

If the CBD is dilated and the patient is jaundiced, the next step is a magnetic resonance cholangiopancreatography (MRCP) to define the cause. Depending on the findings on MRCP one may need to proceed to an interventional ERCP.

In an acute presentation with jaundice, the cause is likely to be stones in the CBD, especially when a gallbladder is not palpable. (**Courvoisier**)

Causes of surgical jaundice

- Stones in the CBD
- Carcinoma of the head of the pancreas
- Peri-ampullary carcinoma
- Malignancies in the liver
- Pancreatitis
- Cholangiocarcinoma
- Secondaries around the hepatic ducts
- Sclerosing cholangitis
- Strictures of the CBD

If CBD stones are diagnosed, the patient will need to be referred for ERCP for extraction of the stone. The preparation for ERCP must include vitamin K as well as antibiotics as per the hospital's protocol. A sphincterotomy (division of the sphincter of Oddi at the ampulla of Vater) may be needed for removal of the calculus with or without the placement of a stent.

Chapter 17

Pancreatitis

Pancreatic inflammation can be acute or chronic. Acute pancreatitis is a life-threatening disease. Chronic pancreatitis presents entirely differently and will not be discussed here other than to highlight the different presentation at the end of the chapter.

The revised *Atlanta classification* requires that two or more of the following criteria be met for the diagnosis of acute pancreatitis.

- Abdominal pain suggestive of pancreatitis
- Serum amylase or lipase level greater than three times the upper normal value
- Characteristic imaging findings on CT or MRI

Causes of pancreatitis

- Gallstones
- Alcohol intake
- Post-endoscopic retrograde cholangiopancreatography (ERCP)
- Hypercalcaemia
- Hyperlipidaemia
- Microlithiasis in pancreatic duct
- Hereditary causes
- Autoimmune pancreatitis
- Peri-ampullary and pancreatic tumours
- Anatomical abnormalities – pancreatic divisum

The most common causes of pancreatitis are gallstones and alcohol intake (not dose-dependent). If they are excluded, then rarer causes need to be evaluated.

Acute pancreatitis: Presentation

- Sudden onset of abdominal pain
- Vomiting is almost always present
- Tachycardia
- Tenderness localised in epigastrium or generalised all over the four quadrants with peritonitis
- Temperature with pyrexia > 38°C
- Known history of high alcohol intake
- Known history of gallstones, a common cause
- Elevated inflammatory markers
- Elevated serum amylase or lipase

Pathophysiology

Although hidden in the retroperitoneum behind the stomach, the pancreas is a major player in the *control of blood sugar and digestion.*

It has a significant *endocrine and exocrine function.*

The exocrine function of pancreas plays a role in digestion by secreting enzymes such as *amylase, protease* and *lipase.*

- Amylase digests *carbohydrate to glucose*
- Protease digests *proteins to amino acids*
- Lipase digests *fats to fatty acids and glycerol*

The enzymes *amylase* and *lipase* are markers for inflammation of the pancreas. These enzymes do not digest the pancreas because they are secreted as proenzymes that are broken down only in the alkaline succus entericus or enteric fluid in the duodenum.

An increase in the intra-acinar pressure leads to rupture of the acini, leading to pancreatic *auto-digestion* inflammation, and pancreatitis. It is postulated that gallstones that block the pancreatic duct can increase the back pressure on the main pancreatic duct acutely, leading to rupture and release of enzymes. Much as gravel in a jar does not block the flow of water (filtration of drinking water depends on this), stones in the common bile duct will allow flow of bile down the duct unless it is impacted at the outlet at the ampulla of Vater.

The exact mechanism by which alcohol does that is still not clear, but spasm of the sphincter of Oddi around the ampulla leading to obstruction may be a factor.

Jaundice does not always accompany pancreatitis. It is presumed that the stones, after causing the pancreatitis, have passed into the intestines after a transient blockage (**Figure 1**).

Serum amylase

- When serum amylase is elevated to three times the normal value, a diagnosis of pancreatitis is most likely in conjunction with clinical findings
- The serum amylase may be raised in other conditions too, and it is non-specific
- It is raised in peritoneal inflammation of any cause
- In acute pancreatitis, the level rises rapidly and falls rapidly. Serum amylase may thus not be elevated if the patient presents late.
- *In pancreatitis, it rises within 3 hours and decreases in 3 days.*
- In late presentations, serum lipase is a useful marker because it stays elevated for longer after an acute attack.
- Increased amylase *with associated abdominal symptoms* is seen in:
  - Ectopic pregnancy
  - Post-ERCP
  - Peptic perforation
  - Bowel ischaemia
- Increased amylase *without associated abdominal symptoms* is seen in:
  - Congenital hyperamylasaemia
  - Chronic alcoholism
  - Liver failure

Once diagnosed as acute pancreatitis, the management is primarily non-operative.

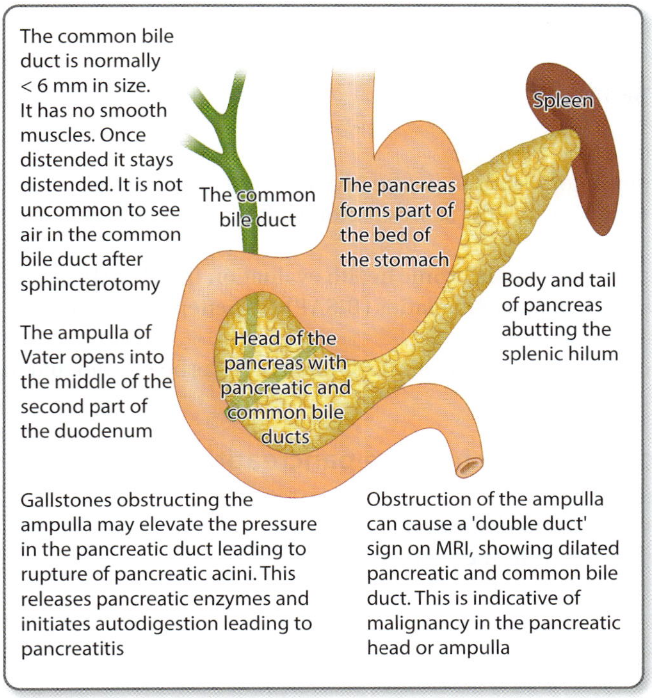

Figure 1 Pancreatitis and gallstones.

At presentation, it is difficult to predict the course of the disease. A small proportion of patients deteriorate and are a likely to need management in a critical care unit.

Ranson's criteria

In 1974, Ranson introduced 11 factors which were significant prognosticators of severity of pancreatitis. This was modified to 10 parameters for gallstone pancreatitis.

Five factors were of significance at presentation and five at 48 hours.

Parameters at presentation

1. Age above than 55 years (alcoholic pancreatitis) and 70 years (gallstone pancreatitis)
2. White blood cells (WBC) count above 15×10^9/L
3. Blood glucose above 10 mmol/L (non-diabetic)
4. Lactate dehydrogenase (LDH) above 600 IU/L
5. Aspartate aminotransferase (AST) above 200 U/L

Parameters at 48 hours

- Corrected calcium < 2.0 mmol/L
- Blood urea above 16 mmol/L (normal previously)
- Arterial pO_2 < 8 kPa (60 mmHg) (alcoholic pancreatitis)
- Metabolic acidosis
- Decreasing haematocrit after 48 hours

Serum amylase is not an indicator of severity.

Positive criteria and mortality

- 0–2 <5% mortality
- 3–4 15% mortality
- 5–6 40% mortality
- 7–10 100% mortality

It is obvious that deteriorating physiology leads to progressive increase in mortality.

A limitation of the Ranson's criteria is that the score cannot be determined till 48 hours have elapsed.

Other criteria such as acute physiology and chronic health evaluation II (APACHE II) and bedside indicator of severity in acute pancreatitis (BISAP) are better prognostic predictors.

BISAP permits early identification of severity within 12–24 hours. It has been validated in two cohorts of 18,000 patients with pancreatitis.

BISAP – bedside indicator of severity in acute pancreatitis

- *B*lood urea > 25 mg (8.9 mmol/L)
- *I*mpaired mentation Glasgow coma scale (GCS) < 15
- *S*ystematic inflammatory response syndrome positive
- *A*ge over 60 years
- *P*resence of pleural effusion

Each of these factors scores a point.

- 0–2 points: <2% mortality
- 3–5 points: >15% mortality

C-reactive protein

Increasing C-reactive protein (CRP) is also an indicator of worsening prognosis.

Cullen's sign

In some patients presenting with severe haemorrhagic pancreatitis, there can be visible evidence of haemorrhage in the form of bruising around the umbilicus. The blood from the retroperitoneum seems to track via either the falciform ligament or the mid-umbilical ligament along the attachment of the urachus.

Grey Turner's sign

In rare cases, similar bruising can be seen in the flanks.

Respiratory problems such as acute respiratory distress syndrome (ARDS) arise due to digestion of surfactant, a mucopolysaccharide that keeps the alveoli open due to surface tension. This occurs due to the action of pancreatic enzymes that leak into the thorax. Once the surfactant is decreased, the alveoli collapse, causing a shunt due to a ventilation, perfusion mismatch. The compliance of the lung decreases due to oedema and deposition of products of inflammation within the alveoli. The lungs stiffen, and patients drop their O_2 saturation despite adequate delivery of oxygen. It may progress to lung injury and ARDS (non-cardiac pulmonary oedema) with a need for ventilation and possibly positive pressure ventilation.

Calcium levels can drop due to the release of lipase that digests fat to glycerol and fatty acids as the end products of fat digestion. The fatty acids will then react with calcium to form soap. This process is referred to as *saponification* of fat. At operations for pancreatitis (rare these days), *fat necrosis* of the omentum can be visible (The author has seen this on several occasions). Current management makes laparotomies very unlikely, and this finding will probably be relegated to history, although it is good to know of a possible cause for low calcium levels in pancreatitis. It is likely to be multifactorial, however, and involves effects secondary to a drop in albumin levels (Imrie 1978) and refractoriness to parathormone.

Management (Box 1)

The principles of management are the same as for all acute presentations, as discussed earlier. Specifics of management for acute pancreatitis involve confirmation of suspicion that the patient has pancreatitis, noting the baseline severity and providing supportive treatment under constant scrutiny in a high-dependency unit (HDU)-level environment.

Box 1: Management of pancreatitis: Principles

Immediate assessment: ABCDE

- Never forget pulse oximetry

Immediate investigations:

- Urine for nitrates, β-hCG, sugar and blood
- Blood for sugar, full blood count, electrolytes and urea, coagulation profile
- Radiology
- *Comorbidity assessment*: Acute myocardial event, diabetes, COPD, renal status and anti-coagulants

Specific management for pancreatitis:

- Serum amylase and CRP
- Baseline blood gas and monitoring of oxygen saturation
- Liver function tests
- CT scan is best done after 3–4 days as the criteria are best established later than at outset
- MRCP followed by ERCP in the presence of Jaundice
- Coagulation profile prior to ERCP
- Attention to nutrition. No need to restrict fluids and diet unless the patient is unable to retain oral fluids
- No indication for routine antibiotics as the problem is initially chemical than infective but needs careful monitoring

COPD, chronic obstructive pulmonary disease; CRP, C-reactive protein; ERCP, endoscopic retrograde cholangiopancreatography; hCG, human chorionic gonadotropin; MRCP, magnetic resonance cholangiopancreatography.

Immediate management

- Initial treatment is limited to:
  - Assessment
  - Monitoring
  - Support of fluid balance
  - Provision of adequate analgesia
  - Ensuring oxygenation
  - Providing oral fluids as tolerated
- Nasogastric tube is seldom needed unless the patient has ongoing vomiting
- Antibiotics are not introduced early but may be needed if there is evidence of necrosis on CT
- CT scan is optimally performed after 72–96 hours after initial diagnosis. There may be a need for an earlier CT scan where there is a doubt about the diagnosis
- If the patient deteriorates, the level of support will increase. In the UK, it is necessary to discuss further care in a specialist hepatobiliary unit. A transfer to the unit may be necessary if further interventions are needed
- Ventilation with positive end-expiratory pressure (PEEP) may be required if there is lung injury
- Endoscopic retrograde cholangiopancreatography may be needed to remove obstruction at the level of the ampulla
- Radiological or surgical drainage of collections may be necessary
- Necrosectomy (either open or minimally invasive) may be needed if there is evidence of pancreatic necrosis on CT. These are best done in specialist centres
- Multiorgan failure is a major problem
- Sepsis can occur if there are complications such as necrosis, pancreatic abscess, ARDS and peritonitis. Antibiotics will be needed and dictated by culture of blood, sputum or intra-abdominal aspirate especially in the presence of infected necrosis and chest infections.

Pancreatic pseudocysts are cysts that arise in the peri-pancreatic tissue. They are referred to as pseudocysts because they are not lined by epithelium, as true cysts are, but by mesothelial structures surrounding the pancreas that wall off collections (**Box 2**). Yet some of these cysts may communicate with the pancreatic duct, and when they do, most resolve over time. If the cysts do not resolve after 6 weeks to 3 months, then they can be drained endoscopically through a cysto-gastrostomy. In general, the procedure is safe to perform when the cyst wall shows evidence of being mature and well-defined. Some cysts may

Box 2: Complications of pancreatitis

- *Pancreatic abscess*: This occurs after 2 or more weeks
- Pancreatic pseudocyst occurs after 3 weeks
- Pancreatic fistula
- Pancreatic insufficiency
- Diabetes
- Chronic pancreatitis

not be accessible for this non-invasive procedure and may need radiological or surgical drainage.

Greater than one-third of patients tend to have mild pancreatitis that resolves in a week.

When the pancreatitis is secondary to gallstones, then a *cholecystectomy* is recommended within 2 weeks of the acute episode, and preferably in the same admission subject to comorbidities and other limitations. This can be a technically challenging procedure in the early days.

Chronic pancreatitis

This presents with symptoms that are quite different to that of the acute episode. Chronic pain can be disabling and needs to be addressed by a multidisciplinary team involving the gastroenterologists and pain team.

Chronic pancreatitis presentation

- *Diabetes:* Loss of endocrine pancreatic function
- *Diarrhoea:* Due to loss of exocrine function
- *Chronic pain:* Neuropathic secondary to chronic inflammation of retroperitoneum

Chapter 18

Bowel obstruction

Acute presentation with obstruction to the large or small bowel is a common cause for admission to the hospital.

Four pillars of presentation of bowel obstruction

1. Constipation or obstipation (not passing stools and flatus)
2. Abdominal distension
3. Abdominal pain
4. Vomiting

The presentation tends to vary depending on the level of obstruction.

The lower the obstruction, the more likely that the patient will present with all the four signs and symptoms.

The higher the obstruction, the more likely that vomiting will be the predominant feature rather than distension or constipation.

Common causes of bowel obstruction

- Adhesive bowel obstruction
- Hernial obstruction
- Malignant bowel obstruction
- Perforated viscus and peritonitis
- Postoperative or paralytic ileus
- Ischaemic and inflammatory bowel disease
- Bands causing obstruction
- Volvulus of caecum or sigmoid
- Internal herniation
- Radiation strictures
- Foreign body causing obstruction
- Gallstone ileus
- Pseudo-obstruction

Adhesive bowel obstruction is perhaps the most common cause of acute obstruction of the bowel. It usually follows earlier laparotomies. Most patients will have a scar of an abdominal incision, though sometimes with the passage of time, the scars in the groin or supra-pubic area may not be clearly visible.

Adhesive obstructions due to bands do occur but are less frequent.

A hernia of one type or another, but more commonly a femoral or inguinal hernia can be a cause of intestinal obstruction, is another common cause of bowel obstruction.

Incisional and para-umbilical hernia may also present as acute obstruction. In most of these presentations, the hernia will be clearly visible. In some patients, it may have been irreducible for a considerable length of time.

In the elderly patients, a superficial examination of the abdomen may entirely miss the presence of a femoral hernia.
No examination of the abdomen is complete unless the groin and genitalia are examined.

Malignancies of the bowel

These can cause bowel obstruction depending on the location of the tumour. In the case of the right colonic cancers, it is the caecum or ascending colon that is the cause of the blockage. It will, therefore, present with small bowel obstruction.

A malignant tumour in the left colon and distal colon are more likely to cause colonic obstruction.

Right colon cancer causes small bowel obstruction. Left and distal colon cancers cause colonic obstruction.

Sigmoid volvulus is a condition where the sigmoid colon tends to rotate in an *anti-clockwise direction* around a mesentery that has become elongated over time. The mesenteric base of attachment to the posterior abdominal wall is narrow. A narrow base with an elongated mesentery facilitates rotation around the fixed point. It is common in elderly patients and in patients in long-term care and those on psychiatric medications. The presentation is one of large bowel obstructions.

Caecal volvulus is uncommon but occurs in the presence of a mobile caecum that is not fixed to the retroperitoneum. The caecum in these conditions will be noted in the left upper quadrant of the abdomen on imaging associated with small bowel obstruction. It can also follow congenital malrotation or congenital Ladd's bands associated with malrotation.

Diverticular stenosis and *extrinsic pelvic pathology* can also present with obstruction.

Inflammatory bowel disease such as Crohn's and ulcerative colitis may present with obstruction; these are now seen only following failed response to primary medical management. Patients with Crohn's disease are prone to multiple stricture formation in the bowel.

Pseudo-obstruction is obstruction in the absence of a defined mechanical cause. In this condition, the colon and small bowel, in the presence of an incontinent ileocaecal valve, will be distended. Pseudo-obstruction of the colon is exactly what it means. This is common in institutionalised patients and those with serious underlying electrolyte and metabolic irregularities. If accompanied by perforation, the mortality rate can be high.

Paralytic ileus is an obstruction due to the loss of normal motility of the bowel. It generally occurs in the postoperative period due to *electrolyte or protein imbalance.* In patients with low albumin, the bowel wall becomes oedematous, and the peristaltic process is impeded.

Small bowel tumours are very rare. This is possibly due to the rapid transit and liquid contents that do not stagnate.

Management (**Box 1**) follows the same protocols, as seen earlier.

Box 1: Principles of management – bowel obstruction

Universal principles of care:
- Immediate assessment
- Immediate investigations

Specific principles of care for bowel obstruction:
- Nasogastric decompression in cases with persistent vomiting
- Intravenous fluid replacement
- Monitoring of intake and output
- Radiology with CT scan of the abdomen replacing the formerly common erect and supine X-rays of the abdomen
- Gastrografin or soluble oral contrast imaging of bowel
- Imaging is needed prior to surgical intervention

Radiological investigations

The *supine X-rays* [**Figures 1a and b**] of the abdomen will be able to define the level of obstruction, but this is increasingly supplanted by CT scan as the main radiological investigation because the CT scan can pinpoint not only the level of obstruction but also the cause of obstruction.

Once the diagnosis is confirmed, the treatment is either:
- Interventional *surgical management*
- Non-interventional but *active medical management*

Active medical management may be needed due to the presence of comorbidities and rests on the fitness of the patient to undergo major interventional surgery.

Non-operative management in adhesive obstruction

A non-operative management may be adopted in patients with adhesive obstruction because recurrent surgical operations may cause more harm. At any point of time, surgical intervention may be needed in surgically fit patients if the obstruction fails to resolve rapidly.

Role of gastrografin

In adhesive bowel obstruction without ischaemia or strangulation, a wait and watch policy is justified. *Gastrografin or soluble oral contrast swallow* is used to assess the feasibility of non-operative management. The gastrografin have a chemical called tween 80, and this can decrease the oedema in the bowel wall, leading to relief of obstruction showed by progression of gastrografin to the distal bowel distal to the area of obstruction. In many patients with adhesive small bowel obstruction, this can be used as a radiological test of suitability for conservative management with the goal of resolution of obstruction without intervention.

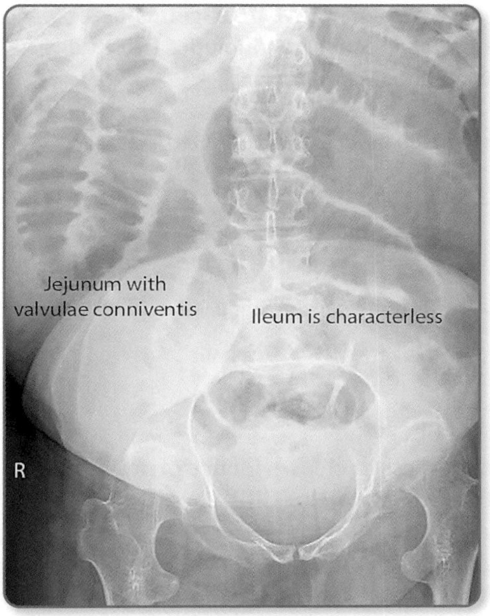

Figure 1(a): A supine X-rays of the abdomen.

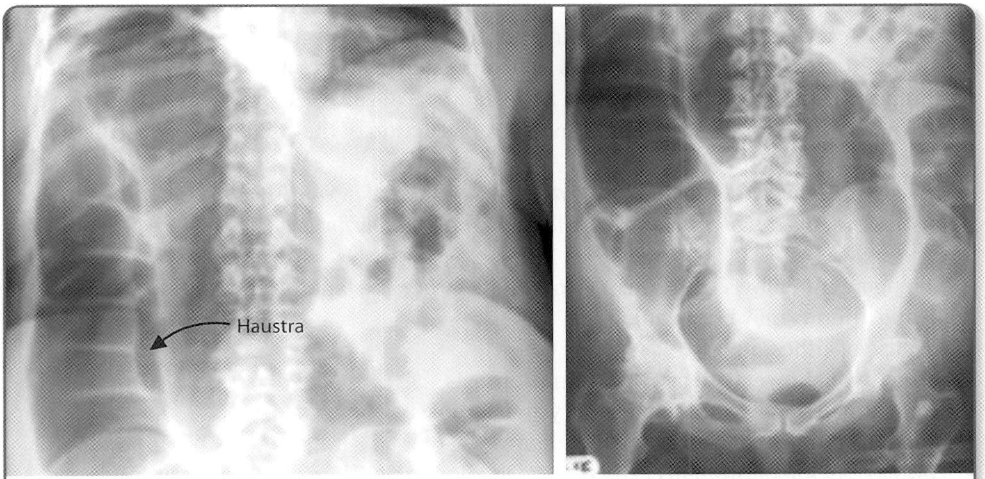

The pattern of colonic mucosa on X-rays is different from that of the jejunum. The mucosal fold lines unlike that of the jejunum, do not go fully across the width of the bowel but stop short of touching the opposite wall. These are called 'haustra'

In these X-rays, the haustra are seen clearly. This patient had a volvulus

Figure 1(b) A supine X-rays of the abdomen.

Regular and repeated assessments are needed if a non-operative management is followed. The management, though not interventional, is active and includes twice daily review of the patient till a satisfactory outcome is reached.

Prolonged obstruction without resolution leads to associated complications with nutrition and metabolism.

Surgical Intervention

Sometimes surgical intervention is inevitable, as in patients presenting with evidence of:

- Ischaemia
- Strangulation
- Perforation
- Peritonitis

These may be clinically clear with generalised tenderness or clear evidence of peritonitis. An extremely high white blood cell (WBC) and C-reactive protein (CRP) should alert one to the possibility of impending bowel ischaemia or strangulation.

In colonic obstruction due to left-sided malignancies of the colon, the area of tenderness may be found over the caecum. *Caecum is the thinnest part of the colon that has the maximal diameter.* In distal colonic obstruction, as the wall of the caecum is thinner than the rest of the colon, it tends to distend early and more rapidly.

Laplace's law states that the pressure on the wall of a tube is greatest where the radius is largest. The caecum, being the widest and thinnest, is the easiest to distend with increasing pressure. Progressive distension causes ischaemia due to stretching and may lead to caecal perforation. This distension is maximal if the ileo-caecal valve is competent. When the valve is incompetent, the presentation may involve obstruction of the small bowel obstruction.

On radiological imaging, if the caecum is distended beyond 12 cm, it should raise suspicion of impending ischaemia or caecal perforation.

Management follows the principles outlined earlier. If a laparotomy is undertaken, the following options may be feasible.

- Release of adhesions
- Resection of bowel with a primary anastomosis
- Resection of bowel without a primary anastomosis
- Stoma formation – ileostomy or colostomy
- Drainage of the peritoneal cavity may be needed in purulent or faecal peritonitis
- Laparostomy when primary abdominal closure is not feasible or in the best interest of the patient

Laparoscopic release of single band obstructions may be possible in selected cases bearing in mind that the distension of the abdomen may preclude access to the peritoneal cavity laparoscopically.

Chapter 19

Diverticular disease of the colon

Diverticulosis commonly affects the sigmoid colon but can affect any part or all the colon.

Pathophysiology of colon (Figure 1)

Diverticula (**Figure 2**) form when the peristaltic pressure in the colon traps a colonic segment full of flatus between succeeding waves of peristalsis, akin to squeezing a balloon at both ends.

The bowel has circular muscles and longitudinal muscles. Circular muscle contraction lengthens the bowel which then goes it to a spasm squeezing the contents. This is followed

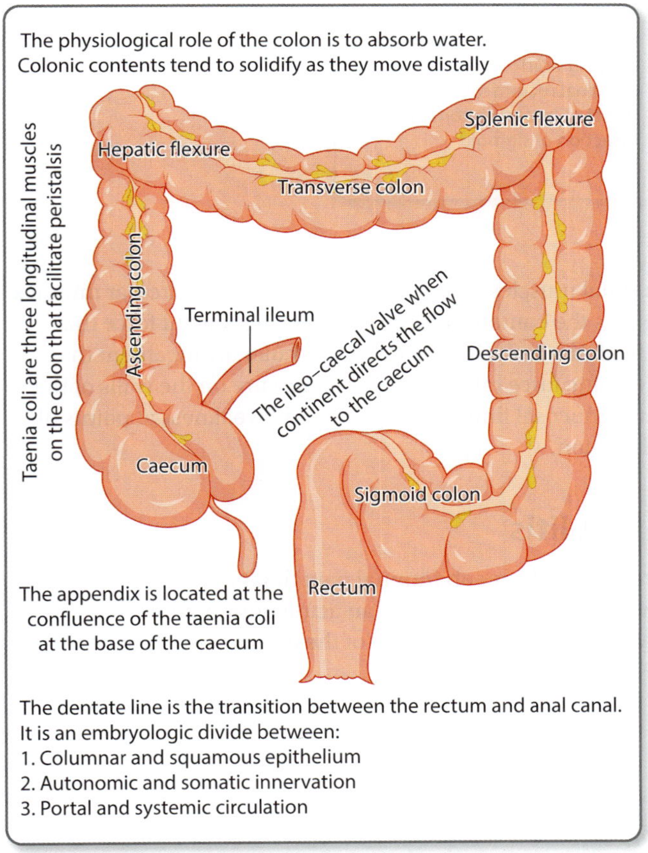

Figure 1 Anatomy of the colon.

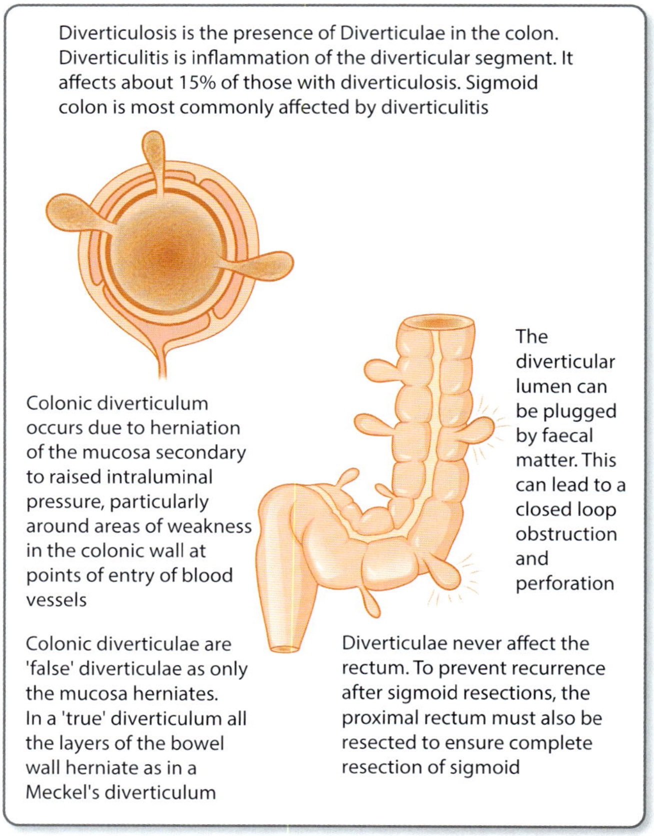

Figure 2 Pathophysiology of diverticulosis.

by the contraction of the longitudinal muscles along with relaxation of the circular muscles. This shortens the bowel and propels the contents distally. This is a significant force that should not be underestimated. Evolutionarily, it is a similar muscular arrangement that propels the earthworm! This peristaltic force raises the lateral pressure on the walls of the colon and causes herniation of the mucosal lining through areas of weakness at points of entry of the blood vessels into the colon.

Presentation of diverticulitis

The most common presentation is one of lower abdominal pain that has gradually increased in intensity over a few days. In some, it may be an acute presentation.

The signs and symptoms vary depending on the extent of the disease and include the following:

- Abdominal pain, which may be localised to the left lower quadrant of the abdomen
- Tenderness
- Nausea and vomiting
- Pyrexia
- Constipation or, in some patients, looseness of stools
- Occasionally retention of urine with abdominal pain in men

- Excessive vaginal discharge in women due to colo-vaginal fistula formation
- Passage of flatus in urine or lower urinary tract infection due to colo-vesical fistula
- Rarely, peritonitis that is localised to the lower abdomen with pelvic abscess
- Generalised peritonitis
- Bowel obstruction due to diverticular stricture (**Box 1**)

CT staging of the extent of the problem will help to determine if the patient can be treated as an outpatient or inpatient.

The CT scan identifies patients suitable for:

- Conservative management
- Interventional radiological drainage
- Interventional open or laparoscopic surgery

CT staging Hinchey classification

- *Stage 0*: Minimal diverticulitis with thickening of colon
- *Stage 1*: Peri-colic inflammation or mesocolic abscess
- *Stage 2*: Distant or deep pelvic abscess with diverticulitis
- *Stage 3*: Purulent peritonitis with or without free gas and diverticulitis
- *Stage 4*: Faecal peritonitis – findings similar to stage 3

The complications of diverticulitis (**Figure 3**) are as follows.

- Diverticular bleeding
- Diverticulitis
- Obstruction
- Perforation leading to localised or generalised peritonitis.
- The 4 P's are:
  - *P*ericolic abscess
  - *P*aracolic abscess
  - *P*elvic abscess
  - *P*eritonitis

When the perforation is contained locally, it manifests as an abscess around the colon. In the absence of containment, either due to the failure of the omentum and adjacent loops of bowel to isolate and wall off the collection or due to an overwhelmingly large perforation, it manifests as generalised peritonitis.

Box 1: Principles of management – diverticulitis

Universal principles of care:

- Immediate assessment
- Immediate investigations
- Comorbidity assessment

Specific principles of care for diverticulitis:

- CT scan of the abdomen to stage diverticulitis
- MRI may be needed to define the presence of fistula to vagina, bladder, or small bowel
- Colonoscopy (not at the acute phase) to view the mucosal aspect and exclude the presence of polyps that may be coincidentally present

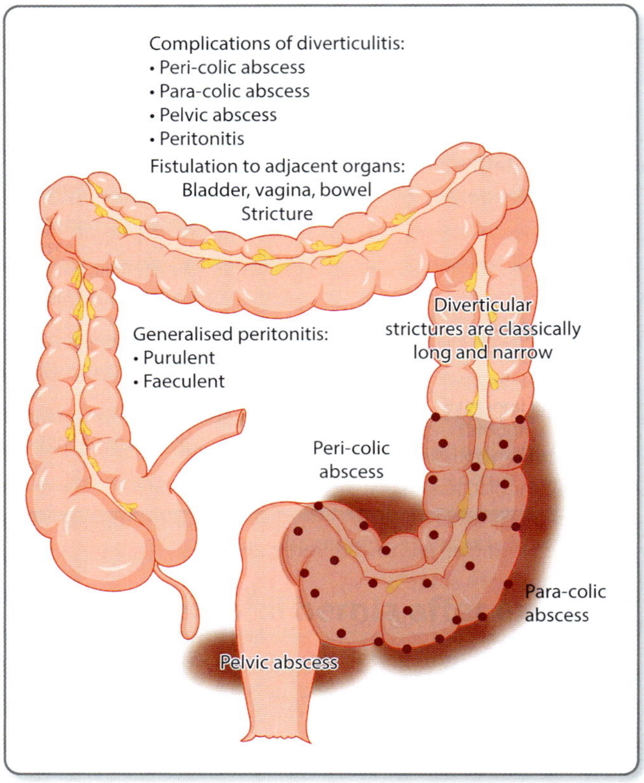

Figure 3 The complications of diverticulitis.

The management of the patient depends upon the severity of presentation (**Box 1**).

Patients with free perforation and peritonitis will be unstable and in a state of sepsis. The sepsis protocol must be implemented at once.

Early intervention saves lives.

Once stabilised and the results of the investigations are available, further treatment options will need consideration. As always these include several options. Many of these patients are elderly and are likely to have multiple comorbidities, including dementia. The decision to progress to surgery must be made after discussions with the patient (if able) and family or surrogates when the patient is unable to interact.

Treatment options

- Feasibility of an operation is not an indication for its performance. Treatment is defined by careful assessment of every patient
- Non-interventional versus interventional options should be based on comorbidities and quality of life
- Wishes of the patient and family should be taken into consideration where the quality of life is poor
- Best interest meeting may be needed to decide on the management in the absence of capacity

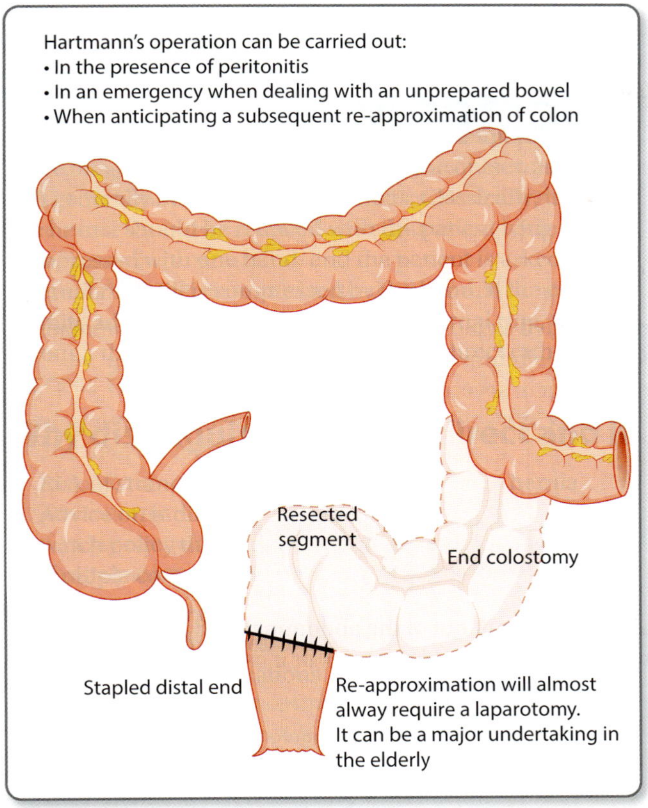

Figure 4 Surgical management, Hartmann's procedure.

- Non-operative management with antibiotics and monitoring will remain a possibility for some
- Non-operative management with radiologically placed drainage (i.e. interventional radiology) may need consideration in selected cases
- Surgical resection with or without primary anastomosis after resection may be an option for fit patients
- Always involve other specialities, especially critical care teams to define level of care peri-operatively
- End of life team will need to be consulted if that is the most appropriate decision for the patient

Surgical management could be laparoscopically aided, open drainage, or resection. This will include primary anastomosis or end colostomy with a Hartmann's procedure (**Figure 4**). After resection, the proximal end can be brought out as an end colostomy. The distal end can be stapled and left within the pelvis, allowing for the possibility of re-approximation of the two ends at a later stage. The operation, therefore, becomes a two-stage procedure.

All patients may not be suitable for this staged re-anastomosis because it will include further anaesthesia and surgery and may increase the morbidity if not the mortality. Some may be more willing and accepting of a permanent stoma.

Chapter 20

Colostomy

Opening of the colon to the exterior is called a colostomy much as opening of the stomach is a gastrostomy, the ileum an ileostomy, jejunum a jejunostomy, and the caecum a caecostomy. The colon can be brought out in several ways.

Types of colostomies

The three common types are:

- End colostomy
- Defunctioning colostomy
- Loop colostomy

In an end colostomy the proximal end is brought out of the abdominal wall as a stoma. The distal segment is either stapled, as shown earlier (Hartmann's), or it can be brought out of the abdomen when it is referred to as a *mucous fistula*.

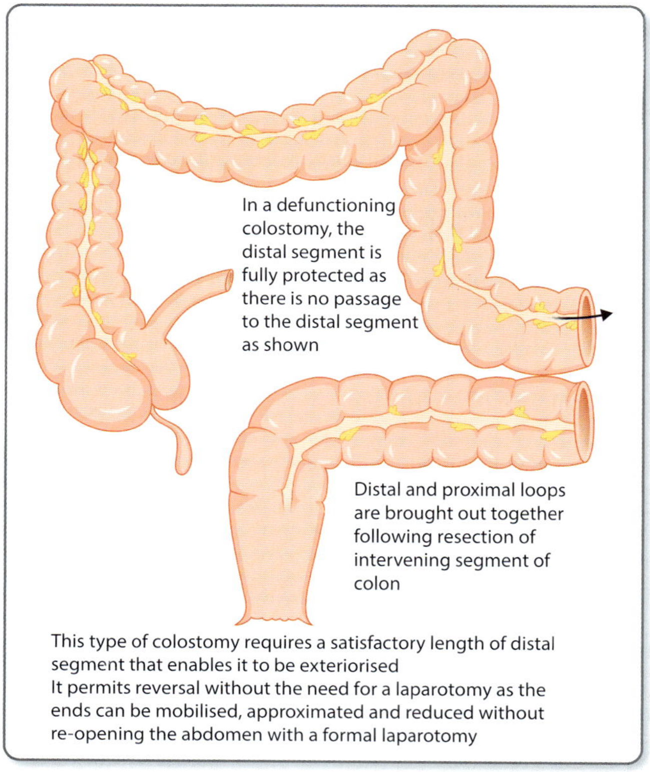

Figure 1 Defunctioning colostomy.

In a defunctioning colostomy (**Figure 1**), the two ends are brought out side by side after complete resection of the intervening colon. This enables re-approximation without the need for another laparotomy. It defunctions the distal bowel, and there is no possibility for ingress of faeces into the distal segment as the intervening bowel has been completely divided.

In a loop colostomy (**Figure 2**), a loop of bowel is exteriorised in continuity without division or resection. It may not technically defunction the distal segment as faeces can flow through to the distal segment since continuity is retained. The advantage of this procedure is the ease of carrying it out in an emergency and the relative ease of reversal.

In certain situations, the terminal ileum can be exteriorised, and once again it can be either an end ileostomy or a loop ileostomy.

Complications of all types of stomas include the following:
- Retraction due to mucocutaneous separation
- Prolapse - protrusion due to peristaltic force
- Stenosis - due to narrowing
- Parastomal herniation
- Loss of blood supply causing ischaemia

Reversal of colostomy depends on:
- The health and fitness of the patient
- The wishes of the patient. Some patients may not want reversal of the stoma

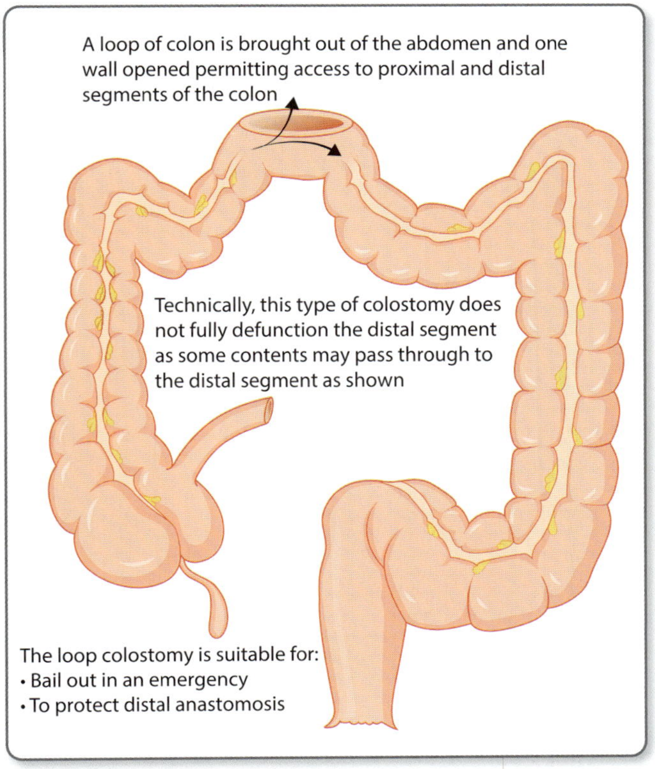

Figure 2 Loop colostomy.

- The acceptance by the patient of the increased risks of the procedure. The operation may fail
- The length of the distal segment. Very short rectal segment may lead to increased frequency of bowel movements up to several times a day
- The quality of the rectal sphincters. This may be a problem in the elderly, especially women leading to problems with continence

Chapter 21

Rectal bleeding

Causes of rectal bleeding

- Haemorrhoids
- Fissure in ano
- Proctitis and inflammatory bowel disease
- Cancers and polyps of the colon and rectum
- Diverticular disease
- Trauma

Haemorrhoids commonly present with rectal bleeding. The presentation is very often one of painless and at times copious bleeding, causing anxiety.

The key points about rectal bleeding:

- A good history is important in elucidating the cause of the presentation
- Haemorrhoidal bleeding is normally bright red and painless
- In haemorrhoidal bleeding, the stools are typically separate from the blood
- Blood may be noted on paper, on wiping or in the pan
- Blood in the pan can appear to be a lot more than the actual amount due to dilution
- Blood in the paper could be due to fissure in ano, haemorrhoids, polyps, low rectal or anal cancer
- Mucous with blood is common with inflammatory disease.
- Constipation is a precursor in many cases of fissure and haemorrhoids but not always
- Diverticular bleed can be profuse
- Malignant tumours and polyps may cause bleeding in isolation or be mixed with mucous
- Polyps or cancers of the rectum can present as haemorrhoids
- Painful bleeding is often associated with fissure in ano
- Typically, in painful rectal bleeding, where the pain lasts after voiding, is consistent with a fissure in ano
- In patients with a fissure in ano, the patient may volunteer the information that voiding stools is like passing glass!
- The fissure may be visible on inspection, often being located just at the anal verge at 6 or 12 o'clock positions
- Most fissures are located posteriorly
- Anterior fissures are more common in women
- Thrombosed haemorrhoids or a perianal haematoma can present acutely with a painful lump
- Perianal haematoma presents with acute pain that is followed by a lump in the perineum. The lump is due to a bleed into an external skin tag or into the skin

- A digital rectal examination is mandatory. This may assist in defining the cause of the bleeding. It might not be possible in patients with fissure in ano as the acute condition is very painful
- Where there is doubt an examination under anaesthesia is needed urgently to exclude other causes such as a painful malignancy
- Proctoscopy is needed in all patients presenting with a clear history of bright red rectal bleeding that is separate from stools. Proctoscopy, in these situations, will in most cases define the site of the bleeding and assist in planning further treatment
- Sigmoidoscopy or colonoscopy is needed to confirm the diagnosis and exclude other causes
- Colonoscopy may be needed if the cause of the rectal bleeding is not obvious. This is likely to be the case, when the patient is older and offers a family history of bowel cancer. It may also be indicated when the type of bleeding is thought not to be related to anorectal pathology based on the history
- Lifestyle changes will need discussions with the patient including avoidance of constipation where haemorrhoids are present
- Faecal immunochemical test (FIT) is clearly not necessary when the bleeding is obvious. The indication for it is more in patients with recent change in bowel habit when there is a need to exclude neoplastic lesions
- Faecal calprotectin is a marker of inflammation of the bowel. This may be needed in patients who present with rectal bleeding associated with change in bowel habit

Chapter 22

Anorectal problems

Anatomy of the anal canal

Refer to **Figure 1**.

Haemorrhoids (Figure 2)

Haemorrhoids are defined as mucosal cushion defects in which the vessels become prominent and present like varicosities of the veins.

Haemorrhoids usually occur at 3, 7 and 11 o'clock positions due to the distribution of the superior rectal vessels. In some, there may be haemorrhoids, in between and alongside the classical location forming an almost continuous ring of haemorrhoids. These are referred to as accessory haemorrhoids or secondary haemorrhoids.

Precipitating factors

- Constipation
- Loose stools

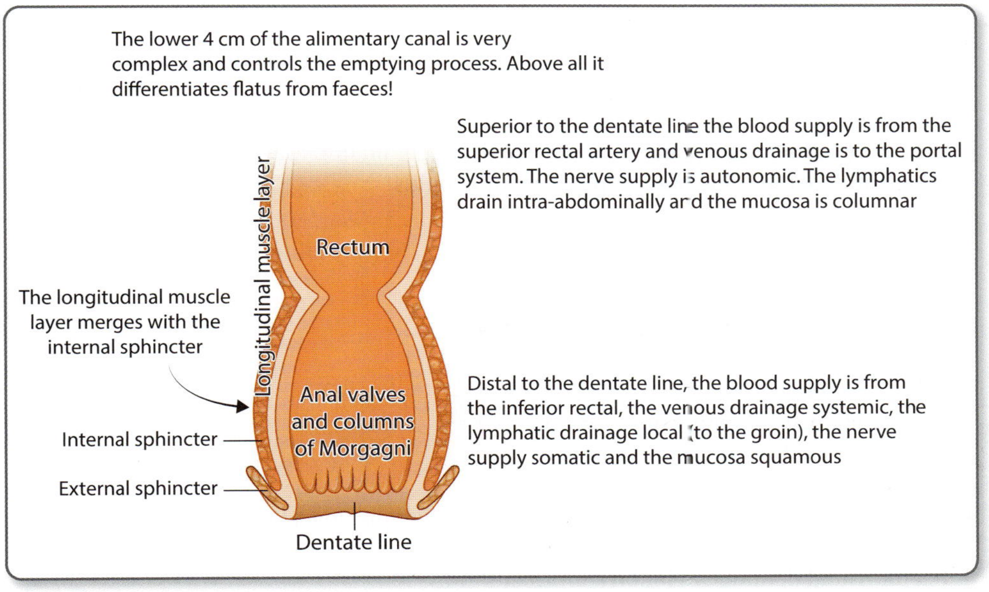

Figure 1 Anatomy of the anal canal.

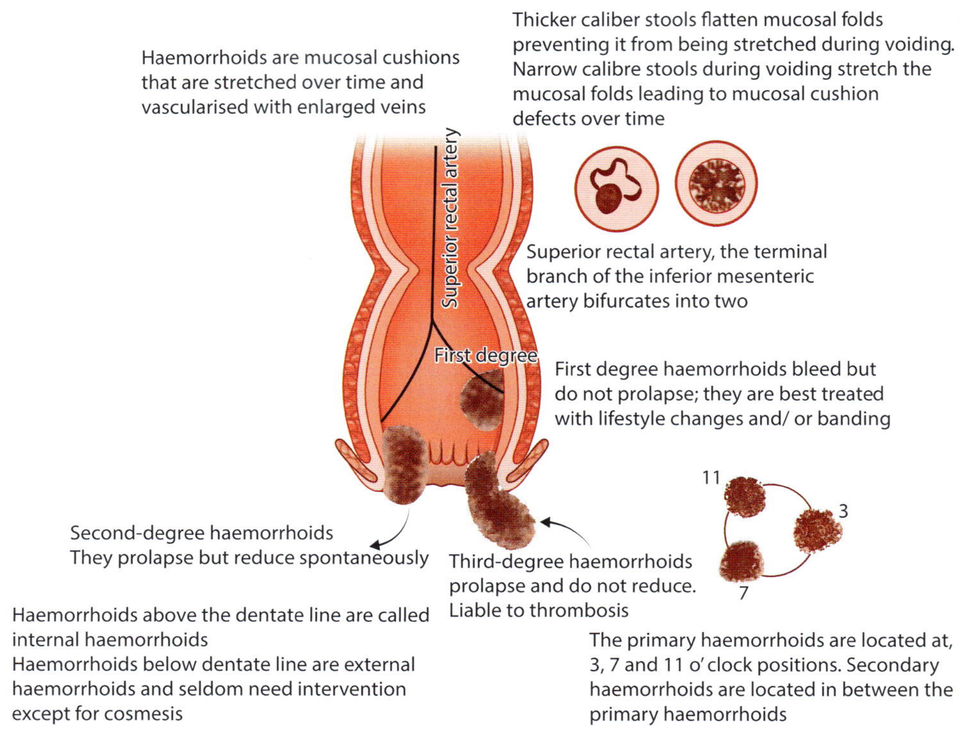

Figure 2 Haemorrhoids.

- Pregnancy, due to increased pelvic pressure
- *Portal hypertension* – the ano-rectal veins are areas of porta-systemic anastomosis. The superior rectal veins drain to the portal vein, and these do not have valves. The hydrostatic pressure is, therefore, transmitted vertically from the portal vein and there is communication with the inferior rectal veins that drain into the vena cava. This leads to varicosities of the veins presenting as haemorrhoids.
- Posture
- Patients on anticoagulants

Management of haemorrhoids

First degree

- Dietary changes to avoid constipation
- Laxatives to reduce straining at stools
- Reassurance that it is self-limiting in most
- Banding of haemorrhoids if persistent. This involves placing a tight rubber band on the base of the haemorrhoids above the dentate line to prevent pain. Over a few days, the haemorrhoid denuded of blood supply falls away

Second degree

- Banding of haemorrhoids similar to the treatment for first-degree haemorrhoids
- Haemorrhoidal artery ligation operation (HALO), where the feeding vessels are identified by ultrasound and ligated under anaesthesia, is another less invasive procedure when the bleeding is persistent. The success rate is variably predicted at 70%. In case of recurrence the procedure can be repeated.

Third degree

These will need a traditional haemorrhoidectomy (Milligan and Morgan). The internal sphincter is identified and kept out of harm's way. The haemorrhoids are then excised and would be left open or closed depending on the type of operation favoured. The procedure is painful postoperatively, and first-bowel movement after operation can be very painful.

Skin bridges must be maintained between excisions to ensure that fibrosis does not result in an anal stenosis. Increasingly these are less commonly done, with early intervention being the norm.

Classically, the primary haemorrhoids are found at the 3, 7 and 11 o'clock positions. The secondary haemorrhoids are found in between the primary haemorrhoids. When there are multiple haemorrhoids, (accessory haemorrhoids in between the standard locations) the adage, 'If it is a clover, the story is over, but if it is a *Dahlia*, it is a sure failure.' is likely to be true. Secondary haemorrhoids can be difficult to treat.

Thrombosed haemorrhoids

Occasionally, when a patient has third-degree haemorrhoids, the vessels in the prolapsed haemorrhoids may get occluded. This can lead to painful thrombosis.

The presentation can be acute with a perianal lump that is very painful and tender. There is unlikely to be any bleeding, and pain will be the most common presentation, along with a persistent prolapse.

Management with rest, elevation, and cold packs may relieve the pain and temporise the situation, allowing for an elective haemorrhoidectomy later.

Patients in whom the symptoms do not resolve, may benefit from immediate haemorrhoidectomy.

Emergency haemorrhoidectomy in the days prior to the advent of antibiotics was a dreaded operation leading to complications of portal pyaemia and sepsis. It is necessary, therefore, to provide these patients with appropriate antibiotic cover prior to emergency haemorrhoidectomy.

Perianal haematoma

Perianal haematoma presents with acute pain that is followed by a lump in the perineum. The lump is due to a bleed into an external skin tag or into the skin. It swells and becomes painful due to the pressure that builds in the contained space. Release of tension by opening the haematoma resolves the pain; if, on the other hand, a non-operative approach is followed, the relief occurs with resorption of the haematoma that normally takes place in about 5 days; this is, thus, referred to as the *'5-day painful condition.'*

It settles down spontaneously in most, leaving just a skin tag. If the pain is very severe, bisecting the lump and evacuating the thrombus relieves the pain instantly.

Fissure in ano

A fissure in 'ano' is a tear in the anal mucosa exposing the internal sphincter. The presentation may be acute with severe pain on defaecation; there may be associated blood on the paper but seldom if ever in the pan.

On examination, the tear is seen on inspection at the anal verge on just spreading the buttocks. When the problem is chronic, there may be a skin tag extending from the lower limit of the fissure, which is referred to as a sentinel tag. In general, the tear occurs posteriorly at about the 6 o'clock position. In about 40% of women, the tear may be anterior at the 12 o'clock position.

The pathophysiology is thought to be constant stretching and straining at voiding constipated stools, causing an area of ischaemia, which then gives way leading to a fissure.

It can also occur during childbirth and after anal intercourse. Ageing may also be a factor, although constipation is more likely to be the cause of the tear.

Management of fissure in ano

The principle here is to relieve pain mostly by reducing the spasm that follows voiding. This is done by:

- Softening the stools
- Local application of local anaesthetic such as lidocaine 5%
- Relieving smooth muscle spasm with smooth muscle relaxants such as rectogesic (glyceryl trinitrate or GTN) or diltiazem
- Injecting botox if the above treatment options fail. This is given in small quantities in the intersphincteric plane. Temporary loss of continence may occur, especially for flatus. This will need addressing during consent
- Lateral sphincterotomy is the gold standard but it is increasingly less commonly performed. The sphincter is divided at about the 3 o'clock position away from the 6 o'clock position, the common location of the fissure. In women, especially those who have had children, it is best to assess the status of the sphincter with an ultrasound examination prior to surgery; there is an increased risk of problems with continence.

Perianal Crohn's disease

This is a difficult condition to treat surgically. In most cases, there will be a history of Crohn's disease. In the perineum, there is likely to be thickened fleshy tags with persistent discomfort. Surgery is not indicated, but a biopsy may be needed in some to confirm the histology and start medical management.

Problems with anal continence

This is an area where specialist expertise is needed. The problem is not uncommon in the elderly and very often affects women. Many patients present in their seventh and eighth decades.

The loss of continence can arise in the following:

- Women who have had protracted and prolonged labour in years past
- Patients with neurological problems such as multiple sclerosis

- Patients who have had perianal trauma
- Patients who have had complications of surgery such as sphincterotomy and haemorrhoidectomy
- Those who have laxity of neuromuscular mechanisms

Mechanism of anal continence

Fistula in ano (Figure 3)

Fistula is an abnormal communication connecting two epithelial surfaces, lined by granulation tissue. In the anal canal the fistula arises from the anal glands which anatomically open only interiorly. When these glands become inflamed or obstructed, they find a way to the exterior leading to a fistula in ano.

Where the internal opening is in squamous epithelium and not in the columnar epithelium, the fistula is deemed to be low. These are, therefore, sub-sphincteric fistulae. Recall that, the squamous epithelium is below the dentate line and columnar above.

Fistulae that are not sub-sphincteric (see **Figure 4**) have been classified by Alan Parks as:

- Intersphincteric (most common)
- Trans-sphincteric

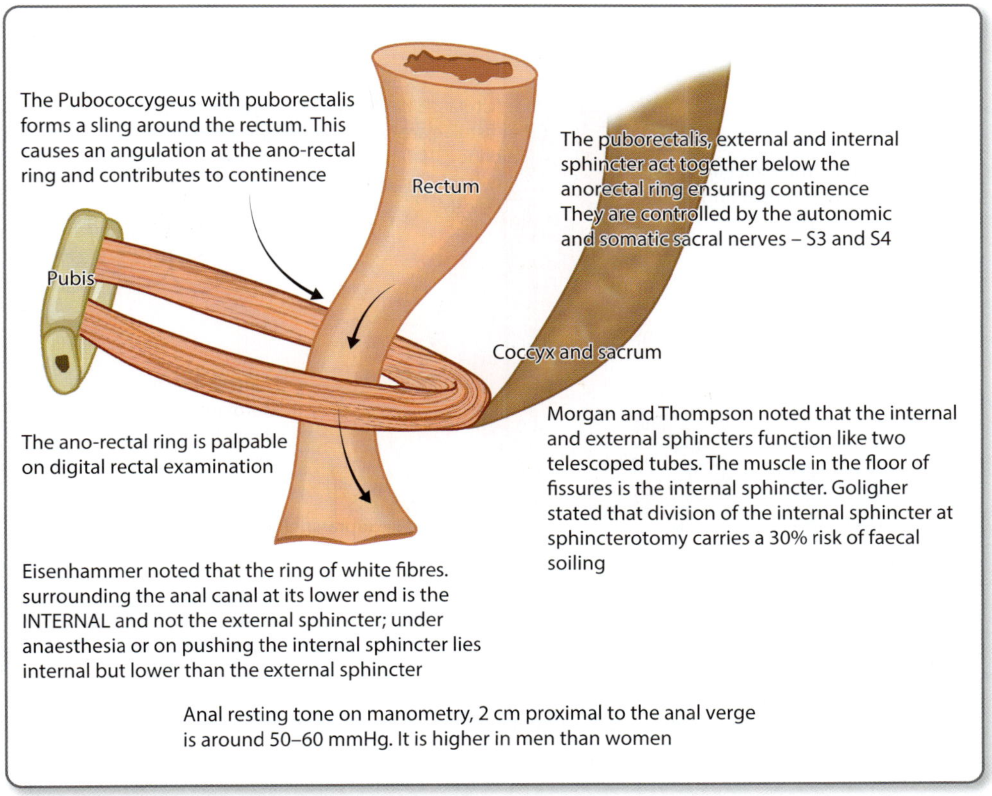

Figure 3 Mechanisms of anal continence.

- Supra-sphincteric
- Extra-sphincteric

Goodsall's rule (see **Figure 4**) applies most of the time unless the cause is traumatic or a surgical complication.

- Anterior fistula < 3 cm from anal verge opens directly into the anal canal
- Posterior fistulae are horseshoe-shaped and open in the midline

Classification of fistula in ano

Refer to **Figure 4**.

Presentation

- Perianal abscess
- Peri-anal irritation due to inflammation of external opening
- Peri-anal discharge
- Pruritus

When presenting as a perianal abscess, bacterial cultures must be taken. Growth of *E. coli or Klebsiella,* as opposed to *Staphylococcus* (skin organism) favours a fistula as the probable cause of the abscess.

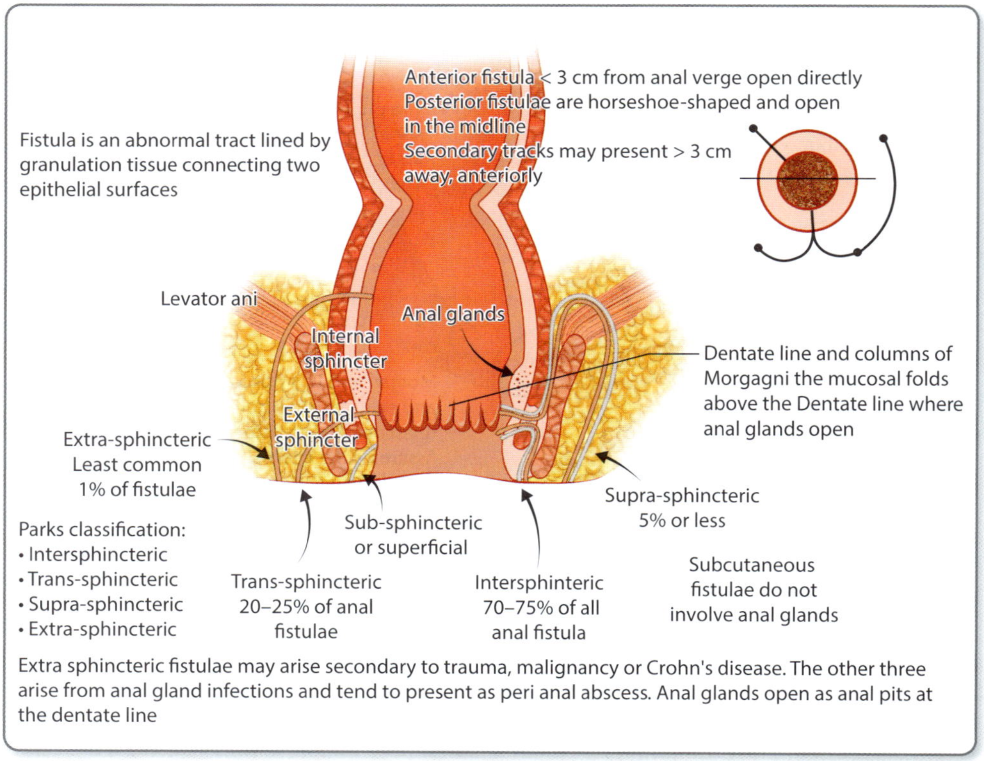

Figure 4 Classification of fistula in ano.

Investigations

The current practice is to request a magnetic resonance imaging (MRI) of the anal canal. The result needs to be discussed with the radiologist. This will allow proper planning of the operation and enable discussion with the patient prior to surgery.

Low fistulae can be laid open as the risk of problems with continence is negligible.

High fistulae will need the placement of a cutting seton or a draining seton in the expectation that the fistula will close by fibrosis over time.

Lift procedure, where the fistula is excised, and injection of glue have variable results even in expert hands.

Perianal abscess

This presents as:
- Painful tender lump that may not be fluctuate
- Fever

The predisposing causes:
- Fistula in ano
- Crohn's disease
- Diabetes
- Anal intercourse

Management

- Surgical relief is provided with an incision and drainage
- As there may not be any fluctuation, a needle insertion and aspiration will act as a guide to the placement of the incision.
- A cruciate incision must be made and intervening skin excised
- Skin should be sent for histology to exclude Crohn's disease
- A limited sigmoidoscopy may be done to document evidence of fistula in ano if an internal opening detected
- A culture and sensitivity of the pus must be sent and result reviewed. Enteral organisms favour a fistula in ano as the cause. This may predict a recurrence of an abscess unless the fistula is addressed. Growth of *Staphylococcus* favours a skin pathology.

Chapter 23

Abdominal trauma – damage control surgery

Abdominal trauma is of two types:
1. Blunt injury
2. Penetrating injury

Blunt injury is common after road traffic accidents. Penetrating injury is fortunately less common and follows stabs and gunshot injuries, accounting for less than one-fourth of abdominal injuries.

When confronted with major abdominal trauma, the damage is done due to bleeding and hypothermia, leading to the 'lethal triad (**Figure 1**)'.

The mortality rises exponentially as the lethal triad sets in, and it is thus important to prevent it where possible by controlling blood loss and hypothermia. When uncontrolled, coagulation cascade is affected, leading to more bleeding. This was recognised in the 1980s during operations for trauma (Stone 1983).

The term 'damage control surgery' was coined by Rotondo and Schwab (1993) to describe a three-stage management of patients with major abdominal trauma.

Damage control surgery

Phase 1: Control of bleeding
Control of contamination
Closure – temporary

Phase 2: Restoration of physiology (ITU)
Early blood transfusion
Avoidance of crystalloid overload

Phase 3: Re-operation
Restoration of anatomy
Re-establishment of bowel continuity

Phases 1 and 2 may be concurrent.

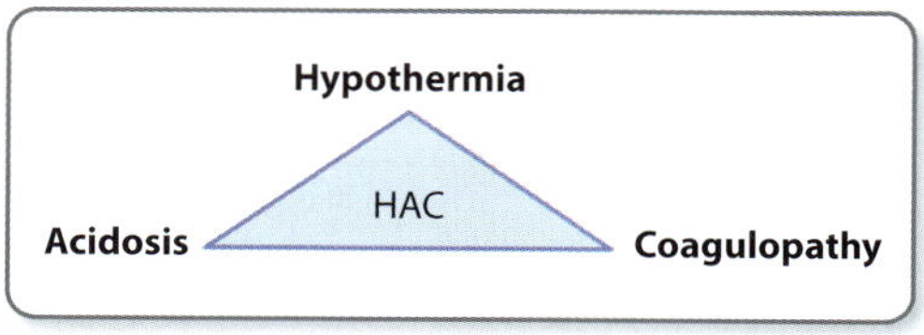

Figure 1 The lethal triad in a major abdominal trauma.

Damage control resuscitation

- Early blood product transfusion
- Immediate control of ongoing haemorrhage (temporary intravascular shunts/balloon tamponade)
- Restoration of blood volume
- Restoration of physiology
- Restoration of haematological stability

Damage control resuscitation (DCR) addresses the early coagulopathy of trauma, avoids massive crystalloid resuscitation and leaves the peritoneal cavity open when a patient approaches physiologic exhaustion without improvement.

Rapid initial surgery is now referred to as 'abbreviated laparotomy' and includes the following:

- Control of the bleeding sites that are obvious with ligation
- *Pack and pause:* If bleeding sites are many and immediate control is not feasible then packing with big pads works well in allowing time for homeostasis to play its part and blood to be transfused
- Splenectomy will need to be carried out if the spleen is ruptured
- Mobilisation and packing of the liver (including the diaphragmatic surface) if there is a major injury
- Exteriorisation of the bowel ends if perforation/s are obvious
- Thorough lavage
- *The abdomen must not be closed:* The abdomen is not closed fully to avoid intra-abdominal hypertension

In the 1980s, it was noted that sustained intra-abdominal hypertension rapidly led to renal dysfunction. By leaving the abdomen open, the physiology can be restored. In certain situations, (the author has done this) a colectomy can be done and the ends stapled and instead of being exteriorised the ends can be left within the abdomen. After a lapse of 48 hours on return to theatre the ends can be anastomosed. This may obviate the need for a colostomy. Re-establishment of intestinal continuity can be achieved without the need for a stoma.

The key principle: Correct the physiology prior to pathology.

- Stabilise the patient in the intensive care unit
- Correct the physiology in the first 48 hours
- Prevent rise in compartment pressure by not approximating the abdominal wound
- Return to theatre and rectify the pathology

Criteria for initiating massive transfusion protocol

1. Systolic blood pressure < 90 mmHg
2. Heart rated > 120 beats/min
3. pH = 7.24 or less
4. Focussed scan for trauma (FAST) positive suggesting intra-abdominal haemorrhage

Massive transfusion protocol – MTP (UK trauma protocol manual)

- Haemorrhage is the most cause of death in the first 24 hours after trauma
- Transfusion ratio of plasma - platelet - red blood cell (RBC) ratio of 1:1:1 reduces exsanguination
- Cryoprecipitate and tranexamic acid (1 g in 10 minutes) may need to be considered
- Delay in reaching targets increases mortality
- Reaching targets within 6 hours saves more lives
- 'Going big early' decreases the need for more blood products and is beneficial in the overall management

Massive transfusion is defined as:

- Transfusions > 10 units in 24 hours,
  or
- Transfusion of three units in 1 hour

When massive blood transfusion is needed it is important to involve the haematology team at the outset to ensure that the complex coagulation process can be supported from the outset and not be allowed to be consumed, leading to consumption coagulopathy. This requires not only volume by way of fluids but also coagulation factors, platelets, and RBCs to transport oxygen in the presence of ongoing haemorrhagic shock.

In haemorrhagic shock, there is an inability of the physiological system to meet the needs of the oxygen demand of the organs. As a ready rule of thumb, 200 mL of packed red cells will increase the haematocrit by three in the absence of continued bleeding.

Stages of haemorrhagic shock (Table 1) in a 70 kg adult

The principles of management are the same as outlined previously, but senior staff from multiple specialities will need to be involved from the outset.

Table 1 Stages of haemorrhagic shock in a 70-kg adult

Parameter	Class 1	Class 2	Class 3	Class 4
Blood loss (mL)	<750	750–1,500	1,500–2,000	>2,000
Blood loss (%)	<15	15–30	30–40	>40
Heart rate	<100	>100	>120	>140
Blood pressure	Normal	Orthostatic hypotension	Hypotensive	Severely hypotensive
Mentation	Normal	Mildly anxious	Confused	Confused withdrawn

Further reading

1. Ball CG. Damage control resuscitation: history, theory and technique. Can J Surg 2014; 57:55–60.

Chapter 24

Blood transfusion – principles

Karl Landsteiner, an Austrian biologist, distinguished the various blood groups in 1900. Subsequently, he also defined the Rhesus group.

Blood groups

There are four blood groups: A, B, AB and O (**Table 1**). The discovery of Rhesus (RhD) rendered these groups RhD positive or negative, thus increasing the number of blood groups to a total of eight. Karl noted that blood of different persons agglutinated on contact. This was due to the reaction in the serum.

- Rh-negative blood can be given only to Rh-negative patients
- Rh-positive blood can be given to both Rh-positive and Rh-negative patients
- *AB group*: They can receive blood from all groups.
  Universal recipient
- O *negative group*: They can be given to all groups.
  Universal donor

All the blood groups are genetically inherited.

Blood transfusion rules:

- *30-minute rule:* RBC units that have been left out of controlled storage should not be returned for reuse, if unused
- *4-hour rule:* Transfusion should be completed within 4 hours of removal from controlled storage

Major haemorrhage: Definition

- Bleeding that results in a systolic blood pressure of 90 mmHg or a heart rate > 110 beats/min in non-β-blocked adults.
- Loss of one blood volume in 24 hours (>5 L in 1 day in a 70-kg adult)

Table 1 ABO system

Blood group	Antigen in red blood cells	Antibody in serum
A	A antigen	B antibody
B	B antigen	A antibody
AB	A and B antigen	No antibodies
O	No antigens	A and B antibodies

- Loss of 50% of total blood volume in 3 hours
- Bleeding > 150 mL/min in adults

Alternatives to blood transfusion

- Cell salvage
- Tranexamic acid
- Erythropoietin
- Intravenous iron
- Oral iron

Transfusion thresholds: These are the haemoglobulin levels below which transfusion is recommended. National Institute for Health and Care Excellence (NICE) guidance:
- Restrictive blood transfusion threshold of a haemoglobin of 70 g/L. Not to be used in major haemorrhages or in patients with acute coronary syndrome
- Transfusion threshold of 80 g/L after coronary syndrome
- Individual thresholds of haemoglobin concentration for chronic anaemia
- The threshold in chronic anaemia is variable and the requirement for transfusion changes according to the clinical situation

Chapter 25

Breast lumps

Breast lumps are common and most of them are innocent. They cause a lot of anxiety and will need early review and assessment. They may be linked to the menstrual cycles in younger women. Benign disease is more common than malignant disease.

Breast lumps are due to:

- Fibroadenoma, a benign tumour common in young girls and young women. It is typically very mobile and because of its mobility it slips and moves away from the palpating hand. It is referred to as a 'breast mouse'
- Fibrocystic disease classically presents with multiple cysts and areas of thickening and represents a benign spectrum of disease
- Subareolar lumps can be due to duct ectasia or dilated ducts. Rarely, they may be due to a duct papilloma or carcinoma
- Fat necrosis may arise following recognised or unrecognised trauma. They may mimic a breast cancer
- Breast abscess is an acute presentation with a painful and warm lump
- Phyllodes tumours (from leaflike in Greek) arise from connective tissue of the breast.
- Gynaecomastia in males
- Breast cancer typically has a firmer consistency and may be fixed to the skin, with tethering of the skin or deeper structures such as the pectoralis major muscle.

Nipple discharge

Nipple discharge is not uncommon in women and occasional discharge is noted by many women from time to time.

It can be:

- Clear
- Greenish
- Purulent
- Bloody

Discharges from the nipple need attention, if:

- It is persistent from the same breast
- If it is bloody
- If it is foul smelling
- If the woman is over 50 years of age
- If it occurs in a male

Fibroadenoma

They are common in the age group of 20–30 years but may occur in teenagers and elderly women on hormone replacement.

A confirmatory cytology with either ultrasound or mammographic imaging may be needed.

In young patients, a non-operative management may be followed but, in most women, surgical excision and histological confirmation will be necessary.

Fibrocystic disease

These patients present with a pain-free lump that sometimes seems to occur overnight. When the cysts are due to blocked ducts, they may feel hard due to the tension on the wall of the cyst from fluid within akin to a tense water-filled balloon. Although they cause a lot of anxiety, they are seldom malignant.

Imaging with ultrasound followed by aspiration and reassurance suffices in most.

When the aspirate is clear there is seldom a need for confirmatory cytology although it may be needed to allay the anxiety; however, if the aspirate is bloody, cytology is needed.

On aspiration most of these cysts disappear and if they recur further aspiration may be needed.

Subareolar lumps

These are noted in the areolar tissue and do not involve the nipple. Commonly they are due to the dilatation of the ducts with retained collection sometimes leading to tethering.

When due to duct papilloma they may present with a bloody discharge and will need identification and excision of the appropriate duct.

Fat necrosis

This can mimic a breast cancer. It is due to trauma and sometimes follows surgical lumpectomy or biopsy. Since the necrosis pulls in the fatty tissue around it, very many of these lumps may feel hard. To confirm the diagnosis, they will need cytology or in some even an excision biopsy.

Breast abscess

Presentation is normally acute and may occur in lactating women. The lump is tender and may in a few be accompanied by fever. If the exhibition of antibiotics fails to promote resolution they will need aspiration, sometimes multiple times or incision and drainage.

Phyllodes tumour

The diagnosis is generally made histologically as they may present like a fibroadenoma. Sometimes they grow rapidly and involve the whole breast.

These are almost always benign with about 10% of the tumours undergoing malignant change to a sarcoma as the origin is the connective tissue and not ducts.

In most, a lumpectomy should suffice but a mastectomy may be needed in a few when the tumour is very big.

Gynaecomastia

This is due to enlargement of breast tissue in men. It occurs due to hormonal imbalance between testosterone and oestrogen.

The imbalance can occur during puberty and in men as they age and the testosterone level decreases.

It can occur in infants due to the high levels of maternal oestrogen. Medications such as cimetidine and proton pump inhibitors (PPIs), spironolactone, 5-α reductase blockers, verapamil, nifedipine, opioids and drugs for human immunodeficiency virus (HIV) have all been implicated.

Breast cancer

Malignant breast disease is mostly of ductal or lobular origin.

These can present with:

- Palpable hard lumps
- Changes in the skin with tethering
- Retraction of the nipple
- Lump in the axilla

They can also be screen detected with microcalcification that is more commonly noted in ductal carcinoma.

Lobular cancers are harder to detect on mammograms. They may present as a mass or soft lump.

A detailed review is available on snippets in surgery volume 2.

Chapter 26

Gynaecological emergencies

Gynaecological emergencies relate to *pelvic inflammatory disease and ectopic pregnancy,* which may masquerade as lower abdominal or right iliac fossa pain.

These patients may present directly to the surgeons. It is worth reiterating that in all young women, the routine protocol to follow must always include urine for nitrates and β-human chorionic gonadotropin (HCG).

If nitrate is positive, then a mid-stream urine sample must be sent for culture and sensitivity prior to starting antibiotic therapy as per the hospital's protocol.

If the β-HCG is positive in the presence of abdominal pain, then the gynaecological team must be informed at once about the patient and action initiated.

If there is a suspicion of a pelvic pathology, then a pelvic ultrasound examination must be arranged urgently; this is mandatory if the β-HCG is positive because ectopic pregnancy must be excluded.

Tubo-ovarian abscess or mass

In women in the reproductive age who are sexually active upper genitourinary infection may lead to adnexal pathology and manifest as pelvic inflammatory disease. If the history is unclear, it may be difficult to determine if there is a pelvic pathology such as a tubo-ovarian abscess (TOA)/mass or an appendicular pathology. More so, if the mass involves the right adnexa.

Classically, TOA may arise as a complication of pelvic inflammatory disease (PID).

The presentation of TOA:

- Pyrexia
- Adnexal mass
- Leucocytosis
- Pain in the pelvis
- Vaginal discharge

These classical symptoms may not always be present. The presentation may mimic acute appendicitis or an appendicular mass. The patient may show evidence of systemic inflammation, and this should raise the possibility that there may be a TOA. Rupture of the abscess can lead to sepsis.

It is best to work in conjunction with the gynaecologists, and at times a *combined emergency laparoscopy* may be needed.

Rupture of ectopic pregnancy

This can present as an acute emergency. As stated earlier all young women presenting with acute abdominal pain must have a β-HCG. A positive pregnancy test should raise the possibility of a ruptured ectopic pregnancy.

Expeditious assessment and immediate action with referral to the gynaecologists is required.

The symptoms of rupture include:

- Acute abdominal pain
- Shoulder tip pain due to diaphragmatic irritation
- Dizziness due to blood loss
- Nausea

In young women with acute abdominal pain the protocol should include:

- Urine examination for nitrates
- Urine or blood for β-HCG
- Ultrasound examination of the pelvis
- Discussions with gynaecologists
- Laparoscopic assessment

Chapter 27

Urological emergencies

The common urological problems (**Figure 1**) that present to acute surgery are as follows:

- Renal colic
- Haematuria
- Retention of urine
- Torsion of testis
- Epididymo-orchitis

Renal colic occurs due to the progressive movement of kidney stones along the ureter.

The common stones are as follows:

- *Calcium oxalate stones* – Most common, small, and spiculated like a *mulberry seed.* Spicules can cause microscopic haematuria as they move down the ureter. It is not associated with urinary infection, and the urine is more likely to be acidic. This type of stone presents classically with colic from loin to groin. With each episode of colic, the stone moves down the ureter

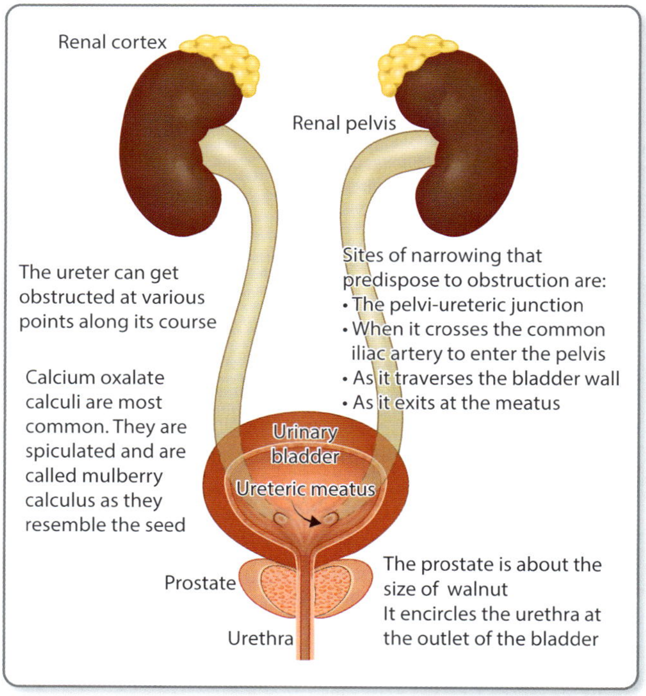

Figure 1 Common urological problems.

- *Triple phosphate stones* – These may not cause symptoms and can occur silently. They can lead to bilateral obstruction and renal failure. They can occur during pregnancy as there may be urinary stasis. They are very often associated with urinary infection. The urine is likely to be alkaline. Normally, they progress slowly and occupy the entire renal pelvis and calyces, appearing like the horn of a stag hence, called the *stag horn calculus.*
- *Urate stones, cystine xanthine* stones are less common and occur due to metabolic problems.

The principles of management relate to pain relief followed by diagnosis and referral to the urologists. Non-steroidal anti-inflammatory drugs (NSAIDs) are the drug of choice [National Institute for Health and Care Excellence (NICE) guidance]. If NSAIDs are contraindicated, then intravenous paracetamol or opioids can be prescribed.

- 90% of *renal stones are detectable on plain X-rays*
- 90% of *gallstones are invisible on plain X-rays*

Examination of the urine for nitrates and blood is mandatory.

If ureteric colic is suspected, a low-dose, non-contrast CT urogram must be arranged urgently. If this is delayed, the opportunity to make the diagnosis may be lost if the stone passes.

Treatment depends on size and site of the stone.

- Wait and watch policy is acceptable for stones smaller than 5 mm
- Medical expulsive therapy can be tried with α-blocker for lower ureteric stones smaller than 10 mm
- Extra-corporeal shockwave lithotripsy (ESWL) can be used for larger stones. This breaks the stones and allows for natural passage
- Percutaneous nephrolithotomy (PCNL) is a procedure that is used when the stone is in the kidney or upper ureter and is too large to be broken by other techniques. It is carried out with a tiny incision in the flank with percutaneous cannulation of the kidney and ureter under radiological guidance. The stone is extracted through this procedure or broken down with a lithotripter and extracted in pieces
- Surgical extraction with open surgery is the last resort

Serum calcium levels must be assessed to exclude hyper-parathyroid disorders.

The *urinary calcium* must be estimated in all with recurring colic. They may be voiding more calcium in the urine (hypercalciuria) and may benefit from *diuretic therapy.*

Prevention of recurrence may be assisted by advising the consumption of more water. While it is nice to advise 2 or 3 L of fluids a day, it may not always be practical as patients vary in weight. Asking a patient to drink enough to ensure that the colour of the water that is passed nearly approximates the colour of the water that is drunk works well in principle. It ensures that the urine being passed is dilute.

Haematuria

The presence of blood in the urine can be *non-visible or visible.*

Non-visible haematuria (NVH) or microscopic haematuria can be due to:

- Urinary tract infections
- Benign prostatic hypertrophy
- Ureteric calculi

Visible or macroscopic haematuria are mostly due to urological tumours such as bladder polyps and malignancies in the kidney, ureter, bladder or prostate.

Management is through the haematuria clinic or the 2-week wait pathway under the urologists.

Urinary retention

Common causes:

- Prostatic enlargement
- Post-operative/post-spinal anaesthesia
- Urethral stricture
- Drugs

Urinary retention can be acute or chronic. Acute retention is a common problem and can be due to prostatic enlargement, leading to obstruction of outflow through the urethra. It can also occur following surgery under *regional anaesthesia* such as spinal or even after general anaesthesia. It can follow from drugs such as *tricyclic antidepressants* and *sympathomimetics.* These can affect the function of the detrusor muscle of the bladder. Urethral strictures can also cause outflow obstruction.

Prostatism

Commonly, patients with prostatic hypertrophy will have symptoms of outflow obstruction sometimes leading to acute retention of urine in the bladder.

The symptoms include:

- Nocturia
- Hesitancy
- Precipitancy

These symptoms could have been present for a considerable time prior to an acute presentation with retention of urine. While *acute retention is painful,* many patients with *chronic retention* may have a very distended bladder without any symptoms.

The treatment is by catheterisation and referral to a urology service. Once catheterised, a trial without a catheter can be initiated after treatment for 48 hours with an α-adrenergic blocker such as Tamsulosin. Once again urinary cultures are needed to ensure early and appropriate treatment of infections. The cause of the prostatic enlargement will need to be ascertained.

Testicular pain

Epididymo-orchitis and *testicular torsions* present with testicular pain **(Figure 2)**. **In cases of suspected testicular torsion, evaluation** with a physical examination will lead to a diagnosis with the use of colour doppler ultrasound studies when the diagnosis is not very clear. In this regard the TWIST scoring system that has been validated by many studies can be used to determine the presence of testicular torsion

The TWIST scoring system is based on:

- Hard testis – 2
- Swelling – 2
- Nausea/Vomiting – 1
- Absent cremasteric reflex – 1
- High riding testis – 1

- Epididymo-orchitis is inflammation of the testis and epididymis
- Onset is likely to be gradual and may be associated with urinary infection, (mostly bacterial in the older age group
- It must be distinguished from torsion which presents acutely in the younger age group

- Intravaginal torsion occurs when a testis with a horizontal lie and a mesorchium undergoes torsion within the tunica vaginalis
- The horizontal lie of the testis—'clapper in a bell position' can be recognised clinically when not acute

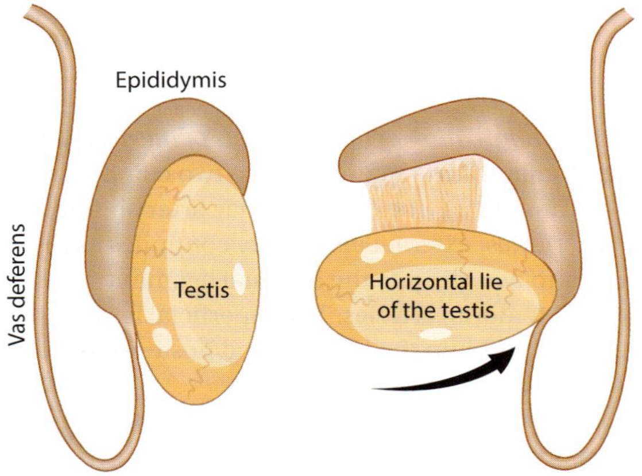

- In all patients presenting with acute testicular pain when torsion is suspected surgical intervention is preferable to a Doppler study. All investigations have a false negative rate and it is preferable to explore surgically immediately than wait for investigations
- Intravaginal torsion may present with right iliac fossa pain mimicking appendicitis

- Extravaginal torsion involving the testis and epididymis is more common in infants with an undescended tostis
- This may present a tender groin lump and an empty scrotum in an infant
- Testis has a tiny 'appendix'—the hydatid of Morgagni, which may also undergo torsion. Where the testis is nontender and the presentation is one of acute testicular pain an immediate Doppler study may show a normal blood supply to the testis
- Infantile scrotal oedema is a condition where the testis is nontender but there is scrotal oedema

Figure 2 Testicular torsion.

When the score is high the probability of a torsion is high and as time is of the essence, it is best to proceed to a surgical exploration directly. When the score is low, an ultrasound scan can be arranged and it has a high specificity and sensitivity.

The differential diagnosis includes:

- Epididymo-orchitis especially in older patients
- Testicular injury and hydrocoele
- Testicular tumour
- Infantile scrotal oedema in the very young

In infants, *infantile scrotal oedema,* a condition where there is oedema of the scrotum with normal testes can present acutely with a swelling causing anxiety to parents. An ultrasound is needed to reassure the parents that there is no torsion.

Chapter 28

Vascular emergencies

*There is a common pattern of bifurcation of major vessels of the aorta (the conducting vessels) (**Figure 1**).* The abdominal aorta bifurcates into two common iliac arteries just below and to the left of the umbilicus. The common iliac artery bifurcates into two, the internal and external iliac arteries; external iliac artery continues as the common femoral artery, and this bifurcates into two, deep to the inguinal ligament, to the superficial femoral and deep femoral (profunda femoris) arteries. The superficial femoral artery continues as the popliteal artery and trifurcates into the anterior and posterior tibial arteries, with the posterior tibial giving off the peroneal artery.

Vessels of conductance are the main vessels that conduct blood to the body from the heart. These bifurcate all along the limbs. At points of bifurcation, turbulence affects streamline flow and causes intimal damage, which becomes the focus of *atherosclerosis.* The process, therefore, affects the large vessels.

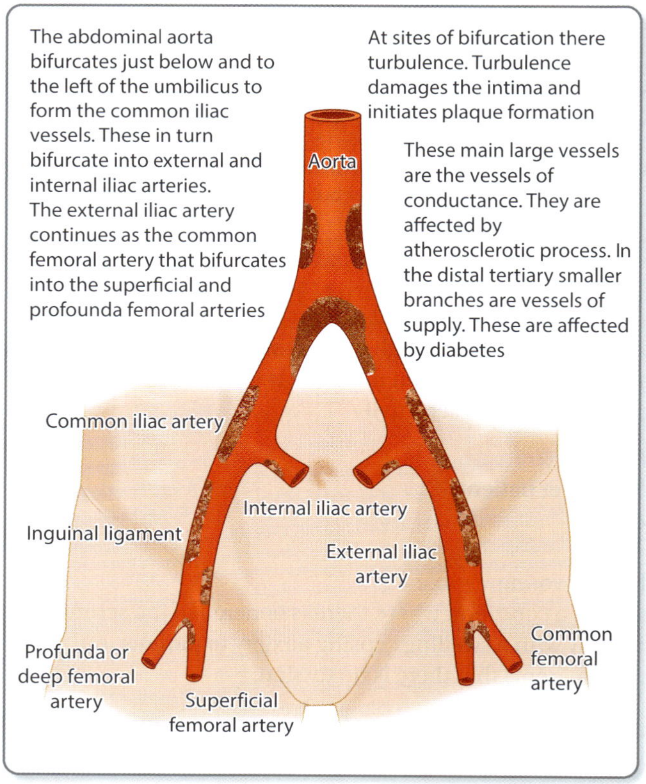

Figure 1 Bifurcation of major vessels of the aorta.

Vessels of supply are the small vessels that take blood to the muscles branching off from conductance vessels. They are typically affected by *diabetes.*

Peripheral arterial disease *(PAD)* predominantly affects the vessels of conductance, the proximal vessels. The presentation can be acute or chronic, the latter being more common.

Predisposing factors

- Smoking
- Obesity
- Hypertension
- Diabetes
- Hyperlipidaemia

Patients with chronic limb ischaemia are invariably smokers or ex-smokers, and a history of smoking must always be obtained.

Only 1–3% of patients with PAD present with critical limb ischaemia with a threatened limb. This manifests as rest pain that does not respond to opiates. The vascular society has suggested a different scoring system for assessing the threat to the limb. This is the *W*ound (*W*), *I*schaemia (*I*) and *f*oot *I*nfection (*fI*) (WIfI) system that can be used to evaluate patients with PAD.

Chronic critical lower limb ischaemia – CLI (**Box 1**).

Critical limb ischaemia

Progressive intermittent claudication is an important symptom, and this history must be elicited. Claudication is pain precipitated by activity such as walking, and *Fontaine* is credited with the staging.

Box 1: Chronic critical lower limb ischaemia – CLI

- Rest pain in the foot for >48 hours despite opiate analgesia. This is typically affected by inflow disease of the major vessels
- Tissue loss – necrosis or gangrene
- Absolute Doppler pressure of <50 mmHg in a non-diabetic or 30 mmHg in a diabetic patient
- Limb-threatening ischaemia that requires amputation within 6 months if revascularisation is ineffective

Threatened-limb ischaemia WIfI

- The era of diabetes has necessitated a different approach to the management of limb ischaemia. This system takes into account:
  - Wound grades such as ulcers and gangrene ischaemia based on CLI
  - Infection in the foot.
  - This enables definition of the severity of the threat to the limb.

Stage I: 'Walk through' calf pain. The pain in the calf resolves on walking as increasingly *collateral vessels are recruited to deliver more oxygen* to the peripheral tissues and wash away the metabolites of anaerobic respiration. The pain is in the muscles of activity, the calf in the lower limbs.

Stage II: Rest relieves calf pain. The recruitment of collateral vessels is insufficient to deliver the needed oxygen to the tissues. The muscular activity must, therefore, come to a stop to allow the tissues to rest and regain aerobic respiration.

Stage III: Foot pain at rest. The pain is in the distal most part, the foot. The oxygenation even at rest is inadequate to supply the peripheral requirements. The foot which is farthest from heart is unable to receive enough oxygen for its metabolic needs. This manifests as constant and severe pain.

Acute thrombosis and acute embolism

This distinction is easy to explain, but it may be difficult to judge clinically. The management of the two tends to be different and, hence, it is a crucial decision to make clinically albeit aided by investigations. This will enable delivery of the right care.

When acute limb ischaemia (**Figure 2**) is suspected, the vascular specialists must be informed and involved in further care. Suffice it to know that with *acute embolism,* the presentation is classical and the onset, sudden. Many patients will have abnormal cardiac rhythms, with the most common being *atrial fibrillation. Thrombotic episode* is more gradual with a history of claudication and rest pain.

Acute limb ischaemia (Figure 2)

Embolism is associated with changes in cardiac rhythm, and in any acute presentation, atrial fibrillation or frequent ectopic beats may be present and must be looked for actively.

Investigations in vascular surgery are guided by a balance of principles that determine, if the:

- Patient is safe for surgery
- Surgery is safe for the patient

Acute limb ischaemia
- Embolism
- Thrombus
- Trauma

Presentation – 5 P,s
- *P*ain or *P*araesthesia
- *P*allor
- *P*ulselessness
- *P*erishing cold
- *P*aralysis

Figure 2 Acute limb ischaemia.

Ensure that the patient is safe for surgery.
Check all cardiovascular risk factors. *'Head over heart over heels'* is the often repeated statement that reiterates the fact that *cerebral* and *cardiac* systems must be examined and assessed along with the limbs. Most patients are arteriopaths with the process of atherosclerosis extending to all vessels in the body. Many will have *comorbidities* such as earlier transient ischaemic attack (TIA), cerebrovascular accident (CVA), myocardial disease, hypertension and diabetes.

Ensure that surgery is safe for the patient.
There is little point in carrying out a major operation when a lesser procedure will suffice, such as an angioplasty as opposed to a major bypass. Safe surgery always depends on choosing the right patient for the right procedure.

A *map of the vascular tree* by way of an angiogram, MR angiogram, or duplex scanning is almost always needed.

An *ECG* and *coagulation* studies are routine investigations in all patients presenting with vascular symptoms.

If there is critical limb ischaemia, consider one of two options.

- *Limb-saving* vascular reconstructive procedure
- *Life-saving amputation,* which may be below or above knee

Gangrene

Gangrene is defined as macroscopic death of tissue with putrefaction.

The key distinction is that gangrene is macroscopic as opposed to necrosis, which is microscopic death of tissue.

Gangrene occurs at the distal extremities when there is loss of blood supply. This can occur due to the following:

- Peripheral vascular disease
- Raynaud's disease
- Vasculitis
- Diabetes mellitus

Gangrene may occur in peripheral arterial disease (PAD). The gangrene can be wet or dry (**Table 1**).

Dry gangrene is associated with peripheral vascular disease. These patients present with constant foot pain if the vessels of the lower limb are affected. They may have a low-grade pyrexia. There is *no infection*, and the treatment will be directed towards the management

Table 1 Types of gangrene

Dry gangrene	Wet gangrene
Atherosclerotic PAD	Diabetic PAD
Well-defined line of demarcation	Ill-defined line of demarcation
Aseptic line of demarcation	Infected line of demarcation

PAD, peripheral arterial disease.

of the associated limb ischaemia followed by an amputation of the gangrenous toe or part of the limb.

Wet gangrene is generally infected and occurs in the distal aspect of the foot in diabetic patients. These patients may benefit from antibiotic therapy, but eventually most will need an amputation. In many patients, there is sensory loss, and the cause of the gangrene may be a trivial trauma to the diabetic foot, leading to infection in the presence of a decreased blood supply.

Aneurysm of the abdominal aorta – key points (Figure 3)

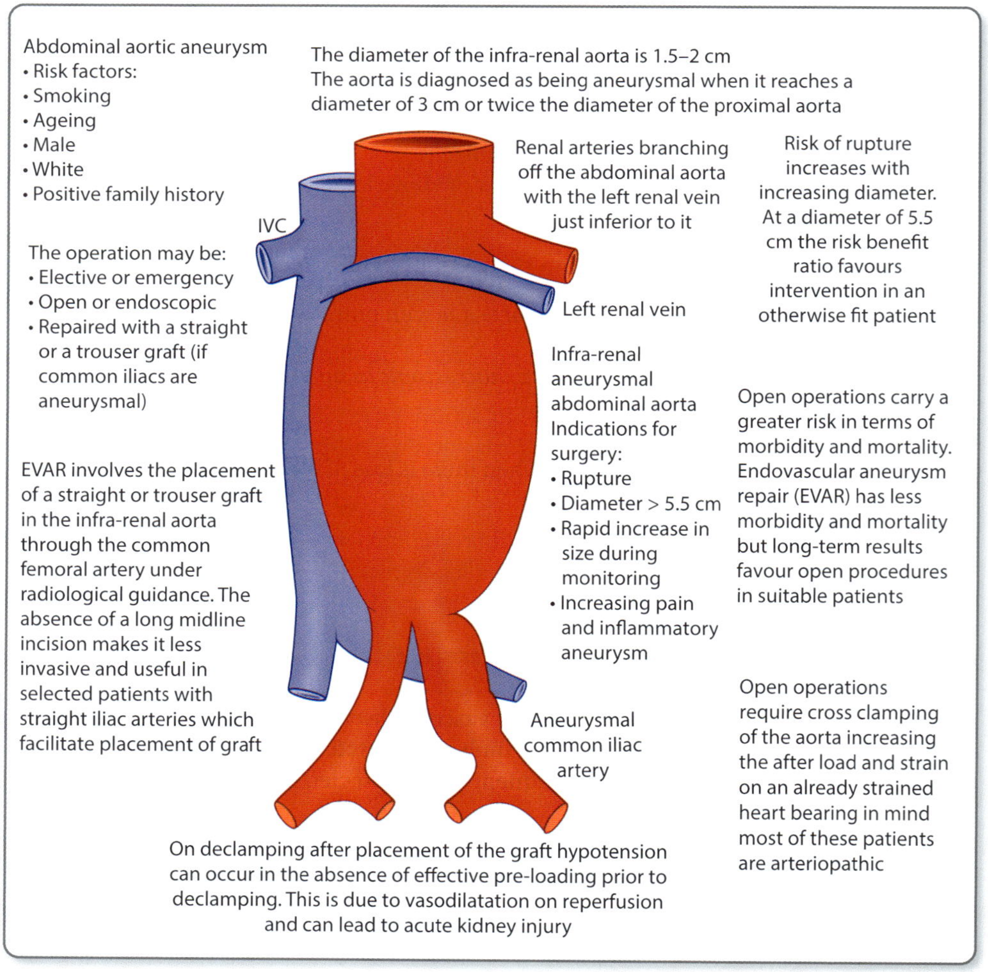

Figure 3 Aneurysm of the abdominal aorta – key points.

Chapter 29

Abscess, boils and carbuncles

No surgical discussion can overlook the common skin problems that are confronted by surgeons. Most skin infections are caused by bacteria, such as *Staphylococcus* and *Streptococcus* (**Box 1**). MRSA (**Box 2**) is another bacteria that causes skin infection. It is associated with systemic symptoms and can be resistant to treatment with commonly used antibiotics.

No surgical discussion can overlook the common presentations that are confronted daily by surgeons (**Box 1**). Abscesses can occur anywhere in the body but are common in areas subject to friction such as axilla, groin, perineum, and natal clefts.

Classically, abscess is defined as a cavity containing pus lined by granulation tissue and surrounded by cellulitis.
Boils or furuncles are infections of the root of hair follicles.

Box 1: Cause of skin infections

Coagulase positive Staphylococcus aureus

- *Causes skin infection*: ABC – abscesses, boils and carbuncles
- Coagulase production by the *Staphylococcus* helps it to break down fibrinogen to fibrin on encountering blood. This coats the bacteria and prevents its recognition and phagocytosis
- *Aureus*: Latin for gold, because of the golden yellow colonies surrounded by β-haemolysis it produces on blood agar plates
- β-*haemolysis*: It is the breakdown of RBC by haemolysin produced by the bacteria. Many bacteria produce haemolysin, particularly *Staphylococcus* and *Streptococcus*

Box 2: Methicillin-resistant *Staphylococcus* aureus (MRSA)

- Methicillin is a type of penicillin and bacteria that are resistant to it are also resistant to many commonly used antibiotics making it difficult to treat them
- Colonisation or staphylococcal carriage must be suspected when patients present with recurrent and multiple infections
- Decolonisation should be considered only when there is no infection, and it involves clearing nasal and cutaneous carriage by application of *Hibiscrub* for skin and *Naseptin* (hibiscrub and neomycin) for nose

When multiple boils occur in close approximation, it is referred to as a carbuncle. It involves the subcutaneous tissue and is accompanied by sloughing. These occur in the nape and back and are associated with diabetes.

When the hair follicles get inflamed due to shaving or friction, they infect the sweat glands in the skin and are referred to as hidradenitis. If it suppurates, the condition is referred to as hidradenitis suppurativa. Once again these occur in the axilla, groin or perineum.

Pilonidal abscess occurs commonly in the natal cleft of the perineum. These occur due to infection of a pilonidal sinus. *Pilonidal sinus* is the presence of sinus in the skin due to friction and maceration in moist parts of the body such as the natal cleft and perineum. Pilar means hair and nidus, nest. It is a nest of hair at the base of a sinus. Typically, it is formed of hair that has entered this 'nest' from exterior, noted by the fact that the roots of the hair are superficial with the ends being found deep. This shows that the hair is a 'migrant' and not a local! Mostly hair that falls from the neck collects in the natal cleft area. It was noted to be common among American soldiers in the Korean War in the 1950s and came to be called the 'Jeep bottom'.

Perianal abscess can be secondary to a fistula in ano, or it can arise from the perianal skin. When associated with a fistula, the type of organism confronted is likely to be those that are commonly present in the bowel and not the skin. If the cultures grow *E. coli, Klebsiella,* or *Bacteroides* then a fistula should be suspected. These will recur unless the underlying pathology is addressed. If, in contrast, *Staphylococcus* is grown, it is more likely to be a cutaneous problem.

Hilton's method of incision and drainage of an abscess

All large abscesses need surgical drainage in the presence of fluctuation. In the perineum, it is best not to wait for fluctuation, and the abscess must be drained when the patient presents with acute perianal pain, preferably after localisation by aspiration under anaesthesia followed by incision and drainage. In areas where there are underlying nerves and vessels, the skin over the abscess is incised superficially in the direction of the underlying structures; the deep fascia is then punctured with a 'sinus forceps' that has a blunt tip, the cavity is entered, and locules are broken down. The wound is left open and packed lightly.

Role of antibiotics

Antibiotic treatment is not needed for abscesses that are incised and drained, however, they may be needed in some circumstances as follows:

- Abscess that occurs in the face. The danger triangle of the face is an area encompassing the corners of the mouth to the bridge of the nose. Although rare, it is possible that infections in this area can spread to the cavernous sinus in the brain through the facial veins and cause thrombosis or meningitis
- In diabetic patients, they may find it difficult to clear the infection without antibiotics
- If a patient is systemically unwell because of the abscess
- In immunocompromised patients
- In the presence of cellulitis

Cellulitis

This is defined as acute inflammation of the dermis and subcutaneous tissue.

Classically, it affects those with comorbidities such as obesity, diabetes, and immobility. It affects the elderly with skin that is prone to break after minimal trauma with reluctance to heal.

The common infecting organisms are *Staphylococcus aureus* and *Streptococcus pyogenes* (Group A *Streptococcus*, or GAS).

The *presentation of abscess and cellulitis* has been recognised for millennia. The signs were outlined by Celsus in his work *De Medicina* in the first century CE.

- *Calor* – warm
- *Rubor* – redness or erythema
- *Dolor* – pain
- *Tumour* – swelling (blisters)
- *Functio-laesa* – loss of function (added by Galen)

Eron classification (Box 3)

Box 3: Eron classification of cellulitis

- *Class 1*: No systemic toxicity or co-morbidity – can be managed with antibiotic treatment without need for admission
- *Class 2*: Systemically well or unwell but has co-morbidity such as obesity, venous insufficiency or peripheral vascular disease or diabetes. These patients will need intravenous antibiotics as short stay for 48 hours followed by outpatient ambulatory antibiotic therapy where available
- *Class 3*: As above but with a positive quick sequential organ failure assessment (qSOFA) such as tachycardia, hypotension or altered mentation
- *Class 4*: Severe life-threatening infection such as necrotizing fasciitis [based on National Institute for Health and Care Excellence (NICE) guidance]

Necrotising fasciitis (Box 4)

Necrotising fasciitis (NF) is a life-threatening bacterial infection caused by Group A *Streptococcus* and amplified by anaerobic bacteria. The amplification of the original infection occurs because of synergy between the infecting organisms. Therefore, this is also referred to as synergistic gangrene. One of the postulated mechanisms is that the aerobic organisms proceed to cause an anaerobic environment as they invade and inflame the tissues. This secondarily allows the growth of a cohort of anaerobic organisms. The mortality rate varies from 20% to 40%.

Box 4: Necrotising fasciitis (NF) classification

- *Type 1*: Poly microbial. One set of aerobic bacteria utilises the locally available oxygen and facilitates the growth of a second anaerobic organism causing local thrombosis and haemolysis
- *Type 2*: Group A *Streptococcus* (GAS) infection
- *Type 3*: Clostridial infections – causing gas gangrene
- If this is suspected a rapid Gram's staining of tissue will help with the diagnosis
- Largely, these are clinical diagnoses, but ultrasound, CT and MRI can help to assist the diagnosis if gas locules are noted in the subcutaneous tissue
- Rapid and ruthless excision of all necrotic tissue is the most important part of the management along with critical care management and antibiotic care in consultation with microbiologists
- *Fournier's gangrene*: It is necrotising fasciitis affecting the perineum and genitalia; while it is common in men and it can also affect the genitalia in women
- *Meleney's synergistic gangrene*: Affects the abdominal wall after surgery and can be rapidly fatal if not recognised and treated immediately

Chapter 30

Skin lumps

The skin is the largest organ of the body.

It has:
- A superficial layer, the *epidermis*
- A deeper layer the *dermis* that has the blood vessels, nerves and fibroblasts
- Deep to the dermis, the *subcutis* has the collagen and fat cells
- Deep to this is the *subcutaneous* tissue

The epidermis has three layers
1. *Stratum corneum* containing the protein keratin and dead layers that flake off. Keratin provides 'the water proofing'
2. *Keratinocytes layer* of living cells that mature and move superficially
3. *Basal layer* where new cells are laid out

Skin and subcutaneous lumps

Superficially, palpable lumps in can be classified as being:
- Intradermal
- Subcutaneous
- Subfascial
- Intramuscular

Lumps can arise from structures in those planes.
- The dermis – *Pilar or 'sebaceous' cysts, implantation dermoid* or congenital *angular dermoid*
- Subcutaneous fat – Lipoma
- Nerves – Neurofibroma
- Lymphoidal tissue

Dermal lumps

These are in the dermis of the skin and not in the subcutaneous tissue.

They are therefore not mobile. Pilar or sebaceous cysts may have a punctum; the edge is well-defined. These are in parts of the body with hair and when these cysts become large the hair over the cyst is typically absent. They arise from the pilar glands at the root of the hair follicle but are commonly and incorrectly called sebaceous cysts rather than pilar cysts.

Management

Surgery is required if the cyst is painful or increasing in size. On occasions the cyst can get infected, and the contents may discharge spontaneously leaving nothing more than a residual nubbin of tissue. This can be left alone or excised if necessary. As these cysts are most often present in the scalp there may be a tendency to increased vascularity leading to bleeding. The need for meticulous haemostasis is therefore paramount.

Lipoma

These are commonly subcutaneous. They have a well-defined *edge that slips under the palpating hand* unlike the dermal cysts. Classically, when they are in the subcutaneous plane the mobility is obvious; however, lipoma may be in different planes under the skin.

Location of lipoma:
- Subcutaneous
- Subfascial
- Intermuscular
- Submuscular

Management

Merely the presence of a lipoma is not an indication for surgery. The duration of the lipoma and its behaviour determine the indication for surgery.

Many lipomata tend to grow slowly and remain asymptomatic over a long period of time. Surgery may be needed:
- If there is, however, a change in its rate of growth
- If there is an increase in symptoms such as pain

Neurofibroma

These are benign neural sheath tumours. As they arise from the nerves, their mobility is restricted to one plane along the long axis of the nerve from which they arise.

Types:
- Localised
- Diffuse
- Plexiform

Multiple neurofibromatosis NF-1 (von Recklinghausen's disease) is a congenital genetically transmitted condition that should be suspected if more than six café-au-lait spots are noted. It is quite common for children to have one or two spots but six or more must raise the suspicion of NF-1. NF-1 presents with:
- Café-au-lait spots
- Freckles
- Optic gliomas

Neurofibromatosis-2 (NF-2) is another presentation that is less common.

These may present as nerve tumours, such as *acoustic neuroma (vestibular schwannomas)* and involve hearing and balance.

Lymph nodes

They are subcutaneous and located in areas where there is nodal drainage, such as:
- Axilla
- Supra-clavicular fossa
- Groin

When noted the area that is draining to these nodes must be inspected for inflammation or malignancy.

Inspection and palpation

It is advantageous to follow a protocol when examining these lumps. This is referred to as the six S's and helps to define the lumps clearly.
1. *S*ite
2. *S*ize
3. *S*hape
4. *S*kin overlying the lump – healthy, colour – red and dusky
5. *S*urface – smooth, bosselated and engorged veins
6. *S*urrounding area/structures – increased vascularity

An organised examination and thought process is not only impressive, but it reflects an organised mind with a sound approach.

Palpation helps to define the nature of the pathology.
- Acute
- Inflammatory
- Indolent

This is important for planning the management.

Other benign lesions of the skin:
- Naevus
- Haemangioma
- Arterio-venous fistula

Naevus

A naevus is a benign proliferation of melanocyte. This can be *congenital* or *acquired.*

Congenital naevi are of many different types. 'Café-au-lait' spots are commonly seen in fair-skinned persons.

Naevi are classified depending on the site of location within the skin.
- *Dermal naevi* are a collection of naevus cell nests in the dermis
- *Junctional naevi* are nests at the junction of dermis and epidermis
- *Compound naevi* have naevus nests in the epidermis as well as in the dermis

Dermatoscopy has given rise to newer classification.

Sun exposure may lead to the formation of naevi. Some acquired naevi involute with time and others may fade.

Currently, the preferred management is a referral to a dermatologist for management rather surgical removal.

Melanoma of the skin

- Arises from melanocytes
- About 30% of them arise from pre-existing moles
- The most common risk factor is exposure to the sun
- Many are pigmented and look black or brown
- Some rare ones can be amelanotic

A pigmented lesion is suspected of being a melanoma based on the ABCDE guidance of the American Association of Dermatologists.

- *Asymmetry*: Halves do not match
- *Border*: Edges are not smooth
- *Colour*: Mottled and uneven, with shades of brown, black, white and pink
- *Diameter*: The spot is greater than the tip of a pencil eraser (6.0 mm)
- *Evolving*: New lesion or change in size, shape or colour

Management

The early recognition and management are now carried out by dermatologists. The staging is based on the TNM system, but Clark's and Breslow's staging are also used to prognosticate. Radical surgery, nodal dissection and systemic chemotherapy may be needed for advanced stages of melanoma.

Clark's staging is based on the pathological depth of invasion.

- *Level 1*: In situ lesion in epidermis
- *Level 2*: Superficial dermis
- *Level 3*: Deep dermis
- *Level 4*: Reticular dermis
- *Level 5*: Subcutaneous tissue

Breslow's staging is based on the numerical depth and correlates strongly with survival. The more superficial the lesion the better the survival. The levels are:

- Level 1 - Up to 0.75 mm
- Level 2 - 0.76–1.5 mm
- Level 3 - 1.51–4 mm
- Level 4 - Greater than 4 mm

Types of melanomas

- *Superficial spreading melanoma*:
  - Most common type of melanoma
  - Occurs more commonly in the fair skinned persons
  - Usually flat and superficial as the name indicates
  - The edges are irregular with variegated colour of different shades of black and brown.
- *Nodular melanoma:* These are typically modules that grow into the deeper layers I tend to occur mostly in the *torso and limbs*
- *Lentigo maligns melanoma:* These melanomas develop in *Hutchinson's melanotic freckle.* These are found in areas exposed to the sun such as face and neck.
- *Amelanotic melanoma*

- *Acral lentiginous melanoma* occur in the *palm and sole of the feet.*
- *Subungual melanoma* is a subtype that occurs as a pigmented lesion in the nail and can be mistaken for a haematoma.

Squamous cell carcinoma

These are present in areas of the body exposed to sunlight. They are seldom life-threatening.

They also occur in parts of the body that are not exposed to sunlight such as the anal canal suggesting the presence of causes other than exposure to ultraviolet rays.

It presents as an ulcer or a new skin lesion.

They may also arise in old scars when it is referred to as a Marjolin's ulcer.

They tend to spread in contiguity to the deeper layers and to the regional lymph nodes. When recognised early and confirmed histologically they can be treated by:

- *Curettage* and *electrodessication* of the base for small cancers
- *Mohs surgery* after Frederick Mohs. This is a laborious microscopic clearance layer by layer until malignancy is cleared. The procedure is applicable in parts of the body where skin is at a premium such as around the eyes, nose, etc. Elsewhere in the body its value is questionable.

Excision and primary closure

For advanced cancers as in common with other skin cancers the surgical treatment is directed towards wide *'tri-dimensional'* excision and *clearance of regional nodes* if they are involved. *Skin grafts or rotation flaps* may be needed if there is a large defect to bridge after excision.

Basal cell carcinoma

These are skin cancers arising from basal cells of the epidermis. The basal cells replenish dead cells. The DNA of these cells are susceptible to mutations when exposed to ultraviolet rays. They occur as tiny transparent lesions or ulcers in parts of the body exposed to the sun like the face, ears, neck, etc., ageing and immuno-suppression are other factors. Much of the principles of treatment is like the management of early squamous cell cancers.

Chapter 31

Postoperative care

The length of stay is a key surrogate marker of good care. The stay is lengthened if there are postoperative complications. Complications increase the overall stress levels among the carers and the cared. It is, therefore, necessary to monitor and prevent complications by regular assessment of the patient clinically using physiological parameters. Early detection of abnormal parameters followed by immediate action is beneficial and puts the patient on the road to a complication-free recovery. It prevents progression down a slippery slope towards increasing levels of care and death in a few (**Figure 1**).

Actions that enhance care

- Daily or twice ward rounds (twice daily for some ill patients)
- Review of:
  - National early warning scores
  - Haematological, biochemical and radiological results with appropriate action
  - Daily fluid balance, total intake, urine output and output from drains
  - Review of all medications
- Adhere to the antibiotic and deep vein thrombosis (DVT) prophylaxis policy of the hospital
- Address pain. The effects of pain on recovery and lung function cannot be overemphasised

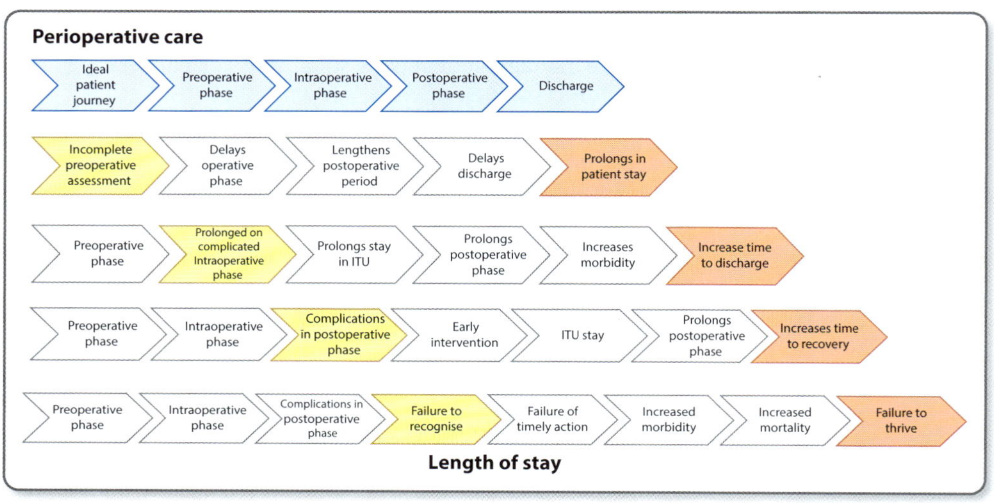

Figure 1 Perioperative care.

Abdominal pain after surgery leads to *shallow breathing.* The dead space air (residual air from the alveoli to the oral cavity following expiration) has a higher proportion of expired air that is rich in CO_2. Shallow breathing simply moves the dead space air to and fro, leading to a drop in oxygen saturation. Shallow breathing will also fail to fill the alveoli, which may then collapse, leading to *atelectasis* and/or pneumonia.

Intra-abdominal factors for the cause of pain, such as peritonitis or even anastomotic leak, will lead to shallow breathing and a drop in oxygen saturation.

Excess opiate analgesia can also suppress respiration.

The other effect of pain is tachycardia, and it can have a significant impact on cardiac function, especially in the elderly. *With tachycardia, the diastolic period is shortened.* Coronary perfusion occurs during diastole, and thus a rapidly beating heart is less well perfused. The implication of this is obvious. Tachycardia tires the heart!

Nutrition is a crucial factor in the postoperative period. With minimally invasive surgery, most patients can start feeding enterally quite early.

If it is expected that a patient is unlikely to be suitable for enteral feeding for 5 days or more, then total parenteral nutrition (TPN) may need consideration.

Discussions must be had with the nutrition team to initiate TPN. This may well be needed in patients with a bowel fistula or those recovering from peritonitis. In these situations, the ileus is prolonged, and parenteral nutrition may be needed. Albumin, a negative acute phase reactant, is a good indicator of progress. Low levels of albumin do cause oedema of the small bowel, leading to prolonged ileus. It is seldom corrected rapidly by parenteral or enteral protein. Ileus leads to vomiting and respiratory complications such as *aspiration pneumonia.* This will certainly lengthen postoperative stay.

The buzzwords are target and trigger.

If hypoxia is noted [more common in the obese, smokers, the elderly, and those with chronic obstructive pulmonary disease (COPD)], this must raise the possibility of respiratory problems such as atelectasis in the early postoperative period or infections later.

Sepsis and shock of any aetiology and diabetic ketoacidosis must be borne in mind.

Blood gas assessment will be necessary if the saturation remains low despite remedial action.

If the hypoxia is persistent, the cause of the hypoxia must be determined. At the outset, oxygen is delivered to the maximum possible level in the ward, disregarding COPD. More people come to harm from hypoxia than from the cessation of the hypoxic drive that may manifest as respiratory acidosis and increasing CO_2 levels.

Repeat of blood, *ECG,* and (if cardiac problems are suspected) *troponin* may be needed. If the problem is purely respiratory in the postoperative period, a CT thorax or a *CT pulmonary angiogram (CTPA)* to exclude pulmonary embolism may be appropriate. An examination of the abdomen along with the chest will exclude sub-diaphragmatic mischief, which can manifest as poor respiratory function. A CT scan in those cases will need to include the abdomen and pelvis as a CT thorax, abdomen and pelvis (TAP).

Postoperative *anaemia,* when present, may need correction with transfusion. The transfusion trigger of 70 g/L may not apply in postoperative states. The targets vary as patients with coronary syndrome postoperatively need a higher level of haemoglobin than a patient with known chronic anaemia. Oxygen carrying capacity is dependent on the level of haemoglobin and the FiO_2. This will need discussions with other clinicians, including the haematologist and the consultant in charge of the patient. The locally agreed policy should be implemented.

In the postoperative period, an increase in respiratory rate may be the earliest manifestation of an impending complication. A fall in urine output can be an early indicator of impaired cardiac output.

Chapter 32

Postoperative complications

Postoperative complications can arise after any operation. Complications arise due to five factors.

1. Patient related
2. Presenting problem related
3. Technique related
4. Technology related
5. Treatment related

Patient-related complications can arise due to comorbidities and mental status. In elective cases, actions to mitigate these must be taken prior to listing a patient for surgery and at the time of preoperative assessment. Recognition and anticipation of problems due to comorbidities must be highlighted at the *'WHO time out'* before every operation. It is now mandatory with the worldwide introduction of the *WHO checklist*.

- Diabetic patients, those with hypertension, and those on anticoagulants can be overlooked leading to stress for both the patient and the practitioner
- Cardiopulmonary exercise testing (CPET) is a surrogate marker for fitness and is useful for predicting problems
- The American system of classification into American Society of Anesthesiologists (ASA) grades 1–5 is useful but subjective. Likewise, the calculation of morbidity and mortality as well as assessment of frailty all remain subjective
- Mental problems of patients such as one that swallows countless needles or hairpins repeatedly needing recurrent laparotomies may also lead to postoperative complications
- High or low body mass index (BMI) patients are liable to more complications than those in the normal or the overweight range.
- Drug users who present with ischaemic limbs make reconstructions difficult which contribute to postoperative complications
- Ultimately, the matter of proceeding to surgery in a patient that is unfit must be based on discussions with the patient, their family, the surgical, critical care and anaesthetic teams

Presenting problem–related complications are sometimes difficult to prevent – for instance, the patient who has a faecal peritonitis due to colonic perforation. The operation may be successful, and there may even be no primary anastomosis. Antibiotic cover may be adequate, yet the patient can succumb to overwhelming sepsis. This also applies to patients presenting with peritonitis that follows appendicular abscess or peptic perforation. Preventing it may not be possible as the time of presentation may be too late for a successful outcome.

Anastomoses may break down if the vascularisation is poor or oxygen delivery is decreased due to chronic obstructive pulmonary disease (COPD) or cardiovascular pathology despite technically well-fashioned anastomoses.

Technique-related complications can be reduced by regular practice under guidance and seeking assistance when needed. There are many possible complications that relate to technique. A few are highlighted here.

- Repair of a large incisional hernia of the abdominal wall with inappropriate sutures
- *Approximating tissue under tension*
- Devascularisation during the mobilisation of the bowel
- Not using the mesh in the proper plane
- Insufficient mobilisation of the bowel for a tension-free anastomosis
- Anastomotic technique such as *not everting the vascular anastomosis*
- Anastomotic technique such as *not inverting the bowel anastomosis*
- Rough handling of sutures that may fracture later
- Diathermy damage to bowel
- Inadvertent perforation of bowel during laparoscopic procedures or port insertions
- *Not placing drains when needed, delaying detection of complications such as bleeding*
- Early postoperative feeding despite the presence of ongoing ileus, leading to problems such as vomiting and aspiration injury to lungs
- Not controlling bleeding at the time of surgery and hoping that the bleeding will stop
- Not checking and ensuring that the procedure has been completed safely

Technology-related complications should be mitigated by attention to detail, but sometimes they may be unpredictable.

- The incomplete firing of a few staples in a stapled anastomosis
- Fracturing of a diathermy needle tip during laparoscopic surgery
- Failure to ensure that the proper gas supply systems are in place for anaesthesia
- Wrong type of operating table, such as one not suitable for a Lloyd Davies position, that prolongs surgery
- Failure of laparoscopic camera/light systems (rare these days)
- Diathermy burn due to improper placement of diathermy pads
- Diathermy injury due to improper setting of the intensity

Treatment-related problems are complications such as the following:

- Bleeding in patients on aspirin or clopidogrel
- Not bridging anticoagulants when needed, leading to postoperative cerebrovascular accident (CVA)
- Not ensuring preoperative medications are prescribed, such as antihypertensives, potassium, digoxin, etc.
- Excessive opiate analgesia leading to sedation and respiratory complications
- Not changing antibiotics based on available results of cultures and sensitivity
- Not considering kidney function in prescribing aminoglycosides and non-steroidals
- Not using the proper urinary catheter for long-term use

This list is only a partial list; there are many such problems that one needs to be aware of always.

The postoperative complications fall into three groups:

1. Wound-related complications
2. Intra-abdominal complications
3. Extra-abdominal complications

The *principles of care* are universal:

- Examine the whole patient before the part
- Systematic examination of the patient
- Examination of the part in concern
- Resuscitation of the patient based on findings
- Rapid appropriate investigations
- Timely action and call for help

Wound-related complications include wound infection and dehiscence. The infections can be limited to the wound or deep space such as pelvic collections. Where there is a deep wound infection, dehiscence is a possibility. The management follows the principles laid out earlier and starts with assessment of the patient as a whole and then the part that is affected.

The consultation with microbiologists starts at the time of recognition of the infection. Recognition of infection is facilitated by daily ward rounds and attention to detail, including small changes in observations and minor complaints. Would dehiscence can be an emergency especially if the bowel is exposed. Where possible, intra-peritoneal collections must be excluded preferably by a CT scan prior to surgical intervention.

Intra-abdominal complications after surgery commonly involve presence of blood, bile, or faeces; there can also be ischaemia of the bowel or fistula formation due to small or large bowel injury.

Where there is no drain placed after surgery, one must be aware of the possibility that diagnosis of the collection can be delayed.

Changes in the National Early Warning Score (NEWS) with respect to oxygen requirement, tachycardia, temperature and mentation will need evaluation. If necessary, radiological imaging must be arranged after routine bloods that will include C-reactive protein (CRP), urea and electrolytes, blood sugar and full blood count.

With ongoing bleeding, the haemoglobin will drop. If there is a drain, then indication for surgery is dictated by the quantity and rate of loss of blood. If there is persistent drainage of blood, the blood must be cross-matched prior to return to theatre.

When there is drainage of bile after gallbladder surgery, immediate imaging and discussions with the gastroenterologist will be necessary. The patient may need an urgent endoscopic retrograde cholangiopancreatography (ERCP) and stenting if bile duct injury is noted. If there is a common bile duct injury, the problem needs escalation to a specialist hepatobiliary team. Cystic duct stump leak can be managed with the stenting of the common bile duct.

Bile-stained drainage could be due to bowel injury, and as in patients with faeculent drainage, the patient can become rapidly septic. Timely resuscitation will include not only fluids but also antibiotics after sampling blood for culture. Irrespective of the time of day, the patient will need assessment with respect to immediate management, which will include surgical intervention.

Extra-abdominal complications fall into the following broad categories:

- *Wind-related (Lungs)*: Pyrexia from days 0 to 5
- *Wound-related*: Pyrexia from days 5 to 10

- *Water-related [urinary tract infection (UTI)]*: Pyrexia from days 10 to 15
- *Wall-related (Vein wall)*: Pyrexia from days 10 to 20

Early pyrexia is mostly due to respiratory problems. Wind and pump complications are related to lungs and heart. The problem with the lung tends to occur early; when early, it is likely to be related to a mucous plug causing atelectasis. The clinical manifestation may only be a drop in oxygen saturation or rise in temperature. Very often these occur in the first couple of days and are best treated with physiotherapy.

Cardiac problems in the postoperative period are generally due to four factors:

1. Hypotension and hypovolaemia
2. Hypoxia
3. Hypokalaemia
4. Hypomagnesaemia

These should be corrected. Oftentimes, the preoperative medications such as digoxin and potassium may have been missed, or the potassium not supplemented.

Wound infections are common after emergency operations for peritonitis. Normally, the wounds will show evidence of infection later than 2 days. A subtle sign may be a slight elevation in temperature. They manifest in a progressive manner as follows:

- Erythema
- Cellulitis
- Serous discharge
- Purulent discharge

Urinary infections may follow the use of catheter. *When no direct cause is evident for a patient's pyrexia, urinary infection or line sepsis must be suspected.*

Deep wound abscesses can also manifest at this stage and the adage 'Pus somewhere, pus nowhere, pus under the diaphragm' needs to be changed to 'Pus somewhere, pus nowhere, pus in the lines' such as central lines.

'Pus somewhere, pus nowhere, pus in the central lines'

When fever is unaccounted for, all fluids including blood, pus, sputum and urine must be cultured not only for bacteria but also *for fungal infections!*

Symptomatic deep vein thrombosis (DVT) in the postoperative period can be reduced with preventive measures but even that may be difficult when the cause is pathological such as on-going pelvic malignancy. *Thrombo-embolic deterrent (TED) stockings* are beneficial to the extent that one needs to apply these stockings in just seven patients during the perioperative period for one major benefit! The *n*umbers *n*eeded to *t*reat *(NNT)* is therefore seven. This is an excellent benefit for such a non-invasive measure. It works by compressing the superficial leg veins thus directing a greater flow to the deep veins of the leg.

It is now unequivocally recognised that after orthopaedic joint replacements and pelvic cancer surgery, some form of anticoagulation for a period of 28 days in the postoperative period is of benefit in reducing the number of patients presenting with postoperative DVT and possibly pulmonary embolism. Patients must therefore be prescribed fractionated heparin or oral anticoagulants (which may prove to be even more beneficial), for this period.

Chapter 33

Antithrombotic medications

Clot formation after injury to the vessel has three basic steps:

1. *Vessel constriction or spasm*: This is an immediate effect and the reason behind the effectiveness of 'pack and pause' when there is excessive bleeding
2. *Platelet aggregation* at the site of injury follows soon with an attempt to stop the bleeding by forming a platelet plug
3. *Fibrin mesh (clot)* is laid out on the plug the activation of the coagulation enzymes cascade which strengthens the plug till the time healing occurs after which the clot is taken down by macrophages. *Fibrin the basic structure of the clot is formed by the action of thrombin on fibrinogen.* Thus, inactivation of thrombin by increasing antithrombin activity reduces clotting. Heparin and low-molecular heparins work this way.

Unfractionated heparin

Heparin is a fat-soluble anticoagulant that increases the activity of antithrombin. Antithrombin activity of heparin, by stopping the formation of fibrin prevents clot formation and clot extension. *It does not assist in clot resolution.* Heparin acts on the coagulation cascade by activating antithrombin (previously called 'antithrombin III') which inactivates the coagulation enzymes thrombin (factor II), factor Xa and IXa.

One of the side effects of heparin is *HIT, or heparin-induced thrombosis.* It, thus, appears to promote the process that it is supposed to prevent! This is an autoimmune response manifested by decrease in platelet count, thrombosis and skin allergy. If this is clinically suspected or confirmed, stop heparin at once, contact the haematologist, switch to another anticoagulant such as warfarin, and ensure platelet count returns to normal.

Fractionated heparin – low molecular weight heparin

This is a synthetic derivative of heparin. Its actions are more predictive and controlled. They are more effective than vitamin K antagonists. Drugs such as dalteparin, enoxaparin and tinzaparin are now in common usage. They can be used for prolonged periods up to 28 days after major surgical procedures.

Oral anticoagulants

- Vitamin K antagonists (VKA)
- Non-vitamin K antagonist oral anticoagulants (*NOACs*)

Vitamin K antagonist anticoagulants

These act by decreasing the activity of vitamin K dependent coagulation factors 2, 7, 9 and 10 as well as coagulation proteins S and C (www.ncbi.nlm.nih.gov).

The commonly used ones are:
- Warfarin (Coumadin)
- Dicoumarol
- Acenocoumarol

Warfarin

Warfarin acts as an anticoagulant by inhibiting vitamin K–dependent clotting factors 2, 7, 9 and 10. It also inhibits proteins S and C. Warfarin is usually prescribed for patients with atrial fibrillation or recurrent deep vein thrombosis. Warfarin level needs to be monitored by regular INR, also known as prothrombin time.

Non-vitamin K antagonist oral anticoagulants

- Apixaban
- Dabigatran
- Edoxaban
- Rivaroxaban

These drugs unlike warfarin, which can be reversed with vitamin K, do not have any antidote except for dabigatran. Their usage has increased as there is no need for intensive monitoring with international normalised ratio (INR), as in the case of warfarin and other coumarins.

Reversal of anticoagulants

Minor bleeding when overt, as from skin injury, is easy to treat with pressure and without long-term consequence.

Major bleeding may not be overt and can be dangerous with excessive blood loss; the haemoglobin count can fall rapidly.

For minor bleeding with any of the above drugs, desmopressin can be used if simple measures fail. It modulates the levels of factor VIII. It also increases platelet adhesion.

Where there is major bleeding, then reversal may be carried out as shown (**Table 1**).

Table 1 Major bleeding reversals

Aspirin/Clopidogrel	**Platelet transfusion**
Heparin	Protamine sulphate with complete reversal
LMWH	Protamine provides partial reversal PCC may be of benefit
Warfarin	Vitamin K/PCC if needed
Dabigatran	Idarucizumab, 5 g
NOVACs	4 factor PCC

LMWH, low-molecular weight heparin; NOACs, non vitamin K antagonist oral anticoagulants; PCC, prothrombin complex concentrates.

PCC – 4 factor prothrombin complex concentrate

This is a complex of factor 2, 7, 9 and10. It is better than *fresh frozen plasma* but more expensive. It is especially useful in major clinical bleeding, especially when surgical intervention is needed. *Octaplex* is the one of the commonly used complexes.

Bridging anticoagulation for surgery

Many patients scheduled for surgery will be on anticoagulants such as warfarin. Some may be on NOAC's. When elective surgery is needed for patients on anticoagulants, consideration must be given to the need for bridging with low-molecular-weight heparin (LMWH). It is best to follow the hospital protocol or to discuss with the anticoagulation team.

Bridging is needed if, after risk assessment, the risk of thrombo-embolism is high.

It is needed in patients who have had the following:

- Venous thromboembolism (VTE) within the previous 3 months
- A VTE while taking anticoagulants
- Atrial fibrillation (AF) and transient ischaemic attack (TIA) within the last 3 months
- Atrial fibrillation and earlier TIA with risk factors such as:
  - Cardiac failure
  - Diabetes
  - Hypertension
  - Elderly over 75 years of age
- Mechanical heart valves

Chapter 34

Deep vein thrombosis

Deep vein thrombosis (DVT) contributes to a considerable number of preventable deaths. Strict adherence to the identification of persons in need of prophylaxis and implementation of local prevention policies are beneficial. Preprinted risk assessment forms help to decrease the risk of DVT.

Virchow's triad is a theory that explains the three main factors that contribute to the development of blood clots, or thrombosis (**Figure 1**).

The following categories of patients are at risk:
- Above the age of 60 years
- Smokers
- The obese
- Those with a history of DVT
- Young women on contraceptives
- Those with varicose veins
- Those with a recent abdominal cancer
- Orthopaedic lower limb surgery

Thrombo-embolic deterrent stockings

These simple stockings do the trick. These stockings offer compression of the calf at pressures of 20 mmHg or less. The compression is graduated being greatest at the ankle and decreases over the calf muscles. This compresses the superficial leg veins, the long and short saphenous veins, and therefore directs the flow to the deep veins, thus increasing the rate of flow in the deep vessels. As slowing of flow is one of the triad

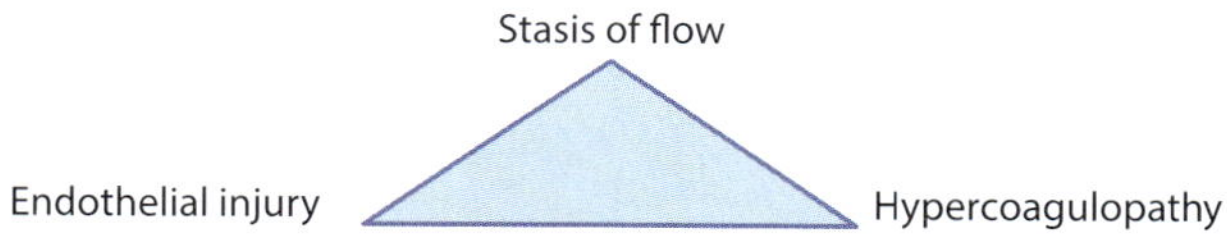

Thrombosis is intravascular clotting. When the flow is slow and in the presence of endothelial injury and increased tendency to clot the platelets adhere to the endothelium at sites of injury or near valve sinuses. This initiates the process of thrombosis

Figure 1 Virchow's triad theory.

of pathological changes that lead to DVT, increasing the rate of flow in the deep veins decreases the risk of clotting.

The numbers needed to treat (NNT) with thrombo-embolic deterrent (TED) for one benefit is just seven!

Prevention and early detection of DVT reduces the risk of pulmonary embolism (PE), which is thought to be as high as 10% in patients with DVT. PE is responsible for a significant proportion of hospital deaths.

High index of suspicion helps in the diagnosis of DVT, especially in patients with the stated risk factors.

Dorsiflexion of the leg, causing pain, is noted in *<50% of patients* (Homan's sign).

Phlegmasia cerulea dolens, painful swollen leg, is seldom seen.

Venograms and duplex Doppler studies may be normal in many. If the index of suspicion is high, anticoagulant therapy is advisable at the outset till investigation confirms or confutes the diagnosis.

Pulmonary embolism occurs due to clots getting dislodged from the limb veins and moving to the heart and on to the pulmonary artery. This leads to a *ventilation perfusion mismatch* as ventilated areas may not be perfused due to the absence of blood flow. It imposes a cardiac strain and may manifest initially as *reduced oxygenation in postoperative patients.*

An ECG may show:

- *Abnormal rhythm in 70% of patients*
- The classical changes are less commonly seen.
  These are in certain leads referred to as 'S1Q3T3'
- More commonly, they present with signs of *right heart strain and a new right bundle branch block (RBBB)*
- A new onset of *atrial fibrillation (AF)*
- Inverted T waves across the anterior chest leads, V1–V4.

If the clot is large, then it can lead to death.

If the PE is suspected, start the patient on high-flow oxygen through a non-breather mask and arrange a CT of the pulmonary artery (*CTPA*).

D-dimer is unlikely to be useful as it may be raised in the immediate postoperative period.

If confirmed, immediate anticoagulation will be needed.

Thrombolysis is not likely to be an option in patients who have had major surgery as the risk of bleeding is high.

Further reading

1. Beyth RJ, Cohen AM, Landfield CS. Long-term outcomes of deep-vein thrombosis. Arch Int Med 1995; 155:1031–1037.

Chapter 35

Acute kidney injury

Acute kidney injury (AKI) is often confronted in the surgical wards. There are three criteria, three categories and three stages.

Criteria for acute kidney injury

The AKI is an abrupt (within 48 hours) reduction of kidney function, manifested by *any one* of the following criteria.

1. An absolute increase in serum creatinine of 0.3 mg/dL (≥26.4 μmol/L) or greater
2. A percentage increase in serum creatinine of 50% or greater (1.5-fold from baseline)
3. A reduction in urine output, defined as <0.5 mL/kg/h for >6 hours

Categories of acute kidney injury

Acute kidney injury may be classified into three general categories:

1. *Prerenal:* An adaptive response to severe volume depletion and hypotension, *with structurally intact nephrons*
2. *Intrinsic:* Response to cytotoxic, ischaemic, or inflammatory insults to the kidney, with *structural and functional nephron damage*
3. *Postrenal*: From obstruction to the passage of urine

While this classification is useful in establishing a differential diagnosis, many pathophysiologic features are shared among the different categories.

Staging of acute kidney injury (Table 1)

The acute kidney injury network (AKIN) has proposed a staging system for AKI. In this system, *either* serum creatinine *or* urine output criteria can be used to determine stage.

Table 1 Staging of acute kidney injury

Stage	Serum creatinine (SCr) criteria	Urine output criteria
1	↑ ≥0.3 mg/dL (≥26 μmol/L) or ↑1.5- to 2-fold	<0.5 mL/kg/h for >6 hours
2	>2- to 3-fold ↑ from baseline	<0.5 mL/kg/h for >12 hours
3	>3-fold ↑ from baseline, or if baseline SCr ≥ 4 mg/dL (≥350 μmol/L) then an acute ↑ of SCr ≥ 0.5 (≥44 μmol/L mg/dL)	<0.3 mL/kg/h for 24 hours or anuria for 12 hours

Patients who receive renal replacement therapy (RRT) are considered to have met the criteria for stage 3.

Acute kidney injury network classification/staging system for acute kidney injury

A patient can fulfil the criteria based on either serum creatinine or urine output or both.

Another clinically useful classification is the *RIFLE* (**Table 2**).

Classification which grades the renal function according to levels of deterioration of renal function leading to end-stage renal failure.

RIFLE classification – *R*isk, *I*njury, *F*ailure, *L*oss of kidney function and *E*nd-stage kidney disease (RIFLE) the Second International Consensus Conference of the Acute Dialysis Quality Initiative (ADQI) Group.

Oliguric and non-oliguric patients with acute kidney injury

- Patients who develop AKI can be oliguric or non-oliguric
- Can have a rapid or slow rise in creatinine levels
- May have qualitative differences in urine solute concentrations and cellular content
- Approximately 50–60% of all causes of AKI are non-oliguric

Classifying AKI as oliguric or non-oliguric based on daily urine excretion has prognostic value.

Oliguria is defined as a daily urine volume of <400 mL and has a worse prognosis, except in prerenal injury. Anuria is defined as a urine output of <100 mL/day and, if abrupt in onset, suggests bilateral obstruction or catastrophic injury to both kidneys.

Stratification of renal injury along these lines helps in diagnosis and decision-making and can be an important criterion for patient's response to therapy.

Table 2 RIFLE classification

Class	GFR	U/O
*R*isk	↑ SCr × 1.5 or ↓ GFR > 25%	<0.5 ml/kg/h × 6 hours
*I*njury	↑ SCr × 2 or ↓ GFR > 50%	<0.5 mL/kg/h × 12 hours
*F*ailure	↑ SCr × 3 or ↓ GFR > 75% or if baseline SCr ≥ 353.6 μmol/L (≥4 mg/dL) ↑ SCr > 44.2 mmol/L (>0.5 mg/dL)	<0.3 mL/kg/h × 24 hours or anuria × 12 hours
*L*oss of kidney function	Persistent ARF (loss) is defined as need for renal replacement therapy (RRT) for >4 weeks	
*E*nd stage	ESRD is defined by need for dialysis for longer than 3 months	

ARF, acute renal failure; ESRD, end-stage renal disease; GFR, glomerular filtration rate; SCr, serum creatinine; U/O, urine output.

Assessment in acute renal failure

- Urine dipstick for protein/blood
- Urine biochemistry check Na and osmolality
- Urine culture and sensitivity before starting antibiotics
- Renal ultrasound
- Chest X-ray to exclude pulmonary oedema
- Non-contrast CT

In pre-renal failure, the kidney is pathologically normal and continues to concentrate the urine. The ability to concentrate the urine means the following on *urine examination:*

- High osmolality
- High urea
- Low sodium

In intrinsic renal failure or acute tubular necrosis (ATN), obviously the intrinsic renal function is lost and this means the following on *urine examination*:

- Low osmolality
- Low urea and creatinine
- High sodium
- Presence of casts (typical of ATN)

A renal ultrasound may show a normal-sized kidney or a small kidney that is <9 cm with bright echo in parenchyma. A small-sized kidney suggests chronic damage whereas a normal-sized kidney is suggestive of acute renal failure, with bright echo due to oedema.

The principles of management are to ensure a tight-fluid balance and enable delivery of oxygen to the tubules. This can be done by ensuring oxygen saturation > 95% with levels of haemoglobin > 7 g/dL.

A further principle is to *exclude any toxins* that are being prescribed, such as the following:

- Non-steroidal anti-inflammatory drugs (NSAIDs)
- Aminoglycosides
- Angiotensin-converting enzyme (ACE) inhibitors
- Beta blockers
- Opioids

Chapter 36

Cardiac problems in surgical patients

Common cardiac problems in surgical patients are:

- Hypotension (the most common)
- Tachycardia

These generally follow from the four H's:

1. *H*ypovolaemia
2. *H*ypoxia
3. *H*ypokalaemia
4. *H*ypomagnesaemia

Other problems are as follows:

- Primary pump pathology such as myocardial infarction
- Excessive volume infusion and cardiac failure
- Changes in rhythm leading to atrial fibrillation (AF)
- Pulmonary embolism

As always, absolute values are less relevant than trend over time.

The warning signs that should alert one to the possibility of cardiac complications are as follows:

1. *Increased respiratory rate (early marker of the ill patient)*
2. *Progressively decreasing urine output (early marker of poor cardiac output)*

Urine output is a surrogate marker for cardiac output because a hypoxic kidney cannot work at its best!

The medullary nephrons are even in normal conditions working at the boundaries of hypoxia. Any further decrease in oxygen delivery rapidly tilts the balance.

Atrial fibrillation is common in the elderly. Very often, correcting the fluids and electrolytes will enable reversal to a sinus rhythm. It is also likely that the patient's drugs, such as digoxin (a rare prescription these days) or a β-blocker may have been missed out in the peri-operative period and restarting them will aid in rate control.

Tachycardia may be due to hypovolaemia. Tachycardia tires the heart; older the heart more rapid the onset of tiredness leading to myocardial infarction. Never underestimate the importance of tachycardia especially in the elderly. Recall that the heart is perfused during diastole and tachycardia by shortening the diastole affects coronary blood flow. Tachycardia may be due to hypovolaemia.

- Assess the drains for blood loss
- Assess adequacy of fluid replacement

Bradycardia is rare in the surgical patient, and when it occurs, it could be due to:
- Pain
- Beta-blocker therapy
- Myocardial infarction

The risk of cardiac problems in non-cardiac surgery patients is proportional to the pre-existing cardiac disease.

High risk

- Myocardial infarction (MI) within 6 months has the highest risk
- Unstable angina
- Severe aortic stenosis
- Decompensated cardiac failure
- Uncontrolled hypertension
- Cardiac arrhythmia

Lower risk

- Myocardial infarction >6 months prior to surgery
- Stable angina
- Compensated cardiac failure or valve disease
- Cardiomegaly

Pacemaker

- All patients with pacemakers need a recent cardiological assessment to ensure pacemaker function prior to surgery
- Diathermy earthing at the time of surgery must be placed away from the pacemaker
- Short bursts of diathermy rather than continuous bouts are preferred
- Bipolar diathermy is safer in these patients than monopolar diathermy

Chapter 37

Haemorrhagic shock

The definition of shock:
- An acute circulatory failure
- Leading to inadequate tissue perfusion
- Cellular hypoxia
- Cellular damage
- Dysfunction and failure of organs

In the shocked state, autoregulation sets in and directs blood to the kidney and cerebrum at the cost of skin and bowel.

Types of shock

- Hypovolaemic – due to loss of blood volume
- Distributive – or vasodilatory as occurs in sepsis, anaphylaxis, neurogenic or endocrine shock
- Cardiogenic – due to cardiac pathology
- Obstructive – due to non cardiac pathology such as PE, tension pneumothorax, pericarditis, cardiomyopathy

Stages of shock

1. Less than 500 mL blood loss
2. 500–1,000 mL loss
3. 1,000–2,000 mL loss
4. Greater than 2,000 mL loss

Hypovolaemia (**Figure 1**) is the most common cause of shock in surgical patients.

Hypothermia must be avoided because it contributes to bleeding diathesis, as noted in the discussion on the lethal triad.

Exsanguinating patients need immediate definitive action and surgery. Successful resuscitation with 10–20 mL/kg of fluids crystalloids or colloid immediately will improve the outcome. The type of fluid infused is not as important as the rapidity of action. Crystalloids in excess may cause oedema, while colloids can have anaphylactic or allergic reactions. A combination of colloids with crystalloids may be acceptable.

Blood should be given when needed, however, if a patient is exsanguinating, it is imperative to control the bleeding before infusing blood, as with ruptured aortic aneurysms or major trauma.

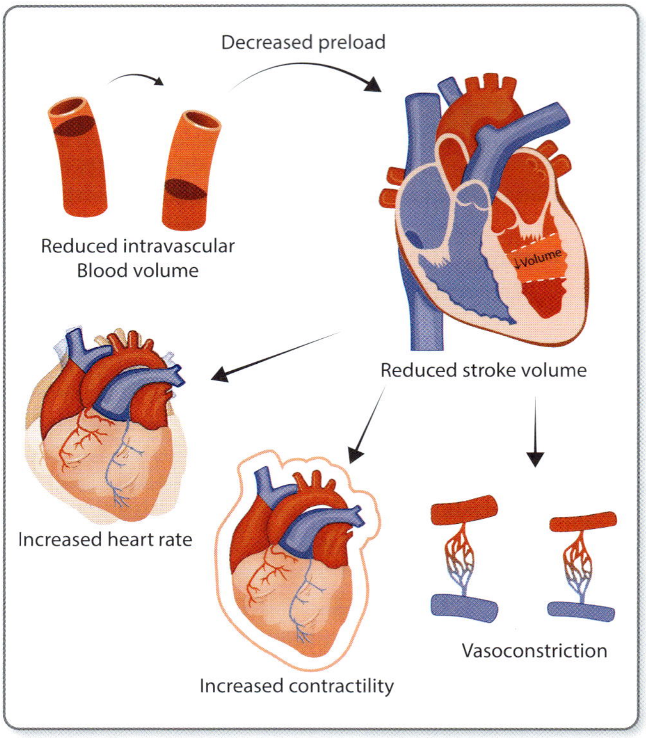

Figure 1 Hypovolaemic shock.

Distribution of fluids between compartments is determined by osmotic forces generated by solutes in the solution. The extracellular fluid is supported by its cation, sodium (Na). Intracellular fluid is supported by its cation, potassium (K).

The Na^+/K^+-ATPase pump functions to exclude sodium from the intracellular compartment. Water can diffuse across a selectively permeable membrane along a gradient, flowing from an area of higher to a lower concentration along the slope by osmosis. This process helps to maintain isotonicity with between the compartments.

Chapter 38

Postoperative fluid management

Any major operation will activate the endocrine orchestra led by the pituitary. Prime among the various responses, with respect to fluid management (**Figure 1**), is that major body cavity surgery initiates the *antidiuretic hormone (ADH)-aldosterone system*. The ADH does exactly what the name implies: it retains water and sodium.

A reduced urine output immediately after a major operation is a natural response to injury.

The daily fluid intake normally equates to output
Intake: Food, water, small amount from metabolism
Output: Insensible loss from skin and breathing, sweating, urine and faeces

Daily volume replacement postoperatively must include daily maintenance fluids plus fluids lost from drains and urine

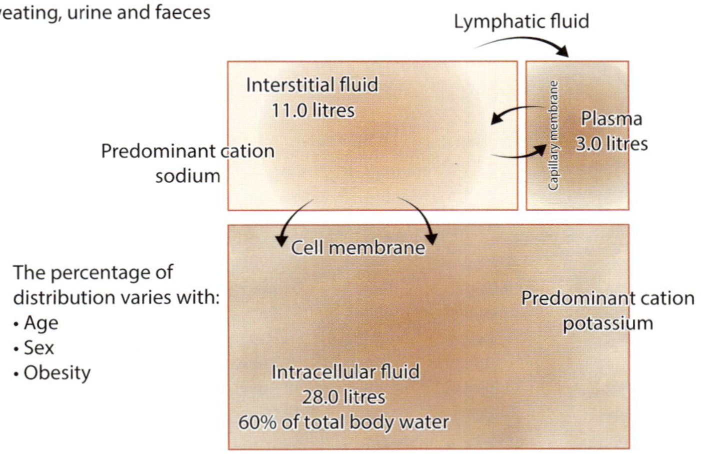

Total body water in a 70-kg adult is 42.0 litres
Total blood volume is 5.0 litres with plasma constituting 60%, the rest is cellular

The types of fluid are **crystalloids** and colloids. The crystalloids diffuse between plasma and interstitial fluid
They stay where sodium stays.

Colloids and blood stay in the plasma. They help to build up volume rapidly

Dextrose and water diffuse through the entire body water. Most useful in replenishing **intracellular** compartment in conditions like **diarrhoea**

Figure 1: Fluid management.

Here are some points of note in fluid balance postoperatively.

- *Insensible loss* is often not appreciated. It can be as much as a litre depending on the presence of fever or the provision of dehumidified oxygen
- Strict intake output chart must be kept, and the loss must be replenished over and above the daily requirements
- Minimally invasive procedures and fast-track recovery will need careful management, as oral fluid regimens may be set up early
- The body retains water and sodium postoperatively
- Basal water requirement is 30–40 mL/kg/day
- Daily sodium requirement is 60–100 mmol/day
- Daily potassium requirement is 40–60 mmol/day. This must not be ignored and must be included from the immediate aftermath of a laparotomy.

Overlooking hypokalaemia can lead to cardiac problems.

Chapter 39

Enhanced recovery after surgery

Recovery is a process that takes time. Individuals recover at different rates depending upon their state of fitness. It is dependent on several factors that include the following:

- Preoperative health of the patient
- Intraoperative procedural process
- Perioperative care
- Postoperative convalescence

If the problems outlined are assessed and addressed at each point, it is felt that the process of recovery can be accelerated. This has been termed 'enhanced recovery'. Currently, many hospitals have protocols for the patient's journey that facilitates recovery.

The *preoperative phase* concentrates on the maintenance of optimal health prior to surgery. This includes:

- Optimising physical and nutritional fitness by regular exercise and activity
- Increasing protein intake
- Ensuring an adequate carbohydrate load prior to an operation to decrease postoperative insulin resistance
- Suspending or decreasing smoking and alcohol consumption prior to surgery

Carbohydrate loading moves the patient to a *'fed' or anabolic state,* while the earlier system of starvation prior to surgery moved patients to a catabolic state. With insulin being an anabolic hormone, the anabolic state sets in prior to surgery with preoperative carbohydrate loading. According to some studies, this preserves insulin sensitivity postoperatively and hastens recovery. This remains to be proven conclusively.

Intraoperatively, principles include the following:

- Decreasing bleeding during surgery and using minimally invasive techniques
- Titrating the intravenous fluids to requirement and not 'drowning' the patient with fluids
- Decreasing use of opiates and providing good analgesia by way of epidural or rectus sheath catheters

Postoperatively, the provision of adequate analgesia with epidural or rectus sheath infusion of local anaesthesia facilitates early mobilisation.

It allows for sitting the patient for at least 6 hours on day 1 to standing by the bed and walking with assistance early.

This is facilitated by use of fewer tethers such as drains, urinary catheters, and intravenous fluids. Anecdotally in our hospital, walking the patient as soon as possible was contributory to a more rapid recovery.

The vertical nursing

This is the principle whereby a patient is nursed in a sitting position by day instead of being nursed flat in the bed. This along with daily chest physiotherapy benefits the lung function.

It is worth stressing that the patient must be examined daily by clinicians with help from physiotherapists and the pain team.

Early introduction of diet must be very carefully titrated by senior clinicians lest it pushes some patients into paralytic ileus and worse still, aspiration.

After discharge, there must be regular communication and coordination with the nursing team.

Nutrition, physical activity and deep vein thrombosis (DVT) prophylaxis remain key factors.

The rapid recovery process moves away from the traditional model where we used to:

- Stress the patient
- Starve the patient
- Drown the patient with intravenous fluids
- Rest the patient increasing exposure to the effects of immobility

The rapid recovery process involves less starvation and stress, early mobilisation and attention to overall adequate fluid balance, and defined discharge criteria. The policy, when successful, decreases the length of stay.

Chapter 40

Cardiopulmonary exercise testing

Cardiac and pulmonary status play a key role in recovery from non-cardiac body cavity surgery. Oxygen demand increases after surgery. An efficient 'pump and pulmonary' system is necessary to deliver this increased demand.

The functional capacity of a person is graded in terms of METs or metabolic equivalents of task. A person sitting and typing this, is using the equivalent of 1 MET. More active movements like climbing a flight of stairs and carrying out independent normal life activities is about 4 METs which is the reserve that will be needed for recovery after surgery. A fit athlete will have a MET of 10.

The cardiopulmonary exercise testing (CPET) is a surrogate marker for cardio-pulmonary fitness. The reason for a person's breathlessness may vary from being unfit to having lung, cardiac, haematological, and circulatory problems. Traditional assessment is unable to quantify the cardiopulmonary status as well as the CPET can.

Cardiopulmonary exercise testing is a non-invasive test that measures the cardiopulmonary status of patients at rest and during exercise.

The actual test commonly involves subjecting the patient to physical exercise on a bicycle or treadmill (**Figure 1**). The patient breathes through a mouthpiece. This allows concurrent

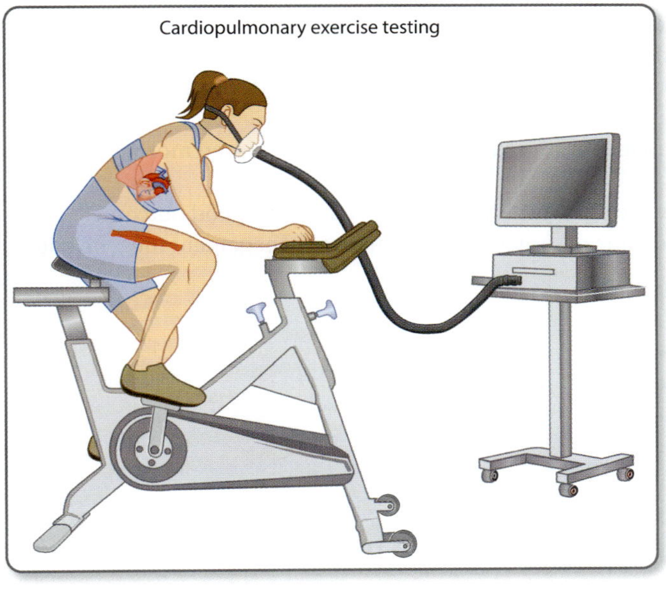

Figure 1: Cardiopulmonary exercise test.

monitoring of oxygen utilisation as well as the carbon dioxide output. ECG, heart rate, and blood pressure are recorded simultaneously. The ECG tracing is done throughout the procedure much like the cardiac exercise testing, and the procedure is stopped if abnormality is detected on the ECG. The threshold at which the metabolism switches from aerobic to anaerobic metabolism can be calculated; this is the anaerobic threshold (AT).

Anaerobic threshold

The AT is that point during exercise when the rise in lactate due to exercise can no longer be buffered by bicarbonate.

At this point, there is an increased production of CO_2. The base excess goes down, and the lactate and CO_2 increase sharply. Technological progress has made it possible to immediately measure this change. Computerisation provides an easy-to-read report. The test is normally performed and reported by consultant anaesthetists with the report suggesting levels of fitness and suitability of the patient for different types of surgery. If the AT is very low, the patient may be deemed unsuitable for surgical intervention.

The oxygen demand goes up after surgery and stays high in the early postoperative period. Knowing the level of activity at which a patient switches from aerobic to anaerobic metabolism will help in:

- Postoperative planning
- Delivery of surgical treatment
- Delayed delivery of surgical treatment
- Non-delivery of surgical treatment

Aerobic capacity is a marker of the ability of the patient to meet the higher oxygen demand that will be necessary after surgery.

The patients who might benefit from this assessment are as follows:

- Patients who are scheduled for major non-cardiac operative procedure
- Patients in need of assessment of lung and cardiac function
- Evaluating recovery for rehabilitation after surgery

The cardiopulmonary exercise test is done a week to 2 weeks preoperatively, giving time to decide on the type of intervention that will be of benefit to the patient.

It must be appreciated that *prehabilitation* may help to improve the performance of some patients and deny surgical treatment to some.

Poor functional status can manifest as cardiac problems and increased mortality in the postoperative period.

If the patient does not meet the demands that will be needed for a good outcome, discussions about risks and benefits of surgery and alternative management must be had with the patient.

Chapter 41

Suture materials

The suture materials used for surgery fall into the following categories:

- *Absorbable*:
  - Braided
  - Non-braided
  - Organic
  - Synthetic
- *Non-absorbable*:
  - Non-synthetic
  - Synthetic

The current generation of absorbable sutures are strong and thus have contributed a lot towards replacement of non-absorbable sutures with reduction in 'stitch sinuses' that used to be a complication of non-absorbable sutures such as thread and silk.

Absorbable sutures

These sutures 'dissolve' over time due to proteolytic action. They do not need removal when used for approximating skin. The story began with *catgut* made from the mucosa of young sheep (kid) intestine. They are still in use in different parts of the world. *The plain catgut gets absorbed in seven days.* To make it resistant to dissolution by the proteolytic enzymes of the body, they were chromium-coated and labelled 'chromic catgut'. *Chromic catgut is normally absorbed in 21 days.* Sometimes they take longer.

Currently in most parts of the world, the absorbable sutures used are synthetic.

They are as follows:

- Polyglycolic acid – Dexon
- Polyglactin – Vicryl
- Poly-dioxanone – PDS
- Poliglecaprone – Monocryl

These can be used for abdominal wound closures and for approximation of subcutaneous tissue and skin.

They may be physically detectable in wounds for up to 6 months however they lose their strength over time.

The wounds are only half as strong as normal tissue at 42 days after surgery, and they are 90% as strong as the normal for that patient in 6 months. They are also weakest at 8 days, the time when traditionally patients used to be discharged.

In patients with recurrent laparotomies, it may be preferable to offer them external support such as an abdominal corset for up to 6 weeks after surgery.

Non-absorbable sutures

Non-absorbable sutures are used when it is important to ensure that the wounds remain stronger for longer. One needs to reflect on the fact that approximating paper with steel will only tear the paper! Finally, it is the nature of the tissue and the process of healing and degree of mechanical support that will determine the strength of the wound. The sutures merely bring edges together so nature can build a bridge.

Commonly used non-absorbable sutures are as follows:

- Polypropylene
- Polyester
- Nylon
- Silk (rarely used now)

Chapter 42

Postoperative pain control

Postoperative pain control and analgesics

The presence of pain in the postoperative period is detrimental to postoperative progress.

Postoperative pain may be a manifestation of *prolonged surgery* and provision of poor pain control.

The consequences of pain especially after laparotomy affect the respiratory system and then the cardiovascular system. The most obvious manifestation of postoperative abdominal pain is *shallow breathing.* Shallow breathing leads to restricted pulmonary movements. This circulates *dead space* air which is richer in carbon dioxide than freshly inhaled air. It is not just the rate that matters but also the depth of respiration. *Deeper the breathing greater the oxygenation.* Increased rate of respiration with shallow breathing may yet lead to hypoxia because of breathing dead space air that is low in oxygen and thus with low FiO_2. The shallow breathing can also lead to atelectasis and in some elderly patients to subsequent pneumonia, sepsis and cardiac failure.

The opiates that are the queen of analgesics need to be used appropriately to enable early mobilisation and improved chest movement.

Paracetamol

Reduces pain and pyrexia but not inflammation. The mechanism of action is unclear. Pain is due to the production of prostaglandins following injury. Prostaglandins potentiate pain that is caused by inflammatory mediators such as histamine and bradykinin. They sensitise the nerve endings and manifest as pain. It is believed that paracetamol must act in some way to decrease the effect of prostaglandins possibly by suppressing cyclo-oxygenase-2 (COX2). The mechanism of action may be a combination of central and peripheral effects. *Paracetamol also acts on the hypothalamus to bring down the temperature.*

Non-steroidal anti-inflammatory drugs

This group of drugs includes aspirin, ibuprofen and diclofenac sodium. They are classified into non-selective and selective NSAIDs based on their action on cyclo-oxygenase (COX).

They *reversibly* inhibit these enzymes unlike aspirin which *irreversibly* inhibits the enzyme thus affecting platelets for their lifetime of 8–9 days. This is the reason that aspirin effects take a week to be abolished.

Cyclo-oxygenase 1 (COX-1): This enzyme has a physiological protective function on gastric and intestinal epithelium, renal and platelet aggregation function. As is obvious, the organs involved in the side effects mirror the inhibition of the protective function of this enzyme. Thromboxane A2 is synthesised in platelets through COX-1 enzyme activity causing vasoconstriction and platelet aggregation. Aspirin inhibits this irreversibly, reducing platelet aggregation and production.

Cyclo-oxygenase-2 (COX-2): It is unexpressed normally but it is driven by *inflammation and is referred to as inflammatory* prostaglandin.

Inhibition of COX-1 and -2 in a non-selective or selective way provides relief from pain. Selective COX-2 inhibitors do not cause gastric symptoms but their side effects include cardiac and cerebrovascular accidents (CVAs) related problems.

Opiates

Opiates are derivatives of opium. Morphine is the queen of analgesics. There are many types of opiates, but the commonly used ones are *morphine, pethidine (demerol) and codeine. Fentanyl and heroin* are other types in use for sedation and analgesia.

The opiates act agonistically on specific receptors called *Mu, delta and kappa.* Presynaptic Mu receptors inhibit release of excitatory neurotransmitters like P substance and glutamate. Post synaptic Mu receptors inhibit neuro transmission by hyper polarisation of the post synaptic neurons. By acting agonistically, morphine enhances these effects. Morphine and derivatives act on μ-receptors present in the *dorsal horn of the spinal cord* and the central nervous system especially in areas related to pain such as *thalamus* and *peri-aqueductal grey.* These receptors are also found in the respiratory system and gastrointestinal system (hence respiratory depression and constipation are side effects of morphine). Codeine, though less effective than morphine, is less addictive and is more commonly used.

In the postoperative period, morphine can be prescribed as a PCA or patient-controlled analgesia. This is possible only when the patient has capacity and does not have any mechanical problems such as arthritis or neurological deficits that restrict movements of the hands. It is very useful in patients who can understand the principles of PCA. Language may thus be a barrier.

Prescription writing for these drugs is very stringent requiring the dosage to be written in words as well as in numbers. Always refer to the national formulary prior to writing it and follow the protocols required for the respective country.

Gabapentin

This is an anti-convulsant which also benefits neuropathic pain such as post-herpetic pain.

In 2018, a meta-analysis showed that it was of no benefit for sciatica but had benefitted the spasticity of multiple sclerosis. It must be appreciated that gabapentin is not an analgesic in the routine sense of the term.

Patient-controlled analgesia

When a patient controls the amount of analgesia needed, it is more effective than non-patient-controlled analgesia.

Patient-controlled analgesia can be instilled through:

- Central lines
- Peripheral veins
- Epidural lines
- Through skin, i.e. fentanyl patch with a button to press.

The system was introduced in the 1970s but has evolved to different types of pumps to deliver the medication through the various lines.

The main *components* are:

- Patient-controlled button – for self-delivery
- A mechanical pump
- Medication chamber – containing either opiate alone or opiate and a local anaesthetic, normally, bupivacaine
- Programming screen – for minimum effective dose to be run in the background with lock out period
- *Locking device* – to prevent overdosing by the patient or by proxy by relatives

The *contraindications* to its use:

- Lack of capacity on the part of the patient
- Inability to comprehend the system – language barrier
- Inability to use the hand to manipulate the button, e.g. rheumatoid arthritis
- Allergy to medications
- Chronic renal failure, anti-thrombotic therapy, sleep apnoea and bleeding disorder

Further reading

1. Pastino A, Lakra A. Patient-Controlled Analgesia. In: StatPearls [Internet]. Treasure Island (FL): StatPearls Publishing, 2025.

Chapter 43

Local anaesthesia

The most common agent is *lignocaine,* also called 'Lidocaine and xylocaine'.

- It has been in use since 1948
- It is the most used local anaesthetic throughout the world
- It acts by inhibiting sodium channels and when infiltrated close to nerves, it closes the sodium channel and thus stops propagation of nerve conduction. In the heart, the same effect decreases the rate and, hence, it is useful in managing ventricular arrhythmias when amiodarone is contraindicated
- It acts more rapidly than bupivacaine
- Bupivacaine, however, is longer acting

Combining lignocaine with adrenaline:

- Reduces bleeding
- Doubles the duration of action due to the accompanying vasoconstriction leading to slower absorption
- Doubles the quantity that can be used from 3.5 mg/kg body weight to 7 mg

Toxicity is manifest as *central nervous system (CNS) and cardiovascular system (CVS) effects.*

- *Central nervous system:* Circumoral tingling and numbness, anxiety, agitation and seizures leading to confusion and coma
- *Cardiovascular system:* Hypotension, bradycardia, arrhythmia and cardiac arrest
- *Other side effects:* Tinnitus and urticaria

Management of toxicity is by recognising excess dosage, stopping the infusion of local anaesthesia (as in epidural analgesia) and giving immediate *intravenous lipid emulsion* infusion.

Other local anaesthetic drugs

- *Bupivacaine hydrochloride*: Slow but longer action compared to others
- *Prilocaine hydrochloride*: It has a low toxicity

Epidural analgesia

According to the faculty of pain management of the Royal College of Anaesthetists, epidural anaesthesia is very effective in the management of postoperative pain.

- Continuous epidural analgesia has major implications and so needs an informed consent
- There must be 24-hour access to expert care and advice
- Anticoagulant usage prior to inserting epidural, during insertion and removal and initiating treatment while epidural is in use can all have complications, leading to haematoma and worse, paralysis

- Aseptic principles apply from the time of insertion to removal
- Some degree of sensory block may occur
- Monitoring complications while the epidural is in use will promote early action
- *Complications*:
  - Infection
  - Abscess
  - Haematoma
  - Hypotension: Other postoperative causes such as bleeding and myocardial infarction need to be excluded
  - Post-epidural headache
  - Increasing motor blockage (Bromage scale)
  - Urinary retention
  - Pruritus if opiate is used
  - Neuropraxia or nerve damage
  - Total spinal – a sinister complication with respiratory arrest and cardiovascular collapse. The patient will need supportive therapy in the ITU.
  - Failure of analgesia

Bromage scale scores the degree of block:

- Complete paralysis
- Foot movement alone
- Foot and just able to flex knee
- Full range of movement

When there is complete paralysis, overdosage or pressure effect due to haematoma or abscess must be suspected.

Chapter 44

Epidural infusion care

- Epidural infusion bags will need replacing every 24 hours even if not fully used
- The epidural catheter is removed in 3–4 days to prevent the risk of infection and sepsis
- Aseptic care must be always provided even at times of manipulation of kinks or disconnections
- The infusate is typically normal saline with added local anaesthetic and/or opiate:
  - *Standard infusion* with fentanyl 2 μg/mL in 250 mL of 0.1% bupivacaine
  - *Opiate free infusion* – 250 mL of 0.125% bupivacaine

The infusion rate can be titrated to control pain. It will vary from 2 to 15 mL/h.

Respiratory rate must be monitored as excess dosage will suppress respiration. If respiratory suppression due to excess dosage is suspected, naloxone 400 μg must be given immediately and titrated with incremental dosage till there is a reversal of respiratory suppression.

Rectus sheath catheter

- This avoids complications of epidural anaesthesia as the effect provided is limited to the abdominal wall
- There are very few systemic effects other than those related to the local anaesthetic infiltration
- The procedure is carried out under vision prior to closing the abdomen
- The catheter is inserted posterior to the rectus muscle but anterior to the posterior sheath
- This plane is easy to access during the first laparotomy
- Finding this plane in re-operations may be difficult

Infusate

Normally 400 mL of 0.125% bupivacaine is infused at the rate of 10 mL/h.

Transabdominal plane block (TAP block)

- This block is instilled in the anterolateral abdominal wall in the intermuscular plane between the internal oblique and the transversus abdominis
- When instilled under ultrasound guidance in the correct plane, it blocks the dermatomes (T6 to L1) of the mid and lower abdomen from the midline to the mid-clavicular line
- It is effective for up to 24 hours
- Instillation is done at the time of surgery

Chapter 45

Antibiotics and surgery

Currently, most of the hospitals have guidelines on the use of antibiotics in different circumstances. There is also a greater input from the microbiologists in most hospitals. Management of postoperative infections or sepsis will require discussions with microbiologists. It is important to follow-up on culture and sensitivities that may have been requested during surgery as very often results are not reviewed in good time and this may lead to further complications or increased length of stay. In certain hospitals, the need for intravenous antibiotics does not restrict the patient to inpatient stay but an outpatient facility which is nurse driven allows the patient to continue treatment at home.
Briefly the antibiotics are divided into two groups.

1. Bactericidal
2. Bacteriostatic

Bactericidal drugs – these kill the bacteria by destroying the cell wall or damaging the cell content.

- *Beta-lactams (penicillin, cephalosporin and carbapenem)*: Amoxicillin, cefazolin and meropenem
- *Aminoglycosides*: Tobramycin, gentamicin and amikacin
- *Fluoroquinolones*: Ciprofloxacin, levofloxacin and moxifloxacin
- *Glycopeptides*: Vancomycin
- *Nitroimidazoles*: Metronidazole (strictly not an antibiotic as antibiotics are substances that are made by live organisms against other live organisms. Many antibiotics nowadays are synthetic. Metronidazole has an important role managing anaerobic infections)

Bacteriostatic drugs – these slow the growth of bacteria but do not kill them.

- Chloramphenicol
- Tetracyclines
- Clindamycin
- Ethambutol
- *Macrolides*: Erythromycin, clarithromycin and azithromycin
- Nitrofurantoin
- Novobiocin
- Oxazolidinone

Antibiotic resistance – WHO statement:
Bacteria, not humans or animals, become antibiotic-resistant. These bacteria may infect humans and animals, and the infections they cause are harder to treat than those caused by non-resistant bacteria.

- Antibiotic resistance is one of the biggest threats to global health, food security and development today
- Antibiotic resistance when acquired by an organism can affect anyone, of any age, in any country
- Antibiotic resistance occurs naturally, but misuse of antibiotics in humans and animals is accelerating the process
- A growing number of infections – such as pneumonia, tuberculosis, gonorrhoea, and salmonellosis – are becoming harder to treat as the antibiotics used to treat them become less effective
- Antibiotic resistance leads to longer hospital stays, higher medical costs and increased mortality

Antibiotic resistance can be reduced by sticking to guidelines and prescribing only the appropriate dose for the appropriate length of time.

If antibiotic resistance is noted on culture and sensitivity, it must be notified to the surveillance committee in the respective hospitals.

Above all the most important factor in surgical patients is to always ensure strict hygiene and sterilisation thus reducing the chances of infection.

Gentle surgical handling and reduction of haemorrhage during surgery will contribute to decreased postoperative infections.

Chapter 46

Proton pump inhibitors

H2-blockers and proton pump inhibitors

These are used universally, and a working knowledge of these powerful drugs that have changed the face of surgery is essential.

The discovery of H2-blocker, cimetidine by Sir James Black at GlaxoSmithKline in the mid-1960s, and its introduction in 1976 changed the management of dyspeptic disease, peptic ulcer disease and gastro-oesophageal reflux disease (GORD) forever.

H1-blockers are the usual antihistamines that block responses to common problems such as hay fever and common cold. They are anti-allergic.

H2-receptors are found in the parietal cells of the stomach.

H2-blockers block the histamine release-related acid production in the stomach. They have now been surpassed by the most efficient *proton pump inhibitors (PPIs)* such as omeprazole and pantoprazole.

The *proton/potassium pump* is a membrane pump that is located in the gastric mucosa. As its name suggests, it exchanges hydrogen (proton) for potassium and releases the hydrogen into the gastric lumen forming acid.

Blocking this is the most effective way of reducing acid production in the stomach. It has superseded the H2-inhibitors purely because of its effectiveness with almost complete blockage of acid production.

Uses of proton pump inhibitor

- Short-term treatment of peptic ulcer disease
- As part of the treatment of *H. pylori* eradication
- Gastro-oesophageal reflux disease
- Prevention of non-steroidal anti-inflammatory drugs (NSAIDs)-related peptic ulcers
- Dyspeptic symptoms - short-term use for 4 weeks

Many people take PPIs over the long-term without appropriate indication.

Patients who are treated with the PPI while an inpatient continues to take it on discharge. These drugs are available over the counter. The implications of long-term treatment are becoming clearer now.

Long-term effects are:

- Calcium and magnesium malabsorption
- B12 deficiency
- *Clostridium difficile* associated disease (CDAD)
- Chronic kidney disease (CKD)
- Dementia

Calcium deficiency can lead to fractures with a 35% risk in hip fractures in women who used PPIs regularly for 2 years.

Table 1 Proton pump inhibitor (PPI) doses in the management of *dyspepsia* symptoms

PPI	Standard dose	Double dose
Omeprazole	20 mg/day	40 mg *once a day*
Lansoprazole	30 mg/day	30 mg twice a day
Pantoprazole	40 mg/day	40 mg twice a day
Rabeprazole	20 mg/day	20 mg twice a day
Esomeprazole	20 mg/day	40 mg *once a day*

Magnesium deficiency has a prevalence of 1% in those using PPIs long-term and it can lead to cardiac arrhythmias.

Dial and colleagues conducted a multicentre case control study to determine whether gastric acid suppression increases the risk of *Clostridium difficile-associated disease (CDAD).* Compared with patients who did not take a gastric acid suppressant, those taking the PPI had a 2.9-fold increase in developing CDAD.

Clostridium difficile is killed in an acid stomach, but it colonises an antacid stomach and can thus lead to infections in some patients.

Lazarus and colleagues evaluated the association between PPI use and the incidence of *chronic kidney disease (CKD).* Their analysis was performed in a long-term running population-based cohort and replicated in a separate healthcare system. In the running cohort, patients receiving a PPI had a 1.45-fold greater chance of developing CKD. In that same cohort, patients on the PPI had a 1.72-fold increased risk of acute kidney injury (AKI). Similar outcomes were seen in the replicated cohort. However, the replicated cohort did observe that *twice daily dosing* of the PPI had a *stronger association with CKD* than once daily dosing.

***National Institute for Health and Care Excellence (NICE) Guidance 2019**: **A proton pump inhibitor** should be prescribed for appropriate indications at the lowest effective dose for the shortest period **(Table 1)**; the need for long-term treatment should be reviewed periodically.*

The recommended doses of PPIs for the *H. pylori* eradication therapy.

Omeprazole	20–40 mg twice daily
Lansoprazole	30 mg twice daily
Pantoprazole	40 mg twice daily
Rabeprazole	20 mg twice daily
Esomeprazole	20 mg twice daily

Proton pump inhibitor usage in gastro-oesophageal reflux disease:

In reflux disease, the maximum damage occurs at night and the optimal level of acidity of pH > 4 is reached 6 hours after the intake of the PPI. In the author's view a dose prior dinner may be more desirable. The standard recommendation is for PPI to be consumed before or after breakfast. Pre-prandial dose has been shown to be of marginally greater benefit.

Further reading

1. Lehault WB, Hughes DM. Review of the Long-term effects of proton pump inhibitors. Fed Pract 2017; 34:19–23.

Chapter 47

Diabetes and surgery

In terms of ward care, the get it right first (GIRFT) programme in the UK found that *people with diabetes undergoing surgery had an excess length of stay of 3 days.* This is related, at least in part, to suboptimal inpatient diabetes management. The implications of insulin resistance have been discussed in an earlier chapter.

The suboptimal level of inpatient care for diabetics increases the duration of their inpatient treatment.
The capillary blood glucose (CBG) in the perioperative period should be maintained between 6 and 12 mmol or 110 to 210 mg/dL.

The discussion here is based on the perioperative management of the surgical patient with diabetes 2015 (Nathanson MH, Dhatariya K) (Reviewed in 2020).

The following are some of their *key statements and recommendations:*

- Studies have shown that high preoperative and perioperative glucose and glycated haemoglobin (HbA1c) levels are associated with poor surgical outcomes. These findings have been seen in both elective and emergency surgery
- One study showed that the adverse outcomes may be due to *failure to identify diabetes* or hyperglycaemia, *polypharmacy* with unrecognised errors in prescription, as well as presence of *comorbidities* including *micro- and macrovascular disease.* The adverse outcomes in such patients include:
  - Greater than 50% increase in *mortality*
  - 2.4-fold increase in the incidence of postoperative *respiratory infections*
  - Doubling of *surgical site infections*
  - Threefold increase in postoperative *urinary tract infections*
  - Doubling in the incidence of *myocardial infarction*
  - Almost twofold increase in *acute kidney injury*

Paradoxically, there are data showing outcomes of patients with diabetes may not differ from non-diabetics if diabetes is recognised and addressed before surgery. The reasons for this may be due to increased vigilance surrounding glucose control for those with diabetes.

Recommendations

- Glycaemic control should be checked at the time of referral for surgery
- Information about duration, type of diabetes, current treatment and complications should be made available to the secondary care team
- Preoperative testing should include urea and electrolytes and ECG for all patients with diabetes; however, a random blood glucose measurement is not indicated

- *Surgery should be scheduled at the start of the theatre list* to minimise disruption to the patient's glycaemic control
- With appropriate guidance, patients with diabetes should be allowed to retain control and possession of, and continue to self-administer, their medication. *Many patients will have several years' experience and be experts in self-medication*
- The aim is to avoid hypo- or hyperglycaemia during the period of fasting and the time during and after the procedure, until the patient is eating and drinking normally
- *All patients must have their CBG (capillary blood glucose) checked on admission on the day of surgery*

Guidelines for patients on *insulin* for operations with short starvation period with *no more than one missed meal*

Those on *once daily dose* with drugs like Lantus insulin:
- Reduce dose by 20% on the day before surgery
- Check blood glucose on admission
- If a patient requires *variable-rate intravenous insulin infusion (VRIII)* (see below) then continue at 80% of the usual dose

Those on *twice daily insulin*, short-acting, (Novorapid and humulin S), and long-acting insulin
- No dose change needed on the previous day
- Halve the usual morning dose; check blood glucose on admission; leave evening meal dose unchanged
- If VRIII is being administered, then stop the insulin

Guideline for perioperative adjustment of oral hypoglycaemic agents (short starvation period - no more than one missed meal) is also available on https://doi.org/10.1111/anae.14663

Drugs that require omission when fasting due to risk of hypoglycaemia:
- Drugs such as sulphonyl urea (e.g. glibenclamide, gliclazide and glipizide)
- Take normally on the day before surgery
- For *morning operations* if once daily dosage, then *omit the morning dose.* If on a twice daily dose, then omit the morning dose
- For *afternoon operations* omit the drug for the day
- If VRIII is being used, *stop* oral medications until eating and drinking normally

Drugs that require omission when fasting *due to risk of ketoacidosis*
- Sodium-glucose cotransporter-2 (SGLT-2)
- Similar to management of sulphonylurea

Drugs that may be continued when fasting:
- Metformin, acarbose, dipeptidyl peptidase IV (DPP-IV) inhibitor [e.g. sitagliptin, glucagon-like peptide-1 (GLP-1) analogue (e.g. exenatide, and pioglitazone)]

Use of a variable-rate intravenous insulin infusion

- Variable-rate intravenous insulin infusions are preferred in patients who will miss more than one meal
- Those with type 1 diabetes mellitus undergoing surgery who have not received background insulin

- Those with poorly controlled diabetes (defined as a HbA1c > 69 mmol/mol, 8.5%)
- Most patients with diabetes requiring emergency surgery
- Variable-rate intravenous insulin infusions should be administered and monitored by appropriately experienced and qualified staff

Glycaemic control in patients with diabetes is a balance between their carbohydrate intake and utilisation (e.g. exercise). It also depends on what medication they take and how those medications work.

The time of day and the expected duration of the operation need to be considered, as well whether the VRIII will be needed.

Patients with continuous subcutaneous insulin infusions only missing one meal should be advised to maintain their CBG at 6–10 mmol/L. If longer periods of starvation are predicted, a VRIII should be used and specialist advice sought.

Further readings

1. Nathanson MH, Dhatariya K. Peri-operative management of the surgical patient with diabetes 2015. Anaesthesia 2019; 74:810.
2. Frisch A, Chandra P, Smiley D, et al. Prevalence and clinical outcome of hyperglycemia in the perioperative period in noncardiac surgery. Diabetes Care 2010; 33:1783–1788.
3. Kwon S, Thompson R, Dellinger P, et al. Importance of perioperative glycemic control in general surgery: a report from the surgical care and outcomes assessment program. Ann Surg 2013; 257:8–14.

Chapter 48

Oxygen

Oxygen should be treated as a drug.

It is perhaps the most common drug that is used in surgical emergencies.

It should certainly be one of the first drugs in sepsis and shock. In most acutely ill patients, an oxygen saturation of 94–98% is desirable.

The delivery of oxygen can be:

- *High concentration oxygen therapy (high flow)* is used in patients with sepsis, pneumonia, hypotension and anaphylaxis. In these patients, there is little risk of CO_2 retention. The respiratory rate is high. Both the oxygen and CO_2 levels are likely to be low. The oxygen saturation target should be above 94% saturation
- *Low concentration oxygen* is used in patients with chronic obstructive pulmonary disease (COPD). The oxygen delivery is targeted with a Venturi mask providing 24% or 28% concentration oxygen to maintain the saturation between 88% and 92%.

The modes of delivery are discussed in the chapter on 'sepsis'. Suffice it to say that commonly, they are delivered by:

- Nasal cannula
- Non-rebreathing mask
- Venturi mask
- Incubator
- CPAP – continuous positive airways pressure
- Intubation and ventilation

Hypoxia is defined as reduced tissue oxygenation. This is classified as:

- *Hypoxic hypoxia:* This is the most common type of hypoxia where the oxygenation is reduced due to decreased FiO_2, (high altitude) V/Q mismatch pulmonary embolism (PE), impairment of diffusion [pneumonia and acute respiratory distress syndrome (ARDS)]
- *Hypemic hypoxia:* The oxygen carrying capacity is decreased due to anaemia. Carbon monoxide poisoning is also a rare cause but most quoted
- *Stagnant hypoxia:* The circulation is not able to deliver the oxygen to the tissues as in shock where the circulatory system is unable to meet the needs of the tissue due to reduced circulatory volume
- *Histotoxic hypoxia:* This is seen when the system is wrecked as with cyanide poisoning – more common in the novels of Agatha Christie

Hypoxaemia is reduced partial pressure of oxygen in blood. This can be due to:

- Hypoventilation
- Low inspired PO_2

- V/Q mismatch
- Right-to-left shunt
- Impairment of diffusion

Low saturation may be noted when there is:
- Tachypnoea
- Dyspnoea
- Apnoea
- Tachycardia and hypotension
- Confusion and memory loss

Extra-corporeal membrane oxygenation (ECMO): This is used in the intensive care unit in patients with cardiopulmonary complications of sepsis that fail to respond to various ventilatory manipulations. It can also be used as a bridge prior to cardiopulmonary transplantation. The ECMO machine has a membrane oxygenator, which acts as an artificial lung and exchanges oxygen and carbon dioxide from blood.
- *Venoarterial ECMO*: In this type of ECMO, the blood bypasses the heart completely. The blood is drawn out of a major vein and pumped back by the ECMO machine into a major artery
- *Venovenous ECMO*: This supports lungs alone when cardiac function is unaffected

Chapter 49

Fat embolism

Fat embolism occurs after any long bone fractures. Early treatment of long bone fractures may decrease the incidence of systemic presentation referred to as the *fat embolism syndrome (FES)* a triad of involvement of lung, kin and brain.

While emboli of fat have been noted close to the site of orthopaedic injury in a high proportion of patients, the systemic manifestation is less common. There are no diagnostic tools and it remains an empirical diagnosis based on the multiorgan effects.

The organs most affected are:

- *Lungs* – manifests as hypoxia requiring support with oxygen or even ventilation if it proceeds to acute respiratory distress syndrome (ARDS)
- *Brain* – anxiety or irritability and decrease in Glasgow Coma scale (GCS). This is due to cerebral oedema
- *Skin* – petechial rashes.

Pathophysiology

- *Fat emboli theory:* Fat embolises to venous sinusoids during reaming or at the time of injury. These emboli move to pulmonary capillaries and cause hypoxia due to ventilation perfusion mismatch.
- *Biochemical theory* was advanced because *emboli* have been found in the systemic capillaries and that is difficult to explain by the above fat emboli hypothesis alone. It is thought that inflammatory response to trauma releases free-fatty acids from the marrow and this leads to hypoxia.

Risk factors

- Young age
- Closed fractures
- Multiple fractures
- Conservative therapy for long-bone fractures

Management

- It is essentially early recognition based on clinical suspicion and initiation of *supportive therapy*
- Steroids have been tried but with little effect on mortality and morbidity
- Ventilatory support may be needed for a length of time. This will also assist with the management of cerebral oedema

Prevention

- The early fixation of long-bone fracture is important to prevent or to decrease the severity of FES
- External fixation or fixation with plate and screw produces lesser lung injury than nailing the medullary cavity and venting the medullary canal during nailing, reduces the number of emboli

Further readings

1. Nixon JR, Brock-Utne JG. Free fatty acid and arterial oxygen changes following major injury. A correlation between hypoxemia and increased free fatty acid level. J Trauma 1978; 18:23–26.
2. Behrman SW, Fabian TC, Kudsk KA, Taylor JC. Improved outcome with femur fracture: Early VS delayed fixation. J Trauma 1990; 30:792–797.
3. Wheelwright EF, Byrick RJ, Wigglesworth DF, et al. Hypotension during cemented arthoplasty, relationship with cardiac output and fat embolism. J Bone Joint Surg Br 1993; 75:715–723.

Chapter 50

Post-splenectomy care

Splenectomy increases the lifelong risk of overwhelming infection both in children and in adults. *The risk of the post-splenectomy septic syndrome is not abolished by vaccines.*

Non-operative management of haemodynamically stable patients with isolated splenic injury and splenorrhaphy in patients requiring laparotomy are options that need consideration because of all the risks of splenectomy.

Splenic autotransplantation and lifelong prophylactic antibiotic therapy have been used but their effectiveness is not established.

Post-splenectomy specific complications relate to:

- *Thrombocytosis* – which presents as deep vein thrombosis or in patients with liver disease, portal vein thrombosis. Platelet counts after splenectomy have been reported to increase 30–100%, with a peak reached at 7–20 days postoperatively. The thrombocytosis may need antiplatelet therapy if platelet level keeps rising. The risk of stroke rises with thrombocytosis. Platelet counts >1,000 k/μL will need antiplatelet therapy but there are no agreed levels at which the treatment needs to be initiated. The author favours treatment if trend over time shows platelets rising beyond 500 k/μL. Low-molecular weight heparin may also need.
- *Predisposition to bacterial infection,* commonly encapsulated bacteria. These are *Streptococcus pneumoniae* (*Pneumococcus*), *Neisseria meningitidis* (Meningococcal) and *Haemophilus influenzae.*
- *Other complications:*
  - Intraoperative haemorrhage
  - Pancreatitis
  - Pancreatic fistula
  - Pulmonary embolism
  - Atelectasis and pulmonary infections
  - Postoperative infections and abdominal sepsis
  - Death

The infections are more common in children and in the first 2 years after surgery. Adults are less prone but there is the potential to develop *overwhelming post-splenectomy sepsis,* and this justifies the need to take preventive measures. This includes:

- *Patient's education:* About the risk of infections.
- *Vaccinations:* The British Haematological Society recommends the following vaccinations from 2 weeks prior to surgery to 2 weeks post-surgery:
  - Pneumococcal
  - Meningococcal C, A and B
  - *H. influenzae* B conjugate
  - Seasonal influenza

- *Antibiotics:* Penicillin or erythromycin if allergic to penicillin. Lifelong in adults, but if compliance is a problem for at least 2 years. In children, it is needed till the age of 16 years or at least 2 years.

Further readings

1. Shatney CH. Complications of splenectomy. Acta Anaesthesiol Belg 1987; 38:333–339. PMID: 3327338.
2. Greer JP, Foerste J, Lukens JN, et al. Wintrobe's Clinical Hematology, 11th edition. Philadelphia: Lippincott Williams & Wilkins, 1981:1128–1134.

Chapter 51

Hypothermia

Hypothermia (**Figure 1**) is defined as a temperature of <35°C or a core temperature <36°C.

Hypothermia is dangerous because it affects multiple organ systems such as the central nervous system (CNS) and cardiovascular system (CVS) leading progressively to loss of consciousness, cardiac arrhythmias and if uncorrected to death.

Body heat is lost during surgery by:

- *Conduction:* Heat loss by direct contact with the operating table
- *Evaporation:* Open abdominal wound under warm theatre light. Fluid is lost by transformation to gas. Excessive sweating is another cause
- *Radiation:* It is the most common. The body emits electromagnetic energy to the surrounding cold bodies in theatre
- Respiration
- *Vasodilatation:* Sepsis or anaesthesia-induced dilatation circulates warm blood to cold peripheries from which fluid may be lost

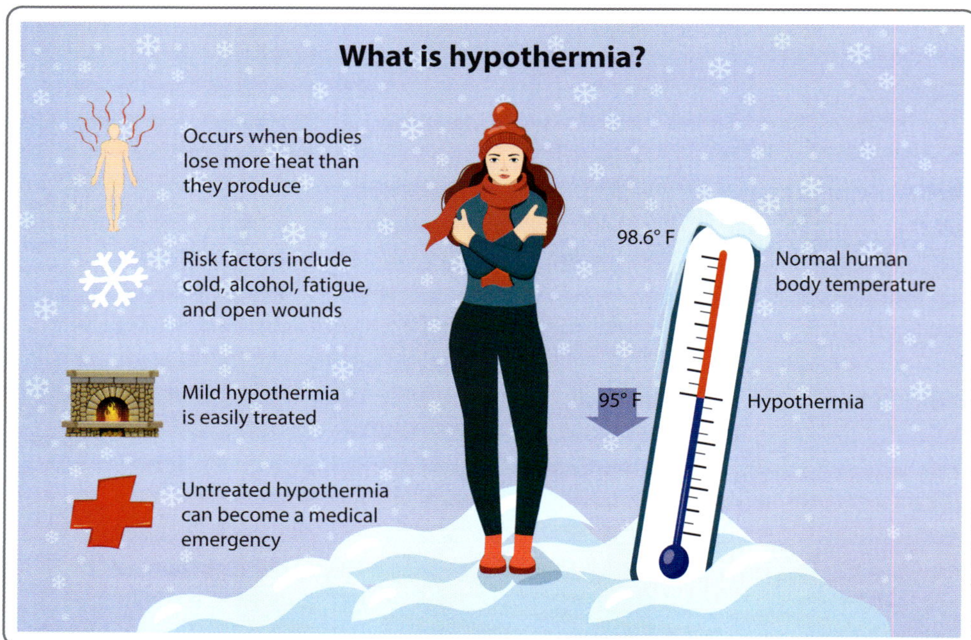

Figure 1 Depicting hypothermia.

During prolonged operations these factors must be borne in mind as hypothermia can lead to coagulopathy and bleeding due to impaired platelet function.

Hypothermia may also precipitate myocardial ischaemia.

Risk factors for hypothermia

- The elderly
- Infants
- Mentally ill
- Under clothed hikers

Hospital treatment is directed towards rewarming of core temperature by:

- *Passive warming*: Covering the person with blankets and giving them warm drinks
- *Blood rewarming*: Warming with warm intravenous fluids or even a haemodialysis machine in extreme situations
- *Airway rewarming*: Applying humidified oxygen through a mask or nasal tube
- Irrigation of the body with warm salt water

Chapter 52

Surgery and hormones

Every type of surgery causes a stress response that in many patients understandably begins well before the actual operation. *The magnitude of the response is proportional to the severity of the surgical intervention.* Minor operations like hernia repair may show little evidence of the phenomenal hormonal response that comes into play after major operations, complications and sepsis. This has been addressed in the chapter on metabolic response to surgery.

The hypothalamus, pituitary and target glands of adrenal, thyroid and gonads play a major role in a beautiful negative feedback system (**Figures 1 and 2**). These systems are classified as:

- *HPA* – hypothalamus–pituitary–adrenal axis (**Figure 2**)
- *HPT* – hypothalamus–pituitary–thyroid axis (**Figure 2**)
- *HPG* – hypothalamus–pituitary–gonadal axis

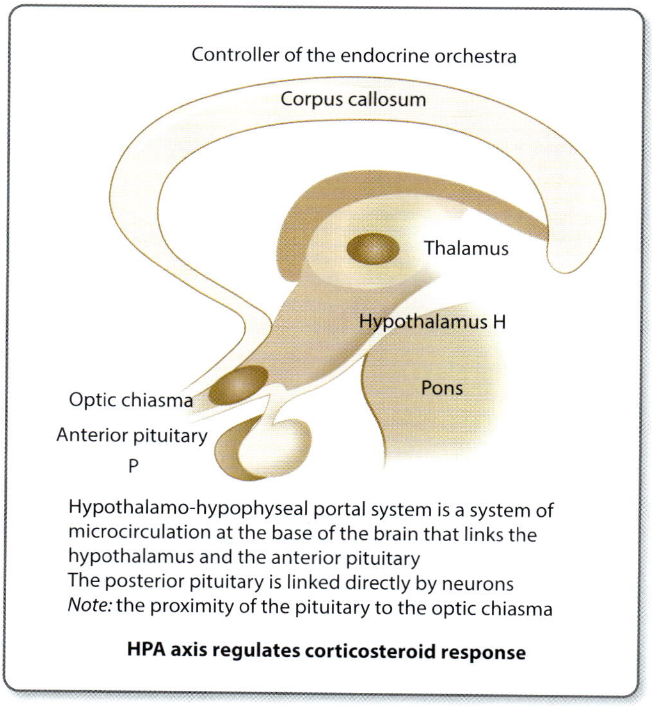

Figure 1 Corpus callosum and hypothalamus–pituitary–adrenal (HPA) axis.

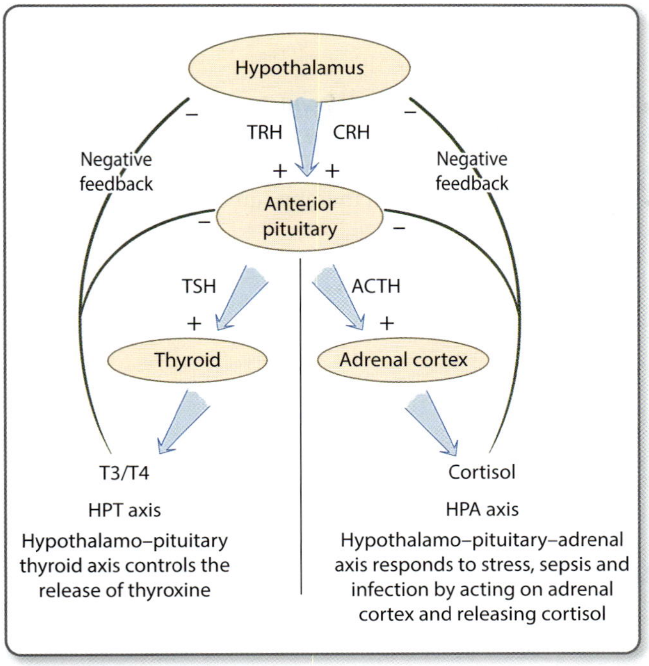

Figure 2 Hormonal regulation via the hypothalamic–pituitary axis (HPA).
ACTH, adrenocorticotropic hormone; CRH, corticotropin-releasing hormone; HPT, hypothalamic–pituitary–thyroid axis; TRH, thyrotropin-releasing hormone; TSH, thyroid-stimulating hormone.

Four of the key hormones in surgical response are:

1. Adrenaline/Noradrenaline
2. Glucocorticoids
3. Insulin
4. Thyroid hormone

The other hormones that need attention because of their role in clinical management are:

- Parathormone and its role in calcium homeostasis
- Calcitonin
- Oestrogen and its expression and modulation in breast disease

The adrenal gland

It has a cortex and a medulla.
The cortex has three zones – *GFR*.

1. *G*lomerulosa – produces aldosterone
2. *F*asciculata – 75% of the cortex produces glucocorticoids
3. *R*eticularis – produces sex hormones

The medulla: Embryologically, the medulla is part of the sympathetic system and functions like a sympathetic ganglion. It relates purely to the adrenergic response of 'fight and flight'. Medulla produces adrenaline and noradrenaline.

The *four S's and trauma* stimulate the hypothalamus and initiate the endocrine response.

- *S*urgery
- *S*tress

- *S*epsis
- *S*ympathomimetic drugs
- *T*rauma

Patients on long-term steroids will need replacement therapy with hydrocortisone. *The dosage of prednisolone at which the replacement therapy should be initiated is in fact quite low, as low as 5 milligrams a day.* Failure to manage this can lead to an adrenal crisis.

Omitting steroid replacement in patients on long-term therapy can suppress the HPA axis leading to hypotension and cardiovascular collapse.

Clinical manifestations may be:

- Fatigue
- Abdominal pain
- Low Na^+
- High K^+
- Hypotension
- Adrenal crisis manifests by confusion and coma
- Death, if unrecognised

Hormones and calcium

Calcium in plasma

- 55% is unbound, free and filterable
- 45% is bound to plasma proteins
- Plasma proteins bind to both hydrogen ions and calcium ions
- In alkalosis, there is less hydrogen ions. More calcium is, therefore, bound to plasma proteins. This can cause *tetany* because there is less free calcium.

Three hormones regulate calcium levels and maintain calcium homeostasis.

1. *Parathyroid hormone (PTH)* (***Table 1***) secreted by the parathyroid glands
2. *Calcitonin* (***Table 1***) secreted by the parafollicular *C cells* in the thyroid gland
3. *Calcitriol* is produced by the *kidneys.* This is the effective form of *vitamin D (calciferol).*

Table 1 Hormones regulating calcium levels

Parathyroid hormone (PTH)	**Calcitonin**
Produced by parathyroid glands	Produced by parafollicular 'C' cells in the thyroid gland
Increases calcium levels	Decreases calcium levels
PTH production is increased in response to low-calcium levels	Calcitonin production is increased in response to high-calcium levels
Stimulates osteoclastic activity	Inhibits osteoclastic activity
Inhibits osteoblastic activity	Stimulates osteoblastic activity
PTH also acts on the kidney to retain calcium	
Stimulates calcitriol production and increases absorption of calcium from the small bowel	

Parathyroid hormone moves calcium out of the bone by a *slow and rapid process.* The slow process acts on osteoclasts to *increase bone resorption.* The rapid process pushes the calcium out of the bone fluid into the plasma.

- Calcitonin opposes the action of PTH
- Calcitonin decreases serum calcium levels
- Calcitonin is released by a feedback system when the serum calcium increases
- It *stimulates osteoblasts* and deposits calcium into the bone; it also *inhibits osteoclasts* thereby reducing calcium coming out of the bone

Calcitriol is produced by the kidney.
It is the active form of vitamin D.

Vitamin D is obtained from:

- Exposure to ultraviolet (UV) rays of the sun
- From foods
- From supplements

It is inactive.
Activation requires two hydroxylations.

The first 'hydroxylation':

- Occurs in the liver
- Converts vitamin D to 25-hydroxyvitamin D [25(OH)D]
- This is known as *calcidiol.*

The second 'hydroxylation':

- Occurs in the proximal convoluted tubule (PCT) of the kidneys
- Forms the physiologically active 1,25-dihydroxyvitamin D [1,25(OH)2D]
- This is known as *calcitriol*

Calcitriol elevates calcium levels by promoting absorption of calcium by enterocytes.

Calcitriol thus enhances the PTH effect on bone.

Chapter 53

Brain-stem death

*Brain-stem death (**Table 1**) or brain death* is legal death. A person who is brain-dead cannot survive without artificial support. In such a patient, the damage is irreversible.

The brainstem is responsible for autonomic functions of the heart and lungs. It is the track that links the body and the brain in a two-way system with input and output of information leading to awareness and consciousness. Without a functioning brainstem there can be no consciousness.

To declare a person legally dead absence of a functioning brainstem must be established.

*Vegetative state (**Table 1**)* is different from brain death. Unlike brainstem death, the person in a vegetative state has an intact brainstem but no awareness or consciousness.

Brain death is diagnosed when there is:

- Coma
- Absence of brainstem reflexes
- Apnoea

Tests of brain death are:

- Absence of light reflex in both eyes
- Absence of corneal reflex
- Absence of dolls eye movement in a comatose patient
- Absence of eye movement on insertion of cold water into each ear
- Absence of gag reflex
- Absence of response to painful pressure over forehead
- Absence of spontaneous breathing on removal from ventilator

Table 1 Brainstem death versus vegetative state

Brainstem death	Vegetative state
No functioning of brainstem	Functioning brainstem
No consciousness	Some consciousness
No spontaneous respiration	Spontaneous respiration
No possibility of recovery	Slim possibility of recovery
No awareness	Awake without awareness
No response detectable on brain scan	Some response detectable on brain scan

Chapter 54

Ethics

Management of any patient must be tempered with compassion and empathy. The first principle is *primum non nocere*, which translates to 'First do no harm.' To this, I would add, 'Do the best you can.' Always.

The following are factors that need consideration.

- Loss of autonomy
- Withholding or withdrawing treatment
- Futility and frailty
- Consent and capacity
- Combined decision-making
- Deviation from the norm

Loss of autonomy

This is quite difficult to understand, but as you gain experience, the work will teach you. When working in a place of authority, the position confers a degree of authority to the treating healthcare workers. Many patients find it difficult to challenge authority even if its recommendations differ from their wishes.

When a position confers authority, it is necessary to use it with care. Many patients will agree to most things if they like the treating doctor, and they will try to oblige by giving the answers that the doctor expects rather than disagree. Very often, discussions with surrogates and next of kin may help in divining what the patient really wants.

The General Medical Council (GMC) guidance: Withholding and withdrawing treatment is available online.

The possibility of over and under treatment needs careful assessment and clarification with the patient and surrogates. An investigation or treatment need not be provided just because it is available, *but only because it is of benefit to the patient.*

It is also clear that the professionals and patients want more guidance on what is considered ethically and legally permissible in this area.

The patient and their families want greater involvement in making these decisions, with better arrangements to support them when facing these distressing situations.

Futility and frailty

When it comes to futility and frailty, they can be classified as follows.

- Physiological futility
- Anatomical futility
- Social futility

In physiological futility, possibility of *imminent death* is included. An old surgical adage, now implemented with political awareness, is that 'If a patient is dying imminently or recovering rapidly, do not intervene.'

Nature must be allowed to take its course, for instance, after a second cardiac arrest on the ward after a failed resuscitation. Seldom if ever do patients survive a second cardiac arrest. Physiological futility is a situation where the Glasgow Coma scale (GCS) is <5, and there may be little point in attempting heroic interventions. There are always exceptions to all rules, and that must also be borne in mind.

Anatomical futility is a situation when, after a road traffic accident, the body is so badly mangled that it cannot be meaningfully reconstructed.

Social futility is difficult to judge. There are situations when a patient cannot be returned to the same lifestyle as the patient was used to prior to admission to the hospital for treatment. Take, for example, an elderly patient with dementia who presents with a colonic perforation. It is likely that the carer is an equally elderly partner. In these situations, it is more than likely that following the operation, the dementia may worsen, leading to inability for the carer to look after the patient at home. The patient may then need to be admitted to a nursing home with major implications for the future. These situations merit discussions with the next of kin and will require the *best interest meeting* to aid the decision-making process. In times of emergency, the latter may not be feasible, and it may be best to be guided by surrogates. *Consenting for surgery* will also require the 'best interest meeting.'

Frailty

The ageing process takes its toll, and unfortunately there is no return to a better state of health that is possible for most. (Nortin Hadler in 'Rethinking ageing').

Frailty is a recognised factor that increases morbidity and mortality after any type of surgery.

A quick rule of thumb for assessing frailty is the following.

- Hand-grip strength
- Sitting to standing time
- Walking speed

Rockwood clinical frailty score

1. *Very fit*: Exercise regularly/robust
2. *Well*: Exercise occasionally/no active symptoms
3. *Managing well*: Controlled medical problems
4. *Vulnerable*: Symptoms limit activities/independence
5. *Mildly frail*: Slow with inside and outside activities
6. *Moderately frail*: Help with all outside activities
7. *Severely frail*: Full dependence for personal care
8. *Very severely frail*: Approaching end of life

Rockwood score in dementia

1. *Mild*: Forgetting recent events; repeating stories and questions
2. *Moderate*: Recent memory very impaired; attend to personal care with prompting; recall past events well
3. *Severe*: Cannot do personal care without help

Capacity and consenting

Capacity is the cognitive function that allows us to:

- Take in new information
- Retain that information, and
- Weigh the pros and cons of that information
- Prior to coming to a decision about whether the information is in keeping with one's judgement

Capacity is not binary; it is a spectrum, and the grey area may involve assisted decision-making or co-decision making, with legal implications. Capacity cannot be taken for granted in the ill patients because it is quite likely that illness itself has taken away capacity.

The loss of capacity may be transient due to an illness such as sepsis, or it may be an established loss due to dementia or other illness.

It is always necessary to assess capacity, and if a patient is thought not to have the capacity to make a judgement, then one must involve the family or surrogates in the decision-making process. It may be necessary to call for the best interest meeting with surrogates to decide on the most acceptable modality of treatment, which may include non-treatment. Capacity merits careful consideration along with frailty and dementia. It may be acceptable in certain situations to agree to a surgical intervention for a time-limited period, defer the final decision for a period of 48 hours after surgical intervention, and then convene a meeting to make a final decision depending on the progress that has been made by the patient.

Consultation with colleagues, anaesthetists or a critical care team in these situations is invaluable. Avoiding conflict with the family and carers is pre-eminent.

Consent to intervention of any sort forms part of the same discussion. Some patients may already have considered aspects of end of life and decided on levels of care that they would like implemented.

This may be presented as an *advanced directive.* The advanced directive is a legal document that clearly outlines the wishes of the patient about future medical care. It may state the level of care that the patient would like implemented including, 'Do Not Attempt Resuscitation' *(DNAR)* orders. As it is a legal document, the stated wishes of the patient must be implemented.

Note the feasibility of an operation is not an indication of its performance. Every patient must be assessed from the point of futility and risk of mortality and morbidity for any operation.

Breaking bad news

- This is best done by doctors with experience and knowledge of the situation
- Bad news may not always be life-threatening, but it may change the future for the patient, family, friends, and relatives
- The manner of communication must be considered genuine and well meaning
- Bad news is unpleasant, and the behaviour of the informant must reflect the seriousness of the situation with due preparation and planning about the manner of information delivery and inclusion of appropriate staff members

Practical principles

- Ensure that every patient is reviewed daily
- Consider the care of the patient as a contract between the two individuals, carer and cared.
- Deal with every patient as one would like to be dealt with oneself
- Apply these principles universally
- The treatment of patients should be guided by standard principles because any deviation from the norm can lead to disaster

King Edward VII was being treated for cor pulmonale by Bertie Dawson of the London hospital.

The King asked him how he proposed treating him.

'Sire' replied Dawson 'I shall treat you like any of my patients in the wards at the London Hospital'.

Chapter 55

Now test yourself?

Questions

This section has multiple choice questions. Most of the questions are based on real-life scenarios. Each question has an explanatory answer.

1. A 65-year-old man is unable to do routine work but can take care of his activities of daily living. His WHO performance status is:

- **a.** Two
- **b.** Zero
- **c.** One
- **d.** Three
- **e.** None of the above

2. You are called to assess an elderly lady with cellulitis in the leg. After assessment, you conclude that the patient could be in a state of sepsis because:

- **a.** She has a temperature of 37.9°C with a painful inflammation in her right foot
- **b.** Her respiratory rate is 22 breaths/min and systolic blood pressure is 85 mmHg
- **c.** The pain in the leg is very severe and she needs more analgesics
- **d.** She is walking about with limp because of the inflammation
- **e.** She says it started with a thorn prick when she was gardening

3. Patients with septic shock can be identified by:

- **a.** A systolic pressure of 95 mmHg or less
- **b.** Persistent cough for >2 days
- **c.** The need for intravenous fluids to maintain a mean arterial pressure (MAP) of 100 mmHg lactate of 3 mmol/L
- **d.** Need for vasopressors to maintain a MAP of 65 mmHg or greater and a lactate of 2 mmol/L or less
- **e.** Need for vasopressors to maintain a MAP of 70 mmHg or greater

4. A 14-year-old boy presents with pain that started in the umbilicus the previous evening. At the time of the ward round, he has severe pain in the right lower quadrant of the abdomen and the consultant makes the diagnosis of appendicitis. The reason for the change in location of pain is:

- **a.** Increased flatulence at the time of onset
- **b.** Inflammation of the appendix at the tip and not the base of the appendix

c. Inflammation of the parietal peritoneum extending to the visceral peritoneum
d. Inflammation of the visceral peritoneum extending to the parietal peritoneum
e. Somatic pain proceeding to autonomic pain

5. An 82-year-old lady presents with acute onset of pain and tenderness in the right iliac fossa suggesting appendicitis. Actions prior to consideration of surgical intervention must include:
   a. Assessment for fitness for surgery
   b. CT scan to exclude carcinoma of the caecum or other pathology
   c. Discussion with the anaesthetist
   d. All of the above
   e. None of the above

6. At laparotomy for a right iliac fossa mass thought to be due to appendicitis, the surgeon finds a thickened reddened distal ileum with a normal caecum the options include:
   a. Suspect Crohn's disease and proceed to biopsy a lymph node
   b. Appendicectomy
   c. Suspect tuberculosis and proceed to an appendicectomy
   d. Suspect that it is a Meckel's mass and proceed to resection of small intestine
   e. Suspect Crohn's disease and biopsy a lymph node for diagnosis and appendicectomy

7. What are the possible positions where the appendix can be located?
   a. Pelvic
   b. Retro-colic
   c. Para-colic
   d. Pre- or post-ileal
   e. All of the above

8. At operation of appendicectomy, there is a Meckel's diverticulum located in the distal small bowel. The complications of Meckel's diverticulum include:
   a. Bleeding
   b. Perforation
   c. Obstruction
   d. Peritonitis
   e. All of the above

9. An 84-year-old patient is admitted with features of acute appendicitis. 6 hours later the patient's temperature is 38.5oC, heart rate is 106 beats/min and respiratory rate is 24 breaths/min. The white cell count is 1,50,000 cells/μL and C-reactive protein (CRP) = 160 mg/L. On examination, she is tender all over the abdomen. The cause for the rapid progression is because:
   a. She is old
   b. She is possibly constipated
   c. The omentum is attenuated, and localisation has failed
   d. Previous hysterectomy has prevented localisation
   e. She has cystitis

10. A 65-year-old man presents with a history of nausea and upper abdominal discomfort for weeks. On examination, he has clinical jaundice with a non-tender palpable mass in the upper right quadrant of the abdomen that moves with respiration. On the basis of the clinical findings, the most likely diagnosis is:

- **a.** Acute cholecystitis
- **b.** Acute pancreatitis with sub-hepatic abscess
- **c.** Common bile duct (CBD) stones causing jaundice
- **d.** Pancreatic malignancy
- **e.** Hepatic flexure carcinoma

11. A 63-year-old man presents with jaundice and upper abdominal pain. An ultrasound confirmed the presence of multiple small gallstones, but the common duct could not be visualised. Magnetic resonance cholangiopancreatography (MRCP) showed a CBD that was 12-mm dilated and a possible impacted stone at the ampulla.

- **a.** Proceed to a MRCP
- **b.** If MRCP shows a common duct stone, an endoscopic retrograde cholangiopancreatography (ERCP) and extraction is the next step
- **c.** Check coagulation status prior to ERCP
- **d.** Warn the patient about possible complications of ERCP including pancreatitis
- **e.** All of the above

12. The location of the fundus of the gallbladder is important when assessing acute cholecystitis by eliciting the Murphy's sign.

- **a.** It is located at the tip of the right ninth costal cartilage in the transpyloric plane
- **b.** It is located at the tip of the left ninth costal cartilage along the mid-axillary line
- **c.** It is located parallel to the umbilicus on the right
- **d.** It is located in the right flank
- **e.** It is located just to the right of the xiphisternum

13. Following a difficult laparoscopic surgery on a 74-year-old man with previous history of pancreatitis there is evidence of bile-stained discharge of over 350 mL on the second postoperative day. Your options are:

- **a.** Examine the patient clinically, exclude peritonitis and request routine bloods and liver function tests
- **b.** Arrange immediate imaging CT or US
- **c.** Discuss with gastroenterologist and arrange an urgent ERCP and stenting if needed
- **d.** Inform the patient that you suspect injury to the bile or cystic duct
- **e.** All of the above

14. A week after day case of laparoscopic cholecystectomy, a 54-year-old lady presents to the acute surgical unit with jaundice. Clinically, the abdomen is soft. She has no tenderness. The full blood count and CRP are normal. Bilirubin is 90 mg/dL and alkaline phosphatase is 160 U/L. Rest of the liver function tests are normal. The most likely diagnosis is:

- **a.** Injury to the CBD
- **b.** Injury to the cystic duct
- **c.** Injury to the liver

d. Movement of small stones to the CBD during dissection needing ERCP and extraction
e. Hepatitis

15. A 39-year-old lady presents with typical features of biliary colic. The ultrasound examination has failed to demonstrate any abnormality in the gallbladder or liver. The liver function tests and routine bloods are normal. You proceed to a CT scan of the abdomen after discussions with the patient and this is also normal. She continues to have transient postprandial pain lasting for up to 6 hours at times. It is always located in the right upper quadrant. There is no change in bowel habit and no bloatedness to suggest irritable bowel. The next step could be:

a. Reassure and discharge the patient
b. Ask her to see if she can come to terms with the discomfort
c. Prescribe buscopan as an antispasmodic
d. Arrange a hepatobiliary iminodiacetic acid (HIDA) scan of the gallbladder
e. Ask her to take proton pump inhibitors daily

16. A 60-year-old lady has pelvic pain. The gynaecologist arranged an ultrasound scan of the abdomen. It shows normal adnexal and pelvic contents but has picked up multiple stones in the gallbladder. She is referred for surgical opinion regarding the next step.

a. Discuss operative and non-operative options with the patient regarding management of asymptomatic gallstones
b. Advise proceeding to laparoscopic cholecystectomy
c. Manage expectantly and repeat ultrasound scan in 6 months
d. Arrange a CT scan
e. Reassure and discharge her

17. A 63-year-old man presents acutely with clinically detected jaundice. The full blood count shows a haemoglobin (Hb): 144 g/L; WBC: $11.9/10^9$/L; bilirubin: 160 mg/dL; and alkaline phosphatase: 240 U/L. Aspartate aminotransferase (AST) is normal. On examination, the abdomen is non-tender and there is no palpable abnormality. Ultrasound examination has shown tiny gallstones, but the CBD could not be visualised due to overlying bowel. The jaundice could be due to:

a. Stones in the CBD impacted at the lower end
b. Stones in the cystic duct
c. Hepatitis
d. Pancreatic malignancy
e. Hepatic flexure carcinoma

18. A 58-year-old man presents with a 3-day history of increasing pain in the left lower quadrant of the abdomen. He does not have pyrexia. There are no urinary symptoms. He has been passing flatus. On examination, he is very tender in the left the lower abdomen. Routine bloods show a WBC count of $20.0/10^9$/L. Provisional diagnosis is acute diverticulitis. The next step is:

a. A CT scan of the abdomen
b. Urgent laparotomy
c. MRI of the pelvis

d. Laparoscopic examination of the abdomen
e. Supine abdominal X-ray

19. A 77-year-old man presenting with abdominal pain and tenderness has a CT scan that shows a large localised pelvic collection without evidence of free gas. There is evidence of diverticulosis in the left colon. The radiologist reports that this is a localised diverticular abscess. The options for further management could be:

a. Drainage under imaging control
b. Proximal colostomy and drainage
c. Laparoscopic lavage and drainage
d. Hartmann's procedure
e. Any of the above

20. A 73-year-old lady who had a low anterior resection 8 days ago is increasingly unwell. The oxygen saturation is 94% and the heart rate is 110 beats/min. A National Early Warning Score (NEWS) is 6. Chest X-ray (CXR) on day 7 was normal. On examination, her abdomen is distended and tender. She has had one loose bowel movement. The clinical diagnosis that must be considered is:

a. Pneumonia
b. Postoperative cardiac event
c. Atelectasis
d. Anastomotic leak
e. Bowel obstruction

21. A 65-year-old man had a coronary artery bypass graft 4 days ago. The operation was difficult. He has been started on fibre rich enteral feeding on day 2. He now has a distended abdomen that is non-tender. He is not passing flatus. A supine abdominal X-ray shows dilated colon and small bowel. His haematological and biochemical parameters do not suggest sepsis. You arrange a CT scan and that rules out mechanical obstruction and the radiologist reports it as a possible pseudo-obstruction. The management is:

a. Intravenous fluids
b. Correction of electrolyte imbalances
c. Endoscopic decompression and exclusion of mechanical cause
d. Surgical decompression if refractory to conservative management
e. All of the above

22. A 75-year-old man had repair of bilateral inguinal hernia laparoscopically. He returns with abdominal pain, tenderness, and vomiting 48 hours after surgery. Supine abdominal X-ray shows distended loops of small bowel. The possible diagnosis is:

a. Inadvertent bowel injury
b. Retained carbon dioxide causing distension
c. Analgesics causing constipation
d. Recurrent hernia
e. Eating very soon after surgery

23. Five days post-total colectomy for ulcerative colitis in a 39-year-old lady, her progression has been slow. This is attributed to the steroids that she had been on prior to surgery for acute colitis. The abdomen is tender. The stoma is dusky. The WBC was $16/10^9$/L 2 days previously, but now it is $25.0/10^9$/L. Platelet count is $35.0/10^9$/L. CRP is 215 mg/L. The possible cause of this deterioration is:

a. Increasing opiates for pain
b. Previous steroid therapy
c. Not continuing the antibiotics
d. Paralytic ileus
e. Ischaemic stoma and distal small bowel

24. A 53-year-old lady presents with adhesive obstruction following a hysterectomy when she was 39 years old. At the operation, she needed resection of the terminal ileum and a right hemi-colectomy with release of other adhesions in the proximal bowel. 5 days later, she remains distended and has not opened her bowels or passed flatus. Her abdomen is not tender, and she has not needed opiates for the last 2 days. Hb is 123 g/dL. WBC is 13.5 cells/mm^3. Albumin is 18 g/dL. She is apyrexial. What is the probable cause?

a. Paralytic ileus
b. Bowel injury
c. Anastomotic leak
d. Pelvic abscess
e. Intra-abdominal bleeding

25. A 42-year-old male with a strong family history of carcinoma colon is referred on the fast track with looseness of stools and a positive faecal immunochemical test (FIT) test. The quantitative analysis is 210 μg/g. The next step in management is:

a. Reassurance, that he is too young to have a serious problem
b. Arrange an ultrasound scan of the abdomen
c. Arrange an immediate colonoscopy and prescribe bowel preparation
d. Arrange a CT scan
e. Arrange a flexible sigmoidoscopy within 3 months

26. A 42-year-old lady is referred with complaints of aches and pains in both wrists, right knee, left hip, and lower back. She complains of increasing tiredness and thirst. She has lost 10.5 kg in 1 year. Ultrasound scan shows a 21 mm × 15 mm complex solid nodule just deep to the right lower lobe of the thyroid gland. The rest of the neck is normal. The possible diagnosis is:

a. Parathyroid hyperplasia
b. Parathyroid adenoma
c. Thyroid nodule
d. Vascular haemangioma
e. Pyramidal lobe

27. A 49-year-old lady with ultrasound detected parathyroid adenoma confirmed on a Sestamibi scan is likely to have:

a. Low-corrected serum calcium levels
b. High-corrected serum calcium levels

c. Low parathormone level
d. High calcitonin level
e. Elevated serum phosphate

28. An 80-year-old diabetic lady complains of severe abdominal pain 6 days after an anterior resection. On assessment, she has a temperature of 38.4°C; a pulse rate of 98 beats/min, respiratory rate of 24 breaths/min and a poor urinary output. Oxygen saturation is 87% on 100% oxygen delivered through a re-breathing mask. The most likely cause for her tachypnoea is:

a. Opiate analgesia prescribed for pain
b. Increased delivery of oxygen
c. Intra-abdominal sepsis leading to metabolic acidosis
d. Poor control of blood sugar postoperatively
e. Massive intra-abdominal haemorrhage

29. A 32-year-old alcoholic presents to the surgical assessment unit with a 6-hour history of vomiting and abdominal pain. On assessment, the pulse rate is 98 beats/min; respiratory rate 22 breaths/min; oximetry shows 92% saturation. The abdomen is very tender with guarding in the epigastrium. CXR is normal. The WBC count is 16.3×10^9/L. Serum amylase is 656 U/L and CRP is 88 mg/L. The possible diagnosis is:

a. Gastritis
b. Right basal pneumonia
c. Cholecystitis
d. Hepatitis
e. Acute pancreatitis

30. One day after a major laparotomy for intestinal obstruction you are requested by the surgical high care to write up a fluid regimen. The baseline requirement over 24 hours for a 70-kg man is likely to be:

a. Three litres of normal saline with 20 mmol of kcl/L
b. Two litres of normal saline with 20 mmol of kcl/L and 1 L of 5% dextrose saline
c. Three litres of dextrose saline with 20 mmol of kcl/L
d. One litre of normal saline and 2 L of 5% dextrose with 20 mmol of kcl in each litre
e. One litre of gelofusin and 2 L of 5% dextrose with 20 mmol of kcl/L

31. A 57-year-old male presents with severe abdominal pain and vomiting of 12 hours duration. A clinical diagnosis of pancreatitis is made. The severity of the disease can be assessed by which of the following parameters?

a. Glasgow score of 14 or more
b. C-reactive protein > 150 mg/L
c. Elevated serum amylase
d. Elevated serum bilirubin
e. Body mass index (BMI) > 30 kg/m^2

32. Which of the parameters in the above patient would indicate the need for ERCP and sphincterotomy?

a. Serum bilirubin of 130 mg/dL

b. Serum amylase of 1,120 U/L
c. C-reactive protein of 300 mg/L
d. WBC count of 11.0 cells/mm^3
e. Serum calcium of <1.4 mg/dL

33. A 29-year-old man presents with abdominal pain of 8 hours duration. There is no history of previous pain, and he is not on any medication. On clinical examination, the abdomen is rigid, and he is in a state of systemic inflammatory response syndrome. The patient continues to deteriorate and is scheduled for surgery as he is found to have free gas in the erect CXR. The anaesthetist requests a blood gas analysis. It is likely to show.

a. Pulse rate of 80 beats/min
b. Respiratory acidosis
c. Tachypnoea > 20 beats/min
d. WBC count of 4.0×10^9/L
e. Metabolic acidosis

34. An 84-year-old lady presents to the emergency ward with upper abdominal pain of 24 hours and pyrexia. On examination, she is tender in the upper abdomen. A diagnosis of acute cholangitis is made as she is jaundiced. What type of bilirubin is likely to be predominant in the bloodstream?

a. Unconjugated bilirubin
b. Conjugated bilirubin
c. Immediate ERCP
d. Intravenous fluids and antibiotics
e. Ultrasound scan

35. A 72-year-old man presents with dry gangrene of his right big toe. Diabetes has been eliminated as the cause. Previously, he had an angioplasty of the right superficial femoral artery with some improvement in his symptoms. The foot is warm. Dry gangrene is characterised by which of the following factors?

a. A clear line of demarcation between the gangrenous and non-gangrenous tissue
b. Presence of cellulitis proximal to the gangrenous toe
c. Presence of infection in the toe
d. Watery discharge
e. Purulent discharge

36. The gangrenous toe in the above patient needs to be addressed by which of the following options?

a. A bypass graft to improve blood supply
b. Medial compartment fasciotomy
c. Lateral fasciotomy
d. Immediate amputation is not necessary
e. Forefoot amputation is preferable as it heals well

37. A 30-year-old woman presents with severe diarrhoea and vomiting of 1 day's duration. The water loss that follows is from which of the compartments?

a. Likely to lose water from both intra- and extra-cellular compartments

b. Likely to have a greater loss of water in the extra-cellular compartment
c. Thirst is generated by osmoreceptor activity in the hypothalamus
d. Parasympathetic activity is responsible for repletion of water
e. Likely to have a greater loss of water in the intracellular compartment

38. A 45-year-old lady with a BMI of 32 kg/m^2 presents with a history of intermittent upper abdominal pain mainly located in the right upper quadrant of the abdomen. The pain was first noticed at the outset of 6 months ago after dinner and kept her awake for most of the night. It settled by the morning but has recurred intermittently. She has had no fever. It is increasingly more troublesome and affects her quality of life. She is likely to have:

a. Acute cholecystitis
b. Acute cholangitis
c. Biliary colic
d. Crohn's disease
e. Renal colic

39. A 40-year-old man presenting with a lump in the back overlying the scapular region on the right of over 10 years' duration. The lump has been slowly increasing in size. It is not painful but increasingly it is becoming awkward. It is 10 cm in length and 7 cm in width; mobile and non-tender. The skin over it is healthy and there is no evidence of any punctum.

The most likely diagnosis is:
a. Subcutaneous lipoma
b. Epidermoid cyst
c. Pilonidal cyst
d. Hidradenitis
e. Carbuncle in the back

40. A 16-year-old lad presents with pain in the left shoulder and left upper quadrant of the abdomen following an injury to the left upper abdomen while playing football. He was seen in the accident and emergency (A&E) and sent home with paracetamol. He came back the following day with more pain. Hb was 100 g/dL and the heart rate was 110 beats/min. A CT scan was done immediately. What is possibly happening here?

a. A small capsular tear with a subscapular haematoma
b. A complete laceration of the spleen
c. Devascularisation of >25% of the spleen
d. Normal spleen
e. Perforation of colon

41. Post-splenectomy protocol consists of:

a. Immunisation against encapsulated bacteria
b. Antibiotic prophylaxis for life
c. Recognition that severe infections are most likely to occur in the first 2 years after splenectomy
d. Implantation of splenic tissue into the omentum after traumatic splenectomy
e. All of the above

42. A 77-year-old man presents to accident and emergency in a state of collapse. A fast scan shows the presence of free-fluid and an aortic aneurysm. He is resuscitated with fluids and an urgent ultrasound confirms the presence of an abdominal aortic aneurysm (AAA) of 6 cm with tortuous iliac arteries indicating the need for an open repair of a ruptured AAA rather than endovascular aneurysm repair (EVAR). His quality of life is good, and performance score is 1. In the past, he has had a myocardial infarction with placement of a stent. He is not on anticoagulants. At operation, when the infra-renal aorta is cross-clamped, his blood pressure drops. This is due to:

a. Increase in after load
b. Increase in preload
c. Acute renal failure due to blood loss
d. Due purely to hypovolaemia
e. Not having taken his usual medications

43. In the above patient on completion of the operation, the aortic clamp is released, and this establishes flow to the distal segment. On declamping, the aorta on the operating table there is an immediate possibility of:

a. Hypotension
b. Hypertension
c. No change in blood pressure
d. Hypoxia
e. Renal failure

44. A 57-year-old diabetic patient presents with a progressive painful left foot. On examination, the big toe is dusky and there is an area of cellulitis around it. He has no sensation around the distal foot. The popliteal pulse is palpable, and the lower leg feels warm. His glycated haemoglobin (HbA1c) is 78 mmol/mol. This must raise the suspicion of:

a. Wet gangrene
b. Dry gangrene
c. Femoral embolism
d. Diabetic nephropathy
e. Popliteal aneurysm

45. A 9-year-old boy presents with acutely worsening pain in the lower abdomen on the right. He had been to school in the morning, but the parents were called at lunch time as he was vomiting and complained of pain. On examination, the abdomen is non-tender. The pain is increasing and the WBC count is 15 cells/mm^3. The next step is to examine:

a. The scrotum and to rule out a testicular torsion
b. Check the urine for infection
c. Examine the back
d. Examine the hips
e. Reassure his parents and discharge him

46. A 33-year-old man is seen in the acute surgical unit with a painful lump in his natal cleft. He is hirsute and has a BMI of 35 kg/m^2. On examination, he has a red and tender swelling in the upper part of the natal cleft. The likely diagnosis is:

a. Ischiorectal abscess
b. Fistula in ano
c. Pilonidal abscess
d. Perineal haematoma
e. Abrasion and inflammation

47. A 27-year-old man presents with an acutely painful left testis of 12-hour duration. He has had dysuria for 2 days. The management involves:

a. Urgent Doppler scan of the scrotum to exclude torsion of testis
b. Urine dipstick to check for nitrites
c. Urine dipstick to check for sugar
d. Considering a diagnosis of epididymo orchitis
e. All of the above

48. A 39-year-old lady presents with severe pain in the right loin for 12 hours. It seems to be radiating to the groin. The urine dipstick is negative for nitrites but positive for blood. This must raise the suspicion of:

a. Ureteric colic due to an oxalate stone
b. Ureteric colic due to a triple phosphate stone
c. Renal failure
d. Cystitis
e. Dysmenorrhoea

49. A 49-year-old man presents with a painful swelling in the perineum progressive over 2 days. There is no change in bowel habit and no history of rectal bleeding. On examination, there is induration with tenderness in the ischiorectal fossa area on the left. This is likely to be:

a. A perianal abscess
b. Anal Crohn's
c. Pilonidal sinus
d. Perianal haematoma
e. Acute haemorrhoids

50. Methicillin-resistant *Staphylococcus aureus* (MRSA) infections are due to:

a. *Streptococcus pneumoniae*
b. *Staphylococcus* infections that are sensitive to penicillin
c. *Streptococcus* infections resistant to methicillin
d. *Staphylococcus* infections resistant to methicillin
e. Multi-resistant *Streptococcus*

51. A 60-year-old lady presents with acute abdominal pain and vomiting of 8 hours duration. The serum amylase and lipase are raised. She is known to have gallstones. The abdomen is tender. A diagnosis of pancreatitis is made. Corrected serum calcium is 1.2 mmols/L.

a. Low calcium is due to poor intake of milk
b. High calcium is a good prognostic sign
c. Amylase digests fat and is elevated suggesting fat necrosis and low calcium
d. Lipase digests fat and low calcium is a marker of fat necrosis
e. Low calcium is not an indicator of severity

52. A 58-year-old man has pancreatitis. The severity of the presentation can be graded by the Glasgow criteria if:

a. Three or more factors are abnormal at 48 hours
b. Two or more factors are abnormal
c. If a patient over 55 years of age presents for the first time with pancreatitis
d. If the amylase is more than three times normal limit
e. If the PaO_2 96% or lower

53. 8 weeks after being treated for pancreatitis a patient presents with being unwell. There is no pyrexia or vomiting. On examination, he has a large mass in the upper abdomen.

a. This is likely to be a pseudocyst of the pancreas
b. This is a pancreatic abscess
c. This is likely to be a gastric outlet obstruction
d. This is typical of a mucocoele of the gallbladder
e. This patient needs an urgent nasogastric tube insertion

54. A pseudo-pancreatic cyst:

a. Is a cyst around the pancreas walled off by adjacent structures
b. Is a pancreatic cyst lined by epithelium of the columnar type
c. Is an organised haematoma
d. Is a distended duodenal diverticulum
e. Never resolves spontaneously

55. A 63-year-old lady presents with non-specific upper abdominal pain. Clinical parameters are normal, and the abdomen is not tender. 7 years ago, she had cholelithiasis for which she had an ERCP and sphincterotomy followed by a laparoscopic cholecystitis. Gastroscopy was normal and CT scan shows air in the biliary tree and a dilated CBD. Air in the biliary tree is due to:

a. *Clostridial* infection
b. Anaerobic gas forming organism causing infection
c. Previous sphincterotomy
d. Laparoscopic cholecystectomy in the past
e. Biliary fistula

56. A 73-year-old lady presents with bilateral pedal oedema that presented acutely. Duplex scan of the legs did not show deep vein thrombosis (DVT). CT scan of the abdomen shows bilateral hydronephrosis and a retroperitoneal mass. The serum creatinine is 312 mg/dL. Urea is 22 mmol/L. She immediately needs:

- **a.** An urgent laparotomy
- **b.** Bilateral stenting of the ureters
- **c.** Catheterisation of the bladder
- **d.** Laparoscopy
- **e.** CT urogram

57. A 74-year-old man with a history of cerebrovascular accident (CVA) 3 months ago presents with bowel obstruction. He has had no abdominal operations in the past. CT scan of the abdomen shows a small bowel obstruction caused by a band. Options for management include:

- **a.** Discussion with anaesthetist regarding suitability for surgical intervention
- **b.** Considering the temporary discontinuation of anticoagulation if any
- **c.** Weighing the risk of intervention with further complications of CVA
- **d.** Gastrograffin orally to evaluate need for surgical intervention
- **e.** All of the above

58. CT scan in an 83-year-old man presenting with obstruction confirms left colonic obstruction with a distended caecum > 15 cm. The patient's performance score is 0. He is not on any medications other than pantoprazole.

- **a.** Wait and watch progress over 48 hours
- **b.** Colonoscopy and confirmation of diagnosis
- **c.** Urgent laparotomy
- **d.** Liquid paraffin orally
- **e.** Stenting the area of stenosis

59. A 69-year-old lady on warfarin for atrial fibrillation (AF) presents with acute obstruction confirmed on CT scan. International normalised ratio (INR) is 3.6. This patient should have the following prior to surgical intervention:

- **a.** Discussion with haematologist regarding management of anticoagulation prior to intervention surgically
- **b.** Vitamin K orally for 3 days with regular monitoring of INR
- **c.** Stop warfarin for 48 hours prior to intervention
- **d.** Stop warfarin and bridge with clexane
- **e.** Cryoprecipitate infusion prior to surgery

60. An 80-year-old lady with dementia presenting with lower abdominal pain, distension of abdomen and a palpable mass in the left groin. Supine X-ray of the abdomen shows distended small bowel loops.

- **a.** The best interest meeting will be needed to determine further management
- **b.** An urgent laparotomy to relieve obstruction
- **c.** Analgesics and antibiotics intravenously
- **d.** Non-operative management
- **e.** Percutaneous endoscopic gastrostomy (PEG) to assist with fluid management

Answers

1. **A.** If a person can take care of their daily activities but finds working difficult the score is 2. It is worthy of note that the patient is active for >50% of the day. Increasing scores denote decreasing performance. As the performance decreases, the physiological response to injury of any type decreases. Frailty as a person, age is a good determinant of suitability or otherwise for major interventions.

2. **B.** Quick sequential organ failure assessment (qSOFA) is a quick method of assessing the possibility of organ dysfunction and sepsis and enables early recognition. The qSOFA is a bedside method for rapid identification in the ward or primary care setting of adult patients with a focus of infection that when positive indicates poor outcome. qSOFA is positive if two of the three parameters that follow are identified: a respiratory rate of 22 breaths/min or greater, altered mentation, or systolic blood pressure of 100 mmHg or less.

3. **D.** Mean arterial pressure (MAP) is defined as one-third of the pulse pressure added to the diastolic pressure. The pulse pressure when the BP is 120/80 mmHg is the difference between the systolic and diastolic – 40. MAP is therefore 83 (80 + 13.3). The new definition of septic, simply put, is that once the volume is repleted, if a vasopressor is needed to maintain a MAP of 65 mmHg and a lactate of 2 mmol/L the patient is deemed to be in septic shock.

4. **D.** As discussed earlier, the migrating pain of appendicitis is driven by the depth of inflammation. At the outset, the inflammation involves the visceral peritoneum that is tightly enveloping the appendix. Progression of inflammation involves the parietal peritoneum. This increase in severity is manifested by moving to an area of somatic nerve innervation from an area of autonomic innervation. Visceral to parietal. Autonomic to somatic.

5. **D.** Image before invasive intervention. CT scan is more sensitive and has a greater positive predictive value than ultrasound scan. Depending on availability and feasibility, use of CT scan reduces negative appendicectomy or removal of the 'Lilly white' appendix that used to be common when wholly based on tenderness at McBurney's point or the Psoas test. CT scan has the drawback that it exposes younger patients to radiation and insult of contrast. Imaging before invasive intervention has now become acceptable for acute appendicitis as it avoids needless intervention and defines alternative pathology such as malignancy and tubo-ovarian disease.

   Ref: Reich B, Zalut T, Weiner SG. An international evaluation of ultrasound vs. computed tomography in the diagnosis of appendicitis. Int J Emerg Med 2011; 4:68.

6. **E.** Imaging before invasive surgery will avoid this scenario; however, imaging is not universally available. Controversy exists in these situations, if appendicectomy should be done when Crohn's or TB is noted. TB normally involves the caecum, but Crohn's has skip lesions that may be noted at surgery. If the caecal base is macroscopically normal, it may be safe to proceed to an appendicectomy. The histology must be checked postoperatively. There may be a small risk of a fistula in any operation for Crohn's disease. Current trends do not favour immediate resection as medical management may obviate the need for surgical resection in Crohn's where preservation of the bowel is of paramount importance.

7. **E.** Retro colic and pelvic positions are the most common. Pre- and post-ileal are the least common.

8. **E.** Meckel's diverticulum, it is often stated is present in 2% of the population; 2 ft from the ileocaecal valve and has two complications. Bleeding and obstruction: Bleeding, when it occurs, is due to ulceration at the tip of the diverticulum and often in these situations there is a separate blood vessel from the mesentery reaching across the bowel from the mesenteric border. If any young person has melaena and the gastroscopy and colonoscopy are normal, one must exclude Meckel's. I have done with gratifying results on three occasions!

9. **C.** In the very young, the omentum is undeveloped and in the very old it is atrophied. The omentum is a phenomenal organ that is referred to as the 'abdominal policeman'. It seeks areas of mischief and contains it by wrapping around areas of inflammation. If it is underdeveloped the process of containment fails leading to the spread of inflammation. The absence of containment must also be borne in mind in patients who are immunocompromised and those on steroids.

10. **D.** This classically supports the Courvoisier's law. Jaundiced patients with a palpable gallbladder have a high possibility of cancer of the pancreatic head. Bear in mind that double impaction with a stone in the cystic duct and another in the common bile duct (CBD) may also cause findings similar to this as would a Mirizzi.

11. **E.** It is important in jaundiced patients to check the coagulation profile prior to ERCP. In some, the malabsorption of vitamin K can affect the coagulation.

12. **A.** This surface marking is quite important when examining a patient suspected of having acute cholecystitis. In general terms, surface marking relates to bony structures than soft tissue as adiposity and ageing are confounders.

13. **E.** In these patients when there is bile in the drain, it is always necessary to ensure that the patient is not in sepsis. Here, the patient has had a drain, but in situations where there is no drain and the patient presents unwell a couple of days after laparoscopic cholecystectomy, it is expedient to proceed to a CT scan followed by drainage and ERCP. The key principle is that patients must progressively get better day by day after laparoscopic surgery and when the recovery is not progressing as per expectations immediate intervention with imaging and even laparoscopy is indicated.

14. **D.** During laparoscopic cholecystectomy, there are times when small stones are noted in the cystic duct as it is being dissected or clipped. In those cases, when the stones in the cystic duct are appreciated, it is best to milk the stones back to the gallbladder and clip the cystic duct distal to the stones.

15. **D.** Hepatobiliary iminodiacetic acid (HIDA) scan. This involves injecting a radioactive tracer intravenously. This is taken up by the liver cells and excreted into the bile ducts and intestine. The bile with the radioactive tracer collects in the gallbladder if the cystic duct is patent. On detecting a full gallbladder, the patient is given a fatty meal (a MARS Bar or Sandwich), the gallbladder, in response to a fatty meal must contract and empty the contents to the intestine. If there is delayed emptying or lack of emptying, it may suggest a physiological dysfunction. In these situations, some patients also reproduce their symptoms. The problem may relate in some to a hold up by gravel in the spiral valves of Heister, that represents mucosal folds in the cystic duct.

16. **A.** This situation is not uncommon. When the gallstones are asymptomatic, the decision to proceed to a laparoscopic cholecystectomy versus expectant management is often an informed decision by the patient. An argument can be made for a laparoscopic cholecystectomy in a fit young patient because of possible complications over a period of time. This may not be the case in an unfit or elderly unfit patient. The final decision to proceed to a cholecystectomy must be a joint decision with the patient after clear documentation of the discussion.

17. **A.** Common things are more common and rare things are rarer. Multiple diagnosis is more common as one ages! Here, the presence of tiny stones in the gallbladder obviously favours the suggestion that some of these stones may have moved to the cystic duct. Jaundice is normally caused when the outlet is obstructed impeding the flow. In some patients, stones in the cystic duct may not cause jaundice. Furthermore, large stones in the gallbladder may not be able to move down the cystic duct. Small stones can and do.

18. **A.** CT scan is very useful in determining the extent of the disease; is it just an inflammation, is it pericolic, paracolic or generalised peritonitis with free fluid? Each one of these can be managed differently. If peritonitic, the distinction between faeculant and purulent may be difficult purely on imaging and, in fit patients, immediate surgery is needed.

19. **E.** The type of treatment offered to every patient is dependent of the individual circumstances. All these options need consideration. In certain situations, a laparoscopic drainage with a more definitive elective resection at a later stage may obviate the need for a stoma which a Hartmann's will certainly require. In some, a stoma may be altogether the best option for the patient.

20. **D.** While all the other options are feasible, anastomotic leak is the one that generally occurs between day 4 and 8. Respiratory and cardiac problems occur earlier. A drop in oxygen saturation at any stage must be taken seriously and investigated thoroughly. It is also the harbinger of poor cardiac function and often leads to poor renal function as the nephrons deep in the medulla do not take kindly to decrease in oxygen levels as they are normally functioning at the limits of sufficient oxygen.

21. **E.** This situation is not very uncommon. Very often the cause is unclear, but it is essential to exclude electrolyte abnormalities. I have seen this after early introduction of high-fibre diet in some patients, but this is anecdotal. The prime method here is decompression endoscopically and sometimes more than once. The process of endoscopic decompression also tends to exclude unrecognised mechanical factors such as coincidental stenosis or malignancy.

22. **A.** Bowel injury after transperitoneal laparoscopic hernia repair, though rare, tends to occur from time to time. The key principle here is that if a patient fails to progress after laparoscopic operation of any type, especially after day case operations, one must ensure adequate assessment and investigation. These may include further laparoscopy or imaging prior to intervention. The key message here is not to ignore the patient who returns with symptoms following day case laparoscopic surgery.

23. **E.** A raised white cell count, low platelet and elevated C-reactive protein (CRP) in a postoperative patient, especially one that is on steroids must raise the suspicion of ongoing sepsis and the need for imaging and assessment prior to intervention. A dusky

ileostomy may be evidence of full thickness ischaemia and die back ischaemia of the terminal ileal segment within the abdominal cavity. This will require re-operation and formation of another stoma with good blood supply.

24. **A.** In the absence of return of bowel function from the time of surgery, it is safe to presume on going paralytic ileus. This is more likely when the preoperative period has been protracted and optimal nutrition has not been possible. Whenever a patient is unlikely to start feeding within 5 days of surgical intervention, it is best to discuss nutritional supplementation parenterally from the outset.

25. **C.** Age is not a consideration to delay investigations in the presence of evidence of red flag signs. FIT test, when positive, must be investigated thoroughly prior to exclusion of pathology leading to it.

26. **B.** A single nodule in the presence of the history is suggestive of an adenoma rather than hyperplasia. Adenocarcinoma is also possible but it is very rare (1%). When it is a single adenoma, successful minimally invasive surgery will provide rapid relief of symptoms. Further biochemical monitoring till return to normal is mandatory.

27. **B.** Parathormone drives the calcium out of the bone by increasing osteoclastic activity. It is a disease categorised by: Bones, stones, groans and psychotic moans!

28. **C.** Acidosis and sepsis go together. Seldom, if ever do we see metabolic alkalosis in surgical post-operative patients. As stated in the text, oxygen debt is the prime cause of metabolic problems. When there is tachypnoea, there is shallow breathing and recirculation of dead space air that is richer in CO_2 than O_2.

29. **E.** In acute pancreatitis, the amylase rises rapidly within 6 hours; it also falls rapidly thereafter and is not a measure of severity. It is worthy of note that in some patients with severe alcoholism, the pancreas may be damaged, and the amylase may not be very raised. In patients with peritonitis, ischaemic bowel and ectopic pregnancy the levels can be raised. Normally, when the level rises to three times the normal value for your laboratory, pancreatitis is likely.

30. **C.** The sodium retention after surgery usually means that the baseline requirement of sodium is only 90 mmol a day. This is adequately provided by 3 L of dextrose saline. Each litre contains 31 mmol of sodium. It is a combination of half normal saline (0.18% Na) and 4% dextrose. A litre of normal saline contains 154 mmol of sodium; Ringer's lactate and Hartmann's solution contains about 130 mmol of sodium. The baseline potassium is 60 mmol/day and this is often forgotten, leading to low potassium and cardiac arrhythmias in some elderly patients as a consequence.

31. **B.** C-reactive protein is a good indicator of prognosis. The point to note here is that serum amylase, however, high the level is not an indicator of severity.

32. **A.** Patients with acute pancreatitis should have an endoscopic retrograde cholangiopancreatography (ERCP) with sphincterotomy within 72 hours if they have jaundice, cholangitis or a dilated CBD. Sphincterotomy with stent placement is needed in the presence of cholangitis to allow for drainage.

33. **E.** Metabolic acidosis is a manifestation of oxygen debt and sepsis. In the presence of cellular hypoxia, there is a shift from aerobic to anaerobic respiration leading to the

production of lactic acid and a marked decrease in ATP. The acid enters the red cells which contain carbonic anhydrase. The carbonic anhydrase catalyses H_2CO_3 in a reaction than can proceed reversibly in two directions; one forms HCO_3 and H^+ and the other H_2O and CO_2. The system tends to compensate with increased respiratory rate in an attempt to blow off the excess carbon dioxide.

34. **B.** Conjugated and water-soluble bilirubin. It is conjugated with glucuronic acid, a fatty acid to form a salt.

35. **A.** Dry gangrene has the following characteristics: a line of demarcation; the demarcation line is aseptic; the gangrenous area is shrunk and shriveled.

36. **D.** Generally, immediate intervention is not likely to be needed in this patient as the foot remains well perfused. Assessment for critical limb ischaemia must be made and, in the absence of critical limb ischaemia, a referral to vascular team can be made. This need not be immediate.

37. **A.** When the body loses water, in patients with cholera, fluid is usually depleted from both the extracellular and intracellular compartments. A range of compensatory responses come into play leading to stimulation of the renin–angiotensin–aldosterone system and activation of the sympathetic system in an effort to preserve the body fluid volume and retain the sodium. Changes in osmotic pressure lead to stimulation of osmoreceptors in the hypothalamus and increases thirst. In conditions like haemorrhage, the extracellular fluid (ECF) volume is decreased selectively. This, in turn, causes a fluid shift from the intracellular compartment to the ECF. The body to brain messaging attempts to preserve the interior milieu with many tricks. The immediate activation of the sympathetic system is the major player, as it struggles to maintain the cardiac output and decreasing blood pressure. It shifts the fluid and increases the venous tone and heart rate. It also improves the force of contraction of the heart. Subsequently, with the renin angiotensin mechanism, the sodium is retained and along with that the water. The latter part is a slower process than the former.

38. **C.** Biliary colic is a misnomer in that the pain lasts much longer than a colic does. It is highly likely that the pain occurs due to movement of gallstones when the gallbladder contracts in response to a fatty meal. The stones may get impacted in the cystic duct causing pain and as the gallbladder relaxes, it falls away from cystic duct with relief of symptoms. These types of patients are best undergoing cholecystectomy at the same admission. It avoids the possibility of recurrence and more harm.

39. **A.** The presence of a lump with a palpable edge that slips under the palpating hand and mobile in all directions makes it a lipoma. Lipomata can be located at various levels such as subfascial, intramuscular, submuscular, etc. but a subcutaneous lipoma is freely mobile. Neurofibroma in the subcutaneous plane are also mobile but only in one axis and that is perpendicular to the direction of the nerve from which it arises. Epidermoid or sebaceous cysts, on the other hand, are not mobile as they are intradermal. Any lump that is mobile, is therefore not an epidermoid cyst.

40. **A.** In this case, there is a small capsular tear with a contained subcapsular haematoma. In young people, most splenic injuries can be managed conservatively as long as the patient remains haemodynamically stable. Repeat radiological assessments can be by ultrasound examination but the primary investigation needs to be a CT scan with

grading of the type or rupture. Even in adults, splenic tears up to grade 3 may be managed non-operatively as long as haemodynamical stability is maintained.

41. E. Patients who undergo splenectomy are at increasing risk of overwhelming sepsis possibly for life. The risk, however, is greatest in the first 2 years after splenectomy. The risk of infection from capsulated organisms such as *Haemophilus influenzae*, *Streptococcus pneumoniae* and *Neisseria meningitidis* dictates the need for vaccination against these preferably at the time of discharge from the hospital. Antibiotic prophylaxis with penicillin/erythromycin is recommended for life.

42. A. These patients are generally 'arteriopaths' as very seldom does vascular disease affect a single vessel in isolation. Despite being able to carry on activities of daily living, an imposition of additional strain on the heart is likely to affect the cardiac function. A left ventricular ejection fraction of >30 is beneficial for recovery from this type of surgery that requires cross clamping; with cross clamping of the aorta, the heart is suddenly placed under increased strain against which it has to pump.

43. A. On declamping of the aorta, there is a sudden outflow of blood to the peripheries. The distal tissue would have been hypoxic during the period of cross clamping and on reperfusion there is a release of products of metabolism into circulation causing peripheral vasodilatation. This leads to a fall in blood pressure referred to as declamping hypotension and consequent injury to the kidneys leading to acute tubular necrosis. Volume loading the patient prior to declamping and gradual establishment of flow distally, such as declamping one limb at a time may be of assistance. Renal failure may occur, but it is not immediate. Another possibility is the occurrence of 'trash foot' due to the release of debris down the leg. This can be avoided by ensuring that trapped air and debris are released externally prior to restoration of flow.

44. A. Typically in wet gangrene as opposed to dry gangrene, there is no clear zone of demarcation. The transition zone between the area with no blood supply and area with some blood supply in wet gangrene is referred to as a zone of septic separation. The fact that popliteal pulse is present and shows that diabetes is a disease of the small vessels.

45. A. In young boys with acute lower abdominal pain, the examination of the abdomen is not complete unless the scrotum is examined. The possibility, when the abdomen is non-tender in the presence of pain, must be to exclude torsion and renal colic.

46. C. Pilonidal sinus is common in the hirsute and individuals with high body mass index (BMI). During the Korean war, this used to be common among young GI's and was referred to as 'the jeep bottom'. The hair in the sinus is always directed in such a way that the root of the hair is superficial indicating that the hair is from extraneous sources and not intrinsic.

47. E. The dictat used to be that acute testicular pain in the young adult is likely to be due to infection and in the child due to torsion. There are always exceptions to the rule and so it is important to exclude torsion in all acute testicular pain with immediate Doppler scan.

48. A. Oxalate stone is also called a 'mulberry calculus'. The mulberry seed is tiny and spiculated. As this stone moves down the ureter, it abrades the transitional epithelium of the urinary tract and causes microscopic bleeding. The stag horn calculus, however, is soft and smooth and creeps up on the patient asymptomatically and even bilaterally.

49. A. Perianal abscess may present without the typical fluctuation that is seen in abscesses. There is normally induration. Acute tenderness in this region dictates examination under anaesthesia that will normally include an incision and drainage along with a rectal examination to document the presence of an internal opening of a fistula in ano; fistula in ano are commonly associated with perianal abscess. A culture swab must be taken. Staphylococcal infections suggest a cutaneous origin. The presence of *E. coli* or *Klebsiella* raises the possibility of a fistula as the cause of the abscess.

50. D. Methicillin-resistant *Staphylococcus aureus* (MRSA). These areas are a type of *Staphylococcus* bacteria that is resistant to many of the antibiotics commonly used to treat patients with *Staphylococcus* infections. They tend to occur in the community or in healthcare settings. Healthcare workers may contribute to transmission in healthcare settings; infections may follow invasive procedures increasing complications and length of stay. Vascular grafts and joint replacements may be infected by MRSA leading to increased morbidity and even mortality. In the community-acquired infections, the spread is by skin contact.

51. D. Lipase is the enzyme that digests fat. With pancreatitis, the exocrine digestive enzymes are released. These are protease that digest protein to amino acids, amylase that digests carbohydrates to disaccharides such as glucose. The lipase digests the fat. The end products of fat digestion is fatty acids and glycerol. The fatty acids bond with calcium and form soap. The substrate for life page to act upon is the fat around the pancreas and the omentum and this can manifest as fat necrosis. A decrease in calcium level is therefore a sign that indicates severity of the pancreatitis.

52. A. Classically, the severity of pancreatitis is assessed on the basis of laboratory findings. Day criteria being very varied, it is necessary to refer to the guidelines before civility can be assessed. The reason for the assessment is to ensure that the patient gets the appropriate treatment at the appropriate place. The addition of clinical along with laboratory findings make this task relatively more straight forward. When the stability index is positive on laboratory and clinical findings the mortality rate can be quite high even as much as up to 30%.

53. A. A pain-free lump >6 weeks after pancreatitis is likely to be a pseudocyst rather than an abscess. In this patient's case, there is no vomiting and that rules out a gastric outlet obstruction. Abscesses present earlier and tend to be very tender. A pseudocyst encysted and walled off by the surrounding tissue. Some cysts may communicate with the pancreatic duct and these may resolve without intervention. The management of pseudocyst is dependent upon the findings on imaging. If the cyst is thick-walled and it fails to resolve with conservative management, it can be drained endoscopically. When it is multiloculated and failed to resolve it may need surgical drainage.

54. A. As noted above the pseudocyst is walled off by surrounding structures. As such the lining is mesothelial and not epithelial.

55. C. In the presence of a previous sphincterotomy, air from the intestines can be seen in the biliary tree. The biliary duct is open to the duodenal contents. This can on occasions cause cholangitis. The biliary tree ducts do not have smooth muscles. Once it is dilated, for whatever reason it remains dilated always.

56. B. This lady needs immediate treatment from the point of view of the failing renal function. Subsequent assessment needs to be made regarding the cause of the retroperitoneal abnormality. The distinction is between a lymphoma and retroperitoneal fibrosis. The latter is better defined with lymphoma being irregular in structure and outline. In this particular case, it turned out to be a lymphoma. Contrast imaging is contraindicated because of the poor renal function. It is not recommended unless it is followed by immediate filtration.

57. E. The feasibility of an operation is not an indication for its performance. In this particular case, we were able to get away with a laparoscopic division of an adhesive band with almost immediate recovery. In most cases, however, we need to make a careful assessment of the benefits versus the risks of surgery and discuss the management with the patient and his surrogates.

58. C. In this patient's case because he is fit, an urgent laparotomy is the best course to adopt. In certain situations, where the patient may not be fit for surgery but suitable for intervention endoscopic stenting is a possibility; however, gas needs to be instilled into the colon. This may lead to further distension, perforation and peritonitis.

59. A. These patients will need to be discussed with a haematologist as in certain situations surgical intervention may be required sooner rather than later. It is not appropriate to wait for 48 hours as the obstruction may worsen. Reversal may require the use of octaplex.

60. A. These are difficult situations and a decision needs to be taken on an individual basis. It is mandatory to make an assessment of risk versus benefit with regard to surgical intervention. This discussion must be had with surrogates especially in the presence of lack of capacity on the part of the patient.

Index

Note: Page numbers in **bold** or *italic* refer to tables/box or figures, respectively.

F

G

H

Q

R

S

T